D1245784

# AROUND AFRICA
## ON MY BICYCLE

*'A performance which will inspire the youth of
the continent!'*
Nelson Mandela

Riaan Manser was born in 1973 in Pretoria. He grew up in
Zululand and attended John Ross College in Richards Bay.
After studying Human Resource Management he took a
job in the medical industry.

He has been a lifesaver, a surfer and a rugby player. His life
changed dramatically when he made the decision to ride
around Africa on his bicycle and made a commitment to do
something entirely extraordinary with his life.

On his return he became an author and a motivational
speaker and his book *Around Africa on my Bicycle* continues
to enjoy huge success.

In August 2008, Riaan set out to become the first person
to kayak, alone and unaided, around the world's fourth
largest island Madagascar. He hopes to complete his
journey around June 2009.

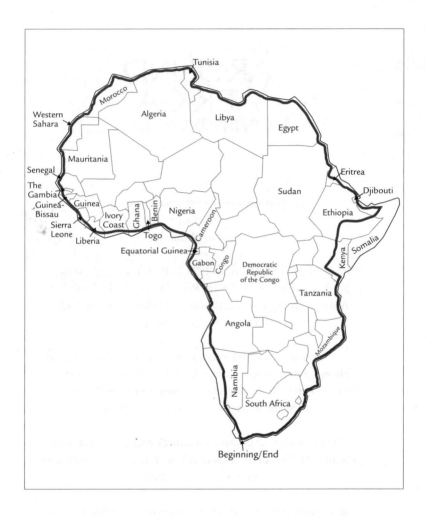

# AROUND AFRICA
## ON MY BICYCLE

**Riaan Manser**

*To Kathy*

*enjoy Africa!*

JONATHAN BALL PUBLISHERS
Johannesburg & Cape Town

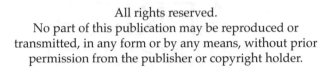

© Riaan Manser, 2007
©Photographs – the bulk of the photographs are from the
author's private collection.
The rest are acknowledged in the caption for each picture.

First published in trade paperback in 2007
by Jonathan Ball Publishers (Pty) Ltd

Reprinted twice in 2007
Reprinted three times in 2008

This new paperback edition published in 2009 by
JONATHAN BALL PUBLISHERS (PTY) LTD
P O Box 33977
Jeppestown
2043

ISBN  978 1 86842 351 4

Reprinted once in 2010

Edited by Willem Steenkamp and Frances Perryer
Cover design and reproduction by
MR Design, Cape Town
Typesetting by Triple M Design & Advertising,
Johannesburg
Set in ITC Legacy Serif
Printed and bound by CTP Printers Cape Town
ISO 12647 compliant

# CONTENTS

# FOREWORD

Do you ever dream of giving up the rat race and doing something completely different? Most people do at some time or other, but almost none ever get down to it. There's always a reason to put off the dream, isn't there? Too busy, too poor, too lazy. For most people, me included, it's really a case of being too scared. That's why for the majority these fantasies remain daydreams rather than fulfilled ambitions or even attempted ones. Then we get old and regret the fact that we never went for it. 'When I get old I'll wear purple.' Remember the message in that book?

Occasionally we learn of people who decide not to die wondering. These are the minority who actually undertake the adventures, the ones who go for it. Some feel resentment towards these adventurers. Why is that? Maybe it's a manifestation of underlying jealousy. That's wrong. We should embrace these stars and celebrate the spirit of adventure winning through. In fact, through them we can in a way fulfil our own fantasies. We can employ imagination and travel with them.

We heard about Riaan Manser as he set out on his epic bike ride around Africa. We spoke to him early and learned of his ambitious plans. It was cool but just another interview on 702. After a few weeks I was amazed at all the e-mails and sms's we were getting asking about his progress. We called again. He painted vivid word pictures and gave us observations that were fascinating and unusual. He was objective but a wonderful optimism shone through, even at the worst of times. Once again people pestered us for more. We listened and decided to regularly hook up and, in a way, adopt his odyssey. It was one of the best decisions we made. You see, through Riaan many of us have now cycled from the Cape around the entire continent of Africa and back again.

Now it's time to put even more flesh on the bones. His book, as promised, has arrived. His achievement is spectacular and a tribute to all people who above all fear being ordinary.

*John Robbie*
2007

\*   \*   \*

The great African explorers were the superstars of their time. They captured the imagination of people tied to their quotidian labours and inward concerns by economic necessity and limitations on travel. Now technology has enabled the masses to know more than ever before about what is out there and where it is. But it's a superficial, two-dimensional knowledge that still requires latter-day explorers and adventurers like Riaan Manser to breathe life into it.

The Capetonian who took two years of his life to circumnavigate his continent might never achieve the acclaim of Livingstone or Stanley. His name should nonetheless be added to that distinguished roll of seekers who have enabled us better to understand our continent. Happily this roll remains open to additions. Even as this book is published, Kingsley Holgate's team is driving around the continent, their vehicles retracing many of Riaan's pedal strokes. Billy Benchley and Christine Henchie are riding horses down the length of Africa.

Very few of us understand what drives an explorer. The old adage goes that someone who asks how much a Maserati costs can't afford it. In the same way, those who question what drives the explorer to put it all on the line simply do not get it.

The best way of getting to know our continent is with a small bag on the shoulder and an unjaundiced eye. Riaan adapts this by carefully distributing his basic requirements for survival and travel about a bicycle. More importantly he demonstrates the imperative for equal measures of grit and humour. And he shows how important it is to maintain the critical balance of these.

Inveterately a glass-half-full man, he has a modesty and earthiness underpinned by stubbornness and dogged determination. Often he tries in vain to find redeeming features in people who on the face of it do not merit such sympathetic understanding. He sees the best in situations when most people tell him to expect the worst. He encounters the most lamentable when he has every reason to anticipate much better.

Great explorers are perforce not fazed by hazards and fears that might deter the ordinary. Riaan's phlegmatic approach transcends the ages. The perils he survives are not dissimilar to those that might have faced his predecessors in hobnailed boots and pith helmets. These included possible death by kudu, spaced-out Liberian rebels, dehydration and feral dogs. Unlike the explorers of yore who headed out with a file of porters, performed their deeds of derring-do and wrote about them afterwards – suitably bathed, shaved and fed – from the comfort of their studies, Riaan is forced to work with more immediacy. En route, he uses a palm top, e-mail and mobile phones to deliver regular newspaper columns and interviews with radio and television.

I spent an interesting weekend speaking to common acquaintances mentioned in his book as benefactors. Without exception they were even more fulsome in their praise of his qualities than he was about their generosity. He seems genuinely surprised that people should show him kindness and largesse when it is clear that all they wanted to do was to be part of his magnificent adventure.

Riaan shows an admirable set of priorities. Dalliances with roundball games occur for diplomatic reasons. His passion for the altogether more seemly game of rugby makes him keep pace with the fortunes of his provincial and national teams in the most unlikely places throughout the two-year epic.

The book is a mélange as varied, tasty and often frightening as the range of cuisine he experienced. It is bright, entertaining and insightful travel writing about a continent that sorely needs a good press. It is also motivational stuff for aspirant explorers and people seeking purpose and direction through testing themselves to the limit – and, of course, it is an informative instruction book on cycling and athleticism.

We can never have enough books examining our continent – particularly by Africans themselves. Equally we can never tire of illustrations of the triumph of the human spirit – particularly by a compatriot who makes us very, very proud South Africans.

*Jean-Jacques Cornish*
2007

# CHAPTER 1

# SUNDAY DREAD – MONDAY LIES IN WAIT

*What must it have been like for the explorers of old to get on a ship and sail into nowhere? The thought of leaving everything you are familiar with and heading for places you know nothing about is nearly inconceivable to most people. I think that in most cases they simply relied on the boat floating and the wind blowing, and took things as they came. I kept telling myself that I was in a way more favourable position because I knew — sort of — where I was going.*

It all started with a dream, and dreams are powerful things that can come true, no matter how unlikely they might seem to some people. But it was not easily brought to fruition, and between the first dreaming and the eventual return a great many things happened to tell you about. I had much to learn when I set out from Cape Town, and I learnt all of it the hard way, which is actually the only way.

Why did I do it? Well, it started with a moment of revelation in Newlands Forest outside Cape Town. My girlfriend, Vasti, and I were in the habit of taking our dogs and meeting up there on Sundays with a few close friends, then going for a long walk among the trees and streams of the picture-perfect forest. I am sure anyone seeing us would have taken us at face value, a bunch of young people enjoying themselves in blissful unconcern about the week that lay ahead. If so, it would have been a misreading of what really lay in our minds. Most people I know dread a Sunday because it means that Monday lies in wait, with five days of toil ahead before the liberation of 'TGIF' (Thank Goodness It's Friday).

I was one of them then, and I was about to burst out of the safe but confining straitjacket of the five-day week; I just didn't realise it till we stopped on the bank of a stream and slumped down to rest while the energetic dogs enjoyed a cool-down in the cold mountain water. Sitting on a large boulder, I drifted into thought while my friends chatted. Although I started by admiring the beauty of the scenery and my good luck in having such friends, quite suddenly I was surprised to find I was bluntly asking myself how happy I really was at this stage of my life. No hippy thoughts here, mind you – just whether I was having a life that I would one day be able to look back on and consider a good one. That was one unspoken and unbidden question. The other was whether I was looking forward to going to work next day.

I was dismayed to discover that I couldn't answer 'yes' to either question. All I could say for sure was that I had every prospect of earning more money. I had worked for the same national primary health-care company for five years, first as an employed manager and then later as an independent consultant, selling their 'product' instead of managing it. The money was good and was likely to get even better. But I was not happier than I had been five years ago, just wealthier. And that is when, as I sat on that boulder with my companions' voices echoing faintly in my ears as though they were far away, I faced up to the crunch questions. Did I want to change this feeling of empty inevitability? Yes! When did I want to do so? Soon! And that was when the decisive moment dawned.

If you make a decision now, it's up to nobody else but yourself, I thought. You cannot lie to yourself or postpone things. If you take this decision now, Riaan, it will mean that you have to start acting NOW. Your life will have to change, NOW. Not later, NOW! All this was silent, of course, because it was going on strictly inside my head, but I could feel the movement of every cell in my body, I could feel each one of them being converted to thinking this way. I could feel that my life was about to change.

I was already on to the next question: WHAT? What was I going to do to deliver on this radical change in my life-commitment? Simple, I thought, something that my future family and I can look back to one day with huge pride. Something that will make history, that in turn will inspire others to change their lives.

But of course it wasn't that simple. Having accepted that vision, I had to turn it into reality, into something do-able.

It would have to have something to do with travel. I had always wanted to travel, even as a child, and see exotic places. One of my childhood heroes was Indiana Jones with his whips, temples of doom and lost arks – this scary stuff had instilled a thirst for adventure in me. So next day I bought a world atlas and started studying each corner of our globe for places unventured to. I told no one about this first step on that journey of a thousand leagues that the old Chinese saying talks about: that would come when the time was ripe and I had something substantial to present. So for the moment it was strictly between myself, my new atlas and the tingling feeling that suffused my mind and body, waiting for a bush to start burning or a lightning-bolt to strike.

It took a while, because I wanted to go everywhere. But as time passed and I scratched through my atlas I realised that I kept coming back to Africa. On the face of it this was the worst possible choice, because Africa was in even more of a mess than usual. Media reports were full of things like the truly savage wars in Liberia and Sierra Leone, Jonas Savimbi's assassination in Angola, the conflict between Ethiopia and Eritrea, the genocidal slaughter in the Great Lakes region. The war in Iraq was unfolding, with all that that implied regarding ripple-effect religious extremism in the North African Maghreb countries. Somalia had no government and seemed to be totally committed to its long process of self-destruction. The killing business was so overwhelming that poverty, famine and disease were way down on the list of calamities, even though malaria alone was wiping out more people every day than HIV/Aids. Even less highlighted were the efforts of President Thabo Mbeki to launch his brainchild, the New Partnership for African Development, or NEPAD, which he had been pushing since his days as Nelson Mandela's deputy.

So Africa seemed to be poised for another century of degrada-

3

tion, death and dishonesty. And that was my first choice?

But I had come to have a very different view of that sprawling chunk of earth, and every time I thought about it I became more convinced that my adventure could only take place in Africa. The final decision came one morning as I sat at my kitchen table, my third large cup of coffee in one hand, poring over a page in my atlas which showed the contours of the continent in detail, a great stretch of orangey, desert sandy shade which was almost tangible.

I sat there, virtually staring the page into submission. I wanted to do something great for Africa and in Africa, something no other person had ever attempted. I wanted to make history. And then, as if by magic, the way forward opened up. Would it be possible to circumnavigate this continent as the old-time sailors had circumnavigated the globe, travelling through each of its coastal countries till, eventually, I was back where I had started? In principle, yes.

Then the next question: how would I do it? By boat, or on foot? Well, neither. Sailing was old news, walking would take too long.

And then: OK, I'll go by bicycle!

I took a couple more sips of coffee. They tasted odd, and I realised that I wasn't thirsty any more, or even hungry. At the same time I was thrumming with sudden energy. Things had to start happening – right away! I called my work colleague, Bernard, and told him I would be very late that day. He said OK, completely ignorant of the pot of adrenalin bubbling away at the other end of the line.

The first thing to be dealt with did not involve dramatic physical action: I had to satisfy myself as to whether anyone else had circumnavigated Africa on land as I intended to do. This entailed spending days on the Internet, riding the Google search engine till it was swaybacked – if someone had pipped me at the post I would surely find a reference to it somewhere!

To my joy and indubitably selfish relief I found nothing. There were accounts of cycling the well-beaten Cape-to-Cairo route and many references to a venturesome girl who had walked from Cape Town to Tunisia. But it looked as if I had a clear run for my world-first essay into the unknown.

It might be hard to believe – and later many of those who heard my story were frankly incredulous – but it never occurred to me to check all 33 countries in detail to see if they were passable by road (in fact they weren't, as I subsequently discovered, to my cost). But even if I had known that right away it would have made no difference. For better or worse, my main character traits are tenacity and optimism. I take no credit for this – it simply happens to be the way I am hard-wired (which is just as well, because anybody who tackles Africa on a bicycle needs both these qualities in abundance).

Plotting the route would just provide a guideline. Essentially the 36 000 km trip, as I saw it, would take me from one large coastal village or town to the next, through each of the countries touching the sea. The first major segment of the journey would end with the left turn into Nigeria, the second at Africa's westernmost point, Dakar. I expected the western side of Africa was going to be the most daunting because of the wars and language and road problems, and I wanted to get them out of the way while my spirits were still high … and while the bicycle was still new and in good shape. Once I had emerged from the 21 countries of western Africa and arrived at Tunis, the northernmost point, I would head eastwards along the northern shoreline of the continent till I got to Egypt, and – my motivating vision from day one – the pyramids at Cairo! The Horn of Africa would mark the fifth segment, arriving at the South African border the sixth, and home to Cape Town the seventh. With a decent estimate of distance I could work out roughly how long the journey would take me. My original guesstimate was about a year, and I grandly christened my scheme the Africa365 Project.

It was soon to become clear that this estimate had been very, very ambitious … but that was exactly what the project needed: unlimited ambition. Though this realisation should have come as a dash of cold water I was getting more excited about the whole thing with every passing moment.

When I plunged into the nitty-gritty of the project I found that I would need every scrap of self-generated excitement. There were three main problem areas: visas, money and sponsors.

The mere thought of applying to almost three dozen different countries for transit visas came close to extinguishing my enthusiasm. Some of them did not even have representatives in South Africa, and I was pretty sure that even those which did have would not necessarily greet my approaches with outstretched arms.

I turned out to be dead right about that. I made innumerable and seemingly endless telephone calls to what felt like – and probably was – more than half of the African diplomatic corps in South Africa, explaining my grand idea, then followed up each call with faxes, deliveries and e-mails. I had never in my life regurgitated one story so frequently and so fervently.

The response was a deafening silence from one and all. So I followed up on each application individually. This elicited various responses, but still with zero results. Some embassies simply told me that my application had been refused. Others said that I would have to have proof of official business which had been sanctioned by the South African government. The most favoured grounds for rejection, however, were that the application was incomplete because I had not given specific dates for my entry and departure. In the end I had to face the facts: I had wasted one whole month of my life. No one had understood what I wanted to do and so no one had been listening to me. After all those endless telephone calls I was now addicted to throat lozenges without having one visa to show for it.

In my chagrin I could imagine my quest becoming a topic of conversation at embassy parties: 'Did you hear about that white boy who wants to cycle around the continent? Ha ha ha ha ... Let's have another drink on that! Ha ha ha ha! Cheers!'

Right. Lesson number one had been learnt. I had more chance of scooping all the water out of the Atlantic with a teaspoon than of getting visas through the official channels. So I decided on a simpler but more drastic approach. I would simply head northwards. Getting into Namibia would not be a problem, because South African citizens are issued visas at the border. So I would cross over, and when I reached Windhoek I would see about getting further visas along the route.

This sorry episode provided a graphic illustration of the difficulty I was going to have convincing anyone besides myself that the journey was possible.

Then there was the question of money. There were two components to my financial calculations. The first was travelling expenses, including expenditure on visas, accommodation, repairs to my equipment and so on. The second was the cost of the bicycle and various bits of camping and other equipment.

A daily budget of US$15 for food and accommodation seemed reasonable considering my intention was to sleep in a tent as often as possible. This came to $5 500 for the 365 days (I was still working on my original time-line at this stage). Visas per country were budgeted at an average of $150 each, which included possible contingency expenses for such things as accommodation and food in case of any issuing delays. In total this would cost about another $5 000 for the 33 countries through which I would pass.

I also had to make provision for keeping the home fires burning while I was away in the wilds. Vasti would move into my house and make sure my futon, photo albums, cat and two dogs were all there when I returned, but there were insurance policies, personal accounts and staff to be paid regularly while I was abroad, all of which would come to roughly $1 600 per month, or about $19 000 for the year. When I had finished making my sums the grand total of my estimated expenditure came to $31 500; at the exchange rate of that time this equalled about R236 000. Needless to say, this did not take into account the considerable loss of income for the year I would be away and the year leading up to my departure.

As far as I could determine, my personal savings would see me through to the end, or at least to near the end. But the decision to use them for the trip was a painful one. I had been putting money away for my own piece of land, the foundation of a good marriage and a secure family environment. I had set my heart on a lovely piece of mountainside in Gordon's Bay. It had vast views of False Bay, with the towns of Fish Hoek and Muizenberg visible on the far side on clear days; Table Mountain in winter was an awesome partner to the setting sun in the magical ritual of every day's end.

I had lived with this dream for so long that in my head I carried around detailed mental blueprints for a small cottage of logs and rocks, with an outside deck for good weather and a fireplace for the cold times of the year. But the blueprints had been drawn by my mental pen before the idea of the great adventure had come into my life. Now they would have to be filed away for the time being.

I also knew that there were likely to be a number of slips betwixt cup and lip, so contingency plans were going to be the order of the day, especially when it came to money. Given the number and variety of possible contingencies, I decided the only reasonable approach was to get a considerable way with what I had, by which time it would not take much to persuade one or other company to assist me for the remainder of the journey. People would be more impressed with physical results than mere verbal commitment and expressed intentions. I sincerely believed that, and I was right ... partly.

I calculated that I needed about $1 500 for the bicycle and camping equipment, plus another $500 for probable bicycle repair costs. My tactic here was to approach various sports and outdoors equipment companies for sponsorships; I was convinced that these companies would be keen to supply the necessary – after all, if I completed my trip and made it back in one piece they would have been part of a historic event and would have proof of just how good their equipment was. Considering my modest needs it was not a bad deal, I thought.

Wrong again. For example, about six months before my planned departure date I contacted a Johannesburg-based bicycle company; they seemed interested, and I flew up there at my own expense to see them. My request was nothing earth-shaking – all I wanted was one of their standard bicycles (if that was what they wanted to advertise) and all the spares I would require en route – and they confirmed that they were definitely interested, promising to get back to me before the end of the month.

Well, three months later I was in Johannesburg again, this time to see people from the Palm company, and while I was there I followed up on the bicycle people. They were still adamant that they wanted to be involved, but I needed a clear commitment, so I asked them when I could collect the bike and accessories. They said they would let me know within a week. Almost three years later I am still awaiting their call (perhaps they believe in the scriptural injunction about a day being as a thousand years).

Two months before my planned departure I gave them up as a bad job and went out to see if I could get a suitable bike locally, even if it meant buying one – which I was hesitant about doing, because although I had some spare cash, things were tight and getting tighter. Soon I found myself in the offices of a Cape Town-based bicycle supplier, literally begging the guy in charge for help and explaining how a $150 investment on his part would result in worthwhile returns, since people would know that his product was the only bicycle in the world to have conquered Africa.

It worked, after a fashion. I eventually paid $400 (R2 800) for a bike with computer and helmet that would usually retail for double that amount. Although I would have appreciated more, I was highly relieved and grateful, yet also slightly humiliated. I had prostrated myself in the dust for a couple of thousand rands. Somehow it didn't feel worth it. I could see so clearly what I was putting into this, what I was risking and what the opportunities were. But other people couldn't. Like beauty, opportunity is also in the eye of the beholder.

I got good vibes, though, from a company called Trappers Trading, whose people were keen to help me with the camping and survival kit I would need. I walked out of there with a treasure trove, all supplied at no cost and without hesitation: a two-man tent, sleeping mat, sleeping bag, paraffin stove, aluminium paraffin canister, Leatherman WAVE survival knife, carbon fire-lighting stick, 45-litre backpack, headlight, waterproof torch, three pairs of thick woollen socks, two pairs of tough adventure trousers (the ones with the removable legs), balaclava, medical kit and 200 water-purifying tablets. I almost laid in a fancy catapult as well, in case I had to shoot myself some dinner along the way.

All this sounds like a lot of kit, and it certainly amounted to quite a weight for one who wanted – and needed – to travel light. But not one item was a luxury. I expected I would have to really rough it; I would enjoy luxuries on the road if and when they presented themselves. Past experience had taught me that the smallest thing could lift my spirits when the going got tough, and I knew it would be the same this time. Besides, I was the guy who hoped to do 36 000 km on a bicycle, so the lighter the better.

One area in which I did not stint myself was medical supplies. I needed as comprehensive a first-aid kit as I could organise, and would also have to make provision for hospital care in case this became necessary – which meant money and communications.

For the health maintenance and repair side I consulted the experts at the Travel Clinic in Cape Town. For a start they recommended that I get re-inoculated for everything from hepatitis to polio, very sound advice in an area where the continent-wide collapse of health services has given the old pestilences a new lease of life, so that Capetonians embarking on nothing more adventurous than a weekend in the Kruger National Park now routinely take anti-malaria precautions after decades of free to-and-fro movement. They then stocked me up almost to paramedic level with everything I would conceivably need. This included prophylactic tablets for malaria, to be taken weekly (these tablets are notorious for side-effects such as nightmares, headaches and other flu-type symptoms, but the alternative was far worse, so I didn't complain).

By the time they were done my now-bulging medical kit contained waterproof sticking plasters (singles and rolls); one-inch and two-inch bandages; gauze squares; Steri-Strip; pre-packed wound dressings (good for burns); elasticised tube gauze; vials of Mercurochrome; antiseptic; Betadine gel; plenty of gloves; alcohol swabs; syringes; needles; a drip needle; a suture kit; scissors; tweezers; a CPR mouth valve; Persivate lotion; ophthalmic lotion; re-hydrating powder; aspirin and paracetamol; Diclofenac; Co-Trimoxazole; Metoclopramide; Metronidazole; Hyoscine Butylbromide; Chlorpheniramine; penicillin; an aggressive antibiotic; a five-day immediate anti-malarial treatment course; five malaria test kits; glucose lozenges; and a space blanket. They even gave me a laminated card inscribed with personal details such as my blood type.

Now for the money and communication aspect. In a health scenario which needed more than my well-stocked medical kit my chances of survival would obviously be enhanced by speedy hospital treatment, but I reckoned that without some serious cash in reserve for just such an eventuality I would have little chance of even getting so much as a pat on the back. So I put aside $1 000 to leave at home as an emergency medical reserve, and set about acquiring a satellite telephone for use primarily in times of absolute emergency (which naturally, as any idiot would realise, would also include calls to my Vasti).

Actually acquiring the satphone turned into another forlorn-hope mission. I sent out the usual begging letters, in which I explained as clearly as possible what I planned to do, and Telkom evinced signs of interest. I dug into my ever-shallower pocket and flew to Johannesburg to see the responsible person, which I reckoned would also be proof of my commitment. It was rather fun checking out the different satphone types and even testing them; I had a mental image of myself in a dense jungle, down on one knee, trying to make contact in true 'Shipwrecked' or 'Survivor' style.

But once again things fizzled out, with promises which turned out to be as empty as I anticipated my pocket would soon be. Sorry, Riaan, I told myself, you're going to have to rely on the old trusty street map for direction and the local radio stations for chitchat. I was also beginning to accept that I could not take everything I wanted with me. Space and weight were the obvious limiting factors, but I realised now that the personal safety aspect had to be considered as well. The more I had to show off to the baddies, the more popular I – or rather my possessions – would be with them. Considering the numerous pockets of lawlessness I would be traversing, I might well end up losing more than just my goodies.

I had another stroke of good fortune. Ideally I should have had a support team, with one crew back home and one following me along the route. That was out of the question, but a good friend of mine named Mark – who, incidentally, is a stand-up comedian, which some people might say is an apt profession for someone mixed up in as crazy an enterprise as this one – introduced me to a small but energetic IT and marketing company. Initially the company wanted simply to host the trip's website, but after some subsequent meetings approached me about managing the entire project from start to finish. This was a wonderful offer, because it would relieve me of one of my major burdens.

Probably the most difficult part of the preparation was breaking the news to Vasti. It had been easy enough to explain to her the adventure concept and my interest in it, but the task of conveying the actual level of commitment I had made required a daunting amount of cold guts.

The first time I mentioned the journey to her she nodded and frowned simultaneously, then muttered: 'That sounds interesting,' before changing the subject to a considerably more immediate matter; I remember that moment very vividly because it took place at the same spot in the Newlands Forest where I had originally decided that the circumnavigation of Africa was going to be my goal.

Telling her the full story required much more effort. Disappointing or upsetting her was the last thing I wanted. To me, the not-so-perfect boyfriend, she was everything I could rely on. Everything I cared for and considered secure was essentially centred on her. The fact that she was extremely beautiful and sexy had some relevance, of course, but it went far beyond that.

Without the luxury of a traditional family support base, I relied on my friends to fill the gap. I knew that while they might be worried about the dangers involved they would generally be extremely positive, among other things because the trip would make me more interesting. But Vasti was a different matter. She was my life, but what I planned to do was certainly not the traditional route into a successful relationship. The stakes on this wager were becoming uncomfortably high.

My trip would also mean a long separation from my two thoroughbred Boxers, Murphy and Jester, and my amazing cat, Jumangi. I reckoned they would deal relatively well with the separation as long as the meals were warm and always on time, but it was going to be tough on me. I had a very close relationship with them, because in my heart I believe that my animals have had a part in moulding me into a better man. That was why my pets had a right to sleep on my bed with me and always had at least the offer of a seat at the dinner table, and why I considered it bizarrely abnormal not to have lengthy conversations with them.

Eventually I bit the bullet and got Vasti and the pets together one evening when the mood was right, and then I let it all hang out, sparing no detail. No one was overly stressed, although I think some debate did hover around who would now sit in my seat while watching TV. Even so, I did take too much for granted, as I was to discover to my shame.

As time went by and I became more and more immersed in my preparations, I found myself mentally digging ever deeper towards the core of my motivation. Was my achievement only going to be about the physical? Was I going to achieve anything for a cause greater than my own? I didn't want to have people to think of me only as the guy who raised money for something. I wanted to be known as an adventurer whose ability to do something good for humanity would be compounded according to his exposure and success. At the same time I think my negative side was whispering into my subconscious, reminding me that I might suffer ignominious failure. I didn't want a big hoo-ha about one specific cause, and then to find my quest didn't work out: better that the whole thing should be just about me and my personal quest. Perhaps I was simply making sure that I would only have to deal with the disappointment of one person – myself.

I am a firm supporter of the 'African Renaissance' concept and I wanted to have a link with something that promoted South Africa's excellence and simultaneously the potential dormant in Africa's jungles and deserts. This is why the 'Proudly South African' campaign was so important to me. It was promoting what all of Africa should be doing naturally. We need to promote our excellence in our own industries and in so doing cultivate loyalty to our own economy. With economic freedom and growth will come education, the key to our continent's problems. My philosophy is simple.

A child who has a choice will not choose the wrong answer when he has been given a decent education. How do you choose when you have no alternatives? 'Proudly South African' reinforces the foundation of our country's success.

What must it have been like for the explorers of old to get on a ship and sail into nowhere? The thought of leaving *everything* you are familiar with and heading for places you know nothing about is nearly inconceivable to most people. I think that in most cases they simply relied on the boat floating and the wind blowing, and took things as they came. I kept telling myself that I was in a way more favourable position because I knew – sort of – where I was going.

In the meantime I had to promote my journey in some way. Thanks to the guys at the IT company I would have a functioning website, but it would be more useful during my trip than before it, and so I took every opportunity for a radio or newspaper interview that would point people in the direction of the website where, I hoped, they would follow each episode as it unfolded. It was not as though I had website sponsors to please, so if I made the right moves I would have supporters who were interested in my effort for exactly what it was – a young guy with a huge dream and the enthusiasm to match.

I was convinced that one-on-one interaction was going to be the only way to draw people into my project, to get them hooked on following my travels and travails, and thus more inclined to tell others and persuade them to check out the website. I didn't want to go to the length of setting up a roadside stall, then hailing passing cars and pedestrians. Instead I contacted the public relations people at various shopping malls and set up appointments to see them. My idea was to have a stand inside each mall, with my tent, camping gear and bicycle set out as I imagined they would be during the journey; while an assistant handed out pamphlets, I would explain what I had planned for the next year of my life.

I chose four major regions – Pretoria, Johannesburg, Durban and Cape Town – as the focus areas, hitting two or three malls in each. Trappers Trading loaned me some extra kit for the stands and local cycle stores in each region let me have the use of a bicycle or two. What really gave the stands an air of professionalism, however, was the huge banners, measuring three metres by two metres, sponsored by USS Graphics in Cape Town. Each banner consisted of a large satellite image of the continent of Africa, together with a blow-up of my ID picture and the website's address. The best word for these banners is 'inspirational': for once I could stand back and actually show people what I was planning to do, and what and where I intended going with only a bicycle.

I never tired of looking at those banners, imagining where I would be and when I would return home, and each time I got the same rush of feeling that had launched me into the project in the first place. Wow! I was going to accomplish something great with my life – I was actually going to pedal my way all around the edges of this huge continent instead of just thinking about it and eating my heart out in frustration.

Eventually I had commitments from the Menlyn, Rosebank, Eastgate, Westgate and Fourway shopping malls in Gauteng, and in Durban the Pavillion, Sanlam Centre in Pinetown and Westville malls bought into my ideas. Now I was ready to hit the show-business trail.

All these preparations had been paid for out of my own pocket, and I decided to approach a few companies with a view to getting them to sponsor some of the major expenses, especially transport and accommodation. I telephoned all the major hotel groups; most said that they would get back to me after they had considered my request. Once again I found it odd that at least some of them did not leap at the chance of being associated with such an amazing project when it landed in their laps. I understood the concept that talking was one thing, and doing it was something else again, but my counter-argument was that supporting a person who has done something remarkable is much more expensive than backing someone who plans to do it.

Having said that, a shining exception was the Protea Hotel group. The group marketing manager was so taken with the originality of my project that he showed immediate enthusiasm and did not hesitate to offer me assistance. As a result I was provided with accommodation in the various cities while I was on tour. That solved the sleeping problem. The transport problem fell away when the Avis car-hire people were kind – or bold – enough to provide me with the necessary wheels.

The road shows were simultaneously exciting and daunting. I had to go and share with people face to face and publicly. My starting point was Gauteng, where I hit three malls in rapid succession. All were busy, with crowds streaming past until 10 pm at Menlyn Centre in Pretoria. Many of the people were interested in my journey and my ideas, while most would chat for a few minutes and then wish me lots of luck before leaving. Not all, though. Some people thought I was raising money and waved me away as I approached to give them a brochure. But I laughed off the occasional rude rebuff; such miserable people damaged themselves and those who had to live around them, not me. I was amazed at how they stood out like sore thumbs among the thousands who passed my stand, positively radiating negativity, and I remember thinking that I didn't want to be like them – regardless of what they might have had in terms of material wealth, I wanted to be on the other side of the equation as a human being! I became even more convinced that there had to be more to my life than just decades of hitting the nine-to-five circuit.

The highlight of the Gauteng road show was a friendly chat I had with a very senior citizen in one of the malls. He waxed lyrical about his youth and its associated dreams and ideas, and added that in the late 1950s he and a friend had planned to do exactly what I now proposed, almost half a century later. Lucky for me that they had not gone through with it! This pleasant encounter provided me with some new food for thought about the reactions of the various age groups. Young people would come up to me and show amazement at the fact that I was willing to leave everything behind and risk my life for something that they did not consider important. Older people, on the other hand, were envious and keen to share their 40-year-old dreams with me. So you had one generation that knew what it had missed and regretted it, and another that was trying its best to find excuses to miss it.

Durban was next on the list, and here, too, things went smoothly. By this stage of the game I had wised up and recruited two assistants, each manning one table while I handled the third. Warren and Christopher did me proud. They understood what I had set out to accomplish and were determined to do their best to get my story across to every stranger they confronted, handing out pamphlets and chatting so enthusiastically to passers-by that they put me to shame.

I remember Warren's technique. He would say: 'See that guy? He's going to cycle around the whole of Africa with this bicycle in one year.' He would then pause, gauge the response to this forthright approach and wade right in with the rest of his spiel if it looked as if he had hooked a fish. The people loved him – but, more importantly, they wanted to know how they could follow me on the journey.

Only the Cape Town leg was a disappointment. I could not get exact dates from the shopping malls, and by this time my departure was a week away, which meant I had to focus my attentions on more important things. So in my home city not one banner or one tent was put up in honour of my upcoming adventure.

By this time my mind was racing 24 hours a day as I grew more and more tense, an astronaut counting down to launch date. I found myself trying to analyse my feelings and isolate the main ingredients.

Fear? Well, yes and no. I knew I was planning to go through some undeniably lethal parts of Africa, and only a fool is fearless. I didn't know how brave I was, but I was willing to face the unknown dangers that lay ahead.

Dread at the inevitability of my departure? That wasn't it either. I knew that at 6 am on Tuesday, 9 September 2003, I would be cycling out of the Waterfront in Cape Town and heading up the west coast of Africa. I would have a good bicycle to ride, I was strong and healthy, I had some money, I had a tent to sleep in and food to eat, I had people who cared for me. Most of all, I would be setting out on an adventure for which I had been preparing for a long time and which was very important to me.

I concluded that 'anxious' would be the best description of what I was feeling. I was impatient to get going; every remaining day at home was another delay before I got back, having made my little bit of history. More planning, more thinking, more preparation would not improve my chances of achieving my goal; what I didn't know by now I would surely learn along the way.

My closest friends arranged a farewell dinner for me on the Saturday night before my departure, a small but festive affair which gave each of them a final opportunity to confirm whether I knew what I was doing. It felt rather odd, sitting there at the dinner table, constantly reminding myself that this dinner was being held for a guy who was planning to circumnavigate the most dangerous continent on earth on a bicycle ... me.

My friends said a few good things to me. None went as far as saying what at least some of them thought, and might never have had the opportunity of saying again. Instead there was concern mingled with admiration. More than one said something like: 'If anyone on this earth is going to complete something like this, it will be you' – my good friend Shane (marketing genius Warren's brother) actually said while toasting me that he would not worry too much because he definitely expected me back, and advised the others to do the same – and I knew he was sincere in what he said.

At the end of the day, the fact is that you need the support of friends and family if you plan to achieve anything of real significance in your life. At times we all do things that sound or look odd to some people. I suspected that some of those around the table didn't quite agree with the Africa365 project, but because of their friendship with me they had put their doubts aside and come out in full support.

As we went home that evening I thought: four more sleeps and I'm gone. I was filled with a mixture of exhilaration and disbelief.

Vasti was at law school at that stage, attending half-day classes at the University of Cape Town, and thanks to minimum attendance requirements she could only take off the Monday, the day before my departure. We spent a truly awesome couple of days, compounded of sadness and joy and excitement ... and last-minute preparation scrambles when she discovered that in the general rush I had neglected to finalise a few small but important things. These included buying my pannier bags, fetching my trail clothing from First Ascent, testing out the bicycle with its full load and, most importantly of all, giving her signing powers on my bank account. Then we found some other small things I had not got around to doing. As any good South African would say: *Sjoe!*

We did some quick prioritising and put aside acquisition of the less important items, which Vasti would bring with her when she and some of my friends met me along the way on my birthday, a few days away. Then we concentrated on the things that I was going to need from the word go.

At Vasti's suggestion I baptised the tent by erecting it in the garden, after which we occupied it during a night of pouring rain and howling winds. Part of Vasti's precious free Monday was spent on going to Cape Town and buying a set of panniers and matching side carry-bags. They looked a bit fragile and were very expensive; since my juices were really flowing by now, I decided to tell the shop-owner what I was about to do and see if I could wheedle a discount out of him. He found my story interesting but not the question of a discount. Oh, well, win a few, lose a few.

I still had to find a carry-bag for the top of the pannier that could also double as a day bag, and we set out on this task as soon as we had been to the bank to sort out the various financial issues. We trekked all around Cape Town but failed to find anything that even remotely resembled what we wanted. We were getting pretty desperate by the time we landed up at the V & A Waterfront and found a shop with a bag that was ideal size-wise but just the reverse money-wise. I consulted the shop-owner about the possibility of getting a sponsor for the bag. This didn't work, but he got a good laugh out of the situation. Later I realised why: here was someone who planned to cycle 36 000 km around an entire continent, and less than 12 hours before his departure was still short of a crucially important item.

We returned home to find our neighbours milling about in front of our house, apparently bent on a sort of early send-off. They were very supportive and the males among them were quite proud of me. One of them, Robin, a veteran of the Rhodesian bush war, proved to be a source of much practical advice; one piece that particularly struck me was that I give underpants the skip – they served no real purpose, he said, and ventilation would be hugely improved. Robin's wife, Hazel, went one better by promising to look after Vasti in my absence, which I really appreciated.

With this farewell out of the way, we visited some other friends who lived close by, my friend Mark's mother, Gwen, and his father, Gary. This was a very practical goodbye visit because it involved all sorts of last-minute preparations. Gwen patiently hand-sewed my sponsors' logos on to my shirts while Gary and I were trying to find a way of mounting the rear panniers, since my bicycle did not have mountings for the pannier rack. This meant we had to be creative – and when you eventually manage to pull a lot of things together using only cable ties, *that's* being creative. Time and distance would tell how well our essay into unconventional creativity would last, but we reckoned it was sufficient unto the day.

To my discredit I had not taken full cognisance of the strain the project had placed on my relationship with Vasti. She had been hugely positive in every respect since I had broken the news to her nearly a year earlier, and had never expressed any doubts or demurrals. But I should have been aware that inevitably tensions would build up that would need to be dissipated. In my selfish preoccupation I had done nothing in this regard, and that final night the storm broke. She started to cry in the middle of a discussion relating to some packing problem, catching me totally by surprise. Was I doing all this just as a stratagem to get away from her and break up our relationship? Feeling both guilty and relieved, I explained slowly and with every atom of sincerity in me that this was *not* the case, that I was doing it for totally the opposite reason, that she was in my future for keeps, and that the trip was actually part of reaching that future. After a while we were back on the same wave-length, but it saddened me immensely to realise how humans can misunderstand one another, even those who share their lives.

A fair amount of the blame lay at my door. I am always full of ideas of one kind or another, some a bit crazy and others not, and it turned out that when I had first told her of my decision she had gone along with it, believing that it would be played with for a while and then forgotten, like so many other schemes – bright or otherwise – that I was always coming up with. It was only considerably later that she realised I had not been fooling that day in Newlands Forest.

Laughingly she reminded me of another bright (maybe) idea of mine which had gone nowhere. At the time we had known one another for only a few weeks. We were travelling back to her house in Stellenbosch one midwinter's day when I decided to air my latest idea. It was extremely cold and most people had wood fires going in their houses to keep warm, often going through several bags of firewood a day. Now, you could see people alongside the roads all day long, either buying or selling wood, so there was definitely a market for my idea, which was to get together a number of clients to whom I would regularly deliver enough firewood for their needs.

Vasti's car was old and fairly noisy, but I explained this whole scheme in some detail. She listened very carefully and smiled periodically, although I could see a rather strange look on her face, and, when I asked her what she thought of it, she replied that she thought it would definitely work. That was good enough for me, although I was still puzzled about those strange looks.

I didn't find out till a couple of months later, by which time the firewood scheme had been pushed into obscurity by something more interesting, that due to the car noise Vasti had understood me to be talking about *fireworks*, rather than firewood. She could not have been blamed for considering me completely psycho, with my plan to go from house to house and convince people to buy a certain number of bags of fireworks each month. What made it worse was that in elaborating on the basic concept I had pointed out that winter would be better for business as people could use my product to warm up their houses, and that I personally knew people who used five to six bags in just one night. We could get advertising slogans on the bags to subsidise costs, I happily burbled on – Blitz Fire Lighters might be interested – and with any sort of luck my scheme would soon spread from the Cape right across the country.

Well, could I be surprised at her apparent readiness to believe that I really meant to cycle all around Africa?

What was definitely a bit psycho was that the bike was only properly packed and loaded on that very last night. But that's how it was, and my one and only test run consisted of cycling a few kilometres around the neighbourhood at two o'clock in the morning, about five hours before my departure. Everything worked all right, but for the record, this is not the way to set off on a circumnavigation of Africa or anywhere else.

But there it was. We left the bike groaning under the weight of its load – a weight which would soon be increased by myself – and crawled off to bed for a couple of hours' exhausted sleep. Tomorrow and destiny awaited.

# CHAPTER 2

# I'M OFF ...
# UP THE CAPE WEST COAST!

*I was beginning to accumulate a detailed record of my jour-*
*ney, writing a daily report on my Palm handheld computer. No*
*scribbling with a leaky pen or blunt pencil for me! All I had to*
*do was flip open my full-sized keyboard, clip the handheld into*
*it and start typing away – easy as falling off a log. So it was no*
*sweat to note down every day's adventures and mishaps, de-*
*scriptions of people, the smells of places, the taste of the food I*
*ate ...*

We woke up exhausted after two and a half hours' sleep and packed
my gear into the car in pitch darkness, because we had to be at the
V&A Waterfront in Cape Town, a 45-minute drive, by 6 am. This
took some doing, since the car was not large and my overloaded bicycle distinctly bulky. Around us our neighbours still slept, but the
guinea-fowl were starting to chatter in the trees above and the dogs
were excitedly sniffing everything that was going into the car, no
doubt convinced that we and they were going somewhere.

Saying goodbye to Murphy, Jester and Jumangi was a very hard
part of my departure. I would miss them dreadfully and the worst
was that I would not be able to tell them that I was coming back. I
would just disappear from their lives, leaving a gaping void that was
beyond their understanding. And if worst came to worst they and
I might never be reunited – the thought kept intruding, no matter
how hard I tried to block it off.

Trying to put the pain of parting behind me, I climbed into my brand-new trail clothes and gelled my hair for the last time, and then with a final greeting to my pets jumped into the car. I did not look back at them as we left, as I normally would have done, but I made them a silent promise: I'll be back. Vasti and I knew that we would meet again on my birthday in five days' time, and we kept falling back on that whenever the conversation veered over to how much we would miss each other.

Of the trip through the darkened streets of Cape Town I recall only a vague maelstrom of a million thoughts. The dense mist was rising gently off the ground and the sea as we arrived at my jumping-off point, the clock tower at the V&A Waterfront, near the new Nelson Mandela Gateway, which was where my journey would end as well. I committed the scene to memory, because for many months to come it would be my lodestone. There I greeted my friends as they emerged from the mist, among them Colin and his cameraman, who were going to follow and capture the start of my journey on film.

Colin was enthusiastic in spite of the ungodly hour, and this helped to put me at ease. After so many months of ever-increasing responsibility, it felt good to be able to shrug off part of the burden and just focus on myself and the fact of my trip. I felt immensely grateful to him and all the others for coming to show me their support. I wanted to tell them all this, let them know that I considered them part of the entire historic journey, but I don't think I succeeded: I just could not express my feelings adequately.

Colin interviewed me for a few minutes on-camera while we waited for some late arrivals. Among them should have been the CEO of Proudly South African and an SABC-TV crew, but it seemed that the allure of a warm bed and duvet had held them hostage. Once upon a time their non-appearance would have left me with a feeling of deep disappointment, but now I felt none of that. In the past year my values had altered so much that I was more than content to have with me the people who really mattered in my life.

The interview over, it was finally time to go. I checked, re-checked and re-adjusted every buckle and cable, lifting the bicycle a few times to confirm the weight I was planning to carry for 36 000 km.

It felt very, very heavy; it was almost impossible to lift it with one arm, and a committed dead-lift stance was needed to get the rear wheel an inch off the ground. This didn't concern me too much. My operating philosophy was 'each kilometre, each day', namely, doing what was necessary to see me through each leg of the journey. As long as the bike was moving in the right direction, whether speedily or slowly, I would be on the way to successfully completing the trip. To this end I had decided that when I finally started pedalling I would not stop till I had left the city, no matter the temptation: the first 5 km had to set the tone for me mentally.

I finished hugging and shaking hands twice over with all present, then tied on my helmet, a strange feeling of unreality gripping me. Was I really here, straddling my bike on the threshold of a trip around Africa? Yes, I told myself, you are. This is the great challenge, and without challenge there can be no achievement. There is no turning back now. I took a final mental snapshot of Vasti and my loyal friends standing next to the clock tower in the cold dawn light, with Table Mountain peering down on us through a veil of low-lying cloud. Then I stood on the pedals, nudged the handlebars to put me into a slow 90-degree turn and set off, followed by Colin and his cameraman on their motorbike. Soon the others were out of sight, and I forced my mind into strictly functional mode.

My most immediate task was to get my mental attitude right. I wanted my mind to be prepared for any possibility, because what I feared most was mental vulnerability. Most tangible things can easily be repaired and most problems solved, but any battle is lost or won in the mind. So I gave myself a short, sharp, very intense pep talk. The time for theorising was past. This was the real thing. The journey had begun, and I was going to plug through to the end, no excuses permitted!

Later on many people asked me if I could remember the specific moment when I realised what I had got myself into – presumably early on in the trip. But it didn't happen that way. At no time did I ever tell myself 'this is it' and really understand for the first time what that meant. It was always real to me; the dividing line was between my visualisation of what lay ahead and the moment when visualisation was no longer necessary, because I had actually set off, and nothing lay ahead except the moment when I would cross the 'finish line'.

During the first 30 km out of Cape Town I attracted plenty of friendly attention from motorists heading to their work as I slogged along with Colin and his cameramen alongside. The commuters hooted and waved as they passed us. I doubt if most of them knew who I was or where I was going; mostly, I think, they just knew that here was a bloke setting off for some obviously distant destination, and somehow it lifted their hearts as they headed in for another eight hours of the same old routine.

I fed off their enthusiasm, using it to create and reinforce permanent positive thoughts for use along the way when I hit rough spots, for when I would feel downhearted, for when there would be no smiling faces, no cold water and no warm food. And, probably most powerful of all, was the mental image of myself returning one whole year later, with throngs of people waving and smiling as I rolled proudly up to the very spot from which I had started. These fabricated pictures warmed and motivated me more than anything I could tell myself; the vigour with which I looked forward to the finish was so strong that sometimes I would actually speed up for a few kilometres without realising it.

My game-plan for the first few days was to get a feel of what energy I could exert continuously over a particular space of time – not hours per day, therefore, but rather the number of days in the week.

Having parted company with Colin, I made it to Malmesbury on that first day and turned in for the night at a bed-and-breakfast, exhausted and a little anxious, my last thought before I conked out being how my overworked body would feel next morning. I was all in – and I had covered a mere 75 kilometres! There was no doubt that I could carry on, but I was not at all sure about what pace I would be able to maintain over a long period. Essentially I needed confirmation from my body for my mental calculations.

The second day did not start auspiciously, because the route out of Malmesbury consisted of a seemingly endless succession of long rises, and the weight I was carrying on my bicycle made them seem even longer … did I say 'seem'? It didn't help that on top of everything else I was carrying about eight litres of water, an extra burden I did not begrudge because getting stuck would be OK as long as I had something to drink. I remain convinced that it was the right approach, but damn, that water was heavy.

My second day's destination was the small mountainside town of Piketberg. Piketberg was only 70 km from Malmesbury, but it felt more like 100 km, and I swear that if an enthusiastic young cyclist named Johan had not joined me for the last 20 of them I would never have made it before sunset. That red-headed 16-year-old didn't realise it, but he saw me through a tough time. And it was only the second day of the trip! It was a disturbing thought.

I booked in at the immaculate old Piketberg Hotel, worked my way through a big plate of home-cooked food whose flavour I remember to this day, then massaged as much Deep Heat as possible into my thighs, which were providing plenty of confirmation about what I could expect while engaged on my self-imposed task. Then I crawled into bed and, as they say in detective novels, after that I remember nothing.

The following morning I had breakfast with the proprietors and the other guests. Some had seen Colin's footage of my departure on the TV news, or heard one of the live radio interviews I did in the first few days, all the interviewers asking questions I was still asking myself, things like 'Why are you doing this?' I had no difficulty fielding the questions, but I knew that my actions were going to speak much louder than words. They were going to have to. Anyone can share their ideas and, dare I say, their macho bravado, but not many can or do deliver.

One middle-aged couple, I remember, were very complimentary of my intentions and, I sensed, envious of what I had tackled (they had done some touring of their own in their younger days, although not by bicycle). I told them that I thought I possessed some ability to communicate with animals. I didn't really believe this, but thought about it whenever I passed a flock of grazing sheep. I had perfected some of their bleats and would loudly greet the flock in passing; they would always turn and face me, and some would even interrupt their snacking to talk back to me. Cows were a bit snootier and would respond only when it suited them, while with ostriches you were lucky if you got a cold appraisal from one bulging eye.

I thought of something else as I sat there, working my way through the ample breakfast. Before my departure, most of those who had understood what my journey was about had emphasised that I was going to meet many new and interesting people, and it certainly had been an accurate prediction so far. After only two days on the road I had already been introduced to more new acquaintances than I would have met in a normal month at home.

The third day – from Piketberg to the Pikeniers Kloof Hotel – I had designated as an easy day. I had my birthday coming up in two days and Vasti and my friends were planning to join me at Clanwilliam, so I decided I need not rush myself but rather try to understand what my bicycle and I were comfortably capable of. Physically I felt good, though tired, but I wanted to be sure I knew how to pace myself. At this stage, I believed, there would not be much to report as regards the bike, because it was new and so far had been going very well.

This last was not quite how it turned out. Midway I suffered the first of what would be many punctures on my trip. I repaired it, feeling very satisfied with the result, but I knew I had a more serious problem, because the tube was being punctured by internally protruding spokes and these would have to be attended to in the near future. But sufficient unto the moment. I reached the foot of Piekeniers Pass and then tackled the climb with renewed vigour and showers of sweat. The pass was my first real test: although it was only a few kilometres long it was steep in most places. I would not be looking to break any records; it was more important to work out the best way of tackling such situations in the future. The heavier your bike, the harder the struggle, and the advice of veteran cyclists, reinforced by my own limited experience, was that in spite of popular belief to the contrary you actually exert more power staying in the saddle than standing on the pedals. So what I did for this entire uphill stint was to stay seated and not stop once, not even for water.

It worked, but I suffered as I battled upwards, loudly telling myself that it had to end sometime, and that when I got to the top I would have a pleasure of a long downhill coast. I finally reached the top around midday, muscles screaming to high heaven and as dry as a piece of Kalahari biltong. I made serious inroads into my water supply, then decided that I deserved a treat and stopped at a small roadside farm stall to buy a 1.5-litre bottle of cold Stoney ginger beer. By the time I was full the ginger beer was looking pretty feeble and I had a belly like a 44-gallon drum.

While I rehydrated on the ginger beer I chatted with some people who said they had seen me on TV, and they told me something very interesting. Earlier they had passed another long-distance cyclist, who was also heading north. From what they said he was about 20 km behind me, so I decided to wait a bit and see if he caught up. Then, perhaps, we could ride together. But after an hour he had not yet arrived, and since I still had to do a few more kilometres I set off again.

Now I was heading in the right direction on any mountain pass – down – and I could enjoy the scenery and indulge in reveries about things past. One of the latter concerned a spot near the top of the pass where there had been a defining moment in my relationship with Vasti. We had known one another for about a month when she agreed to pick up a friend at the town of Klawer and asked me if I would go along, since she didn't feel like undertaking the 350 km round trip alone and at night.

For me it was like a holiday: Vasti drove while I ogled her, made conversation and fed her with bits and pieces from our collection of snacks. Everything went pleasantly till we got over the summit of the pass and saw that a large thatched building near the road, part of a hotel and farm-stall complex, had been engulfed by a huge fire, the resulting clouds of thick smoke billowing over the road in such profusion that passing traffic was at a standstill. Fortunately we hadn't yet driven into the centre of the smoke, and I persuaded Vasti to turn around so we could go and offer assistance.

We drove to the main entrance, where we could already feel the heat of the flames leaping up from the building. I watched the giant flames for a couple of seconds while collecting my thoughts, then went into action. I started by moving three cars that were almost encircled by flames and then focused my attention on the evacuation of people and their belongings from the burning building, which was the hotel guests' breakfast area with an attached kitchen and some staff accommodation. Soon I had the staff organised into a bucket chain, throwing water from the swimming pool on to the thatch to try to stop the flames from leaping over on to the roof of the main residential building. By now my shirt was off and I was concentrating totally on saving the residential building.

While I was doing my Rambo stunt Vasti talked to various on-lookers, one of whom turned out to be the owner of the complex. Earlier on I'd seen this character as well, and in spite of my urgings he had seemed totally uninterested in helping to save the main building. Later I wondered why I and the others risked our necks to stop the conflagration when those with the most to lose didn't seem particularly interested. I haven't worked that one out yet.

Cycling past this place on top of the mountain evoked vivid memories of that night – and brought home to me once again the realisation of how much I would miss Vasti in the days ahead. She had been with me on that first adventure, but this vastly bigger one I would be tackling alone.

But then it was time for my first real downhill stretch, and I achieved my first 'personal best' of the trip by clocking an impressive 66 km/h; no mean feat, considering that the vehicle was a top-heavy and overloaded bike whose all-up weight was something like 50 kg – any falls would have had catastrophic consequences, particularly since I had retired my helmet by now because it was simply too hot and constricting. Now, I am all in favour of wearing a helmet – they can save your life, especially if you happen to come off while travelling at the speed I reached on the downhill part of the Piekeniers Pass – and the pictures in this book showing me without one are not to be misconstrued. But I don't have much in the way of a neck, and the straps were not as accommodating as they would have been on the graceful slopes of a typical slender cyclist's neck and chin.

The sun was beginning to set now, and there was still no sign of my phantom cyclist, who should have caught up to me by this time. As I neared the bottom of the road I had two choices: I could turn off right to the town of Citrusdal or head on, banking on the chance of finding some accommodation further along. I chose the latter option, and after a while began to question the wisdom of my decision, because the road was none too smooth and consisted of just one lane either way, which brought my inexperienced self into nerve-wracking proximity to the cars, bakkies and huge trucks plying to and from Cape Town.

But then I lucked on a backpackers' lodge lying half-hidden behind some trees right next to the road. It was a considerable relief to both my mind and my muscles. The lodge was well populated that night, among others by a group of Belgian tourists. The Belgians' tour guide, a South African girl who had no affiliation to the lodge management, gave me the rates and pointed out the beer fridge, saying: 'Fill the book in if you have a beer, and then just leave the money under the book with your camping fee before you leave.' It was refreshing to be in such an environment.

At this stage the mystery cyclist came into view, pushing his bike up the gravel driveway, the first road-friend I made on my circum-navigation of Africa: a dark-haired, slightly built guy. His Lycra tights, broad leather bike-seat and frayed, weather-beaten cap were clear evidence that, unlike me, he was an old hand at this sort of thing. He smiled when he spotted me (I assume people he had met earlier had told him about me, just as they had told me about him) and when we got close enough we shook hands.

He was another Belgian, named Frank Decoumbrey, and he had been on the roads of the world for three years now. So far he had covered 30 000 km and traversed four continents. He had cycled through Afghanistan, and crossed the USA from east to west – nearly dying of heat and thirst in the notorious Death Valley – and was aiming to reach Tanzania in time to fly home for Christmas. He had had enough now, and he wanted to see his family again.

Eagerly I absorbed his stories as we ate our supper, which consisted of canned fish on some bread he dug out of a side-pannier. It was not the traditional sliced item South Africans are used to, but Belgian-style bread balls that were surprisingly fresh in spite of being several days old. Between us we ate every scrap. Isn't it lovely how good even the simplest food tastes when you're really hungry? By the time we had finished I had decided that he was a real hero. At first glance he was a gentle character who did not seem to be the type of man who could survive really tough conditions in places so unlike his own gentler-natured country. But he was, and had – one of those naturally resolute people whose appearance belies the sheer cold guts inside.

We rounded off our repast with a couple of beers and then gave the warped table-tennis table a test run. Here I had the upper hand, and Frank graciously conceded defeat, although he made it clear that I would have to work hard for any advantage when we hit the road next day: he knew he was a strong cyclist and couldn't wait to show me. Next morning we were up before the sun, quickly breakfasted on bananas and a couple more bread balls, then packed our tents and were on our way. Our first destination would be Clanwilliam, where Frank would have a pit stop and I would have repairs carried out on the snapping spokes of my rear wheel before meeting Vasti.

I learnt some valuable lessons from Frank during the 50 km ride to Clanwilliam. He was very powerful for such a slightly built guy, and would fly up the long hills – I had been averaging between 18 and 19 km/h for the first few days, but now it was well over 24 km/h – and I noticed that he continually varied his sitting and standing positions, the point being, as he told me, to be comfortable at all times. Another handy tip was to maintain as much momentum as possible when going uphill, because it was always transferred into the ensuing downhill rides ... simple stuff to take on board, but not always easy to follow! Frank also lubricated all the little things on my bike and showed me some tools he felt were crucial to a long journey's success, and which, needless to say, I had not even thought of bringing, partly out of ignorance and partly, I suppose, because when you have a new bike you can't even imagine having to repair it.

When we arrived at Clanwilliam, we dropped our bikes off at the bicycle shop – mine to be repaired and Frank's for safekeeping. Here I learnt something else, namely that the job always comes first. The previous evening Frank had washed his undies, but they had not had time to dry out, so right there, in full view of all the customers and staff, he spread the well-worn unmentionables over his handle-bar before we went on walkabout. I laughed and asked if he was not embarrassed about letting it all hang out, so to speak. He laughed back even louder, asking what he had to be embarrassed about. So off we went, leaving our fascinated audience behind.

Over lunch I picked his brain a little more, storing away a number of items of know-how which eventually I incorporated into my own travel routines and procedures. Then, to my regret, we had to part company. Frank had a long way to go and a tight schedule to keep up with, while I was expecting Vasti and my friends.

In due course they arrived, and we spent the day in Clanwilliam's renowned botanical gardens, the joy of our companionship un-dimmed by the fact that there had been such a severe drought that almost none of the millions of tiny flowers that normally carpet the gardens had bloomed. The midday heat was such that the icing on the chocolate cake that my friend Dorothy had baked ran like water and the candles took on a variety of strange droops and angles.

The finality of what I had undertaken finally hit home next morning when they left for Cape Town. This really was goodbye; packed up and ready, I waved a last farewell and then set off for Klawer, my next destination, the road ahead blurred by tears. Then, scarcely five minutes later, they re-appeared, because Vasti had discovered in the nick of time that she had taken my bank card and money with her. So there was a second goodbye, and I was sorry that they had found me with tears still rolling down my cheeks.

Well, the best remedy when you're feeling down is to do something that will take your mind off the subject. The long haul through the mountains north of Clanwilliam before reaching Klawer did the trick this time. That, plus the powerful winds that buffeted my tent where I pitched it outside the local truck stop. Altogether I spent an uncomfortable night. Mosquitoes – non-malarial this far south – queued to get a piece of me, and being new to the game I had taken no chances about internal security, dragging the bike halfway into the tiny tent and sleeping uneasily with a can of pepper spray clutched in one hand.

This was not exactly the ideal preparation for the next stage of my journey, 90-odd km to the railway junction at Bitterfontein, through the great undulating arid plain known as the 'Knersvlakte', or 'grinding plains'. I was now in the lower reaches of Namaqualand, so-called after the Nama clans which, along with the hunter-gatherer Bushmen or San, were its original inhabitants, and I had also crossed the provincial border into the Northern Cape. It was a different world, with a harsh beauty of its own.

It was a hard slog, but at such an early stage of my journey, when I had yet to reach the sinewy endurance developed by Frank in his wanderings, that was to be expected. What I did *not* expect was leg trouble. Up to this stage my legs had been holding up well to the stresses and strains I was imposing on them, and I had made sure they stayed that way by giving them a good massage every evening. But part of the way to Bitterfontein I developed a truly excruciating ligament pain in my left knee. I tried to ignore it and battle on, but that simply didn't work, and I covered the last 30 km pedalling only with my right leg. That night, having pitched my tent in the lee of a farmer's tractor, I knew that I stood before two choices, neither of which I fancied very much. One, I could rest a while and then try to go on. Two, I could carry on in one-legged style till my painful knee recovered or my sound leg gave in as well. A third alternative, to pack up and go home, was not even in the running. There was nothing to be done till next morning, however, so I took an anti-inflammatory tablet and went to sleep.

When I woke up I found that overnight the problem had more or less solved itself. The knee was so much better that I packed up and carried on to Springbok. Somewhat to my surprise I did so well as I threaded my way northwards past the long Kamiesberg mountain range that I logged my first 100-plus day – 128 km, to be precise.

I met some interesting people in Springbok. One of them was Jopie Kotze, proprietor of the Springbok Lodge, who put me up for free when he heard my story. That, so I was given to understand, was pretty typical of Jopie Kotze. He is a force to be reckoned with in those parts – at the local tourist office they said he was 'Mr Springbok', and added that he was reputed to own half the town.

Mr Kotze was plainly intrigued by me and my mode of travel, which differed quite radically from those of the hordes of tourists to whom he has played host over the years. A sly humourist, like many Namaqualanders, he came up with a number of deadpan jokes at my expense – mainly to entertain his guests, I think – and gave me lots of good advice, not always comforting in nature. Among other things he told me that after I crossed the border I would deserve a medal if I made it to my first Namibian destination, Grünau, because even the powerful beer trucks had problems when climbing to 1 200 metres above sea-level.

I took note of all this but was not disheartened, and concentrated on getting the bicycle serviced and replacing the front wheelrim, which was slightly out of shape. While I was engaged in this I was happy to meet up with two other northward-bound cyclists, a boyfriend/girlfriend team who were heading for Zambia and positively oozed a contagious spirit of adventure. They were also noticeably more paranoid than I was (despite the pepper spray) about the security of their bikes. In my opinion an unfair focus by the media on what was, after all, a worldwide problem had created this exaggerated fear of theirs, and I would have liked to clear up some of their misconceptions, but there simply wasn't time to get into lengthy discussions because I had so many other things to do. One of them was to get rid of non-essentials. Shedding even a kilo or two can make an amazing difference to a heavily laden long-distance cyclist, and I had realised that I was carrying too much clothing. The tourist office kindly offered to arrange for the return of my extras to Cape Town.

By now I was beginning to accumulate a detailed record of my journey, writing a daily report on my Palm handheld computer.

No scribbling with a leaky pen or blunt pencil for me! All I had to do was flip open my full-sized keyboard, clip the handheld into it and start typing away – easy as falling off a log. So it was no sweat to note down every day's adventures and mishaps, descriptions of people, the smells of places, the taste of the food I ate, the daily distance covered, the names of towns, villages and hamlets, the places where I laid my weary body at night (believe it or not, I did not plan on documenting my journey in book form; all I wanted was to have the proof of where I had been and what I had encountered). My greatest lack was that I did not have a camera, because the promises of support from the camera companies I had approached had not materialised. Colin had also had to back out unexpectedly, so I knew I would have to make a plan to overcome the lack of pictorial coverage en route; what I didn't know was how I would be able to do it without inflicting serious harm on my none-too-generous budget.

By now I was beginning to fall into a natural rhythm. The winds, the cyclist's arch-enemy, were not too bad in those early weeks, and the almost orchestrated variation between flat and hilly terrain was a perfect training ground, so that I was growing confident in my cycling ability. My body was learning to accommodate the physical exertion and adapting without any serious injuries, and I had managed in excess of 100 km in one day, in spite of the semi-crocked knee.

I was also getting used to my new type of accommodation. Camping was always an option, but if something better came up, I was willing to negotiate around a price of up to R25, the equivalent of about five US dollars, and in the days ahead I soon lost any feeling of embarrassment about asking for a discount. If I got one I splashed out on food. I was now well on the way to a staple diet of bread and sardines or other tinned fish, with some bully beef or whatever might be thrown in if I had made a saving on accommodation.

From Springbok I headed to the Steinkopf mission station, and from there set off for Noordoewer (literally 'North Bank'), the border crossing over the Orange River. It was all of 70 km, but it took me just two and a half hours, meaning I had achieved an average speed of just under 30 km/h. This was a sure sign of how I had toughened up in just a few days. I also had a strong motivation. I simply had to reach Noordoewer by lunchtime on the Saturday, because the Currie Cup rugby championships were in full swing, and there would be a whole afternoon of exciting rugby to watch on television. So I had to arrive well in time to seek out a suitable TV venue.

It seemed, though, that my prospects of an afternoon's sporting bliss were not going to be achieved, because I soon discovered that the only television set in Noordoewer capable of picking up a satellite signal was in the campsite bar, which meant that most of the locals would be gathering there to watch the regular weekly Namibian soccer broadcast. So I did one of the bravest things of my life, given that southern Africans are not people to be trifled with when they are deprived of their Saturday sport. I stuck around in that bar, sipping on my beer and making sure everyone knew that I was here specifically for the rugby. At first this was OK, but as the soccer kick-off neared people started streaming in, and they began to get tense about my hogging the TV set.

I didn't budge, however, and kept my eyes and attention firmly focused on the screen, ignoring as best I could the increasingly aggressive remarks coming from behind me. Eventually the barman, who was growing nervous, apprised me of the situation. I replied firmly that I was a client of his establishment and I reckoned I had preference when it came to watching TV … unless, of course, the other people present were also staying there. The barman caved in and I went on watching the rugby. This did not go down really well with the increasingly agitated crowd. But I stuck to my guns and my beer, right to the end. That game was by far the tensest one I have ever sat through. But I'm not talking about the actual rugby match, which we won easily enough.

Having escaped with a whole skin, I asked the manager for news of Frank. He said Frank had stayed there two nights earlier, taking the luxury indoor option (by our stripped-down standards) because he had not been feeling well. I was disappointed, but I reckoned that if I averaged 100 km a day and he took one day's rest along the way I might catch up with him in Windhoek before he turned eastwards towards Caprivi.

I turned in that night with a peculiar sense of satisfaction. The border crossing had done me some spiritual good because it had finally wrenched me out of my basic South African comfort zone. From now on I would really have to fend for myself.

CHAPTER 3

# OVER THE FIRST DOTTED LINE:
# NAMIBIA

*Notes on my Palm handheld: Pedalling up long and dusty roads through kudu country. It's been hot! The heat has been my sole welcome to Namibia as I pedal away into her flat and barren landscape. I had imagined what it would feel like to visit so many countries. As a kid I had a couple of odd beliefs. Such as the idea that the sky in London would be a different colour to ours. Also that they did not have bright colours but rather that everything was a shade of grey, just like in the olden-day movies. Would I be breathing different air, I wondered?*

It took me eight tough days to ride the 800 km or so between Noord-oewer and Windhoek, a persistent headwind my constant companion. The toughest of them was the 150 km stretch from the Orange River to the town of Grünau. I left Noordoewer a bit late, approximately 10 am, and so wasted the valuable cooler morning hours. My previous night's commitment to only stop when I had reached Grünau remained intact, but it was not easy to hold on to. It was hot, hot, hot, the road always looked as if I was going slightly upwards and the headwind was constantly picking up steam.

The ride to Grünau didn't provide much in the way of scenery, because the view in all directions was exactly like the previous day's when I was still on South African soil, heading for Springbok. When you cross a border you imagine it's going to look different on the other side, which it hardly ever does in terms of topography, and this was the case here as well. The road ran as straight as an arrow, and a permanent mirage of sweltering heat waves scrambled the images of even the big beer trucks that passed me on their way south. No doubt Jopie Kotze in Springbok would have suggested I was seeing that mirage because I had been sampling too much of what these big trucks were carrying!

I covered the distance in eight and a half hours of continuous effort, my only time off the bike being five minutes or so to rest and eat a hasty three-course meal of sorts, consisting of biscuits, liquorice allsorts and Super C's. Then I rolled up to the Grünau campsite, knocked out by my efforts but full of self-congratulation at having reached my first target, even though the total distance I had covered so far was minuscule, compared with what still lay ahead.

I celebrated by going into discount mode and persuading the manager to waive the normal R30 fee, although I then rather ruined this little financial triumph by going into the bar and spending more than that on food and soft drinks. Having pacified the inner man, I turned in and slept like a log. Next morning early I was on my way again.

I made good time in the next few days. The road was great, the only hindrance being the wind, which blew continuously from the front and slowed me down as I pedalled through the wide, flat plains. But I was experiencing too many sensations of sight and sound to let this dishearten me, and the huge trucks that thundered close past gave me a little boost of wind every time they overtook me. Any seasoned cyclist will tell you that this is not actually a desirable scenario, but in my naivety I rejoiced innocently about this dangerous help. I also discovered another of life's smaller secrets while pedalling along those endless kilometres of die-straight road: there were only two kinds of motorists in the world – those who waved at me and those who didn't.

I soon fell into a night-time camping routine. My mental list of non-negotiable priorities included no-go areas regarding my health and that of my bike – eat well and don't be too brave with local food, because if the bike's 'engine' (namely myself) was not working properly the trip would be going nowhere, and make immediate repairs if something went wrong with the bike, so that a small problem didn't turn into a big one. But my main concern was security, and finding a good spot to pitch camp without an audience was always the focus of the last hour of cycling every day. A foreigner on a bicycle is an obvious target for criminals anywhere in Africa. So if I was near a town I would put in the extra effort to get there that night, and if I was in view of people or had been noticed by passers-by I would either change my intended campsite or boldly go and pitch my tent right next to the onlookers' houses.

I soon discovered, however, that human beings did not necessarily pose the greatest threat to my safety: Namibia being the equivalent of one big game park, my roadside resting-places resulted in a close encounter with the local wildlife which I could have done without. I had decided to bed down for the night next to one of the many concrete flood-channels under the highway to the north, and wedged myself, the tent and the bike in between two thick thorn trees, watched by some huge kudu bulls silhouetted against the setting sun. Those thick thorn trees surely saved my life that night, when the kudu, panicked by something or other, came stampeding through my campsite. It was terrifying: imagine being abruptly woken from your sleep by a herd of huge antelope which looked even more gigantic when viewed from near-ground level through the tent's peephole. Lions, elephants and hyenas – they were supposed to be the real danger to me, not what I had assumed were Bambi-style grazers. But suddenly one was coming straight at me, and there was nothing Disney-like about him.

Fortunately my feet were facing the area that was being trampled, and not my head. I got up – although this didn't mean much, since I had to squat hunched over because the roof of the tent was so low – and stood ready with the little canister of Mace spray which was all I had by way of protection, while my heart pumped away at about 200 beats per minute. I was painfully aware of the fact that this was more to reassure myself that I was ready for anything than an actual defence plan, and it felt as if the canister was getting smaller with every passing second. It didn't take much imagination, as I tried to peer through the tent's ventilation gaps, to generate a mental image of a half-naked me vainly squirting pepper spray into the face of a rampaging 400 kg beast in well-nigh pitch darkness.

Well, it didn't happen and the kudus went about their business; I settled down again, thinking what a great story a near-fatal encounter would have made, but all the same I was glad I would not have to tell it.

In due course I arrived at the town of Rehoboth, 96 km south of Windhoek. A warm rain was making the road slippery as I emerged from the surrounding mountains, and I celebrated my arrival in grand style by coming off my bicycle, which provided considerable entertainment for the various local inhabitants who were hanging around outside the roadside bottle stores and cafés. It was my first noteworthy fall since leaving Cape Town, and it forced me to come to terms with two more new realities: firstly that I was going to fall a lot more in the coming months, and secondly that I would have to learn to live with the audiences that such unscheduled acquaintances with the ground automatically attracted.

Having survived the fall without much damage to anything except my dignity, I booked in at the campsite belonging to Rehoboth's main attraction, the hot springs, then watched some rugby and made new acquaintances. I spent an entertaining evening – perhaps 'entertaining' isn't quite descriptive enough – eating at a sports pub with a local man, his wife and her sister. They were a boisterous, amusing trio who drew humour from everything, and what made them even more interesting was that I could sense a tension of unknown origin underlying the merriment.

That strange undercurrent finally manifested itself in three separate incidents. The first took place before we had even eaten anything. The husband had crossed the room to chat up another woman; the wife took exception to this and threw her chair at him. The chair fell well short and landed on the heads of some younger people who, I suspect, had come to the pub looking for a bit of excitement – although not of this exact kind, I'm sure – and while they were sorting themselves out the husband and wife had a grappling match. This seemed to clear away any confusion or misunderstandings between them, because after a couple of minutes, once the hair-curlers and tracksuits had been straightened out, we were all viewing our menus in anticipation of ordering food like any other big happy family.

My hosts ordered a plate of mixed bar snacks that included samoosas, sausages and chips, and insisted that I help myself when it arrived (which I did with reasonable restraint, if I say so myself). Before the food arrived, however, the evening's second bit of excitement launched itself when a black man who had been sitting at the bar on his own came over to our table to introduce himself. He said his name was Saul and explained that he was a regular at the pub.

Thinking the conversation was over, I picked up my conversation with my hosts, but Saul not only stuck around but actually ordered a beer on my tab. When he had finished the bottle he ordered another, also on my tab, at which I explained to him that I couldn't afford to pay for his afternoon's entertainment. Saul accepted this but seemed very disappointed. But when the platter with its load of great-smelling food arrived he cheered up and started to help himself with a lavish hand, probably believing me to be the sponsor of the meal. This was a big mistake on his part, because the wife's sister promptly took drastic action. Saul's hand was just leaving the plate with a piece of sausage pinched between his fingers when she stabbed at it with her steak knife. Fortunately for all concerned she missed and buried the knife's point in the table-top, at which stage the husband and wife grabbed her before she could try an encore.

Saul was shocked and loudly questioned her actions. She, in turn, made her feelings very clear about his uninvited attention to our food and drink. Saul replied that he had thought we were all one group, and that I was his friend – the implication being that I had invited him to join in. Up to then I had minded my own business as if unaware of the entire fracas – the rugby game had been exciting, but not half as adrenalin-laden as this! – but the fence-sitting was obviously past now, and with the correct amount of tact I made it known how well I actually knew Saul.

I had hoped that this would end the scene, because I wanted the spotlight off me as soon as possible. Instead there followed a political argument which was directed specifically at Saul. The thrust of it was that Saul, being an Ovambo (the largest ethnic group in Namibia) expected everything for nothing and got it because the president, Sam Nujoma, was also an Ovambo. Although Saul was in the wrong I felt sorry for him, and realised for the first time how easy it was for an argument to end up focused on a person's race, culture or religion instead of the actual issue. South Africans are relatively advanced when it comes to considering others' differences and being sensitive to them, but plainly this approach was not as fully developed elsewhere. This afternoon was turning out to be an unforgettable one, all right, albeit for the wrong reasons.

Then, to round off the evening, the sister – a very large woman with enormous breasts – decided to make a move on me. Having manoeuvred herself into a position where she had me in a corner, she set about persuading me to let her spend the night with me in my tent. Quite apart from the fact that there was no way on earth that both of us would have fitted into the little tent, I had absolutely no desire to get involved with her. Since it was impossible to advance either of these arguments without giving serious offence, I explained that I intended to get my head down as soon as possible because I intended to leave Rehoboth very early next day.

This didn't slow her down at all, and eventually she actually had me draw a map of where I had pitched the tent at the campsite. Obviously confident that I had now succumbed to her charms – I had mentioned Vasti regularly to her earlier the afternoon, but certain sectors of her memory-banks had obviously faded along with the daylight – she started whispering in my ear, telling me exactly what she had in mind, and what she would let me do to her.

I was deeply stirred by all this, but with fear rather than desire, because I was petrified about what would ensue once she understood that I was not interested in a one-night stand. In the meantime I kept telling her that it would be nice, but that my back was hurting and I was suffering from uncontrollable cramps. To my dismay I realised that these protestations were having only a temporary effect, and heaven knows what might have transpired if her newly reconciled sister and brother-in-law hadn't decided that they all needed to go home immediately. I parted company with them, deeply grateful for this unexpected rescue, and spent the rest of the night giving my very tired body a blissful rest.

Next morning I was up early (I hadn't been lying about that), spent a soothing hour lazing in the bubbling water of the warm springs and then set off for Windhoek in the mellowest frame of mind I had enjoyed since starting my solitary two-wheeled trek.

I arrived in Windhoek feeling emotionally charged at completing the first long-distance leg of my journey. My first priority was to find some cheap but reasonably secure accommodation, since I couldn't accurately forecast my departure date. I was about to tackle the thorny problem of getting a visa to enter Angola, and my earlier experiences hadn't left me with much optimism about a fast result.

The accommodation problem more or less solved itself in the pleasantest way when the people at the Windhoek tourism office arranged for me to stay free of charge in a lodge directly across from the city's showgrounds, and I turned my mind to the other things I wanted to do. I wanted to meet a few well-known Namibians like Stefan Ludick from the 'Big Brother Africa' TV show and the Namibian rugby team, and I needed to make contact with the Namibian Broadcasting Corporation to stir up some PR coverage. So I pumped up my persistence quotient and got going, trusting to the intervention of good fortune along the way. And intervene it did, thanks partly to the friendliness and helpfulness of many Windhoekers who went out of their way to help me. (Some people might not understand why I wanted to meet a BB housemate, but I had sound reasons. I wanted to meet people outside the norm, because I believe that everyone has something worth passing on to other people – getting to know Stefan would be a good start to the process.)

Getting the visa proved as difficult as I had anticipated. By now I had amended the route through Angola that I had planned in Cape Town with the help of my atlas, because I had been advised that it would be far wiser to head north by way of the port city of Benguela rather than simply pumping it up the main road which led to the capital of Luanda. But that was the easy part. Actually securing a visa for Angola plunged me into a bureaucratic nightmare of the first order. I had to return to Pretoria, the Angolan staffers told me – not once but repeatedly – and apply for the visa there. My pleas and explanations fell on deaf ears. Pretoria first, and that was that. Since there was no question of doing this, I decided to camp outside their front door, as it were, till I managed to break them down to the point where they would give me what I wanted, if only to get rid of me. I didn't actually put up my tent outside the embassy, but that was how it must have appeared to the embassy staffers when they arrived for work every morning and found me wrapped in a blanket, waiting for them at the front door.

My strategy was of the most elementary kind. Sooner or later the ambassador (I didn't even know who he was) would have to use the front entrance, and when he did he would have to step over or around me to get inside. Then I'd take the gap and do some fast talking, flourishing my main weapons, supportive letters from the South African embassy and the Proudly South African Campaign. It would only be a matter of time, I stoutly believed, before the right people inside the Angolan embassy would connect their South African colleagues' letter with the homeless guy sitting on their front steps!

My free accommodation was a great help here, but even so I had very little financial elbow-room – which is why I heard opportunity knocking loudly on the door when the Namibian Broadcasting Corporation people asked if I could cycle to their studios with my bicycle for an interview, one of several I was to do for them. Needless to say, I answered 'yes' and in due course I set off for my appointment with fame and (I hoped) assistance in pursuing my mad quest. This turned out to be more easily said than done, since I couldn't find the studios in spite of having been given comprehensive directions. Eventually I called them on my cell phone, and this did the trick. Could I see the Namibian Brewery towers from where I was calling (the towers are such distinctive landmarks that I suspect the Windhoekers use them as general reference points, the way we Capetonians do with Table Mountain)? Yes, I certainly could. Well, then, that was the direction I should go in, and we'd meet there.

A few minutes later I was strolling into the brewery's reception area. The TV people had obviously sent word that I was on the way, because I was immediately made to feel comfortable while I waited for the camera crew. Then the good fortune for which I was hoping so fervently dropped from the sky. After I had been there for a couple of minutes a man walked past, glanced back at me, then turned and asked if I was 'the cyclist'. My traveller's persona wasn't firmly in place yet, and with a degree of confusion I owned up to possessing a bicycle, but felt constrained to add that 'whether I'm "the cyclist", I don't know'.

It turned out I was, or at least I was the cyclist he was looking for. He introduced himself as Dixon Norval, the brewery's marketing director, said he had heard me on the radio and thought what I was doing was commendable. Would I mind him seeing my bicycle? Well, of course I had absolutely no objection and I showed him my bike, telling him a few stories in the process. This obviously flicked some switches in his market-orientated brain, because he asked: 'What can we do for you? Can we give you a couple of cases of beer or cool drink?'

I really appreciated his offer, but of course I couldn't take him up on it, for the same reason that I had turned down similar offers from other companies in South Africa: I wasn't driving a delivery truck and there was no way I could haul such heavy stuff along with me. With regret I declined, but then took my courage in both hands and added in the same breath that I did have some requirements which could only be solved by spending some money. This being the case, I went on, 'can you guys help me with some finance?'

This is usually the conclusive enthusiasm-quencher, but Dixon only paused for a moment and then said: 'Riaan, wait for me in my office, I have a couple of things to sort out, and then we can chat.' I spent a somewhat dazed 10 minutes or so in his office. Then he walked briskly in and said: 'How much do you need, and for what?'

This left me even more dazed, but when I had recovered from my surprise I told him that if Namibian Brewery would cover all my visa-related costs it should see me comfortably through to the very end of the trip. Dixon liked the idea, handed me a blue notepad and said that he had to go off again, but when he returned he would like to see a specific figure.

I did some feverish figuring after he had left. I had an approximate figure in my budget for visas, but I had not made provision for collateral expenses caused by bureaucratic delays like the one I was currently experiencing, and which I now saw would happen again further along in the journey. I calculated the likely additional visa-related expenses and came to a final figure, which I jotted down in a state of extreme nerves. Maybe it was too much, and he would turf me out empty-handed. Maybe I should ask for less, and take my chances further up the road if I came short ...

I was still fighting with myself along these lines when Dixon returned. Full of trepidation I handed him the notepad, sure now that he would show me the door with the request that I close it from the outside. Instead he studied the product of my calculations for a couple of minutes and then looked up and said: 'We'd be honoured to be involved with your efforts; this amount is fine, but it will obviously come with some conditions. Will you accept?' Damned right I would! Which is how the 'Windhoek Light' logo ended up on all my official cycling shirts.

Thanks to Dixon's unexpected mission of mercy I could now fill the most important gap in my equipment, the digital video camera I needed to record the rest of my trip, not just for posterity but also to bore my grandchildren with one day. Even better, my Angolan visa actually came through soon afterwards, and I paid for it with the first instalment of the Brewery's largesse – $80, to be precise.

In between all this I also managed to achieve my other aims. Thanks to another intervention by the patron saint of crazy cyclists, I was introduced to Stefan Ludick when he and I both happened to be at the NBC studios for radio interviews. He was an impressive chap, down to earth, sincere and extremely honest. We chatted about life in the BB house, and I certainly found out some interesting things, not only about events in the BB house but also about how he was selected for the show from the thousands of Namibian applicants. He had been called into the interview room, he said, went through the normal greetings and then nervously asked the interviewer if she would mind if he took off his pants for the interview because it helped him think more clearly. She agreed, and the rest – the boxer shorts, 'Big Brother' and a role on the top-rated soapie 'Egoli' – is history, as they say.

In turn I told Stefan about a unique taxi ride I had taken in Windhoek, during which he had been the centre of attention even though he wasn't there. He had been the main topic of conversation, and being proudly South African, I started singing *Nkosi Sikelel' iAfrika* and ended off my rendition with a little of the Namibian anthem. The driver's response was: 'You're wonderful, you're just like Stefan; you love black people!'

Stefan didn't see himself as a celebrity, in spite of being mobbed by crowds and receiving the odd marriage proposal, but he didn't let any of it go to his head, and he was well aware of the responsibility that rested on his shoulders. White people in Namibia and South Africa have to make an extra effort to win black people over to understanding how we young people really think.

I also got to meet the Namibian World Cup rugby team when the Multi-Choice pay-TV service provider invited me to a breakfast with the team on the day of their departure to Australia at which the Namibian Prime Minister was the guest of honour. It was a great experience to be with the players and absorb their positive vibe and attitude – among those who especially impressed me were the captain, Sean Furter, prop Kees Lensing and iron man Wolfie Duvenhage.

It also gave me a rare opportunity to see at first hand the unpleasant spectacle of politics being stirred into sport, an effort as futile as trying to mix oil and water. This was in the shape of an alarming speech by the president of the Namibian Rugby Union, who peered at the players through his John Lennon glasses and gave them a distinctly aggressive talking-to that reminded me of a schoolmaster addressing a crowd of unruly pupils. One of his remarks that sticks in my mind was 'I will not warn anybody on this trip. If you as much as stick your head out of the bus, I'll send you home immediately.'

The players' reaction to gratuitous remarks like these filled me with pity. What an honour it was for Namibia to have men like these representing it, and how embarrassing it was for them to be publicly addressed like this by the head of their sporting code! Of course the need for discipline both on and off the field was a non-negotiable, but the matter should have been discussed internally and, most importantly of all, at the right time. Even the forwards – traditionally less sensitive to verbal brickbats than the other players – were offended. The Prime Minister, thankfully, had a clearer focus on the matter at hand, and his remarks were appropriate to what the occasion was actually about, namely the players and the country.

With the appearance of my visa I was finally set up and ready to go. All going well, I could be crossing the border by the following Sunday, just five days away. After that? Well, time and circumstances would tell. Local bikers had warned me that there were no bicycle shops till Luanda, but what the hell; I was fit and so was my bike, not to mention my finances. A man couldn't ask for more.

I have to admit that in spite of all this optimism I felt a little nervous as I left Windhoek behind me. I was, after all, heading for a country which 99 per cent of people would classify as distinctly dangerous, not to mention hampered by an infrastructure which had been crippled by decades of civil war and, for the most part, not repaired after peace had made its belated appearance. Of course, things would have been worse without my newly acquired visa and sponsorship, but that still left my frame of mind in a far from comfortable state.

My spirits were not lightened by my experiences as I travelled deeper into the Ovambo tribal territory. The closer I got to the border, the less friendly or helpful the people seemed to become, a great contrast to what I had experienced further south. I particularly remember the night I spent at a remote garage which was said to be owned by President Nujoma himself, which was certainly the most unpleasant I had had so far, and that included the encounter with the stampeding kudu herd.

I had put in a very long, hard stint to reach the garage, which according to my informants was the only structure for at least 100 km.

I had hoped to reach it by nightfall, but the clock got away from me, and as dusk began to fall I was still peering ahead through the gathering darkness in hopes of seeing the lonely cluster of lights that would tell me I was within reach of my destination. For the first time I felt genuine anxiety, and craved the company of fellow human beings who might have some slight interest in my well-being.

I finally reached my long-anticipated oasis, but my welcome was anything but warm when I approached some of the petrol attendants for assistance. All I got was blank stares whose message was very clear: they weren't interested in me and did not give a damn whether I lived or died. Maybe it was racial tension, which I had been warned about – and which I reckoned that, being a South African, I would be almost over-qualified to handle – or simply wariness of strangers, especially oddities like myself; maybe it was a bit of both. But whichever it was, it taught me another little lesson, namely that stereotypes are useless, because you have good, bad, friendly and unfriendly people wherever you go.

Anyway, I didn't feel safe that evening. I chained my bicycle to the only lamppost available and pitched my tent right next to it so that I could guard my scanty but precious possessions, and there I spent a distinctly uncomfortable night. The garage was the watering-hole of what appeared to be every serious beer-drinker in the vicinity, and I was awakened almost hourly by inebriated individuals stumbling over and demanding to know who I was and what I was up to. Some staggered off after I had told them, while others were abusive and told me to pack up and move somewhere else. Instead I entered into protracted gesture-filled debates with each visitor.

When I think back to it now I can't help smiling. Isn't it amazing how a person's normal approach is altered when he is tired and irritable? But hindsight is a wonderful thing. I wasn't feeling philosophical right then, because what I needed was some rest, not rambling, inconclusive debates with a stream of drunken and sometimes hostile fools. So it will not come as a surprise when I say that I was up and packed an hour before sunrise, and on my way, tired but relieved, as soon as there was enough light for me to see where I was going.

Another pretty unorthodox overnight stop was at Oshivelo, where I was allowed to pitch my tent in a back room of the local police station. My only companion was a local who had been arrested for drunkenness and spent the night lying lights out on the concrete floor with a car tyre for a pillow. The night was freezing cold, but next morning he didn't seem to have come to any harm, which says a lot for his constitution or the amount of booze he had swallowed, or maybe both.

My final Namibian stay-over was at Ondangwa, 60 km from the border and formerly home to a sprawling air force base during the 1965–1989 'border war'. The Rugby World Cup was in full swing, and I arrived in time to see South Africa take on England and Namibia tackle Australia. We lost badly to England that game, and this quenched my obsession with seeing *every* World Cup game in which South Africa was involved: I reckoned I needed all the motivation I could get, so I could do without the feeling of depression engendered by a rugby loss, especially to England.

I regretted having to by-pass the famous Etosha National Park, but I simply could not let myself go off at a tangent in any sense. My journey was not about seeing everything but rather about experiencing everything, 'everything' being defined as all that came my way, not the stuff listed in the typical tourist itinerary. That didn't leave much room for diversions; if I stopped at every place of interest, I'd probably have to break my journey at some point to receive my senior citizen's card.

# CHAPTER 4

# ANGOLA: LANDMINES AND SAMARITANS

*It took me a while to get my mind around the concept of a country where millions of active mines, just waiting for the pressure of someone's foot, were a part of everyday life. I thought back to my placid First World existence and tried to superimpose a situation where as simple a thing as walking to school, going to fetch water or just taking your girlfriend for a romantic stroll was a gamble where a wrong step could leave you dead or mangled and unemployable in a fraction of a second ... and I failed.*

Passing through the Namibian customs was a formality, although the officials did express surprise at my intention to travel through Angola armed with nothing except determination and an overloaded bicycle (I didn't say anything about my pepper spray, just in case). 'The animals will get you if the robbers don't,' one of them told me with a broad smile. I smiled back, hoping he was joking. Then I was pushing my bike through the gate.

Entering Angola was a little scary. I didn't know what to expect and could only, like everyone else, prepare to plunge into the bowels of the war-ravaged nation depicted in the South African and world media. But the Angolan immigration guys were charming and eager to have me there, and in no time I was stamped and ready to go. I wasted no time crossing the 50-metre concrete slab to the entry-gate, eager to stamp on those butterflies in my belly.

A sort of welcoming committee was waiting for me, made up of teenaged boys dressed like the rapper Tupac Shakur and, as I soon found, speaking imitation gangster-rap English which they had obviously picked up from the same source as their fashion sense. The leader of the group informed me that he and his associates would assist me while I was in Angola. I responded with a sincere 'thank you', but explained that someone was waiting for me. I am not a very accomplished liar, and so I was caught slightly unawares when one of the youths asked: 'Where is dem waitin'?'

'Er ... down there,' I said, pointing to one of the streets, although I had not the slightest idea of what sort of people it housed or where it led. The group didn't respond immediately and I headed for my 'destination' right away, hoping that they would forget about me. I wasn't actually afraid, I remember, but I was unsure of the new environment. It was crucially important to find a secure base to work from – make a real friend, find a safe place to sleep, learn some Portuguese, that sort of thing. I noticed now that Tupac Shakur's adherents had decided to follow me, and I put some more weight on the pedals so as to out-distance them. Unfortunately I had not taken note of the fact that I was about to hit thick sand, and when I did I lost control and came off with a thump. I bounced up and started dusting myself off, noticing that my following had doubled in the blink of an eye.

The fall seemed to have knocked my worried feeling away, which might have been a bit premature, but fortunately my unscheduled dive had attracted the attention of a young hotel worker, who gestured to me to come his way and then led me to a hotel entrance, well-barricaded and painted orange. It was a humble establishment which had no running water or electricity, but made up for both with an abundance of kindness. It was a good start to my venture into Angola.

Early next morning I was on the road again, arousing great interest among the stall-holders on either side, and I got another dose of unsolicited Angolan kindness when one of them took the trouble to shout: 'Wrong side ... wrong side ...' as I passed him. At first I didn't understand what he was talking about, then realised I was on the wrong side of the road! South Africa, like just about every other former British possession in the world, drives on the left side of the road, as does Namibia, which picked it up during the South African mandate, while Angola follows the European fashion.

This was no small favour on the stall-holder's part, seeing that traffic in Africa tends to be a survival exercise at the best of times. So I would just have to get out of my left-handed habit of the past 2 000 km or end up as roadkill. I waved my thanks and swung over to the right-hand lane, realising that my rear-view mirror was now on the wrong side, so that it was going to be impossible to keep an eye on vehicles coming up behind me. Oh, well, I'd just have to keep glancing back and make a point of keeping my ears open for sounds like roaring truck-engines.

Having found the path of vehicular righteousness, I commenced my cultural acclimatising process for exotic Angola. What this grand phrase actually means is that I put my head down and cycled through 155 km of landscape. I had always been intrigued by the name 'Angola', although I hadn't allowed my mind to be dominated by all the stories of war and degradation I had been hearing for so many years. My thoughts ran more to lots of jungle and fertile soil, but I didn't spot any right away. It started off pretty flat and open, just like the landscape on the other side of the border, but gradually the dry veld began to make way for bush, dotted with baobabs. This really pleased me. The baobab is the most visually distinctive and amazing tree on the planet, full of personality, charm and unmatched individuality, and I was thrilled that sooner or later I would have the opportunity of having myself photographed next to one.

But that would come later. Right now the most prominent roadside objects were the wrecks of tanks and other armoured vehicles dating from the Angolan civil war, which started in 1975, when the Portuguese abruptly withdrew and left three guerrilla movements to fight it out for supremacy. It didn't end till the 1990s, by which time it had become a Cold War battlefield involving everyone from the South Africans and Russians to the Americans and Cubans.

Some of the vehicles were total wrecks, while others were still in reasonable condition, although they had obviously been stripped of anything useful during the war, either for spares or to prevent them from being used against their former owners. There was a sort of horrible fascination about them, and I found myself sitting on one of the shot-up tanks, trying to imagine what it must have felt and sounded and smelled like to be an armoured trooper in action. It was a sobering thought to realise that a lot of them must have been considerably younger than I was.

In Xangongo I met an interesting family who provided some hope for the future of Africa. Their backyard was dusty and cluttered with various odds and ends, but I was content to pitch my tent there, and afterwards I had a long and interesting conversation with the de facto head of the household, a very attractive and sympathetic young woman of 24 named Deore.

Deore showed what a gutsy, determined woman could accomplish even in a country as battered, poverty-stricken and graft-ridden as Angola. She not only supported her mother and two children of her own but was also a student in Windhoek, which meant that she had to travel back and forth at regular intervals to keep both sets of home fires burning. Yet as I chatted with her – she spoke perfect English – I never had the sense that she felt herself to be disadvantaged. She was satisfied with her situation because she had taken control of her life and was making something of it. It gave me something of a different perspective when I thought of students at home moaning about examinations and peer pressure, or the general fondness for using a disadvantaged background as a one-size-fits-all excuse for one's own lack of enterprise and determination. I also couldn't help thinking how good it would be if we were all to take the time to get to know people beyond the 'hello, how are you?' stage. I decided I would have to make some plans to come back and visit people I had met and wanted to see again.

From Xangongo the road took me northwestwards, and I enjoyed crossing the big rivers while wending my way through hilly and rocky terrain. I had picked up a very basic Portuguese vocabulary by now, and to spur myself on to greater effort I used it to play a game with myself. 'Bom dia' meant 'good morning' and 'boa tar-de' good afternoon, and the locals weren't afraid to correct you if you went one 'good morning' too far. So I made it my daily personal goal to have at least 70 km on the clock before I got the first correction of my greeting. This represented a natural half-way mark for the day; after 70 km the sun had usually reached and passed its peak, so that covering the remaining 50 or 80 km seemed a breeze.

By now I had developed a sound routine for camping. There were many tiny villages alongside the road, usually between 10 and 20 km apart, the most popular sites being near a river bank or on top of a hill near a river bank. Maybe there was a good reason for the latter choice, but it must have been pure torture to maintain a supply of water, since the hills were usually very steep and the customary water containers didn't have handles. I couldn't help thinking that spitting out the water after brushing one's teeth was probably just about a capital offence in the hilltop villages.

Anyway, about an hour before total darkness every day I would harness this new-found knowledge to logic – and, if I was lucky, the sound of human activity within earshot – to find a campsite that was invisible from the road. Having done that, I would start to clear a patch of earth and pitch my tent on it. This had to be done as near to total darkness as possible to make sure that no passer-by would spot me. It was easy to camouflage my tent so that it wouldn't show up in the headlight beams of passing cars easy. Sometimes I would find a couple of mounds of sand where road-workers had started to level out the ground, and that would be enough to hide the tent completely on one side. On the other side I might pile rocks up to about shoulder height till the tent disappeared from view.

Every hour or so a huge truck would pass by with a load of people squashed willy-nilly into the back. From their elevated view they could see me, of course, and often shouted incomprehensible bursts of Portuguese at me. Sometimes this worried me. Were they shouting 'Hey, white guy! We'll come back to get you! Don't fall asleep! We know where you are!' Or were they simply making Jopie Kotze-style jokes? I couldn't tell, of course, and my interpretation depended on my state of mind; thinking the worst is not difficult when you have no one to share your concerns with. At such times the only remedy was to go to sleep as soon as possible.

One night I was particularly nervous, for a reason I have forgotten now. I had selected a spot on a patch of cleared land, about half a hectare in extent and containing a man-made dune about 4 metres long and 2 metres high. I pitched the tent directly behind the dune, but because the clearing lay on a hairpin bend in the road I needed almost 360 degrees of shelter, the particular problem being that it was visible to any people passing either end of the dune.

I took some extra precautions, waiting for complete darkness before pitching the tent and only eating supper – a tin of bully beef, washed down with Game energy drink – once I was inside, having stripped down to my shorts because it was extremely hot and humid now that the daytime breeze had dropped. I remember how quiet it was that night: in the Angolan bush everything seems to go on 'pause' in the first few hours after sunset.

When I had finished eating I lay down for the most enjoyable time of day, bed-time. But I felt uneasy this night and so I slept patchily and uneasily. Every little sound would have my heart pumping louder and harder as I lay with the can of pepper spray on my chest, trying to persuade myself that I was dozing off. But I couldn't get rid of the vision of someone attacking me during the night, and most of the time I lay awake, rehearsing an aggressive response if the circumstances called for it. A robbery attempt, or worse, was sure to happen at some stage of my journey. Would it be tonight? It got to the point where I would sit bolt upright (as far as the tent allowed it) if I heard voices, real or imagined, from out in the night.

Then I heard a voice just a few metres from the tent, and the unmistakable sound of feet stepping on rocks and disturbing the sandy gravel of their beds. Act, Riaan, don't just sit there! I thought. Heart racing, I unzipped the two tent zippers in one fluid motion, and a moment later I was outside, aiming the torch's beam in the direction of where I reckoned my attackers would come from and aiming it high so that the light would be in their eyes. 'Boa noite!' I said loudly. I wasn't frightened any more; revved up on the adrenalin flowing freely into my veins, ready to defend myself with tooth and claw.

Somewhat to my disappointment nothing happened. All I could see – far beyond where I had expected my attackers to be – was the dim shape of a man walking away down the road. He didn't acknowledge my aggressive greeting in any way, just kept going till he had disappeared around the sharp bend in the road. I went back to bed, feeling strangely satisfied. I had showed him that he would have had more than a handful if he had tried anything.

Next morning, as I was packing up my tent, a stooped old man came walking along from the direction in which my visitor of the night before had gone. He paused, raised his arm in greeting and said: 'Bom dia, to do bem?'(Are you OK?). I returned his greeting and he spoke some more in Portuguese, none of which I understood, ending off with a big smile. I returned the smile, then ransacked my very limited vocabulary to explain that I hadn't understood. So we tried again, making use of sign language this time, and eventually we worked out that he had been last night's 'attacker'.

It was a small incident, perhaps, but an important one for me, because after that day I never again allowed myself to sink into such debilitating fear, and I had also finally begun to realise that what I had originally perceived to be aggressiveness in the local population was simply a humble boisterousness for which I developed a sincere admiration.

The jungle environment continued all the way to Lubango, Angola's second-largest business centre. Angola was presenting me with the real Africa that I had looked forward to seeing – Capetonians in their pleasant Mediterranean city, so far south that it is barely part of the continent, don't feel as if they are really in Africa. But this was another story. Lubango was a city in the jungle, and I had to work hard to get there, because it was defended (I can't think of a word that is more apt) by 16 long, very intense hills.

My laborious approach to Lubango actually marked the start of my hill-climbing training, and now Frank's advice on the road to Clanwilliam came in very handy. Make full use of your momentum, he had said, and so I put in an immense effort on the downslopes and kept pumping away as my forward rush carried me through the dip at the bottom and up the next rise. Gravity and the weight of the bike worked in my favour for a change, to such a degree that it felt as if the hills were considerably shorter on the upward slopes. Nonsense, of course, but that was how strong the effect of my charges downhill was.

I had no money at this stage, and my first priority on arriving in Lubango was to get to a bank. It was just after lunch and well within office hours, so I didn't foresee any problems – all I had to do was find an ATM booth, and I was well away. Unfortunately it turned out that Lubango didn't have any, so I headed for the Banque de Angola. I anticipated that the bank staff might have a problem if I wheeled my dusty bike into the Temple of Mammon, so I enlisted the help of one of the amputees I saw everywhere.

Lubango was full of them; every street-corner seemed to have a bunch, some on crutches and the others in wheelchairs, and missing one or both legs. I learnt later that the Lubango region had more landmine victims than anywhere else in Angola, which was saying something. Indiscriminate laying of landmines during the civil war has left an estimated 10 million of the infernal machines still in place and waiting for some poor innocent to step on them, and the results were to be seen everywhere.

It took me a while to get my mind around the concept of a country where millions of active mines, just waiting for the pressure of someone's foot, were a part of everyday life. I thought back to my placid First World existence and tried to superimpose a situation where as simple a thing as walking to school, going to fetch water or just taking your girlfriend for a romantic stroll was a gamble where a wrong step could leave you dead or mangled and unemployable in a fraction of a second ... and I failed.

In any case, this particular amputee was sitting outside the Banque de Angola's front door, and he was more of a friendly one-legged unemployed philanthropist than a well-positioned beggar. He loved my bicycle and would only let me park it in one place, right next to him. Having entrusted it to his care, I entered the bank and went in search of someone who could speak English. I struck it lucky with the first staffer I spoke to, and when I had told her what

I wanted she took me straight to the manager's office.

He was an energetic young guy who assured me that wiring money to Angola from South Africa would not be a problem. Could we call my bank and authorise an electronic transfer? He even asked what exchange rate I would be comfortable with (I still don't understand this – surely there is only one rate of exchange for a currency at any one time?). I didn't kick about this, however, and before the signed approval note had even been faxed he handed me a crisp $100 dollar note he had fished out of his pocket. Whooee! How often do you find this sort of bank manager when you really need him? I certainly needed him that day, and it wasn't even necessary to invite him to help. I took the money and ran, so to speak, and to this day I still don't know whether he went as far as drawing the funds from my account.

The immediate pressure on my finances had been lifted, but I didn't let this bonus go to either my head or my pocket, and immediately started looking around for a suitable night's lodging. I soon ran into a student who cottoned on without delay to what I wanted; he said there was a camping area outside the town but he thought that this option was a little risky because it had absolutely no security. However, he added, he knew many people in the town, and we could ask around till we found a place where I could spend the night.

We started to wander about, my new acquaintance visibly amused by my insistence on what I considered suitable quarters. I wasn't fussy; I'd be quite happy to get my head down on a naked concrete slab, as long as it had a fence around it. Eventually I ended up at the garage doors of an unknown family's house. I knocked on the front door, which was opened by the two young daughters of the house, who were seized by such a fit of continual giggling that nothing much happened till their father and brother made an appearance.

The father couldn't speak English and neither could the son, although he could understand it, which isn't quite the same thing. Still, I managed to communicate the essentials. In a flash I found myself sitting at their dining table while the mother of the house plied us with food. And there was more hospitality to come. They offered me a bed, which I gratefully accepted, but when I woke the next morning I found a man of considerably more years than myself curled up on the floor of the bedroom. This was a bit of a shock, and it was even more of a shock when I discovered that the man on the floor was the 65-year-old uncle of the house, and I had been sleeping in his bed!

I felt pretty ashamed about usurping the uncle's sleeping-space, so that he had had to sleep on the floor in his own house, my only excuse being that I hadn't known about it when I crawled in and got my head down. But that's what you call extreme hospitality.

I got another dose of it at breakfast, when I mentioned that I would like to get hold of a small Angolan flag to sew on to my backpack. It so happened that the father was due to meet a government official that morning, so he told me to accompany him to the local administrative headquarters, where he was certain we would be able to find one. But it was not as easy as that. In spite of the fact that eventually he had people from all the departments in the beautiful old colonial-era building looking around, a suitable flag was not to be found anywhere. But then he came on a solution which was completely unexpected and probably wouldn't have happened anywhere else.

As we were walking down the grand staircase at the entrance to this building the regional governor pulled up in his chauffeur-driven official car, from each corner of which flew one of Angola's four traditional national flags. It turned out that my host knew the governor; he introduced me, and in no time I was standing, rather stunned, with one of the flags from the car in my hand.

That day I called home to Vasti for the first time since entering Angola. It did great things for my spirits, although the interest at the other end, I think, was more about how I was surviving the landmines and other after-effects of the Angolan civil war. I told Vasti about everything that had happened to me, about the beauty of the country and the kindness I had received from its people, but I was conscious of the fact that I was not doing justice to either.

I suffered some vehicular grief soon after I left for Benguela next morning. The patchy bit of tarmac that doubled as a highway for the first few hundred kilometres of Angola gave way to a very uneven rocky dirt road that soon took its toll on my bike, and about 10 km out of town I heard a snapping sound followed by a continuous scraping. Inspection revealed one of the legs that attached the carrier to the bicycle's rear axle had broken. It was a pain in the neck but not a disaster, however, and I used three spare cable ties to pull the broken ends of the frame together; this jury rig was sturdy enough to take the full weight on the back of the bike, which at this stage was about 30 kg, not counting my water supply.

While I was still down on my knees repairing the frame I had another of those Angolan encounters when three trucks laden with crates of soft drinks came down the road. When the drivers spotted me they stopped, and one who spoke fairly good English offered their assistance. I had just about finished what I was doing, so I declined their offer with thanks, but chanced my arm and added: 'But I will have a Coke, if you have one.' The English-speaking driver regretfully turned me down, saying it was impossible because a client in Benguela was awaiting delivery of the exact amount of bottles the trucks were carrying. This didn't worry me because I wasn't really that thirsty, and they ground away into the bush after we had exchanged farewells.

I say 'ground', and I mean it. Those three drivers must have had a torrid time keeping their fragile cargo in one piece on that uneven road surface with its lethal combination of potholes, slipperiness and rocks, even a small indentation translating into such violent juddering that I could hear the trucks' metal parts clanging together till they had left me at least one kilometre behind. They had to take it so slowly, in fact, that about 4 km down the track I actually caught up and passed them.

The truck drivers regained some of their professional dignity a few kilometres later, however, when the road improved slightly, although this is strictly a relative term. In the interim they had worked out how to give me – and themselves – a soft drink without falling foul of the recipient, and so we all had a small celebration to toast our third encounter of the day. I didn't ask questions about the how or why of it, just drank my warm Fanta. I was tired and hot, and I had had images of a cold sparkling drink pumping some liquid energy into me. What I got was about the same temperature as a baby's bath-water, but a long road makes you grateful for small mercies.

We chatted a bit while knocking back their unsuspecting client's soft drinks, and I learnt a bit more about the tough trade of Angola-style trucking. Depending on the condition of the road, they said, it would take them three or four days to reach Benguela, since there had been a lot of rain recently, and the road didn't get much maintenance (well, that was pretty obvious). Their considered opinion was that in some areas it was going to be impossible for me to travel on a bicycle. I took note of what they said, because I suspected that things had been a little too easy thus far, but their predictions excited rather than scared me ... after all, was I an adventurer or was I not?

I encountered an unexpected sort of adventure when I passed Quilenges and came to one of the many beautiful small river crossings between the town and Benguela. A metal-and-concrete bridge about 15 metres long spanned the river at that point, and standing around at my end were five strangely dressed men. All wore light blue body armour with chest and gonad protector flaps, and a couple of them held what looked like old-style motorbike helmets with oversized visors.

The men crowded around me when I pulled up and bombarded me with questions, most of which I didn't understand because they were speaking Portuguese. My first reaction, after so many solitary days on the road, was to feel hemmed in and resentful about my personal space being invaded, but when I found out what they were doing my instinctive growliness was replaced by complete admiration: all were members of a mine-clearing organisation known as the Halo Trust – one of its patrons had been Diana, Princess of Wales, who had actually visited Angola a few months before her death as part of a campaign to drum up awareness and support.

Seeing these Halo Trust guys on their hands and knees, slowly crawling forward to lift the mines, was a humbling experience: these fellows were in more danger during every minute of their working day than I had been in my lifetime. Highly educated and experienced bomb experts will tell you that lifting mines in peace-time is a relatively safe procedure. Maybe so, but experts in dangerous pursuits tend to take a calmer view of their jobs than someone like me, a man who has no real understanding of technology, whose only relationship with these lethal devices has consisted of seeing the results of mine explosions on the TV. How could the stress level of a weekly deadline in the 'real world' even come close to what these men in their helmets and body armour – no foolproof defence, by the way, if a mine rendered unstable by long neglect suddenly decides to go off – accepted as their daily lot?

I was so moved that I did something I had not indulged in so far – I took out my digital camera and filmed them at their work. Up to that point I had kept the camera well out of sight because I had not wanted to endanger my project and quite possibly my life by letting the wrong eyes fall on it. But now I was forced to accept a piece of logic I had been dodging: what was the use of having a camera if I didn't use it to record my experiences?

When I'd done, I stood on the bridge, taking in the awesome beauty of the river and its banks, with the water-reeds transmuting themselves into thick bush and clusters of baobab trees ... and then having my admiration jarred by the sight of the de-mining team in their light blue body armour, crawling through the cordoned-off areas, which reminded me that amid all the peaceful natural beauty lurked a terrible man-made danger.

The millions of mines that lurk in ambush beneath Angolan soil are what you might call a self-inflicted wound. South African forces which intervened in Angola at various stages of the border war did not generally use mines very much, and usually charted and later lifted them; most of the Angolan mines were laid by the troops of one faction or another, usually without charting their location and seemingly without any plans for lifting them afterwards, even if anyone still remembered where they were. So now Angola and the international community face a huge problem in making the country reasonably safe again.

Detecting and lifting these uncharted mines is a fantastically time-consuming activity, and fantastically expensive, too, when it has to be done on this scale. The bottom line is that the original mines cost about 50 US cents each to manufacture, but when I passed through Angola the price of removing just one was $20. So enormous sums that could be spent more profitably on other things are poured into the de-mining programme.

I left the Halo Trust men inching along on their dangerous progress and carried on, my mind full of a mixture of sadness and incomprehension that did not dissipate for some time as I toiled along the terrible road. At one stage I passed a convoy of 4x4s which, one of the drivers told me (I don't know whether this is true), were the first on this stretch of road since the war-torn 1980s to carry only foreigners, some of them being South Africans working for companies based in Luanda.

Two car-loads stopped to chat. Standing straddle-legged over my bicycle, I got a kick out of seeing the amazement on the occupants' faces, and I was moved at the sense of pride the South Africans showed as they told their colleagues that this madman was a fellow countryman, that this was how tough all South Africans were. Fortunately I didn't become teary and emotional while sticking my head into the air-conditioned vehicles – that would have ruined the moment, not to mention that reputation for toughness.

I encountered more kindness as I approached the coast, longing to feast my eyes on the sea, which I had last seen while cycling out of Cape Town on my very first day. At one small village, consisting of not more than five huts, I was welcomed so enthusiastically that even though I had only done 91 km that day, less than my commitment, I simply couldn't refuse their offer to rest a while and eat some sugar-cane.

In doing so I turned into an unwitting bringer of death. I was chewing on what I think was my eighth metre of sugar-cane when I noticed a hyperactive chicken, which seemed to be the only one in the village, darting about between the huts. By way of keeping the conversation going (I swear!) I mentioned that at home I really enjoyed eating 'frango' ('chicken' in Portuguese).

The village headman and his wife, who were highly intoxicated, immediately insisted on inviting me to a chicken dinner, brushing off my polite attempt to decline the offer. Next moment just about the entire population of the village was in hot pursuit of the chicken, which did some valiant ducking and diving (perhaps it had had a lot of practice) before it was finally overwhelmed. I should add that the boiled chicken dinner I enjoyed later went down surprisingly easily, considering that it followed about five kilos of sugar-cane hors d'oeuvres. Sheesh! I'd never eaten so much sugar-cane in my entire life. But in that poverty-stricken but hospitable village, shaking your head wasn't accepted as 'no'.

I sang for my supper, so to speak, by setting up my tent in the place of honour next to the headman's hut. This caused a sensation, and every last soul turned out to watch. One individual faced the setting sun, exclaiming 'wow', or the Portuguese equivalent, and the masses, so to speak, responded with an even louder Portuguese 'wow'. I think it would be fair to say that a good time was had by all of us.

I fell asleep to the sound of a loud conversation between the headman and his wife, and at first light I was up again, ready for the next leg. The headman, somewhat hung over, came out to say goodbye, and at his request I got out my camera to take a few photographs of him (there was just enough light) holding a fancy wall clock which was apparently a prized possession. I suppose one could say that this was the closest I have ever got to a personal encounter with Father Time.

Pedalling out of the village and into the rising sun, I wondered whether they would remember me, and whether they would tell their children the story of my visit with as much enthusiasm as I expected to do one day to the children I hoped to have. They left an indelible impression on me, the people of that tiny village which is not even a dot on the Angolan map, not because they were different from others but because of their good hearts. For me they redefined the word 'poverty'. If you asked me now, I'd say that 'poverty' is a relative term and an insult to the 'poor' people I met during the course of my journey. I see them as having more than many people I met later who thought they had everything, yet had less than those who, by their standards, had nothing.

It might sound strange, but as I rode away I – Riaan Manser, fabulously wealthy by their standards – wanted a bit of what they had. It took me a while to figure out what that was. I think the answer is simply happiness, in spite of their poverty, the war and everything else. They knew who and where they were, and, knowing that, were content and willing to extend their contentment to passing lunatics like myself.

My next engagement with the local flora and fauna on the way to the coast was a good deal stranger, although I was so inured to bizarre encounters by now that I handled it, I think, with suitable aplomb.

I was crossing a stretch of fairly level terrain when a 4x4 vehicle appeared about 100 metres ahead, closed in and then went into a controlled skid that brought it to a halt within spitting distance of a petrified me, enveloping us both in a large cloud of dust. Out jumped a muscular Greek-looking guy, hand extended in greeting, while from the passenger seat a young woman, presumably his girlfriend, smiled and nodded in a sort of frustrated but friendly fashion.

He asked me where I was from and where I was going; for some reason he seemed very excited, but he was not in any hurry, so obviously he wasn't being chased by anybody. Anyway, we fell to chatting and he explained that he was heading for Cape Town on holiday and would return in three weeks' time, then took a look at my bicycle and asked me for more details about my trip. In the process he hauled out a crammed cooler box and gave me an ice-cold beer. The beer was very refreshing, and I nearly said yes to a second one, although I knew it was a bad idea to have more than one while I was on the road.

He offered the second beer a couple more times, but I stood fast. Then he had a sudden inspiration, and instead of making another offer of beer asked me if I would like something (I can't remember what). I didn't know what he was talking about, so I just smiled and said: 'Naah, not really, naah.' He must have realised that I didn't understand, so he told me to wait while he fetched something from his cubbyhole. He came back with an empty VCR cassette-holder, which he gently tapped and then opened, holding it closer so that I could get a better look inside. Now I saw that the box wasn't empty after all, but filled with white powder. He dipped his long pinkie fingernail into the powder and held it to one nostril for a long sniff, a big grin on his face. I felt pretty awkward because I realised that he thought I was one of 'the guys'. My new friend, who actually seemed a genuinely nice guy, was snorting cocaine in the middle of the Angolan bush, and was offering me a hit!

I said thanks, but no thanks, and I was ready to promise that I hadn't seen what he had just done. But he wasn't worried about that. 'This makes me very awake,' he explained. 'I can drive through the whole night and not be tired. You take this and you will be strong.'

Jeez! I thought. Who does this guy take us health-loving bicycle adventurers for? He would probably snort the equivalent of some small, poor African country's GDP up his nose before he even got within sight of Table Mountain. To steer the conversation away from his coke and my nose I asked him what he did for a living.

'I am ... er ... how you say? A drug ... god?'

'Oh ... a drug LORD?' I replied with a cackle of nervous laughter. It's not every day that you meet up with a self-confessed magnate in the drug business.

'Yes ... yes ... yes ! A drug lord!' he laughed back.

My earlier feeling of unreality returned. Was I really chilling out with a genuine drug lord in the jungles of perilous Africa while he snorted cocaine off his car's bonnet? Well, yes, I was, although he did admit that he only drug-lorded part-time, since he had a day job with the local operation of a well-known South African company. I resolved silently to keep the information to myself, just for safety's sake, even though I would be long gone by the time he got back from Cape Town.

Anyway, I didn't end up in the middle of the road in a pool of blood, which I had always believed was more or less the usual result of meeting up with a drug lord. I waved goodbye as he roared away with his frustrated girlfriend, after giving me some valuable advice on which roads and towns to look out for. What a strange country! Now I was even keener to see what other weird and exotic adventures it was saving up for me.

I kept going, feeling ever more light-hearted as I got nearer the coastline, and then, just before I actually laid eyes on the sea, I had another one of those strange and heart-warming Angolan encounters. A black Land Rover Discovery came up alongside me and stopped. Inside were five Angolans with their eyebrows scrunched together in confusion at the sight of me. Where was I going? One of them could speak some English, and I managed to pass on my place of origin, nationality and destination.

Another of the five, whose name turned out to be Paulo Rangel, was more interested in me than the rest and kept feeding the English-speaker with more questions to bounce off me. When he had satisfied his curiosity he wanted to know if there was anything he could do for me. I said that I was fine, although a bottle of cold water wouldn't hurt. But they didn't have any, for which they apologised profusely, apparently very sorry for anyone doing something as ludicrous as pedalling a heavily loaded bicycle on such a very hot and humid day.

They wished me well, and after repeated goodbyes took off for Benguela again. I put my head down and struggled on through the intense midday heat, sure I would never see them again. But about 22 km from Benguela town the Discovery came back and stopped in front of me. I stopped, too, not knowing what to expect. What I got was a pleasant surprise that left me as astounded as I was thirsty. They had driven back all the way to bring me three litres of ice-cold water, four Cokes and two Sprites!

It was like blood to a vampire, and I gulped down an entire 1.5-litre bottle of water, followed that up with a delightfully fizzy Coke and then went to work on a Sprite. But after the second sip I realised I should have gone slower on the water – my stomach felt as if it was about to burst, and not even some awesome burps could alleviate the pressure. In spite of the discomfort I managed to answer a few more questions they had forgotten to ask me earlier, then the chief questioner found a small piece of paper, scribbled a note on it, added his telephone number. 'Call me, call me,' he said through his makeshift interpreter, and then they were off again.

I spent a few minutes recovering from my over-indulgence and then carried on. One puncture and several hills later I had the sea-view for which I had been hankering so much. It was a fantastic moment – 'out of body' is probably the best way to describe it without being too dramatic. I thought to myself: So what they draw on the maps is probably true. Africa really *does* look like it appears on paper! Seeing had become believing.

Seeing the sea for the first time since leaving Cape Town proved very motivational for me. In my mind's eye I could rebuild my end-vision, which had become a little tattered from all the new impressions I had taken on board, of how Table Mountain would look when I rolled up to the Nelson Mandela Gateway again. For 3 000 km I had travelled in unknown territory, but now I really had my bearings again. Without looking at a map I knew I was making progress. I knew I could do this trip.

The sea constantly in view from the corner of my eye, I cycled the last few kilometres to Benguela and soon had the town in view. Then I ran into a road-block, manned by some soldiers, which was set up near a complex of large barrack-type structures visible on my right. I approached the road-block with some relief, because it marked my entry into the town precincts.

I hadn't anticipated any problem, but I ran into some communication difficulties right away. The first soldier I spoke to gabbled away at me in Portuguese of which I understood next to nothing. He got a trifle irritated by my lack of comprehension, but smiling and showing him my passport got me through to his superiors. This didn't help as much as I had hoped; even with one person translating, it soon became clear to me that they didn't understand what I was talking about either, and were highly suspicious of both my intentions and myself. I tried to look calm, which I was definitely not. Then I remembered the note from my good Samaritan of earlier, Paulo Rangel, hauled it out and asked them to call him.

In an instant the entire situation changed. My erstwhile interrogators escorted me out of the office with great courtesy, and next moment I was heading for Benguela in true VIP style, with a military jeep, machine-gun and all, ahead of me and another behind, sirens wailing full blast and lights flashing spectacularly on both of them. Whoever this Paulo Rangel was, I concluded as I battled to keep up with the lead jeep, he obviously drew a lot of water in those parts (it turned out he was, in fact, governor of Benguela, the second-largest state in the entire country). Talk about sheer damn-fool luck!

I didn't have a lot of time to think about these things because I was very busy trying not to be run over by my rearguard. These guys had obviously not done much cycling in their time, because we were averaging nearly 30 km/h for the last few kilometres into the centre of town. This might have been slow for them but not for the guest of honour. The normal practice is that if you cycle 100 km or so, the final five are a warm-down rather than a stamina-building event. Since my escort didn't know this, I think I sweated out every drop of all that liquid I had consumed earlier just keeping up with them.

My arrival caused a sensation. The locals dropped what they were doing and lined the streets to see me enter the town, emitting a barrage of whistles and shouts that got louder with each passing metre. Those who knew a couple of words of English shouted them at me, the spirit being more important than the actual meaning. I waved to them and replied with as much dignity as a dirty, sweating, bicycle-riding VIP like me could muster.

We screeched to a halt in front of an impressive old colonial three-storey building, complete with large gardens full of tall palm-trees, and two armed soldiers saw me inside for another meeting with my eminent acquaintance. Mr Rangel was busy with other things just then, it appeared, and after waiting for about half an hour I decided to persuade my entourage, the armed guards included, to let me go off and rehydrate my parched body.

Hearty handshakes and a few repetitions of 'muito obrigado' (thanks very much) did the trick, and they dropped me off in the town centre at an open-air coffee bar that looked a bit like an oversized hot dog stall, indicating that they would come and fetch me when the governor was ready to see me. That suited me fine, and I got down to pouring some fluid into myself. Then, as I sat there saving my own life, none other than my other road-friends, the three Coca-Cola truck-rivers with whom I had drunk someone else's soft drinks, rolled into the main street. I was pretty surprised. We had all left Lubango at the same time, four days earlier: had I actually beaten them to it? Impossible, surely!

They thought so, too. The driver who had given me the warm Fanta hung out of his window when he spotted me, shouting: 'You take vehicle here, huh? Yes?'

'No, bicycle,' I said, pointing at my bike, which I had leaned up against the hot dog stand.

'No ... never, never, never!' he said, unable to believe that a guy on a bicycle could have covered such a distance quicker than a truck. I could understand his amazement, but I knew why I had managed it: for me it was easy to avoid the countless small bumps that pitted about 75 per cent of the road, because I was close to the ground, but the only way they could make progress without smashing their cargo was to slow down to about 2 km/h.

When my entourage came and took me to Paulo Rangel he treated me as an official state guest. He was obviously a wealthy man and, unlike some wealthy men, he was also extremely generous. He insisted that I stay over for three nights so that he could show me the town and arrange for an interview on Angolan TV, and they were great nights. We ate at the most popular Benguelan restaurants, and I got to meet all the right people in town, because everybody seemed to know him and rolled out the red carpet when they heard he was coming. Naturally he put me up at his official residence, a veritable small palace with at least six spacious bedrooms, solid marble floors and a spiral oak staircase, as well as the most spectacular bathrooms I had ever seen, positively reeking of opulence. Each had red-brown marble walls and floors, and a walk-in bath at least five times the normal size.

But the palace also spoke of the long, hard struggle that still lay ahead for Angola as it recovered from the decades of war and lack of good governance. Thick layers of dust partly obscured the twinkle of the crystal in the beautiful chandelier over the staircase, and there was no running water, so that I had to use a bucket and a cup to shower every morning and tip a litre or two into the toilet-bowl after doing my business. It was a sad thing to see, as sad in its way as the de-mining operation I had passed earlier. We tend to take a lot of things for granted in South Africa, where we have managed to come through the storms of decades without having our country laid in ruins.

While in Benguela I met an interesting couple whose story showed how different the Angolans' approach was to some other African governments. They were Zimbabwean farmers who had been violently tossed off their farm by the Mugabe regime, which basically told them to find some other means of making a livelihood, adding that if they emigrated they would only be allowed to take their most necessary personal belongings and would have to leave all large assets or substantial amounts of cash behind.

The two placed a fairly liberal interpretation on the definition of 'large assets' and left in their privately owned cargo aircraft, which they flew to Angola. There they soon secured a contract to fly government officials around (a good idea, I reflected, recalling my battle with the road from Lubango). I really felt sorry for them; they had had a bad deal from a racist tyrant who had wrecked his country simply to cling on to power. But they were anything but morbid about the whole disgraceful business – all they talked about was the good things that they believed the future held in store for them. They didn't know how long their contract with the Angolan government would last, but that didn't seem to worry them too much either. All they kept saying was that they were happier and safer than they had been in Zimbabwe – and, more than anything else, how relieved they were that they could still find a home in Africa.

I was sad to leave Benguela and Governor Paulo Rangel and his people. I could have done something in this town. People everywhere knew about me because of him and greeted me as I moved about.

I felt as if I could have created a little home here, and I might have stayed on if I had not had my personal quest to complete. I have often dreamt of surprising Mr Rangel with a more orthodox visit and repaying his generosity and hospitality in true South African style. I received many kindnesses from the people I met, but he was my first real Angolan friend, and he capped the favourable opinion of Angola with which I left for the next leg of my adventure.

I pedalled through some amazingly beautiful country after leaving Benguela, stopping regularly just to absorb my surroundings and try unsuccessfully to find something to compare them to. But I didn't neglect the pleasures of the flesh either, such as they were. In the town of Sumbe, for example, I had the good fortune to corner the only person there with digital satellite TV, and got to see the Currie Cup final being played in South Africa – no small treat for a rugby fan like myself.

It was another of those laid-back Angolan episodes. There I was, sitting in a complete stranger's house while he and his family went about their usual business and I emulated my countrymen on a typical Saturday afternoon – lounging on a couch in front of the TV, absorbing a never-ending flow of snacks and drinks. The only difference was that this particular South African didn't even know the name of the person who was supplying the couch, TV, snacks and booze, and the person in question probably didn't realise why I was getting so excited, although I suppose he must have understood. But that was Angola for you.

I nearly got involved in the guano business while in Sumbe ... well, I suppose bat droppings would qualify as guano. It involved a retired or converted preacher (I wasn't quite sure which, or why his ecclesiastical status had changed) and a politician friend of his, and between them they convinced me of the leading role bat guano was going to play in the potting industry. The idea fell on fertile ground, so to speak, but my entrepreneurial instincts had to take second place to my date with the rest of Africa. Perhaps it was just as well.

Sumbe did not let go of me easily – not because it was particularly tourist-friendly but rather as a result of the excruciatingly long, steep hill that bordered it to the north. I was also not feeling too good, because I was on the verge of suffering from a serious bout of dysentery, my first real illness so far. It had started gently enough with nothing more serious than the effect of a big bowl of stewed prune. But then my digestive system kicked up a few notches, so that anything I ate seemed to pass through me very quickly and have an altogether different consistency. At first I didn't get too excited about it, believing that my body would soon understand what was going on and adapt, and that more vegetables in my diet would help. I suspected that my problem originated from the river water I was drinking en route, sometimes without bothering to use purification tablets, because the water in many Angolan rivers is so clear and refreshing that at times I was lulled into a false sense of security.

Once I was cycling through a particularly beautiful stretch of what looked like virgin jungle with the music of running water constantly in my ears, and as I had done before, I decided to fill up with some of it. I waited until the water-sounds were very loud, laid my bike down on the track and clambered down to the rocks past which the river ran. The water was so fresh and cold that I drank a litre of it right there before returning to my bike with my bottles filled to the brim.

Then, only a couple of kilometres further, I stopped after a long, rough, winding hill-climb to have another drink and heard human voices very near by. I pedalled another 50 metres or so and there they were: about 30 people scattered along the river's rocky banks, some washing clothes, others bathing ... and yet others casually squatting to relieve themselves in the water.

I stared at this unexpected scene while my brain clicked through some hasty calculations. The water I had been drinking a couple of kilometres downstream might have been sweet and cold, but it had certainly not been untouched by human hand, to put it delicately. Then I laughed, unscrewed the cap of my bottle and unhesitatingly took another large gulp. That was how I was going to deal with this journey – head on. Quite probably I had already unknowingly drunk or eaten much worse things. My motto would be 'what doesn't kill you will make you stronger'.

Maybe so, but that was not to guarantee that the strengthening process would be painless or without embarrassment. But with dysentery you soon reach the point where it is less about avoiding embarrassment than selecting the option which is least embarrassing.

About 40 km outside Lobito, for example, the need was on me and I turned in at one of the innumerable roadside villages. We went through the usual sign-language and occasional words routine, and they showed me where I could pitch my tent for the night, not realising that what I really wanted to know, with ever greater urgency, was where the facilities were. Eventually I pulled one man aside, simulated a quick squat and put on a 'where is it?' expression. He got the idea right away and pointed to a path, intimating that I should follow it for about 100 metres, after which the object of my desire would be on the left.

I headed for the path without further ado, but after 100 metres by my reckoning there was no place of easement in sight and I simply couldn't wait any longer, so I took a quick look around while barely holding on to my sanity and dignity. I spotted a sheltered place on the other side of the path and went into the obligatory crouch with all haste, remembering just in time to sit facing outwards so that if someone came walking past I would have time to take evasive action. What happened then, apart from the obvious, brought me to a new depth of embarrassment. Having done my deed – for the time being, that this, this being the nature of the beast – I was able to pay attention to the sounds of the bush around me ... and what I heard was enough to wipe the smile of momentary relief off my face. To wit, the unmistakeable giggling of children just a few metres behind me.

I whipped around and there they were, about six youngsters (I wasn't capable of coherent counting just then). One boy was leaning comfortably on a stick with his foot fitted into the hollow at the back of his other knee, while others were stretched out on the ground, resting their heads in their hands and grinning at me and one another. They didn't run away when they saw I had spotted them, just stayed right there, watching me finish and pull up my shorts, as if they were watching a TV show ... and I suppose it was rather comic in a horrible way. To me, quietly dying inside by this stage, each moment seemed to last a lifetime, and when I walked away with as much dignity as I could muster (which wasn't much just then) I know that I had plumbed depths of embarrassment that I sincerely hoped I would never reach again.

Things didn't improve as I neared Luanda, psychologically stronger but going steadily downhill physically. Every so often I would jump off the bike without even bothering to stop and then slide headlong down the bank of the road (most Angolan roads are above ground level because of the rains), desperately fighting to get my shorts off before I really disgraced myself. It must have looked like a scene from a Jim Carrey movie, and like Carrey I sometimes had an appreciative audience, like when a typical slow-moving bus came chugging past at a climactic moment. Then all the passengers would hang out of the windows to find out where the owner of the bicycle had got to, see me in extremis behind a bush (if I was lucky) and pass on the news to their fellow-passengers. Oh, well, at least I provided a lot of Angolans with some welcome free entertainment.

# CHAPTER 5

# TSETSE FLIES AND OTHER PEOPLE'S BEDS

*One local man told me that when he was in the army he soon discovered how to distinguish between a tsetse and an ordinary fly. When you swatted an ordinary fly, he explained, it keeled over and fell off you. But when you swatted a tsetse it just did 10 push-ups and then flew away. This was a joke, of course, but in the days to come I couldn't help wondering if there wasn't a grain of truth in it somewhere.*

I'll never, ever, forget the last leg of the journey to Luanda, which stretched my physical and mental endurance far beyond anything I had encountered so far. Everything seemed to be against me – the terrain, the weather and my general state of wellbeing. About the only thing in my favour was that I was travelling on a tarmac road surface again.

My troubles started when I spent the day before my arrival cycling grimly through torrential rain which came down with such force that when I rode directly into a shower the fat drops actually hurt my face and hands. Eyes screwed half-shut, I alternated between squelching over stretches of wet tarmac and planing through pools of water whose surface was lashed into opaqueness by the downpour. Needless to say, I was soaked to the skin, and the dysentery did nothing to help either.

I worried constantly about the lack of visibility – not only was it difficult to see ahead through my half-closed eyes, but there was also no way I could check out approaching puddles to see if they were safe to ride through – and, sure enough, it brought me to grief. Or perhaps I should say 'added grief', considering what I had been going through and how lousy I felt already.

The grief arrived when I was going down one very long hill and giving it all I had left in me; I figured that downhills made up at least half of every day's distance (if the day's overall attitude stayed the same, of course!), so upping my downhill efforts would in turn up my daily average speed, cut down on my overall travelling time and allow me to arrive much earlier at each day's destination. The trouble with calculations like these, of course, is that reality tends to intrude on theories. Thanks to the driving rain I didn't spot some sharp object which lay in ambush in one of the puddles, and suddenly after a tremendously loud bang closely followed by the sound of scraping metal there I was, wetter than a drowned rat, squatting next to my up-turned bike to fix the latest of the many punctures I suffered then and later. It was such a bad one that a complete change of tyre and tube was needed, and the slashed tyre was such a wreck that I decided to keep it as a souvenir.

The tyre fixed, I pushed on, feeling worse and worse with each passing kilometre. I had no definite stay-over point in mind for this leg, so I was trusting to luck to save me from having to pass what would definitely be a miserable night in my tent. And once again Lady Luck came to my aid right on schedule. Near dusk I came to a large army tent next to the road which proved to be the guard-post at the entrance to a nature reserve and resort. I was a sad sight, completely drenched to the point where my shoes made slimy squishing sounds, and the guards were quick to take pity on me. They gave me a place to lie down and somewhere to hang my wet clothes out to dry. This latter was a great boon, because most of my luggage had got thoroughly wet while I was repairing the puncture, and now weighed several extra energy-wasting kilos.

Next day I needed every scrap of energy for that interminable last stage to Luanda, just under 100 km away, because I was really suffering. The dysentery was having another go at my innards, so that half the time I was scouting ahead for a suitable site instead of admiring the scenery, and I had developed severe flu symptoms. I had a pounding headache and the bright light shot arrows of pain into my head which only stopped when I closed my eyes, which is obviously not something you can do very often while riding a bike.

It got worse as the day wore on and the temperature rose with each passing hour; my vision was blurred and I found myself becoming dangerously drowsy. By the time I reached a viewing spot on the edge of a cliff about 50 km from Luanda I was so far gone that I could barely keep my eyes open, so I stretched out on one of the small benches along the cliff's edge and slept for an hour. I woke up feeling slightly better and less blurry in the eyes.

Then, as I cycled away from the lovely view – which I was not really in a condition to enjoy, to be honest – I ran into another nastiness in the form of bugs the size of bumble bees. What they were I don't know, but they were there in huge numbers, flying every which way and scoring one direct hit after another on my face and body. Many of them were mating in mid-air and covering long distances with their bodies firmly attached to each other. It looked like a pretty uncomfortable way of getting one's ashes hauled, but what do I know about the way bugs prefer their carnal pleasures? Although I admit I did feel a bit guilty about some courting couples which got scrunched in no uncertain terms while doing their thing directly under my front tyre. My main concern, though, was to keep my mouth closed so that I wouldn't have to place an extra strain on my unhappy guts by requiring them to digest a loving couple or two. That was definitely *not* one of the traveller's tales I wanted to take home with me.

As I got nearer and nearer the city centre the traffic took on what I can only describe as a quality of poetic madness. People, cars, motorbikes and bicycles weaved past each other with aggressive ease. I wasn't one of those death-defying cyclists, however, I was just too damned sick, with the combination of fatigue, malaria tablets and dysentery leaving me extremely weak and light-headed. My exotic appearance also threatened to bring me to grief. At least a dozen mini-bus taxis drove up alongside me at various times and slowed down so that their passengers could have a good look at me, the result being that more than once I came close to ending up in a pothole or down a steep gutter filled with sewage. There was just too much happening around me for my fevered state to handle, and it was clearly just a matter of time before my movable show included a fall.

The time came all at once when a huge double-axle truck started reversing towards me against the flow of traffic. Being in the same lane, I tried to manoeuvre into one of the neighbouring lines of vehicular chaos as soon as I saw what it was doing. But as you might have guessed, the next taxi full of sightseers was taking its place alongside me, keeping pace while the passengers squashed their noses against the windows or hung half-way out to get a better view, all flashing broad Angolan smiles at me.

I had other things on my mind than smiling back, however. The truck was getting ever nearer and the taxi was blocking my only escape-route, to the left. Then the truck's large metal bars clipped one of my handlebars and made solid contact with my right shoulder and chest. The bike stopped dead, but I became airborne and then nose-dived down towards the concrete road-surface with its generous layer of sewage. I tried to break my fall with my hands, but it didn't help much, and I remember thinking, as I slid through the filth with the world upside down around me, that I really didn't deserve this after everything that had happened to me so far.

That fall just about finished me. My knees were grazed and bleeding, but even more painful were the strips that had been ploughed neatly into my hands by the rough road surface, and I was so spent that I couldn't even summon up the energy to curse the mini-bus's driver. One thing was sure: I was not going to forget my entrance into the Angolan capital for a long time. 'Memorable' is not nearly strong enough a word.

To make it worse I had to pedal an additional 13 km – which felt more like 130 km in my present condition – to reach the South African embassy. Finding the right area was not too difficult, however, and once I had reached the traffic circle I had been directed to it would have been impossible not to see the embassy's large South African flag. It made a bright rainbow of colour against the backdrop of approaching grey rain-clouds, and even in my exhausted state it seemed to be saying to me: 'Don't worry – it's not that bad!'

Inside the embassy's reception area I perched myself on the edge of one of the couches, afraid of soiling its lovely leather with my distinctly unlovely self. Not to put too fine a point on it, I was filthy, a horrible amalgam of dirt, sweat of various vintages and unspeakable grime collected during four showerless days and my little roll in the street. My body odour was so fierce that even I noticed it, in my numbed condition. I felt even more embarrassed when I realised that what I was smelling was myself.

But when Mr Niven Naidoo came through the big security doors to greet me he didn't faint, retch or even bat an eyelid. A stocky guy from Durban, he had a big smile on his face and welcomed me with total aplomb, as if noisome, ragged and bloody long-distance cyclists, half-dead of flu and dysentery, staggered into the embassy every day of the week.

Mr Naidoo had been told about me and wanted to know if he could assist in any way. I told him I was ill and would like to see a doctor, then have a good bath and a long sleep. No sweat! Almost before I knew it I was in an embassy 4x4 and heading for the Park Hotel, where the military attaché had arranged free accommodation with the owner, who was a friend of his. Later I heard that he had done all this in between trying to deter a local from decamping after driving into his 4x4. Talk about multi-tasking!

The hotel was on the other side of the city, and getting there took us about two hours because we had got tangled up in homebound peak-hour traffic. Luanda's population is estimated at 13 million, but its current infrastructure is only designed to cater for only 3 million, so there are some obvious commuting challenges. One of these is that there are only about four or so main routes in and out of the city, and this time of the day all were bumper-to-bumper. And I *mean* bumper-to-bumper. In fact, sometimes it was even bull-bar-to-tail light or driver door-to-rear passenger door. In Luanda, it seemed, the only traffic rule was that there weren't any traffic rules.

Not that there weren't any traffic police, but their interpretation of their duties seemed a little unorthodox, as I soon discovered in an encounter right outside the embassy. There was a traffic circle next to the embassy, and like much of the rest of Luanda at that time of day it was packed solid with vehicles, so much so that various motorists had temporarily given up and parked along the side of the street.

The driver and I decided that we needed to load my bicycle into the back of the 4x4 before we set off for the hotel, so he parked on the side of the street like the others and we got busy. We had loaded the bike and were just squeezing in my loose kit when a female traffic cop came running over to us from the traffic circle's control-point, shouting (so the driver translated the conversation for me later) that our car was illegally parked and would have to be impounded.

The driver laughed at the idea and pointed out that all the other cars were parked in exactly the same way and had no intention of getting going any time soon, while we were actually planning on moving off. The cop was not interested in this observation and demanded his driving licence and the car's registration papers. This was bad news, because it meant that we wouldn't be going anywhere till we had paid a fine. The driver put up a good fight, persisting with his demand to be told why the other law-breakers were not being threatened with impoundment, and eventually the traffic cop giggled and whispered that he was not to worry, obviously the 'stranger' (which is also the word for 'foreigner' in Portuguese) would pay.

Unfortunately the 'stranger' couldn't pay, since I had absolutely no money on me. So the driver coughed up the equivalent of 12 US dollars and the traffic cop returned to her post, where everything had gone to hell in a handbasket during her 15-minute essay into bribery and corruption.

The driver told me that the money came out of his own pocket because the embassy did not cover what you might call operating expenses of this type. I felt very bad about this, seeing my bike had caused the problem, but I really had no money with me. And to be honest I was not interested in paying a bribe. Along the way I had treated the odd policeman to a beer or a soft drink to cement relations or repay a kindness, but being held to ransom like this was a different matter – I would rather sit in a jail and be charged with something than help to support the worst criminal of all, a cop who had gone rotten.

Anyway, we finally got to the Park Hotel, physically if not financially intact. I had a wonderful bath and a not-so-wonderful time washing the muck out of my hands and knees – the stinging seemed to reach almost every part of my body, damaged or undamaged – then went to bed, too tired even to think of eating.

I passed out cold and slept like a dead man, but got up earlier than I would have liked because I hadn't met the owner yet and felt that it would be common courtesy to say hello to him. But I hung around the reception area like a spare part till lunchtime without laying eyes on him, then discovered that he was elsewhere in the city that day.

That evening, though, I met the owners' two sons, Gilberto and Paulo, and had dinner with them. My appetite was still misfiring, but I took their advice and had some of the hotel's renowned cabbage soup, and enjoyed talking to them. They were cut from very different cloth. Paulo was a smooth dresser with a sophisticated approach, while Gilberto was more the relaxed, macho man's man type of guy – one of his stories was of how he had wheelied his BMX all the way from the hotel to the beach front. Jissie! As far as I was concerned that was a long way. I had travelled two hours in traffic just to get here, and he had *wheelied* it!

In the course of our dinner I met a number of other people. One was the tallest man I was to meet anywhere on my trip; I have big hands, but when I greeted him I realised that his were a good few sizes up from mine. Somehow it was no surprise to learn that he was the captain of the Angolan basketball team, which had recently won a gold medal at the African Games in Nigeria. Another was a South African named, I think, Johan, who was doing work for the family and joined us at the dinner table. Johan was a man who, in late middle age, had discovered that in booming Angola there was a new land of opportunity. His actual job was as a consultant on the construction of a brick-making plant whose products would be

85

used for erecting the housing complexes in what Angolans called 'the new city' on the outskirts of the original Luanda.

My first priority was, of course, to start organising visas for the countries that lay immediately ahead, but the weekend had arrived, so nothing could be done till the following week. The delay was actually the best thing that could have happened to me, because it gave me the opportunity to rest up and get in lots of sleep. I needed both because I had not yet recovered my normal good health. I wasn't very hungry, which was not like me, and the dysentery kept dragging me down. It was obvious that I needed serious help. The South African doctor to whom I was sent by the embassy concurred emphatically and immediately put me on a course of antibiotics.

Niven called from the embassy to say that many of the South African crowd in Luanda would be watching the Springboks play their World Cup quarter-final game against the All Blacks that Saturday, and some of the guys were keen to pick me up and take me to one of their houses so that I could watch the game with them. It was a very nice gesture, but the day didn't turn out too well. The Springboks got thumped and I was too sick to really enjoy the occasion. I couldn't even do justice to the amazingly fine-smelling breakfast, so that one of the women present remarked very audibly to a friend that 'for someone who cycled from South Africa this guy isn't very hungry'.

By the Monday, however, I felt much better and launched my assault on the unsuspecting embassies of my target countries, which included the Republic of Congo, the Democratic Republic of Congo, Gabon and any others that were willing to assist me at short notice. But whatever else I got, the non-negotiable ones were Congo, the DRC and Gabon, because Libreville was the next capital I intended to visit.

I sallied forth, full of hope and expectation; it was only later that I realised how over-confident I had been in my belief that obtaining the visas would be a mere formality. But I believe that that very over-confidence also helped me. I never entered an embassy simply to apply for a visa; I arrived expecting to walk out with it in my

Above: The bicycle just before I had it spray-painted to look old and less attractive to robbers. Right after the spray a passer-by stopped me and asked where I had bought such an amazing bike and how much it had cost. Crazy!

Top: Saying goodbye at the Cape Town waterfront: Don't worry, I'll be back in one year (365 days)! And leaving Cape Town: only 6 km on the clock! (Four photos courtesy of Dorothy von Olsten)

Above: My first birthday on the road: friends and flowers at Clanwilliam (photos courtesy of Shane Smart, Dorothy von Olsten).

Right: A promo pic (courtesy of Dorothy von Olsten).

Cape Town, South Africa

Above: Remote in hand, capturing the horizon in Namibia. Wind and harsh sun reflected off white ground were a problem: a week later my top lip's entire skin painfully peeled off. See how weatherbeaten the little flag was after only a week or so.

Above right: The heat was so intense in the Namibian flat plains that my tyre imprints were visible in the melted tar.

Above: Early paranoia in Namibia: bicycle chained to lamppost.

Left: Tabard or gin – your choice: a night with a drunk in a mosquito-infested room at the Oshivelo police station.

Aaah, biltong! Namibian meat is incredible in price and quality.

When 130 km was still a lot. This day I did 157 km to see the Springboks play rugby the next day.

Above: In my opinion, Angola was the most beautiful country out of the 34, with forests of baobabs lining the strong-flowing rivers. Nothing beats nature.

Right: Blowout! Three eloquent comments on the roads served up to me in Angola.

Below: Father Time: my host insisted on being photographed holding his clock.

Below, middle: Good night! Clearing the surrounding thorn bushes and stick grass by stamping the ground was the wrong thing to do in an area still littered with unexploded landmines, but I was too tired to think clearly.

Right: Relics of war litter the roadsides: the tank's defunct, but the landmines need disabling.

Angola

Top left: A focused driver: waves were breaking into the small speedboat that took us across the 16 km mouth of the Congo River from Angola to the DRC.

Top right: Taking bike for walk. On the way to the Cabinda border the choice was between pushing in thick sand or pushing in thick sand. This was the best that it got.

Left: Cabinda to Congo – my first big river crossing by dugout. Wobbly and wet but safe.

Above: Photos taken by remote in the Congo jungle. This was the road in its entirety: a strip of thick mud flanked by impenetrable growth from which, said the WWF representative, the lions watched you go by.

Below: Crossing the river from Congo to Gabon, clean-shaven and in good spirits! In addition to its human passengers, the boat from Congo to Gabon carried antelope, fish, chickens and my eventual dinner that evening, crocodile.

DRC, Cabinda, Congo

Top Left: The jungle wasn't only of the leaf and tree variety. In Libreville the traffic was just as tricky to negotiate and proved way more dangerous.

Top right: Crossing the line! A 30-second break in bucketing rain allowed a Gabonese passer-by to take his first-ever photo.

Right: I'm in Gabon ... but let me rather text you the place's name, OK?

Left: Cameroon, near the Equatorial Guinea border. The former mayor of the town allowed me to camp on his front lawn, where he sat a metre away just like this, overseeing all my movements.

Above: TV interview in Douala, Cameroon.

Gabon, Cameroon

Top left: A tranquil scene in chaotic Nigeria tells of the hustle and bustle to harvest fish.

Top right: The Onitsha Bridge – a proud landmark for Nigerians.

Right (above): 'No food for lazy man' – Owerri, Nigeria; (below): Africa Cup of Nations, Nigeria 4: SA 0.

Below: Religion's a commodity in Nigeria: most of the adverts lining the road are for churches. My imagination could only begin to conjure up reasons for the strange request at the bottom.

Right: A fellow cyclist in Togo, 'inside' the scene I wanted to be in. The mist in the picture is actually dust clouds created by the Harmattan.

Nigeria, Togo

Grand Popo, Benin, where the abolition of slavery is celebrated by a dramatic statue and the nearby Hotel Mandela reinforces the point!

Face-to-face with a large python on the outskirts of Cotonou, Benin.

Breakfast with a petrol smuggler in Cotonou, Benin. Oversized scooters are driven to Nigeria to collect fuel which is then sold in Benin.

Benin/Togo border: I didn't film much at this time, having been threatened and harassed so much that I was nervous about whipping out my video camera in front of people.

Taken by a friend of the general manager outside the DSTV office in Accra, Ghana.

Near the Salt pans in Ghana a school's motto was 'Be Up and Doing.' No better advice or mantra anywhere!

Benin, Togo, Ghana

Top left: A rat seller on the freeway heading north out of Abidjan. A healthy size, these city rats ... well done on an open fire, spread on fresh baguette with plenty chilli ... that's the way!

Top right: From this tree I shot fruit bat dinner for a local petrol attendant and his family. Where I stayed in Treichville, gangster suburb of the city, bat was the freshest thing on the menu.

Above left: I did not take many pictures in Liberia, for obvious safety reasons. This wrecked vehicle was one of many that I went past that were riddled with bullets, tipped over and lying in pools of gun shells.

Far left: I'm never keen to take photos of people suffering but these two in Sierra Leone encouraged me to tell their story.

Mid-left: Truth comes to you in many ways. I personally believe to my core that women make our country and its people. In Sierra Leone the UN army had this message at the exit of their camp.

Bottom: There was something eerily intimidating about these ritually decorated guys in Guinea-Bissau. Our interaction was one-sided: they got all they asked for.

GIVE ME A GOOD MOTHER
I WILL GIVE A GOOD NATION

Ivory Coast, Liberia, Sierra Leone, Guinea-Bissau

hand. I wasn't aggressive in my approach, just confident and determined ... and it worked.

The South African embassy was the plushest and most efficient of those I visited – a couple consisted of no more than a small room, and the way they functioned in comparison with ours was sometimes downright unprofessional; in fact, I would go so far as to say that some were embarrassments to their countries. The poverty of the country concerned – and poverty is a fact of life in so many parts of Africa – can't be used as an excuse in this case. Even a poor country's embassy can have willing and helpful staff who project some sort of positive image, even if it just says: 'Yes, we know we have such-and-such a problem, and we're trying to do something about it. In the meantime, go and have a look for yourself.'

The antibiotics were now kicking in, and within a few days there was a noticeable turn-around in my physical condition. After a week I could finally tuck into the food with something like my normal gusto, and the large Angolan portions suited my newly regained appetite very well. I was feeling so much better that I was silly enough to make the oldest mistake in the book and didn't take the pills as regularly as the prescription required.

Almost everywhere I went I was the recipient of unexpected kindness. For example, look what happened to me at the very first bank I went into, my aim being to get them to transfer money from South Africa, as I had done back in Lubango. Instead of being ushered to a teller's desk I was led to the boardroom and asked to wait. Ten minutes later the man I had first spoken to returned with $100 US and told me it was a gift from the staff!

It was one of those moments when you really wonder whether you're dreaming, then realise to your amazement that you're not. I mean, these people didn't know me at all and had no reason to want to help me. I was really moved by these guys, and the goodness they were spreading by helping me, because the great thing about people doing good things for strangers is that it puts the recipient under tons of positive pressure to go out and spread some of the kindness among others. I was beginning to owe many people, that was for sure.

There was also a public holiday while I was in Luanda, and to celebrate it Johan, Paulo and Gilberto took me and a cooler box full of beer out for a day at the famous Ilha de Luanda, a narrow peninsula cluttered with beachside bars and hotels. It was jam-packed with locals and foreigners, all enjoying what the Luandan beaches had to offer. This included hordes of very sexy and sophisticated girls, both in and out of the water. There seemed to be an infinite number of 20-year-olds wearing bikinis that they had probably received as tenth birthday presents, since the cups often covered little more than their nipples. This sounds pretty good, and it was, actually, but it was definitely not what I had expected from my original researches.

So if you expect to find vaguely rural-looking girls (whatever they look like) in Luanda you would be mistaken. It's like a girl from Texas losing the boots and hat when she arrives in New York. Luandans are in love with Brazil – many locals even jokingly said to me that Angola is just another Brazilian province – and the influence shows clearly in the way they dress.

Seeing that I had time to spare, what with dysentery and the visas, I managed to meet one of Angola's sexiest singers, Bruna, who had developed quite a following in South Africa as a participant in the 'Big Brother Africa' show. She has an angelic voice and I loved her singing, and when I went to see her at a function where she was performing she actually sang a couple of songs especially for me. OK, they were part of her warm-up, but at least she asked me which songs I wanted to hear.

In the middle of the second week in Luanda, on the very night Bruna sang for me, my casual attitude towards the antibiotics came back to bite me in the backside – almost literally. After seeing Bruna I went straight back to the hotel, but not to dive into bed. My innards went into a state of total anarchy and I spent the entire night propped up on the toilet because I didn't dare lie down in case I suffered the ultimate embarrassment while asleep.

When morning eventually arrived I went back to my doctor, who told me what I already knew: 'Always complete your entire antibiotic course. Always!' He prescribed Cypro and another three days of rest before setting off again. I swore to stay on the straight and narrow this time – and I did, because that harrowing night had been a warning that if something like this happened again when I was out of reach of medical treatment I might not survive. My kind hosts had no problem with the extension.

I had now been in Luanda for 10 days, far longer than I had intended, but I was still awaiting a positive response from the Nigerian embassy. I used some of my spare time to go hunting for an Angolan sponsor, and struck it lucky when I hit the De Beers Corporation building, the biggest in the city. I had been thinking about this for some days, although I realised that it was foolishly optimistic, even for me, because all the South African staff had gone home after a squabble between De Beers and the Angolan government.

The basis of the dispute was an allegation by the government that De Beers had continued to buy diamonds from the late Dr Jonas Savimbi's UNITA group, its main opponent, which it accused of continuing to foment violence after losing out in what UNITA described as a fraudulent general election. UNITA controlled most of Angola's diamond-fields in the north-eastern part of the country, and by buying diamonds from it, the government said, De Beers was an accessory to the continuing violence.

It didn't look awfully promising, therefore. On the other hand, De Beers was a very large and famous corporation, and the departure of its South African staff hadn't closed down its Angolan operation. Nothing ventured, nothing gained! And, after all, I was supposed to be an adventurer. So I talked my way into the stringently guarded building and ended up in the office of a man by the name of Toy Yoanda. We chatted for a while, and I told him of my project and the great kindness I had received so far from Angolans of both high and low degree, about which I intended to tell everybody I met when I got back home.

Toy asked me to come back and see him the next day, and I left in a happy frame of mind. This was considerably better than nothing – at least he hadn't summarily tossed me out, which meant that I would be able to press my case for a spot of sponsorship. I hadn't even brought up the subject of money on that first visit. When I returned next morning he wasn't available, but I was astounded and deeply moved to be given a crisp white envelope he had left for me, containing $600 US in even crisper notes. And I couldn't even thank him!

Actually I never saw Toy again, but I did manage to telephone him and express my gratitude. I don't know exactly why he did me this great favour, but I suspect he took it on himself, on behalf of all Angolans, to show support and in a way to thank me for my intention to throw a more positive light on his much-misunderstood country.

I got another boost – spiritual rather than financial this time – when the local operation of the South African Grinaker construction company asked me to address the pupils at its private school. It was huge fun for me as well as the kids, and a number of them, having heard of my self-designed adventure, didn't take long to tell me what they were planning to do with their lives. Some of these plans might have sounded absurd by conventional adult standards, but I knew them for what they were: dreams that could come true if they dreamt hard enough. Both children and adults think big, but the difference between them is that adults think big within certain boundaries and children think big without any boundaries at all. I think I scored the most out of that meeting, because those bright-eyed children encouraged me to keep dreaming without letting myself be hampered by self-imposed boundaries.

I left soon afterwards, nearly two weeks after I had wobbled into Luanda more dead than alive. I received a final farewell gift from strangers, as unexpected as all the others, when the Luanda branch of the South African Shoprite/Checkers grocery chain told me to help myself to provisions for the trip ahead. I took full advantage of this great favour and filled up with the same sort of well-known brands as I had bought in Cape Town, although I had to be firm and stick to the sort of things that wouldn't weigh me down too much – pasta, energy drinks, canned fish and the like.

Now I was as ready as I ever would be. I held a farewell braai for my friends at the Park Hotel and called Niven to tell him I was leaving next morning, and also to thank him and his colleagues at the embassy for all their help. Gilberto dropped me off on the outskirts of the city that Thursday morning. As I cycled off I could see him waiting by his car to make sure I had got off safely. I was eager to get going, of course, but I was sad to leave Luanda. It's chaotic and rather battered at the moment, but the vitality and good nature of its people may help it to become one of Africa's great cities again.

The kindness of Angola's human inhabitants, I have to add, is not detectable in its insects, and I refer especially to the tsetse flies. The tsetse is not impressive to look at, but the dreaded sleeping sickness contracted from its bite has probably done more to keep Africa from fulfilling its potential than any other disease with the possible exception of malaria. AIDS gets the world's headlines, but the unspectacular silent killers like malaria and sleeping sickness have been inflicting far worse damage for many generations.

On top of that the tsetse is as tough as old boots. One local man told me that when he was in the army he soon discovered how to distinguish between a tsetse and an ordinary fly. When you swatted an ordinary fly, he explained, it keeled over and fell off you. But when you swatted a tsetse it just did 10 push-ups and then flew away. This was a joke, of course, but in the days to come I couldn't help wondering if there wasn't a grain of truth in it somewhere. And here I was, heading straight into an area so infested that passing hunters and other travellers habitually roll up their windows to keep out the tsetses and the equally vicious horse flies, blissfully unaware that the bright blue of my shirt was a colour notoriously attractive to the tsetses for some reason. I had read in the 'Lonely Planet' guide that tsetses were attracted to brightly coloured, large, slow-moving objects, and that pretty much described me as I toiled along in my blue shirt. So I was a catastrophe looking for a place to happen, and I think it was out of sheer pity for what I was about to endure that passing travellers plied me with cool drinks and snacks.

In my ignorance I was not too alarmed at first, although irritated by the tsetses' bites, each of which left a painful bump. But it got to the point where I couldn't sleep well at night because of the growing number of painful bumps on my back. I still wasn't seriously concerned about what I had got myself into, although by now I had got into the habit of continually slapping my back to chase away the hordes of tsetses which kept landing there for a quick bite of something. But then the true horror of my situation was brought home to me in a strange and terrifying way as I forged along on the dirt road which had taken over from the tarmac leading out of Luanda.

Before I had left Cape Town a photographer had taken some very imaginative promotional pictures of the various shadows thrown by my bike and me, and late one afternoon, with the sun fast approaching the horizon, I remembered her images and looked around to see if my shadow looked any different up here. But the shadow I saw was like something out of a horror movie trailer. There was my and my bike's combined shadow neatly light-painted in black on the rich soil, and I saw my shadow-arm coming up to slap my shadow-back, and when it did so another shadow arose from my body and flew off, looking exactly like the soul departing my body at the moment of death. Instinctively I turned to inspect my baggage, and a wave of my hand sent hundreds more tsetses rising up from the black saddle-bags. It was horrible.

It was then that I started realising just how severely I had suffered so far. My entire back was covered in lumps, new ones on top of old ones. When I lay down at night it felt as if I was lying on a bed of small round pebbles, and even a minor movement could trigger a sharp stab of pain inside one of the lumps. In addition to these I was bitten behind my knees every time I stopped, although the bites here were not as badly inflamed as the ones on my back. My only consolation was that sleeping with the dysentery had been worse, and in a way I was almost glad to have an irritation which distracted me from the ever-present worry about being attacked and robbed during the night.

I took what precautions I could as I toiled over the endless hills. On the way up I would try to time my movements so that I could slap my back every now and then without losing rhythm or speed, and downhill I would go as fast as possible, which helped to lose some of the hitch-hikers. I also stopped only to sleep and relieve myself, and shed the blue shirt (which didn't help much, since the only other colour I had was white), wore a T-shirt under it in spite of the heat to stop some bites from penetrating and smeared insect repellent over my back and shoulders.

All of these stratagems made an immediate difference, although the bitter-enders stayed on. But I now had a greater concern. Sleeping sickness starts showing up about a week after one has been bitten, and at my present rate of progress I would be somewhere in the middle of the Democratic Republic of Congo's jungles by then. It was a frightening thought. By all accounts the DRC – rather an ironic name, seeing that it seemed to have become a family business, with the new President, Joseph Kabila, taking over when his father was assassinated – was in a terrible state. Decades of dictatorship and warfare between its various robber barons had left the official government's writ non-existent outside a few centres and completely collapsed the infrastructure.

I tried to put these forebodings aside as I pressed on, because there was no turning back now. So, slapping and pedalling, I reached the little seaside fishing village of Nzeto, where I had a contact of sorts. A passing hunter had written me a note of introduction to one Costa and assured me that everyone in Nzeto knew the 'branco' (white man). And that's exactly how it was. Costa? Sure! Within minutes I was knocking on the salt-encrusted front door of his little beach cabin.

After about five minutes of knocking Costa finally opened it. I didn't know quite what to expect – a ragged, bearded beach-comber, perhaps, waiting to be rescued after a shipwreck. But apart from being deeply tanned, Costa didn't look like that at all, being a fit-looking middle-aged man with an irrepressibly smiling face. He made me comfortable and told me that he was originally from Portugal, but had married an Angolan girl and was very happily settled in his cluttered little cabin. Then we sat at his table and ate some fruit (more than I should have eaten, actually) which was completely foreign to me – large things, with light yellow flesh textured like a pawpaw and pips like a pumpkin's, only darker. Apparently it was very nutritious, because when I had finished Costa said that what I had eaten had as much Vitamin C as a large bag of oranges. I was certainly learning something new every day!

It was a fascinating place, cluttered, like all those fishermen's cottages that you see in TV films, but with the difference that a lot of the clutter consisted of what one can only call conversation pieces of historical importance. The very table at which he sat, he said after showing me some pictures of his family in Portugal, had once had the current president and various of his sworn enemies around it, not eating fruit but talking peace.

In spite of his fairly humble circumstances Costa was friendly with many of Angola's top businessmen and, like them, wanted to see an end to the decades of civil war that still rumbled on in places. That was another thing about Angola. Here was a humble Portuguese fisherman living in an obscure little village, many kilometres from anywhere, but on occasion he walked with people in high places and was not overawed by them.

Costa invited me to stay over for the night, but I declined because it was still too early in the day. I reckoned I could easily fit in another 40 km before sunset, camp for the night and next day cycle to Soyo. From there I would cross the Congo River's mouth into the DRC.

It didn't work out that way, though. The brakes of my back wheel had been rubbing against the outside wall of the tyre and finally wore right through to the inner tube, which didn't take long to burst. I was not too worried at first. The day was young and I had a reasonable stock of spares – two tyres and five tubes. But it wasn't as simple as that, as I soon discovered. Firstly, a tube could be repaired if the hole wasn't too big, but it invariably started leaking air before very long; secondly, even if I put two large patches on the inside of the tyre's ruptured wall the tube would somehow manage to force its way through.

By noon I was becoming distinctly worried. Soyo was still 70 km away, and I was running out of time – I had already had to make two repairs, each eating up about an hour. More importantly, I was running out of spares, particularly tubes. So now I was down to my last tyre and second-last tube. I tried to keep my mind off my problems by watching the landscape go by.

The little dirt road had hugged the coast the entire way so far and the views had been invigorating companions, but when I came to the tiny village of Manga Grande, sitting on a plateau on top of a hill which then fell gently away towards the sea, covered with palm and banana trees, it beat everything else I had seen that day. A couple of hundred metres from the village I announced my arrival in spectacular fashion when my rear tyre burst with a noise like a cannon-shot. I was as amazed as the inhabitants, and it was only when pedalling instantly became about a hundred times harder that I realised what had happened.

While the inhabitants stared, open-mouthed, I hopped off and inspected the damage. What my inspection told me was that I was going to have to push that damned crippled bike all the way to Soyo, 70 km away, unless a lift miraculously appeared from somewhere … and not one vehicle of any kind heading in the right direction had passed me that entire day. What the hell was I going to do?'

Then good fortune made its appearance in the shape of the village policeman, whose main job, so he explained, was to search passing vehicles. I showed him what had happened and asked his advice in my very broken Portuguese. He thought the idea of pushing my bike to Soyo was preposterous and suggested that I leave the bike in a safe place, take the next vehicle that passed through, whenever that might be, and fetch spares from Soyo. In the meantime he would keep the bike in his own bedroom, the safest place in the entire village.

I accepted and pushed it in, then started worrying about the next stroke of good fortune I needed, a vehicle with an amiable driver and room to spare, going in the right direction. And would you believe it, scarcely five minutes later a Toyota double-cab bound for Soyo pulled up, carrying grocery supplies and a number of passengers including an elderly couple and a woman who was breast-feeding her baby.

My police friend and I negotiated with the owner-driver, one Tyson, and he found me a space next to the breast-feeding lady and her baby. It wasn't the most comfortable seat I'd ever had – she seemed to have retained a few kilos from her pregnancy, which made things a bit tight – but it certainly beat pushing the bike to Soyo. Just as well, I thought, that by this time my travels had sweated off every bit of extra baggage on my body.

It was a long, long trip to Soyo, because the road was challenging even for a rugged 4x4 like the Toyota, not to mention a mortal danger to our spinal cords – in some places it was so bumpy that at times we would be shaken right out of our seats. We bounced along as if the Toyota had square wheels and got slung back and forth as Tyson zigzagged between the more insurmountable sections, the shock-absorbers crying out as if in mortal pain.

To add to my troubles I was having problems with the baby. My part of the seat sagged down, so when I relaxed my head was level with the breast-feeding lady's shoulder and the baby was practically eyeball-to-eyeball with me. When the road bumped us loose from our seats it would also dislodge the baby's gums from nature's primary feeding interface, and I would get splattered with liberal amounts of breast-milk and saliva.

My first inkling of what was happening was when I became aware of a strange sensation, something like warm yoghurt being flicked at me from the end of a school ruler. I investigated with some difficulty, since my arms were virtually clamped to my sides and moving my head also meant moving it in the direction from which the yoghurt-like stuff was coming. Which was, of course, the baby, whose head and upper body hung upside-down right up against me, mouth wide open. No one looks at their best upside-down, and from the look of him we were equally bewildered by the whole business.

I didn't want to make a fuss, so I concentrated on trying to scrape the worst of the gunk off me, but I take it that I made some exclamation of horror in the process, because now the other passengers saw what had happened. Before long everyone was in fits of laughter except the baby and myself. I wore a rather feeble smile, not wishing to seem a spoilsport, and he cried fit to burst.

I managed to improve my situation very slightly when we were flagged down by a handful of villagers who, I was later told, wanted Tyson to take a very sick old man to the Soyo hospital for urgent medical attention. Tyson pointed out that the Toyota was full to bursting point already. The villagers retorted that one simply didn't leave a sick man to die. There was no denying the truth of this, or the fact that the old man was obviously very poorly. I remember him so well: small and slender with a grizzled beard and moustache, dressed in a brown suit and clutching a brown hat in one hand and a walking-stick in the other which was more a decoration than anything else, because he could hardly move. But there was still the space problem to solve, and the discussion went on and on.

Eventually the penny dropped, and I was ashamed that it had not dropped sooner. I was the only person in the Toyota who was not old, breast-feeding or otherwise encumbered or engaged. Common decency compelled me to make a suggestion to Tyson. I would get into the back and complete the journey standing up amid the cargo; this meant that the passenger sitting in front next to Tyson could cram himself into my seat, and the sick man could take his place. This was an acceptable compromise. I got on the back and the front-seat passenger shoe-horned himself in next to the breast-feeding woman (and good luck to *you*, my friend, I thought). Then the villagers eased the sick man into the Toyota and put his hat and medical papers on his lap. He just sat staring into the distance, still holding his useless walking-stick.

It was another 40 ghastly kilometres to Soyo, and I spent them hanging on to the cab, which wasn't much of improvement on my previous situation, except that I had free use of my arms again and had escaped from that damned baby's fall-out. I passed the time by thinking about the sick man. At his age, I thought, a man would want to retain something even more precious than good health: his dignity and the respect of his family. Then my thoughts wandered off to the wonderful Angolans I'd met, and how the lack of something I had always taken for granted, good medical care, impacted on their lives.

With all due respect to traditional remedies, someone like this old man needed modern First World medicine to survive ... and the people out in the jungles and other remote places of Africa didn't have the choice available to someone like me who lived in a stable, fairly developed country.

I kept wanting to say it was unfair, but then I felt that to say so would be to degrade the value of living a family-orientated, loving, peaceful and natural existence. The people here had something we didn't have, something 99 per cent of the 'privileged' world will never have. Learned books full of jaw-breaking words could be written, explaining our innate desire to return to nature, but the words would not capture the essence. There was a great conundrum here. We wanted what they had – and they wanted what we had. Yet neither group could achieve its goal without running the risk of destroying the real advantages it already enjoyed.

Nearer to Soyo the road was tarmac and the going was quicker and easier. An amazing number of oil shops, all bearing the logo of the Angolan national oil company, Sonangol, lined the approaches, and this gave me more food for thought. Having your own business was great in many ways, but what concerned me was that you needed to think twice about opening your own little oil dispensary when every other neighbour in eyeshot was doing the exact same. Oh, well, there was no easy answer, and I needed to concentrate on my own problems.

After four very long hours on the road we finally rolled into Soyo, just in time for another glorious sunset. A sunset is a very special thing. We all know that the sun will rise tomorrow and set again gently in the very late afternoon. We all know sunsets are beautiful and sometimes positively awe-inspiring. We all know that we take them for granted. We *don't* all know that in the average lifetime there are only about 25 000 opportunities to really enjoy them. I decided, then and again on many later occasions, that I would often remind myself of where I was now and where I probably could have been.

It felt good to know that I was on the coast of Angola, looking out over the Atlantic Ocean, instead of knocking on another client's door. It was a reminder to myself that I was doing the right thing. It's a simple exercise which everyone should do. The problem is that you have to be honest with yourself, which not many people are.

The main street was one long stretch that ended near the harbour area, with a hotel on the right near the bottom end and, to the left, the turnoff to a security compound where the local expatriate workers lived. Tyson offered to put me up for the night at his house, then take me to the expatriates' compound in the morning. Gratefully I took him up on his offer, so he dropped me off at his house in the local township and left me with his strictly non-English-speaking wife and sister while he went off to the hospital with the old man.

The township was like a lot of others in Africa – little houses almost on top of one another, children playing in the streets, teenagers giggling in groups and adults peering out of the windows. What they were peering at, I soon discovered, was me, and I knew what question they were asking themselves: 'What's this white guy doing here?'

I spent my time greeting as many people as I could and even playing with some of the younger children, but before too long I could feel the atmosphere begin to change. Disgruntled-looking adults who obviously had nothing better to do confronted Tyson's wife and demanded to know what I was doing here.

Although she had been dropped in at the deep end she kept her cool, explaining (as far as I could make out) that her husband had picked me up along the way and had then left me with her. I didn't understand all the words being flung back and forth during the increasingly heated exchanges, but one I did recognise was 'stranger', meaning foreigner. Then some of them demanded that I show them my passport, which I politely but firmly refused to do, meanwhile keeping a sharp eye open for Tyson. Where the hell was he? Mentally I berated myself for not asking him to take me directly to the expat compound. In the meantime I applied my only strategy – smiling and focusing on the more sympathetic-looking ones – while trying to work out an escape plan to put into action if Tyson didn't roll up soon and save me from his neighbours.

Then things got a stage uglier when some of my original tormentors returned with a couple of policemen. I didn't feel too good about this. Here I was facing a hostile crowd and two presumably equally hostile cops in the dark in a foreign country, and I didn't even know enough of the local language to explain my situation with any clarity. So I did the only thing I could: I took out my passport so that they could see who I was and offered a Portuguese-as-he-spikked type of explanation. To my relief the policemen were very understanding and actually apologised for interrogating me. This didn't please the grumpy ones; some of them, I think, would only have been happy if there had been a public lynching ... an outcome which, I need hardly say, wasn't one I favoured much.

Then, at last, Tyson appeared; it turned out that he had visited some of his friends on his way home. I didn't care – I was wiped out, and simply didn't have the energy left to struggle with conversation. Tyson saw my state and without further ado showed me to my bedroom. This was actually his sister's, he said, but her husband was away, and so she had offered it to me. There it was again, that special kindness to strangers that I had come to expect of Angola.

Tyson and I spent the following morning browsing among the wooden stalls in the town market, looking for bike spares. There were plenty to be had, but the tubes were French-made rather than the common American ones I was using, which meant that my pump would be useless, and we simply couldn't locate a replacement anywhere. The replacement tyres were not exactly what I needed, either, because the tread was meant for smooth road surfaces and the tyres themselves were too narrow for my mountain bike's rims.

Getting back on the road was going to be a case of easier said than done. But I wasn't perturbed. There had to be a solution somewhere, and I would find it – I hadn't come this far to be defeated by some narrow tyres and tubes with the wrong valves. So I actioned Plan B, which was to throw myself on the mercy of the South Africans in the expat compound.

Being a local, Tyson wasn't allowed into the barricaded village, so he dropped me off at the entrance and I asked the gate-guards to put me in touch with any South African who happened to be available. They verified that I was who I said I was and then passed on my request to the head of security. Twenty minutes later he arrived in person, and once again the gods of good fortune smiled on me. He was a South African named Johan Goosen, otherwise known to all and sundry as 'Goose', and was very friendly and ready to help. I told him my story and explained my needs, and almost before I was aware of what was happening he had arranged a warm shower and a plate of hot food, just to get things off on a good note.

Some of the South Africans and other staff would be very interested to meet me, Johan said, and would I like to stay the night as a guest of the compound? As you can imagine I didn't turn this offer down, and I had a very pleasurable evening, during which I made some good contacts for the future. My hosts were all involved in the local oil business. They included Junior, the local head of the Texaco operation and the man who had actually authorised my stay (I was amused to see that he was the spitting image of Andre Watson, the famous South African rugby referee); my temporary room-mate Evre, who skippered the boat that patrolled around the numerous rigs rearing up from close inshore to as far as 30 km out to sea; and employees of a de-mining company that had been contracted by the oil industry to clear away unexploded ordnance.

John and Co easily found tyres and tubes in their storeroom that fitted my bike and next morning I headed for the town's market, from where Tyson had said all transport back to Manga Grande left. This time I had to pay, but at least it ensured a comfortable seat with enough room for my elbows and no next-door baby. The policeman was pleased to see me and helped with replacing the tyre and tube. This was followed by a small farewell party, and then in the late afternoon I cycled away as the setting sun washed everything – the bush, the people, the clay walls – in a wonderful deep orange glow.

This is not normally a good time to start a day's journey, but I planned to cycle through the night, because I had just made the rather unnerving discovery that the visa which had cost me so much time and energy was due to expire that very day. I felt like kicking myself for such slack planning. And it was only my second country! I knew it was going to be a tough night, especially on that excuse for a road, but I didn't deserve to have it easy after such a blunder.

Darkness came quickly and brought with it a silence interrupted only by the rasping of my tyres on the gravel. I could see the closer oil rigs clearly now: the yellow flames that wobbled above each one were so bright, even from what looked like 10 km away, that at times they actually cast some flickering light on to the road in front of me. I couldn't help thinking of the threat from possible oil disasters. I didn't know – and still don't know – anything about the safety measures in place in that part of the world, but I believe that one bugger-up would be all that would be needed to cause a pollution disaster, and I fear for Angola's coastline, so spellbindingly beautiful, yet so fragile.

Easy come, easy go ... What have we humans done to deserve this splendour? What have we done to preserve it while harvesting its bounty? The oil industry represents the investment of huge quantities of effort and expense, and there is always the temptation to the people with their hands on the levers of power to give the harvesting top priority, with preservation coming a poor second. It was a gloomy thought, but I was to discover that the situation wasn't quite as gloomy as I thought while I toiled towards Soyo that night.

'Toil' is the word for that progress through the murk. There wasn't much of a moon and the flickering light from the rigs became obscured by the thickening bush on either side of the road as I bumped along at an average of about 5 km/h. I made a quick calculation: all going well, of which there was no guarantee at all, it was going to take me at least 14 hours to reach Soyo.

They were already proving to be tough hours. Every now and then I would ride off the road because I couldn't see where I was going. That meant bumps and scrapes, but those I could handle – my main concern was mollycoddling the bike till I got to my destination. But I arrived at a sort of epiphany when I reached a rise and struggled up it while straining to make out where the path was going. Unbeknown to me I had lost my way again and was now riding up an embankment which, I think, had been left over from the original road-construction work. I discovered my mistake when my tiny world suddenly came apart – literally. The bike bogged down in some thick sand while I kept going and tumbled down the rocky remainder of the embankment.

This latest tumble forced me to take stock of my situation and face a fact that I had ignored up to now because I had been so strongly focused on reaching Soyo: I had set myself an impossible task. I had been cycling since sunset and now, past midnight, had managed only about 30 km. I had had several falls, but had managed to avoid serious damage to either myself or my bike. But the next fall could change all that. The only logical conclusion was that I should stop while everything was still in one piece.

I ran my mind back through my recollections of the trip in Tyson's Toyota and suddenly realised where I was: on a sharp bend where the road broadened considerably. I also remembered that less than a kilometre past this bend we had passed a very small village, and I decided to push on to it.

I pedalled on and within a few minutes reached the centre of the village. At this time of the morning everybody was sleeping except a few young men. One of them came up to greet me and we held a tortured conversation – he had learnt some Portuguese at school but often had to pause while he tried to recollect sentences from his text books, while I knew considerably less than that. After some false starts I finally understood what he was saying, namely that the road ahead was better than the bit I had just covered (I remembered that vaguely myself), but that it would be better to wait for daylight before going on.

Well, there was no arguing with that advice; my little adventure with the embankment had shown me the folly of trying to carry on in the dark. And then I got another dose of good fortune and Angolan hospitality. Would I like, he asked, to get my head down at his home? Once again there was no sense in disputing the wisdom of his suggestion, and in no time at all I was at his house and looking forward to some much-needed sleep.

Like their compatriots of earlier, these Angolans didn't fool around when it came to hospitality, and to my horror I found that they planned to give me the bed belonging to the family's grandmother. This was much worse than the case of the 65-year-old uncle, and as tactfully as possible I refused the offer, saying I would be happy to sleep on the floor. When the night-owl and his family eventually understood my objection they led me to another room, where she was snugly tucked into a bamboo bed, to show that she wasn't suffering. With this my objections fell away, and they made me comfortable with a blanket, a lamp and a few mangoes to snack on. Once again I went to sleep filled with wonderment at the sheer goodness of these people, who had so little themselves, compared to many South Africans, yet were willing to share it with a total stranger.

I slept like a log for a regrettably brief time, because I was on the road again before the first ray of sunshine made its appearance. The first stretch was a struggle, of course, but at least I could see where I was going, and eventually I reached the tarmac and was able to crack on the speed. People stared at me as I came puffing into Soyo, which was hardly surprising, considering that I wasn't the sort of sight one saw much, if at all, in that part of the world. I didn't pay any great attention to this public scrutiny because I was keen to get to the expat compound. On the way, though, I stopped off at the hotel to say hello to the owner, to whom Tyson had introduced me during our wanderings.

This little social visit landed me in some totally unexpected complications. I was waiting outside the hotel while one of the staff went to find the owner when some of the locals milling in the street came up and asked who I was and where I was going. Mindful of my experience in the township two days earlier, I was as friendly as possible, but they weren't having any of this, and when they saw that the conversation was going nowhere they fetched two uniformed immigration officials.

One of the officials demanded to see my passport and visa, and for a moment I didn't know what to do. I had not even thought about a possible complication like this and hadn't worked out a strategy to get out from under it. And now here I was, looking into the muzzle of the immigration people's gun (figuratively speaking, of course), with a sizeable crowd, including the hotel-owner and his staff, looking on to see what would happen next.

I decided that my only way out was to make this guy feel bad about the way he was treating me, so that peer pressure would keep the level of aggression down. So I respectfully asked why he needed to see it. He replied that it was his duty, and I went on to inquire – more for the onlookers than for him – whether immigration offices were not meant for people moving between two countries, rather than the interrogation of an innocent tourist in the middle of the town, and whether all strangers were questioned in this manner.

I concluded by explaining that I would be happy to show him my passport, it was just that this would mean unpacking my entire kit to get to the dry parts, starting with unwrapping the plastic sheet I had strapped over everything to keep my baggage dry. He stood firm, however, and I started unwrapping, making a bigger issue of the effort than it really was. I began getting nervous as I got near to where my passport was packed away, because I knew I was on really thin ice. What would he do when, filled with remorse about hassling me, he discovered that I had an invalid visa? He'd probably take me by the collar and drag me off to the cells.

Anyway, I finally reached the passport and handed it to him, deliberately leaving all the little notes and small photos I kept inside it – maybe this would distract him and he wouldn't notice that the visa was one day into expiry – and I made a point of drawing his attention to the other visas I had, detailing my completed route and describing the one ahead. Then I waited, with my heart in my throat and my stomach in a twist.

To my immense relief he failed to notice the date on my expired visa and headed briskly back to the immigration office at the harbour without even hanging around to watch me re-pack my kit. The original trouble-makers showed signs of disappointment at being thwarted of their entertainment, so I decided to forget about the socialising and get on to Johan right away. I rang him from the national telephone company office across the road, and after a tense half-hour or so his driver was there to pick me up.

As we put my persecutors behind us the driver, also a South African, apologised for the delay, explaining that he had not been given a description of me beyond the fact that he had to pick up a white man on a bicycle. As a result he had followed another white man on a bicycle and after discovering his mistake had been given a wrong lead by one of the locals. He had then spent the next 20 minutes driving around and getting a bit frantic and beginning to doubt the accuracy of his instructions before Johan called him, wanting to know why I was still waiting at the telecoms office.

The people at the expat compound were really kind, and everyone wanted to help me on my way. Junior was able to offer some particularly important help in the shape of his aluminium welding shop, the only one for hundreds of kilometres in any direction. The shop was installed on a maintenance ship anchored in the harbour alongside some pristine mangrove swamps, and Junior arranged for it to tackle my broken carrier-frame the next afternoon; Evre promised he would take me out there before one of his routine patrols.

That night we got together at the small five-star hotel in the security compound for a few drinks with an evaluation team which was doing an environmental assessment of Texaco's work in Soyo, and I realised for the first time how good business people were at putting whatever they had available to good use. This group's members really knew what they were doing, having visited many such sites before, and having me as a guest allowed them to take a little time off from saving Mother Earth. Having been born and brought up in Zululand, I knew a little about mangroves (as a kid I'd always been fascinated by the way the sea-snails moved up and down the stems in unison with the tides), and I was able to contribute a few pennyworths with my story about how the local community at St Lucia had rallied and fought against the destruction of the estuary and its mangroves.

The time I spent with these people gave me yet another new perspective, because they were so different from the average guy, who doesn't even know what lies beyond his garden's back wall. They were living a life that was teaching them new things every day. You can be an engineer in an environment you grew up with and are accustomed to, and you can continue with the daily and repetitive influences that develop you as a person till you retire. But these fellows had left behind what they knew in preference for what they *didn't* know, and I concluded that this was largely the reason why all of them took to me and my intended journey with such enthusiasm; they had also done and were doing something extraordinary.

I spent the next two days eating large quantities of breakfast, lunch and dinner, in between which Johan and Evre looked after me with great dedication. This included showing me the sights, which included such unusual things as the bullet-holes in the lampposts from a rebel attack a couple of years earlier. At dinner the second night Johan also had a bit of fun when he took some of my pictures of Vasti and me to show everyone how my eyes closed when I smiled. He couldn't believe how plump I had been before I left. Looking at the photos, I couldn't believe it either.

The Texaco welding shop made a more than thorough job of my bike. The rear carrier strut that had snapped while I was leaving Lubango was now stronger than ever, because they not only welded the ends together but reinforced the crucial areas with plate aluminium. They even found a spare tyre that was more conducive to off-road conditions and a better fit on the rims. The only thing I hadn't found yet was a pump suitable for the French-type valves – and, of course, a solution to my visa problem.

After much discussion the consensus was that I should chance my arm with the visa. If I was caught out it would probably mean having to go back to Luanda for an extension, but it was worth trying to wriggle through by saying nothing and then pleading ignorance if anyone noticed the expiry date.

Johan dropped me off at the dilapidated excuse for a jetty and even more dilapidated immigration office, which was made of reeds and consisted of a waiting area and a more private room where the actual business of immigration took place, such as stamping passport pages and, I assumed, taking backhanders.

Before driving off Johan took out a folded note and handed it to me, saying in a strangely diffident way: 'Take this, you'll need it more than me.' I only discovered the reason for his uncharacteristic shyness when I opened the note and found $100 tucked inside. Not for the first time on my journey I was deeply moved. That hundred-dollar handshake sprang from more than just his natural kindness. It signified that at least some people believed in me and my journey; it was not only about myself any more.

Buoyed up by Johan's vote of confidence – not to mention the very welcome cash boost – I marched into the immigration office, ready to do battle about my bum visa. But it could not have been simpler, and it is refreshing to tell this story, which is the antithesis of all the tales about buying off corrupt officials – usually true – that come out of African travel tales in such profusion.

The official asked me if I had enjoyed Angola, to which I replied with exactly what I felt. He was pleased, although he made it clear that he considered me crazy to venture into the very undemocratic Democratic Republic of Congo, stamped 'sortie' on my passport and hailed the captain of the boat that would take me over the river mouth – no minor excursion, since it is the widest in Africa. We manhandled the bike into the boat and I sat there in solitary splendour, waiting and praying for other passengers to come soon so that we could get going. The Congo was waiting for me, although it didn't know it yet.

# CHAPTER 6

# ROADBLOCKS AND ANTHEMS
# – INTO THE DRC

*I recall distinctly the feeling of vulnerability we all had when we encountered groups of soldiers manning roadblocks on the way to Boma. A few of the roadblocks were official, but others were actually just small drinking and bribe-taking parties. On that journey to Matadi – and on the return – I saw more drunken soldiers than I could have imagined. In Angola I had seen soldiers drinking to cool down, but here, it seemed, soldiers drank to fall down.*

The long wooden motorboat chugged steadily across the 16 km stretch to the Democratic Republic of the Congo with me, my bicycle and about another 10 passengers. The day was overcast and calm, but the closer we got to DRC soil the windier and choppier things became as the two opposing forces, the mighty river and even mightier Atlantic Ocean, collided with one another. Soon we were contending with heavy swells and even some breaking waves, so that at times the boat would become airborne for a few moments before smashing down again, to the accompaniment of loud creaking from the hull.

The confidence I had talked into myself at the start of the journey began to evaporate as the boat bounced around, and, looking at the faces of my fellow passengers, I wasn't the only one. I tried to hide the concern building up by keeping a smile on my face and letting off the occasional cowboy-style whoop, but this didn't help much. One consolation was that the boat's captain, unlike the rest of us, didn't look worried; his impassive gaze remained firmly fixed on the horizon, even when my video camera was aimed at him. Not without some effort, I convinced myself that if we were in danger his poker face would surely exhibit signs of alarm.

Till that happened there was nothing to do but hang on, and the trip seemed to be taking a long time, much longer than I had expected. I had thought that we'd zip across quite quickly – after all, the DRC shore was clearly visible from the Angolan side. I only realised how far we had to go when, after about half an hour, I began making out trees and buildings, some of them quite large, on what had been merely a featureless line of river bank when we had set off.

My main concern, though, was not for myself but for my bicycle if the boat were to sink. To ease my mind I tied a cord around my foam bed-mat and knotted the other end to the bicycle's frame. If the boat *did* sink, I told myself, and the water was not too deep, the mat would be a sort of a buoy to mark my treasured bike's temporary watery grave. It wasn't a very good idea, but it was all I could think of at the time.

I also had rather mixed feelings about what lay ahead. When I left Angola for points north I was fully aware of how lucky I had been so far, and particularly on this very day in getting through customs with an outdated visa. But I was a bit nervous about entering the DRC. It was the first French-speaking country of my trip, of course, but I also knew there wasn't much that was democratic about this allegedly democratic republic. It was notorious for some distinctly undemocratic things. There was a horrific war of genocide in progress on the eastern borders, and when President Laurent Kabila was assassinated he was succeeded in monarchical style by his son Joseph, the world's youngest head of state at the age of 27. I also knew that the DRC had the world's largest deployment of United Nations troops, which tells you something.

My introduction to the DRC was inauspicious, although highly visible. The locals started getting worked up about my arrival while we were still off-loading the bicycle, and the nearer I got to the immigration office the worse it got. When I finally reached the little bamboo structure my passport was intently scrutinised, to the accompaniment of disapproving frowns. I kept my cool while these puffed-up roosters on their very small dung-heap crowed as loudly as they could to impress me with their importance, and since I was completely at their mercy I went along with the show and gamely played my usual role.

But that wasn't good enough, and I was told to unpack all my goods. By now the border-control operation was literally paralysed because its entire staff of about 10 officials had their attention focused on me. To ensure minimal loss of gear at the hands of this dodgy crew I tried to unpack and re-pack one compartment at a time. It was an uproarious process. Every last one of them was pointing at me and shouting commands which might have been loud but were also incomprehensible, since they spoke about as much English as I spoke French, which was hardly a word.

They strip-searched me and poked into every corner of my kit, even looking inside my toiletry bag and feeling my toothpaste tube to check if there were any hidden objects. Soon the small table on which they made me put my unpacked belongings began to get distinctly crowded, so that it became difficult for me to remember exactly what I had taken out and put back again. By now the small immigration hut was in a condition of near-chaos. Almost deafened by the shouts and incidental laughter, I was as busy as a one-armed piano player trying to take things back – sometimes quite forcibly – from some of my interrogators and return them to my baggage. At the same time I went to some trouble to keep in with the guy who appeared to be the most influential.

After about 45 minutes of this circus they finally stamped my passport and I was directed to the nearby village of Muanda. I was pretty glad to get away, but my mood would have been a bit less buoyant if I had known that the crooks at the immigration office had taken advantage of the chaos to help themselves to items that they obviously believed I did not need any more. Their loot included some of my CDs and, most important of all, the charger for my Palm handheld. This latter would be a serious blow. A handheld of those days lost everything stored on it if the battery wasn't recharged within seven days of depletion. All the daily notes I had made so far would be at risk. All I could do would be to switch it off and hope that I would find a replacement charger before the battery died on me (this wasn't my only encounter with informal shopping in the DRC – a bit later my cellphone also came under new management – but that is another story).

I didn't know it yet, but all this was pretty much a foretaste of what was to come as I battled along roads that degenerated from bad to awful to terrible, got soaked and re-soaked by torrential rain and had to deal with a population which was, for the most part, extremely unfriendly. Still, I persevered in a reasonably good frame of mind, because it was only about 50 km before I reached the oil-rich Angolan enclave of Cabinda. And – what a surprise – I was actually greeted by a narrow tarmac road which ran along the water's edge. I looked back many times; Angola was hidden in a hazy mist now, but I afforded myself the opportunity to evaluate my experiences since leaving Cape Town, and gloat a little. This trip was still young, but already it had been far more than I had dreamed it would be.

But what an unknown 50 km that was! Before long the road turned into a soft powdery track whose surface consisted of two deep wheel-tracks. Gee, great to have a choice! I could push my bike along one wheel-track, and if I got tired of that I could push it along the other wheel-track. What I could *not* do was ride in either of them. So I chose my wheel-track and started pushing, no easy task in that soft sand.

After a few notably difficult kilometres I was faced with another choice when I arrived at an intersection of sorts. To my left and slightly below me was the long coastline, extending north and south, punctuated by burning furnaces from which flames at least 10 metres high jumped into the air – giant silver chimney-like contraptions that, I had been given to understand, were apparently burning off the gases expelled from the oil within the pipelines. They were very much like the flares I had seen near Soyo, the only difference being that this time I had a better view of them.

I eyed them with some misgiving. I could not help thinking how dangerous it was to bring even a lighted match near a petrol station's fuel pumps. Here the massive flames seemed to be in contact with the oil itself, and I had been warned about the pipelines that ran along the surface in these parts. Were people ever hurt by them? I didn't know, but I didn't like the look of them. In any case, I had the choice of going straight on or turning right and going inland, and I didn't want to make the wrong one. I could have asked for directions from various groups of people I encountered at the roadside, but after my experiences at Muanda I was disinclined – I think I believed that asking for help would have shown my vulnerability and ignorance. But it was late in the afternoon by now, and I could not afford to waste even 10 minutes, so I decided to turn right, for no other reason than that a truck had just come from that direction and the tracks looked well used, whereas the road that went straight ahead had some unmarked patches of dried mud which indicated that it did not see much traffic.

My choice of road led me to another four-way intersection and another decision as to the way ahead. By now sanity had prevailed and I decided that I would ask for directions from the next truck driver who passed me. My situation was becoming somewhat desperate, because the sun was heading for the horizon, there was a distinct absence of trucks from which to ask for information and my map did not show any of the tracks before me. So I applied my basic when-all-else-fails procedure, which was to keep moving in more or less the right direction and hope for the best. I also experimented with trying to ride the bicycle when the wheel-rut was heading downhill, and found that if I managed to generate enough momentum I could get up to a speed of about 10 km/h. The only problem here was that sooner or later – usually sooner – the front wheel would bog down without warning in a patch of very thick sand and then the bike would propel me over the handlebars in one violent lunging motion.

In this stop-and-start mode I covered a few kilometres, but not many, and all the time it was getting darker and darker. The terrain, too, had changed from savannah-type bushveld to a more jungly type, and, having seen on TV the sort of things that went on in the DRC, I couldn't help thinking about the possibility that I might be captured by rebels and held for ransom, or worse. It was amazing to see how quickly one's mind could start running on negative vibes – from moderately brave man to fear-ridden child: all it took was for Mother Nature to flick the switch and turn light into darkness. But I had no option except to carry on, and when I came to a long downhill stretch which looked a little more promising than the ones on which I had come to grief earlier I decided to try again. I started off well, and before long I had gained an impressive turn of speed. But the end was inevitable. As I neared the bottom of the slope I felt the front wheel beginning to pick its own direction. Before I could do anything the wheel bogged down with great finality and once more I was catapulted over the handlebars.

This was my worst bit of involuntary flying so far, and my worst landing. I ended up on my stomach, my face and sweaty body covered in what felt like 10 times more sand than I had acquired during any of my earlier falls. For a moment I just lay there, overcome by fatigue and despair. Then I noticed something that put new life into me: an approaching bakkie with a canopy. At last!

The bakkie, which was crammed with people, was upon me before I had even got both feet on the ground. I managed to make eye contact with the driver and signal that I needed assistance. But he had no intention of stopping, and I could see why – the only way to avoid getting stuck in that sort of sand was to keep moving, and he was faced with toiling up a steep hill.

The bakkie struggled part of the way up, its momentum drastically reduced and the passengers in the back in a frenzy of shouting and gestures, then stopped. Two guys jumped out and aimed blank stares at me while they waited for a third person to make his way out of the back. He turned out to be a short, plump, grumpy-faced man who headed for me. Since I couldn't speak French to any extent and was still wiping the sand from my tongue and eyes, our conversation didn't get off to a smooth start. Using up almost all of my scanty French vocabulary, I asked whether he spoke English. He ignored this little bit of outreach, although one of the bystanders picked up on it and said he could understand a little. All I could think of doing was to ask: 'Who are you?'

The fat man was obviously not interested in satisfying my curiosity, though. He kept shouting at me about unspecified 'documents'. Hoping that he wanted to see my passport, which was all I had to justify my presence in the DRC, I started digging it out of my baggage. If he was expecting something else, my welcome to DRC was going to be a very, very official one. But my luck was in. The man who had told me earlier that he understood English said: 'passport ... passport,' adding: 'He is immigration man.'

Having taken possession of my passport – which made me a little uneasy – the 'immigration man' started firing questions at me. What did I have in my bags? Where was I going? Was I alone? Where had I come from? Thanks to my interpreter, I was able to give him the information he wanted, but he would not accept my answers. Each time I started to explain he would stare at me aggressively and then, before I had finished, ask another question.

After a bit of this I became impatient, and asked our interpreter to ask the fat man whether I had done anything wrong and why he was detaining me. This question, too, was ignored. At this stage I got help from an unexpected source. The other passengers understood what was going on and started speaking to him. I couldn't understand much of what they were saying, but I gathered that they were embarrassed by the way he was treating me and wanted him to shut up. In between all this the interpreter made use of the opportunity to explain to me roughly where and how far ahead the border offices were. It turned out that I only had three or four kilometres to go in the direction of a pronounced hill in the distance.

This was both good and bad news. Although the border offices were quite close, there was no chance of my getting there before sunset, because the light was almost gone now and the fastest time I could make – and then only with considerable effort – was about 5 km/h. Well, I would just have to push on and take my chances. After some difficulty I extricated myself from the fat man's fit of officious nonsense and trudged on, wrestling my bike through the wheel-tracks all the way.

About an hour and a half later, as the last shreds of light began to fade, I could see small paraffin lamps in the road ahead of me. In the gathering darkness I did not attract too much attention from the people wandering around at the border post, but it didn't help me much, because all of the officials had long since gone home. I was acutely aware that I was on a slightly sticky wicket, because my visa for the DRC was valid for only five days, and the chances of my Angolan visa not being accepted as a multiple-entry visa were high. This meant that I would have to find an ally among the immigration officials, or some other influential person, to stand by me if things went wrong, which appeared to be a distinct possibility.

Once again the gods of good fortune (or perhaps madmen) smiled on me, in the shape of a very friendly immigration official called Pablo, an unusual name for a Congolese. Pablo took me around the small market, arranged dinner for me at the bamboo-walled local restaurant, took me for a stroll on the other side of the border and even offered me one of the immigration offices to sleep in. The office was pretty poor accommodation. It had a concrete floor and peeling walls, both fitfully illuminated by the flickering orange lamplight (there was no electricity). But I wasn't complaining – it was a lot better than the next best alternative. I got Pablo to teach me a few phrases of French, so that I could ask for some fish to eat or enquire whether it was going to rain, then laid myself down on the concrete floor and slept in a pool of sweat.

'Slept' is possibly not the right word to describe how I spent the night. I was attacked by the worst plague of mosquitoes I had come across so far. Thinking back now, I can't remember actually sleeping; what I do recall very clearly is spending hour after hour scratching mosquito bites in a vast variety of places on my body. It would be wonderful one day to understand what insects think or don't think when they descend on a helpless victim such as I was that night. Why do they aim for those little spots when veins are in such ready supply?

Thanks to all this, waking up early was no problem. Not that it served any purpose, since the border only opened around 8 am. But Pablo was up early, too, so at least I had pleasant company while waiting for the bureaucracy to start grinding. In due course, by which time some more people had arrived at the immigration office, some of Pablo's colleagues gathered on the open land about 20 metres away, accompanied by a few soldiers, one of whom carried the DRC national flag and the other a portable hi-fi. The soldier hoisted the flag and the one with the hi-fi started pumping out some brisk military-sounding music which I assumed was the national anthem, since everybody around me stood to attention and sang along, while Pablo braced up and saluted vigorously as the flag reached the tip of the pole.

I stood up too, and in the spirit of the occasion saluted the flag as well, which caused some surprise. I could see Pablo straining to get a better view of me from the corner of his eye without stirring from his martial pose, and I saw one young girl cover her mouth with her hands in what looked like a gesture of shock. When the music ended Pablo and the soldiers dropped their salutes, with me following suit. I noticed people giggling and chatting, obviously about this weatherbeaten stranger who had turned up and joined in the daily national festivity. That I had made a good impression was confirmed when Pablo turned to me, shook my hand firmly and said: 'Merci beaucoup, mon ami,' to which, lacking the necessary vocabulary for 'you're welcome', I responded with a smile and a nod before re-applying myself to my now lukewarm mug of tea.

Then it was down to business. To forestall a possible problem with my Angolan visa I enlisted Pablo's help in exploring my options with his superiors. The exploration bore fruit, because the DRC immigration staffers were more than helpful. They stamped me out of their country without any fuss, didn't bother about checking my baggage and even accompanied me across to the Cabinda/Angola side to see if they could negotiate their way around my visa predicament. But here we ran into a problem, and after a long discussion the chief Angolan immigration officer said I would have to return to the DRC and go to the town of Matadi to speak to the Angolan consul, the only person who would be able to help me out of the squeeze. I couldn't help thinking that things might have turned out differently if I had had the opportunity of singing and saluting with the Angolans as well.

The Congolese hospitality didn't end there. The chief DRC immigration officer made it his personal task to find transport to Matadi, which was about 220 km away, and also to secure my bicycle during my absence in the safest of all places, right behind the chair in his office. With my daypack filled with essentials and irreplaceables – and my heart with gratitude for all this unexpected kindness – I set off along the banks of the awesome Congo River in a small passenger bakkie. Outside Muanda I transferred to a Mercedes truck carrying a mighty overload of various goods for the next leg, 102 km and 15 hours to the former rebel stronghold of Boma. The road out of Muanda was of the thick, soft variety I had experienced earlier, but there was a bright light at the end of the tunnel – from Boma, I was told, there was a tarmac road all the way to Matadi.

I recall distinctly the feeling of vulnerability we all had when we encountered groups of soldiers manning roadblocks on the way to Boma. A few of the roadblocks were official, but others were actually just small drinking and bribe-taking parties. On that journey to Matadi – and on the return – I saw more drunken soldiers than I could have imagined. In Angola I had seen soldiers drinking to cool down, but here, it seemed, soldiers drank to *fall* down.

I soon found myself drawing unwelcome attention from the soldiers. At each roadblock there would be shouts of 'le blanc, le blanc!' to attract my attention. I knew this meant 'white one, white one', but I also knew what would happen if I responded in the way they expected. Instead I worked out a rather different strategy, which was to make them see me as part of the group, rather than as a lone white man. So when we approached a roadblock I would start a conversation with one of the other passengers. I also made sure not to seem nervous or intimidated by the soldiers' shouts, and responded to even the most aggressive approach with a broad smile, as if I did not understand a word of French, which was pretty much the case anyway.

This worked quite well. My fellow passengers were paying bribes left, right and centre, but I never handed over a cent – not that I had much in the way of ready cash, because I had hidden the bulk of my money inside one of my shoes and retained only a few dollars on my person. My theory was that if I was held up the robbers would have to go to the length of stealing my socks before striking the mother-lode, such as it was. I don't intend to imply that the entire DRC military consisted of robbers, but I had no doubt that these guys with AK-47s over their shoulders and beers in their hands were the most threatening of all DRC citizens.

And threatening they were. As I sat on top of the overloaded truck with about 30 other people while it bumped and swayed in the darkness of what had now turned into dense equatorial jungle, I found myself wondering, for the first time since setting off from Cape Town, just what the hell I was doing. This was not what I had imagined it would be like. But we eventually reached Boma, although we were in a pretty sad state after 15 hours of non-stop, gnat-infested, cold, no-rest travel.

Boma was absolutely nothing to write home about, but so low had my expectations sunk by now that it was a memorable occasion to find that the miserable place actually had electricity. What I needed now was as much rest as possible, and with the help of two fellow-travellers I found the most dilapidated hotel I had ever seen. In all fairness I think I could have done better, but for my insistence on affordability. At 2000 CFA francs a night the price was reasonable in theory but not for what I was getting, or rather not getting.

It turned out that the electricity I had been so excited about was off most of the time and only available to a certain hour. This meant that the fan over the gigantic but dilapidated bed was little more than a decoration, a serious problem considering the intense humidity. The rest of the room matched the bed as far as condition was concerned; it exuded neglect and decay, and at two of the corners the ceiling hung forlornly down. I was too tired to care, however, and went to bed right away, covering myself with the thin blanket provided. It was not a particularly comfortable sleep. The humidity in the middle of the night was shocking – I am sure that not many other countries in the world could have dished up worse heat discomfort – and within 10 minutes the thin knitted-type sheet was glued to my damp body ... well, at least it all helped to protect most of my body from the voracious mosquitoes, although they made merry with whatever bits stuck out.

It goes without saying that I was up early and ready to start look-ing for a ride to Matadi as soon as possible. From what I heard, the road was tarmac and would take no more than an hour to traverse. But first I needed a thorough wash, and I received a short, sharp lesson in DRC-style ablutions. The hotel had a toilet and shower area at one end, but in the absence of running water you were given a bucket of cold water and a cup with which to sluice it over you. Soon I was in a shower cubicle with my bucket and cup, stripped stark naked and blissfully washing the grime away.

Then I realised that sluicing sounds were also coming from an-other cubicle diagonally opposite. I looked across to see who my early-morning companion was and saw to my shock that it was a girl in her early twenties. Years of adulthood were stripped away in an instant, and I felt like a schoolboy who discovers that he has ac-cidentally wandered into the girls' changing-room. Judging by her reaction – a broad nervous smile, made even broader by the array of white teeth against her very dark skin – she had also suffered an abrupt reversion to childhood. I laughed from pure anxiety, grabbed my towel and bucket and shot into the cubicle next to me. It was directly in the line of sight of the hotel's only passage and in-creased the distance between us by little more than a metre, but in the circumstances it was the best I could do. Such was my abrupt introduction to the principle of unisex showers. Aikona!

After absorbing helpful directions which indicated that Matadi lay at 10 different points of the compass, I finally got a lift from an old man in a Peugeot sedan who knew the right way, and in due course we arrived at my destination. Matadi was spread out along the banks of the Congo River and looked amazingly like a typical seaside town, harbour and all, which quite amazed me because I knew we were so far inland – South Africa has many marvellous sights to see, but not one river as mighty as this. I decided that I simply had to take a picture from the bridge that led to the town, but my driver advised strongly against it, obviously aware that any repercussions would affect him as well, so I stayed my hand.

My first imperative was to find the Angolan consulate, seeing that I had only a day and a half left on my visa, and the DRC was not the sort of country in which one wanted to fall foul of the bureaucracy. Well, less than five minutes after my arrival I was knocking on the consulate's door and then explaining my predicament in very broken Portuguese and even worse French. This didn't work too well, and it was only when I cemented this shaky edifice with some English that the penny dropped. After that everything went smoothly, and two hours later I was heading for the taxi-rank with a five-day visa in hand and my heart full of happiness, although my pocket was considerably lighter because the visa fee had turned out to be $80 more than I had anticipated. Still, I was on my way, and keen to get back to Boma that same evening. My legal time in the DRC had now doubled, but I still had to retrieve my bike and get through the border. Any delays en route and I would most certainly not make it in time.

Two sedans were waiting to leave for Boma, but each had secured only one passenger so far. I explained to both drivers that I would go with the first car that was ready to leave, then went off to sample my first Congolese beer, which I reckoned would be well-deserved balm for my nerves. I took my 'medicine' in a charming beer garden where I might have been tempted to spend considerable time, except that one of the drivers I had spoken to came to pick me up before I was half-way done, having filled up with passengers long before either of us had expected.

I arrived back in Boma in a sanguine mood, had another session in the unisex bathroom (no embarrassing encounters this time) and got ready for an early night, so that I could be up at dawn to catch the first truck back to the border. For some reason the town seemed quite different from what I had seen during my earlier stay, with the streets and the roadside cafés full of loud young men – although very few women – and I decided that before going to bed I would mingle with the vibrant crowds to eat something and read up on Congolese history to prepare myself for what I suspected I would find awaiting me in the next few days.

That is exactly what I did, though not without generating some unintended excitement. It hadn't struck me that there was no question of my blending into the crowds, since I was obviously one of the few white blokes the locals had seen in a decade or so. It didn't take me long to discover my mistake. I was sitting in a dimly lit street café, reading my 'Lonely Planet' guide and waiting for my order of two scones and a Coke to arrive, when I became aware of a nearby group of fairly sozzled beer-drinkers with bandannas around their heads who were trying to attract my attention. I pretended not to notice them and started reading.

Having skimmed the introduction to the DRC chapter, I made my way to the sections on Boma and Matadi, which were not exactly comforting. The paragraph on Boma was short and succinct: 'If Boma was on your itinerary then now would be a good time to remove it. Boma is the new home for the displaced rebels from the war-torn north-eastern DRC. Avoiding here would be a good idea!' Coming on top of the attention of the bandanna boys, this did nothing for my peace of mind; all I wanted right now was to get back on to my bicycle.

I started working out an escape route back to my hotel. It was only about 20 metres away, but the street was almost empty, so it was going to be just about impossible to use the traffic to camouflage my movements. I should have gone straight to bed, I reproached myself. But no, I had to go and look at the bright lights, and now I had well and truly painted myself into a corner. What the hell was I going to do now?

I decided that speed and surprise were my only weapons. I calculated what I owed the waitress, counted out the exact amount, so that when I was ready I could pay her and head for the hotel with the speed of light at the first opportunity. And then providence once again reached out a helping hand. As she put my scones and Coke on the table the electricity went out. Immediately I was on my feet, and I streaked across the darkened street, book under my arm, one hand holding the snacks and the other feeling for my room-keys. Long before the bandanna boys could have had an inkling of my disappearance I was unlocking the door to my room. I plunged inside and subsided on to the bed ... and about two seconds later the lights came on again. Phew! I sighed with relief – and the next thing I remember is waking up about four o'clock next morning.

By 4.30 I was waiting at what I had been told was the departure point for trucks heading for the border. No vehicles of any kind were in sight, so I sat down on a concrete block and ate one of the muffins from the night before, feeling pleasantly refreshed by the early-morning air and confident that I would soon have a lift. But nothing came by. The hours passed, and still I waited; but the only vehicle to come through – a Land Rover at about eight o'clock – was so fully loaded that I didn't even try to flag it down.

I began to worry. If I didn't get a ride this morning I wouldn't make it to the border in time, with all that that implied. But there was nothing I could do except wait and watch the passing parade – hordes of kids heading for a school near by, shopkeepers arriving to open up for the day.

As if the fruitless wait wasn't bad enough, I eventually attracted some unwelcome attention from two aggressive men who insisted on seeing my passport. I tried to act confused and explained that my passport was back at the border, but all this did was visibly irritate them. After a while, however, they let it go, but only after hunting up a scrap of paper and a chewed-up Bic ballpoint pen so that they could take down my particulars. I was pretty sure that they were just trouble-makers rather than officials, but I answered their questions truthfully, just in case, and meantime hoped they would go away when they had had their fun, which they did.

It was a taste of what the locals had to put up with in this virtually lawless town, and the wisdom of my approach was justified when a young fellow in his twenties introduced himself in rather basic English as Ronsard Ngoma and offered to help me. We went into his little cool-drink bar he and his wife ran, with a photocopying machine as a sideline, and he explained that the men who had been questioning me were dangerous types who were best avoided.

I spent the rest of the day with Ronsard and his wife, learning more French phrases from them as I waited for a truck to arrive. One finally pulled in that afternoon, but the driver still had to pick up some cargo, and it was almost sunset before he returned, by which time his vehicle was loaded to the gunwales with goods, with a substantial number of passengers perched on top. I said goodbye to Ronsard and his wife, elbowed myself into an inadequate bit of space and finally left Boma behind me.

Among my fellow-passengers was a Congolese with whom I soon struck up quite a friendship, which suited us both because if one of us needed to relieve himself during one of the stops the other could look after his bags. The journey back, like its predecessor, lasted 15 hours, and my new friend helped to make it as pleasant as possible, even talking me through each roadblock, where I was almost invariably harassed by the police. He was very impressed by my cellphone, although I had been discreet about showing it around until I trusted my new travelling buddy. He wanted to know exactly how it worked and what features it had, saying that one day he would like to have exactly the same model.

When we arrived in Muanda I gave him a big hug – which is very uncharacteristic of me – and told him that I was honoured to have met him and that I felt he was like a brother. I meant it sincerely, because I could not understand how someone could have unselfishly protected a stranger like he did with me. He returned the hug and went swiftly on his way, presumably as pressed for time as I was. Or was he? Seized by some unfraternal doubts, I searched my bag and found that my cellphone had gone.

It was the greatest disappointment of my trip so far. But I took it philosophically, hoping for just two things as regards my former brother. Firstly that he would learn a similar lesson one day, and secondly that he would have a long period of bad reception.

My onward passage to the Cabinda border post was uneventful, barring two more roadblocks where we were interrogated and searched in true Congolese fashion, and I arrived in time to pass through. Pablo the immigration officer was visibly relieved to see me (obviously he knew all about the sort of things that might happen in Boma), and after I had picked up my bicycle he stamped my visa and escorted me safely across into Angolan territory. This time we didn't salute and sing the national anthem.

# CHAPTER 7

# MUD, SWEAT AND TEARS
# IN CONGO'S JUNGLE

*Amid all this misery I was, nevertheless, conscious of the amazing edge the jungle around me gave to my city-dulled sense of smell. My nose was subjected to a no-holds-barred sensory assault which somehow did not dull it but actually made it more sensitive. Every new thing I saw had its own unique scent as well. The mud and thick grass had their own smell, which I can recall at will whenever I think back to that day.*

First impressions, so they say, are lasting – and Cabinda, which would be part of the Congo except for an accident of history, certainly presented me with the best one that any cyclist who has just gone through vehicular hell could hope for: a tarmac road stretching as far as the eye could see!

This was very good news indeed. I knew that if the road stayed the same I could make Cabinda town before sunset, and that, in turn, meant that I would be able to reach the Congo Republic border the very next day. I also knew by now that it was from such anticipation, the excitement of pausing for a moment and visualising where I would be the following afternoon, that I drew much of my strength. The more exotic the destination, the better it felt. How many others in the world were thinking about the same thing as me at the same time? Few, very definitely few, I was convinced. Maybe even none.

My day-dreaming had to go on hold for a moment, however, while I steeled myself to deal with a panic situation that was beginning to develop, thanks to the fact that I had not been able to find a pump to fit the new tubes I had acquired at Soyo. I had accepted the situation reluctantly, knowing that sooner or later I was going to suffer a flat tyre, but powerless to do anything but hope for the best. Hope is but a doubting faith, however. The dreaded event had come along sooner rather than later, and in its most agonisingly drawn-out form, a slow puncture.

I didn't have to spend much time considering a way out of this predicament, because there wasn't one. Unless I could find a way of pumping up the tyre, or catch a lift on a passing vehicle to wherever I could get help, the only thing I could do was ride on till it was totally flat, and thereafter push the bike all the way to Cabinda. The only light spot in this dismaying scenario was that because it was the front tyre it would take longer to empty itself than the rear one, which bore the main burden of my body (90 kg) and baggage (30 kg).

I pushed on, gloomily contemplating the wreckage of my immediate travel schedule. Then after about 5 km I came up to a clump of grass huts. Barring the occasional chicken scratching around, the only sign of life consisted of two young boys sitting on the dusty ground next to the huts, looking terminally bored. I was so desperate that I decided to take a chance (well, it wasn't a chance – it was everything) and see what help I could get out of them.

I stopped in front of them and pantomimed a wheel-pumping session, appropriate sound effects and all, throwing in a 'por favor' after every fourth or fifth 'shhhh'. This comical non-conversation made perfect sense to these sons of Africa, the continent where the bicycle is the poor man's Mercedes; the elder of the boys led me to one of the huts and woke the occupant from his siesta. The recently woken one must have been the village bicycle man, because he had my puncture fixed and the wheel pumped up in 20 minutes flat. What made it even more impressive was that when it turned out that he did not have the correct valve fitting either, he simply improvised an alternative that worked just as well.

Thanks to the ingenuity of this roadside bike boffin I made it to Cabinda town before sunset, right on schedule again. I used the cushion of time I had gained to take action on the accommodation referral the Soyo oilmen had given me to their Cabinda colleagues. I cycled off the main road to the airport, where their offices were located alongside the runway, and made my pitch. To my surprise the reception I got was anything but warm. I became the afternoon's main topic of conversation while they shunted me from one office to another without explaining what was happening.

Eventually, however, they loaded my bike and myself into their bakkie and set off. I decided that this looked promising in terms of accommodation and a plate of warm food, but was I ever wrong! They drove me straight to the police station, dropped me off and went on their way, leaving me to the tender mercies of yet another over-suspicious policeman. I had been well and truly dumped.

I was flabbergasted. I had expected these guys to show me the same hospitality as their colleagues in Soyo, but instead there I was with the bakkie literally driving off into the sunset and the policeman shouting into my right ear, ordering me to put the bicycle into one of the police station's holding cells. Before I had even got around to lifting my bicycle on to the pavement, however, he had moved on. Where was my passport? I began to reach for it, but by the time I had it out he had moved on yet again. What was I doing in Cabinda? Where was I going? Coming at the end of the day's efforts and anxieties, it was exhausting.

When the policeman had examined my passport and received answers to his questions via an interpreter he transferred his attention to my panniers, which he ordered me to unpack. I did as I was told, feeling anything but charitable towards the oil company people. What had they told this fellow? But the gods of good fortune came to my aid again in the shape of the interpreter, a gentle guy with whom I immediately formed a good relationship which, I am pretty sure, saved me from spending a night in the cells. After about two hours of rigmarole the policeman told me that I was free to go, apparently having satisfied himself that I was not a threat to the nation. He must have been very satisfied, or maybe he had just tired himself out, because he seemed quite blasé about letting me wander out aimlessly into the darkness to do heaven knew what.

'Aimless' is the word, since I didn't yet know where I was going to sleep that night. But I did know that I was very hungry, and so I headed for a restaurant I had spotted diagonally opposite the police station, right up against the Cabinda radio station's broadcasting studio. I flopped down to order some food and simultaneously enquire about accommodation opportunities. I got both. The burgers were not the greatest, but the friendliness was top-notch. The waiters, all apprentices at the radio station, made my problem theirs. They approached the manager for assistance, and he rose to the occasion with a proposition I couldn't refuse. I could put up my tent on the radio station's grounds and he would give me a few T-shirts, while in return I would give the station a live interview.

Deal! Next thing I was in the studio, with an interpreter turning my words into understandable Portuguese. Afterwards I set up my tent in full view of all the other restaurant-goers, to whom this was clearly the most exciting thing to happen in Cabinda in recent memory. Now that's what you call live entertainment.

My departure next morning was less spectacular, seeing that I had to start very early in order to reach the border before day's end, and I was out on the road to welcome the sunrise. The highway was as good as it had been south of the town and I settled down to enjoy it, since I had a shrewd suspicion that things were going to be considerably different when I crossed over into the Congo Republic, about 75 km away. My night's destination was Pointe Noire, about 36 km on from the border, and I anticipated that at best this stretch would be very slow going.

Once again I was wrong. The highway to Pointe Noire was as neat and tailored as a meticulously chiselled piece of art – the best road I had encountered, in fact, since I had left Cape Town, 4 000 km to the south. In sad contrast was the terrible poverty of the people living on either side. It had become an all-too-familiar sight in the past two and a half months. But that is Africa for you – the Third World rubbing shoulders with the First World, and neither seemingly affected for better or worse by the other.

I had left my tyre with the off-road tread on the rear wheel in anticipation of having to face bad roads, but this tailored stretch of highway was so smooth that it felt as if I were riding on slicks. I didn't take time to swop tyres, however. The sun was two hours away from the horizon and I was in a tearing hurry, so I stepped up a gear and bore down on the pedals, and covered the 36 km to Pointe Noire in just over an hour, having averaged nearly 30 km/h.

My arrival meant I could pack away my hard-won bits of Portuguese and get on with 's'il vous plaît', 'merci' and the other words and phrases in my very sparse collection of French. That wasn't the only thing that had changed: I couldn't help but notice how reserved the Congolese were in comparison to their Angolan neighbours. People chattered among themselves when I cycled past, but very rarely called out to me, as Angolans would have done. I don't know whether this was due to courtesy – a reluctance to become involved in someone else's business without being asked – or simply unhelpfulness, but the immediate result was the same: I had difficulty in finding accommodation, my first priority, when I reached the outskirts of the town.

Time after time I went up to people who were either moving along the road like me or sitting at a roadside stall, introduce myself with a friendly 'bonjour' and then follow this up with: 'Pardon, je veux hotel pour dormir, s'il vous plaît', by which I meant, 'excuse me, I want a hotel to sleep, please'. Mostly their response was to frown in confusion and then just turn and walk away. After a bit I began to have some doubts about the efficacy of this approach. Maybe it needed some fine-tuning, although I wasn't sure about which part of it was falling short.

But once again the gods of good fortune smiled on me and sent a young student with books tucked under his arm to approach me and ask, in reasonably good English, if there was any way he could help me. Naturally I had no problem telling him exactly what I needed, and within 10 minutes I was booking into a cheap hotel room. I was a bit tired and aimed to get to bed early, but before that I repaid my rescuer for his kindness by standing him to some locally brewed beer.

Now, I'm No 1 when it comes to enthusiasm, as anyone who knows me will tell you, but this guy was so energetic and enthusiastic that I was actually taken aback. He was all fired up to take me on a comprehensive tour of the town right away, but I managed to persuade him that it would be better to enjoy our beer and then meet up again next day. Before we parted company I asked my student friend to translate a few more key words for me, one of which happened to be 'glacé', which is French for 'iced', which I reckoned would come in handy when asking for drinks or water as I headed into the large swathe of French-speaking Africa lying ahead. As it turned out, I used 'glacé' before I even got to my room, although not with any great success.

The hotel's receptionist, who was also the barman and handyman, asked if there was anything I wanted before going to sleep. I was still extremely thirsty because the beer had not been nearly enough to replace all the moisture I had sweated out, so I asked him for water with ice. Well, that was my intention. What actually happened when I tried to explain that I wanted 'de l'eau with glacé' was, I suppose, comical in a horrid sort of way.

He didn't get the message and I resorted to sign language, the basis of which was that my saliva represented water, while the nearest hard surface represented ice. It must have scarred this guy for life to see me pulling blobs of saliva from my mouth, repeatedly saying 'de l'eau, de l'eau' while pointing to the congealed spit, then rapping with my knuckles on the wall or table to the tune of 'glacé, glacé' to explain that in the de l'eau there should also be 'hard' water, namely ice. After a bit of this I realised from the look on his face that he believed he was dealing with a lunatic. So I gave up and went to bed thirsty, no doubt to his great relief.

My plan was to spend a day or two in Pointe Noire so I could gather information about what lay immediately ahead and also to catch up via e-mail with things at home in Cape Town, which included writing my fortnightly article for the *Cape Times* newspaper. By now I was getting a surprising response from the *Cape Times* readers, which buoyed me up and left me feeling strangely relieved. One supporter actually contacted the Laureus Sport Awards organisation to make them aware of my circumnavigation attempt (another South African had won the 'Alternative Sportsman of the Year' award in 2001).

Like most outsiders I had not expected much of Pointe Noire, considering the Congo's notoriously ruinous general state, but it turned out to be surprisingly well developed and in fairly good shape. The streets were reasonably well maintained, the electricity was regular and the town even had a supermarket. But these were merely luxuries: for me the most important thing was that the town had an Internet connection.

I wandered around with my student friend showing me the sights and introducing me to people who could offer sound advice on what I could expect when I headed further north. It appeared I had two choices. The first was to go directly north and the other was to head eastwards to Loubomo and from there northwards to Gabon, each of these options having advantages and disadvantages that I would have to consider.

One consideration was my feeling that the less time I spent in the notoriously unstable Congo the better. The road straight north would see me in Gabon after only 200 km, while the Loubomo-Gabon route was a longer one. On the other hand, my maps showed no roads whatever for the northern route, although the locals – among them members of the Lebanese community – reckoned that a man on a bicycle would have no problems. The trouble with this advice was that it was all third- or fourth-hand; no one I spoke to had ever been that way themselves.

But what the hell – was I an adventurer or wasn't I? And in any case I had got this far in spite of having started with zero advice. So I swallowed my doubts about the accuracy of the information and opted for the blank-space route.

The Lebanese were a generous bunch, and the fact that I had a Lebanese surname warmed their hearts even further. One of them, named George, owned a cellphone shop and was eager to help me after he heard about my loss along the Boma road. He got on to some friends who worked for the Congolese national cellphone network, CellTel, to organise a sponsorship, and that same afternoon I was sending SMSs to Vasti from a new Ericsson handset.

I hit the road early next morning, my first destination being the town of Madingo Kayes, the last way-station of any substance, if my maps were to be believed; 200 km might not be all that far, but I had no idea of what I was heading into, so the safest assumption was that my ride wasn't going to be either smooth or fast.

The outskirts of Pointe Noire had an exceptional vibe. Twice I stopped and backtracked to find the source of beating drums and what most foreigners would consider 'African' music. At one place a group of children and one older boy were putting out a sound that would have had audiences on their feet anywhere in the world, although their 'instruments' were nothing more than a collection of plastic and metal containers of various kinds which they were beating with their hands. They were a bit shy about being filmed, but I got into the spirit of things, and although I am generally not one for dancing I returned the favour by wiggling my head and hips in time to the beat. It's amazing to see how music can unite people from totally different worlds!

In spite of the blank space on the map this road, too, was world-class, and I was so impressed that I had to take photographs of it, although I wasn't sure how I was going to explain pictures of endless kilometres of tarmac when I got home again. This being the Congo, I would not have been surprised if it had ended abruptly after a few kilometres, but it didn't, and after a good day's stint with some great views and further snatches of vibrant home-made music along the way I cycled into Madingo Kayes about 30 minutes before sunset.

The rapidly fading light meant I had to find some accommodation as soon as possible, so I accosted the firstly likely-looking people I came across, a group of schoolboys playing alongside the road. The Madingo Kayes people were far friendlier than the ones in Pointe Noire, and within minutes the boys had me in conversation with their school's headmaster, a Roman Catholic priest. He spoke English fairly well, so I had no trouble explaining what I was doing and where I was going, and he proved to be a generous soul – I would have been content to set up camp on his front lawn, but he would have none of this and offered me a bunk bed in the school hostel. I spent a memorable evening with the schoolboys. We cooked porridge on the passage floor; ran impromptu French classes (including tests) for my benefit and then fell asleep to the violent but strangely therapeutic hammering of heavy rain on the building's tin roof.

I remember one part of the 'French class' particularly well. It involved reading from a book of speeches by Julius Nyerere, Tanzania's first president, and his message came through loud and clear. Africans must take charge of their own lives; Africa must feed itself and otherwise provide for itself. Africans must restore their pride on their own terms. I concluded that he was a visionary, a man with the real Africa in his heart and her problems weighing heavily on his shoulders (and also, incidentally, the only African president in his time ever to voluntarily step down from power).

When the boy who owned the book saw how captivated I was by what I was reading he tried to give it to me as a keepsake. I declined his generosity with great reluctance; I knew it would have given me hours of enjoyment and positive reinforcement on the road ahead, because I felt exactly the same way about Africa's future.

The kids were up bright and early and so, of course, was I. We said a hearty goodbye and went our separate ways, they to school and myself towards the unknown, with the non-stop rain beating down on us all.

I hope they had a better day than I did. The headmaster had warned me not to expect the fine road to extend much beyond Madingo Kayes, and that was an understatement of note. The world-class road didn't deteriorate, it just vanished, and I was condemned to a path which was not a thoroughfare so much as a continuous muddy disturbance of the vegetation, winding through the sort of jungle that I had only ever seen on TV. Just as well, I thought, that growing up on the north coast of KwaZulu-Natal and frequently visiting the dense, humid mangrove forests found in St Lucia had prepared me for what my eyes were absorbing.

The track was so indistinct that at times I wondered whether I was not creating an entirely new one of my own. Cycling was impossible: at best the track was nothing but soft mud, overgrown with plants, and at worst it was completely washed away. I began to get a sinking feeling that I had made a serious mistake in my choice of route.

That night I pitched my tent only a metre or so into the bush. That was enough – the vegetation was so dense that even someone walking slowly past would have had difficulty in seeing my camp. The local wild life was not even on my list of concerns, and they must have known this, because they made sure I 'enjoyed' another memorable night. I discovered that almost as soon as I lay down to sleep soon after sunset, having eaten a can of sardines for dinner. It was a dark and eerie night, but not a silent one. Baboons and monkeys set about raising an unearthly racket, while the insect population's musicians turned their volume up to full blast, and whenever there was a lull it was filled by the endless rustling of the foliage.

The upshot of all this was that I was not exactly enjoying a relaxing evening in the bush. Wilderness areas in Europe and elsewhere are comparatively safe, with few predators of the life-threatening type, so that a lone camper's greatest danger usually derives from his own stupidity in not taking basic precautions, but in an African wilderness the operative part of the word is 'wild'. Between my edgy nerves and the extreme humidity there was not a spot on my body which was not irrigated by perspiration. I didn't have a waterproof fly sheet to cover my tent with – fortunately it had stopped raining – and as a result I had a great view of the night sky to fall asleep to when I eventually drifted off.

It was an uneasy sleep, though. As the night hours passed the baboons and moneys slowly plucked up the courage to make a closer acquaintance, and at intervals I would be woken by their stealthy footfalls on the other side of the tent's walls. I stayed where I was. They were doing me no harm, and in any case it was too dark for me to make out anything in the jumble of trees, vines and branches all around me. In addition I was feeling the effects of the malaria medication, so that it felt as if I was wearing ear-plugs and everything around me was moving in slow motion.

All very strange. But something even stranger was yet to come. About an hour before sun-up I felt a gentle yet forceful movement underneath my right shoulder-blade. At first I thought that it was just the product of my imagination in combination with the environment and the malaria pills, but it wasn't, not by a long shot. I was lying on top of what was obviously a fair-sized snake of unknown identity.

How I had landed in this predicament was a mystery. My only explanation is that somehow the snake, seeking warmth, had insinuated itself in the space between my body and groundsheet and the bed of roots and leaves underneath. My reaction to this dodgy situation was to move my weight on to my left shoulder, away from the snake's continuous circular motion. This did the trick, and once the snake was snugly in a cosy position of warmth it stopped moving.

Now, I am sure that some people would think me mad for not reacting in a slightly more positive way – beating the snake over the head, perhaps, or propelling myself out of the tent like an anti-tank rocket, or both. But mine was a reasoned response, apart from the fact that I had nothing to whack the snake with and that the tent wasn't designed for speed-of-light exits. Firstly, I usually wake up drowsy in the mornings, which militated against a knee-jerk reaction. Secondly, I used a level-headed approach once my drowsiness started dissipating. The big question was whether the snake had the strength to force its way through the groundsheet and into the tent itself. I decided it did not. This being the case, it was a matter of letting sleeping snakes lie, since all it wanted was a warm place to curl up in.

So I left the snake severely alone and the snake did likewise with me, and the two of us enjoyed another 45 minutes' lie-in before the new day forced us out of the sack. This peaceful co-existence didn't make me careless, however. When the time came for me to crawl out I did so very carefully, shoes on and a watchful eye out to make sure that the serpent was not disturbed.

All this went without incident. Now I had to collect my gear without initiating hostilities. So I made sure I had visual contact with the lump below at all times while I quickly but gently collapsed the tent and then slowly pulled the groundsheet towards me. And there was my late sleeping partner in full view. Being colour blind,

I don't know exactly what its colours were, but there was definitely a blocky yellow-and-black pattern on its body. That was the sum total of my observation, because I didn't hang around to do any gawking – the muddy track with all its horrors was suddenly a very attractive place to be.

The attractiveness didn't last. The route ahead was just like the previous day's – overgrown and permanently waterlogged, almost invisible where it was not actually non-existent – and after a while I came to the conclusion that a hovercraft conversion on my bike would have been handy. I had hoped that because it had not rained the previous night the strong sunlight would dry up the remaining puddles of water and the going would be dryer and easier. Well, I was wrong, mainly because the growth was so thick overhead that the sun's rays had no chance of reaching the ground; at times it actually became so dark that it was difficult to navigate.

There was no question of cycling. I tried a number of times, always in the lowest gear, and each attempt ended in a spectacular – and spectacularly dirty – crash-landing, although at least the mud meant that I had a fairly soft touch-down. It didn't take me long to accept that this was the name of the game, and I buckled down to the back-wrenching task of pushing the bike through seemingly endless kilometres of slippery mud, always hoping against hope that a recognisable road would appear around the next bend.

Amid all this misery I was, nevertheless, conscious of the amazing edge the jungle around me gave to my city-dulled sense of smell. My nose was subjected to a no-holds-barred sensory assault which somehow did not dull it but actually made it more sensitive. Every new thing I saw had its own unique scent as well. The mud and thick grass had their own smell, which I can recall at will whenever I think back to that day.

Eventually patches of hilly grassland, bathed in welcome sunlight, began to appear between stretches of jungle, and it occurred to me that so far this sort of terrain had usually been in the vicinity of my Atlantic Ocean sightings. But right now I had no time for mental meandering. It was very hot, and I was running out of water. Where would I find a new supply? I hadn't seen one clean-looking stream, or any sign at all of human activity. So I did the only thing I could: I struggled on, hoping for the best. Every so often I would have a view of the ocean on my left, and gradually the grassy hills with their dark jungle borders gave way to endless miles of beaches and majestic tracts of turquoise sea.

I began to grow slightly delirious, and gradually my remaining energy and mental clarity became focused not on finding potable water but on going for a swim in the surf. All these sightings were from elevated positions which gave a false impression of the difficulty that would be involved in actually leaving the track to venture towards the water, but just then the 'how' was not relevant. What *was* relevant was the silky slip of the sea-water over my body, washing away the muck and sweat that had accumulated on me during that terrible day.

I passed a rusted, sun-faded warning sign that warned passers-by (so I gathered, although I couldn't understand the French too clearly) about the possibility of encountering leopards, lions, elephants and buffalo. I mention those specifically because they were all depicted on the sign ... I suspect that the artist who had painted it had been given some simple instruction, such as 'paint on this piece of metal the animals you see around you every day,' then left to his own devices. And there it was, years or decades later, still warning all those passing through.

The sign didn't upset me, and wouldn't have even if my mind had been totally clear. I was not spooked by the thought of encountering threatening wildlife, especially those that would enjoy a human hors d'oeuvre. I developed a mental image of being attacked by a lion, gouging out his eyes and then flipping him over and subduing him with a half-nelson ... all this after I had sprinted down the valley for a few kilometres like a man possessed. Seriously though, the thought of animals *did* scare me. But I also knew that I would be disappointed if did not meet up with a lion or elephant somewhere along the route: without at least one such encounter my adventure would not be a total success.

In the meantime I was still intent on making that dip in the Atlantic into a reality. I was close now, very close, so that at times the crash of the waves was louder than the sound of the banana trees' huge leaves flapping in the wind. Using the sound of the waves as my lodestone, I staggered down a little path leading towards the ocean. Then, for the first time that day, I saw signs of human habitation – a small straw hut perched somewhat uncomfortably on the only dry-looking square of land to be seen.

The occupant of the hut was a diminutive, wrinkled old man who now came out to greet me as I advanced slowly on his home. He was in scarcely better condition than I was, whether from age, some unknown debilitating ailment or too much palm wine I couldn't say. Whichever it was, he was barely able to keep a straight line as he walked over to me, or even aim his handshaking hand with any precision. But we managed to connect, and after an extended and enthusiastic pressing of the flesh I manage to convey by sign language firstly that I was desperate to have a swim and secondly that I was equally desperate for some water to drink.

This took some effort, given my companion's distracted state, but he finally got the message and let me park my bike inside his hut. That done, he handed me a plastic container full of murky water, which I gratefully poured down my throat. Then he led me through a patch of waist-high reed grass. Within 50 metres the sound of the sea had become perceptibly louder, and I was growing more and more excited, not only at the prospect of a swim but also by the thought that it would be in Congolese waters, another small 'first' for me. When would I have another opportunity to do this, if ever?

By now the old man had been joined by a teenage boy, and when a leguaan or amphibious lizard at least two metres long came splashing at top speed past us, only a few feet away, they laughed with identical raspy, phlegm-ridden gargles. But I was startled, not concerned. Leguaans were a common sight when I was growing up in Zululand, although we never saw ones as big as this. The average person there feared a leguaan more because it bore a strong resemblance to a crocodile than for any logical reason.

We kept moving briskly through the remaining section of the swampland – even in my fevered state, I remember, I couldn't help wondering what other surprises might eventuate on the return journey – and then the beach came into view as we cleared a small dune that flanked the wetland. I could feel the cool sea breeze against my face. At last! It was my first close contact with the ocean I loved so much since leaving Cape Town in September.

I stepped on to the beach under the beady-eyed gaze of its permanent inhabitants, thousands of crabs. I took off my shoes and socks, then ran down to the water's edge with the joyous abandon of a child, accompanied by the crabs. An aerial photograph taken during those ecstatic moments would have been interesting, because the army of crabs totally encircled me, yet never came closer than about two metres at any time. I felt a little like Gulliver arriving on the island of Lilliput.

I wasted no time getting into the water, clothes and all. The sea was relatively calm, compared to what I was used to, but not calm enough to tempt me into going too far out. I lay back, treading water and looking landwards, and I wish I could have taken a photo with my eyes and brought it back to show everyone what I saw: the beaches with their dugout canoes giving way to beautiful and natural greenery which in turn stretched to the horizon to meet with a sky that was the colour of the water in which I was floating. Sea, sand, earth, sky, then sea again, a full cycle of colour.

The old man and his young friend were models of tactful tour guides. They reclined on the beach as though it was perfectly normal for an exceedingly dirty white man to appear from nowhere, gabble to them in words they couldn't understand and then hurl himself fully clothed into the sea. Who says that you have to study tourism, anyway? The best tour guides are the ones who have real love and respect for the land they are showing you; representing the land you are showing is more important than always having all your facts in order.

I felt a little stab of shame as I lay back in the water, filled with bonhomie. Instead of leaving my money in my shoes, which is what I would have done normally, I had put it into my pocket before running into the sea. Any sensible person would say that that had been simply a prudent precaution. Yet all of a sudden it seemed ludicrous. Had I expected the old man and the boy to steal from me while I was in the water? Why would they want to do that in such an isolated part of the planet, never mind Africa? So why had I acted in this way? Sure, there was the obvious answer. But I wanted to *trust*, to feel the liberation and exhilaration of complete trust in someone. If I couldn't have it here, in this ideal time and place, when and where would I *ever* have it?

I decided to postpone the debate with myself to another day; I still had a long trek ahead and no way of doing it at any speed. Refreshed to a degree I could not have imagined just an hour earlier, I pulled my socks on over my sandy feet, filled up my water bottles with Congo murky, said goodbye to my companions and headed into the jungle again. I left with a strange feeling of regret. This was the sort of place where I'd be willing to devote my life to being a hippy, loving the planet and its people all day long.

But the planet – or this little bit of it, anyway – didn't love me back just then. It started raining soon after I left and didn't stop. I had done only about 15 km up to lunch-time and was determined to double that miserable figure at the very least, but at 4 km an hour through ghastly mud I ended up changing the measurement of my progress to celebrating every kilometre completed.

By dusk I was still struggling along, dismally aware of how little progress I had made and at a loss about where to spend the night. Then I was lucky enough to come across another trackside hut. This family was rich in nothing but hospitality, and although I had not planned to stay over I really had little choice. I pretended not to understand their offer to put me up for the night, then felt terribly ashamed when the family elder lay down and imitated a sleeping puppy. Well, that was the end of my prevarication; the last thing I wanted to do was show disrespect to these warm-hearted people, who had so little but yet were prepared to share it with a total stranger.

So I ended up reluctantly spending the night in a borrowed bed. Reluctantly? Well, yes. It might seem an offer no exhausted guy could refuse, but I knew very well that the bed would harbour an over-population of bugs which would seek permanent refuge on me. That was why I always reckoned that my tent was the best option. It eliminated the chances of picking up unwanted fellow-travellers and it could be extremely comfy; if possible I usually set it up on a surface that was a dense twining and mixture of roots, branches, leaves, twigs and mud. The plant debris created a very soft suspension system and also left space for a minor air-flow. You might find yourself with an unscheduled room-mate, however, as I had discovered the previous night.

Through no fault of my hosts I spent another uncomfortable night. The bed's population was as numerous and aggressive as I had feared – the result being a bug, lice, flea and gnat problem that was to plague me in the days ahead – and the humidity was almost claustrophobic, although I managed to fall asleep eventually in spite of swimming in a pool of my own sweat. The oddest thing about the heat, I noticed once again, was that I seemed to perspire *more* rather than less once I had calmly settled down for the night. The dark hours were always the worst. I usually enjoyed the days, even when the going was tough; it was the nights that were often anything but enjoyable.

Next morning I got my flea-bitten self off to an early start and plunged back into the middle of nowhere, surrounded by hundreds of identical grass hills, with the dark jungle now, thankfully, well off to my right, so that I steered clear of it most of the time. The going was not as difficult as the day before, but it wasn't much better, since the mud had been replaced by the only slightly lesser evils of soft sand and thick bush.

An additional problem was that there were frequent lethal ravines between the hills, three metres or more in depth, which had been dug out by years of heavy rains; they were almost impossible to see in time and bade fair to inflict serious damage on me or my bike or both if I nose-dived into one of them. My way through this perilous maze didn't help either. It varied between a 20 cm wide footpath, unused car tracks and then my personal favourite, absolutely nothing. I soon learnt that when the path pulled this last trick I had just two options. If I was lucky I would be able to spot where it picked up somewhere ahead. In more difficult cases I had to settle for using my logic and following likely-looking gaps in the foliage. One way or another, these stratagems always worked.

At this stage yet another buggeration factor made its appearance: my bicycle's brake-pads gave up the ghost, totally worn out. I now had zero stopping power, which was no joke when I considered those lethal ravines. I tried a little creative engineering with an attempt to re-position the brake-pads so that I could extract a final bit of use out of the remaining half a millimetre of rubber, but this didn't work. Yet another complication came along when I reached the foot of one hill and found that the single sandy footpath I was on had split into two, each heading 90 degrees away from one another – one in the direction of the sea, the other sharply inland. I consulted my maps; needless to say, neither of the branches was marked. So I sat and thought the matter through, the process being more or less that, firstly, I had to make a decision, and secondly, I had no information on which to base that decision. This being the case, the chances of going the wrong way were equal – although the consequences of a wrong decision would *not* be the same.

I considered my options and decided to take the inland-pointing track. My reasoning was that it had taken considerable effort of the five-steps-forward-and-four-steps-back variety over very rough terrain to reach this altitude above sea-level. If I went seawards and found I had made a mistake, the climb to regain my present altitude of about 200 metres above sea-level would be pure torture – in terms of sheer effort, one kilometre on this terrain was roughly equal to 50 on a tarmac road. So I would be far happier knowing I had made a mistake but did not have to backtrack inland from the coast.

The decision might have lightened my mind but it did nothing for my ease of travel. My sole diversion in the hours of struggle that followed came when I saw the only signs of life I had encountered that entire day, two women with clay pots balanced on their heads, going in the same direction as I was. They were so shocked to see me – and who can blame them, considering what I must have looked like by then? – that they didn't respond to my greeting at all. They just stared in disbelief, then got well out of my way.

As I passed I asked if this was the road going to the border of Gabon. No response, just more goggling. So I decided to spare them any further trauma and continue on my way, I was confident (for some reason or no reason) that I was on the right path. Then, when a gap of something like 50 metres had opened up between us, they broke out of their paralysis and started shouting something. Although I didn't understand exactly what they were saying I realised that they were pointing in the direction of the Gabon border. I was going in the wrong direction! I thanked them and stopped for a drink of water before continuing, while the women wasted no time in moving on.

Now it was decision time again. I could struggle back over those hellish 10 kilometres to where the path forked and start all over. Alternatively, I could risk heading westwards, directly across country through the thick grasslands, and with luck and maybe a bit of logic I would eventually meet up with the coastal track.

It didn't take me long to decide. I was *not* willing to retrace my footsteps; it would take me five or six hours and necessitate another night in the jungle, which I would prefer to avoid. Also, my water-supply was low and I knew that there was none to be found along the way I had just come. So it was straight to the west, shit or bust.

It came close to being bust. For all its defects, even the path I had been following was better than nothing. Now I was pulling my bike out of large holes and dragging it up 10-metre-high banks of muddy grass, sweating like a fountain and watching my water get less and less. Soon I had only about 500 ml left, and I sat down to rest. I was gazing into the distance, asking myself the sort of questions you ask when you have painted yourself into a corner, when I saw a familiar object hanging from the branch of a small tree. A guava! In fact, many guavas! In a split second I had one in my mouth. It wasn't entirely ripe, but it was juicy and I could feel it putting new strength into me. So I climbed in, and I think the true depth of my desperation became clear when I found myself repeatedly saying out loud: 'Imagine that ... imagine that ...' in between bites.

Having wreaked genocide among the guava population, I set off again, my optimism restored to such an extent that I was convinced that the other track was just over the next hill. Precisely what that belief was based on, I don't know, since I was quite literally in the middle of nowhere, armed only with a useless map and a feeling that I would soon link up with a track which might or might not exist. All I *did* know for certain was that if I kept heading westwards I would run into the Atlantic Ocean sooner or later – unless, of course, I conked out along the way.

Conking out was not such a remote possibility. It was becoming more and more difficult to move at any sort of reasonable speed and it was obvious that I was going to have to set up camp within a few hours. I was also down to the dregs of my water supply, and I re-evaluated my strategy as I took the final sips. The best – really the only – thing to do was to leave my bike for the time being and head westwards as fast as I could, the aim being to find either a source of water or the seaward track. Ideally both, but either would be sufficient reward. So I bade a temporary farewell to my faithful steed and set off.

Walking without the hard labour of pushing my overloaded bike was a strangely liberating experience, and at times I even broke into a steady run for the sheer freedom of it. But I didn't find either water or track, and after going over four tall hills I knew that I would soon have to start retracing my steps, because the further I went the more difficult it would be to find my bicycle again. I had a last look-around before actually turning back, using my video camera's zoom facility in lieu of binoculars. To the west, as before, there was nothing. But when I swung the zoom more to the north I picked up what looked like a track running over the centre of a hill. At last!

I reversed direction and got going, already making plans for when I had retrieved my bike. It was going to take concentration and strategy to get back to this point. Travelling on foot, the route I had taken would not necessarily be suitable for a bike, so I would have to deviate in places from the mental track I had laid down – but I had to get back to the exact spot from where I had spotted that faint, distant path. Then I would aim for a point between the visible track and due west. That, surely, was my best guarantee of success.

The knowledge that I was closing the distance to the Gabonese border once again sped me on. If I got back to my turn-around point and hooked up with the track I had spotted, I was virtually there!

By good luck as much as anything else I got back to where I had left my bike and successfully back-tracked again. Yep, there was the track in the distance! Choosing a landmark to keep me heading in the right direction wasn't easy because ahead the jungle was creeping back again and no feature of the terrain really stood out. I decided I would select a new landmark every time I topped another hill.

But my plans proved unnecessary; fortune really does favour the brave, or at least those willing to act bravely. As I reached the level ground at the end of my first northwesterly downhill I came upon the Congolese version of the Holy Grail: two faint parallel tracks, running north, the same tracks that I had spotted in the distance. Although the tracks had obviously not seen use for a long time and consisted largely of soft sand, it was wonderful to be following something more tangible than merely my instinct. I was literally back on track!

A new type of obstacle reared its ugly head as I toiled nearer and nearer to the Gabonese border: rivers. In the rainy season rivers in that part of the world tend to be large and swift-flowing, far too powerful for a man with a clumsy overloaded bicycle. But I was beginning to come across fellow human beings who could help me ... although sometimes at a price, as I learnt when I made my first real crossing.

I was faced with a roaring river 35 metres wide, so full that there were no banks visible on either side, and the only way across was by way of an ancient rusty barge which looked more dangerous than the foaming torrent heading seawards. It must have been an impressive boat once upon a time, but that time was long past. Now it was a mere shell of its former self. The heavy-duty cable which formerly drew it back and forth across the river was long gone, the housing cages which had guided it rusted down to anonymous blobs, and had been replaced by a thick but mouldy-looking rope. The barge 'captain' was obviously no wild-eyed optimist, because he positioned the rope in such a way that if he and his crew lost their grip we would not be washed downstream. This done, they started pulling us across.

In spite of the dodgy circumstances he and his crew were cheerful, and the laughter and bantering never stopped while they bent themselves to their task. I enjoyed the companionship, although not the heavy toll fee, which cost me a handful of CFA francs. (This is a common currency shared by about half a dozen former French colonies in the region, and according to my informants in Pointe Noire is also far and away the most stable currency in West Africa.) My personal definition of a stable currency is one that remains in my own pocket, but now a temporary instability set in as the 'captain' named his price for getting me over the river. Fortunately for all concerned I had not yet got a satisfactory grip with the exchange rate; it was only later that I discovered to my horror that I had paid him the equivalent of $30 US, which was pretty extortionate, even when one considers the circumstances.

But what the hell, I was getting closer to the border all the time. According to my map the last village before the border was called Nzambi, and after that it was just 30 km before I finally crossed the line. My game plan now was to get to Nzambi before sunset, sleep over and then knock off the final 30 km next day.

I arrived at Nzambi on schedule, and found a place which would stay on in my memory long after I had moved on. It consisted of a small collection of huts next to a deep-blue lake nestling between the hills, which the setting sun had turned to gold in a manner startlingly similar to some of Leonardo's paintings. It looked familiar for another reason, and after a second or two I realised that I was reminded of the hills that had surrounded Marcus Aurelius's house in the film 'Gladiator'. I tried to capture this wonderful ambience with my camera, and of course I failed, because part of it was in my mind and emotions.

My reception was not hostile but it wasn't cordial either. I hadn't expected any particular welcome, but likewise I had not expected everyone to steer clear of me as if I were carrying the plague. I was somewhat puzzled by this till I saw some men in uniform – army, police or immigration officials, I wasn't sure which – approaching me. Then the penny dropped. This was a border town of a country that had reason to be wary of insurgents, and all power resided in the men with the uniforms and guns.

In spite of this unpromising beginning, though, the formalities proceeded smoothly in the wreck of an immigration office, although the officials pulled the good-cop-bad-cop stunt – one was surly and barely acknowledged my existence, while the other asked friendly questions and gave me advice about the Gabonese roads. I didn't know whether this was standard operating procedure or whether they were just bored and indulging in a little play-acting, but I played the same game as always, which was to engage with the friendly guy and avoid a confrontation with the grumpy one.

In due course the grumpy guy stamped my passport, confirmed in his own charming way that I would leave the Congo the following day and departed. Once he had gone the friendly one, whose name was Luke, tried a quick scam. Would I like to unpack my luggage so that he could see what it was that made my bike so heavy? Needless to say, I replied that I would prefer not to because repacking wasn't so easy, and suggested he make a few spot checks. Luke came back with a counter-suggestion. If I paid him 2 000 CFA I wouldn't have to unpack a thing. This, he claimed, was a standard formal procedure: you could either unpack your bags or save yourself the trouble by paying a stipulated fee.

I did not bite on this dubious claim and started unpacking without waiting for his instruction. Luke kept an eye on me till some hunters came by with a selection of small monkeys and large squirrel-like creatures. Then he lost interest in what I was doing and told me to pack up again so that he could get down to negotiating for his dinner.

In spite of his somewhat flexible moral approach Luke was a pleasant fellow who bore me no ill-will for my lack of co-operation, and invited me to spend the night in the dilapidated military barracks. The four soldiers inhabiting the barracks were very friendly and bartered their turtle eggs and squirrel stew for a few mouthfuls of my Jungle Oats porridge. No doubt this would have surprised most people from South Africa, where Jungle Oats porridge is a staple breakfast dish, to realise that to these Congolese it was more exotic than things like turtle eggs.

Knowing little about turtle conservation, I did not realise what a delicate situation they were in along the West African coastline, so I had only a few small qualms about eating the eggs. I reasoned that the vast majority of hatchlings didn't even make it to the sea anyway, so as long as I didn't make a habit of eating the eggs, it was OK. Dinner over, I went to bed and endured another long and partly sleepless night, which was made even worse by Nzambi's hyperactive mosquito population and the swollen, itchy horse-fly bites I had collected during my journey there.

Torrential rain escorted (or perhaps I should say 'washed') me out of the Congo next day, so fierce that I turned into a contortionist in my efforts to stay on the track as I trudged northwards, pushing my bike. The going alternated between thick, sticky mud and slippery clayey rock which sometimes had my bike and me heading in different directions. Now and again I could freewheel on the downslopes, but only at great risk, because the only way I could brake was by holding the sole of my shoe firmly against the front wheel. During all this I encountered a fellow pilgrim, flip-flops in hand and dressed only in a pair of tight shorts, who passed me along the way as I was traversing some thick jungle. I greeted him as he passed and would have loved to ask him where he was going, but he was in full stride and I was too puffed, so I'll never know.

I was relieved to eventually cross into Gabon at Ndindi, a picturesque town on the banks of the Banio lagoon – not so much because I hadn't enjoyed travelling through the Congo (yes, in spite of everything) but because it marked a concrete return for my efforts. It was an almost startling transition. One minute I was freewheeling through dense jungle, the next moment it fell away and I was on the banks of the lagoon, with nothing between myself and an unscheduled swim except the sole of my right shoe.

A stocky grey-haired man saved me by warning me about the

chances of imminent immersion and then he and his son paddled me over to the other side in their half-sinking dugout canoe, two more of the many Congolese who had appeared out of nowhere to offer timely assistance during my ride through their country. It made me think about the priorities of the First World environment from which I came as I sat back and ate their gift of fresh pineapple under the gaze of the son, who was fascinated by my appearance, by my bicycle and the way I was eating the pineapple.

Most of the jungle people I had met in the past week had been good human beings who did not deserve to have the doubtful benefits of what we like to call modern civilisation inflicted on them. The fact was that they didn't really need a road through their jungle, or any of the other 'help' we consider so necessary. They led contented and reasonably stable lives and could do very well without outsiders intervening to 'save' them.

They dropped me off on the Gabonese bank and went on their way, and this final act of kindness from total strangers ended my arduous trek through the Congo. I waved goodbye and got on the bike. Now for Gabon, and whatever awaited me in the fifth country of my journey, not only into Africa but into my very soul.

# CHAPTER 8

# KINDNESS AND CORRUPTION IN GABON

*I pulled out my Leatherman survival knife, flicked open the seven-centimetre-long saw blade with its razor-sharp saw teeth and went at the bites with it. I started with restrained, carefully calculated sweeping motions, but this didn't last long, and eventually I was literally scraping away the itching, the blood dripping off my toes on to the floor.*

The feeling of bonhomie generated by my Congolese friends' act of goodwill lasted only till I met the local Gabonese immigration official. No 'good-cop, bad-cop' thing here: it was strictly 'bad cop'. Whether he was that way by nature or because he had taken an instant dislike to me for some reason, I didn't know. What I *did* know was that I found myself outside the immigration shack, unpacking my possessions in the mud and rain while he stood high and dry on the verandah and barked instructions at me, completely indifferent to the unnecessary misery he was inflicting on me.

Confrontation was not an option, so I hung on to my self-control and stayed patient, smiling at all times. It didn't do anything to soften his attitude. He insisted on looking through everything, including my family photos, letters and maps. It was completely uncalled-for harassment, and the only good thing I can say about it is that I rediscovered some things that I had packed away so well that I had not been able to find them for some time.

Only people who have undertaken this sort of trip will fully understand how it feels to be totally alone in a strange country with only a very sketchy knowledge of the local language, and to be abused by people one would normally look to for help. One's first inclination is believe one is in a country run by callous officious idiots like my unwanted Gabonese acquaintance. But on reflection it might be that people like these have never done any travelling of their own and have no idea of what it feels like to be a tourist in a foreign country. His approach might have been different if he had had a similar personal experience.

But these first impressions did not last, because although I didn't realise it as I wallowed about in the mud with my personal possessions scattered about me, I was about to meet the first person of emotional significance on this journey. He was a Senegalese named Mahmoud, a very laid-back guy in a caftan with a big smile on his chubby charcoal-black face. He owned the only shop in the village and came to my rescue in many ways. I had to wait three days for the weekly motor-boat that would take me up the lagoon to my next destination, the town of Mayumba, and during that time Mahmoud and I were constant companions.

Mahmoud included me at his table, where I was introduced to his wife's delicious traditional Senegalese dishes, including a type of shortcake biscuit she called 'croquet', and rented me a comfortable room for almost nothing. It was a solid wooden structure that was furnished with a reed bed, mattress and side-table, and it came with some interesting extras, in the form of a giant rat population. By 'giant' I mean not the number of rats but their size – some were as big as small cats. And they were not backward about coming forward.

My first night there they pulled over the side-table to get at the last of my Senegalese biscuits, and it was nothing unusual to have them galloping over me during the dark hours, looking for any leftover food. If they woke me up at night I would take my torch and flash it around, which sometimes revealed slightly hair-raising sights; one time the torch's beam showed up about 10 extra-extra-large rats scurrying around on the floor and along the wooden walls. I didn't get worked up about it, however. As far as I was concerned I didn't mind sharing the room (they had been there first, after all) as long as they didn't run over me while I was awake. Some people might find this puzzling, but I wasn't going mad, it was just that I had picked up the soldier's and traveller's knack of being able to sleep in even the worst conditions.

During the day I hung out with Mahmoud in his shop, learning more French while we swopped stories about our respective homelands (among other things I learnt that he had gone to school with the famous Senegalese musician Baba Maal, in the coastal town of St Louis). In the process I cultivated a distinct liking for tjeboudienne – fish, rice and an oily spice-laden sauce – which his wife served up for lunch every day, and was glad to hear that I was going to be eating a lot of it when I reached his home country.

During this time I became really aware of how far the ripple effect of a specific event can reach. Mahmoud liked to spend his day in relaxed style, chatting with his feet propped up on a chair when there was no immediate business to transact. Being a good Muslim, he prayed five times a day at the pre-ordained times, but he was always prepared to acknowledge the arrival of a customer, even in mid-prayer. Then one morning we had tea earlier than usual and an unusually serious Mahmoud explained why, impatiently struggling with our mutual language barrier: in faraway Iraq Saddam Hussein had been captured by the coalition forces. I listened in wonderment. Iraq was half a world away from this obscure Gabonese village, but news of the dictator's fall had penetrated here as well.

A new fervour crept into Mahmoud's daily routine of worship. His prayers were considerably louder, and if customers came in while he was on his knees they were totally ignored till he had finished. I never discovered the details of who or what he was praying for, but the change definitely had something to do with Iraq, and it definitely did not go down well with some people in the community. That's politics for you.

How it all ended I don't know, because the boat finally arrived and I embarked after fond farewells to Mahmoud and his wife. It was an interesting ride as the boat zigzagged along the picturesque shores, picking up other passengers. Quite a number brought livestock with them for sale to restaurants, ranging from chickens and fish to reedbuck and a couple of crocodiles, and it soon became clear that Gabonese attitudes towards animals, wild or domestic, differed somewhat from South Africa's.

I knew that the animals were doomed to end up on someone's dinner-table, but I couldn't help trying to alleviate their suffering in the ferocious sunlight. The crocodiles in particular were having a very hard time and seemed to be dying by inches, so I used a scoop I found on board to splash water on them. One of the crocodiles didn't make it, but the other reached Mayumba alive. It was a pretty pointless exercise, I suppose, given where the animals were headed.

After my battles with the Congolese jungle the Gabonese roads were a pleasure when I set off from Mayumba: although not tarmac they were actually surfaced, and they actually went somewhere specific. Not that conditions were ideal. The graded surfaces were covered with a slippery layer of clayey mud which made turning corners very tricky. I soon found that the bicycle, its wheels locked into tracks carved into the mud by previous vehicles, headed in only one direction: straight ahead. I could try to turn – and there were a lot of turns because the road meandered all over the place – but the bike and I wouldn't change direction. We would still forge straight ahead, only upside-down.

I also encountered certain problems with stream-crossings, which were very basic – five or six huge logs laid side by side, with broad planks nailed across them to accommodate larger vehicles' wheels. It would have been the equivalent of vehicular Russian roulette to try riding across these contraptions. The gaps between the planks were three times my tyre width and threatened to swallow my bike even when I was pushing it carefully along.

The land was very mountainous, and this caused further frustration. I couldn't risk getting up any speed on the downhills because my defunct brakes meant that I had no way of significantly reducing my speed when I reached the bottom where one of those dangerous log bridges lay waiting. So I had to work hard to get up each muddy uphill and then creep down the other side, slowing myself as best I could by holding my shoe-sole against the front tyre. This wasn't doing my sole any good.

Anyway, late that afternoon I came up to a couple of huts along-side the road, totally populated by senior citizens. Why, I don't know, but there wasn't one child, teenager or youngish adult any-where. But there was nothing wrong with the old folks' hospital-ity, and while I was pitching my tent they prepared a bed for me in one of the huts. I declined their offer with thanks, spinning a story about why I planned to sleep in the tent but adding that if it rained I would take them up on their offer.

The fact was, of course, that I could hardly tell them the real rea-son for my choice, namely the bed-bug problem, which had be-come worse because an additional species had now enlisted in my legion of tormentors. The late arrivals were minuscule flies the lo-cals called 'foeroe', and they were all over me, biting and causing a rash of a thousand bumps to my calves and forearms. There was no getting away from them: they were everywhere in numbers so enor-mous that there seemed to be a perpetual haze in front of my eyes, and every piece of pineapple I cut had a horde of passengers riding on it into my mouth. They bogged down in my sweat, so that I had a sort of grainy bug paste on my forehead and neck. And how they could bite! Biting flies? In other circumstances I might not have be-lieved it, but I was soon converted. I never could understand how they were able to wreak such havoc – after all, how big could their mouths be if their bodies were less than a millimetre long?

Fate was against me. That night it *did* rain, so copiously and con-tinuously that eventually I gave up and moved in with my hosts – more for the sake of keeping my kit dry than anything else, since the downpour had relieved the humidity. But I paid dearly for my concern about my luggage. The 'foeroe' flies swarmed over every piece of exposed skin they had gnawed on earlier, while the squad-rons of mosquitoes in the room joined hands with the bed-bugs to well and truly finish off the back of my legs.

The itching went to a level I had never experienced so far, and my grim determination to go to sleep proved absolutely fruitless against the onslaught. About the only good thing to come out of this was that I was ready to hit the road at least two hours earlier than usual, and I was keen to get going, not because I felt fresh and full of beans (I didn't) but because I knew that movement and activity would distract me from my afflictions.

The going wasn't easy – in fact, it was harder than on the previous day. The terrain became even more mountainous, which meant in turn that the hills became steeper and the turns sharper, and I found that my left shoe's sole was wearing out from its braking activities. I should explain that stopping the bike by shoe was a tricky business which involved removing my foot from the sticky cleat mechanism and on to the front tyre without throwing myself off balance. The timing had to be exactly right or disaster would follow, and as I was using traditional cycling shoes with cleated soles, this meant that the parts involved in dislodging my feet, usually smoothly, became stickier.

My first serious fall came because of a momentary lapse in concentration. I found myself bearing down on a 90-degree turn to the left of a rock-face, going too fast and with my foot still in the pedal's clip. Desperately I tried to free my foot, but it refused to come away from the clip, and I knew that if I didn't stop in time I would make direct contact with the wall at over 60 km/h, with serious and possibly even fatal consequences.

There is nothing like a life-and-death situation to accelerate the decision-making process. I had about five seconds left before I hit that wall of rock, and I decided to try to ride through the turn instead of merely bracing myself and hoping for the best. It was a valiant try, if I say so myself, and it was a pity that it ended in total failure. I am still not quite sure of the sequence of events, although it would have made very good footage in any film. I assume that the bike slid into some sort of skid, hooked and flipped up into the air and then slammed into the rock.

When I had more or less collected my scattered senses I started by checking my body to see if I had sustained any serious injuries (I wasn't feeling any pain yet because I was still in shock). I palpated my vital organs and then swivelled my neck around without finding any signs of malfunction in anything. So far, so good. Then I checked my head. It was bleeding profusely from a cut, but head wounds tend to bleed a lot and it appeared to be working all right.

Further checking revealed that, apart from an extravagant number of grazes and bruises, plus a sprained ankle which was puffing up at great speed, my only major injury was a deep cut about three centimetres long on my right elbow. The shock was beginning to wear off now, and from the first throbs of pain I knew that this cut was going to give me lots of grief.

I was too relieved at having survived fairly unscathed to worry about what was to come, however, as I opened my medical bag to clean out the muck and bandage my arm (I didn't have any sutures). It was a painful business and perhaps I wasn't as thorough as I should have been, so it's quite possible that I am still carrying some Gabonese gravel around with me. To make this experience even more unforgettable the 'foeroe' flies were swooping on my exposed arms and legs throughout the doctoring, making further inroads on my plentifully chewed-up body.

When I had patched myself up, I turned my attention to my bike. Somewhat to my surprise it had not suffered fatal damage either, although the front tyre had burst and some metal parts had been bent out of shape. I changed the tyre, wrestled the bent bits into shape again and set off for my destination, the town of Tchibanga. I hoped they had a hospital or clinic there, because I calculated that my roadside repairs needed to be followed up by some expert help.

My spirits were very low as I set off, and for the first time I had what South Africans would call a 'tjankbalie' moment. Tears started to roll down my face as I thought about my friends, my family and my girlfriend in South Africa, so very far away, whom I hadn't spoken to for two weeks. I was hurting physically, it was true, but what really stabbed into me was the feeling of being utterly alone in the world. Man is a gregarious animal, after all, and I missed my own people and needed them here with me.

But my weeping did me a power of good. Some people might think that a crying jag leaves you feeling weaker and even more dispirited, but in fact it was exactly the opposite. When I had cried myself dry I wiped away the last of my tears, and along with them all the negativity in me. I pedalled with renewed energy, because my mind had cleared and I had a specific object in mind. I would get to

Tchibanga as soon as possible, I would get myself and my bike fixed up, and I would contact my loved ones.

It was a huge relief when Tchibanga hove into view. It was a medium-sized town for that part of the world, with both electricity and running water, and a local shopkeeper, an Indian man, showed me to a hotel where I could get cheap, clean and quiet accommodation, even being so kind as to actually negotiate the most economical rate. In any case, I wasted no time in repairing the damage inflicted on mind, body and bike, and believe me, the repairs were badly needed. My elbow had a lump the size of a tennis ball, the bug-wounds had gone from being an irritation to a definite threat and the glands on my inner thighs and under my arms were seriously inflamed, indicating that I had an overall infection of some kind. I started a course of penicillin for my elbow, but in fact it was needed for other things as well.

My bike needed some serious attention for more than the damage suffered in my collision with the rock, because the chain was slipping in 90 per cent of my gear selections. That would be my first priority in the morning; my shopkeeper friend had told me to pass by his shop early on and he would give me directions to a reliable bicycle mechanic.

My hotel room's shower and ceiling-fan proved critical to maintaining my sanity that first night. The perspiration poured from me even when I had towelled myself dry after a shower. But my worst problem was the itching of the bug-bites and stings that covered much of my body, and which became more unbearable with every passing minute. The shower's running water had soothed them a little, and so had the movement of the air over my wet body from the fan. But it still took every bit of willpower I possessed to restrain myself from scratching the bites, and of course when I fell asleep my reflexes took over, so that I would wake up to find myself raking at my ankles and my legs. All I could do was get some water and sluice the most troublesome areas down, which gave some mild relief but didn't solve the problem.

I managed somehow, though, till the electricity went out in the middle of that dark Gabonese night. Suddenly the soothing down-draught from the fan was gone, and so was most of my protection against the legions of mosquitoes waiting to drink my blood. It was just too much, and I began to scratch with all the force I could muster. It was a crazy thing to do, but suddenly all my rage and frustration at my endless torment broke through my restraint.

I scratched and scratched without achieving much, then pulled out my Leatherman survival knife, flicked open the seven-centimetre-long saw blade with its razor-sharp saw teeth and went at the bites with it. I started with restrained, carefully calculated sweeping motions, but this didn't last long, and eventually I was literally scraping away the itching, the blood dripping off my toes on to the floor. I remember that the pain was a crisp stinging sensation that blended with and finally overpowered the itch.

I scraped away, vaguely realising but disregarding the knowledge that what I was doing was totally illogical. I had a more urgent priority, saving my sanity. The scraping eventually slowed back into the original gentle sweeping motion as I started to nod off. I wasn't so sleepy that I didn't realise that putting my feet back on the bed would ruin the sheets and surely spoil my chance of staying a second night, so I slithered to the floor. It was cooler there in any event, and I was so tired I could have slept anywhere.

But the bliss did not last. After some time on the floor – I don't know how long – I was roused by renewed itching, as bad as it had been before ... and even worse, because in addition to being sticky with partly congealed blood my legs and feet were so sore from the scraping that I couldn't touch them, even with my bare hands. Now I knew what it felt like to be tortured! Not that it was something I really needed to know.

I lay there for a while, then dragged my messed-up self into the shower and turned it on, full force and cold water only. Almost immediately I felt total relief, and was ready to sleep once more. But I dared not turn off the shower because I was afraid – *knew* – that the itching would return in full force as soon as I did. So I stood there and stood there, and I assume my abused body finally just shut down, because next thing I knew I woke up and found myself sitting naked on the floor of the shower cubicle, legs stretched out, while the cold water cascaded down on me.

Eventually I forced myself out of the shower and got dressed. It wasn't a pleasant process, but I had things to do. My first priority was to get my bicycle repaired and, if possible, leave later that afternoon. So with the sores on my feet weeping through the socks – although strangely enough my shoes felt reasonably comfortable – I set off for my friend's shop. My legs were hurting fiercely from my attack with the Leatherman, but at least the pain was dulling a lot of the itching. Some remedy!

My friend was as good as his word – in fact better, because when I arrived at his shop the mechanic was waiting there for me. The mechanic, one Christopher, was a bloke who really tried, but I didn't have too much confidence in him, because he seemed to be what you might describe as a hammer-and-pliers mechanic. Watching him operating on my bike was a painful business. Being a typical polite South African I let him carry on for quite a while (who was I to offer help and advice in any case? I'd never repaired this type of bike either), but eventually I called a halt and questioned him directly about whether what he knew what he was doing.

The critical moment came when Christopher set about trying to force the rear derailleur's factory-fitted screw in at a different angle from the receiving hole. Christopher said he reckoned that the original position of this crucial part was the problem, not the possibility that the worn-out sprocket teeth or the chain could be the cause of the slipping gears. I disagreed vehemently with this diagnosis and the gear problem stayed unresolved. Christopher put the bits back together again, his feelings hurting as much as my feet did, and I said goodbye to my Indian friend. Almost immediately after leaving Tchibanga I faced a really testing mountain pass several kilometres long, but I didn't mind. The tougher the cycling, the less time I had to think about my painful arm and the ever-present itching.

I spent all day on the road and stayed the night with a most interesting jungle family. We couldn't understand each other except for the odd French word we had in common, but they grasped my essential needs – a sheltered area under which to pitch my tent, and some sleep – and saw that I got both.

That family had character. The father was very flamboyant, giving loud orders to anyone who crossed his line of sight. His wife was a very haggard lady with a smouldering pipe permanently in one hand and a Marge Simpson voice with which she uttered a stream of grunts and growls of disapproval about the actions of the other family members. I am sure that she would have scared the daylights out of most kids. Was this the traditional Gabonese culture and the average sort of woman? I didn't know, but decided that if she was the Gabonese men must be a henpecked lot.

Her daughter didn't look older than about 16, but she was already breast-feeding a baby, and I thought of the old Afrikaans saying 'vinnig ryp, vinnig vrot!' (early ripe, early rotten). Still, the baby powder came in handy next day to soothe some of the irritation on my feet, which later shocked passers-by when I made an early lunchtime stop at the next village, Ndende, and took off my shoes and socks to air them. The crusted objects were not a pretty sight.

I wasn't feeling too bad, though, all things considered, and reckoned that this was because I had started the penicillin at the right time, or my body would have packed in by now. It just goes to show that timing is everything. The road was still a bumpy dirt track, but it had improved and the terrain had flattened out, so that my problem with the slipping gears wasn't as bad as it might have been, and I could maintain a steady pace without knocking myself out.

I spent the night with a family whose members communicated in much the same way as my previous hosts. The older women smoked their pipes and didn't speak so much as belch out their words. The men all ended up sitting around a fire, drinking, I think, palm wine. All in all a real barrel of laughs, but there was no faulting their hospitality.

The younger boys took me to the river to watch me bathe (hoping, I suspected, that I would be attacked by one or other wild river creature from which they would have to protect me). I would have loved to plunge in and let the river soothe my constant itching, but the fear of contracting a water-borne disease through my open scratches niggled at me, and with deep regret I only did what was absolutely necessary.

By the time I got back to the family the womenfolk had prepared a dish of rice and cassava. I did justice to it, hunger being the best sauce, although it wasn't awfully exciting in comparison with the meals Mahmoud's wife had served up. Cassava is basically a giant banana-type vegetable that tastes somewhere between potato and cardboard; it is a staple food in Gabon, but I doubt whether everyone is mad about it.

As I had done with my hosts of the night before, I greeted everyone before I went to sleep. They were circled around the fire and became silent at my approach from the dark. '*Bonne nuit*' (good night) I said, lowering my head slightly and lifting my hands, palms exposed in the universal sign language of goodwill. I was hoping that the international language of manners and respect would overcome the linguistic, not to say cultural, barriers, but the only response I got was a couple of frowns and confused looks. I gave up on building bridges and went off to my tent for another uncomfortable night.

My hope at this stage was that the gears would keep working after a fashion till I got to the Gabonese capital of Libreville, but the next day's journey proved that I hoped in vain. It became impossible to find a gear that would hold any sort of pressure, even though the terrain had flattened out even more. My hopes revived slightly when I got to the town of Mouila, because although it was pretty much like Tchibanga it seemed to have more of a military air and therefore, logically, it should have had a bit of technical back-up. I was dead wrong; Mouila had nothing to offer, so I consoled myself with a sit-down lunch and set off again.

About all I can say about Mouila is that I was able to give some of its inhabitants a good laugh, although not by choice, because I wasn't feeling very humorous at the time: I was frustrated because the bike was going badly, my body was raw and itching, and I still hadn't spoken to my friends and family. But life picks its own moments to provide some free comedy, as I proved yet again while making my way slowly and carefully to the outskirts.

The last building I came to had a large water-pump in front of it, raised about 15 cm above the ground on a concrete slab which was covered in bubbles and foam. Around it was a bunch of children, all awaiting their turn to fetch water or wash themselves or whatever laundry they had brought with them. This domestic scene reminded me that I hadn't filled my water containers yet, so I freewheeled up to the pump, my feet still clipped into the pedals. My intention was to pull my feet out of the clips just before I came to a complete stop in front of the pump, but I couldn't get them out fast enough and down I went into the slushy grime of the run-off water, which had collected in a pool that smelt awful. I fell into this noisome stew with some force, one shoulder totally submerged and my head thoroughly washed, if that is the right word. What I mumbled while I was filling up doesn't bear repeating, but the kids, bless them, enjoyed every moment.

I passed through the town's outer police point and got going. By now my spirits had recovered from my encounter with the run-off and I was full of get-up-and-go. If the damned bike wouldn't do its job, I would push it all the way to Libreville, more than 300 km away! Filled with this fine feeling of resolve I struggled on for about 20 km before realising that I wasn't thinking clearly. The bottom line was that I had to get to Libreville by other means, somehow get the necessary parts and repair my bike, then come back here and set off northwards again.

The problem with all this was, of course, that there was a clear lack of 'other means'; in the entire hour and a half since I had left Mouila not one vehicle had passed me in either direction. I turned around, cycled back slowly to the police post and started explaining to the officer in charge that my bike and I needed a lift to Libreville. I was still trying to get this across to him in my fractured French when, out of the blue, a truck pulled up. I could scarcely believe my eyes.

The chief cop had obviously grasped the essence of what I was trying to tell him, because he immediately addressed himself to the driver. From the look of him the driver wasn't really inclined to give me a lift, but the policeman convinced him that he was going to play good Samaritan that day, whether he liked it or not. Needless to say the atmosphere was a little icy as we pulled away from the police post, but it was a long, hard journey and we became better acquainted when the driver saw that I was willing to help with loading and off-loading his cargo, and once with changing a tyre.

I liked his attitude. His job was to transport wood to Libreville from the rural parts, and he embodied the spirit that brings success in spite of all obstacles and challenges. I don't know if 'challenges' or 'obstacles' are strong enough to describe the sickening corruption he had to work his way through. I had had some exposure to it, but nothing on this scale. It is surely the cancer that eats away at Africa and holds it down from achieving anything like its full potential.

It appeared that he needed permits, real or imaginary, for almost everything. Just about every official this guy came across had to be slipped a few notes to ensure that he wasn't fined for one silly thing or another. He had to pay off one official to prevent a fine for transporting people (me) without a taxi licence. Another had to be bribed to overlook the fact that some of the planks in the back were slightly longer than his manifest stated. And so on.

The crooked official I remember best was the one who objected to my presence. He was lying back in his chair under a large shady tree about 20 metres off the road, chewing a piece of grass and alternating between shooting aggressive glances at me and threatening to confiscate the truck's load because the driver was giving a foreigner a lift. We were at that roadblock for over an hour while the driver negotiated his way through this cesspool.

Then when I went to collect my passport the official refused to give it to me unless I paid him $10. His stare was as aggressive as ever, but it was now aimed past me because he refused to make eye contact. I took this gap and laughed, telling him that there was no way a poor guy like me on a bicycle could afford to support a man like him. Then, still laughing, I leaned forward and took my passport from his hand. I thanked all the other people around him and told them I would return. It was not that I wanted to see this swine again, but I wanted to recruit some allies before I returned here all alone on my bicycle. Then I would be a sitting duck.

Eventually we reached Libreville, and as in Luanda the South African embassy staff were really helpful. I ordered the parts I needed from South Africa because none were available locally. This meant that I would be staying over longer in Libreville than I had expected, because the advent of the Christmas–New Year period meant that they would take five days longer to arrive. One of the staffers, a lady named Katrina, went out of her way to help me and even offered to put me up at her home. Needless to say I accepted with gratitude, not just because it helped me to conserve my funds but also because it was only a few days before Christmas, and that is the one time of the year when nobody wants to be alone.

The time I spent with Katrina really opened my eyes to the reality of the glamorous lifestyle that diplomats are perceived to enjoy. Travel the world, see places most people only dream of, meet extraordinary characters and so on. But there is another side to the coin. Here was Katrina, for example, a very attractive and charming woman, yet still without a life partner. Choice or circumstance? I could hardly ask her, since it was none of my business. But our time on earth is so limited that if we choose to commit in one direction we do not always have time to re-direct. And, I reminded myself, we don't all want the same thing. I envied Katrina, no pity involved here.

The talk about life being short makes me think about a joke a friend of mine, a stand-up comedian, used to make. He would say that he didn't understand what people were on about when they said that life was short because 'how can life be short? Life is the LONGEST thing you and I will ever know. Nothing in your life could ever be longer than your life. Come on, forget it! Life is not short.' For the record, I don't agree with him there.

I made good use of the extra time to smooth out bureaucratic bumps in the path ahead; Albert, the embassy driver and all-round good guy, took me around Libreville on a quest for visas to enter the next few countries, and we managed to get them for both Equatorial Guinea and Cameroon. This meant that I had a clear path till I got to Nigeria.

I also learnt another lesson that you don't see in travel books:

Never stash your dollars inside your sweaty socks. I picked this up when Albert and I marched confidently into a bank to exchange $200 into CFA francs. Albert was well known and soon had us in the correct queue. But before we had moved even one place the teller beckoned us closer and wagged an index finger, saying: 'No, no, no, no!'

No? We were baffled. But then the teller took my dollars and compared them to another dollar note he had with him. Now we saw that my dollars were brown in colour, as opposed to the light green of the teller's note; he must have been truly eagle-eyed to have spotted the difference from so far away.

Anyway, now I had a real problem because according to the teller no bank in Libreville would be willing to exchange those strange brown dollars of mine. So there I was with $600 of the wrong colour. What the hell was I going to do now? I toyed with the idea of getting hold of a black market currency dealer. Albert didn't like this idea, pointing out that it was illegal and probably dangerous. But I didn't see any alternative, so once Albert had dropped me off for the day I started asking around. My enquiries eventually led me to a shopkeeper who not only took the money I had on me without blinking an eye but gave me a better exchange rate than the bank! He was keenly interested when I said I had more dollars to exchange, and next morning I went back and got rid of the rest of my funny-coloured money. I hope he didn't have a problem trying to exchange it himself later on.

I also set about looking for a local sponsor or two, but I had no luck – nobody in Libreville wanted to spend any money, although everyone wanted to interview me for TV. I did get a couple of free gifts from a cell phone company, including some very pretty wax printed material which I sent home to Vasti via DHL. But that was about all, which left me feeling rather disappointed. I hadn't expected miracles, but found it inconceivable that *not one* Gabonese company was interested.

Katrina and I had Christmas lunch and New Year's Eve dinner at other embassy staffers' homes, and even though my journey was still at an early stage, the diplomats were very taken with my adventures so far, with my tales of Angola and the two Congos holding them spellbound.

I had quite a funny conversation with an aunt of mine on Christmas Day. She asked how I was and so on, and I told her a few stories about what had befallen me so far. Then she asked: 'Haven't you gone far enough now?' It took me a moment to realise that my aunt, like a lot of other people, had not truly comprehended the scope of my ambitious undertaking and didn't realise that I was not out on just another long-distance cycling holiday.

I hastened to disabuse her. 'No,' I said, 'it's not far enough. I have a long way to go, actually.'

My aunt was not baffled by this response. She had brought me up during my difficult teenage years and knew exactly how headstrong and self-willed I was. So to her my answer was exactly in character. It felt so good to know that, and to know that there were people concerned about my wellbeing.

My new sprockets arrived after Christmas and I had them fitted to the bike by a local mechanic who knew what he was doing – I had discovered that not all of Libreville's numerous bike mechanics worked on what they called 'American parts'. They used spares of French and Indian origin, my mechanic explained, because 'American' bicycles were too expensive.

With the sprockets in place, I was ready to set off on New Year's Day. I was in fine fettle after my layover, but I had a small problem. My generous hosts were under the impression that I was heading straight for the Equatorial Guinea border, whereas my intention was to go back and do that stretch of over 300 km that I had not covered. I had intended simply to say thanks and goodbye and then be on my way, but Katrina and her colleagues decided to make an outing of it by escorting me safely out of the city and some of the way north towards the border.

I was too embarrassed to mention my backtracking plans, so I cycled behind their car to the village of Ntoum and then northwards for another 25 km. It was the first time I had travelled with a support team and it was a pleasant way of doing things – people to chat to along the way, who would lean out the car window from time to time and pass you a sandwich or cool drink. *That* was the way to circumnavigate Africa!

Around the 25-kilometre mark the road had worsened to the point where it was almost impassable, so obviously the time had come for us to say goodbye before things got to the point where I would have spend valuable travelling time helping to push their vehicle out of a donga. It was sad to have to bid farewell to these good people who had done so much for a total stranger, and I thanked them with all the sincerity in my heart. Then we parted company.

The way I had it planned now was that I would carry on to the border with Equatorial Guinea and then somehow find transport back to Mouilla; if worst came to worst I would cycle back to Mouilla and catch a return lift to the border. This might sound slightly harum-scarum, but I wanted to savour that stretch I had missed, and I didn't want to waste any more time waiting for external factors to come into play.

The recent rains had made the road very muddy, but it was relatively easy to avoid the sticky patches, and in the Congo I had discovered how to avoid bogging down in a puddle spanning the width of the road: hit it at some speed and keep going at all costs. Naturally my baggage and I got wet in the process, but not as wet as would be the case if I were to bog down and fall over, or had to dismount and push myself out.

The feeling of being somewhere exotic and unventured-to was more evident here. Gabon had always been an exotic name for me, and now I was going through jungle terrain to get to a country called Equatorial Guinea. And on a bicycle! I was amused by the looks of surprise on locals' faces when I went by them, which gives an indication of how often identifiable foreigners passed through that part of the world on two wheels instead of four.

Katrina had given me a French/English dictionary as a farewell present, which emboldened me in my scrappy dialogue with the locals and led to an impromptu French lesson at the hands of the locals that would later come back to haunt me and evoke amusement during the rest of my journey through West Africa. People shouted 'Bonne Année!'(Happy New Year!) as I passed them on the road. There was still a distinct carnival atmosphere with a sort of Valium haze around it, and although the locals were hung over and tired, they still made the effort to welcome me into 2004, Gabonese style. I filed 'Bonne Année' away in the back of my mind: it should be good for general-purpose greetings for at least a fortnight, and I would remember it easily because it sounded similar to the evening greeting of 'bonne nuit'.

I made good time, and reached the outskirts of the border town of Cocobeach just after lunch. From here there were plenty of pick-ups – overloaded, naturally – making their way back to Ntoum, so I picked up a ride much earlier than I had expected. But getting further south proved to be more difficult: all I could find was over-priced, uncomfortable, overloaded and clearly unroadworthy buses with 'we go when we're full' schedules. So I actioned Plan B and set off on my own two wheels. It was a bit late in the afternoon, but I wanted to make a start.

The start turned out a bit differently from what I had expected. I hadn't got very far when a 4x4 came hurtling past, but I could see the driver looking back at me in his rear-view mirror, so I waved enthusiastically. He got the message and reversed back to me. He turned out to be a Frenchman called Pierre who was MD of a com-pany in the town of Ndjole, further south and about 80 km off the highway, and he was perfectly willing to give me a lift as far as he was going.

This was an offer I had no intention of refusing, and we manhan-dled the bike into the back of the 4x4, although with considerable difficulty and at the cost of some wear and tear on the upholstery. I felt so guilty about the damage the bike was doing that I actu-ally offered to call it quits, but Pierre would have none of it and even persuaded me to sleep at his house in Ndjole, after which, he said, he would drop me off on the highway again. I needed no fur-ther persuasion, because in addition to a comfortable night's rest I would be able to find out where the giant logs came from which I had seen being transported into Libreville.

So off we went, and for the first time, having nothing to do, I could appreciate the country I had been struggling through. Gabon has a majestic feel about it, a natural magnificence which was both humbling and intoxicating. Pierre didn't realise how unusual it was for me to sit silent as we wound through the mountains, threading our way past giant trees up to 40 metres high. I contemplated them with awe, mixed with fear that without official protection they would not be there if I ever returned, because according to people I had spoken to there was a huge amount of uncontrolled greed-driven logging taking place without any thought for the environment. The same thing had happened with oil, I was told. Now the oil was drying up and more and more attention was being given to exploiting the forests.

Next morning Pierre kindly drove me all the way to Lamberéné, the place made famous by Dr Albert Schweitzer's hospital, where he felt I would be able to find formal transport at the taxi-rank. But this was exactly what I wanted to avoid: such places were overrun with touts, all promising the earth and ready to squeeze every cent out of your pocket. So I asked Pierre to drop me off outside the town. There I said goodbye, and he gave me a farewell in the form of a bag of the lemongrass he had used to make tea for us the night before. I waved till he was out of sight and then got ready to go my own way, in my own way.

Going my own way didn't bring immediate results. After spending an unsuccessful hour alongside the main road out of town I decided to go to the police roadblock I had remembered from the original trip up from Mouila and see if I could scare up a little help here. This wasn't the infamous 'bribery under the tree' place of my earlier trip, so I reckoned I might run across some goodwill, official or otherwise. There wasn't much to the roadblock, just a rather shaky official hut next to a square, extremely well-made wooden house. I parked myself outside the wooden house and fell into conversation with the elderly owner, who was extending it in order to add a shop; the police would never stop halting passing vehicles, he joked, so obviously he was missing a valuable opportunity regarding the passing trade.

Seeing that he was doing the extensions all by himself, I offered to help. He accepted gladly and we sawed a few dozen beams to the right size for the addition's verandah railing, then nailed them neatly in place, giving the humdrum dwelling something of an air it had not previously possessed. I reckoned he could not fail to do well out of his shop, and if I had had the time and money I would probably have taken a few shares in the enterprise.

The old man paid me for my efforts by helping to persuade the driver of a pickup (overloaded with people and baggage, need I add?) to take me along as well. The driver tied my bicycle to the top of the canopy-shaped metal frame on the back, I climbed up on the bumper and we set off southwards through the mountains and jungles. It was a precarious perch, but hey, this was how they did it in Gabon. I knew that as passengers got off I would gravitate slowly but surely towards first prize, an actual place in the back where I could sit down, while a less fortunate newcomer would take over my space on the bumper.

I have two clear memories of that trip. The first was my initiation into how one carried a dead monkey. For this I had to thank (?) several hunters from whom the driver bought fresh-killed monkeys, porcupines, rats and deer. The way to carry a monkey, I saw, was to make two holes in the top of its skull, into which its tail was then threaded, the result was a sort of shoulder-bag with four limply hanging legs. It was certainly practical but pretty gruesome to look at, and I couldn't help wondering what sort of reaction I would get if I paraded this jungle fashion in the streets of Cape Town or Johannesburg. Presumably I would be arrested without further ado, if I wasn't beaten to death on the spot by an irate animal lover.

The kilometres passed in the customary bumpy fashion, and in due course my patience was rewarded with a seat up against the rear flap. But there was a price to pay, because the occupant of this seat was also the guardian of the meat, the driver told me; it would be my duty to see that passengers did not help themselves when getting off at their destination. So there I sat with my feet on the carcasses, a situation I did not really enjoy. I did not realise that the carcasses and I were scheduled to meet again that very night. But more of that later.

The second unforgettable moment involved something worse – and even sadder – than mounting guard over the heap of dead animals. Sitting on my right was a poorly clothed girl in her early teens who appeared to be in some discomfort for a reason I didn't know, and after a while she shifted her weight on to my right foot in a bid to ease whatever was bothering her. We sat like this for a while and then the cause of her discomfort became horribly and embarrassingly obvious when, without any warning, she urinated on my shoe and the floor on which we were sitting.

The poor kid was distraught and started to cry as the nauseating fumes of warm urine rose up to engulf us. I felt very sorry for her, and leaned forward to pat her on the shoulder as a token of sympathy. Wrong move! As I leaned forward the full force of the stench travelled up my nose, and before my hand even reached her shoulder I was gagging. I managed to hold on to my breakfast, but it was touch and go for a while.

She got off at the next village and dashed away into the darkness, but we who remained behind had to suffer the consequences of her overfull bladder for many kilometres to come. None of the other passengers were aware of what had happened and wanted to know the cause of the miasma. I just shrugged and ignored the urine sloshing back and forth with every movement of the vehicle. It didn't matter now, and in any case I was still playing 'down, boy!' with my innards, because the smell and the jarring had formed a deadly alliance.

We arrived in Mouila about an hour after sunset, and when the driver had dropped off his cargo of meat at one of the restaurants he took me to the police barracks and asked them to look after me. The cops were amenable to this and put me in a room with a corporal whose partner was away on leave. He was a friendly soul who made sure I had everything I needed and even took me on a walking tour of the town, so on the way back I stood him to supper at – you've guessed it – the very restaurant to which the meat had been delivered earlier.

We ate the plat du jour, rice and sauce with a few chunks of meat on top. I didn't ask what type of meat it was – sometimes it's better not to know what you're eating – but I couldn't resist enquiring as to whether the meat was fresh. Oui, oui, the meat was very fresh, the proprietor said enthusiastically. Killed that very day! I couldn't resist going a little further and insisting on a discount on the grounds that if I had not been a vigilant meat guard all this lovely stuff would not be in his larder for me to eat.

And so to bed, for which I was more than ready after my day's exertions. My brain couldn't have been as tired as my body, because at one stage I was talking so loudly in my sleep that I actually woke myself up. Fortunately my room-mate the corporal was a heavy sleeper, and he did not stir a finger during my unplanned oration. A very nice guy; I regret not having been able to contact him after I left there, but the police barracks and facilities were very basic. I can understand that a country like Gabon might not be able to afford high pay for its cops, but at least it could provide them with a PC or two and access to the Internet!

We were up at army time next day, and before long I had said goodbye to the hospitable policemen and headed off into the sunrise with my bike now going like a dream, mightily relieved to be heading in the right direction once more. On my way out I kept my eyes open for the scene of my swim in the sewage. Fortunately, perhaps, it was too dark, and I can't say I was very sorry. By this time, incidentally, I was well acquainted with Gabon's public toilet system, or rather the lack of it. In a nutshell, if you had to go you went, and you had the whole countryside to choose from. Well, it wasn't quite as simple as that, because in this part of Gabon the bush and jungle were so dense that darting off the road for a quickie was well-nigh impossible. As a result it was quite likely that you would be squatting in the road in the classic position, pants around ankles and going at it, only to have a whistling hunter or other pedestrian suddenly make his appearance out of dense clouds of mist.

When travelling by bicycle this element of a journey becomes a crucial management factor; regular bowel movement is something you hold thumbs for. My own routine was to do the necessary about three kilometres into the day's ride. It's amazing how fast your inhibitions curl up and wither away. In no time at all you wouldn't give two hoots if a whole phalanx of hunters came up at a jog-trot, chased by a rogue elephant; you assumed the position and placidly had your daily strangle while reading the next chapter of the 'Lonely Planet'. Of course, only a real adventurer would understand what I'm talking about.

It took me two days of mingled happiness and regret to get back to Lambérené. Happiness because the road was top-class (for some reason I had not noticed this earlier), so that I made good progress; regret because the ambience of the older, more natural Gabon had got left behind.

I retain some vivid mental snapshots of the older Gabon, however. There was something almost surreal, for example, about the sight of the hunters – usually old men, for some reason – materialising out of the thick morning mist like so many ghosts of the past, each with a shotgun broken open and hanging over his shoulder. Then they would dematerialise again, and as the mist lifted you would hear shots ringing out in the distance and the screaming of a mortally wounded animal: the sound of the endlessly repeated cycle of life and death from which people of the West have become divorced but which in Africa remains as close and as real as an old friend. This is why, when people ask me what the benefits are of cycling through a country, I can reply in all truthfulness that a cyclist sees and hears more than a traveller using any other form of transport could ever imagine.

Although situated in the back of beyond, Lambérené remains famous, decades after the death of Dr Albert Schweitzer, who lived here for 52 years and built a hospital which was to become famous around the world. To Western eyes it seemed to be a chaotic and probably insanitary mess, with all sorts of odd features like patients eating meals prepared not by a hospital dietician in a squeaky-clean kitchen but by their own families in a three-legged pot over an open fire in the yard. What they didn't understand is that Schweitzer knew that patients did best in familiar surroundings, eating familiar food and surrounded by their loved ones. So the hospital endured, and is still in use today, while his home and grave continue to draw visitors, even though both are run-down and unkempt.

Lambéréné stands on either side of the lake and river and is very beautiful. I spent the night at a lakeside lodge that was one of the two major urban attractions. The accommodation was meagre, but the impromptu entertainment provided by kids playing the Gabonese version of tag was top-notch.

As I was not going back to Libreville but still had some urgent things to deal with regarding sponsors and the medical supply business I had left behind in Cape Town, I stayed over for an extra day in Lambéréné, most of which I spent holed up in the Internet café next door to my lodgings.

I sent and received a barrage of vital e-mails. Some were to keep my sponsors happy (among other things, Mongoose had sponsored a bicycle as a prize for the person who forecast the exact date of my arrival in the DRC). More importantly, however, I had to deal with a crisis that had arisen regarding my business's income. I had left the running of the business to Vasti, but combined with the demands of her law school internship it was a burden no one person could carry.

The crux of my business troubles was that I had no representation at crucial meetings when issues and problems regarding the medical plans were raised. Some of my larger corporate clients had become accustomed to 24/7 hands-on treatment, and the leaders of employer unions needed constant assurance that their needs were a priority. Being a medical-based service, it meant the nature of our work and interaction was intrinsically emotional. The people who were sick complained about accounts not being paid, while the healthy complained that they were wasting their money.

When I had decided that this journey was what I wanted to do with the next year of my life I had also conceded that I would not be able to keep everyone in my business happy, but I believed that those who remained in my company would be the type of people I wanted to work with in the future. What I had *not* anticipated was that certain people whom I had trusted would try to sabotage an agreement which brought in R15 000 a month and was not only the basic life-blood of my journey but also paid my staff's salaries.

I wrestled with this unforeseen disaster and decided that the only thing I could do was to stall the cancellation of the agreement, thus giving myself and my staff a fair opportunity to make alternative financial plans. This is where companies like Windhoek Light did not understand the real life-saving impact that they were having on my circumnavigation. Their help reduced or eliminated stresses that I really did not need at a time when all my energy and concentration were needed to deal with immediate problems.

Having done what I could, I had another good night's sleep and then a lakeside breakfast of tea and egg rolls before putting my wheels on the fine tarmac road again and heading out into the dense, beautiful forests. Once more I was struck by the awe I had felt when travelling with Pierre to Ndjole, except that the emotion was even more tangible this time.

Looking at these jungle giants, it was hard to credit what I had heard about the indiscriminate logging operations, or the warning not to be fooled by appearances, that in many places one had only to go about 100 metres into the jungle to see thousands of hectares of forlorn stumps where the great trees had been cut down. I didn't stop to check out this claim. Maybe I didn't want to see the corpse of a forest. But I had a legitimate reason for not wasting any time. That night I planned to sleep smack on the Equator. I had driven over it in a vehicle, but that meant nothing. This way was the real way.

There was nothing dramatic about the Equator, just a sponsored sign at the roadside and a few huts on the 'exact line', inhabited by a few families that made their living from what passing tourist traffic there was. But that didn't matter. The drama of it came from within me; I had travelled a long, frequently painful road to stand here with my toes on the Equator.

The locals offered me their entire stock-in-trade, which consisted of a choice between bottles of warm beer and a walk through the forest. I was game for either but finally settled for the warm beer and a photograph, then quickly set up my tent, because the thunder grumbling overhead was providing fair warning that a rainstorm was imminent. Sure enough, in no time torrential rain was belting down to the accompaniment of the heavenly artillery. By then I was comfortably ensconced under cover right in front of the Equator sign, drinking my warm beer and eating a pineapple. Life did not stop for one second in spite of the rain, though. Schoolchildren went back and forth from one hemisphere to the other as if it was an everyday thing, which, of course, it was. So did men on bicycles and women carrying wood.

A thought struck me and I asked the unofficial tour guide: 'Is this exactly where the equator is?'

'No, not exactly,' he replied with commendable honesty. 'The equator is about 100 metres wide, so you're inside it right now.'

It had me wondering whether that was actually how the equator works, if it is an area rather than an exact line. The earth, after all, is not exactly spherical. I thought of another South African who had completed an extraordinary modern-day adventure which was part of my motivational make-up – Mike Horn, who had circumnavigated the entire planet along the equator in 18 months just after the millennium, without any motorised assistance.

'Here our paths cross for the first time,' I thought. 'The next time will be in Somalia or Kenya.' Those two countries seemed a long way away, which of course they were – particularly by the coastal route I had chosen.

What people like Mike prove, and what I hoped to prove as well, is that the amazing thing about adventure in our modern world is that there is still so much to discover. It may not be about venturing into unknown lands of fables and folklore, but rather about facing the more dangerous prospect of going into places where the risks of death and disease are known and well documented.

By morning the rain had stopped and I had a clear, easy run from the Equator to the town of Ntoum, which I reached several hours before sunset. Ntoum was a crossroads, a sort of nodal point for travel in several different directions, and I knew that there would be plenty of transport opportunities. The only thing I had to do was make sure that I didn't get taken to the cleaners – a get-rich-quick transportation tout in that part of the world can pick up even the faintest whiff of desperation, and judging by their behaviour that afternoon I must have positively reeked of it.

I had reckoned that the name of the game was to play it laid-back, making frequent jokes about the price, while asking questions about what time the transport was leaving the next day. Well, it didn't work; those fellows had seen all the attitudes and heard all the lies. So with bad grace I paid the inflated price my driver of choice demanded and loaded my bicycle on to the back of his bakkie.

But far worse was to come, as I discovered when we reached a little village which I estimated was no more than half-way to Cocobeach. All of the passengers who hadn't departed at destinations along the way got off and went their several ways ... except me, since I was going on to Cocobeach, of course! Some of them laughed as they looked back to where I was still perched on the back of the vehicle, keen to get going again.

Now I got worried and I tackled the driver in a distinctly unfriendly mood. He shrugged, smiled and said over and over: 'We no say Cocobeach. We no say Cocobeach, of course!' This was the end of the line; I had been taken for a ride in more ways than one. I didn't waste any of my precious time in what I knew would be a futile argument about a refund, so I got my bike on its wheels and pedalled off northwards – after all, I had been over the road ahead a week earlier and it held no fears for me, and maybe I would find some other transport before nightfall.

I got over a few difficult kilometres without meeting any other traffic and then arrived at a little village called Mitembie which I remembered from the previous week's trip. There was no transport here either. Seriously disgusted with myself about being taken for a sucker, I started looking around for a place to overnight: Equatorial Guinea would simply have to wait till the morrow.

Mitembie's total business community consisted of one small wooden shop run by a gregarious and humorous woman, half Portuguese and half Gabonese, who was delighted to play host to a visitor. She made me a meal of sour beans with rice and invited me to pitch my tent inside her shop after she had closed up, but I preferred to set up next to it because Gabonese closing times tended to be pretty elastic, and I suspected she would be open till late into the night.

I might have been wrong about the lift, but I was quite right about the closing hours. An astonishing quantity of warm beer was consumed by the villagers that night, and I couldn't help thinking, as the sounds of wassail filled the night, that she would be able to double her turnover at the very least if she acquired a fridge.

That night it rained copiously, which allowed me to test a new rain-sheet I had bought in Libreville. In my opinion tent manufacturers should not make any advertising claims about a product till they have subjected it to a night of equatorial rainfall. That is what separates the men in the jungle from the boys in the laboratory.

The next day's stretch to Cocobeach was a bit messy – lots of mud and pools of water everywhere, to the point where I doubted if my farewell escort from Libreville would have got very far. What I remember best about this section, though, was that I started getting attacks of itching again.

I was taking time off for a much-needed roadside scratch when help arrived in the unlikely form of an old man who happened to see this sad sight. I was going about it the wrong way, he informed me, shaking his head as he imitated my frantic nail-raking. What I needed was (and he demonstrated again) a patting and stroking movement. My first thought was that the oldster had no idea of what I was going through, and that if he had seen me attacking myself with the Leatherman a few nights earlier he would have called for the Gabonese equivalent of the little men in white coats.

But the old boy knew what he was talking about, and the pat-and-stroke technique worked wonders. On reflection it made perfect scientific sense. Any sting or insect bite jolts your body into releasing histamine, which makes you want to scratch even more and sets the itching-and-scratching cycle in motion. So the best approach is to avoid further irritation as much as possible, which in turn means that less histamine will be released. This was real folk-medicine, based not on systematic scientific research and fancy medicines but on the accumulated empirical knowledge of countless generations.

Cocobeach wasn't much to look at, being mainly a collection of beachside huts, but it had two solid structures which answered my purposes, a hotel and an immigration office. Having arrived earlier than I'd expected, and knowing that the trip to Equatorial Guinea was merely a boat-ride away, I headed straight for the immigration building.

Before I had left South Africa I had heard and read about travellers' difficulties with immigration offices, which were said to be mostly unmarked and frequently impossible to find, but I had come to realise that this was all nonsense. My wanderings had taught me how simple it was to find an immigration office. Firstly, ask around to make sure you're actually in the town you think you're in. Secondly, make sure you know the word for 'immigration' in the local language. Thirdly, ask anyone for 'immigration'. For locals living in a border town the gateway to the neighbouring country is part of their lives. If you are a local and over the age of five and haven't been across the border at least once, the only possible explanation is alien abduction.

By this stage I had also discovered that immigration officials at exit points were often friendlier than the ones at entry posts. Perhaps it's because they reckon that you've have had your time in their country and are simply on your way out. In other words, you have spent your money. I certainly had no trouble with the local immigration man, who stamped me out without hesitation and instructed me to wait on the beach for the next departing powerboat. I parked myself on a patch of grass between the office and the sea and settled down to a bit of pleasant loafing, at which stage I saw a rare thing in this neck of the woods, another white person who was walking around on the waterside rocks.

My ethnic equivalent was a pale thin guy with a chunky camera around his neck who went down on his knees from time to time to take close-up photographs of something or other. I introduced myself and we got to talking. He turned out to be a Canadian named Brent Hoffman, who had just graduated with a degree in zoology and was now doing research for his master's thesis.

Brent was not the type of guy I would have imagined meeting

here in Cocobeach on the rough, tough Gabonese border. I suppose one could best describe him as an intellectual – certainly not the type of Canadian who drank lots of beer and periodically got mashed against the outer glass wall of an ice-hockey rink. Be that as it may, Brent and I decided to form a temporary alliance to smooth our way through this no-option environment. Brent was clearly not what you might call street-wise and was maybe a little naïve about the way he was perceived by the locals and the immigration staff. But he was no fool, and I learnt one valuable lesson from him: always try to stay below the radar!

I saw how this worked when we found ourselves on the periphery of a commotion in the immigration office, when a heated altercation broke out between the boatmen and drivers on the one hand and the officials on the other. From what I could gather the boatmen were being forced to pay unofficial taxes. One driver said he believed that the reason for immigration's sudden interest in his colleagues and himself was our presence in Cocobeach – the officials believed that the boatmen would over-charge us and profit individually. The boatmen, needless to say, scoffed at this idea.

We soon had an opportunity to put Brent's radar-avoidance tactic into action when two boatmen began preparing to leave in defiance of stentorian warnings from the officials to stay put. Brent and I were offered seats in one of the boats, but in view of our foreign status and the official weaponry on display – not to mention the fact that the immigration officials had our passports – we both declined. I then unilaterally voted Brent in as the official liaison officer of MPLFGEG (the Movement of Peace-Loving Foreigners from Gabon to Equatorial Guinea). His first task was to gather facts about the possibilities of our moving safely across the river mouth, and after conferring with the officials he reported that today would be impossible, but we were guaranteed seats on the first boat next day, which would leave at sunrise.

That was that. Brent and I booked into a double room at the hotel, making sure that we would be ready bright and early. This close proximity resulted in his seeing the damage that the bugs – not mention my Leatherman – had inflicted on me, and he gave me a bottle of special Canadian bug-repellent containing, he said, a special ingredient called DEET (I forget what the letters stand for). DEET worked by disguising your scent from the bugs, its only drawback being that it burnt your skin and clothing if it was too strong.

In any case, after a good night's sleep we were up and packed before any of the locals was stirring – sunrise is the best reward for an early start to a day, I always think – then took our bags and my bicycle down to the beach, where we waited for our transport to arrive, patiently but a trifle apprehensively, because we wanted to be well away before the previous day's unresolved problem with the boatmen escalated. We knew that it would be easy for us to end up as unintended hostages because the immigration officials still had our passports, so they wielded absolute power over us.

After a while two boats pulled in and the driver of one of them beckoned to us to start loading our goods. Brent double-checked with the driver that it was all right for us to embark, then went off at my urging to see about getting our passports back. He returned empty-handed, however, saying that the immigration officials had told him to be patient and wait some more. I decided to try again and bearded the immigration chief in his den, asking why our passports were being withheld. He apologised, said Brent had misunderstood his staff, and handed over the passports. Not long after that we were chugging towards Equatorial Guinea.

This little encounter gave me some food for thought. Desperation, I concluded, was a mobile factor in the eternal equation of supply and demand; the closer the demand side moved towards desperation, the more insistent it got, and often this resulted in a corresponding decrease in the resistance of the supply side. This morning's episode had demonstrated how my theory worked. In spite of a local upheaval we had managed to get away by dint of an insistence which overcame the fact that it was communicated only by way of some garbled French and bits of the local language.

How you implement this theory varies, of course, from individual to individual. Brent was unperturbed by the whole episode, whereas I was close to frustration meltdown.

My day's emotional trauma had not yet ended, as it turned out. When we disembarked at a large concrete jetty, all the passengers were instructed to lay out their baggage so they could receive their 'quotes' for the journey. Now the driver who had been so helpful in getting us into his boat turned instantly into a combination of Scrooge and Satan as he scribbled his passengers' individual 'quotes' on to pieces of cigarette carton, sour in the face and avoiding eye contact.

Not a good sign, I thought, and when he handed me my piece of carton I saw I was quite right. This waterborne highwayman wanted to gouge 25 000 CFA out of me, the equivalent of $50 US, or about R350 in South African money. Mamma mia! The average bill for the other travellers was about 1 000 CFA. We were being mugged!

I couldn't quite figure out his financial logic, since Brent was charged considerably less, although our luggage took up similar amounts of space, but concluded that my bicycle must have accounted for the extra. Not that any of this mattered. The bottom line was that I wasn't going to cough up $50, even though I was very tired emotionally and really did not want to get enmeshed in a drawn-out argument. So I emptied my pockets in front of him and said that that was all the money I had on me (about 19 000 CFA, say $35).

The boatman-mugger believed me, sullenly took the money and peremptorily waved me off the jetty. I refused to leave unless he let Brent go too. This made him furious, and I think he would have assaulted me if the immigration officials had not been watching the proceedings. Instead he called on them to remove me by force.

As it happened, one official could speak some English, and he promised me that he would make sure nothing happened to Brent. This pacified me a little, and I moved about 20 metres down the jetty, but I still refused to go on to dry land till Brent was out of the boatman's clutches. I could see that Brent was nervous – which was understandable, considering what a famously law-abiding country he came from – but he kept his cool and offered the same excuse as I had. After much grumbling the boatman took what Brent was offering, 10 000 CFA, and he joined me. We walked off the jetty together, vastly relieved to have the episode behind us but a little concerned about what lay ahead after this less than happy introduction to Equatorial Guinea.

# CHAPTER 9

# TOUGH TIMES IN EQUATORIAL GUINEA – AND HOSPITALITY IN CAMEROON

*The policeman paged through my passport, his bottle and his rifle clamped between his legs, mumbling as if very disgruntled about something in it. Then we got to the core of the matter: he looked at me and made the universal signal for money, the rubbing together of the forefinger and thumb.*

While growing up I was always being reminded of the fact that no matter how badly done by you felt, there were always people out there who were even worse off than you were. And this was certainly the case at the Equatorial Guinea border post, where I had a tough time, but not half as bad as Brent did.

In fact, 'tough times' just about sums up my journey through Equatorial Guinea. I didn't know much about the place, except that it was in two pieces, a large island and a piece of mainland, pretty small by Africa's sprawling standards – just over 25 000 square kilometres, was very rich in oil and was run by a notorious kleptomaniac dictator named Obiang Nguema Mbasogo, who had elected himself president in 1979. But further enlightenment came thick and fast.

Our troubles started almost immediately after we walked off the jetty to the immigration building near by. Up to now the immigration offices I had encountered had ranged from modest to humble in size and appearance, but this one was huge, with a facade of Corinthian pillars at least 10 metres high which made it look like an ancient Roman temple. In its glory days it must have been a very impressive structure, but when we got closer we realised that those days were long past. It looked as if it had been bombed at some distant time and then left to rot; the once-magnificent pillars were chipped and broken, the walls cracked and sun-parched and the foundations exposed by what looked like soil erosion. For the first time in my life I was really scared of having a building collapse on me.

The building rose straight up into the sky from the roadside, and to me it looked impossible to get my bike inside, so I left it for the time being and took only two bags full of kit for the immigration officials to check. Brent, on the other hand, dragged everything he had with him. Just getting up to the ground floor was a mission, because the outside stairs were in such a ruinous state that in some places Brent and I had to pass our baggage up hand over hand before ascending ourselves.

The entrance hall was a huge, gloomy, nightmarish place, dark and getting ever darker because all the light fittings and even the wall-switches were long gone. A crowd of people wandered around in the murk, going in and out of a multitude of doors bearing faded signs in Spanish, the inherited colonial language. I could understand the signs more or less because of the similarity to Portuguese, although of course I had no idea whether they were still a reliable indicator of what went on behind them. Judging by what I was seeing, it didn't appear as if much of Equatorial Guinea's oil revenues went into maintaining the infrastructure – I expect the president couldn't spare a lot from his offshore bank account. Anyway, the whole place was beyond creepy, and I remember thinking: If you're a tourist, this is the sort of place you don't want to be alone in.

The semi-somnolent immigration officials on duty showed a marked rise in enthusiasm and energy as soon as they spotted us. Fresh meat! They led us into one of the forlorn offices and demanded our passports. I followed my usual strategy of identifying someone who could speak some English and then explaining where I had come from on my bicycle and adding that I was very keen to see his country. It didn't seem to work this time, and we were moved from one department to another without any explanation being asked or given. We gained the distinct impression that they were trying to separate us, and constantly assured them that we didn't mind waiting for each other.

But it was not to be. My kit check went much faster than Brent's because I had brought less with me. The officials were a little puzzled when I assured them, lying swine that I was, that I had only the two bags. They went through them quickly but carefully, pausing only to ask about some items that interested them. A traveller who wandered around with only one set of clothes but plenty of electronics and toiletries! That intrigued them, but there was nothing in my bags to give offence. Having cleared this hurdle, I hovered near Brent while they rummaged through his kit to ensure that we stayed together.

At this stage the immigration guy who had been escorting us around returned to check on our progress, and asked me to go back to the office we had started from to sign some forms they had prepared for us. I was keen to get away from the baggage-hounds while the going was good and said yes, arranging with Brent that we would meet up again when the officials had finished with him.

Back in the original office I found my passport stamped and ready, but not Brent's. When he eventually arrived – which took longer than I expected, because they turned his bags inside-out with such thoroughness that it took him an hour to repack everything – his visa turned out to be no good. Some absent-minded clerk at Equatorial Guinea's embassy in Libreville had put the wrong date on it – January 2003 instead of January 2004. For the time being it was the end of the line for him.

I offered to wait with him till the next morning to see his problem solved, and suggested possible solutions to the problem. Could they not communicate with their foreign affairs department and confirm the mistake? After all, it was obviously just a clerical error, since our visa numbers differed by only a few places and must thus have been issued very close to one another. Brent was surely not a national risk, and should be allowed to travel to the capital of the mainland chunk of the country, Bata, to get the matter straightened out. And so on and so on. Brent kept his cool, but it was a trying time, and I could detect the anxiety in his voice and eyes. He did not want to be left on his own with these guys, that was clear, and I couldn't blame him.

But once again fate intervened. While we were scouting out some accommodation we were approached by a boatman, a friend of the English-speaking immigration official, who told us that he was about to take a load of fish across to Aclayong, a town located a few kilometres down towards the river's mouth, which was the starting-point of the road to Bata. Would I like to come along?

This offer left me in a quandary. If I went with the boatman I would be able to hit the road to Bata first thing in the morning. On the other hand, I had promised to stand by Brent and I couldn't simply shrug that off. Now Brent showed the stuff he was made of. Knowing how valuable this head-start would be for me, and knowing, too, that his problem might take more than just one day to work out, he insisted I leave. The immigration man backed Brent up by promising to look after his interests, and I caved in, although I felt pretty bad about it. We exchanged e-mail addresses and discussed the possibility that in the end he would get to Bata before me, and then I set off into the dark with the boatman.

It took us just half an hour to get to Aclayong, weaving in between islands of mangrove forests under a bright full moon that made the journey unforgettably beautiful. Aclayong wasn't much to speak of, a cluster of only six or seven solid structures, but I had no difficulty in finding a place to sleep – in addition to charging me no more than the locals who had come with us, the boatman arranged for me to pitch my tent on the porch of a house belonging to the village chief, who was away in Bata.

It rained throughout the night, gently but continuously, so it was no surprise that there was mud everywhere on the narrow road when I set off for Bata next morning. I pedalled through dense jungle for some time before I ran across another human being, and the encounter pretty much set the scene for my journey through Equatorial Guinea.

I had come up to a roadblock, although there wasn't much to it, simply a bamboo branch stretched across the slushy road. It seemed to be unmanned, so I ducked underneath it and carried on. But I had barely got going again when an agitated man in a brown overall came running out from the bushes, brandishing a rifle and screaming at me in Spanish, and wouldn't let me proceed till he had subjected my bicycle and me to a lengthy and unnecessary search. I assume he regarded me as a security threat, although why he should think that a spy, saboteur or other bad guy would come riding down the main road to the capital, as bold as brass, rather than sneaking across at some unguarded part of the border, was a mystery to me. But as I say, this was a portent of things to come.

The road firmed up and widened as I reached my first way-station, a ferry-crossing town called Mbini on the Mbini River. I stuck to Brent's modus operandi and maintained a low profile, but things worked differently in Equatorial Guinea, as I was starting to realise. As I stood by the water's edge with some locals, waiting for the ferry, a small boy came up to me and gabbled at me in Spanish, pointing at a type of outdoor restaurant and café. I didn't understand anything he was saying except the words 'go go go', but the other ferry-goers smiled nervously, evidently knowing exactly what was afoot.

As had happened so often in the past, someone who could speak English – a young, well-dressed guy in this case – came to my rescue. 'The boy says that the policeman wants you to go there,' he explained.

'Why?' I asked.

'He wants to see your document.'

Not again! The paranoia in this country was starting to make me nervous, but I had no alternative except to go back up the slipway to where the policeman in question and a couple of his friends were sitting at a table behind a barricade of large beer bottles. Over his shoulder was slung his rifle, which I did not like at all, particularly when he started speaking and waving his arms – even though I had virtually no Spanish, I know drunken slurring when I hear it. I decided that there was no way I was going to hand over any document of mine to this sozzled alleged guardian of the law.

One of the policeman's friends translated as he slurred away at me: he wanted my passport. I told him that it was standard procedure for the border immigration officials to retain it till I left the country again. Instead I handed him a photocopy of my passport which, I said, the immigration officials had instructed me to produce if there were any official queries en route.

The drunkard swallowed this specious explanation hook, line and sinker, then ordered me to buy a beer for everybody at his table. Putting on my customary tense-situation smile. I explained that the customs fees at the border had been more than I had expected, and that I was on my way to Bata to find a bank because I had run out of cash. The cop didn't buy this and moved on to demand some cash money. I responded by politely raising my hands, apologising to his friends and asking if I might be excused, since the ferry had just arrived and I simply had to catch it. Then I slowly retreated backwards till I reached the slipway again, and wasted no time in getting on to the ferry.

Well, one more interrogation down; obviously many still to go. I had a feeling that even though Equatorial Guinea was one of the smallest countries I would pass through, that fact was not going to make my passage any quicker.

Bata was a busy port town with a pretty coastline and ramshackle outbuildings propped up against square, solid structures obviously dating from the colonial era, the most modern ones being the hotels facing the beaches. I was nosing about the beach area for accommodation when I ran into another Canadian, a mid-twenties backpacker named Michael Kreeft. Michael was tall, brown-haired, humorous and good-looking, and he had organised an enviable lifestyle for himself: he spent half of every year in Canada, planting seedlings for the national forestry regeneration programme, and the other half globe-trotting with the money he had earned.

Michael was staying at a cheap hotel in the centre of the town and negotiated a room for me as well. The bucket-and-cup shower I had here was the most invigorating one of my life, not only cooling down my body after three days of non-stop sweating but soothing the last of my self-inflicted scratch wounds.

Michael's approach when it came to interacting with people was a lot like mine. If I bought a soft drink at a shop, for example, I liked to chat with the shopkeeper before leaving, and both of us were always ready for an impromptu game of street soccer. But sometimes, as he freely admitted, Michael's friendliness got him into unexpected situations, and just how easily this could happen I discovered that very night when we went to eat in a fancy (relatively speaking) restaurant.

A stream of local girls went past us on the way to an adjacent disco, and Michael took to smiling at them and then greeting them in a posh British accent. All the girls reciprocated the smile and then continued on their way, except for two who came over and made polite conversation in French and a little English. Michael had no conversation problems, since French is one of Canada's official languages, but I didn't get very far with the girl I was chatting with. I did what I could with what I had, but my new companion lost interest quickly when she became aware of my limitations.

I harboured certain initial suspicions about our new acquaintances, who just seemed to be dressed too skimpily, even for the sultry summer weather. Michael's new friend, for example, wore a dress which consisted of nothing more than two narrow strips of material running down from her shoulders and over her nipples before joining up with her abbreviated skirt.

The girls' intentions soon became clear: they wanted us to buy them beer and then go to the disco with them. I thought this was a bit forward of them, considering our acquaintance was only about two minutes old. In any case I was physically and emotionally tired, and wanted only to get out of Equatorial Guinea as soon as was humanly possible. A party would certainly have been a good safety valve for my internal pressure cooker, but as far as I was concerned it would just be a distraction.

Michael was in better physical and emotional shape and played the girls along for a bit. His companion was totally taken in and began getting very friendly and comfortable (and, he said later, trying to caress him in a very intimate manner, preparatory to going back to our hotel with him). He kept on telling her that the hotel would not be up to her standards, and each time she rolled her eyes as if he was joking with her – which, of course, he was.

Eventually the girls gave us up as a bad job and headed for the disco, where, I am sure, they found more accommodating male friends, while Michael and I strolled through the town to see what else it offered. The cafés were very cosmopolitan and trendy, buzzing with both expatriates and locals, but I was a real wet blanket and we got in an early night.

Next morning I went shopping among the busy street stalls in front of our hotel, looking for either a new pump with which to inflate my French tubes or new tubes which fitted my old pump. To my delight I found the right tubes and bought enough to see me through, so I hoped, to Douala in Cameroon. I also wanted some breakfast, which I got at a funny little place, not a café but a room in a dilapidated house. The head of the household served me and I sat there eating and drinking instant coffee I had made with condensed milk and water that had been boiled over a fire, while around me the other occupants were waking up and going about their business.

For obvious reasons there wasn't much communication between us, but all of them, especially the father, were so artlessly kind to me that I felt like a member of the household myself. I couldn't help reflecting that First World companies which strove to create a family atmosphere in their businesses could have taken lessons from this café, if it was really one, because it had the recipe down to the letter. All it needed was a decent toilet. The only other drawback to this simple but homey establishment was that there was an open-air butchery on the pavement right outside the front door. I missed the throat-slitting but got a close-up view of the bleeding and skinning, which is a bit much for someone who has just had breakfast.

Finding an Internet café before I left – I was feeling homesick just then – proved more difficult ... impossible, in fact, even though

Michael joined in the search. Eventually we gave up and decided to have lunch before I set off. It turned out that Michael was planning on visiting the same game parks as Brent intended seeing, so before hitting the road I asked him to look out for him.

I was feeling pretty good as I set off down the broad, jungle-lined gravel road. Maybe Equatorial Guinea wasn't actually such a bad place after all! Or maybe it was. Fifteen kilometres along I arrived at a dusty four-way checkpoint. Booms manned by at least four policemen barred each entrance/exit gate. I wasn't unduly nervous about this, having acclimatised myself to the vagaries of Equatorial Guinea's officialdom. Patience and compliance with every request, plus lots of smiles: that was the infallible recipe. Except if some of the ingredients were stale, that is.

I entered the central square – a veritable hive of activity, with cars, trucks and people being shunted off to any of four different roads – by the simple expedient of ducking under the first boom I came to, without any objection from the police manning it. Now I needed directions, because I had been under the impression that there was only one main road, heading straight from Bata to the Cameroon border. So I did the logical thing: I went up to the nearest policeman and asked him. Bad mistake.

I gave him a big smile and wished him a good morning in Spanish (well, it may have sounded a little Portuguesey). He responded by fingering his rifle and giving me a blank stare. I tried again, expanding the smile and asking if he spoke any English. More of the blank stare and rifle-fingering. Then he silenced me in mid-gabble with a raised hand. I noticed now that he was scanning my bicycle very nervously, and I began to get a slight sinking feeling. Suddenly he started screaming to other policemen who, I saw now, were lounging on chairs under a sun-bleached bamboo shelter on a grassy mound at one roadside corner. They screamed some instructions back at him and he indicated that I was to leave the bicycle in the road and follow him over to the other cops. I did as I was told, passport in hand but none too easy in mind, because for some reason everyone seemed aggressive and very unhappy with me. *Patience and compliance,* I told myself. *Remember the recipe!*

My mood escalated from uneasiness to anxiety when I got to the other police, two men and a very large woman. I saw now that the shelter was of a more permanent nature than I had realised, because it contained some beds. I also noticed that quart bottles of beer stood at the feet of the woman and one of the men, a sure sign that neither of them was completely sober. *Patience and compliance!* But this time the ingredients definitely *were* stale. All three ignored my smiles and efforts to communicate in any way. All I got was long, aggressive stares; it was a sure bet that they would not be interested in hearing about my journey and what I was hoping to achieve.

The male drinker paged through my passport, his bottle and his rifle clamped between his legs, mumbling as if very disgruntled about something in it, with the woman passing comments from time to time. After a bit the man began talking louder, paging so roughly through the passport with one hand that he was crumpling its pages. Then we got to the core of the matter: he looked at me and made the universal signal for money, the rubbing together of the forefinger and thumb.

Using Portuguese, which was the closest I could come to Spanish, I replied with 'desculpe', meaning 'excuse me'. He repeated the sign several times, to which I laid on some respectful smiles and laughs, very gently explaining that I didn't have any money because the immigration formalities had emptied my pockets. This didn't make him happy, but I stuck to my point. The fat woman broke the deadlock by asking her colleague what my nationality was. He replied that I was a South African.

'Aaaaaaaaggghhhh!' she said, adding in Spanish: 'White racist!' This set off a long discussion which I did not understand much of, although I gathered that she was trying to persuade her colleagues that I was a racist because of my skin colour and nationality. She got so worked up that she started hitting the wall of the bamboo structure with her fist while telling them what sort of person I was and what I had obviously been up to during the apartheid years. I didn't even try to reason with her or refute the accusations she was making against me. That would only add fuel to the flames, because her heart was full of hate – at that moment, specifically for me.

There was an amazing lack of logic to all this, of course. She didn't know anything about me, and what self-respecting white racist would choose to live among black people for over a year in any case? But it was not about logic, of course. Get it out of your system, damn you, I thought, filled with intense dislike by her insults. Yeah, that's the way – get it out of your system! And then let me get on with my trip!

Of course, it was also possible that all this thunder and lightning was merely the run-up to robbing me of my possessions, or worse. But whatever the case, I realised that things had gone from poor to extremely bad; if I did not get my passport back or find a higher-ranking (and sober) official soon, it was going to be a very long afternoon.

The male drinker was now thoroughly worked up. 'Visa, visa, no good, no good!' he shouted, manhandling his way through my passport, which he was holding upside-down at this stage.

We were getting nowhere, and the situation could only deteriorate, so I set about implementing Plan B. Retrieving the passport turned out to be easier than I thought. I shrugged my shoulders every time the male drinker pointed at it and indicated that I wanted to see what was wrong with it. He wouldn't comply, however, and the next time he pointed it at me, shouting more incomprehensible Spanish words, I grabbed with a gabbled 'obrigado, obrigado, obrigado'. I had no idea as to whether 'obrigado' meant 'thank you' in Spanish as well as in Portuguese, but that was all I could think of to convince him that I was not acting aggressively.

By now an interested crowd had started to gather around the shelter, and from their efforts to disperse it I realised that the police didn't want the public to witness what they were doing. Aha! I implemented Phase Two of Plan B. 'Por favor, chef de policia, por favor' (please, chief of police, please) I repeated over and over as loudly and respectfully as I could, to make sure that as many bystanders as possible could hear me and witness my problem.

The male drinker jumped up and ran out at me, screaming in

Spanish. As he came up to me I pulled a sort of 'Plan C' trick and sat down on the ground in front of him. That was obviously the last thing he had expected. He stopped in his tracks, looked around in a bewildered way and then stormed off. At last I'd get to speak to someone more senior! I took advantage of his disappearance to run to my bicycle to collect my letters from the embassy in Libreville and the Proudly South African campaign, then went back to sitting on the ground where he had left me.

After about five minutes the drinker returned with another man. My saviour! I got up and waited for them with my hands folded in front of me. What happened then was the opposite of what I had expected and hoped for. I hadn't even finished saying 'good morning' in Spanish when my 'saviour' had me by the elbow and was pulling me down the mound towards a waiting minivan, like a Colombian druglord kidnapping an informer.

They tossed me into the back of the van like a sack of potatoes. I tried to soften my landing with my outstretched left hand (the right had a death-like grip on the plastic folder containing the letters), but it didn't help much. Immediately the van sped off, where to I didn't know. I saw now that there were several other civilians in the van, obviously feeling as apprehensive as I was. Since they were clearly not plain-clothes cops, I assumed the minivan was a taxi which had been on its way to Bata before being commandeered.

My supposed saviour did not look at me and I didn't dare look at him. I just sat tight with a very dry mouth, clutching the folder in hands that had turned numb with fear. I didn't think I was about to die – or at least not without my country finding out about it – but nevertheless I was obviously in deep trouble. That was confirmed when I heard my un-saviour instructing the driver to go straight to the police station, so it was likely that I would end up in a cell.

On arrival at the police station I was taken by the arm and marched inside, my escort and myself cutting through the loungers outside the building like Moses forging his way through the Red Sea. Once inside, however, I was pleasantly surprised when I was conducted to the station commander's office instead of a cell, and silently recited my patience-and-compliance mantra to myself. But it still didn't work. The good news was that the station commander could speak some English, which meant I could abandon my laboured attempts to explain myself in Portuguese and about 10 Spanish words. The bad news was that my alleged saviour was shouting so loudly that all I could get out was that I was on a bicycle tour around Africa as an ambassador for my country. 'Please read my embassy letters,' I said, 'and call them if you have any problems. I'm sure they'll come and fetch me.' Then we were on the move again.

That didn't take me very far, only to a holding cell whose steel door crashed shut behind me before I had even sat down. I had never been inside a prison cell before, and I was taken aback by my new environment, to put it mildly. About the only good aspect was that there was still some sunlight coming in through the tiny windows, but man, I didn't want to be here in this confined, overcrowded place when it got dark!

I took a long, silent look at my fellow 'criminals' (after my own experience I wouldn't have liked to bet on the chances of them being guilty of anything more serious than spitting on the pavement), trying to project a confident, fearless air. My companions were very quiet, some staring blankly at the ground while others smiled at me. A number looked as confident and fearless as I hoped I was looking, and I decided they weren't putting it on; they'd been in this situation before.

Two hours later the door swung open a crack to reveal an officer wearing a beret, obviously checking to make sure I was in the cell, because as soon as he spotted me the door slammed shut again in spite of the upraised hand and friendly smile I produced with the speed of light. Still, he had had the professional look of a senior rank, neat and well-groomed; maybe I'd made the point that I was nothing more than a harmless tourist.

Perhaps I had. About 45 minutes later the door screeched open again to reveal the station commander, with an army officer at his side. The station commander beckoned me over and introduced me to the officer, who I gathered was a captain. I shook his hand and kept smiling. By this time I had calmed down and got rid of the frustration and anger that had built up in my confrontation with the fat policewoman and her drunken chum. That was mainly thanks to a bit of advice from Vasti before I had set off: when necessary, lose a battle so that you can win the war. Well, I had certainly lost the battle with the cops, but not the war – yet.

The captain apologised for the way the police had treated me and explained that everyone was on guard because there had been reports of spies. Naturally I accepted his apology – well, he seemed to mean it, and I had no alternative anyway, made it plain that I knew it had all been a misunderstanding and then asked him about the safety of my bike and kit, which was my major concern now that I was free again.

The captain assured me the bike was OK and told one of his underlings to make sure I got safely back to the square. On the way the underling bought me a soft drink – probably on the captain's instructions – which was greatly appreciated, because, as you can imagine, I was as dry as a bone after everything that had happened to me. That soft drink was beyond a peace offering, it was an act of sheer diplomacy.

As we approached the square I strained to spot my bicycle, trying to ignore the nagging feeling that it had long since vanished, but to my immense relief it was right there where I had left it, baggage and all. I straddled it, being careful not to look anywhere near my beer-guzzling interrogators, shook hands with my escort and got out of there – fast – without even knowing which road was the one I needed.

I got well away and then consulted my map, which informed me that there were two logical choices. One road would lead me on to a freeway which might or might not be there, while the other was a more direct coastal route which was, however, marked as being no more than a track. I settled for the track because it was shorter than the other road, which meant that if the going wasn't too bad I should be able to get out of the country in 24 hours.

That was the deciding factor: I was still pretty shaken by the day's events and wanted nothing more than to get out of Equatorial Guinea and its lunatic atmosphere without a moment's delay. There was very little good cycling time left before darkness fell, but

I was determined to put in as many kilometres as I could before being forced to call a halt. I could see signs of recent road construction for the first few kilometres, but they slowly faded out till there was nothing left but the muddy jungle road. I kept going as the sun set and the night began to close in on me. About two hours after sunset, though, I had to call it quits because it was completely dark and I had to find a place to make camp. Things didn't look very promising. There were very few cleared spots alongside the road where I could pitch my tent, and the areas that had been graded were very uneven as regards both surface and consistency, heaps of mud and leaves, with large branches sticking out of them. I searched on for about another half an hour, by which time I could not see much of anything. I had to continue in the eery darkness.

Then, as I was rounding a sharp corner, I heard the sound of an approaching vehicle's engine and saw its headlights. If this had been Gabon or even the DRC I would have flagged it down, but Equatorial Guinea had shifted me into true fugitive mode. Without a second thought I flung my bike down and flattened myself on the ground next to it. The headlights lit up everything around me, and it seemed to me that even if the occupants didn't see me they would surely be able to hear my heavy breathing and thudding heart-beat. But they didn't see me, and of course didn't hear me either, and when the car had vanished down the road I got back in the saddle and kept going, even though I couldn't really see where I was going. Even if I managed no more than about three kilometres an hour, it was better than cowering in the darkness, and who knew what might come up?

And come up it did. Though I am a firm believer in Murphy's Law, I don't hold the view that whatever happens will necessarily be something bad. So I was only slightly surprised to see a twinkling of lights around the next bend, not more than 500 metres ahead of me. I didn't know what lay behind the lights, and didn't care either. Sleeping in a village of whatever size beat bedding down in the jungle for both safety and comfort, and it would show whoever cared that I had nothing to hide. So I bumped on, vastly relieved.

The lights turned out to be paraffin lamps hanging in a small cluster of huts which housed an army captain and his men. I showed the captain my passport and told him who I was and what I was doing, not quite sure about his reaction – if Equatorial Guinea had taught me anything, it was to steer clear of anyone wearing a uniform – but this time I was received with the kindness I had encountered in so many of the other countries I had passed through. The captain directed me to a suitable spot to pitch camp, and a soldier in the hut next to the tent cooked a double supper, a very tasty mess of soft, puffy rice with bully beef and corn, so that there would be enough for me as well.

It turned out that I had reached a small military post whose personnel had the duty of searching anyone travelling to or from neighbouring Cameroon. Next to the post were a few civilians who ran a small shop which supplied the military and any passing travellers with food and other necessities. It all seemed very harmless and peaceful. I hung around outside the shop for about an hour because I wanted it clearly understood that I was simply a friendly traveller, nothing more, then greeted everyone still sitting around and went to bed. A peaceful night lay ahead, it seemed.

But about 1.30 am someone rudely awakened me by giving my tent a vigorous shake. I crawled out, dressed only in my shorts. There stood a man in uniform. 'Come, come, come,' he said briskly, and led me towards the sound of idling vehicle engines. I could see blue lights flashing among the trees, and with a pang of concern knew that either the police or the army had come after me.

Two Land Rover Defenders, flanked by armed men, were parked facing each other with their headlights on, the blue flashers on their roofs making strange patterns on the surrounding trees. The Defender on the right had some soldiers standing around it, the most visible one leaning back against the bull bars with a foot resting comfortably up at knee-height. I could see him only in silhouette against the headlight beams, but it was an impressive silhouette. He must have been nearly seven feet tall, with heavily muscled arms bulging against his rolled-up sleeves and an army beret cocked up on his head.

As can be imagined, I was anything but happy with all this: it had that same druglord-about-to-execute-an-informer ambience I had felt before. What made it worse was that no one in the vicinity said anything or made even the slightest noise, as if they were expecting something to happen, obviously to me.

The captain of the base, who was standing to one side, explained that the silhouetted giant was Brigadier so-and-so (in my agitation I didn't take note of his name), who was there to find out more about me. Politely I leaned forward to shake hands with the newcomer. Wham! One of the sentries thumped me on the chest with his rifle-butt, sending me stumbling backwards. The captain explained that a person like me didn't approach the brigadier; the brigadier would approach *me* when he was ready. I apologised with a smile which probably looked as nervous as I felt and then kept quiet.

The brigadier questioned me for about 20 minutes, the captain interpreting, about where I was going and what had happened to me in Bata earlier (he had obviously received a garbled report about my run-in with the vinous gendarmes). It was an unnerving business. In addition to being a modern-day Goliath – you could imagine an army sending him out all by himself to scare the daylights out of any opponents – he had a hoarse, booming voice that sent his subordinates scurrying to do what he ordered. I could just see him ordering his men to execute me and bury me in the jungle. Who would ever know where I was buried, or even that I was dead? Africa has been swallowing up lone travellers for centuries.

When the brigadier had finished examining my passport he said that word had reached him that I was carrying special documents. Special documents? At first I couldn't fathom this question. Then I realised he was talking about the South African Embassy's letter of support, which stated that I was acting as an ambassador for the Proudly South African campaign, and which I had shown around in my brush with the law in Bata.

The brigadier had me fetch the letters and compared them with the information in my passport, and although he remained poker-faced I had the feeling that he was slowly coming to the conclusion that I wasn't a spy but exactly who and what I said I was, and my fear began to subside with every nod he gave to my explanations and answers.

Eventually the brigadier was satisfied (I think that what finally convinced him of my harmlessness was the valid Cameroonian visa in my passport) and ordered the captain to open the shop and feed me whatever I wanted. I wasn't hungry – I'd eaten earlier, and in any case a small-hours interrogation by such a fearsome figure is enough to take anyone's appetite away – but I wasn't about to make any further waves and downed a second supper consisting mainly of a large plate of rice.

In the meantime the brigadier finished conferring with the captain and silently came up from behind, startling me by putting his huge hands on my shoulders. Then he said – in very good English, to my further surprise: 'We apologise for all the inconvenience of today. If you need anything, *anything*, then you speak to that man' (pointing to the captain). 'He will make sure you leave here safely and get to Cameroon. Please visit us again. Bon voyage.'

I was astounded, not so much by the fact that he spoke English as by the invitation to return to Equatorial Guinea. Fat chance! There was no way I was going to set foot in this country of madmen again. It was only a couple of months later that I realised they weren't all that crazy. That was when I heard that several of my own countrymen, along with Cape Town-based Englishman Mark Thatcher, had been implicated in a plot to stage a coup, presumably to install another dictator who was more to their liking – if there actually was a plot, of course, and it wasn't all a smokescreen for something else. But no wonder the suspicion level was so high … although I still think that one guy on an overloaded bicycle would not have been ideal for this type of mission.

Anyway, next day I crossed – at last! – into Cameroon, although not without some final hassles with power-crazy, bribe-hungry border officials. But at last my feet sank into the Cameroonian soil, and I heaved a huge sigh of relief. Grateful though I was to the gigantic brigadier for letting me go on my way, I didn't think I'd be taking him up on his offer any time soon.

I didn't carry on straight away to the Cameroonian immigration office. My experiences in Equatorial Guinea had left a deeper footprint on my psyche than I had realised, and I found myself gripped by a strange reluctance to tackle this new country. I thought about it and came to the conclusion that I was sick and tired of being disappointed by people. Then I took a grip on myself. Disappointments and problems with officialdom were realities that were going to occur and re-occur as I headed north. If I could not accept that, I would fail in my quest. So if I wanted to go one kilometre further I would have to tackle my attitude problem and get it under control, because how much I enjoyed this adventure would depend on how much I could control my own state of mind.

So I gave myself a good mental shake and marched into the immigration office with my usual smile, shook hands all round, told them about my plans, had a few laughs and strolled happily out with an entry stamp in my passport. No demanding of bribes, no unnecessary unpacking of my worldly goods, no mutters about illegal money-changing, nothing. These Cameroonian immigration guys were great ambassadors for their country, telling me about some of the tourist attractions I could expect to come across and warmly asking me to enjoy my visit and to tell others to visit, too. So here goes: Visit Cameroon! You'll have a good time.

My plan for the day was to find a small town where I could get some decent rest. The first village was excuse enough to stop and pitch my tent on the local mayor's front lawn, after which the mayor's matric-student son, Alex, showed me around and took me down to the river for a swim. Then his mom cooked us a hearty meal. Talk about hospitality!

Next day I took time off to have a swim near the town's legendary 'Rocher de Loop', or Loop Rock, accompanied by a local who appointed himself as my guide and joined me in the water. My self-appointed guide explained that when the Germans had originally landed here late last century – today's Cameroon resulted from an amalgamation of the French and German colonies of that name – it was believed that any person who went to the rock and saw its centre never returned, thanks to a curse they had brought with them from their homeland. I didn't have the time to test the truth of this, but it would have taken a lot to keep me from coming back and hitting my saddle again; I had a lot of things to do and a lot of places still to go.

I was back on a dirt road through the jungle when I set off next day, and there were plenty of punctures to keep me occupied. During one of these enforced pauses a World Wildlife Fund employee stopped to ask if I needed help. I said I was OK, but we chatted for a while about the work the WWF was doing, and he made no secret of his amazement when he heard where I had gone on my bicycle. Among other things, he also told me that he and his colleagues had spotted gorillas and big cats east of where we were, animals that till then had been thought to live only across the Congolese or Equatorial Guinea borders.

I took time off to visit a rare sight, the 'Chutes de la Lobe', a freshwater waterfall that flows almost directly into the sea – it drops into a small lagoon about 100 metres short of the breakers. I could also have gone on a boat which took people to visit the allegedly secret pygmy tribes who were probably the first humans to inhabit the area, but some British tourists who had just returned from such an excursion advised me not to waste my money. So I decided that the short people were largely a tall tale and carried on towards my next stop, the popular beach town of Kribi, where I stayed for a couple of days.

The Kribians are used to attracting tourists, and as I approached it seemed that there was an offer of accommodation every 500 metres or so. I finally found a kind-hearted manager who gave me a safe site for my tent for a dollar US a night. I then spent what I had saved on a daily taxi ride into Kribi, my justification being that it was the only place in that part of the world which I knew had an Internet facility, something I needed badly. It was only on leaving Kribi at the end of my stay that I discovered why everyone I had met had raved about it – the road heading north runs along kilometre after kilometre of wonderful unspoilt beaches.

About 15 km outside Kribi I scored another first for the trip, and a pretty unbelievable one at that: I changed the front tyre for the first time since I had left home. Considering that I had covered about 6 000 km by this time, much of it over roads ranging from bad to terrible – and sometimes non-existent – this was a well-nigh incredible feat of endurance. The wheel had been wobbling for the last 500 km, and I had assumed, without actually investigating the cause, that the rim had buckled. But now, after 15 km of pedalling, I was struck by a belated fit of caution and had a good look at the 'buckled' wheel. It wasn't buckled at all – the tube had started pushing out of a hole worn in the side-wall of the tyre. It was this bulge that had been causing the wobble, not the rim.

When I reached the leafy, pleasant town of Edea I reckoned it would be a good place to recharge my batteries, so while having lunch at a roadside stall I asked about suitable accommodation. There was a big hotel on the outskirts, I was told, where only the rich people went. Ha! It would be a good challenge for my haggling skills to see if I could talk the proprietors of this fabled establishment into a cut-rate (or, ideally, free) place for the night, so I headed there, psyching myself into negotiation mode.

It turned out I had revved myself up for nothing. When I arrived at the hotel – which was not a high-rise but sprawled out to an impressive extent – and looked up the manager, a Frenchman named Jean-Pierre, I got the sort of welcome I had come to expect in this country. He was only too glad to offer me a free night's rest with a buffet breakfast next morning, and even invited me to have dinner with him and a Cameroonian teacher friend that evening.

Jean-Pierre was perfect for his job – seeing him in action with both staff and customers was an education in the art of handling people. Again I was not surprised; the other French expats I had bumped into along the way seemed to have been cut from the same cloth. So all in all I spent a pleasant and instructive night at his establishment, and the next day's stint was just as good, because the road surface was tarmac again. As a result I made quick work of the 70 km to my next stop, Douala, although getting through the chaos on the outskirts was a little hair-raising.

The rules of the road seemed to be a subject for debate rather than obedience, and I found myself navigating through a mass of people, cars, motorbikes and goats which were all heading the wrong way without any concern for the fact that they were swimming up-stream, so to speak. I managed to survive all this, though, and when I made contact with the Cameroonian television service and the local representatives of South Africa's DSTV network they made my two-day stay a really memorable one. They organised a room for me at the local Meridian Hotel, put their Internet facilities at my disposal, laid on interviews on the national radio service, introduced me to a bagel restaurant and took me to the French import supermarket, Carrefour, to stock up

Even more importantly, they arranged a meeting with the local heads of Sony Ericsson and MTN Cameroon, who collectively replaced my old cell phone with a state-of-the-art P800 camera phone. The Sony Ericsson man, an Australian named Adam, also gave me a 200 000 CFA donation towards my trip. I really appreciated the cash, but just as valuable was what Adam said when he handed it over: that what I was attempting was inspirational, something that he felt many would want to emulate, while yet others would envy me for what I was doing. It was immensely heartening to know that although some people thought I was crazy, others could see the value in what I had endured thus far.

I enjoyed myself so much in Douala that I actually talked myself into delaying my departure into the unknown. I knew that from here on to the Nigerian border cell phone communication would become very difficult, and subconsciously, I think, I wanted to stay in touch a while longer. But once again I took myself in hand, and as a penance I forced myself on to the road late one afternoon, even though it was only about two hours before sunset.

My Douala luck held, though, and I found a Catholic mission which allowed me to sleep on the porch of the parish office. In the morning I was awoken early by church bells and invited to attend the seven o'clock Mass. I'm not a Catholic, so I turned the offer down with thanks, but I had an uneasy feeling about it afterwards. I had spent the night with a stained-glass Jesus watching over me, and then I had turned down an opportunity to give thanks! Too late, I concluded that I should have attended, Catholic or not. A man going where I was going, and smelling the way I smelt – worse than everyone else in the church rolled into one – needed all the divine protection he could get.

Well, I'd had my chance and blown it, so I wasted no time in getting back on the road, pedalling through huge palm plantations that stretched all the way to the horizon and weren't left behind till I got to a seaside town called Limbe, which has the dubious distinction of living cheek by jowl with an active volcano, and showed it. Thanks to millions of years of successive lava deposits the beaches weren't golden but a lighter shade of soot, the water looked darker than it should and every picture I took seemed to have been digitally altered. The bay with its black sands was a strange but stunning experience, though, and the seafood restaurants were just as striking for their excellence.

I made one of those instant friends I had come across everywhere so far, a man called Nelson, who owned a photo shop where people could have identity and family pictures taken – the sort of place where you can have the Eiffel Tower or Waikiki Beach in the background if you want. Nelson gave me a place to sleep on the floor of his studio, in front of the fan and right next to the Brooklyn Bridge, and outlined Limbe's rather dangerous recent history for my benefit. From his telling the locals seemed to have rather a casual attitude towards their lava-belching neighbour. In 2001, he said, the volcano erupted and entirely destroyed a village near by. Two weeks later the villagers moved right back and rebuilt their houses on the exact same spot. I couldn't help thinking that someone should have informed them that the theory about lightning never striking the same place twice, if it is true, certainly does not apply to volcanoes.

Later, when I left Limbe for my next stop at the town of Idenao – having been interviewed at length by a very enthusiastic and creative journalist named Wilson for the regional newspaper – the volcano made its presence felt in no uncertain fashion when I found myself having to detour around a slab of lava that had flowed down the mountainside and over the road. Wow, where else in the world does someone ever have a close encounter like that?

Rather sadly I had to pass up something I had contemplated while on my trip, the annual foot race up and down Mount Cameroon, which at 4 100 metres above sea-level is the highest mountain in West Africa. But it wasn't due yet, and I couldn't spare the time. Maybe some other time ... after all, I'd like to visit Cameroon again.

When it came to crossing over into Nigeria, I opted to go by boat, a journey of about four hours-plus. All the travel books warn at length against going by sea when crossing into Nigeria from Cameroon. As usual I ignored them. It was not that I didn't believe what the reports said – it is true that the sea-passage is notorious for piracy, and on top of that Nigeria and Cameroon were at war with one another because of on-going quarrels about oil – it was just that I felt most 'Afro-pessimism' came from people who weren't really qualified to pass judgement. Rumour becomes legend and then conventional wisdom very easily, and it often takes no more than a leap of the imagination to turn a surly-looking policeman walking past you with his rifle over his shoulder into a murderous cash-in-transit robber on the way to work.

The driver of our small motor-boat was a fearsomely large man who went by the equally fearsome name of Rambo, and my first impression of him was not a good one, seeing that he wanted to throw two passengers overboard because they were unwilling to pay the whole fare for the trip up front. But, as I learned, it wasn't as simple as that. They didn't have passports, and if they were caught Rambo would automatically be in big trouble, so naturally he wanted some motivation to run the gauntlet with them – even if it was only that he wouldn't have to worry about losing the fare if they were grabbed before they had paid him.

Well, they coughed up and he didn't deep-six them, and we forged ahead through slicks of oil bubbling up from the plentiful underground reservoirs, all of it going to waste because the squabble between Nigeria and Cameroon was hampering further exploration. But the trip itself was uneventful; we came across just one other vessel, a Cameroonian trawler whose crew generously flung some sizeable pieces of their catch over to us; so the only danger I encountered during the crossing was a near-miss from a 10-kilo chunk of tuna.

When I had crossed into Cameroon from Equatorial Guinea a few days earlier a local had warned me about how aggressive and violent the Cameroonians were (ha, he could talk!). He said they would look for a fight wherever you went. Well, that had not turned out to be the case – although I will admit that the folk in Idenao were a little different from the other Cameroonians I had met. They were more aggressive, but they were also far and away more active than many other scary people I had met – so I added a few pinches of salt to what one of my fellow-passengers now told me about Nigerians.

They were even worse than the Cameroonians, he said. They wouldn't even foment a quarrel first, just haul off and hit you. Then I added another handful of salt when he went on to another subject and claimed that Nigeria was far more developed as regards infrastructure and technology than South Africa. 'Get ready,' he warned, 'it gonna shock you.' I stared at him in some incredulity. Was he serious? South Africa was by far the most developed nation anywhere in Africa – this is not a question of bragging, just a simple statement of fact. But he had said it with an absolutely straight face, so I didn't see any point in disputing the matter with him.

In spite of his cautiousness about the passportless passengers, Rambo did not hesitate to call in en route to drop off various people who didn't want to pass through the formality of customs, and in the process I caught glimpses of some very interesting, not to say frequently laughable, lifestyles. On the verandah of one wooden cabin that stood on stilts above the water, for example, was a guy slumped in a chair, a beer on his lap and a fishing rod in one hand – fast asleep.

Another encounter of a closer kind was even more hilarious. The two passengers who had nearly walked the plank at the start of the trip wanted to get off at a certain spot between clumps of reed in an isolated little cove. The boat wasn't very manoeuvrable, so we overshot slightly and found our way barred by a wrinkled old man who was standing stark naked in the water, washing himself all over. Rambo asked him to move over so that we could do a U-turn. The old man ignored us as if we were nothing more than an unwelcome mirage and carried on lathering away at himself with such vigour that he actually splashed us with some of the soapy bubbles that covered him (but not well enough, unfortunately). Rambo tried again. No luck. I wondered if my arrival in Nigeria was going to be delayed because of the need to wait till the stubborn oldster had finished sluicing himself down. Then Rambo had another go at diplomacy. I couldn't understand anything of what followed, but he must finally have produced some telling argument, because the old guy grudgingly moved slightly sideways to let us go on our way.

We didn't meet up with any more difficult old men, however, and eventually arrived at our destination, Oron. We were now very near Calabar, the town to which the murderous self-appointed Liberian president, Charles Taylor, had just been extradited at the invitation of then Nigerian president Olasegun Obasanjo. Taylor had deserved far worse than that, but the African Union had felt that the only way to end the very bloody and brutal Liberian civil war was to persuade Taylor to leave the country more or less voluntarily. Now Taylor would be within a mere stone's-throw of me. This was closer than I fancied being to such a mass murderer and torturer, but I consoled myself with the thought that I didn't plan on staying in Oron for very long.

But these dark thoughts were soon dissipated by the treatment I got from the Nigerian customs. My fellow-passenger's warnings to the contrary, they couldn't have been nicer. Passing through amounted to little more than 'Hi, how are you? I am fine. Hold still while I stamp your passport. Welcome to Nigeria. Have a good time. Goodbye.'

Now, that's what I called good service, and as a gesture of gratitude I bought each of them a cool drink and a handful of grilled meat. It is true that virtue is its own reward, but the good guys in the world should stick together.

# CHAPTER 10

# NIGERIA – PEOPLE AND PREACHERS FOR AFRICA

*The people of Nigeria seemed genuinely desperate for salvation.
But to some wise guys, of course, religion merely represented
a good business opportunity. Nigeria is the only place I know
where you can set up your own discipleship school, with yourself
as the CEO. Those American pocket messiahs with their little
cults of a mere couple of thousand wouldn't last a weekend.*

Here's some free advice. Don't make the most densely populated
country on the continent your first cycling destination. Fortunately, my earlier experiences and advice I had received had given me a
good idea about what to expect on arriving in Nigeria. So I was under no illusions when I landed at Oron. But I have to admit that the
advice fell a little short of the reality.

I had been told that Oron was a small town by Nigerian standards. So it was, but it was still about 10 times the size of where I
came from, Gordon's Bay. I had also been told that it would be easier to get by in conversation with the locals because everyone spoke
English – which is partly true. What most of them seem to speak is
'pidgin', a strange and distorted form of the language. Most South
Africans are pretty good at mangling English, but I saw now that
they were rank amateurs compared to Nigerians.

The fearsome-looking Rambo had taken a liking to me and insisted that I go with him to meet his family; if I wanted to, he add-

ed, I could sleep over as well. I soon discovered that what Rambo meant by 'family' was actually 'extended family', so that he had to borrow a friend's motorbike – something every second person in this city seemed to have – for us to visit all his far-flung relatives. We refreshed ourselves from this gruelling social round with boiled eggs and grilled meat at a roadside restaurant while he related his day's experiences to an attentive crowd. I was beginning to understand now why he was called 'Rambo', but without any negative connotation attached; although big and muscular, he seemed to command genuine respect wherever he went.

Rambo and his wife shared their dwelling with some married cousins, the result being that I found myself a temporary member of a household of nine, a bit of a crush that wasn't helped by the fact that the electricity was off (Rambo explained that he had been late in paying his electricity bill, and the power would only be reconnected the following day). The only spare space in this overcrowded household was the lounge, and there I camped out, sweating my way through one of the most humid nights I've ever survived while fighting off hordes of mosquitoes which simply could not pass up the chance of feasting off a foreigner. My main weapon was Tabard lotion, which repelled the mozzies all right but simultaneously raised my body temperature to furnace-level. You might say I spent the night between a sauna and a hard place (the floor).

But I survived, as I say, and next morning Rambo and his cousin escorted me out of town, although not before my host had had our pictures taken at a photo shop. For some reason Rambo wanted us to pose like boxers who were promoting a fight, clenched fists resting on one another's chins, and then he got even more creative, so that eventually we were shadow-boxing while the cameraman snapped madly away.

Then we were off. Rambo and his cousin rode ahead on motorbikes, clearing a path for me by shouting at people to get out of the way and hurling pidgin insults at those who didn't move quickly enough. In between pumping away at the pedals I kept my ears open for new words in this strange new lingo.

Pidgin is a lazy, shortened gangster version of the real thing, and while it wasn't going to be as tough as picking up Portuguese or French, it was obvious that I would have to work at making sense of things like 'morn you' (good morning to you), 'How da body?' (how are you feeling?) and 'boutter you?' (Fine, how about you?)

Man, this was interesting. I started using my first pidgin before I had even left the town behind me – if I ever did leave it behind me. The most densely populated country in Africa, Nigeria is so jam-packed with people that I seemed unable to go for more than 50 metres without making eye contact with someone. This meant that whenever I stopped a curious crowd would form immediately. The children in particular were fascinated by me; they would sit very close in, eyes glued on my every motion, so that when I had a cool drink their heads would go up and down as I drank from the bottle and then lowered it again.

It got a bit wearing after a while, but typical Nigerian humour helped to rub off the rough edges. When I was mobbed by kids while I was drinking sachets of ice-cold water at a small shop near the town of Aba, an old man who had obviously noticed that I was showing signs of irritation came up and said, absolutely deadpan: 'Don't be concerned at the children's behaviour. They are staring at you for the simple fact that you are so handsome. They can't take their eyes off you.' Since I was anything but handsome just then – sweaty, grimy, red from exertion, hair all over the place where it wasn't plastered down, yes, but certainly not handsome – I would have had to be a real curmudgeon not to squeeze out a grin.

Aba was a large city by any standards – I reckoned it must have had a couple of million inhabitants at least – and for my own safety I decided that I would extend my budget to allow for more secure accommodation than usual. That translated into a seedy little three-storey hotel in the centre of the city which proved right away that its staff sorely needed a crash course in client-crisis management.

My first night there I had no warm or running water, advertised promises notwithstanding. I brought this matter to the attention of the manager and politely suggested that he offer me a discount on the room for my second night, to which he replied: 'That's not the type of business we're into.'

The second night was the real killer, however. I awoke at some unearthly hour to find my room half-filled with black smoke, while sparks and flames ran up the curtains. A hasty investigation showed that the cabling of the air conditioner had been badly repaired and had caused a short circuit. Fortunately I had earlier run water into a bucket and placed it at arm's reach, thanks to some deeply buried but much-appreciated bit of survival instinct. This was not the ideal antidote for an electrical fire, but it was a lot better than nothing, and after making sure that the flames were mostly extinguished and the electricity had been turned off I headed down to the reception desk to report the incident. The receptionist, whom I awoke from a deep sleep, informed me that they did not have another room for me. Later that morning I learned that she had, in fact, had rooms available, but they were upgrades and I would have had to pay more. Unbelievable!

In the morning I tackled the manager. He listened attentively while I gave him a blow-by-blow account, getting angrier and angrier when I considered how casually they were dealing with what might have been a fatal incident. If I had not woken up in time, I pointed out, I could have lost consciousness and either suffocated or been burnt to death, and the hotel would have been toast. The least they could do, I ended, was give me my third night there for free.

When the manager replied I nearly laughed out loud, because his reaction was the very last one I expected: 'God bless you, God bless you. Praise God that He spared you and the hotel. All praise be to God.' Well, I'm as religious as the next guy, but this effusion reduced me to silence.

I had already noticed that the inhabitants of this teeming nation were not what one could call taciturn people, and when I wheeled my bike out of the hotel after my third – and, thank goodness, last – night I witnessed a classic exhibition of Nigerian-style road rage which reinforced everything I had observed so far.

I didn't see the start of it, but when I arrived on the scene a very angry pedestrian was busy shouting fiercely at the occupants of a small, boxy car – father, mother, two kids with school satchels in the back seat. Next thing he grabbed the father-driver and started pulling him out through the window. The father took exception to this, and suddenly fists were flying in all directions. Most of them were near-misses, but the pedestrian connected often enough to lay the father flat on his back. To my amazement – and amusement – the kids in the back took all this with absolute aplomb, gazing straight ahead while Daddy lay there seeing stars. Perhaps he was a fantastically bad driver, and close encounters with enraged pedestrians were a daily occurrence on the way to school? I'll never know the answer to this great African mystery.

A little later, while fortifying myself with coffee and buttered bread down one of the many side-streets, I had an even stranger experience when a travelling circus or zoo – I never found out which – passed by. The first animal I saw was a chimpanzee wearing beach-boy clothes and a Gary Player-type hat, walking upright, human-style. When his handler saw me goggling at this unexpected apparition he tugged at the chimp's leash and said loudly: 'Where's your master? Where's your master?'

The chimp cast his gaze over the people in his vicinity, made eye contact with me and immediately headed in my direction, taking off his Gary Player hat and holding it out for a donation. I dropped a few naira into the hat, not knowing whether it was a polite request or a 'money with menaces' situation, and he and his handler went on their way. It was certainly a nice trick – when the chimp heard the word 'master' he headed for the first white person he saw and put the bite (figuratively speaking) on him. Good psychology, too – whites stuck out like sore thumbs in the sea of black humanity, and were likely to be tourists with a little disposable cash.

I was still contemplating the beach-boy chimp's technique when things got even stranger. A large male baboon stalked past within a metre of me, attached to his handler by a leash which looked to be no thicker than about two millimetres. Right after him came two large fully-grown hyenas – also held in by almost invisible leashes – and growled loud ripples into my cup of fresh coffee as they passed. It was the first time I had seen hyenas at really close range, and they were an intimidating sight – huge chests and massive jaws looking as evil from near by as they did at a distance. My first instinct was to

Above: Banjul, Gambia – Nelson Mandela is everywhere...

Top left: If only they could talk! Trees as companions ... baobabs each have their own personality. This one was in Senegal.
(Photo: Nic Bothma/EPA)

Middle: Dakar, Senegal. He doesn't speak English and I hardly speak French ... perhaps he's laughing because I told him I'd cycled from South Africa! Each day I'd wake up with a guarantee of a hundred of these magic moments.
(Photo: Nic Bothma/EPA)

Bottom: Navigating the traffic on two different main roads in Senegal.
(Photo: Nic Bothma/EPA)

Gambia, Senegal

Right: This Mauritanian camel was as lonely as I was – but nowhere near as far out of his comfort zone.

Above: The horizon was simmering with non-stop mirages that day – 50 degrees and still smiling.

Right: My brain had obviously started boiling in the brutal Mauritanian sun: I set up this scene with great effort, loading the bicycle and squatting in position (no seats) to simulate 'cruising' the desert. The skin on the fingers that held me in position was blistered by the extreme heat of the metal.

Above: How much tea do you want in your sugar? Taking a break in the shade of a thorn bush with Ahmed and assistant. These 'Arab dresses' are amazing at keeping you cool!

Above right: The iron ore train from Zurat to Nouadhibou is the world's longest. People and animals share the space and brave the freezing elements together.

Right: Choum, northern Mauritania, going further into nowhere.

Mauritania

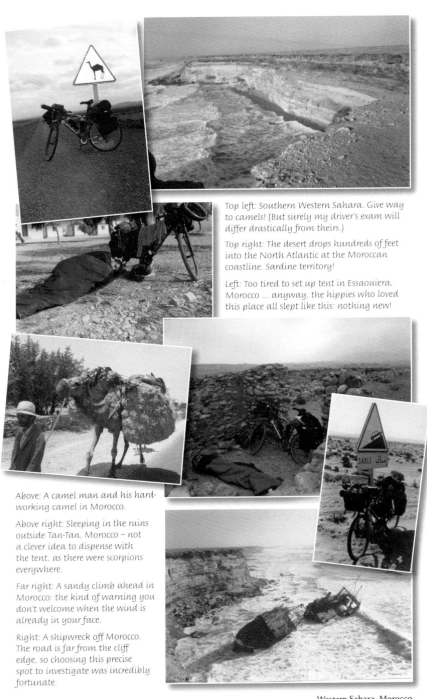

Top left: Southern Western Sahara. Give way to camels! (But surely my driver's exam will differ drastically from theirs.)

Top right: The desert drops hundreds of feet into the North Atlantic at the Moroccan coastline. Sardine territory!

Left: Too tired to set up tent in Essaouiera, Morocco ... anyway, the hippies who loved this place all slept like this: nothing new!

Above: A camel man and his hard-working camel in Morocco.

Above right: Sleeping in the ruins outside Tan-Tan, Morocco – not a clever idea to dispense with the tent, as there were scorpions everywhere.

Far right: A sandy climb ahead in Morocco: the kind of warning you don't welcome when the wind is already in your face.

Right: A shipwreck off Morocco. The road is far from the cliff edge, so choosing this precise spot to investigate was incredibly fortunate.

Western Sahara, Morocco

Top left: The sandstorms around Laayoune would have clogged up the empty space between my ears if not for the essential headgear.

Top right: Early morning mist wraps around a Moroccan castle.

Left: Meknes, Morocco, awaiting other guests at the National Street Rally Championships.

Above: Meeting the mayor at the National Street Rally Championships.

Above: Paparazzi Patrick took this photo of me signing T-shirts in my room in his house in Rabat.

Left: My friend Madani (who took the photo) invited me to dinner with a famous Paris-Dakar rally winner, Patrick Zanaroli, on my right.

Morocco

Top right: My bicycle after 16 000 km and 21 countries' abuse.

Top left: About to board the Tangiers–Algeciras ferry: camera nearly confiscated here!

Left: A photo of me and Vasti – frequently taken out and looked at!

MERIDIEN DE GREENWICH

Above: Algeria: another landmark, the Greenwich meridian.

Left: The Spanish enclave of Ceuta ... trying to get to Algeria via Spain.

Above: Roadside accommodation in Algeria: I can sleep through anything.

Right: Azzaba, Algeria, posing with friends including the baker who loaded my bike with cakes.

Morocco, Algeria

Top left: Al Kala harbour, Algeria, pondering life – and why Tunisia didn't want me.

Top right: An evening with friends in Algeria. The guitar player described himself as an English teacher/pet shop owner/barber/ musician/socialite.

Right: These Algerian villagers welcomed me to their town (where I was eventually locked for my own safety on the roof of a restaurant).

Above left: Get the law to take the pics where it's considered illegal … like coming up to a roadblock.

Above: Impromptu home-making in the Algerian outback.

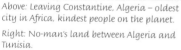

Above: Leaving Constantine, Algeria – oldest city in Africa, kindest people on the planet.

Right: No-man's land between Algeria and Tunisia.

Algeria

Above and below: El Jem: this replica of Rome's Colosseum was used for scenes in 'Gladiator'.

Top left: Tabarka: tourist heaven in Tunisia.

Top right: World War II graves. So much young and precious blood!

Above: Tunisian embassy staff: movers and shakers who found a way into Libya for me.

Hammamet, Tunisia – a two-day getaway while the Libyans pondered approving my visa.

Tunisia

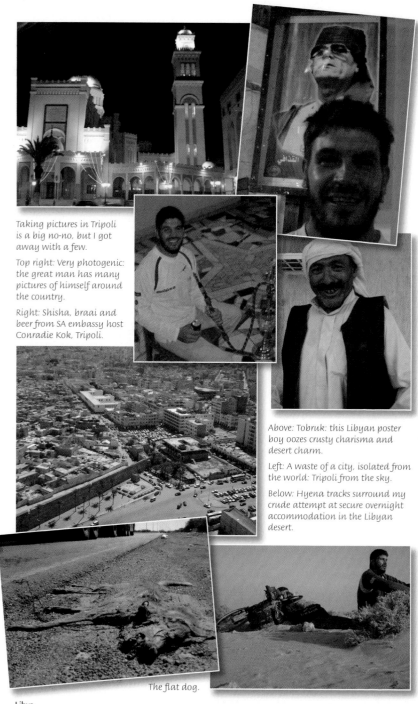

Taking pictures in Tripoli is a big no-no, but I got away with a few.

Top right: Very photogenic: the great man has many pictures of himself around the country.

Right: Shisha, braai and beer from SA embassy host Conradie Kok, Tripoli.

Above: Tobruk: this Libyan poster boy oozes crusty charisma and desert charm.

Left: A waste of a city, isolated from the world: Tripoli from the sky.

Below: Hyena tracks surround my crude attempt at secure overnight accommodation in the Libyan desert.

The flat dog.

cram my breakfast down my throat and get out of there at a rate of knots before something worse came by, but I had second thoughts and stayed put. There was no chance of a quick getaway because the rest of the travelling zoo or circus, or whatever it was, was blocking my escape, and the thought of two large, ill-tempered hyenas chasing after me like a pair of spotted guard dogs was simply too horrible to contemplate.

In retrospect, I shouldn't have been so surprised by the hotel manager's reaction to my complaints. One of the things about Nigeria that struck me from Day One was the huge interest in churches and gospel crusades. Nigeria certainly has more churches per square kilometre than any other place I've ever visited. Nearly every person I met had been, was or wanted to be a pastor. Advertisements for church groups and gatherings lined the roadsides, far outnumbering any other form of advertising. In extreme cases the faithful would sling huge banners across an entire freeway to advertise their forthcoming gatherings, and I remember one that really blew my mind: A NIGHT OF BLISS WITH PASTOR CHRIS. Note that there was no mention of God, although you can be sure His name was often taken by the preacher in question, or there wouldn't have been much bliss during the meeting, Pastor Chris or no Pastor Chris.

I do not believe that this was put-up stuff; the people of Nigeria seemed genuinely desperate for salvation. But to some wise guys, of course, religion merely represented a good business opportunity. Nigeria is the only place I know where you can set up your own discipleship school, with yourself as the CEO. Those American pocket messiahs with their little cults of a mere couple of thousand wouldn't last a weekend in Nigeria.

This is not to say that all the religion has bred much meekness and mildness in the Nigerians. It has so many people, and there is such endless competition to get on or just make a living of some kind, that the people are aggressive by nature. But it is not a grim aggressiveness. Essentially they are a fun-loving lot, and time and again I found that standing up for myself with some humour built into the determination earned me instant respect. The good humour did not extend to relations between the locals and the police, though, and a hair-raising experience I had at a road-block one afternoon while returning from a reconnaissance trip to the troubled region of Port Harcourt stays firmly imprinted on my mind.

The driver of the minibus taxi I was riding in had a serious disagreement with the policeman who was doing the searching: the cop wanted a bribe and the driver flatly refused to provide one. When he was stopped from going through the driver became, to put it mildly, verbally aggressive. The cop, a menacing-looking character dressed completely in black and carrying an AK-47 assault rifle, grabbed the key from the minibus's ignition. Without hesitation the driver grabbed at a screwdriver lying on his seat and threatened to stab him. Next thing the driver had several muzzles peering at him.

It was a tense moment, all right, and not just for the driver. I was seated directly behind him, which meant that the rifles were now also pointed at me. Indirectly, certainly, but that wouldn't make a difference to any bullets that might be fired. It didn't make me feel any better to hear the women behind me screaming as they fought to scramble out through the sliding door. But a smartly-dressed young guy on my right to whom I'd been chatting didn't get his water hot, apart from looking slightly nervous. His advice was to stay put and not give way to panic. 'Do no' worry, maan, dis is apenin all da time,' he soothed me as the cops hustled the driver away to God knew what fate. I nearly replied: 'Oh, well, that makes it OK then!' But an hour later the driver came back, unscathed and with keys in hand. Everybody was smiling and joking as we continued on to the next town, Owerri, where my bicycle had been left in my hotel room. Our spirits were so high that we nearly erupted into full choral rapture, Nigerian revivalist style: 'Now I am free, now I am free, now I am free, He's so good to me!'

But if Nigeria was hilariously scary, it also boasted good tarmac roads, which made my life considerably easier as I worked my way past and over an uncountable number of hills in the next 900 or so kilometres. Which is not to say that Nigerian driving habits didn't make the freeways confusing at times, not to say downright terrifying. For example, it was unnerving to be steaming along a modern two-way freeway, complete with an island separating the lanes, and then suddenly to see a line of traffic barrelling head down straight at you. The reason for this, I soon discovered, was that if your average Nigerian driver found the going too slow on his side of the freeway he would simply find a gap in the concrete divide and use the on-coming lane. This continual dicing with death didn't seem to get people worked up, and there was no hooting or shouting at one other. It was simply the way things were done there.

What with the good roads and plenty to eat, I was in fine shape and covered nearly 1 000 kilometres in just over a week, the best cycling I had done to date. I set off early every morning and paced myself well, which is important on long journeys, so I never ran out of steam. My only problem was that both my big toes were shedding their nails, the result of the constant pressure created by standing out of the saddle. Anybody who has had this problem will know what I am talking about when I say that the really painful bit comes when you have to detach the final live part of the nail.

In the process I also set a distance record, albeit by accident. I had planned to go about 30 km past the city of Onitsha so that my daily distance would be 125 km. When I had gone 15 km past Onitsha, however, a white bakkie stopped in the road ahead of me, and an Irish or Scottish guy (I'm not sure which) jumped out and offered to give me a lift. As I usually did when made an offer like this, I declined with thanks, thinking that this would be the end of the matter. But he went on to offer me accommodation for the night as well. Now that was another matter altogether, and I said I would love to take him up on his offer, as long as the house wasn't too far away, because there was only enough light left for me to go about 30 km at most.

'It's never that far,' he said, went on to explain what landmarks, bridges, railways and buildings I would encounter further along the road and then left, promising: 'I'll be waiting alongside the road with ice-cold beer.' I cycled on after him in a distinctly sanguine mood. How about that! A cold beer or two, a nice plate of hot food and a soft bed after a hard day's work. Perfect!

Well, after 40 km there was still no sign of him, his bakkie or the landmarks he had mentioned. Had I really met him, or had it all been a hallucination? I took no chances, and whenever I saw any sort of white speck ahead I gave it a wave, just in case it was him waiting for me. But it never was, and by now it was dark, with not a sign of human habitation in sight. There was no question of camping out because the sort of open yet secluded ground that I needed for both comfort and security was nowhere to be found.

I looked at my clock: 145 km! It had been a long haul, but there was no end in sight. What should I do? I thought it over and decided that the only logical course of action was to carry on. Who knew what lay ahead? (As you can see, I had not lost my usual cock-eyed optimism.) Maybe he or some other friendly fellow-humans were waiting on the other side of the very next hill!

Well, neither he nor they were, and the clock stood at all of 179 kilometres by the time I staggered into a small town that was built around a freeway junction. In Nigeria freeway settlements like this are common. One can see why. Anybody in such a town is cheek by jowl with not one but several major transport routes. I expect just about everyone living in a town like this can see the bus coming through their shower window, dry themselves off, get dressed, have a cup of coffee and still get to the pick-up point in time.

An extremely kind family of four boys and their parents offered me a place to sleep in their house that night, which I accepted with alacrity, having long since written off my Irish/Scottish acquaintance of earlier in the day. Was he still standing somewhere on the freeway waiting for me while his ice-cold beer got warmer and warmer? Well, too bad; I had done my best to catch up with him. But I was grateful to him all the same for providing me with the motivation to break my distance record.

Before I went to bed I had a large and memorable meal. The bush meat I ate that night was the best I had ever had, although it was monkey meat and in normal circumstances wouldn't have gone down as smoothly as it did. I got on well with the Nigerians' cuisine, and my staple daily diet was meat with a mountain of rice, well lubricated with the pepper sauce they liked so much. If the restaurant I was eating at ran short of rice, I would dig out a couple of handfuls of the South African product I had bought in Angola. I had turned into a real eating machine by now, with a 2 kg bag of rice sometimes lasting me only a day.

Before leaving the following morning I made an important telephone call to Senegal and received news I was expecting but did not want to hear. The next country but one on my list was Liberia, a hellhole by any standards. A very good photographer friend of mine in Cape Town, a German girl named Dorothy von Holsten, had given me the contact details for a colleague, Nic Bothma, whom she knew had worked in Liberia. Nic's name is not well-known to the general public, but during the heat of the fighting in the capital, Monrovia, he had risked his life to take amazing pictures which had hit the front pages of the world's newspapers, and his reward had been to be made the European Press Agency bureau chief for West Africa. There was surely no one better qualified to give me advice on Liberia and what routes to take. And, as I say, it was advice I didn't really want to hear.

'Take Liberia off your list right now,' he said in an emphatic tone which conquered the crackling on the line. 'You will not live to tell the story if you go into that country. There's no law there, and people do unimaginable things to each other. Take another route. Go around Ivory Coast, Liberia and Sierra Leone. A white guy on a fancy bicycle will *not* make it through any of these countries. Head north into Ghana and go via Burkina Faso, then through Mali into Senegal.'

But I didn't really have a choice if I wanted to do what I had set out to do. I *had* to pass through every coastal country of Africa, regardless of what danger awaited me. I wasn't being foolishly macho. I knew that I would be going through some extreme-risk areas, where I would be a sitting duck and from which I might not emerge in one piece, if at all. But I *had* to go, and if I was to have any chance of coming out on the other side I needed sound advice from the best possible sources – people like Nic, who had leopard-crawled under the whizzing bullets in Monrovia to get to where *he* had had to go. Then maybe my chances of survival would jump from one in a million to one in a thousand.

In spite of the crackling line Nic sensed that my mind was made up, and that I remained stubbornly focused on going through Liberia and Sierra Leone, no matter what, and he made a last appeal to my better judgement. 'Riaan,' he said, more softly now, his voice full of concern for me, 'Riaan, don't go.'

Although I simply couldn't take Nic's advice, sound though I knew it was, our discussion wasn't wasted because without being aware of it he passed on some of his do-or-die energy and enthusiasm, the same spirit that I believed was running through me. I would just have to accept that very few people I met would ever understand how I felt.

I was looking forward to reaching Lagos, Africa's second-largest city and the next major milestone after Luanda. I had broken my journey into about seven segments, each ending with a deliberate pause so that I could re-evaluate my schedule, equipment and finances. Reaching Lagos, the start of the second, was an exciting prospect, and it was getting close. Exactly *how* close was not that easy to determine, however, because one thing the West African traveller should not depend on is getting a straight answer regarding distance from any Nigerian.

They tend to calculate distance not in metres, kilometres or miles but in terms of the estimated time it will take you, which naturally depends on their conclusions about what you are capable of. Every time I made an enquiry about distances the person would give my bicycle a thorough inspection before assessing my physical state and perceived energy levels, then finally deliver a calculated estimate like: 'For you ... erm, erm, erm ... I say 45 minutes.'

By the time I had reached the town of Njebu Ode I had had enough of these time estimates. I needed some specific figures because the South African Embassy in Lagos had kindly sent out their resident police officer, Johan Stadler, to escort me in. I should explain that the South African Embassy, like so many others in Lagos, has a permanent on-site police office to combat the criminal traffic which is one of Nigeria's best-known 'exports' to South Africa.

Painful experience had proved that diplomats simply do not have the forensic skills needed to intercept false passports and similar bogus documentation.

In any case, Johan Stadler needed to have a reasonable idea of when I would be nearing the city later that afternoon, and without some figures I couldn't give him any sort of estimate. So, having tried everything else, I decided to tackle the people who should surely be able to give me something solid – the truck drivers, who spend 15 hours a day travelling to and from Lagos. I stopped at the very next filling station, found myself a likely-looking driver and put the question. But after less than a minute the portly driver was inspecting my bicycle, prodding the tyres with his foot, checking the tread and testing the brakes. With a sinking feeling of *déjà vu* I waited for his verdict. Surely not ... ? But there it came: 'Erm, erm, erm ... for you, it will be about an hour ... ya ...an hour.'

Oh, no! But I decided to try again before letting this once-golden opportunity slip away like its predecessors. 'Thank you, sir,' I said, with a big grin on my face, 'and by the way, can you tell me when last you cycled this stretch with an overloaded bicycle?'

'No, no ...' he replied, unruffled by what I now realised must have sounded pretty sarcastic, 'we know how long it takes. We have lived here for our whole lives. Many people use bicycles in Nigeria.'

So there it was. You qualified for your diploma in Nigerian time estimation, cyclist category, by being born there, spending your entire working life overtaking hordes of bicycles and understanding the local psychology. I gave up and hit the road again, and after a while stopped worrying about the distance I still had to cover – firstly because I was obviously getting very close to Lagos now, and secondly because I had something more urgent to worry about, namely the impending self-destruction of my main wheel-bearings.

After carrying an extremely heavy load over mainly horrendous road conditions for more than 6 000 km the bearings had finally started giving notice of their intention to retire, by way of a nerve-racking metal-on-metal scraping noise. When no notice was taken of this warning, the bearings started breaking and seizing up, so that pedalling became harder and harder. When this second warning was also ignored the bearings simply locked up altogether, leaving me with only one option for forward movement: pushing.

To my great relief Johan found me some time later, several hours past my estimated time of arrival. I would like to say that he roared up and rescued me as I was tottering towards Lagos, on my last legs from the exhausting effort of pushing my bike, but actually he spotted me in the bowels of a noisy crowd that had gathered around a roadside television set to watch Nigeria's opening game in the Africa Cup soccer tournament.

Johan introduced me to all the staffers at the embassy and made arrangements for my first temporary passport, the only thing that would avert a break in the continuity of my trip. My passport was nearly full, and would not get me further than Morocco, but processing the application for a new one would take about four months, which I obviously did not have. At the same time the South African diplomats were rightly wary of issuing temporary passports because they were so often used for fraudulent purposes by foreigners – photographs could easily be changed, new information entered and so on. So without Johan as a reference it would have been a battle.

Johan's kindness went even further. After consulting with his wife (this is always a good thing for a husband to do, since he rarely has any clear idea of household arrangements) he invited me to stay with them while I was in Lagos. This was really travelling first class – they lived on Ikoyi Island, the poshest area in Lagos, and home to diplomats, embassies, expatriate workers and various members of the Nigerian elite. It was central, safe and perfect for getting my administration and repairs comfortably done.

I saw some interesting things in Lagos, and I am sure that if I had stayed longer I would have seen even more. One of the things I *did* see was probably the most organised beggar in Africa, if not the world, the epitome of someone who not only made the best of a handicap but with true Nigerian ingenuity had turned it into a business, complete with employees.

This guy's office was at an off-ramp of Lagos's record-length bridge, where he parked himself in his wheelchair every day and exhibited his stock-in-trade, a broad smile and an enormously swollen foot caused by elephantiasis. This fellow had an entire team working for him. His driver, so to speak, was a boy who looked 10 years old, who pushed him from car to car, preceded by his marketing team, a loudhailer-wielding rapper type who encouraged people to be generous in their donations; I think this included gory details about the man and his foot. Accompanying the beggar was another guy whose role I was not sure of – he was either a reserve speaker in case the rapper ran dry or some sort of relative who was there to provide moral support and company.

I don't know which impressed me more, the wheelchair man's smooth operation or the bridge, the longest in Africa at more than 13 km, which connected the islands of Victoria, Ikoyi and Lagos to the mainland. Building it must have been a massive – and massively expensive – undertaking. If this had not been oil-rich Nigeria but one of its poorer neighbours I would have been travelling in a pirogue propelled by a team of paddlers between the tranquil, picturesque villages on stilts which were built alongside the bridge.

Unfortunately their picturesqueness didn't hold up on closer inspection, when the scum of faeces, empty tins and old plastic bags bobbing up and down below them became all too obvious to the eye as well as the nose. One of the embassy staffers told me that he and some of his colleagues had been fishing in the lagoon the weekend before and had come across a floating body. I could believe it.

I had been lusting for some fish and chips after my months of an all-meat diet, but this cooled my ardour, and so I decided to try out a place I had heard a lot about, a burger joint called 'Mr Biggs' which was said to be Nigeria's answer to McDonalds. It was a bit of a cultural shock, because I had got used to eating real West African food in real West African eating-places. Mr Biggs was just the reverse: modern architecture that stood out like a sore thumb among its neighbouring buildings, an interior so neat and clean it felt like a hospital to a road-bashing roughneck like me, and distinctly un-African food, no different from what I would have expected in a US-style establishment. I ate and left with no intention of repeating the experiment. The food had been pleasant enough, but I had got used to stronger meat. I was into reality, not expatriate fantasy.

By now I had also realised that all Nigerians did not necessarily conform to the popular conception of them in South Africa, the gist of which was that they were either crooks who have swindled you or crooks who haven't had the opportunity yet. I discovered this when I went to the Liberian embassy to get my visa. While I was waiting in the garden for the bureaucracy to go through the necessary motions – you would have thought it would take place like lightning, since people weren't exactly queueing to go there, or not legally, anyway – when a boy in his early teens came up to me, introduced himself as Patrick and said that he had heard from some people that I needed a bicycle mechanic.

I looked him up and down and quite honestly liked what I saw. He was obviously poor, but carried himself with an air of pride. He seemed to know a good deal about bicycles and even made a couple of what sounded like sensible suggestions about how the broken bearing problem could be repaired. Then he made me a proposal. He knew a good bicycle mechanic who lived about 5 km away. If I would give him my bike he would take it to the mechanic and return within an hour with a quote for fixing it.

It might sound difficult to believe, but I actually agreed to do just that, and off he went. I must admit that I started to experience a few qualms when I gave the matter further thought, but Patrick was back dead on time with a quote of 120 naira, which was the equivalent of about one US dollar. I was astounded, and asked him why it was so cheap. He grinned and replied: 'Nigeria gets everything cheap,' then explained that the mechanic was his friend. Still somewhat shocked, I gave him the 120 naira, plus a bit extra so that he could buy himself a cool drink and a snack on the return journey.

Off he went again and an hour later he returned, just as the Liberian bureaucracy finally creaked into motion and spat out my visa. I tried the bike; the cut-rate mechanic had done a great job, so that the pedals turned as smoothly as the day I first climbed into the saddle. I felt so good about my bike's rejuvenation that I tipped him 150 naira, a nice bit of change to judge by the broad smile on his face, and I would have cycled back if the embassy driver hadn't turned up just then. As we drove away I wished Patrick all the best: his spirit was the sort Africa needed to pull itself out of its doldrums.

I have another unforgettable memory of my time in Lagos, but not one as joyful as this. If you stay in another country for any length of time you end up sharing some of its hurts and joys. In my case it was the annual commemoration of the explosion of a huge arms cache in the suburb of Ikeja on 27 January 2002, when a fire, apparently oil-related, spread to a large military arms cache. The dump blew up with a blast which caused the deaths of more than 1 000 people – many of whom drowned while trying to flee across nearby rivers – and damaged buildings as much as 10 km away. The people remembered the tragedy with such intensity that they might have been on the spot themselves. The Mandela Hospital next door, they told me, had had to be evacuated after flying debris and fragments had totally destroyed the roof-tiles and windows.

As usual, the victims were mostly the poor and innocent. They died because of incompetence or negligence by the people in charge (and the wealthy who skimmed off so much money that should have gone elsewhere) in failing to secure something as dangerous as an ammunition dump. Nigeria earns a staggering amount from its oil, and it would have cost only a tiny fraction of a percent of this income to make sure that things like the explosion didn't and couldn't happen. Most Nigerians I spoke to felt the same way. Sad, sad, sad, sad!

On a lighter note, the SuperSport programme of South Africa's Multi-Choice satellite television service invited me along to the screening of the South Africa–Nigeria soccer match, one of the other guests being Aby Plaatjies, who had achieved some fame as the South African contender in the 'Big Brother Africa' television programme, and had just finished shooting a Nigerian film in the capital, Abuja. She told me in passing that she had received negative press and reactions at home in South Africa because of her supposed sexual antics while in the Big Brother house. OK, most of us would agree that she could have held out for those few short weeks, but we would also agree, I'm sure, that no one is perfect. She had beautiful skin, and I must say she came across as a very kind and charming girl. The only problem I had with her was that she told the audience at the end of South Africa's 4–0 drubbing that she actually supported Nigeria! But, before all those diehard Bafana Bafana supporters out there ask the question, I stood high and firm behind my team. Proud of the four-goal difference ... well, no. But proud of my country – yes.

The evening included some frank discussions with the Nigerian media which gave me an interesting 'other side' perspective on the world's widely held belief that Nigerian business people are corrupt. 'We know that the way money is sometimes made is considered illegal, but the genius it takes to implement these plans is what we must appluad,' one young man commented. Another one opined that 'at least our people aren't lazy and don't sit around all day begging. They risk everything to make a living for their families.'

This dodgy logic was a bit hard to swallow. Could it be that they really believed what they were saying? It seemed so. No wonder crookery was not only a Nigerian home industry but one of its best-known exports! Jeez, I thought, first their team beats us hollow, four–nil, and then on top of that this beer-swilling bunch of rationalisers expect me to agree to a proposition as ludicrous as this! Next thing they'll be asking for my soul. I felt sorry for the honest Nigerians like young Patrick. What chance did they have in a moral climate like this?

I was learning some other things, and not always via the obvious channels. The DSTV Multi-Choice MD in Nigeria, Willem Hattingh, taught me something about business, stress and life. Just turning 36, he was all alone in Lagos and faced with the fact that a powerful rival company had just started up in Nigeria. It was a big bundle of combined worries to hit anyone. But Willem Hattingh was more than calm. While we ate at a restaurant to celebrate his birthday, he outlined each problem – including his age – and how he would tackle it, all in a completely matter-of-fact way. I was impressed by his mental strength and inspired by it as well. In a way we were in the same boat, taking on big challenges alone and far from home. If he could face unpleasant facts as calmly as this and turn them to his advantage, so could I – Liberia or no Liberia.

And my time for facing *that* little problem was growing nearer. After almost a week in Lagos I had large bold ticks against all the items on my vital-to-do list. Liberia, here I came!

Johan and his perpetually cheerful driver took me back to where they had picked me up; from here I could cycle directly back the way we had come, through the chaos of Lagos and on to the Benin border, or head north and west, then over the border and down to Benin's capital of Porto Novo. I decided on the Porto Novo route, which was a bit longer but had the great advantage of allowing me to avoid chaotic Lagos.

By lunchtime I reached the border and left the vast human ocean of Nigeria behind to enter the country whose main claim to fame was that it was the birthplace of voodoo. The immigration guys were so pleasant that I made a mental note not to model dolls of them into which I could stick pins (I told you I was falling into local habits). Then I rode into Porto Novo, which lay right up against the border.

# CHAPTER 11

# INSIDE A PICTURE IN BENIN, TOGO AND GHANA

*I have a theory which I call 'being inside a picture', meaning sort of blending into whichever local scene you find yourself encountering, so that you become part of it and its flavour instead of being a foreign body looking on but not getting involved. We take photographs of a beautiful scene or a joyous crowd of people so that later on we can look back and revive our memories, but what we remember is what it was like to be there, looking at the scene. What I like to look at is a picture of a scene that I had actually gone into — joining the crowd, climbing the mountain or whatever. Those are the memories that stay the clearest for me.*

Benin is where you want to be if you are a cyclist. That was my conclusion early on in my visit, and nothing happened to change it. It was green and beautiful, like most of the rest of tropical Africa that I'd seen thus far, but the cherry on top was the importance placed on the allocation of freeway lanes for cyclists and scooter-riders.

My first good impression came right in Porto Novo itself, and things got even better from there on. Once I had passed Porto Novo's waterways I was astounded to come out on to a toll road with three lanes, one of which was meant for cyclists and scooter-riders and was barricaded to make sure motorists got the point. Now you will understand the glowing praise at the start of this chapter: after my fell battles with lousy roads and homicidal drivers it was like heaven.

The people of Benin were quite different as well, reserved and polite, and hospitable into the bargain, as I discovered when I set about finding a bed for the night in Cotonou, the national capital. This was contrary to my usual practice of looking around at the outskirts nearest my departure point, the reason being that otherwise it was sometimes difficult to get off to an early start because there were often so many interesting things and people to see in these West African towns that I would spend valuable road time wandering around and gawking.

I made an exception this time and tackled the first likely-looking person I came across. When I had explained my needs in the usual mixture of basic English and fractured French, he escorted me to a mid-range hotel which was on target as regards comfort but out of my normal price range. But I had a chat with the manager, and he gave me one of his 'budget' rooms for a huge discount. This meant that the room lacked some of the usual extras travellers expected, but it had everything I needed or wanted – a comfortable bug-free bed, plenty of warm water to sluice myself down with and a desk and chair where I could write up my somewhat neglected journal.

I made my next new acquaintance when I went out to have a sandwich and try the local beer, and fell into conversation with another diner. We talked about a lot of things, but particularly about a recent air disaster, when a Lebanese airliner had crashed just after take-off from Cotonou's airport, which I remembered hearing about in Libreville on Boxing Day.

This guy took me out to a beach west of the city where, he said, parts of the aircraft had washed up afterwards, and as we strolled along the inviting and now-undisturbed sands I remembered what I had thought that day: You don't know how lucky you are till you think about the pain and misfortune some people elsewhere are suffering. The people of Benin must have felt that way, too, because my new friend told me how disturbed and shocked everyone had been, although most of the victims were strangers. A disaster like that makes us all look at our own lives, and we don't always see the shapes we thought were there.

Getting away next morning proved to be a challenging task, for the usual reasons (oh, well, I had enjoyed a comfortable bed ... so comfortable to my jungle-hardened body, in fact, that I was only up and off an hour and half after sunrise). By that time Cotonou's streets were already alive and teeming with the characters that seem to be the essential fibre of any West African city's economy. The stall-owners were unpacking their fresh vegetables, while café workers were putting out wooden stools and side-tables for the growing number of early-morning customers, and this looked so inviting that I decided on the spot to have breakfast ... less than one kilometre from the hotel, and already I was getting side-tracked instead of heading purposefully for the freeway.

Ordering breakfast was simplicity itself. The customers were shouting for black coffee and bread in the orderly Benin fashion, so I simply pointed to what the people sitting to me were eating and added 's'il vous plaît', then sat back to enjoy that special buzz that seemed to infuse Cotonou's early-morning dive into the day's activities.

I have a theory which I call 'being inside a picture', meaning sort of blending into whichever local scene you find yourself encountering, so that you become part of it and its flavour instead of being a foreign body looking on but not getting involved. We take photographs of a beautiful scene or a joyous crowd of people so that later on we can look back and revive our memories, but what we remember is what it was like to be there, looking at the scene. What I like to look at is a picture of a scene that I had actually gone into – joining the crowd, climbing the mountain or whatever. Those are the memories that stay the clearest for me. People don't always understand this when I try explaining it, but that's how it is, and right now I was in the picture, in this Cotonou coffee shop, cheek by jowl with everyone from businessmen in their jackets and ties to petrol smugglers putting about on their scooters.

'Smugglers' is, perhaps, a bit harsh. Without wanting to sound like the Nigerian journalists I had just left, I think you could describe them more accurately as just businessmen who had adapted to their environment. Their scooters had large custom-made petrol tanks bulging out on either side, and what they used them for was to drive to the nearby Nigerian border, fill up with cheap fuel and then sell it in Benin after decanting it into suitable containers. Petrol was obviously not meant to be sold in this casual and somewhat dangerous way, but they weren't actually doing anything officially wrong, and the law left them alone. I couldn't help admiring the way that the artificially high petrol price, instead of being a damper, had given the spirit of free enterprise a new way of creating self-employment.

Things didn't get any better from the time-wasting point of view after I had finished breakfast and reluctantly dragged myself away from my observer's seat to continue my journey. That proved to be an entire task in itself. There seemed to be no end to the city, even with the help and advice of everyone I met in the process. They showed me which freeways to take and which off-ramps to avoid, while one milk-shop owner even stocked me up on one of my favourite foods, ice cream, in 100 ml sachets in three different flavours. Wow! For a moment I considered replacing my staple food of rice in favour of an ice cream-based diet.

I managed to break free finally, and must have covered about 30 km when I began to see indications that the concrete was about to start fading out. I didn't have time to worry about this, however, because I had just come across a prime distraction, heralded by a sign sticking out from behind a bush which simply announced 'Zoo'.

A zoo out here in the bush, apropos of nothing? Maybe 'zoo' meant something else in the Beninian idiom. Anyway, this I simply had to see. But it was a zoo, all right, a private one which had been founded about 40 years earlier by the current owner's grandfather, so he told me when I had made his acquaintance. It must have been quite attractive once upon a time, when its population had even included some lions. But now it was in a serious state of decline, and the lions were long gone. They had died about three years ago, he told me, because, as he put it, 'they did not have any more meat.'

He still had two large pythons, though, one of them over three metres long, which I eventually had wrapped around my neck. The python must have been very hungry or just plain irritable for some obscure serpentine reason, because when one of the attendants handed me the front part of the snake to hold he lunged at my face.

Not having embraced a snake this size before, I decided to hold him as gently as possible to keep him calm. That was a mistake, because as soon as I had laid him down on the back of my neck he half-slithered out of my grip and bared his open mouth and fangs 10 cm from my face. I decided to ditch any attempt at diplomacy and firmed up my grip on his neck (do snakes have necks?) quite considerably. My state of mind just then was none too calm, as I am reminded every time I see the look on my face in the video footage the zoo keeper took of my conversation with the python.

The saddest moment for me was to see the zoo's crocodiles. They were caged in concrete pens measuring about two metres by three, without a drop of water in evidence anywhere. I asked why this was and the owner said that they were given some once a week, so I invoked my visitor status and asked that the crocs get an immediate dose of their native element. The owner was amenable, and each crocodile got a shower-bath from a bucket. It was pitiable to see how eagerly they lurched up against the concrete sides of their pens, trying to get to the source of the water.

I cycled away feeling pretty sad, knowing that without an advocate like me they would go back to their once-a-week water treatment. It was the sort of place where I would happily have spent a few weeks to help to improve these and the other animals' living conditions, and simultaneously see if I could help the owner to get his zoo back on a more profitable basis. But I had places to go and a rough schedule to stick to, and so I said a mental goodbye to the forlorn little place.

Fortunately there were some wonderful surroundings to distract me. I'll always remember Benin for the beautiful lakes that seemed to surround me wherever I went. The lakes were dotted with picturesque little islands, some of which could not have been more than about 50 cm above the water's surface, but each carrying its share of identical square mud huts.

The lakes might have been beautiful, but they weren't tranquil. The islanders and people on shore made their living here, so there was constant traffic, from water taxis ferrying people back and forth to fishermen plying their trade in elongated dugouts. I admired the boat-handling skills of the fishermen because I knew from experience how difficult it was to keep a dugout stable and pointing in the desired direction. In Malawi a couple of years earlier I'd rented a dugout with which to row myself along the coastline of Lake Malawi, and the entertainment I provided for the folk at Nkhata Bay, my point of departure, must surely still be talked about today. But these fellows knew what they were about, and they cast their nets and hauled them in again without so much as a wobble. I remember one such lake in particular. It was late afternoon, and the sun's rays threw a wonderful golden-red light over the fishermen and reflected off the reeds that framed them on either side.

I ended my day's progress at a town named Grand Popo, more for sentimental reasons than anything else – it had a fine Mediterranean-style hotel named after Nelson Mandela. The hotel was far too expensive for me at the normal rates, but when the owner heard I was a South African he promptly offered to put me up for nothing.

My early stop gave me time to wander around, and in the centre of Grand Popo's only traffic circle I saw an impressive statue, dramatically silhouetted by the setting sun, depicting a slave with outstretched arms, broken shackles hanging from each wrist. It was a symbol of the dreaded trade in human flesh which was so integral a part of West Africa's history, and its eventual disappearance.

Slavery does not cast a dramatic shadow over my home country. It certainly existed, but no native peoples were ever enslaved, all slaves – a comparatively small number, compared to many other countries – being imported from the Far East and sometimes places like Mozambique and Madagascar, and by the time it was officially abolished in the 1830s imports had long since been stopped. But in Benin and some other parts of West Africa slavery was a dominating fact that affected all other aspects of daily life, with everybody involved in it, either as slaves or slavers. Huge numbers of tribespeople, mostly taken prisoner by their fellow-Africans, were brought in chains to the coast and shipped by American and other slave-traders to spend their lives as beasts of burden on the plantations. To forget about slavery would be to forget about a major part of Benin's history. That was the message of that statue, painted red by the dying sun as if dipped in the blood of the innocents who had passed through here.

Next morning I left Grand Popo and my kindly host behind, and within a matter of hours I was crossing over into Togo. Geographically Togo is a skinny little country, and its border with Ghana was only about 45 km – say two hours, more or less – from its border with Benin. There was something unadventurer-like about such a swift crossing of an entire country; I mean, you struggle for thousands of kilometres to reach the place, and when you get there you're almost afraid to blink in case you miss it altogether. It was a bit like that old comedy movie about production-line tourism, 'If It's Tuesday It Must Be Belgium'. So when I had passed through immigration at about 10 am I carried on down the main drag a little way till I reached the capital, Lomé, then stopped for an early lunch and took a stroll through the streets, which I enjoyed in spite of a strongish wind, locally known as the Harmattan.

Lomé is pleasantly situated, with a promenade well equipped with benches facing the sea, and seemed to be a very laid-back place, although it teemed with people riding cargo bicycles in all directions – presumably travelling to or from one or other delivery. One of them took time off to rest on a bench, and I photographed him, and when I looked at the photo later on I was surprised to see that the background looked blurred, as if the day had been misty. But it was dust that blurred the background, not mist, and it was only then that I realised how strong the wind must have been.

I recalled then that someone had told me about the Harmattan while I was still in Nigeria. At that time of the year very strong, very hot winds sweep seaward from the Sahara, bringing gigantic dust-clouds with them. Then when the dust reaches the coast it becomes heavier as its particles absorb moisture from the cooler and more humid coastal atmosphere, and settles to the ground. The early morning is a notoriously bad time when the wind blows, with visibility sometimes being cut to a few metres, as I saw myself. In my opinion (not the Togolese Tourism Board's, let me add) sufferers from asthma or hay fever would be well advised to make sure of their timing before visiting Togo, or they might have an uncomfortable time of it.

Having exhausted Lomé's attractions I got going again, although in slightly desultory fashion. I raced 15 km with a 60-year-old cargo cyclist I met along the road, pulled over just before the border town of Aflao to help some shore fishermen pull in their gigantic nets, and still managed to reach the border by 3 pm. Now that's the way to spend a day productively.

I didn't get across right away, because while I was grappling with the crowded chaos at the border I met some Togolese businessmen who had just returned from Ghana, and they insisted I have a meal with them before going any further. This turned out to be a very long affair and much more than a mere social occasion, because I discovered that they were personal friends of the Minister of the Interior of the Ivory Coast, into whose civil war I was scheduled to ride in the not-too-distant future. This minister, they said, was a former leader of the Ivorian rebels and also had many contacts within the even dodgier destination of Liberia. If I was going to tackle these two countries then it would be a very good idea to have him on my side, and they would personally inform him of my intended visit.

All this took some time, so that the immigration office was long closed by the time our extended lunch finally came to an end. I wasn't too upset, because it meant that I would have to spend the night in Togo like a good adventurer. It turned out to be quite a night, because my new friends introduced me to 'sodabe', a transparent, fuming palm wine which is West Africa's answer to jet fuel.

Sodabe is rough stuff that even the locals tend to avoid, although they like to watch foreigners give it a try. My first taste of it let me know instantly why people other than hopeless drunkards avoid it. It literally burns its way down your throat and then seems to continue right down into your toes. Your body tenses up, your features distort and uncontrollable shivers run up and down your spine. No wonder the locals enjoy watching a newcomer go head-to-head with sodabe – it's more fun than watching TV. And a modest amount of it, I need hardly say, will make you drunk, drunk, *drunk*.

All things considered, it was my good luck that I was able to wake up next morning, happy in the knowledge that I was still alive. But I wasn't in good shape to cycle 100 km – just the opposite, in fact – and so I arrived at the Ghanaian border post very late that morning. In spite of my near-terminal hangover, though, it was a most pleasant experience. Thank heavens for a Ghana on our continent. I knew things were going to be all right from the moment the immigration officials with their cultivated English accents extracted the necessary information from me and proceeded to electronically load me on to their data system.

I was so pleased, in fact, that to celebrate my smooth landing I temporarily abandoned my miserly ways when I stopped at the first service station I encountered, which looked a lot like the ones at home, about one kilometre into the country, and bought each of the three petrol jockeys a cool drink before treating myself to a Red Bull energy drink. This led to a conversation about how much Ghana was like South Africa and included a crash course on our national anthem, an explanation of what 'Bafana Bafana' meant and why Mark Williams doesn't have any front teeth. The jockeys must have thought I was babbling crazy, or perhaps they read between the lines and understood that I was yakking from chronic loneliness.

Then it was off again. The drink and conversation had brought me back quite a lot, but the after-effects of the sodabe were still working their malign magic. I had planned to cover considerable Ghanaian ground after crossing the border, 210 km in two days, but the process of reaping what I had sowed with my Togolese buddies forced me to halt for the day at the first town I came to, Akatsi, which meant that I had to cover 160 km the next day if I wanted to keep to my schedule.

I managed it, although not without effort, and so arrived at the capital, Accra. It was an intimidating city to approach, with the concrete freeway growing ever wider and busier as I came closer. Fortunately for me – and people planning to travel there by road in the near future, please take note – there was a Woolworths around the first corner. There was no debate in my head whether to go in there and ask for directions.

The manager, Karen, was a South African and probably one of the most connected people in Accra. In no time at all she was on the telephone, arranging TV interviews, $200 worth of sponsorship and a glitzy evening at a nearby five-star hotel. I protested feebly that I had nothing anywhere near formal to wear (or even clean clothing of any kind); but she simply told me to select an outfit which I could wear that evening. That was not the end of Karen's shower of largesse – while she was about it, she also arranged accommodation for me at the house of another South African, André.

André was a real character who, like Karen, seemed to know everybody in Accra, and among other things he took me to play some golf with a difference ... the difference being that the course had browns instead of greens, which, he said, was a common phenomenon in countries where water was scarce. Instead of a lush carpet of grass to putt on we had a compacted oily clay mixture that in some places was as hard as concrete; chipping directly onto the brown was something he advised me not to do – but only towards the end of our round. Whoever said that 'all's fair in love and war' should have added 'and golf'. That could have cost him dearly, because in the end it was my birdie and par on the 17th and 18th holes respectively that saved him a bet and some Ghanaian cash.

My stay in Accra wasn't all fun, however. The front wheel-bearings that had been fixed to run with such silky smoothness by my acquaintance Patrick's mechanic in Lagos had been giving me some trouble again, and thinking it was something fairly minor, I took up an offer by a friend of André's, an Australian who owned an engineering shop, to service my bike for me and also check for any non-obvious wear and tear. His telephone call to me was very direct. He said he had both good and bad news.

The bad news was that the main bearings were about to give in again. The ones that the Nigerian mechanic had put in were not the correct diameter, and to seat them firmly he had welded them on to the bicycle's frame. The only way to get these damaged bearings out, he said, was to cut a hole into the frame and then break them out with a heavy-duty chisel. But the good news, the Australian added, was that if he hadn't spotted the problem I would not have got much further, never mind reaching the Ivory Coast. I could see the logic of his argument, although I was disappointed. But strangely enough, I felt sorriest for my bike, and I mentally apologised when I went to fetch her – she really didn't deserve such treatment.

While in Accra I made the acquaintance of yet another good Samaritan whose good offices were to prove critically important during the rest of my trip. He was Mr James Baldwin, chairman of Multiport, an international shipping agencies network with a representative in nearly every port in the world, and he expressed his belief that his colleagues along the rest of Africa's coastline would be only too eager to assist me. Now, when the chairman of a company expresses a belief like that you can lay money on it that it's not just a vague expression of goodwill. As I left Accra I was extremely conscious once again of the fact that without meeting people like Karen, André, Mr Baldwin and many generous locals I would never have made it this far.

I also took with me the memory of something I had never seen before, a day-time swarming bat colony. Bats are shy, nocturnal creatures, or so I had always believed, but at one point while André was driving me around the city on a sightseeing tour he casually pointed to the sky above the city's main park and said 'Can you believe those are bats?' The answer was 'no'. Here were hundreds of bats circling above the park's trees. I was speechless for a moment. Bats are supposed to spend the daylight hours in dark caves, resting up for their night-time jaunts, not swarming around the sunlit sky while below them families are eating their picnic sandwiches and children are swooping back and forth on swings.

The Ghanaian coastline was very touristy, although not that busy for the time of year. But it wasn't all relaxing. I retain an unforgettable impression of visits to the old fortresses along the coast from where slaves were shipped away. In Cape Coast castle, the most famous or infamous of them, I sat in some of the dark, wet cells where they were kept before being herded on to the ships. Sometimes, I was told, they would be crammed in there for months, urinating, defecating and sometimes dying alongside one another, unable to move.

The museum was very informative and quite well preserved. The ballroom retained its original wooden floors, and it was easy to visualise scores of richly dressed men and women moving gracefully through the steps of a fashionable dance while down below the wretched slaves shivered and cried themselves to sleep.

As difficult to forget was the notice, still intact, inside the museum which announced an imminent slave auction. It gave the time, place and then, as though it was a sale of second-hand cars, the names of the slaves and their previous owners. What made it even worse was that the author of the notice made use of the excess space by advertising that rice, beans and sowing equipment would go on the block in addition to the slaves. If ever proof was needed that slaves were mere chattels, this was it.

The tour guide told me that the famous Louis 'Satchmo' Armstrong's great-grandparents had gone to America from Cape Coast. Whether this was true or not – I don't know how such a fact could be established – it really brought the fact of slavery home to me.

Ghana's salt plains were something I had not seen before either. Huge mounds of white salt were dotted alongside the road, with people and their donkey-carts taking small bites away at a time. A small thing that made a great impression on me was the motto I saw outside a modestly sized school in between the salt plains. 'Be Up And Doing'. That was typical of the Ghanaian approach to life. You could sit and rot or get up and live: the choice was yours. The message was that these salt-plain kids, all from poor homes, were taught not to feel sorry for themselves or expect people from outside always to do things for them. They were being taught the most valuable lesson in life, that you must rely on yourself and your own abilities.

Meanwhile I was making good time. The rebuilt main bearings were as smooth as silk again – for the right reason this time – so that I covered 150 km on each of two successive days after leaving Accra, the only delays coming from numerous punctures. Repairing them, I wondered how things would turn out in the Ivory Coast, the thirteenth country so far. Would it turn out to be a lucky number for me – or the reverse? There was only one way to find out, and that was to keep going. Which I did, with a mixture of anticipation and trepidation.

# CHAPTER 12

# IVORIAN ADVENTURES, CULINARY AND OTHERWISE

*You can't always choose your food, and here is a hard-won ad-*
*venturer's tip: don't think about the source of the meat, con-*
*centrate on the taste, texture or smell, whichever is the most*
*appealing to you. Part of life's adventure is to eat. If you eat*
*what you have eaten for 30 years, you are registering negatively*
*on the eating adventure scale. Eat whatever gets put before you*
*and you will set a new benchmark in your life — everything from*
*here on will be easier to consume.*

It might sound strange, but the Ivory Coast's greatest significance for me was not its civil war but the guts its rugby players had shown when trying to qualify for the 1995 World Cup, one of the great sporting events in my life. Like other rugby fans I remembered only too well the tragedy that befell Max Brito, the Ivorian wing, when he broke his neck in a game against Tonga during the tournament. I was hoping to meet with him when I reached Abidjan to offer my encouragement. Needless to say, I was hoping to steer clear of the civil war, about which I was not as confident as I might have led most to believe.

The venture into the Ivory Coast started well, with an easy passage through immigration, after which I headed into the hilly border region, sweating like a fountain in the extreme heat. The first living creature I met was a small yellow snake, which recklessly slithered into my path and, alas, not out again. The next was what looked like a yellow-billed kite, which followed me for more than

10 km, keeping pace with me so that for more than an hour its shadow travelled alongside mine. The third was a teenager, one of a small group of youngsters, carrying on his shoulder what I reckoned must be the biggest pineapple on earth.

It was a monstrous fruit, and when the youngsters saw me gaping at it they stopped, and one of them placed it on the ground in front of him; it was as large as a watermelon and the leaves reached all the way up to his groin. I wanted to take a photograph of this amazing sight (who would ever believe me at home if I couldn't produce some evidence?) but I was still jumpy about machinegun-wielding rebels appearing out of the surrounding bush, so I decided that the best thing would be to keep moving.

Eventually, though, I had to stop, because I had just about exhausted my supply of water, and I hailed a stationary truck-driver to ask for directions to the nearest source. He not only gave me detailed information but also presented me with a sachet of red-coloured ice, saying: 'Besab, besab, très bien!'

I had no idea what 'besab' was, but it was très bien, all right. Later I discovered that besab is a juice made from the flower of the hibiscus plant – the flower is boiled for a few hours, and a heavy dose of sugar is added to the resulting juice, which is then frozen in 100 ml or 200 ml sachets (presumably the freezing is done in Abidjan, since I saw no indication that the Ivory Coast had electricity till I got to the capital). As I went on I was to see similar sachets containing ginger and baobab drinks also being sold at the many roadside stalls, but the besab tasted so great that it partly displaced ice cream sachets as my staple refreshment.

Fuelled by besab and a disinclination for unfriendly encounters, I made good time to Abidjan, but I didn't arrive at the right time or the right place. My earnest advice is to organise your visit so that you don't ride in from the eastern side of the city on a bicycle during a public holiday. This is what I did, and it was a hair-raising essay into a world of anarchy – no lesser word would be adequate.

Cars were drag-racing on the main road, half-clothed youths hanging out of the windows in imminent peril of their lives and screaming at any of the pedestrians on the ragged verges who showed any signs of disapproval. You feel positively naked propelling a push-bike through this sort of situation ... man, I needed a sign from above to let me know things weren't going to get worse! And I got it, in the shape of the biggest traffic jam I had ever seen, with hundreds of revving, hooting cars blocking the freeway in both directions. Which just proves the wisdom of the old Chinese saying that you need to be careful about what you wish for.

When I had finally extricated myself from the traffic jam and got into Abidjan I found myself in an impressively big and sophisticated city. My first attempts to find a reasonably priced hotel in the more expensive part of the city yielded nothing except another day-time bat experience, featuring a colony about five times the size of the one I witnessed in Accra, in the sky above an area called Le Plateau. I also discovered that Abidjanians, unlike the residents of Accra, liked to eat their bats instead of just looking at them. I found this out when I stopped off at a petrol station and saw a young boy and one of the pump jockeys trying to shoot sleeping bats from the trees above us with a catapult. They weren't doing so well, so I offered my services as a marksman, since in my early youth I had been something of an expert at both catty-shooting and 'kleilat', which for those who don't know consists of flinging balls of clay with a flexible branch. My first couple of shots missed, but then I got my eye in and knocked one to the ground, where the pump jockey pounced on it, explaining to me that he was taking it home that evening for his family to eat. I hope they had something to eke it out with, since even a burly bat hasn't got much meat on it.

Then it was back to the search for accommodation, and I finally found a place in a district called Treichville, which the South African embassy staff later referred to as 'gangster land' when I told them about where I planned to lay my head. Well, sometimes it's a good thing to hear unfair criticism when you've already found it is unfair. I say this because while Treichville's denizens were certainly fairly unsophisticated and aggressive, they accepted me with kindness right from the start – starting first thing in the morning, when the owner of the mint tea stall outside the entrance would hail me with a badly mangled version of my name the moment I stepped out of my hotel.

Treichville also introduced me to new varieties of West African cuisine, namely rat and bat dishes. I can't say that in other circumstances I would ever have eaten either if I could have avoided them, but I was an adventurer, after all, and the fact is that there is a lot of truth in the saying that 'meat is meat and a man must eat'. These new departures didn't taste all that different from other forms of animal protein, and in any case I really was not tempted to eat the beef that was on sale on filthy tables at the street stalls. At least I *think* it was beef, but each chunk was covered in such a thick layer of bustling flies that I couldn't be sure.

In between sampling various types of squealers and swoopers I had a live telephone interview with the Supercycling programme of SATV's SuperSport. I must have sounded a bit odd, because it took place in an ancient telephone booth with a similarly aged telephone inside, the result being an echoing, doomy sort of voice that would have served well for dubbing a Dracula film.

I also found some much-needed technical help which provided me with a pleasant and unexpected bonus. Both of the bike's wheel-sprockets were showing considerable wear and needed replacing, and once again the local South African diplomats came up trumps. The embassy's Miss Naidoo knew of the best bike shop in Abidjan, called Rimco, and got my bicycle and myself there and back. Andreas and his brother, the proprietors of the Rimco Company, replaced not only the sprockets but also the chain, which – so I realised for the first time – had put in 9 000 km without any complaint, which was quite astounding. Their 'fee' for the work was a TV interview, and they not only offered to provide back-up for my entire stay in the Ivory Coast but also tried to set up a meeting with Max Brito, which unfortunately didn't pan out because it transpired that he was now living permanently in France for medical reasons.

Leaving Abidjan – courtesy of the giant freeway curling its way slowly out of the city – I learned something new about Ivorian cuisine: It was not just poor people who ate rats. A young guy was standing at the roadside, offering two large rodents, each at least

40 cm long, and he got a lot of interest from passing motorists, but the eventual buyer was a man in a suit driving a 500-series Mercedes. There was a quick transaction which ended with the rats being dropped on to the back seat, after which the suited type drove off, presumably to have his 'passengers' turned into an early lunch. Well, if it's socially acceptable for South Africans to eat uncooked sun-dried meat, dehydrated mopani caterpillars and bottom-feeding crayfish, then the same paradigm surely applies to a well-established Ivorian sinking his teeth into a juicy rat. At least it's been cooked first.

My general state of wellbeing didn't last long. I had only progressed a little way when my newly installed chain snapped. I gave Andreas a call and his driver came out to help me repair it. A few kilometres later the same thing happened. How ironic! For thousands of kilometres I had had no trouble with the old chain, and now a brand-new one had let me down twice within 15 km. Andreas's driver came out again and I made some more progress, but after having covered a total of 30 km I gave it up as a bad job and heeded Andreas's advice to turn back, sleep over for another night and make a fresh start next day. What a wasted effort! But at least I could now repair a broken chain with my eyes closed, which might prove useful knowledge on the journey ahead.

Next day I set out again, pedalling inland through hilly terrain towards the rebel-held city of Man in the north-west. The chain was working OK now, but that was the only good news – I was acutely aware of the fact that I was steadily working my way towards what Abidjanians regarded as a no-go area. Andreas had shown me a photograph of a government soldier whom the rebels had stripped naked, bound hand and foot and then killed, after which they had dumped the body on the verge of this very portion of the freeway to the north as a graphic warning to the government.

I don't know if the government took any notice of this gory message, but the image certainly kept returning to my mind as I travelled, and I found myself pondering the wisdom of what I was doing rather more frequently than usual. My planning at this stage called for me to reach Man in one piece, then make inquiries about the best route into and through Liberia.

That stage of my trek was worrying me more than I had cared to admit to Andreas or anyone else in Abidjan, and in fact I had tried to banish all thoughts of it temporarily because I didn't want to be visibly seized by anxiety and make everyone else nervous as well. But the facade of serene confidence was just that. Liberia was hovering around the edges of my thoughts all the time. It was such a pity that these two countries had been so devastated by war. The Ivory Coast is beautiful and naturally forested as far as you can see, while the people are kind, helpful and, above all, grateful for any tourism. But the war had turned their country from one of Africa's shining examples of peace and prosperity into a nation of despair.

There was much to see and distract me from my gloomy thoughts as I cycled along. I had plenty of company because bicycles are a popular means of transport in the Ivory Coast, and not just for carrying people, either. I passed a man and his son struggling along with a piece of bamboo at least eight metres long draped over the seat, and further along the assistant to a cattle-herder was pedalling along with an exhausted calf draped over his shoulders.

Something a little harder to swallow, so to speak, was the sight of dozens of head of cattle engaged in a nasty modern version of free-range grazing, the nourishment being not grass but a festering pile of processed plastics and rubbish. It was so uniquely horrible that I couldn't resist the temptation of filming it, in spite of a definitely threatening attitude exhibited by the cattle-herders. I got my shots and then pedalled on, trying not to think too much about what I had just seen. I mean, the chances were good that I would end up eating portions of one of those grazers in the near future.

I was really cracking along at this stage at the highest sustained level of effort so far. Although the terrain had lots of ups and down I was averaging 150 km a day, following a routine that I had worked out – start early, cover about 100 km by 1 pm, then spend the remaining five hours or so of travelling time comfortably cruising through the remaining stage. The only drawback was that the new toe-nails I had grown while staying over in Abidjan were giving painful warnings that they were on the way to coming loose as well.

The gods who watch over crazy cyclist-adventurers were kind enough to intervene on my behalf before I reached Man. Their messenger was a captain in charge of a company of United Nations troops I ran into just east of the city. 'Don't go any further north than the village of Duekoue,' he said, 'these guys will kill you for another bottle of beer. Stay away from here.' A gigantic Romanian officer who was also familiar with the general area was even blunter: 'You will die,' he said in thickly accented English. 'You must take aeroplane to Senegal.'

I appreciated their concern for me, but I had a problem with the well-meant advice; they were talking about an area about which they had general but no hands-on knowledge because they were not deployed there. So I thanked them with sincere gratitude but decided to ignore their warnings. Changing my route was out of the question at this stage, and the sooner I dealt with it the better.

As a symbolic, if rather premature, farewell to the Ivory Coast I had my last meal of roast monkey in the town of Blolekin. It was dictated by necessity rather than choice, because a deluge of fleeing Liberians had quadrupled Blolekin's population and led to a scarcity of many things, food included – not that an Ivorian would have seen anything strange about eating monkey meat, of course.

In normal circumstances I would have done some enquiries about the dishes on the menu before ordering, but just now I was beyond such finicky things. The first dusty little restaurant I saw – little more than a bunch of plastic chairs and tables on a tract of patchy grass, enclosed by a picket fence – instantly won a new customer simply by being there. I leaned my bicycle against the fence, took a chair, caught the friendly waitress's eye and got down to business with 'riz et sauce, s'il vous plaît'. This was a generic Ivorian dish, a blob of meat and bone on a bowl of rice with a topping of the ubiquitous pepper sauce. The meat could be virtually anything. 'Bush meat', as the Nigerians called it, was anything that had lost the war with the early-morning shotgun.

My mouth watered as the waitress brought me the bowl of fluffy rice with the meat on top. The rice, soaked in pepper sauce and the meat's juices, smelled irresistible, but because it was a bit hot I decided to start on the meat. It was well done and crispy on the outside, probably from being seared by the flames of the cooking fire, and I got down to it. Being a seasoned Ivorian gourmand by this time, I was not surprised to find that I had to remove two bits of thin nylon rope with which the chunks of meat had been strung together before roasting. But nylon rope wasn't the only foreign body lurking in the meat. I was chewing away enthusiastically in the reasonable but mistaken assumption that there were no further surprises in store for me when my teeth grated on something very hard. Investigation revealed that I had just bitten down on a shotgun pellet. I was a little more careful after that, and found two more, one of which I actually sucked out of a bone. When I told the waitress about it, she explained that the monkey had been shot that very morning and had had to be cooked very quickly for the lunchtime clientele. I suppose you don't get meat any fresher than that.

Suitably distended with rice and monkey meat, I hit the road again with distinctly mixed feelings: Liberia was getting closer with each push on the pedals. This was brought home to me in dramatic fashion a few kilometres from the border, when the tarmac I had enjoyed so far came to an abrupt end and launched me on to a slippery mud-and-clay track winding through the jungle. It was as though the Ivory Coast was saying to me: 'You're on your own now.'

In fact those were the exact words of farewell I got before crossing the line. They came from a young French officer at a military camp a few kilometres down the jungle track, so discreetly tucked away that I didn't see it till I came across a sandbagged bunker with a number of supply trucks and armoured vehicles behind it.

The soldier manning the bunker gestured for me to remain where I was and went off to find someone who could speak English. This turned out to be his platoon commander, who was relatively fluent, and his first question was: 'Where are you going?' He looked fairly puzzled, which was understandable in the circumstances. I told him, and he replied that if I went on I would be strictly on my own, because 'we do not go further than this point. It is too dangerous. We will rather have the criminals attack from where we can see them.'

'I will be very careful,' I said, which was pretty meaningless, since carefulness had nothing to do with it, but I wanted to get well away before he had time to change his mind about letting me go on. The die was cast now, and I didn't want the wind taken from my sails while I still had the resolution to propel myself into the hell-hole called Liberia. I wanted to be left alone so that I could get it over with. Naïve? Stubborn? Yes, and yes. But it was now or never.

I carried on, deeper and deeper into the jungle, feeling very lonely now and completely ignorant of when I would actually reach Liberian territory. I spent my final night on Ivorian soil at a little jungle village called Toulepleu, where I had a sort of dress rehearsal for what lay ahead.

I was parked in a plastic chair against the clay wall of a hut while the 12 village elders gathered around in a half-circle to inspect my passport and question me about where I had come from and where I was going – all this under the rapt gaze of everyone in the village barring newborn babies and the bedridden. I didn't resent any of it; living where they did, the process they were putting me through was not officiousness but simply a wise precaution.

In any case, when the elders had finished questioning me they deliberated among themselves and finally decided that I was no threat to anyone. Would I like to eat with them? Well, I certainly would and did, and when the inner man had been attended to they made sure I had a safe place to pitch my tent and sleep.

I got my head down that night knowing that Liberia was now only a stone's-throw away. I fell asleep hoping that nothing worse than stones was thrown at me in the next few days.

# CHAPTER 13

# LIBERIA ... AND THE WORST DAY OF MY LIFE

*How many people in the world have the privilege of knowing exactly when and how they will die? I knew what was going to be on my tombstone, if anyone ever knew where I was buried: Born 14 September 1973, died 26 February 2004. And at least I would die doing something extraordinary.*

My arrival at the Liberian border was not one of life's dramatic moments, contrary to what one might have expected. Africa's most notorious nation sort of crept up on me as I toiled along the rain-swamped road, not knowing when I was going to find signs that I had actually left Ivorian territory. Battling with the messy road might have been quite a bit of fun for a cross-country cyclist whose bike carried little besides its rider, but it was another matter in my case. So I slogged on, confident that sooner or later a recognisable border post – probably more battered than the worst of the ones I had experienced so far – would come into view.

Strangely enough, I wasn't nearly as nervous as I had thought I would be at reaching the point of no return. Perhaps it was the sheer relief of not having to anticipate the worst any more, or maybe I had just worried the thing to death. But there it was.

After a while the bumpy path slanted down towards a stream with a dubious-looking plank bridge over it, then curved sharply left and dived into the dense bush again. I had stopped darting constant fearful looks around a few hours ago and was concentrating on crossing the bridge, so it was quite a surprise to spot a little brick structure on the other side of the stream. It appeared that I had finally crossed the border – as represented by the stream – and arrived on Liberian soil.

There were no signs of life, and it struck me that perhaps Liberia's immigration control system, like most other aspects of its governance, had simply ceased to function as a result of the civil war. What did that mean for me in terms of the necessary formalities? *Were* there still any necessary formalities in Liberia, a collapsed state if ever there was one? Well, first things first. I devoted my energies to pushing the bike up the incline from the stream, the 'road' having turned into an eroded strip of rock and ditches which could not be ridden by anything except a hovercraft.

After I had gone a few metres, however, it became clear that the post was not devoid of human life after all. A short, stocky guy whose head sprouted a thicket of rigid dreadlocks came sauntering across the track in leisurely fashion and apparently caught sight of me out of the corner of his eye. He made a small, slow turn to get me into full view, but didn't seem at all perturbed or surprised; it was almost as if he had been expecting me.

Now the accumulated fears of the past few weeks returned in full force. He started talking before my adrenalin-level had started spiking, but he wasn't talking to me, which was all rather peculiar till I realised that he wasn't trying to communicate; he was engaged in attracting the attention of others in the building. Suddenly several heads sporting equally impressive hairstyles appeared in the building's one and only window.

I kept moving towards the building with a confident air which was not entirely counterfeit. I was in a ticklish situation, that was for sure, but it was not necessarily a worst-case scenario yet, like an uncontrollable mob hacking up or shooting any person in its path. I would apply the formula that had served me so well up to now (although with only partial success in Equatorial Guinea, admittedly) and see what happened.

Not that I had any illusions about the fact that I was on a distinctly sticky wicket. The owners of the heads, about 10 all told, had now come pouring out and had surrounded me, glaring in what was undoubtedly very unfriendly fashion. I gave them my patented peace-brothers-I'm-just-a-pilgrim smile and asked where the immigration office was. 'Dis is id,' they replied, and then the questions began, some of them almost incomprehensible because Liberians speak a creole of their own which is a jumble of West African pidgin and American English, spiced by hints of a Caribbean accent.

It's amusing to listen to when you hear someone like the comedian Chris Rock speaking this way, but it becomes very threatening when you have a bunch of aggressive young jungle men with crazy hairstyles barking at you at eyeball-to-eyeball range. On later reflection I had a certain understanding of their reaction. If you have spent most of your formative years involved in a country shattered by continual fighting and frequent bloody massacres, and then are suddenly confronted at the border by the first white man you've seen in at least half a decade, the question of who he is and what he is doing assumes great relevance. But just then I wasn't indulging in any reflection. My main focus was on talking my way out of the current predicament.

I decided that the best way to proceed was to stick to my original plan of treating these odd immigration officials just like any of the others I had encountered so far, although obviously more carefully. So I didn't answer them individually; I just kept repeating to the crowd in general that I was on my way to Sierra Leone and that I had heard all about Liberia but wanted to see it for myself. I also told them how far I had travelled and where I still intended to go.

This was risky, since there was always the chance that I would lose credibility because my plan to circumnavigate Africa by bicycle definitely sounded crazy to some people. It might have been my imagination, but it seemed to me that I could detect 'does this guy think we're stupid?' looks on some of the hostile faces surrounding me after I had finished talking about my plans.

After a while the interrogation became a bit more formal, so to speak, when they hustled me into the building – which was basically just one room – plonked me down in a chair and demanded to see all my documentation and also the contents of my bags. I complied, while simultaneously scoffing as humorously as I could at the more ridiculous suggestions and questions. I noticed now that there seemed to be some sort of hierarchy, in the shape of an older guy holding a tattered paper folder, although he didn't take part in the questioning, other than occasionally holding a muttered discussion with the chap sitting directly in front of me.

They didn't seem to know exactly what documents they were supposed to examine, although it appeared that some understood that my passport and visa were involved. I had no problem about showing them everything I had, knowing that both my passport and the visa from the Liberian Embassy were in good order, but I was very worried that they might confiscate both and then demand a big bribe for giving them back. I told myself that they were official government representatives, dreadlocks or no dreadlocks, and wouldn't risk their jobs, but I couldn't really convince myself, given the circumstances.

In the meantime the questions went on, with each man firing off his own in competition with his neighbours. The most frequent one was about whether I was armed. When I replied that I had no guns or any other weapons, they wanted to know how I would defend myself if I were attacked – a not unnatural question in a country where, in Mao Tse-Tung's words, power sprouted from the barrel of a gun. I finally settled this one by getting up and doing some fancy shadow-boxing. This impromptu entertainment distracted them into moving on to another topic, the validity of my passport and visa, the signature on the visa and the fact that I was a white South African being the main issues.

I answered these by flourishing my letter which stated that I was an 'ambassador' for the Proudly South African campaign. There is a world of difference between an ambassador for a buy-local initiative and a diplomat of the Department of Foreign Affairs, but I calculated that this crew of backvelders wouldn't realise that. I was right, and they were definitely impressed by the fact that my 'appointment' as ambassador was on a South African Embassy letterhead.

I made the most of this gap by explaining that as a South African ambassador it stood to reason that my documents would be in order, and invited them to contact the appropriate South African embassy if they wanted to confirm my status, legal or otherwise. Then I mentally held my breath. This was the make-or-break moment. If their intentions were absolutely lawless and they did not feel threatened by the thought of international reprisal, the odds that I would survive would be very bad. If they took heed of what I had said, on the other hand, I would have a chance of getting away.

To my intense relief it turned out to be make rather than break. They told me to re-pack my kit, and the older man set about processing my documents. This entailed producing a questionnaire on a worn sheet of A4 paper from the tattered folder and asking me a series of 'administrative' questions. When that had been done he set about the actual processing, which took place in Liberian style. Instead of putting an entry stamp in my passport he drew up a document such as I had never seen before (and I do not believe has been issued to any other long-distance cyclist). Essentially it was permission to enter Liberia which was issued not in the name of the virtually non-existent Liberian government but under the authority of the MODEL rebel group. I might just as well have saved myself the $50US I had coughed up at the Liberian Embassy in Lagos. Whatever those dilatory diplomats told themselves and others, their writ obviously did not extend to the outer marches of their country.

I wasted no time in getting away from the unofficial border post, even though I knew that what lay ahead might be even worse, but as it turned out, my next brush with unofficial officialdom was considerably more pleasant. This was at a place called Toe Town. Here I had to undergo another interrogation while sitting out in the open on a tattered red sofa under a spray-painted message reading 'Fuck Charles Taylor'. This was not exactly the sort of wall-decoration I had become accustomed to in other official offices, but at least I was left in no doubt as to their sentiments. My interrogators, who introduced themselves as 'the real guys in charge', were altogether smoother than the wild-haired backvelders at the border and understood the big picture; they were convinced that I was actually an international journalist and welcomed my presence in their country, calling out 'please write the truth' as I cycled off.

That was exactly what I intended to do, I thought to myself. The truth and nothing but the truth. And it was a horrible truth I saw around me as I headed for my next destination, Tapeta. As I cycled through the jungly countryside with its vivid red soil I came across scores of burnt-out and ransacked villages. One I remember particularly well had fully packed suitcases, riddled with bullet-holes, lying around everywhere; both inside and outside the clay-walled huts was a litter of discarded shoes, overturned bedsteads, abandoned toys and expended cartridge-cases, both AK-47 assault rifle and 9 mm pistol rounds, so many that sometimes my bicycle's tyres slipped on them. It was not difficult to imagine what had happened there.

It was beyond sadness, and I picked up a few of the cartridge-cases. In Liberia at the beginning of the new millennium these were the real tourist souvenirs. I knew they would always remind me of what I had seen.

I had been warned that Tapeta had been very thoroughly shelled, bombed and shot up, and so it was – a disaster, one might say, which had found a place to happen. But I wasn't complaining, because there was a dilapidated camp which operated under the auspices of the International Red Cross where I was able to spend the night. In Liberia, merely seeing the dawn without having your throat cut or worse was a victory, and I knew that I had only to survive another five or six nights before I could shake its blood-stained dust off my shoes.

I set off very early in the morning for the northern town of Ganta – I had decided that the earlier I left, the less risk I would expose myself to. Even so it was not a very pleasant ride. Every little town I passed through had a few vocally aggressive youths, screaming at me to stop and making derogatory racist remarks. Naturally I did nothing of the sort. Trying to look unconcerned – although my heartbeat invariably spiked – I carried straight on, shouting things like 'I'll come back, I promise. I'm late and I can't stop now,' and throwing in a few words of French for dramatic effect. I don't think anybody believed me, but it always created enough confusion among the ringleaders for me to make my escape.

All these unpleasant encounters, however, were merely the calm before the storm, and an hour into my day, about 15 km from Tapeta, I ran into the real hair-raising Liberia about which I had been warned.

I was traversing terrain which was both hilly and jungly, so that I couldn't see much of what lay immediately ahead. I remember following a long, curving descent, followed by an equally long climb which eventually brought me to a small plateau about 300 metres long. There I was surprised to find a small village of half a dozen huts, with a group of 15 or 20 teenaged boys sitting on stools outside the largest building. They had exaggerated hairstyles like my late interrogators at the border, and were playing some sort of board game while smoking something – I don't know what, all I can say is that they were shrouded in its fumes – from broken-off bottle necks.

I didn't like the look of them, and when they noticed me, which didn't take long, it was obvious from questions like 'Hey, white mudderfugger, whad da fug you doin' 'ere?' that they didn't much like the look of me either.

I didn't reply, just pasted on my smile (with some difficulty) and waved, trying not to make eye contact. This was partly to alleviate their aggression and partly, to be quite honest, because I was too scared of what I might see. It didn't work. 'Stop, stop, stop, stop!' they shouted. 'Stop or we shoot you, mudderfugger!'

I tried the 'I'll come back, I promise' gambit of earlier, my voice a little cracked with anxiety now. The only result was a rise in their decibel volume, and when I looked back to assess the situation I saw the younger boys sprinting after me, although the older ones still sprawled on their stools.

By now I was nearly through the village and could have outpaced them, but the hill was just ahead, and it seemed to me that I had two options. I could keep going and hope I could stay ahead going uphill, or I could confront them. Without thinking too much about it I chose the second and jumped off my bicycle, holding it between me and my rapidly approaching pursuers.

Within seconds they were all around me, glaring at me with

glazed eyes while they screamed more racist insults and laid violent hands on both my bicycle and myself. They grabbed the bike and threw it to one side, then tossed myself and my cap in the opposite direction. One of the boys gripped me by the shoulder and tried to drag me, but fortunately he was smaller than I was. I lowered my shoulder so that it was easier for him to drag me in the direction of the older gang members. This worked, and my bike was taken into the building while I ended up stretched out on the ground in front of the older boys. All of them were drugged to the eyeballs; I still didn't know what they were smoking, but it gave off an acrid smell which left a bad taste at the back of my throat.

What followed could hardly be described as an interrogation. I lay on the ground for about an hour while they fired garbled questions at me, then they dragged me across the road and into the larger building, which they said was their prison. There they threw me into a damp, musty, gloomy cell and the whole chaotic process began once again, while I unpacked my possessions for their scrutiny. The small wallet containing my petty cash soon vanished into the pocket of one of the boys, but my camera and cell phone were still hidden inside my bags, unseen by my interrogators in the gloom.

By this time some sort of hierarchical structure had begun to emerge. The leader of the gang, an older boy, sat to my right behind a medium-sized pine desk, shooting a stream of questions at me. The others made themselves comfortable on some feeble-looking bamboo benches to his right and directly in front of me, and subjected me to a barrage of shouted questions and suggestions about what they should do to me.

Some wanted to imprison me for my unspecified crimes, the general consensus being that I should sit behind their bars for a week. Others urged that I be forced to leave my bicycle and walk to the town of Grey, about 20 km away, and get a letter from their commander. Then when I returned they would let me reclaim my bike and continue on my journey.

I agreed to everything they were suggesting. 'Yes, sir,' I kept saying, 'I'll do that, sir.' It didn't pacify them. One boy in an oversized camouflage jacket who looked no older than about 12 demanded aggresively of me: 'Why you no stop when you see da uniform we wear? You can see we're da police.'

'I didn't see you, sir.' I said humbly. 'I didn't know you were the police. If I had known who you were I would have stopped, sir.' That slowed him down, but I was not out of the woods by a long shot. The strange thing about all this was that although the boys were armed to the teeth they didn't really threaten me with their AK-47s, which seemed more of a status symbol than anything else – or perhaps they had no ammunition for them. I was much more worried about the large hunting knives most of them seemed to have.

One of the taller older boys who was standing next to me had little to say but took to jabbing his knife into the wall within centimetres of my head, the point of the blade sinking deep into the soft clay. Heavily doped like the rest of them, he was swaying on his feet, and it seemed clear to me that before long he would misjudge one of his stabs and sink the knife into my head instead of the wall. In desperation I appealed to the leader behind his desk, but without much success; though the swaying guy moved slightly away he continued his manic activity.

I spent the next three hours or so answering their questions, usually the same ones which got the same answers. During this time I managed to get my anxiety under control, mainly because I was sure that only a relatively calm situation would get me anywhere, so that – or so I hoped – they would begin to regard me as friendly, which would vastly improve my chances of survival. But of course that isn't how hostage situations work, especially in Liberia. Some of them were becoming tired of all the talking and wanted some action. One boy in particular expressed loud discontent with the way things were going and made a suggestion that, I need hardly say, filled me with foreboding: 'Let's gut him, we're wasting our time. Let's kill him.'

This was the ultimate reality check. He and his mates were clearly not interested in what I was doing in Liberia. They weren't even interested in trying to scare the wits out of me. What they were interested in was murdering me. It was a dreadful moment as I faced up to the grim reality of my predicament. The truth hit me like a hammer. Control of my life had passed completely from my hands; I was totally powerless to influence what happened to me now, a mere pawn being tossed about in a sea of witless druggy argument.

I remember staring at the ground just in front of my feet and seeing in my mind's eye the sudden onslaught by this drug-addled pack of beasts in human form, the big knives ripping into my body, the slow and painful death I would suffer after they had disembowelled me. All my priorities – the entire way in which I viewed the world – changed instantly and forever. I am probably still unravelling some of the things I learnt about myself that day.

Nothing happened immediately, however, although the proponent of disembowelment was still rallying support for his proposal, and it looked as if he was gaining popular support ; the discussion about what to do with me and my body had reached an advanced stage.

At this point I was resigned to the fact that I was not going to make it out of there alive. Yet my eternal optimism wasn't quite dead. I actually found myself thinking that even in my current terrible situation I had something to be grateful for – how many people in the world have the privilege of knowing exactly when and how they will die? I knew what was going to be on my tombstone, if anyone ever knew where I was buried: Born 14 September 1973, died 26 February 2004. And at least I would die doing something extraordinary. But I also found myself having a silent personal conversation with God: Why would you let me come this far and then have me fail in this way? Am I supposed to learn a lesson here? Because if so, I don't know what it is.

My mind might have been working this way, but my body wasn't. The fight-or-flight instincts embedded in all of us since primeval times were revving at top speed. I had never before come even close to experiencing this level of fear, and the 'flight' part of those ancient physiological processes was in control. I remember how my legs trembled as I stood next to my bike, unpacking the last of my food supplies, my remaining reserves of machismo leaving me slightly embarrassed that my knees were physically shaking. I tried to make the trembling stop, and of course failed. It was as though I had had a nerve spasm; try as I might, the trembling just went on.

Then I had something of an epiphany as the 'fight' component suddenly overcame the other. This was not the way I was going to leave this world! If they decided to attack me, I would give them a fight such as they had never imagined. A sort of cold, clear rage seized me, and I started to wind myself up, both physically and mentally, for a struggle to the death.

I was very strong and fit after my long journey, and I had spent most of my life playing rough-and-tumble contact sports. They might win in the end, but I would make them pay in blood. I took note of who had knives and how sober they were, where the rifles were lying and which of the boys could reach them in time to do me harm. Now I began to gain confidence and in my head quickly war-gamed a short, bloody battle – one which I could win.

But now rescue came from an unlikely source. While I had stood there, trembling first in fear and then in fighting fury, the leader of the gang had found an old copy of *Time Magazine* among my confiscated documents with a flattering photograph of President Thabo Mbeki on the cover. Now, Mbeki has been accused by some critics of neglecting his citizens, but that day he certainly saved my bacon. The leader might have been totally wasted, but somehow the sight of Africa's leading statesman managed to ring a bell in his fogged skull. 'Tis my friend,' he said confidently. 'Tis my friend.'

It was pretty unlikely, of course, that Mr Mbeki had ever made the acquaintance of any ragged, doped-up teenage Liberian terrorists, since the only time he had ever visited Liberia had been when he called in at Monrovia in the north during the process of exiling the murderer-president Charles Taylor to Nigeria. No doubt the news of his visit had somehow trickled down to this remote village and become part of the leader's personal myth.

Instead of keeping my mouth shut, I nearly blew myself out of the water by remarking that Mbeki had never visited that part of Liberia. Talk about stupid! But I really wasn't thinking too clearly at the time, being as heavily revved up on adrenalin as he was on whatever he had been smoking. Instantly he was plunged into rage at my perceived disrespect in daring to say that and Mbeki were not, in fact, good buddies.

Fortunately my sanity came back in a rush; I pretended to re-examine the tattered copy of *Time* and recanted: 'Aaaah, now I remember! Mr Mbeki *did* come here. Of course you must know him. Please forgive my mistake.' Instantly the guy's rage vanished and he started laughing exuberantly, jabbing his finger at something on the cover. I took advantage of my new status as an FOT (Friend of Thabo's) to move up to the desk and see what he found so funny, and was mystified to find that apparently it was Mbeki's grizzled eyebrows and moustache.

Why these should amuse him so much was a total mystery – Mbeki's eyebrows and moustache, after all, are quite unexceptional – but I found myself cackling along with him. My reason wasn't connected with Mbeki's facial hair, however. In my slightly hysterical state there was something horribly hilarious about the fact that I was standing in a musty clay-walled hut in the middle of the Liberian jungle with a drugged-up rebel, laughing at an old magazine photograph of my country's head of state.

Then he stopped laughing as abruptly as he had started, which pretty much killed my own mirth stone-dead. Hastily I moved back to my bicycle to unpack the last few items on which I'd been holding back, including my cell phone and camera. The leader watched me in stony silence as I unpacked, as slowly as I could. Then without any preamble he said coldly: 'Go, before we kill you.'

Those were the magic words I had just about given up all hope of hearing, and I started hastily re-packing everything that was within reach. Those that were out of reach or being handled by the boys would simply have to stay. I nearly blew it again when I reached for a slightly crumpled but intact box of Jungle Oats which stood on the table, right in front of one of the grumpiest guys. I suppose I should have let it go, but oats are my favourite breakfast food so I leaned over the bike to retrieve the box. It didn't move, and then I noticed that Grumpy had clamped his thumb and index finger firmly around its lower corners.

Whether he, too, was a Jungle Oats fan or simply wanted some loot I didn't know, but I wasn't going to jeopardise my future health and happiness for the sake of a good breakfast, so I just shoved it into his hand and babbled: 'This is for you and your family.' Grumpy didn't bother to acknowledge my gift, but I was not offended. I had to get out of there very quickly before their minds wandered off at a more lethal tangent. I crammed in the last few items of kit and began pushing my bike towards the blessed bright sunlight of the doorway, bits and pieces of clothing hanging out of the bags.

Keeping my eyes fixed on the leader's, I forced my way past the few boys around the doorway, repeating: 'Thank you, thank you, thank you very much.' Then I was in the saddle and going like stink, my mind a misty blur though which faces watched me from doorways.

I love my country and I love my continent, but I'm not willing to give my life for either, I thought as I virtually bent the pedals getting to the top of the hill. No doubt some armchair critics might think that this is unpatriotic. Well, let them try an encounter like that before they shoot their mouths off. This had been, without doubt, the worst day in my life, a day which surpassed all my other personal bad moments rolled into one.

I didn't look back till I had crested the hill. There I stopped to catch my breath and also, I think, to reassure myself that all this had not been merely a sort of daytime nightmare. Having satisfied myself on this score, I let go a few expletives about the whole pack of them and then headed downhill, leaving the wretched cluster of huts behind me forever.

Then, inevitably, the delayed shock of my ghastly encounter set in. I didn't go to pieces; I just felt numb all over. Anyone in his right mind would have decided, then and there, that adventure was adventure but did not include travelling unarmed and alone through a country full of homicidal spaced-out lunatics. Instead I found myself calculating the speed I would have to maintain to reach my next destination, the village of Saclepie, before sunset, as if my hair-raising escape had been just a bad dream after all. What made it even worse was that I was aware of how strangely I was acting; I clearly remember asking myself what I thought I should be saying to myself. I couldn't decide, so I just kept asking myself this same question, over and over, as I headed for whatever horrors awaited me at Saclepie.

But Saclepie brought not more horror but, quite literally, salvation. When I got there a friendly local directed me to the office of the UNHCR (the United Nations High Commission for Refugees). I could not have landed in better hands. I don't know what would have happened to me if it had not been for the wonderfully understanding and caring staffers of the UNHCR. Their ministrations brought me back to some semblance of sanity and probably saved my life into the bargain. They calmed me down, gave me a place to sleep that night and called ahead, arranging accommodation and contacts along the route I was to take. Some organs of the UN might be useless and even counter-productive, but the UNHCR is not one of them, and what it does makes up for the failings of all the others.

My next stop was the town of Bhanga, where an entire brigade of Bangladeshi soldiers was stationed. Still badly traumatised, I rode like a fury to get there before dark, and I made it in good time, because the ratty clay road suddenly acquired a well-maintained tarmac surface which made it possible, with extreme effort, for me to average 27 km/h for the 120 km trip through the hills. I didn't stop anywhere except when it was absolutely necessary: as far as I was concerned, I was cycling for my life.

Often I would be chased by teenagers when I passed through one or other population centre, but I outpaced them every time, and the odd UN roadblock denoted temporary safety. My state of mind can be gauged from the fact that at every encounter like this I would feel my heart pounding, and any loud noise was enough to have me out of the saddle and pedalling away standing up, fatigue and bleeding toenails forgotten till I was alone again. There was no question of enjoying the countryside or ruminating about what I was doing. My thoughts had narrowed down to just one: *Get out of here. That's all you have to do. Just get out of here.*

The Bangladeshi soldiers at Bhanga were somewhat mind-blown to see a lone white man on a bicycle travelling through one of the most dangerous places in the world – the brigadier and his staff made no secret of their amazement that I had got through in one piece, since even the relatively quiet area around Bhanga was considered life-threatening – but once they had got over their amazement they were extremely hospitable. They served me with traditional Bangladeshi curry (made, they told me, by chefs flown in from home for the purpose) and treated me to a showing of the old James Bond film 'The Spy Who Loved Me' on a large plasma screen they had set up.

I got going very, very early next morning for the haul to Monrovia, and didn't begin running the usual gauntlet of pursuers and verbal abuse till about 8 am, by which time I had made considerable progress. The route was more heavily populated than it had been the previous day, but the atmosphere wasn't as tense, probably because the greater UN troop presence encouraged trouble-makers to keep their distance. I took no chances, however, and didn't stop even to fill up with water or eat. I was beginning to regain my mental equilibrium by now, and I noticed that the further I cycled the less nervous I became. I was also able to deal with the fact that this was how it was going to have to be for the next while if I was to make my circumnavigation a reality.

A pleasant surprise awaited me as I approached the outskirts of the badly battered capital, Monrovia, which I did with some trepidation. The driver of a UNHCR goods truck flagged me down, introduced himself as Phillip and said simply: 'They told me to look after you.' I was overwhelmed.

Phillip's instructions were to deliver me safe and sound to the UNHCR offices in Monrovia, but he suggested that on the way we call at his home in the local township so that I could meet his family and have a cup of tea. I accepted with alacrity, not only because a gallon or two of tea would be very welcome after my exertions but because I had recovered enough to begin looking forward to new experiences again, and the township – little more than a kilometre from where the fierce fighting of a few months before had raged – was the sort of place where a locally based foreigner would be unlikely to go.

Over tea Phillip and his friends shared stories about Liberia which told me something about why this small country, which had been founded with great hope and expectation by freed American slaves in the late nineteenth century, had been reduced to such a pitiable condition. One really gruesome story aptly illustrated the fear that had reigned under Charles Taylor. According to Phillip, it was well known that on one occasion Taylor had killed a cousin he suspected of betraying him, then cut the dead man's heart from his chest and taken a bite out of it. In other circumstances I would have tended to roll my eyes in disbelief, but this was Liberia, where any vileness was possible. Even if it was not true, I reflected, it was the sort of atrocity Taylor had made commonplace during his tenure.

Phillip offered to put me up at his home, but I declined with thanks – from a purely logistical point of view it made sense for me to be as near to the UNHCR offices as possible, because riding back and forth on my bike was obviously not an awfully safe option. It was the right decision, and I do not think the UNHCR chief of staff ever realised just how much he really did for me.

The accommodation – a large, luxurious flat, whose permanent residents were a Kenyan woman who shall remain nameless and a wonderful man from the Central African Republic called Guy Guernas – was wonderful, to be sure, but what was even more important was that I had some crucial down-time in which to decompress, clarify my jumbled-up thoughts and refocus my energy for what lay ahead – something very rare and precious amid the chaos of a city which had no government and little else.

My flatmates were an utter contrast to one another, and meeting them gave me much food for thought. Guy Guernas was a remarkable man to whom great personal suffering had brought not bitterness or disillusion but a huge personal commitment. It was both humbling and inspiring to hear the story of his life.

Thanks to the conflict in his own country, Guy had first-hand knowledge of what it felt like to be a refugee, and by the time I met him he was a veteran UNHCR worker who had served in a number of unwholesome places, starting with a voluntary return to the Congo–CAR border regions after his own escape to assist in conflict resolution. And make no mistake about it, that conflict wasn't just a case of two old ladies swinging their handbags at one another; making peace is often much more difficult and complicated than making war, and frequently just as dangerous. Later he was also deployed in Afghanistan, one of the most lethal environments in the world, where peace often means only a temporary state of non-war.

His very tough and frequently dangerous job had not robbed him of his sense of humour, however. When I told him of how some children in the Congo jungle had been struck dumb by the sight of their first white man (me), Guy capped it with an even better one about his first visit to Afghanistan. On landing there he asked to be taken for a quick drive through the affected areas. The UN vehicles were always well received, he said, and when his driver stopped at one spot the vehicle was immediately surrounded by hundreds of children. But the welcome only lasted till Guy got out to smell the environment and meet the people, as he put it.

To his astonishment the welcoming crowd was seized by panic as he straightened up after getting out. The children nearest the vehicle gaped at him in shock, frozen in their tracks, while others screamed in fear and trampled on their friends in a frantic effort to put as much distance between him and themselves as possible. The reason for all this was quite simple: these Afghan kids, products of a homeland which had remained remote from the world in spite of all the communication advances of the twentieth and twenty-first centuries, had never seen a black man before, and particularly a very dark one like Guy!

We had a good laugh about this, and I couldn't help remarking that he must have doubled his work-load just by getting out of the vehicle, considering the counselling and group therapy those Afghan kids probably needed after being introduced to the wider world in such a terrifying fashion.

I felt privileged to have met him. Guy was the best sort of UN representative – committed not to his own interests but to improving the lives of people who, as he knew from personal experience, had not had any choices in determining their lot. I really hope I'll meet him again one day, if only to restore the faith in simple human goodness that daily life tends to kick out of you.

The Kenyan woman, on the other hand, surprised and shocked me by complaining about the living conditions and the fact that she was being paid a daily allowance of only $80 US, over and above her huge salary. It was rather disgusting to listen to her. In my book $7 000 a month would be very good pay even in South Africa, where salaries are probably higher on average than anywhere else on the continent, and the $80-a-day living allowance was not too shabby either, considering what most things cost locally and the highly favourable rate of exchange for a stable currency like the US's. How could she talk like this when she knew at first hand of the dreadful suffering and deprivation all around her, not to mention in some other places in Africa? I was frankly embarrassed to hear a fellow-African taking such a selfish line.

Guy took me under his wing in no uncertain terms. He went out of his way to comfort me and strengthen my commitment to making my own bit of history, and also arranged interviews with CNN and Liberian radio (considering that Monrovia was literally a disaster area, I was amazed that it still had a functioning radio station).

For the television interview the cameraman and interviewer took me through the city to the recent hotspots. It was an eye-opener for me as I cycled past walls with most of the plaster shot off them, which tells you something of the number of bullets which must have been flying around. The famous Monrovia Bridge, the focus of the fiercest fighting between Charles Taylor's army and the LURD rebels from western Liberia, was even more of an eye-opener and brought home the close-up nature of the gun-battles; the very lamp-posts had been turned into a mangled metal maze. If I had been a member of either group I would have been able to stand at one end of the bridge and have my opponents in clear view at the other end. I couldn't help thinking about what the destruction would have been like if either side had had heavier weapons rather than small arms.

Apart from activities like these I was also in consultation with the UNHCR chief about the rest of my journey through Liberia. He told me that the UNHCR deemed the stretch from Monrovia to the Sierra Leone border to be even more dangerous than the route from which I had just emerged. This being the case, he and his staff insisted that I catch a ride to the border on a UNHCR vehicle. Since he was about to repatriate the first batch of refugees to return to Sierra Leone the timing would be perfect. How did I feel about that?

The answer was that I felt very good about it, for more than one reason. Firstly I would not have to cycle through a small stretch of countryside which was obviously deadly dangerous to man and beast alike. This contravened my basic principle of physically covering every centimetre of the route, but my recent encounter had underlined the old truth that you can't always get what you want, and I didn't want to appear to disrespect all that the UNHCR had done. Secondly, the Sierra Leonians were being sent home because Liberia was considered even more dangerous than where they had come from. Logically this meant that Sierra Leone could hardly be worse than Liberia (which turned out to be right, to a certain degree). That did a great deal for my peace of mind, such as it was; I had begun to dread entering a Liberian look-alike.

So I was about to start moving in the right direction again – and, I hoped, towards a more pleasant outcome. Well, time would tell.

# CHAPTER 14

# TALES OF HORROR IN SIERRA LEONE – AND A HERO FROM MY PAST

*There was something dream-like about it all. I had grown up in a fairly stable society where amputees were rarely seen. Here in this camp everything had been turned on its head, and I was the odd man out in a mini-society where an amputated limb and a tale of immense suffering was the norm.*

In spite of my traumatic experience I couldn't help feeling slightly guilty as I bumped towards the border with the UNHCR's truckful of repatriates. As a true adventurer, not to mention a lifelong rebel, I should have spurned their invitation and done the trip (25 minutes by truck, but naturally somewhat slower by bike) on my own two wheels. On the other hand I certainly wasn't consumed by my feelings of guilt, because I had to admit that my encounter with the young thugs had proved that I had very little real choice in the matter. But I didn't spend much time agonising about it. I was on the point of crossing over into Sierra Leone, and I had to stay focused on surviving *that* little jaunt.

Sierra Leone was in a pretty bad state, having recently emerged from a decade-long civil war which had only ended when a peacemaking contingent of 17 000 British and other troops had stopped the fighting and disarmed tens of thousands of guerrillas on both sides. But by then the infrastructure had been wrecked and about 50 000 people were dead, while large numbers of other Sierra Leonians had had their legs or arms chopped off by the rebels. Now the country needed large-scale reconstruction help, and that was only the start, because the poverty, tribal rivalry and official corruption which had caused the war hadn't gone away in the meantime. To make matters worse something like 70 000 allegedly rehabilitated former combatants had been pumped into the job market, or perhaps 'jobless market' would be more accurate.

It was all such a great pity. Sierra Leone has quite a small population – about 5.5 million – and it could be quite prosperous because it is rich in diamonds and used to export rutile, cocoa, coffee and fish as well. But right now the average *annual* income, I had read, was about $220 US, and the average life-expectancy a miserable 39 years.

And here I was, preparing to cycle through this shot-up country where a lot of weapons were still in circulation and a good many people had yet to give up all those bad habits they had picked up during the civil war. It certainly seemed a lunatic enterprise as I pushed my bicycle over the bridge under the incredulous stares of both the repatriates and the officials processing their documents.

An immigration official pretty much spoke for all of them when I finally shuffled up to his shelter of withered banana leaves and handed him my documents. 'What are you going to do in Sierra Leone?' he asked, stopped as if he couldn't get his final words out and then added: 'On a *bicycle?*' It was not an official question, so to speak. He was just trying to get a hold on the mind of a man who would tackle such a bizarre enterprise.

I can't remember what I replied, but it must have sounded pretty lame, because I was beginning to wonder myself. So I did the only thing I could and got going. And the going wasn't easy. I had been warned that the first few hundred kilometres from the border consisted of jungle tracks which were almost impassable in the rainy weather. That was perfectly true, and I was glad to reach my first destination, the town of Zimmi, muddy and wiped out but in one piece.

I looked up the regional UNHCR chief, Igor Sotizovic, and he put me up for the night at the organisation's guest house. Next morning I got off to an early start after being given two valuable gifts by Igor. One was the 'Lonely Planet' guide for West Africa and the other, which turned out to be literally a life-saver, was an official UNHCR cap. Igor knew that, strictly speaking, it was against the rules for me to wear the cap, but he realised very well that I might end up in a desperate situation in which the cap might give an assailant pause before knocking me off.

The people I encountered seemed low-spirited and unenthusiastic, and the general vibe was pretty bad. One could say its main ingredient was tension, but that would not be quite accurate. It was more a sort of desperate 'enough is enough' feeling. The only exceptions were the children, who, like children everywhere, were unfettered by adult fears for the future and managed to have a little fun. In several towns they formed a sort of impromptu welcome committee as I passed through, shouting 'Pakistan, Pakistan, Pakistan!' It took me a while to realise that they were referring to the UN Pakistani troops based in the area, who must have been the only non-black foreigners they had ever seen in their short young lives.

I made it to Bo, Sierra Leone's second-largest city, and with my usual luck met up with an American UN staffer who kindly offered me a bed at a house she shared with some others, and then – which was just as good for me – allowed me to switch the DSTV cable decoder to channel 21 for the entire Saturday so that I could gorge myself watching rugby matches. I wasn't a fan of any of the teams involved, but watching rugby was one of the things I had really missed on my trip. Somehow the games made me feel good about myself and also about my country, and reinforced my resolve to do the rest of the trip as I'd done it up to now – on my own terms.

But the UN staffer's unmotivated attitude towards her job was shocking. The UN's most valuable resource should be a corps of staffers who succeed at what they tackle – or perhaps just manage to make a dent, which is sometimes the best one can achieve, and a lot better than nothing – because they have a personal attitude which does not depend on the resources at hand but on a 'can do' spirit. I didn't see any of that here; to be honest, her salary was wasted money. I reflected that with what she was taking home I could have had three South African girls doing five times as much. In fact, I think the UN should recruit more South African girls for community work in places like Sierra Leone. If South African women of all races have proved anything, it is that they don't shrink from poverty and suffering, and have the mental toughness to get down and do what is necessary, by hook or by crook.

Leaving Bo, I inadvertently set off what would prove to be an amazing chain of events when I cycled past the offices of a security firm called Grey Security, a well-known name in South Africa. Never one to miss taking a gap if I came across one, I stopped in and was told by the man in charge that Grey's national manager, in the capital of Freetown, was a South African named Julius Lloyd. I telephoned him right away and he was very friendly, inviting me to contact him when I eventually got to Freetown. I promised I would, meaning every word of it. Sierra Leone being what it was, being in the bosom of a large security company was about as safe a lodging as I would get anywhere in Freetown.

I spent that night at a town with the odd name of Mile 91, where another Pakistani brigade was based. The Pakistanis were more reserved people than, say, the Bangladeshis, but they gave me a meal and a bed, and they warmed up considerably when I started talking about some of South Africa's more famous cricketers. Long live cricket! It has certainly proved one of the long-gone British Empire's most durable exports.

I remember one thing in particular about Mile 91 and its hospitable Pakistanis. As I cycled out of the camp next morning I went past a sign in the UN colours of light blue and white, reading: 'Show me a good mother and I'll show you a good nation'. That just about said it all, and I thought about the old saying that the hand that rocks the cradle rules the world.

In spite of the ghastly image created by the fighters in the civil war – one can hardly call them 'soldiers', which implies discipline and restraint – the Sierra Leonians I met as I travelled further were generally kind and helpful people, always ready to engage with me on a friendly level. One cyclist I met on the road the day after leaving Mile 91 was so willing to help me in taking some video footage that he climbed high up into a tree to get the perfect shot of me pedalling past, although it took about 20 takes before we ended up with a shot that wasn't all just fingers, leaves and flies.

At the town of Masiaka, about 75 km from Freetown, the road split into two separate directions, one heading north to Guinea, my next national destination, and the other continuing westwards to the capital. There seemed no reason to cycle to Freetown when I planned to head north, so I arranged with the friendly staffers of an organisation called War Child to baby-sit my bike and headed west in a crowded (naturally!) taxi truck.

When Freetown hove into sight I was charmed. It was the prettiest city I'd seen, snuggled away in dense foliage and ranges of hills that came to an abrupt end in long, lovely beaches running into a turquoise sea. If this had been in South Africa it would have competed with Cape Town as the Number One tourist destination. That was from a distance of course; closer in the scars of the recent past were all too painfully visible, and it was a case of 'might have been' or, God willing, 'what might be again'.

The truck dropped me off at Freetown's central taxi rank and I caught another taxi (also crowded, needless to say) into the city to meet Julius Lloyd. It was an interesting excursion, to say the least, not just because of the obvious scars left everywhere by the war but also because of the way the other passengers reacted to me. Surprise at seeing a lone white man sitting so casually among them instead of tooling around in a fancy official vehicle was the common reaction, and some asked me what I was doing there, to which I replied that I was just a tourist. No doubt some of them found this a bit hard to swallow. Why should a tourist want to come to Freetown?

One of them, a one-legged guy on crutches who introduced himself as Jacob, was so intent on making more space that his stump ended up in my lap, which didn't seem to bother him, to judge from his broad smile and easy manner of chatting. He gave me to understand that he was the victim of a rebel attack on his home village, but I didn't ask for details – who was I to stir up obviously painful memories? When he heard I intended to visit the local UNHCR office in Monrovia he almost exploded with excitement. 'Please go visit my friend Mohamed and tell him I say hello,' he said. 'He is the mechanic there.'

The heavily guarded UNHCR office was on the main road and far easier to get to than Julius Lloyd's, so I made it my first stop. There I was met by the human resources officer, an extremely attractive Kenyan woman had heard about me and immediately arranged accommodation for the night at the UNHCR guest house.

I checked in with gratitude and then decided to go out to look at my surroundings and find something to eat. This provided a little more excitement than I had bargained for. I wandered into a definitely dilapidated area and then found myself sprinting in the general direction of the UNHCR building, chased by a group of aggressive young men who were shouting things like 'Stop, you white fugger, stop!' and 'This is our country and you'll do what we say!' Not bloody likely!

I suppose it looked rather hilarious in a terrifying way, and the other pedestrians had a good laugh as I tore past them, no doubt with eyes like saucers, coming close to taking a dive from time to time as I negotiated the uneven road-surface. I didn't become disorientated because I had planned to go on to the UNHCR building anyway, and before long I arrived, gasping for air, at the road which went directly past it. I summoned up my last reserves of oxygen and before long arrived at the front gate. Phew! My Kenyan lady friend was horrified by my narrow shave, arranged for one of the staffers to give me a lift back to the guest house and earnestly counselled me against taking any further strolls. She needn't have bothered; one dash for life was quite enough.

I had two people to meet the following morning: the kindly Julius Lloyd from Grey Security and Jacob's friend, Mohamed the mechanic. I arranged to link up with Mohamed at the UNHCR canteen, little knowing that our meeting would ultimately introduce me to the full horror of Sierra Leone's suffering.

In due course he came energetically bustling in, in spite of the fact that like his friend he was on crutches and missing one leg above the knee. He introduced himself with a white-toothed smile that was every bit as broad as Jacob's and joined me for some tea and buttered bread while I explained who I was and how I had met Jacob. He seemed quite laid back, so I took a chance and asked him straight out how he had lost his leg. Two one-legged bosom friends! There had to be a story there.

Mohamed didn't take umbrage. 'Me and Jacob were together that time, did he tell you?' he asked.

'No, what happened?' I said. And quite calmly, in between bites of bread and sips of tea, Mohamed told me a story of cold-blooded human cruelty so ghastly that I could scarcely believe what I was hearing.

Their village, he said, had been occupied by a group of rebels, well hyped up on drugs, who then proceeded to have their way with both the inhabitants and their property in the time-honoured way of brigands. Jacob and Mohamed had protested about what the rebels were doing, and for their pains the rebels put them up against a big tree and shot their legs off. This was a specific punishment for temerity and disobedience, Mohamed added; in other cases the rebels systematically chopped off the limbs of innocents because, as they liked to explain with gruesome humour, they didn't have money for visiting cards. So they would lop off some arms and legs in a village as evidence that they had come calling.

When I got my voice back I told Mohamed about what had happened to me in Liberia. I realised that, traumatic as it had been for me at the time, it paled into insignificance when compared to his story, and so when he asked if I would be willing to give a talk about my (mis)adventures in Liberia at the UN camp for amputees in Freetown I was more than happy to oblige. We made a date for the following day and Mohamed arranged through his network of UN drivers for me to be dropped off right outside the Grey Security front door.

Julius Lloyd was out, but his wife, who doubled as his receptionist, told me he would be back soon. 'Soon' turned out to mean about an hour and a half, which the two of us passed pleasantly in conversation and consuming coffee – far too much of it in my case. Then he walked in, and my jaw dropped nearly to the floor. Up to this moment I had regarded him as nothing more than the friendly Grey Security manager in Freetown, but when I laid eyes on him I realised who he really was, and an indelible memory of part of my early life came rushing back.

When I was an 18-year-old boy in 44 Parachute Brigade during the dying days of national military service, one of my officers had been Major Julius Lloyd of the Special Forces, a living legend and everyone's model of a good soldier, the sort of man you would definitely want next to you when the bullets were flying. And here, 12 years later, we were meeting again – in Freetown, of all places! To say I was astounded is putting it mildly.

Old habits die hard, and I said: 'Major Lloyd!' The 12 years that had passed since our last meeting might have been 12 seconds. That's the way it is in the army, especially in the paratroops, where real respect must be earned the hard way, and as a good South African boy I had been raised to respect my elders in any case. Julius did not live in the past, however, and told me to call him by his name. Which I did, but I can tell you it took some doing; every ex-soldier will know what I'm talking about.

But although Julius had moved on from the army days he had not forgotten the cardinal principle that an officer looks after his troops first before attending to his own needs, and he and his wife implemented the principle right away by insisting I stay with them for as long as I was in Freetown. I was only too glad to accept, not just because it was great meeting my old hero so unexpectedly but also because I reckoned this would be about the safest place to lay my head in all of Sierra Leone.

The Lloyds then set out to show me around. They took me to dinner at a restaurant called Alex's which was wildly popular with all the UN workers for its great food, showing me the famous beach of Lumley on the way. This was really something to see. The beach seemed to stretch to infinity, and the setting sun turned it into an animated postcard – although I would have had to 'photoshop' out the hundreds of UN luxury 4x4s to get some feeling of tranquillity. It became clear to me that Freetown only had a functioning economy because of the millions of dollars the UN's resident workers spent there every month. This sounds like another instance of the UN wasting money, but on the other hand I suppose it was an essential, if unintended, part of the reconstruction process.

That was only the start of Julius's kindness. But more of that later. I had an appointment at the UNHCR canteen next morning with Mohamed, who would take me to the amputee camp for my talk. I wasn't sure of what to expect as I sat there waiting for him. Should I be nervous? Would they be hostile? Then Mohamed arrived and we set off, and I soon found out what I had headed into: the most heart-rending experience of my entire life.

Needless to say there were amputees everywhere – people of all ages, the stumps of their arms and legs wiggling around as they went about their daily tasks, and young children missing hands or forearms scurrying around behind me, inquisitive about their visitor but shyly hiding behind walls of plastic sheeting when I looked at them. In the meeting area I was introduced to many of the amputees. Women who had just finished doing their washing bounced across to me on one leg to shake my hand; those who had no hands extended the stumps of their arms.

There was something dream-like about it all. I had grown up in a fairly stable society where amputees were rarely seen. Here in this camp everything had been turned on its head, and I was the odd man out in a mini-society where an amputated limb and a tale of immense suffering was the norm.

The most heart-rending sight of all was a young woman named Miriam with a baby about a year old holstered on her hip: a normal enough thing, except that the baby's right arm ended at the elbow. That was shocking enough, but the story she told me while calmly playing with her baby was even worse.

Drug-crazed youths armed with pangas and guns had occupied her village in the middle of the night and selected a group of the inhabitants, who were taken one by one into a hut. There each would be offered the options of 'a short sleeve or a long sleeve', indicating where the victim's arm would be chopped off.

Miriam was one of those selected for amputation, and soon it was her turn. She was dragged into the hut, and she still remembered how brightly the candles had seemed to reflect off the men's faces as she pleaded desperately for mercy. 'I have a 6-month-old baby,' she told the rebel commander as he lounged in a chair and watched the torturing. 'I don't have a job, and I can barely feed her.'

He listened in arrogant ease as she stumbled through her plea, then replied: 'I understand. We won't harm you.' But Miriam's relief was short-lived. As he finished he nodded to a rebel standing on her right, who grabbed her little daughter, threw the tiny child on the table and chopped off her arm.

Then it was time for my talk. I started off barely knowing what to say to these innocent victims of a country that had gone mad. Then I warmed to my task, and all the pent-up emotion spilled out of me. They responded with an outpouring of their own feeling, applauding me by clapping or drumming on the tables with their stumps if they did not have two hands to clap with.

My eyes filled with tears. My sufferings to get this far were pinpricks in comparison with what even the most fortunate of them had gone through. Yet they understood what I was trying to do and they were applauding *me*! It was one of the real defining moments in my life, and I felt a new rush of determination to complete my journey and spread my message; even more determined, in fact, than I had been on the very first day of my journey.

Julius continued to look after his one-time soldier in the most generous way. He gave me $400 out of his own pocket, then went even further by calling his friend James, CEO of Celtel, Sierra Leone's largest cell phone company, and telling him all about me. James promptly gave me a whopping $1 000 – big, big money in Africa. I was rich! I had been anticipating some fairly heavy expenses at Dakar in Senegal, a couple of countries up the line, where I would have to have my bicycle serviced and, no doubt, repaired for the slog ahead. Now all I had to do was get there, and Julius's and James's generosity would take care of all conceivable expenses I might incur.

I didn't take any extreme precautions in hiding the money, just stuck it in the lower side-pocket of my everyday pants. This probably sounds a little crazy, but as far as I was concerned it made sense. I might be called on to unpack my bicycle, as had been the case on so many occasions up to now, but unless I was body-searched the cash would be safe So all I had to do was make sure that I *wasn't* body-searched – and if I was, I would have to take all desperate measures to make sure I wasn't parted from my boodle.

Julius went even further in helping me. In his opinion a lone traveller in these parts needed something a little more decisive than guts and a pocketful of money, and he called another friend, who supplied me with a powerful electric stun gun, complete with a graphic demonstration of how to use it, with my body as a living target (no, he didn't switch it on, so I had to take his word about the effects). The best place to ram the stun gun into before letting it crackle, he advised, was your opponent's solar plexus – 'that will bring an elephant down'.

I was grateful for both the gift and the advice, although I knew that in some situations only a near-miracle or an act of God would help. For example, would the stun gun have helped me in my encounter with the Liberian thugs? Definitely not, I thought. They would have used it on parts of my body I dare not imagine. But Heaven help any elephant, camel or other large quadruped which might feel like walking over my tent from now on. If I wasn't squashed flat in the first few seconds I would see that he had sparks dancing over his belly-button in short order.

I left Freetown with slight reluctance – that might sound funny, but the kindness and intensity of emotion I had experienced there surpassed anything I had felt up to this stage – and caught a ride back to Masiaka. There I collected my bike from the War Child office, thanked the staffers for their help and set off on the north road, raging fires on the mountain ranges bidding me a fiery farewell. I bore down on the pedals: I would have to get a move on if I wanted to reach the Guinean border post at Pamelap the following afternoon.

# CHAPTER 15

# A PUNCH-UP IN GUINEA, AND A SEA VOYAGE TO GUINEA-BISSAU

*I burst through the struggling bodies and snatched the Qur'an just before it hit the floor, then stuck it under my arm and tried to shield Iqbal as he was unceremoniously slung out. Our ejection hadn't ended the fight, however. Iqbal was now penned with his back to the car while the youngsters crowded up close, gesticulating wildly and gabbling what I assumed were blood-curdling threats.*

I didn't expect too much of Guinea, but it proved still to be trundling along in spite of the experts' dire predictions that it would lapse into civil war or stop functioning altogether. The bottom line was that I had not landed in another hornet's nest like Liberia or Sierra Leone, so I could afford to catch my breath and do a bit of pondering before setting off into the relative unknown. The fact was that for me, entering Guinea involved more than just crossing yet another international border. As I rode into the border town of Forécariah I realised that the time had come for me to pause and reflect on the madness I had just lived through, to think about my journey in general and especially to compare what I had initially had in mind with what had actually happened so far, which had turned out to be something very different.

I had not underestimated the physical challenges and so I had not been dismayed at any stage to the point of actually wanting to give up, no matter how hard things had been. But the emotional demands of the kaleidoscope of new experiences – some good, some very bad – had turned out to be a far cry from what I had expected. In the past month I had probably learnt more about myself and human nature in general than I would have picked up in a decade of 'normal' life; my experiences in Liberia and Sierra Leone in particular had permanently changed my entire view of life, and I was determined to share those experiences and new perspectives with other people when the time came.

This western edge of Africa had been a great taskmaster in my education about the real world. Culturally it is unique, a crazy, constantly changing jigsaw puzzle of peoples, languages, religions and lifestyles that seems to bring something new every 50 km or so, with the result that it becomes very difficult for West Africans to understand what makes others tick – not just people from other nations but often their fellow-countrymen.

My struggle with the various languages was a good example, I realised as I paused on the threshold of Guinea. By the mere act of crossing an invisible line I had emerged from a country whose people spoke pidgin English and arrived in one where the main language was French (pidgin French? I couldn't tell). In a few days' time I would cross another dotted line on the map and find myself in a society where the official language was Spanish. And this was not to mention the multitude of indigenous tongues spoken by people whom the colonial and post-colonial eras had touched but lightly.

The confusion and opportunities for trouble-making afforded by this patchwork quilt can be imagined. People can be fed with any amount of propaganda about their allegedly hostile neighbours, or even their fellow-countrymen, and every clod of verbal mud will stick because they are not able – or sometimes even willing – to investigate such claims for themselves. In this regard I couldn't help thinking about how often inhabitants of one country had warned me about the allegedly hostile, unreasonable and intractable nature of the people I was going to meet on the other side, warnings which had almost always turned out to be inaccurate. Different countries certainly had different national characteristics, but that was another matter altogether.

It had just happened again, with Sierra Leonians – themselves barely emerged from one of the cruellest, most atrocity-ridden civil wars in modern African history – telling me to be careful of the Guineans, whom they regarded as the most vicious people on earth, although why this should be so was not clear (needless to say they weren't worse than anywhere else). Now, combine this vast volume of misapprehension with a general lack of education, and continual squabbles are almost inevitable by-products.

It seemed to me that the only solution would be to evolve a universally understood sign language (such as the basic one my circumstances had forced me to evolve), which would not only be highly diverting but would also get the job done. I didn't intend to hold my breath waiting for it to happen, though – I knew it was just one of those bright ideas whose time to be born was still far off, if it was even on the radar at all.

Once again I had a choice of two roads, one heading north and the other going west to the capital, Conakry, 35 km away. My route planning called for me to take the road to the north, but I needed to visit Conakry to send and receive some e-mails. One of them would be my latest newspaper despatch, whose deadline was looming; I had lots of good material, and writing about my experiences would help me to live with my ghastly recent memories.

I looked around for a place where I could safely stash my bicycle while I went off to Conakry and eventually found one at a teleboutique owned by Iqbal, a friendly middle-aged fellow in a loud shirt. He was planning a visit to Conakry himself, and not only got me a lift to the capital that very evening but promised to give me a lift back.

I spent just a day and a half at Conakry, almost every minute of it filled with action. The first thing I did was contact a guy that Guy Geurnas knew from the UN. I found him easily enough, and because his house was full of visitors he put me up at a small hotel at his own cost. Once again I was moved by this unexpected and completely voluntary act of kindness towards a total stranger who could only be judged at face value. The deciding factor was probably the recommendation from Guy, whom he obviously respected as much as I did.

With the usual all-important question settled I went out into Conakry. It was a dusty little city whose streets seemed to have a permanent population of bustling students who soon gave me directions to an Internet café and the local DSTV office. Since it was a Saturday my immediate aim was to get a glimpse of a big rugby match being played in my home-province of KwaZulu-Natal, and I promptly put the arm on the DSTV office manager. He obviously recognised me as a dyed-in-the-wool rugby fanatic and kindly switched the waiting-room TV set from the soccer to the rugby channel.

Having had my rugby fix, I went out to the airport to visit the Internet café. There, to my surprise and pleasure, I ran into Guy Guernas, who had just arrived from Freetown on a UN cargo aircraft which had ferried over some of its staff to connect with an international flight. We enjoyed a pleasant cup of coffee, and then I went to send off my newspaper despatch. It was as if I was sharing my experiences with a bunch of friends, and when I pressed the 'send' button a weight seemed to lift from my soul.

Then I was off to the local sports stadium to link up with Iqbal. It was getting dark by now and people were swarming into the stadium for the Saturday night match, but Iqbal's lurid shirt stood out like a beacon. He ushered me into a light blue Corolla he had borrowed from his cousin, and off we went in some style, neither of us realising that we were heading straight into a bizarre situation that will always make my memories of Conakry a little more vivid than most of the rest.

We were tooling along towards the outskirts of Conakry when Iqbal noticed a new Internet café and telephone shop at the side of the main road, and asked if I wanted to make one last call before heading to Guinea Bissau. Right away I answered yes – this was my chance to have a good heart-to-heart talk with Vasti. So he dropped me off to see some friends while I telephoned Cape Town, serene in the knowledge that calling via the Internet was much cheaper than using an ordinary landline. Or so I thought. My bill came to about

$16, which was something like four times what it should have cost according to my calculations. I didn't know what to do except pay the four teenaged boys running the shop, noting that for some reason they were in a state of visible excitement.

When Iqbal returned and I told him what happened he went off like a rocket. I begged him to forget about it, but he was deeply embarrassed by his young countrymen's actions and stormed inside to demand an explanation and a reduction. When they laughed him off he called the owner of the shop to complain, when this didn't help either Iqbal without explanation strode out and returned about 20 minutes later brandishing a large old leather-bound copy of the Qur'an he had borrowed somewhere, complete with a young boy as its escort. He would demand, he explained, that each of the boys put his hand on the Qur'an and swear to Allah that they had not cheated me.

Wow! This thing had really escalated. I tried to cool Iqbal down by saying that perhaps I had made a mistake, but he had the bit in his teeth now, and no mistake. He marched into the store and the next minute it was wall-to-wall chaos, with fleeing clients trampling one another at the door while the teenagers, one of whom was particularly aggressive, grappled with Iqbal in preparation for throwing him out.

The struggle was so fierce that the Qur'an was knocked from the table where Iqbal had placed it. This was really serious stuff, considering the veneration in which Muslims hold their holy writings, so I lunged into the throng to grab it before it hit the floor. Being bigger and heavier than anyone else there, I burst through the struggling bodies and snatched the Qur'an just before it hit the floor, then stuck it under my arm and tried to shield Iqbal as he was unceremoniously slung out.

Our ejection hadn't ended the fight, however. Iqbal was now penned with his back to the car while the youngsters crowded up close, gesticulating wildly and gabbling what I assumed were blood-curdling threats. This had no effect at all on Iqbal, so infuriated was he by the boys' impudent and discourteous behaviour towards a respectable middle-aged man. I handed the Qur'an back to its guardian, told him to take it home and ask his family for help and then put myself between Iqbal and the boys to separate them and calm things down. But neither Iqbal nor his assailants were in a mood to let things go, and it reached the stage where I had actually pulled out my electric stun gun and had it ready for action, although I was not sure I would be able to use it.

Iqbal saved me from this tough decision by taking matters into his own hands – literally. The youths were still crowding him against the car, gesticulating and shoving their faces into his, to the great enjoyment of a crowd of enthusiastic spectators who had gathered in the dusk and were all agog for the next chapter to unfold. And unfold it did. Iqbal had had enough. He had been an expert boxer in his youth, so he told me later, and he gave the nearest boy a crisp right hook to the ear, which visibly dampened that individual's enthusiasm. This was followed by a flurry of punches which discouraged another of the Internet café boys, leaving only the most aggressive one willing to face him. The two of them settled down to a ding-dong fist fight in which neither seemed to gain any advantage, although Iqbal was definitely the smaller, not to mention older, of the two.

My heart was pumping and my adrenalin was flowing freely now. I didn't want to get involved because I might end up being deported, which would obviously be a great setback for me. On the other hand I had to help my new friend, whose opponent had now been joined by another boy. After all, if I hadn't complained about being overcharged none of this would have happened.

The boy who had taken the Qur'an back had now returned to watch the fun. I gave him my bag and stun gun to hold for me, then threw myself at the more recently joined assailant, grabbed him by the collar and dragged him away from the fight. This startled the main assailant enough to make him stop trying to hit Iqbal, which gave me enough time to put my arm around Iqbal's shoulders and start pulling him towards the car so that we could get away before we attracted official attention.

But it was too late; a couple of police vans had rolled up, their headlights helping to illuminate the scene. I flattened myself against Iqbal's cousin's car, trying to look inconspicuous, which was not easy when it is remembered that I owned the only white skin for miles around. My act certainly did not fool the cop in charge, who sent one of his constables, a gigantic baton-wielding man in black uniform, to collect me. The cop loaded me into one of the vans (Iqbal advising me needlessly to go without making a fuss, and promising to meet me at the police station) and we set off. I checked to make sure that I had all my relevant documents with me, since experience had taught me that I was heading for an 'explain, please' session.

A surprise awaited me at the police station. It appeared that what they did in Guinea when something like this happened was to convene a tribunal of local Muslim leaders, who would then preside over the matter like so many judges and mete out an appropriate sentence in the case of a guilty verdict. It sounded a little too close to a kangaroo court, but once again I was wrong. The tribunal's members carefully questioned all concerned, starting with the chief witness for the prosecution, so to speak, namely Iqbal's aggressive sparring partner. This boy claimed that I had cut his lip open with a punch. I denied this point-blank, the other witnesses backing me up, then told my judges that I didn't wish for any trouble and genuinely regretted the incident.

The tribunal members listened to all this with admirable judicial impassivity, called a 10-minute recess to discuss the matter and then returned to declare me not guilty and tender their sincere apologies for their fellow Guineans' behaviour. Having delivered their verdict, they asked me to wait outside while the more serious related issues were dealt with.

I spent a quiet hour and a half drinking tea and eating croquet biscuits with condensed milk before the judges, Iqbal and his former opponents emerged, the whole lot of them not just tranquil but positively in high spirits. On the way back to Coyah he explained that the boy had been let off with a warning, but he had been fined $20, which he needed to pay within a month, and had also been ordered to cough up for any medical expenses resulting from the affray. I felt a twinge of guilt, having unwittingly been the original instigator, but Iqbal didn't seem too worried about it – I got the strong impression that he had enjoyed giving the obstreperous youth a clip on the ear.

Next day I said goodbye to Iqbal and set off from Coyah towards Boké, my next major destination. I was full of vim and looking forward to putting in a good day's travel, but after a while I started to feel ill, and it got worse with every kilometre that passed. My head felt as if it was going to burst, my body ached all over and all my energy seemed to be draining away. What the hell was wrong with me?

I ran a quick mental symptoms check as I struggled on. My sinuses were congested, but the congestion had started long ago, when I first entered the tropics, so that wasn't it. Dehydration, perhaps? I had upped my water intake early on, when I had first started feeling unwell, and it hadn't helped, so that wasn't it either. Perhaps it was influenza, because one of the few things I wasn't suffering from was a very stiff neck, the sign of malaria or meningitis. I couldn't think of anything else, so I took some paracetamol for the headache and Diclophenac for my aches and pains. That helped, but only a little, and my memories of the excruciating 100 km I covered that day remain merely a blur.

It was still only three o'clock when I finally put down my feet at the bus stand at a small town called Boffa, but I was finished. I remember asking someone about a place to sleep, and being led to a little roadside hotel. I booked into a small room with its own shower, ate a piece of bread and then went straight to bed, hoping against hope that some sleep would help. But a couple of hours after sunset my headache had grown so bad that it woke me up. I knew now that something was seriously wrong with me; I had always suffered from migraines, but this was worse than anything I had ever experienced, and I spent hours huddled in the shower, letting the cool water run over me while I vomited profusely.

It was obviously time to get the heavy artillery out of my medical supplies, and I started with the full malaria kit the doctor in Luanda had packed for me. I didn't think it was malaria because

I had been religious about taking my weekly dose of tablets and had mostly been in good health, but something was obviously badly out of kilter, and a process of elimination might help me to discover what it was.

I did a self-test for malaria, but the result came back negative. I was pleased but also disappointed in a strange way – if it had been positive I would at least have known what was wrong with me. I couldn't think what else it might be, so I continued to dose myself with paracetamol tablets and run cold water over my aching head. Neither made much difference, so it was a very tired and almost terminally headachey adventurer who set off next morning. I wasn't capable of anything more than a slow, steady pace, and it was my good fortune that the dirt road was a good one – if I had had to contend with a real horror I would simply have collapsed. I got to a village named Kolabui around sunset, found a place to sleep and conked out.

Next morning I was feeling much better. Why, I didn't know, and frankly didn't care either; the main thing was that whatever bug had hit me seemed to have shot its bolt. So I had some breakfast while I considered the next leg of my route. I had two options, neither of them really appealing. I could continue inland to Boké or I could head to Kamsar on the coast and board a pirogue for a two-day sea journey to Guinea-Bissau.

I wasn't too keen on the sea trip. It struck me as being the long way around, and if the sea got rough and the pirogue was as rickety as I suspected it would be, there was a good chance of it going down with all the souls on board plus one bike. On the other hand, I had been advised earlier not to take the inland route because the recent rains left the roads impassable.

I decided that this needed further investigation, so before taking a decision I went down to the coast to get some up-to-date information. I had scarcely arrived at Kamsar before I met another of those interesting characters of which the west coast seemed to have such a good supply. In this case it was a pleasantly eccentric Canadian woman named Michelle. She and her son Michael, an Eminem look-alike, had lived for several years in Kamsar, where she worked for the biggest company in the town.

Michelle seemed to know everyone worth knowing, and immediately negotiated a free lodging deal for me at the local hotel. I gathered that she was used to this playing the Good Samaritan for the flotsam and jetsam washed up on Kamsar's shores, so to speak – one of her previous 'clients' was a guy who had apparently set out to travel right around the planet on foot (well, with a little help, since Michelle had helped him to catch an aeroplane flight to his next destination). She told me that he had achieved his goal.

That was just the start. She took me along to the monthly dinner meeting of the expatriates' club – it was very convivial, but I didn't do much talking because I was too busy steadily eating my way through the menu of pizza and pasta – and provided sage advice on the inland route. I could forget about it, she said. The roads were so bad that her company had cancelled all overland trips, so it was the pirogue option or nothing.

Having settled that, Michelle and Michael found a pirogue that was about to leave for Bissau and negotiated a place for me, my role being to stand there looking sorry for myself while they pressed the right buttons with the immigration officials. I might add that the looking-sorry part wasn't completely put on. Most of the passengers were Muslims, and I got the impression that they weren't too happy about sharing the pirogue with a foreigner who was obviously not of the faith. I didn't know enough about Guinea's history to reach any firm conclusions, so I decided that the best thing to do was to try and blend in as much as I could, which I had been trying to do anyway, letting my beard grow and acquiring a Guinean-style caftan which I wore over my usual outfit. I don't think this effort was very successful here, but that was all I had.

In due course the pirogue left, packed with about 25 passengers besides myself. The others were all experienced Guinean travellers and had brought enough eatables and drinkables to last them to Bissau, because this was strictly basic transportation – the captain took your money and steered the boat in the right direction, but that was it. The lack of a dining saloon and cash bar didn't worry me either, since I had lots of snacks on my bike, as well as extra water.

That evening was an unforgettable experience, but for all the wrong reasons. Everyone on the boat made himself or herself comfortable, to the point where some passengers were actually lying down and sleeping. I didn't have that luxury. My bicycle was right next to me, so the pedal dug into my ribs, and I would have had to balance myself on the edge of the hull if I wanted to get any rest. The problem was that this makeshift 'bed' was only about 20 cm wide, and an unexpected roll would instantly toss me into the briny.

But finding a place to lay my body soon became of secondary importance. Not to put too fine a point on it, I needed to empty both my bladder and my bowels. The problem here was that the pirogue not only had no food or drink on board, it didn't have any toilet facilities either, so I settled down to some discreet observation of how my companions were handling the matter.

I soon discovered that their approach was both simple and practical, if not very savoury to watch. If you wanted a piddle you let go over the side, making sure you were down-wind so that you didn't baptise anybody near you, and after the pirogue had anchored for the night the people with more concrete requirements dropped their trousers to their knees and hung their bums out over the water. Well, at least I wouldn't have to try making delicate inquiries in pidgin French. You did it this way or you didn't do it at all. End of story.

My needs were now almost more than flesh and blood could stand, but I managed to hold out till most of the passengers had dossed down before hanging myself out over the side. Thanks to my army days I was no stranger to close-quarter living, but even the army had never got this basic, and I was embarrassed out of my mind. I tried to minimise the inevitable sound-effects by synchronising my contributions with the splashing of wavelets against the hull, together with the occasional crisp cough, but it didn't work very well, and the longer I hung out there the more self-conscious I got. I have never been a publicly demonstrative person, and this was sheer torture, the sort of thing they say builds character and teaches you to be less shy. Bullshit! In my case, anyway, it is more likely to drive you insane. So it was with vast relief of the mental as well as physical kind that I finally got done and used some of the extra water on my bike to wash my nether regions.

We spent all of the next day at sea except for a brief stop-over for refuelling at a tiny inhabited island, and it was a tough day. The sun beat down on us with a vengeance as we sat in a state of semi-hypnosis induced by the droning of the outboard motor and the endlessly repeated splashing of the swells against the boat's sides. The only break in the monotony came during the five daily prayer sessions, when the more devout passengers got down on their knees, although some backsliders found it a bit much and rather shamefacedly missed out on one or two sessions.

The religious activities soon got organised. One bearded man appointed himself prayer leader and took it on himself to activate the other passengers whenever prayer-time neared, then made sure they were all facing in the approximate direction of Mecca and spread out behind him so that they could take their cue from him. What intrigued me was that his style was a nice blend of ancient and modern. He was reciting the old, old prayers, unchanged for countless generations, but he also had a counter, just like the ones cricket umpires use to count balls and overs, on which he recorded each additional prayer he offered that day. This might have looked a bit funny, but the bearded one wasn't joking. He was obviously very serious about his religion, and when one man and a woman passed on the final prayer session the look of disapproval he gave them was so strong you could just about see the little daggers of condemnation coming out of his eyes, like someone in a comic strip.

Our destination for the night was scheduled to be the island of Bubaque, where we would sleep over and next day, all going well, catch another pirogue for the final leg to Bissau. But all did not go well. Near sunset, with Bubaque in plain sight but still something like 10 km away, the outboard gave up the ghost. The captain took it apart and delved around in its innards by torchlight while we sat watching Bubaque's lights grow smaller as we drifted away. I had the horrible feeling that it was going to be a long night with no guarantee of a safe arrival, but the captain knew his stuff, or maybe the outboard was simply an old enemy whose tricks he knew well. In any case, after about four hours he had it back together and functioning again.

We had drifted so far out to sea that Bubaque's lights had vanished altogether, and I was becoming seriously worried (so, I gathered, were the others). Could the captain find the island again? And even if he could, was there enough fuel in the outboard's tank to get us where he wanted to go? But he could and there was, and we finally made it to Bubaque just before midnight. I manhandled my bike ashore with huge relief; spending 38 hours cooped up on a small boat crowded with people I could only smile at was tough stuff. Commuters on the London Underground or New York Subway should try a Guinean pirogue trip, and after that they would never complain again.

The next pirogue to Bissau was not scheduled to leave for two days, so I booked myself in at the local hostelry, Chez Raoul, for the two nights. Chez Raoul was listed in the 'Lonely Planet' guide, a source of pride to the owner, a charismatic character called, naturally, Raoul. He and I clicked right away, and we spent a lot of time talking. Raoul was eager for us to go into business, firstly by exporting besab juice to South Africa and secondly by finding investors for the construction of an ice factory on Bubaque. Being a natural entrepreneur I was soon as enthusiastic as he was, but I don't think that Raoul really understood what I still had planned.

In between discussing juice and factories with Raoul I also did a bit of sightseeing which was anything but strenuous, since 20 km took me from one end of the island to the other on roads such as I had never seen before, a mixture of crushed sea-shells and a hard, concrete-like substance. I had acquired a self-appointed tour guide of sorts, and one of the sights he showed me was a house which had belonged to Amilcar Cabral, the main hero of the independence struggle with Portugal. Cabral was still held in such reverence, he told me, that even now, decades after his death, no one went near it.

Apart from seeing the sights, such as they were, I diverted myself by joining some young children who were catching fish from off the pier. These kids were centuries ahead of me when it came to fishing, but they didn't realise it, and so they watched in awed respect as I ham-handedly tied a knot or tried to release a fish I had caught without harming it. I didn't disillusion them.

Our pirogue finally arrived, considerably later than it should have, and after a further six-hour voyage we landed at Bissau. Getting on shore was a chaotic business because there were no such amenities as gangplanks; how you actually reached the dockside was strictly your personal problem, and it was made even worse by the fact that people on land started scrambling to get on to the pirogue before it had even tied up.

Most of the passengers simply jumped from the pirogue on to the jetty, and one man – I couldn't believe my eyes – actually heaved his young son to some of the other passengers who were already on shore, a distance of at least three metres (the kid didn't seem to mind, so maybe this was standard procedure). I wasted no time in getting ashore. I had had enough of the sea, the pirogue and my fellow-passengers. It felt like ages since I had last done any cycling, and I wanted to see what lay in wait for me.

My planned route didn't pass through Bissau itself, and I didn't turn off to visit the capital. I was in a hurry to make up for the time I had lost on the sea journey, and although it was already late morning I knew I could reach the Senegalese border by sundown if I didn't tarry by the wayside.

It wasn't difficult to adhere to my good intentions in spite of my weakness for being diverted by passing entertainments, because Guinea-Bissau is not only very small (its total population is only about 1.8 million) but almost totally undeveloped, thanks to an economy which is based totally on logging and agricultural products. As a result there was, frankly, not very much to see except what appeared to be full-scale election campaigning in progress. Trucks hung with slogans and crewed by musicians rolled back and forth, pursued by crowds of dancing, singing spectators. Who and what they were campaigning for I didn't know, but the people were clearly having a good time.

I couldn't help thinking that African politics might be less vola-
tile if the general atmosphere was cooled down by a requirement
that election campaigning be restricted to boring speeches, without
voters getting any of the customary free handouts of T-shirts, caps
and concert tickets, or being egged on by campaign managers who
could easily have got work as corporate motivational team builders
anywhere else in the world.

I still don't know what to think of one thing I saw, however.
This was 'WELCOME TO SOWETO' spray-painted in large letters
across the road surface at one place. Soweto? What possible connection could there be between this dusty little country far up the
west coast of Africa and the huge complex of townships sprawling to the south-west of Johannesburg? OK, there was an election
taking place at home just then, but still ... Perhaps there was some
homesick expatriate south African with a spray-can living in Guinea-Bissau. But I pedalled on, so I'll never know.

Around me Guinea-Bissau's landscape underwent a dramatic
change as the kilometres rolled away under me. I had started off
in a region of dense vegetation, but the further north I travelled
the drier it got; I could see the landscape literally turning to desert
under my eyes, and I began to understand some of the factors that
dictated boundaries, colonial and otherwise. Man might propose,
but God disposes by way of rivers, mountains and climatic regions
which form natural barriers and defence lines.

In addition to the 'Welcome to Soweto' slogan, I made another
South African connection, this time a fruitful one, just after I had
taken a ferry-ride over one of the rivers I had to cross. I was pushing my bicycle up the concrete slipway when a blond guy who had
spotted the little South African flag waving from the front of my
bicycle came up and asked: 'Praat jy Afrikaans?' ('Do you speak Afrikaans?') I was astonished to be addressed in my home language
in Guinea-Bissau, of all places. Afrikaans is understood and often
spoken in South Africa's neighbouring countries, but Guinea-Bissau was truly a long way from home.

The blond fellow turned out to be a Dutchman named Johan
who had lived in Durban and Johannesburg for a few years but was

now running his own backpackers' lodge in Banjul, capital of The Gambia, where I would end up in the not-too-distant future. He was going the other way, but gave me his business card and promised me free accommodation if I wanted it when I got there. Not bad!

I hurried on, and as I got closer to the border the atmosphere as well as the landscape began to change. I passed armoured vehicles, artillery pieces and other military paraphernalia, and there was an almost palpable feeling of tension which reminded me a little of Equatorial Guinea, with civilians and soldiers alike showing suspicion at the mere sight of me. I ignored the looks as far as possible. The fact was that to the inhabitants of the more remote parts of West Africa there was something damned peculiar about a lone white guy calmly pedalling around on a bicycle.

Then I was at the border, and ready for my next country.

# CHAPTER 16

# BACK AND FORTH IN SENEGAMBIA – AND AN ALL-IMPORTANT RENDEZVOUS

*I decided that from now on I would make it a rule to wear my caftan while eating and drinking in public. It wouldn't make me blend in with the local population, but it would show, I hoped, that I was respectful of the local culture. The Islamic influence was becoming more visible with every kilometre.*

My entry into Senegal reinforced the conclusion I had reached a little earlier, that sometimes Africans are their own worst enemy, with the citizens of every country warning the traveller about the dangers he could expect from the inhabitants of the next. Being an African myself, I had learnt (and was inclined anyway) to take such gloomy warnings with a pinch of salt, but I can just imagine a first-time visitor from more placid parts coming close to wetting himself on hearing about the cut-throats allegedly lurking behind every rock on the other side of the international border.

I was living proof that this wasn't so. With a couple of exceptions the contrary had been true; if it hadn't, my circumnavigation of Africa would have ended abruptly long before I reached Senegal. Frankly, I think we should stick to inspiring foreigners with caution about the dangerous wildlife they are likely to encounter, rather than the people. Which is not to say that first-time travellers should be totally complacent. It is never healthy to be travelling through a place where there is shooting going on, since an accidental casualty is just as dead as someone killed on purpose.

Casamance, the first part of Senegal I travelled through, was a case in point, visibly recovering from a long but low-level separatist war, but it certainly did not represent the country as a whole. Senegal was lucky enough to become independent in 1960 under the poet and cultural Renaissance man Leopold Senghor, who set the scene by ruling democratically for 20 years and then standing down voluntarily for his elected successor, Abou Diouf. Which just shows what can be done if a nation has wise men at its head instead of the scoundrels who have wrecked so many African countries.

My initial impression of Casamance as I cycled away from the border post was that it was strikingly pretty – the first picture my mental camera took and filed away for later recall was of tall baobab trees on the marshland, silhouetted by the setting sun. On a more prosaic level, I was happy to note that the roads were in good shape and the terrain nice and flat without any killer hills. Unfortunately the wind was blowing in the wrong direction for my purposes, but you can't have everything.

I knew that the moist lushness of the south would give way progressively to desert conditions as I headed further north, but that wouldn't happen right away; first I had to deal with a peculiar product of the colonial era which just about divided Senegal in half, the strange little country – Africa's smallest – called The Gambia.

The Gambia is a tiny tongue of independent territory which is wedged like a dagger into the centre of the Senegalese coastline and literally consists of nothing more than a port, Banjul, at the mouth of the Gambia River, the river itself and narrow strips of land on either bank. Since The Gambia runs across almost the entire width of its 'host' country, there was no way for me to follow the coastline except by leaving southern Senegal, entering and leaving Gambian territory, then entering and leaving Senegal again. Not that I really minded, though – how often do you get a chance of visiting a country which consists mainly of two river banks, has a total population which is less than that of a moderate-sized South African city and earns its living mainly by exporting peanuts?

The Senegalese are crazy about sport, and I nearly persuaded the young owner of a hotel in the town of Bignona to come back to South Africa and try out for rugby. He was big and muscular, although a trifle round, and I calculated he would do very well playing in the front row, where size and strength are prime requirements. He divined the direction of my thoughts and had me know that he had run the 100-metre track event in under 11 seconds. That was pretty impressive, given his general build, and I thought – not for the first time – that Africa with its billion or so population would surely be able to put a world-beating rugby team together. Or perhaps, as a good patriotic South African, I should say 'another world-beating rugby team'.

Passing through the border post brought me, very briefly, back to a country where I didn't have to struggle with a vocabulary that was still nearly as bare as Mother Hubbard's cupboard. Having been a British protectorate from 1888 till independence in 1965, the Gambians spoke English. Happy days! I also found myself, for once, not the only crazy whitey going God knows where on a bike: cycling alongside me was a Dutch family of four – father, mother, son and daughter – whose members explained that this was the way they always went on holiday, although not usually to a place as exotic as West Africa. With some envy I eyed their bicycles and panniers, which were all state of the art; my only criticism was that they didn't have much in those fancy panniers, while mine bulged at every seam. But I suppose that was just sour grapes.

I stayed over at Serekunda, a suburb 10 km outside Banjul, at a hotel owned by a friend of the UN soldiers I had met in the Ivory Coast, who kindly put me up at a discounted rate. By then I had already made a friend of my own, a Malawian named Ron Mponda who was the UNHCR's chief of operations for The Gambia. I had just ridden into Serekunda when I spotted the UNHCR offices, and although it was dusk I couldn't resist pulling off the road and making myself known. Ron was actually on his way out, but he was so overjoyed to see another Southern African that he took me right back inside to chat a little.

It was yet another of those fortuitous meetings with wonderful people which had helped me along my journey. Ron must have been the kindest man in The Gambia. He was so impressed by what I had done so far that he literally emptied his pockets of all his cash as a personal donation to my trip, although I hadn't asked for anything or told any hard-luck stories.

I'm not an intolerant man on the whole, except when it comes to people who spend all their time moaning about how unfair life has been to them without sparing a thought for how fortunate they really are. That intolerance comes from meeting people like Ron Mponda – a genuinely generous person who smiles a lot and tells you about the good fortune in his life, however small .

I spent three days in Serekunda, concentrating on obtaining visas for Mauritania and Morocco, which I mistakenly believed would be easier to get in a country as small as The Gambia. My main form of transport was the local taxis, each of which seemed to have a cassette of South African reggae artist Lucky Dube either blasting out or standing by to be blasted out. Some of those tapes were stretched almost beyond recognition by constant playing, so that you got some mighty slow tribal reggae. I don't know whether he would be amused or infuriated to hear his music played Gambian style, but the fact that I was seen as having a direct connection to the reggae legend himself brought an unexpected dividend, namely that as a VIP I was never overcharged on the fare. One taxi-driver got so worked up, in fact, that he said he was willing to commit himself to hiring the national sports stadium for a concert venue if I could persuade Lucky to visit Serekunda.

A roadside cobbler also solved another pressing problem. The leather Shimano cycling shoes which I had been wearing since the very beginning of my trip were in an understandably ruinous state after the severe tribulations they had been put through, so that the heels were pulling away from the soles, which made pedalling very uncomfortable. The cobbler was not overawed by the prospect of the serious surgery the shoes needed, though. He invited me to sit down on the pavement next to him, then proceeded to sew the shoes into very good shape, *by hand*!

The cobbler, incidentally, was right next to a restaurant which advertised South African wine in a way one could definitely describe as unique. Most of its wines were listed on the menu by name, but the South African vintages were lumped together in two categories. The first was 'South African Wine'. The second was 'Very Good South African Wine'. I was a trifle baffled. Did this mean that the first category should actually have been labelled 'Not Very Good South African Wine'?

I don't think the distinction in quality was very important to the hordes of loud and frequently drunken British package tourists I saw wobbling around Serekunda in all directions. They were there to have some fun, which seemed to consist mainly of soaking up the sun so that they looked like cooked crayfish and chugging down the local booze. Not a particularly edifying sight in many cases, but what the hell, they were enjoying themselves without harming anyone while doing their bit towards propping up the local economy.

I was given to understand that The Gambia is a popular destination for many British tourists making their first acquaintance with Africa – a bit of a turnaround since the nineteenth century, when West Africa was such an unhealthy place to visit that it was popularly known as the 'White Man's Grave' – and Serekunda has become quite a well-known tourist destination. The name means 'the home of the Sere family', whoever they were, and Serekunda once actually consisted of nine small villages which have now coalesced into the largest conurbation in The Gambia. This happened for a peculiarly Gambian reason. Banjul is actually located offshore on St Mary's Island, where it was founded as Bathurst in 1816. No doubt this was because it was less grave-like for the administrators than the humid mosquito-ridden mainland (in those days it was believed that malaria was caused by poisonous miasmas from swamps). As a result there was nowhere for Serekunda to go, and nowadays it is a mass of heavily overcrowded suburbs around the famed Serekunda Market, a loud and bustling collection of shops, craft stalls and street pedlars from all over Africa and a few Arab countries as well, with its own batik factory, which is a tourist attraction in its own right. Serekunda provides another unusual attraction in the form of wrestling matches at the national stadium or elsewhere every Saturday and Sunday. *Wrestling*? For sure. Just about all of West Africa is soccer-crazy, but in The Gambia – and, in fact, in Senegal as well – the national sporting passion is the grapple-and-grunt game.

Having done my tourist thing, I donned my revitalised shoes and cycled down Nelson Mandela Drive to the Banjul harbour to catch a ferry over the river to Senegalese territory. It was a frightening trip which really brought home the reason for all those African ferry disasters. The boat was packed to bursting-point with passengers, goods, cars and freight vehicles, and was so top-heavy that it rolled savagely, so much so that at times it seemed as if the truck next to which I was sitting with a horde of others was about to tip over and turn us all into strawberry pulp. Fortunately we got to the other side before this actually happened, but I didn't waste any time getting off, just in case it decided to roll over and sink at its moorings.

Before long I was on the road to Dakar, where I was due to meet up with Nic Bothma, whose advice about Liberia I had ignored, to my subsequent peril. The roads were conveniently flat, but progress was slow, firstly because of a strong headwind and secondly because of excruciating pains in my knees. I speculated that the extra effort I had to put in as a result of the headwind had over-strained and inflamed certain ligaments, but whatever the cause, I was unable to get up to more than about 10 km/h.

I was in the dry part of Senegal now, and sprawling desert landscapes with golden dunes surrounded me as I got nearer to Dakar. The headwind grew stronger and stronger, but although I was racked by pain from my knees, my self-confidence and motivation were solid as ever. At times like this I wondered how easy it would be for a person to quit. In fact, my pain became the focal point of my determination. I was going to complete my trip so that I would have the whole story to tell, not just half, even if that meant a worst-case scenario of pushing my bicycle for a few hundred kilometres to give my knees time to recover. In any case, Dakar is Africa's western-most city, and that made it one of the trip's special milestones.

When I got to the town of Sindia I found that construction had just been completed on a new road which led directly north to the town of Thiès, a short distance from Dakar. This was good news, considering the condition of my knees, and I celebrated my good fortune with a few bowls of warm camel's milk (what did it taste like? Well, like camel's milk). I decided that from now on I would make it a rule to wear my caftan while eating and drinking in public. It wouldn't make me blend in with the local population, but it would show, I hoped, that I was respectful of the local culture. The Islamic influence was becoming more visible with every kilometre I got nearer to Dakar, and I wanted to make sure that the locals didn't feel I was just another intruding Westerner who was unsympathetic to their folk-ways.

As in Sierra Leone and Guinea, my game-plan was to find a safe lock-up for my bike and kit at Thiès, then take a day-pack and head for Dakar on one or other available form of transport. But I was out of luck, and so there I was, heading for Dakar in a bus with my bike strapped to the roof-rack. I had absolutely no idea of where I was going to put up for the night when we got there, and peppered the driver with inquiries about a suitably economical hotel. When we reached the environs of the capital city he dropped me off outside a hotel which was most certainly not anywhere near cheap – I suspect he got so fed up with my questioning that he simply wanted to be rid of me as soon as possible – and not very hospitable either.

This latter I discovered when I took my usual approach of opening negotiations with the manager about a discount or, at worst, a place to pitch my tent. Having become spoilt by the general generosity I had encountered so far, I was shocked when he not only refused both the discount and camping options but actually had his security man escort me off the property as if he feared I was going to pinch the silver. So there I was, standing by the roadside in pitch darkness with my belongings and shipwrecky knees. Welcome to Dakar!

It takes more than this to discourage me, however, so I braced my aching knees and started pushing the bike towards some bright lights I could see about 5 km up the road. Surely I would do better there! Short of being shot as an intruder, I certainly couldn't do worse. And so it transpired. The bright lights turned out to be another hotel which, at the CFA equivalent of $5 a night, also happened to be within my price range. I could just about feel my weary bones sinking into a humble but comfortable bed.

Then came a crushing and, to me, inexplicable disappointment: payment had to be made in CFA, the night staff said. I explained that I hadn't had the opportunity to exchange some of my dollars for the local currency, and to my surprise they told me to move on. I was at the end of my tether by now, and offered to deposit $100 as a token of good faith. Nope! It was CFA or nothing, and I found myself back on the road, heading towards the next group of lights with my customary optimism somewhat dimmed and my knees shrieking blue murder.

The first set of lights belonged to a garage with a fancy one-stop shop attached. That didn't solve my accommodation problem, but at least I could buy a bagful of my favourite ice-cream sachets. Somewhat cheered by dollops of my preferred trail food, I asked the petrol jockey about accommodation in the vicinity, then started pushing again.

I arrived at the next hotel around midnight, really done in now by the combination of fatigue and pain. This was it, I decided, regardless of the cost; I just couldn't go a step further. But to my dismay it looked as if I would be turfed out of this hotel, too. The owner was on duty himself that night and informed me with some difficulty – he couldn't speak any English and my exhausted state seemed to have brought about a deterioration in my shotgun French – that he didn't have a room free.

OK, worst-scenario time. Would it be possible, I asked, for me to pitch my tent somewhere on his premises? Somewhere things got lost in the translation, and he didn't understand what I was talking about. By now I was getting pretty desperate ... and then, as had happened so often in the recent past, a total stranger arrived to shower me with unexpected kindness. My saviour this time was a French-speaking Ghanaian staffer for the United Nations Development Programme who was staying at the hotel, and he immediately took my problems on himself. He explained my need to the owner and told him about my trip, and with the language barrier out of the way the penny (centime?) dropped. There *were* some vacant rooms, the owner said, but they had not yet been decorated and so he was not renting them out just then. However, I could have one for the night if I wanted. Needless to say, I took him up on his offer with the speed of light. But my new friend wasn't finished with me yet. He was off to Ghana next morning to see his family, he explained, and he was feeling so good about this that by way of celebration he would pay for my room out of his own pocket. I felt humbled again. Where else in the world would you find something like this?

Next day I linked up with Nic Bothma and had a thoroughly good time. Dakar is an impressive city, with oodles of culture and interesting things to experience, and Nic had plenty of good ideas about what to see and do. We roared around on his big scrambler motorcycle, seeing all the sights worth seeing and even riding the waves at Ngore beach, the most westerly surfing spot in Africa.

Ngore was wonderful. I choked and spluttered my way through a couple of the first rides, but soon got my eye in, and eventually I was contemplating (not very seriously, though) the beguiling thought of becoming an ex-adventurer beach bum in Dakar. My general exuberance inspired me to play the first April Fool's joke of my life. If I say so myself, it was quite a good one for a first attempt: a round-robin SMS to my friends and acquaintances, saying that I had had enough of the trip, that I believed I had proved my point and that I would be kayaking back to South Africa with Nic.

After the electronic equivalent of a stunned silence I received some varied and interesting responses. One of my friends who had obviously swallowed this preposterous story without a burp replied: 'Are you sure?' Another friend, Dorothy, bless her heart, believed me, too, and replied: 'You have done well, come home, we miss you.' Vasti, on the other hand, kept her cool lawyerly head and didn't mince her words: 'Get away from Nic. He is making you think like this. Get away from him immediately!'

Well, I didn't get away from Nic. Not only was he a very nice guy, he was also a legend in his own time as far I was concerned, and my respect for the man's sheer guts grew when we talked about his Liberian experiences and looked at some of his photographs; for the first time I fully realised what I had plunged into in my foolish determination to cover every inch of the route on my own wheels. Perhaps the old Arab belief that lunatics are beloved of God has something going for it.

Towards the end, Nic recalled, there were only three photographers still in Liberia covering the war, himself, a Japanese and an American, although for practical purposes there were actually only two, because when the sound of gunfire was heard Nic and the Japanese would head for the action while the American curled up in the shower cubicle for the day.

Nic had some horrifying stories to tell. One that remains in my mind was his description of how some armed boys were shot down around him, while others were kicked and beaten to a pulp without his being able to do anything except take pictures. One of the latter that I remember particularly well showed a nine-year-old 'general' firing his AK-47 assault rifle in pouring rain. Another was of a naked dead man lying face-down, his hands tied behind his back with wire, while past him travelled the first United Nations representative to enter Monrovia. A shiny white 4x4, bedecked with proudly waving UN flags, and a pathetic naked victim of a cold-blooded execution – it was one of those pictures which really do say more than a thousand words.

It was odd that this man, who had seen more brutal and horrifying death and violence than any 100 people would experience in their lifetime, wouldn't even think of riding his motorcycle without a helmet, although the traffic in Dakar was slow-moving and most Dakarians didn't bother. On further reflection I realised that it was not necessarily so odd. Your perspectives and values change after a life-threatening experience. What sense would there be in wasting your life in a senseless road accident just because you were too happy-go-lucky or macho to wear a helmet?

I made other good friends in Dakar. The South African embassy staff went out of their way to help me, and to one of them – Derek Williams, who assisted me with my new visa applications and temporary passport – I owe a huge debt of gratitude for the greatest surprise gift of the trip. One day we sat down together to fill in some documents, and when we were done he casually asked what else I needed while I was in Senegal. Jokingly I said that a visit from Vasti would round off the first 14 000 km of my trip rather nicely. To my surprise Derek immediately got on to the telephone with the South African Airways manager in Dakar, a Mr Dieng, set up an appointment with him and told me how to get to the SAA offices. Now, he added, it was up to me to bend Mr Dieng's ear.

I pumped up my self-confidence as high as I could take it and went along to Mr Dieng's office. Having greeted me, he asked me how he could help. Suddenly all the fancy arguments I had prepared evaporated and I said: 'Please, could you bring my girlfriend to Dakar to visit me?' It was only then that I realised how much I wanted to see Vasti after our seven-month separation.

Mr Dieng didn't bat an eyelid. 'That will be fine,' he said. 'When do you want her to come?' I was speechless. It was actually going to happen! It was difficult to grasp at first, and it only began to sink in as the hours passed.

While I waited happily for Vasti to arrive I spent time marketing my story to more components of the South African media, contacted friends to bring them up to date on my progress and continued my visa-hunting. Most importantly, I made the acquaintance of Mr Thoumas of Multiport, which would stand me in good stead in the future. The only visa that gave me any trouble was the Moroccan one: their embassy staff insisted that the only way of getting it would be to return to Pretoria and have the embassy there issue it. Why? I have absolutely no idea. I concluded that the Moroccan ambassador in Senegal needed to do some swift arse-kicking among his unhelpful staff ... unless, of course, they were acting on his orders.

I was impressed by Senegal, and particularly Dakar. For various reasons Africa as a whole is not a particularly efficient continent, but Senegal seemed to be a gear-notch or two above the rest. Having said this, I should add in all fairness that the hours its private and public sectors keep are impossibly leisurely by South Africa's standards. For example, in Senegal everything closes promptly at noon for a lunch-hour that lasts till 2.30 pm. I could never understand why anyone would need two and a half hours for lunch unless they had to go out and shoot the meal first. Then again, in many cases you could forget about shopping after lunch on a Friday afternoon. Senegal being predominantly Muslim, most shops didn't bother to re-open after lunch because just about everyone would be off to the local mosque for prayers.

On the other hand, the country seemed to function well enough in spite of this strange approach to Western-style teachings on productivity. I expect the answer is that the Senegalese have evolved a system which works well for them because it dovetails neatly with their religion and culture.

Another puzzling thing was that whereas people in Windhoek had been clearly impressed on hearing that I had cycled there from Cape Town, my listeners here in Dakar, which was infinitely further away from my starting-point, somehow couldn't seem to grasp what it meant to make a lone bicycle trip of that extent; it was almost as if they found it difficult to believe me. I thought about this strange phenomenon and decided that it wasn't a case of belief or disbelief, just an inability to understand what it meant in terms of challenges and sheer distance covered between Africa's southernmost and westernmost cities. So if your main aim is to boost your ego, you don't have to cycle further from Cape Town than Windhoek. After that you're bound to be disappointed when you tell people about it.

In the meantime the good luck just kept rolling in as I waited for Vasti to arrive. I had friends in London, Richard 'the German' Hammersen and my best friend Troy Mitchell, who had been following my trip by way of the South African High Commission there, and they were keen to see me after seven months of following my adventures and misadventures. The High Commission, on the other hand, wanted me in London during the tenth anniversary of South Africa's first universal-franchise election for a bit of image-building.

The upshot of all this was a plan which would see me break my journey at Casablanca in Morocco on a certain date, catch a flight to London at the expense of Richard and Troy's girlfriend Katheline, then return to Morocco about 10 days later and continue my trek. I thought it was a wonderful idea (well, of course I did), and even more wonderful because Troy would be celebrating his thirtieth birthday while I was there.

But while it was wonderful, the plan also complicated my life. To make it work I would have to cycle an immense distance to and through a country which was currently impossible to enter legally because of its local officials' insistence that I would have to go back to Pretoria to get my visa. Even if that was sorted out, Vasti was now definitely on the way and most of the two weeks I had allocated for this leg of the trip would be spent on preparations and her actual stay in Dakar. Well, I wasn't prepared to give up either of these great delights, so I decided to take it one step at a time. Somehow I would make it to Casablanca in time for my London flight … I hoped. But first things first.

I got down to hunting after more visas, and suddenly it was time for Vasti to arrive. I was at the airport hours before time, peering at the hordes of people coming in on the off-chance that she might be on an earlier flight. Vasti being Vasti, however, she arrived exactly on schedule. Under my impatient gaze she made the normal slow progress through the customs. I watched her getting ever closer with a strange mixture of joy that she was actually here in Dakar and would be able to see me in the flesh (although not so much of it – I was 17 kg lighter) and sadness resulting from the unbidden feeling that I was not meant to be in Dakar at this moment but should be at home with her. But then she was through, and the sadness was washed away by the joy.

The five-star Le Meridien hotel generously put us up for free for three days and nights, out of which we squeezed as much simple enjoyment as was humanly possible. We loved the hotel breakfasts and made them the extended opening gambit of each morning, we went out and bought snacks in the city, we sat in our room for one whole delightful Saturday watching our teams playing in the Super 12 rugby tournament (they all won!) and I showed off my rather halting ability to communicate in French. I even took Vasti down to the main bus terminal to eat a locally renowned egg and onion sandwich, which she thoroughly enjoyed in spite of the fact that the 'restaurant' was a very dilapidated corrugated-iron shanty.

Vasti's visit was good for me in many ways. Some people had warned me that what I had experienced so far might have changed me to the extent that the 'new' me would be such a shock for her that it would affect our relationship. I had not believed this would be the case, but the proof of everything lies in the eating, and I was delighted to see this gloomy theory blown right out of the water. Things were as good between us as always, and I told her: 'I think with this journey I can only improve as a person.'

Vasti's departure was a tough moment for me. I didn't wait to see her board the aircraft. Instead I sat in a rickety coffee shop outside the main airport building, drinking foul-tasting coffee and repeating to myself: 'You'll be home soon. The worst is over.' I told myself to remember that although Vasti was gone I had at least had the opportunity of spending three glorious days with her. It didn't help. I was sad and beyond sad; the tears rolled slowly down my cheeks as I watched her plane get smaller and smaller, then finally vanish into the blue distance.

That evening, back at my small hotel at Ngore beach, I dispelled my loneliness and sadness by holding an intensive one-man crisis meeting. And 'crisis' was the right word. I had just five days to get to Casablanca, a staggering 3 200 km to the north, through some very tough terrain in which complications of one kind or another were a distinct possibility. There was only one way to do it: I would have to find a safe place to stash my bicycle at the hotel and then catch some form of transport to where I wanted to go.

Oh, yes: and somehow get that bloody visa without first going back to Pretoria and begging at the Moroccan embassy's front door. How I was going to accomplish *that* was even more worrying than the prospect of getting to Casablanca in time.

# CHAPTER 17

# A NASTY EXPERIENCE IN MAURITANIA AND AN UNFORGETTABLE DASH TO LONDON

*The huge mosque was just across the street and some other early-morning worshippers were gathering outside it. I knew then that I could kiss my telephone goodbye. Who were they likely to believe, 'righteous' Mohamed or some foreign infidel accusing their co-religionist of theft right outside the mosque?*

I climbed on a bus for the journey to the Mauritanian border with a small day-pack on my back and a heart brimming with enthusiasm, even though I still had no Moroccan visa. It was a long, long journey, and by the time we came to the border town of Rosso it was past midnight. But the travel gods smiled on me once again: a professorial-looking Frenchman (although how he actually earned his living I didn't know) with whom I had got to chatting on the bus knew one of the local hoteliers and soon organised some accommodation for us in spite of the late hour.

All I had to do now was go to the transit centre next morning for the ferry ride across the Senegal River and I would be in Mauritania. London, here I came! Except that this proved to be a little more difficult than I had anticipated. The first hassle came when a couple of policemen accosted me as I was heading towards the ferry's slipway and peremptorily demanded to see my passport. I produced it for their inspection, after which they had a lengthy discussion about what their next step should be. I played it low-profile, acting ignorant and flourishing my Mauritanian visa whenever it seemed appropriate.

Eventually the cops said I could continue on my way, but only if I gave them photocopies of all the pages in my passport. This was easier said than done. First of all, I had no Senegalese money left to pay for the copies, and secondly there was no photocopier anywhere in Rosso – whether they overlooked this salient fact through ignorance or bloody-mindedness I couldn't tell. But they were unwavering, and in the end I had to backtrack to a town called Richard Toll to get the copies made. The unnecessary expenditure of money wasn't the problem so much as the waste of my precious time, because this unscheduled excursion meant that I missed the first ferry of the day. The only positive thing about this rigmarole was that in the process I had my first real contact with Arab culture.

Northern Senegal is where the western part of sub-Saharan Africa begins to change into the southern reaches of the Arab Maghreb. From here on the black people would gradually morph into the very different Arab-Berber inhabitants of the Maghreb. The border people I came into close contact with here (and I mean *close* contact, since I was one of an inordinate number of passengers crammed into the back of a pickup on the Richard Toll detour) were harbingers of things to come, since they were mainly negroid by race but Arab by culture and religion. I discovered this in no uncertain terms when I was treated to a passionate demonstration of the correct way of folding a turban on one's head. I paid close attention, since it was clear that proper turban-folding was not something to be taken lightly in this part of the world.

Another time-hassle presented itself as soon as I set foot on Mauritanian soil. I was told to stand aside while the other passengers were processed, which went quite smoothly even though most of them didn't have visas to enter Mauritania. Then I was led into a secluded back room, where all the staff officials present surrounded me and fell to discussing my situation with what seemed to be a good measure of discontent. I was virtually ignored during all this in spite of being the guest of honour, so to speak, and I became more and more impatient as the minutes went by without our attempts at communicating in broken English and equally broken French achieving anything. But eventually we got to the actual core of the matter when the official in charge (so I guessed, since he was the one actually hanging on to my passport) started rubbing his forefinger and thumb together in the universal sign-language for 'bribe'.

So that was it! I asked him what the problem was, adding as emphatically as possible that if there *was* a hitch they should contact the South African ambassador in Dakar immediately. It was like flicking a switch. The chief crook's thumb and forefinger suffered instant paralysis and they not only told me to sling my hook but actually escorted me to the nearest taxi to their capital of Nouakchott.

I didn't expect much from Mauritania, which is pretty much of a backwater in all ways. It was a dull, hot, dusty trip through featureless desert to Nouakchott, which was an equally dull, hot, dusty place only a couple of city blocks in extent. And I mean *dusty*, its few streets swamped by sand blown in from the surrounding desert by a horrendous wind which created a permanent dust-haze I could literally taste.

Here I had another try at getting a Moroccan visa. No luck, and the officials at the embassy wouldn't even allow me to communicate with their London embassy. By now I had the bit in my teeth, though; I was on the move, and I was going to stay on the move, by hook or by crook. So I decided to take the only option available and began laying out all the cash I had left on me, about $200, to try to bypass the Moroccan border post altogether and fly direct from Nouakchott to Casablanca.

I took the bull by the horns and went to the local office of the Mauritanian national airline, which happened to be situated just across the street from the Internet café I had latched on to. There I told my sad story to the manager, asked him if it would be possible to fly direct to Casablanca and put in my usual heartfelt plea for a substantial discount. This was a fairly cheeky thing to do, but I was really desperate, and suddenly things began clicking into place. For some reason the manager was intrigued by my story, so after checking my passport to see if I was on the level he offered me a flight to Morocco in two days' time that would get me to Casablanca just 90 minutes before my London plane took off. By great good fortune the London flight was also one of his airline's, and so he was able to offer me a discount which brought the cost of my Casablanca flight down to $120. In addition it meant that the airline staff there would be standing by to hustle me through the transit lounge so that I did not end up trapped by officialdom again.

I accepted like a shot – I had reached the stage where I would have welcomed a seat on the back of a migrating vulture – and he handed me the ticket, earnestly instructing me: 'Do not talk to other people. You and me are the only people who know you have no visa – OK?' Damn right it was OK!

I was in a pretty good mood when I returned to the 'Auberge de la Jeunesse l'Amitié' (or youth hostel) where I was staying. I got on rather well with the place's part-owner, one Mohamed, and we sat chatting at the fire of the security guard, who was also the tea-maker, till the early hours. I told him all about my plans and what I had experienced, and he spent a lot of time talking about how important his religion was to him.

But Mohamed turned out to be a false friend in more ways than one. On the morning of my departure I was packed and ready at 4 am, having already settled my bill in full (no big deal, since the only other guest was a very old, very deaf man). When I opened the door of my room I found Mohamed sleeping on the porch outside my room, which I thought was a bit odd. But I was in a hurry to use the toilet and brush my teeth before leaving, and if he wanted to sleep on his porch instead of in his bed, that was strictly his own affair.

I headed for the ablutions at the end of a dog-legged passage after stashing my pack inside the room and tucking my PDA telephone under it as a precaution, although I didn't bother to actually lock my door because Mohamed was there to keep an eye on things. While I was doing the necessary Mohamed stuck his head in to ask if everything was OK. Of course, I said, why should everything not be OK? He nodded and disappeared. I finished my business and went briskly back to my room to pick up my bag. The PDA phone was gone! Trying to keep calm, I fossicked around just in case I had left it somewhere else and only thought I had hidden it under my pack. But it was gone, all right.

I ran out on to the porch and in the pre-dawn light managed to make out a figure which was definitely Mohamed walking hurriedly across the open plot of land in front of the lodge.

'Mohamed!' I shouted, still trying to remain calm. 'Mohamed, come back. Someone has stolen my telephone!' Mohamed didn't answer, just kept going with his pace increasing from a fast walk to a slow jog. I ran after him – he was now about 100 metres away – calling his name and repeating what I had said. But he took no notice at all.

'Mohamed, why are you running from me? Why?' I shouted, more loudly now, so that some other early risers started staring at us with growing interest. He must have noticed this and replied with arrogance as he started to cross the street: 'I must go to mosque, I cannot talk with you now. Mosque is very important.'

Now I saw the reason for his change from furtiveness to arrogance: the huge mosque was just across the street and some other early-morning worshippers were gathering outside it. I knew then that I could kiss my telephone goodbye. Who were they likely to believe, 'righteous' Mohamed or some foreign infidel accusing their co-religionist of theft right outside the mosque? If I didn't actually come to bodily harm I might well be delayed and miss my all-important flight. And now I remembered my other belongings, still lying in my unlocked bedroom.

The incident disappointed me to a far greater extent than might be thought. The loss of the PDA phone was a serious blow, because it contained virtually irreplaceable information – my daily diary entries and the names and contact details of scores of people I had met along the way; I would have to go back to all the 19 countries I had passed through so far to retrieve what I had lost.

What hurt just as badly, though, was Mohamed's betrayal of the rapport we had built up. He knew what I had gone through to get to Nouakchott and the hardships which surely lay ahead, and even so he had stolen an item of equipment that I was going to need badly in the weeks and months to come. And on top of that he had proved to be a cowardly hypocrite who was willing to misuse his religion to escape the consequences of his dishonesty – the same

man, mark you, who had spent a lot of our discussion time telling me about the greatness of Islam and its importance in his life.
I don't know much about Islam, but 'rob thy guest' is certainly *not*
one of its tenets.

Only people who have made a journey like mine can fully understand how an experience like this can mould one's opinion of
a specific group of people. Whether Mohamed liked it or not, he
was an unofficial ambassador for both his country and his faith in
his dealings with me, and he had besmirched them as well as our
friendship.

I got on the plane feeling stressed and extremely depressed, my
joy at heading for London robbed of its flavour for the time being.
For the time being I had had enough of both Mauritania and Islam. Which made my actions on arrival at Heathrow Airport rather
strange. But more of that later.

I maintained the promised low profile and the flight to Casablanca went smoothly, as did the transfer there to the UK flight at
the hands of the airline staff, who all knew exactly who I was and
the nature of my little problem, and in due course I stepped off
the plane at Heathrow. I realised now that I looked decidedly Middle Eastern with my heavy tan, dark beard and caftan, so I decided
to undertake a stunt that, in retrospect, was pretty rash: if the customs officials and other passengers wanted to take me for an Arab
I would play along with them, to the point of actually greeting people in Arabic. That should help me to divine the truth or otherwise of complaints about the discrimination Muslims worldwide
reportedly suffer at the hands of Westerners.

At the customs we began the customary slow shuffle towards the
counter. I noticed that there was only one other man in the queue
wearing what might be called traditional Islamic-type clothes. He
didn't look intimidating at all! Maybe he was afraid that I was
some sort of fanatic and was determined to steer well clear of me, I
thought with an inward grin.

The queue inched forward. Most of my fellow-passengers were
either blasé or tired, but I was brimming with anticipation, my dis-

appointment with Mohamed temporarily forgotten. All going well, I would be dealing with a young, white, rather unsympathetic official. Not that I wanted hassles entering the United Kingdom, but a real discrimination experience would help me to better understand Islam and its endless friction with the non-Muslim world. But Fate was unkind ... or maybe it wasn't ... and saw to it that I ended up in front of a distinctly Indian-looking official, turban and all, the only one of his kind among the 20 people on duty.

The turban-wearer gave me a friendly smile and greeting, then asked the customary questions about where I was staying, how long I would be in the UK, who I was staying with and what my hosts did. I answered all these questions as briefly as possible. Then, having smacked his stamp on the ink-pad and poised it above my passport, he asked: 'When are you going back to Casablanca?' and I was rash enough to say with pride: 'In 10 days I go back to Morocco and then I'll carry on cycling. I have cycled from South Africa to get here.'

Wrong move. The stamp's downward swoop halted about a centimetre above the passport page. Then the immigration guy slowly lifted it away and said: 'You did *what?*'

Oh no, oh no, oh no! I thought. What had I done? Suddenly I wasn't as keen on a discrimination experiment as I'd been. What had got into me? At the one place so far where it was a sure thing that I would not be bullied, interrogated, arrested, misunderstood or asked for a bribe, I had to go and screw it up! What could I do to get out of this foot-in-the-mouth situation? Well, as it turned out I had to produce all sorts of documentary evidence, including a whole photo album of my travels plus the embassy and Proudly South African letters of support before I was allowed to haul my chastened arse out of there.

An old friend from my school days, Bradley Loubser, was waiting for me in the arrivals lounge, and his eyes popped when he saw the lean, dark, bearded, heavily tanned, caftan-draped character who was greeting him. Bradley was going to put me up and join me at the High Commission thrash, and make sure I got to Troy's birthday party. Apparently the scope of the party was growing by the day, unbeknown to Troy, who was also unaware of the fact that I had appeared to join in the festivities.

Bradley, incidentally, was much more than just host and party-goer. I don't think that there are many people with his multitude of talents who would give up their financially most productive years to assist those who have nothing, but he did. He spent six months of every year working in the northern Ugandan town of Gulu, which was under the de facto control of the 'Lord's Resistance Army', an ultra-violent rebel movement which seemed to have added 'thou shalt kill anyone on a bicycle' to the Ten Commandments in the Bible whose teachings its adherents claimed to follow. Bradley voluntarily faced this terrible danger out of simple religious conviction, accepting the perils as part and parcel of his commitment to God. It was an awesome demonstration of true faith. I have to admit that I didn't have it: I was just glad that my route would not take me through Uganda.

I stayed in my caftan all the way to his house. Bradley didn't mind, but the same couldn't be said for some of the other patrons at a pizza joint where we stopped off on the way. Young and drunk, they showered me with curses and abuse. So I got my discrimination experience after all.

To maintain the element of surprise I lay low for the next two days so that Troy wouldn't spot me; I even sent him e-mails saying how sad I was that I would not be in London to celebrate his birthday. I felt slightly guilty about the deception, even though I knew it was done to add to his joy, because I thought of him as a beloved brother. I had a strange, disjointed childhood, and his family plugged many gaps by treating me as one of their own. I had many other friends, but Troy was special; I knew that if ever we quarrelled he would always have my forgiveness, no matter what. I had seen little of him for quite a while because he had left South Africa to work in the UK, but he had been an unwavering supporter of my journey and a constant source of motivation through all the tough times. So it was going to be a very special moment when I saw him again – even though he would have reached the intimidating age of 30.

The afternoon of the birthday party I met up with the guys who had made my trip to London possible – Richard, Patrick, Clayton and Med, all South Africans. Med (yep, that's his name) helped me with my birthday gift, a voice message on a CD that would leave Troy convinced that I was still in Morocco. This done, we went off to the pub where the party was to take place, and I was stuffed into the broom cupboard to make sure Troy would have no inkling that I was anywhere outside the Moroccan desert. I sat there like – well, like a broom – watching through a small gap as he arrived, and I had a hard job not bursting out of the cupboard to greet him.

The party had been carefully planned to ensure that his surprise present (me) had the maximum impact. First Med would welcome everybody and read out birthday wishes from all over the world. Then the recording from me would be played on a portable CD player, after which Troy would have to slug down his special birthday drink while everyone shouted: 'Down … down … down!' in the traditional South African fashion. At this stage, while his attention was diverted, I would come out of my hiding-place in the broom cupboard and go to stand by his side, so that when he had finished I would be right there next to him as if I had materialised out of thin air. And that's how it went, although I don't think anyone expected the depth of emotion it all evoked.

Troy sat at the centre of a semi-circle of well-wishers, listening to the birthday wishes Med read out. From the broom cupboard I saw his expression soften as Med explained that he was going to play a special message from me. We had gone to a lot of trouble to get the message just right, and I saw now that we had succeeded as I listened to my recorded words, telling him sadly that I was all alone in the desert, but that I would have a party to celebrate his big moment. I reminded him that he was my best friend and that I loved him, and asked him to look around at all the people who were there that night and remind himself of how much they cared about him too. Troy smudged away the tears that had welled up in his eyes and smiled broadly, and it was as if everyone there, myself included, could read his thoughts: *Wow, he managed to get a message to me even though he was in the middle of the desert. Can you believe it?*

Med handed him a large beer mug with his birthday drink, and

Troy started to get it down while I crept up behind him, my heart racing. Troy finished the drink and then sprayed the remaining ice on to the laps of the people nearest him, like a rock star at the end of his concert. I was very close to him by now, and took that as the cue to walk up to his right and put my left arm over his shoulder as if I had been there all the time. Troy was exchanging signals with some people in the crowd and instinctively swung his right arm around me. Then time seemed to stand still as he turned his head towards me. At first he didn't recognise me, but suddenly his eyes sparkled as his thoughts came together and he hugged me, stunned to the point of being unable to get a word out at first. Then he told me how glad he was to see me, how he had been so deeply worried for my life at so many points of my journey. Finally we were both crying with happiness ... I had never experienced anything like that before, and it is a memory I will carry with me to the last day of my life.

I wish I could say that South Africa House's democracy celebration was as much of a blast as the birthday party, but unfortunately it wasn't. The main public event was to have been mass festivities in Trafalgar Square with 30 000 South African flags handed out, traditional foods on sale and so on, and a big evening concert featuring a number of star performers who had been flown in from South Africa and elsewhere in the world. But rain spoilt the outdoors stuff (although Bradley and I managed to get in a few overs in a blow-up bowling net provided by the sponsors of the England cricket team); worst of all, the hugely expensive concert was cancelled in its entirety, and all the performers ended up entertaining a select group of VIPs in South Africa House.

My own role in the festivities dwindled with the rest of it, and eventually amounted to no more than a few interviews with the South African media and a meeting with the High Commission staff. So in the end the celebration reached only a few people instead of the masses. What a disappointment! I couldn't help feeling that some – just a tiny fraction – of the £13 million it reportedly cost would have been better spent on helping me to make history. But of course there are two sides to every story, and my London visit was no exception. I had had a welcome break from the long grind up the west coast, I had gained a little media exposure which could only help me in the long stretch that still lay ahead, I had been able to talk to Vasti without fear of being cut off in mid-conversation, and I had spent a few days with my unofficial brother, Troy.

And that was not all by any means. Another bit of good fortune fell into my lap when I kept a promise to Michel Thoumas from Multiport, Senegal, to visit the organisation's head office in London. This could have been a mere courtesy call, but it turned out to be a great deal more rewarding than that when I fell into the hands of a large, plummy gentleman named Peter Titchener.

Peter was very interested in my travel stories as we sat in his office on Greenwich Quay, overlooking the Thames. He was so taken by the whole enterprise, in fact, that he not only made a generous contribution to my travel budget but took me to lunch at the East India Club. Then he invited me to the international Sea Trade awards ceremony, an annual event which gives recognition to the leaders and achievers in the world's sea-going industry. This year the guest speaker would be Prince Andrew ... would I like to attend and be presented to the prince?

Well, can a duck swim? I reckoned that I would very probably never have another chance to meet one of Britain's royal family, but I had a time problem – I was scheduled to leave London within 48 hours and resume my journey before I lost the momentum I had built up. But hell, I wanted to meet Prince Andrew. So I really chanced my arm. I e-mailed my acceptance – on condition that my meeting with the prince was confirmed. This was damned cheeky of me, because it meant Peter had to contact Buckingham Palace and ask whether I could be included in the six VIP guests who would be pressing the flesh with Prince Andrew at the ceremony. But instead of telling me to go to hell that great and good man got on to the palace – and within minutes had an affirmative reply.

The awards ceremony was held at the historic Guildhall, and of course was a black-tie occasion. It goes without saying that I hadn't brought any formal clothes with me, but nevertheless I rolled up spick and span in a rented dinner jacket that didn't cost me a cent, thanks to yet another fateful meeting. What happened was that while I was nosing around in a clothing-hire shop near the Hendon underground station I fell into conversation with the proprietor, a Nigerian woman. I told her about my trip and mentioned in passing that while in Nigeria I had cycled through a town called Njebo Ode. This happened to be her home town, and she was so tickled that she let me have the evening kit for nothing. It certainly made up for the brutal welding atrocity inflicted on my bike by the bargain-basement mechanic in Lagos.

Contrary to what I had feared, the beautifully cut dinner jacket and black tie actually set off my beard and wild Beatles-style hair to advantage, so I wasn't self-conscious when I was presented to Prince Andrew. His five other VIPs were serious heavyweights – one was the general manager of British Airways and the other the managing director of Rolls-Royce – and I think it must have been a relief for him to be introduced to someone who was very clearly not a captain of industry. After all, as a former naval officer and combat helicopter pilot Andrew was a sharp-end man.

Peter made the introduction and said a few things about what I had been up to, and the prince became very interested in my exploits. Rocking back on his heels so that the wine slopped around in his glass, in a voice that was high-pitched with interest he asked me the standard question: 'Why?'

I explained that my urge to find out new things was exactly the same as the thirst for discovery that had impelled my ancestors to put literally everything they had on the line and venture into the unknown. Andrew understood this urge perfectly, and we chatted a bit about the North African ports he had visited as a naval officer before I had to yield my place to some of the other guests. But before we parted I told him it would be delightful if he could visit South Africa in the near future. And NO, I did NOT bring the subject of Fergie into the conversation.

Things still kept getting better. I went along to the Moroccan embassy to see about the visa which had been eluding me all along and which I now needed desperately or my whole trip would have to go on hold indefinitely. I was, frankly, less than hopeful after the earlier run-arounds the Moroccans had given me – but this bunch issued it to me the same day. Incredible!

Then Troy and the other South Africans involved in my trip held a small fund-raiser which netted me £400 – not a huge sum in London, perhaps, but enough to take me a long way where I was going. I expressed my gratitude to each of them, but I knew that the best 'thank you' would be to complete the trip, regardless of what got slung at me. Bradley made another contribution by taking me on Sunday to a world-famous youth church, Hillsong London. With its constantly repeated theme that one should be grateful for what one had in one's life, the service had an overwhelming effect on me, and Bradley, sensing how much spiritual trauma I had suffered, made sure that I had a copy of the awesome Hillsong soundtrack to listen to while I was on the road.

I even survived a potentially fatal road accident which would have made reality of the 'I was run over by a bus in London, that's why I didn't complete my circumnavigation of Africa' excuse that I had no intention of using.

The day before I left London I set out on some last-minute shopping for videotapes and a spare battery for my video camera. I was walking along Regent Street towards Oxford Circus when I came up to some elderly tourists who were blocking the pavement, which was rather constricted at this point by construction work. I took one small step – no more than about 20 cm – off the pavement in order to get around the tourists, then, without any warning at all, a vehicle (one of the red double-decker London buses, it turned out) ran into me from behind. It was a hard thump which lifted me completely off the ground and sent me flying about 4 metres till I crashed through a triangular warning sign placed on some low scaffolding in the road.

There I lay half-stunned and trying to collect my wits while the bus dragged itself to a halt about 10 metres further on. When I had got my head together, a quick self-check showed that apart from a bleeding hand I had got off scot-free, and to retain some of my dignity I more or less took charge. I gave the worried bus-driver a 'thumbs up' and gestured him on his way, then waved reassuringly to the crowd, although the effect was somewhat spoiled by my injured knuckles, which sprayed blood on the spectators whenever I swung my hand around. But I was genuinely feeling OK, thanks to the adrenalin pumping into my veins, although I knew that I would be stiff and sore after my body had cooled down. When I had cycled out of Cape Town that first day I certainly never envisaged being sent flying by a red London bus, of all things!

Then it was time to return to Casablanca. My mental and physical batteries were fully charged and I was eager for the challenges that I was convinced lay ahead. As I waited to board my flight I bent my mind to making a plan about how I would get to Dakar from Casablanca. Because I was going to finish my trip, come hell or high water, just as quickly as I could. Till now I had never really understood how closely people had identified with me and my quest. Without realising it I had been carrying a lot of individual hopes around with me. That was OK, I had broad shoulders. So there I sat, scheming away amid all the noise and bustle of a society I would soon be swopping for the distant deserts.

# CHAPTER 18

# BACK ON THE ROAD … AND THROUGH THE SAHARA

*I got out of there as fast as I could go without looking like the dead guilty border-jumper that I was. Never again! I thought. This isn't the way I want to enter a country. The right way is the only way. But sometimes a man simply has to ignore his own good advice, then take the money and run like any sensible gambler who has struck it rich.*

With my batteries (not to mention my pockets) topped up and that all-important visa burning a hole in my passport, I was really looking forward to getting back on the road. It was a sure bet that I would run into difficulties of some kind in the next while, but so many good things had happened to me in the last couple of weeks that I was more than willing to take them as they came and see them as a sort of yin-yang balance thing.

My immediate priority was to work out a way, once I landed at Casablanca, to backtrack from Morocco to Senegal via Mauritania without using up my hard-won Moroccan visa. If push came to shove I would have to do so to maintain my momentum, but begging for an extension from the very officials who had insisted I would have to return to Pretoria first was very definitely Plan C, if not D. I didn't even want to think about how slim my chances would be of changing their attitude, and I simply did not have the money or the time for even a quick trip to Pretoria.

As it turned out I didn't have to fall back on Plan C/D. Instead I found myself flying straight back to a reunion with my bike ... for free! I owed this near-miraculous leapfrogging to a combination of two things, a hefty shot of the good fortune which had accompanied me so far, and my ability – well-honed by now – to adapt and blend in with whatever circumstances prevailed.

What happened was that my flight was delayed by five hours, which meant that many passengers who were headed for Dakar missed their connections. Mauritanian Air handled the problem very professionally, passing out dinner and hotel vouchers and assuring everybody that they would be on the next flight to Dakar the following evening. None of this included me, of course, but when a friendly English-speaking official asked if I was part of the Dakar-bound group I took the gap without a moment's hesitation, telling him all about my journey and why I had been in London. His reaction, to my delight, was to include my name on the list of people to be issued with tickets for the next evening's flight to Dakar, plus all the extras. Whether it was because my story touched his heart or whether it saved him tons of paperwork, or both, I didn't know and frankly didn't care. In one fell swoop I had scored a free flight to Senegal, a free dinner and a free hotel bed for the night. Things just didn't get any better than this, I decided.

Since my connecting flight was not leaving till the late afternoon I had time to stroll around Casablanca, gawking at the big mosques and government buildings while simultaneously drinking in the distinctly romantic and exotic feel of the place (OK, I didn't spot anyone resembling Humphrey Bogart and Ingrid Bergman, but I couldn't help being born 60 years too late).

Early next morning I landed in Dakar, where I linked up again with Nic Bothma and began preparing for the next leg of the journey. I spent the day on preparations which included retrieving my bike and fitting the new parts I had bought in London, got a good night's sleep in and set off after thanking Nic for everything he had done.

It felt fine to be on the road again and heading approximately northwards. After a break of nearly four weeks I was definitely not as lean and fit as I had been, but my knees were much better, although still tender, and I knew that a few days' pedalling would tone me up again.

When I got to St Louis, Senegal's second-largest town, I went off to see if I could find a famous musician, Baaba Maal, who lived there, according to my Gabonese (Ndindi) acquaintance. Though everyone knew about him, apparently he now made music overseas – but at least I saw a good bit of St Louis, a pleasantly laid-back fishing town. Then it was on to Rosso and the Mauritanian border.

Rosso had not been very good to me on my first visit, and it wasn't any better this time around, as I discovered when I left my bike in the safekeeping of a security guard at the so-called hotel while I went off on a short errand. He agreed enthusiastically to keep all 'bandits' away from it, but obviously didn't place himself in this category, because when I returned 20 minutes later the front pouch gaped open and there was no sign of my videotapes and Leatherman knife.

I tackled the security guard about it but got nowhere, firstly because neither of us could communicate properly and secondly because he denied everything in an arrogant see-if-you-get-anywhere tone which hadn't been there earlier. I didn't pursue what would have been a frustrating and fruitless process of trying to get him to confess and hand the stuff back. I was bitterly disappointed, not just because the missing items were irreplaceable at that point but also because I had been let down so badly by someone I had trusted. On the other hand, my good fortune of the past few weeks still outweighed this let-down, and he hadn't got any of my money because I had decided to carry it with me all the time.

I had another immediate problem to contend with. At Nouakchott I had had my Mauritanian visa extended so that I could enter a second time, but time had run away with me and it expired at midnight. It was a desperate situation that required a desperate remedy, and so I did something which could have landed me in a doubtless unpleasant Mauritanian jail for an indeterminate period: I locked myself into a smelly long-drop toilet right outside the Senegalese border post, unlimbered my faithful Bic pen and nervously but carefully altered the date by one day. I wasn't exactly proud of this, and it went against all my better instincts, but I have to admit that I didn't feel any significant amount of shame either. I hope nobody in the Senegalese or Mauritanian immigration services reads this chapter.

I entered the Mauritanian immigration office in fear and trembling, and when the immigration official turned my passport's page to get more light on it I calculated the game was up, because to my anxious eyes the forgery stood out like the proverbial canine gonads. I was so nervous that I just about wished he would harass me or dun me for a bribe rather than check my passport. What he actually did was remark 'there is problem here,' adding that he would have to consult with his superiors.

Having dealt with this lot before, I prepared myself to be anything he wanted except defensive, which would have been a dead give-away. Playing the role of innocent tourist to the hilt, I gabbled out an explanation of how I had had the visa extended in the capital and added: 'Hey, I don't know anything about your visas. Speak to your people in Nouakchott, they gave it to me.' The official thought about this and decided it made sense (or maybe he just reckoned it was too much of a hassle to contact Nouakchott about someone as harmless-looking as me), so he unwittingly made up for all the harassment I had encountered on my last visit to Rosso by stamping me through on the spot.

I got out of there as fast as I could go without looking like the dead guilty border-jumper that I was. 'Never again!' I thought. 'This isn't the way I want to enter a country. The right way is the only way.' But sometimes a man simply has to ignore his own good advice, then take the money and run like any sensible gambler who has struck it rich. Perhaps a better word would be 'slog' instead of 'run', because this was what I had to do now. Thanks to all the interruptions I was about six weeks behind schedule, which meant that I would have to make extra haste to traverse long stretches of desert country in which, so I discovered, the terrain was flat but the wind blew in only one direction – towards me.

It was an abrupt transition. On the Senegalese side of the river you travel through relatively dense bush. On the Mauritanian side you plunge immediately into a seemingly endless desert, aching in the heat. Small wonder that Mauritanians swop rumours about the Dakar government deliberately diverting the Senegal River at its source so that they will not have enough water to farm with!

That fierce and unrelenting wind sometimes gusted to what I calculated must be around 30 knots. Two and a half hours later, with night coming on, I had just 17 km to show for my efforts. Luckily I found a safe place to pitch my tent, in the lee of a large concrete block with a manhole in the top. What this block was doing there in the middle of nowhere was a mystery to me, but it was perfect as a campsite because it shielded me from the wind, which otherwise would have squashed my tent to the ground.

It was a sad night, and not just because I had laboured so mightily for so little reward. I knew that in faraway Cape Town Vasti had had to put down my beautiful, big, bold Boxer, Murphy. I loved him so much and had hoped to see him when I returned, but it was not to be. Now the light had gone from his eyes, and I had not been there for him. My Gordon's Bay neighbours, Robin and Hazel, earned my undying gratitude for what they did that day. They went with Vasti when she drove Murphy to the vet for the injection that took him gently into a final slumber, and then volunteered to bury him in my back garden. I am sure that it was not an easy task for them, because they had become his virtual foster parents in the years we lived across from them.

It was the darkest moment I had experienced in my eight months of almost continuous travel, and I realised now the strength of emotion as an ingredient of personal motivation. My relationship with my dogs was immensely important to me, and Murphy's death made me think of the things I was missing out on – things I hadn't given serious thought to before I left home. I didn't want anything to happen to anyone close to me while I was away. Yet I was compelled to undertake this journey because I knew that there would be a permanent gap in my life if I didn't do it. There was no way around it: I simply couldn't be in two places at once. The bottom line was that nothing in life was free. Achievement demanded sacrifice; all you could do was weigh up one set of profits and losses against the other, then make your choice.

That's a strong argument and a sound one. But it didn't console me much as I huddled in my little tent with the wind howling past the door-flap, grieving for my friend and boon companion.

Mauritania was the first country I had passed through which I regarded as truly Muslim, laid-back Senegal notwithstanding. I had imagined it would have a feel something like that of the large Muslim community back home in Cape Town, whose people got on with their lives and their religion while living comfortably alongside the people of many different beliefs and origins that you find in any long-established coastal city. But it wasn't. These were different people with a different view of the world, shaped and polished by a pitiless environment that was a complete contrast to Cape Town with its Mediterranean climate and scenery.

My wake-up call came when I passed a cluster of houses just south of Nouakchott and a girl of about 12 with beautiful frizzy brown hair started throwing stones at me, screaming and showing all the signs of extreme hostility. I was taken aback by her baffling outburst. I had done nothing to provoke her, but it was as if she was possessed. Yet her parents did nothing to stop or rebuke her. They stood watching and actually smiling at her paroxysm of rage.

It was a frightening experience, not because I feared for my life but because I couldn't make out what was going on inside her head, or her parents'. Had my appearance triggered some sort of defence mechanism which was essential to survival in the desert? Or was there an instinctive hostility towards all non-Muslims, born of some long-distant event which had left an indelible footprint on the Mauritanian psyche? I simply didn't know. But as I carried on I noticed that most of the Mauritanians I encountered wouldn't even return a greeting or a smile, and I realised that the tolerance, whether willing or grudging, which South Africans tend to take for granted is a luxury rather than a given.

In a rather battered and dehydrated condition I arrived at Nouakchott, my newly Muslimised eyes noting for the first time that just about all the men there wore virtually identical light-blue Roman-style robes, which they nonchalantly flicked over the shoulders with a gesture made slightly irritating by its constant repetition. I visited the Internet café, renewed my acquaintance with a very kind and gentle man named Mahmoud who ran the Restaurant Phenicia, an excellent eating-place which had been my hangout during my first visit, and debated with myself about the best route to Morocco.

I had two choices, neither of them particularly appealing. I could go directly north to the town of Nouadhibou by way of an incomplete road, a route which had already claimed three foreigners' lives that year – and they weren't even on bicycles! – or I could ride northeast to Atar and then Choum. At Choum I could hitch a lift on the world's longest train – 2.5 km from nose to tail, I was told – which hauled iron ore from the desert town of Zouérate to the port of Nouadhibou. From there I could carry on up the coast. I knew all about highways that ended without warning and didn't much like the story about all those dead foreigners, so I settled on the Atar route. Granted, it was considerably longer in terms of distance, but by now I had absorbed a crucial lesson about West African travel: the time spent travelling between two points didn't necessarily have any relation to the distance covered.

I also did something which most people won't understand – in fact, I didn't understand it so well myself at the time: I returned to the youth hostel run by my thieving ex-friend, the pious crook Mohamed, although I didn't take a room this time but camped outside. He received me sheepishly, which was hardly surprising, since he must have concluded that I was the last person he would ever see again. I think he was even more surprised when I didn't set about beating his head in but simply asked why he had run away that morning. He mumbled that he had been under a lot of pressure from his family at that time and had not been not thinking straight.

Oh, yeah. Poor Mohamed! He had been thinking straight enough to pinch my telephone, though, take sanctuary in the one place I couldn't follow him to and then flog it to the highest bidder. I knew that because Vasti had let me know that she had been receiving some strange calls from Mauritanian telephone numbers. Since she didn't have any admirers in that part of the world, her cell phone's number could only have been retrieved from my stolen PDA. She could not communicate with the callers but, knowing about Mohamed's theft, had saved the numbers and passed them on to me.

This intrusion into our lives really angered me, and I decided to see if I could bring Mohamed to book. I enlisted my restaurateur friend Mahmoud's help and he called the numbers Vasti had saved, inviting the people who answered to visit the restaurant so he could see who they were. But we drew a blank, because as far as we could make out none of the guys who turned up were aware of any theft. In fact, some of them even helped me to search the local market from top to bottom for a second-hand Ericsson P800. No luck, however, and finally I faced the fact that I wasn't going to get anywhere and might as well stop trying.

I didn't tarry long in Nouakchott, but before I left I had two experiences, one shocking and the other horribly funny. The shocking one involved four large Arabs who had accidentally backed their vehicle into a taxi driven by a black man with whom I was acquainted from using his services during my first visit. They refused to accept responsibility for the accident, although it was clearly their fault, and were threatening the black man with physical violence if he didn't move his car so that they could be on their way. He wasn't too happy about letting the perpetrators get off scot-free, but he was badly outnumbered. I had witnessed the incident while walking to the Internet café and knew he was blameless, so I decided to walk over and show the Arabs that they were wrong in their obvious belief that he was alone. I squeezed in between them, grabbed the taxi's keys and told the driver to go and fetch a policeman. The Arabs made no secret of how they felt about this, but I kept a firm grip on the keys and didn't let them see my inward quaking. A few minutes later the driver reappeared with a policeman and I handed over the keys and headed for the Internet café, pleased that I had had been able to help the driver but inwardly dismayed at this nakedly racist incident.

There I was treated to my second unforgettable Nouakchott character, not that he appeared so at first glance, being just another middle-aged Arab wearing the usual blue robes. This fellow was a bit of a pain in the backside; my time was running out and he spent hours in front of the café's only big computer, which I needed to use for downloading larger files and digital photographs. But he didn't budge from his chair except at the customary prayer times, when he rolled out his mat, faced east and vigorously blared out his prayers.

My chance came when he went down for the evening prayers. While he addressed Allah in his usual stentorian voice I slipped into his chair and got down to business. First I had to close down some files he had left open, and to my surprise found myself confronted with page after page of hardcore pornography. So, prayers or no prayers, he was just another dirty old man who passed the time surfing the pornography sites! I was so surprised at this unlikely mixture of filth and piety that I swung around to look at him. He was just rising to an upright condition after genuflecting, and our eyes met. No doubt my shocked face told him the game was up, because he wrapped up his prayer session with all decent haste, grabbed his mat and walked out of the café in a flurry of flapping robes without looking back. I returned to my downloading, perplexed and amused in equal measure; to judge by him and Mohamed, cultivating pious hypocrites was virtually an industry in Nouakchott.

I left Nouakchott without having been able to replace my telephone, but certainly much wiser in the ways of men. The Atar route was much longer than the alternative, but there was an awesome beauty to the endless great mountains of golden sand through which I passed. It wasn't an easy passage, though. The heat stayed around the 40 degrees Celsius mark, so that I began to feel a bit leathery, and the ceaseless wind not only made me fight for every kilometre but actually irritated my skin. The solitude of these unpopulated regions was marvellous, giving me a decent chance to listen to music. The Hillsong CD's second track quickly became the early morning starter to my fuel cells; it had me going like a steam train every time, even before the first chorus ended.

In case you think there can be nothing crazier than someone cycling through umpteen kilometres of virtually uninhabited desert, rest assured that there are worse nut cases, like the fellow I crossed paths with who was *roller-blading* from Atar to Nouakchott for the sheer fun of it (admittedly he had the wind at his back, which must have helped a great deal). He presented a strange figure in his heavy biker's jacket, large elbow- and knee-guards, a balaclava and an umbrella over his shoulder like Mary Poppins. He was very friendly, though, and wanted to know more about me and my adventure while we shared a cup of sweet Mauritanian tea. Maybe he was so inspired that he decided to keep on roller-blading till he reached Cape Town.

The desert wasn't totally unpopulated, however, and as time went by I eventually met some very kind Mauritanians. One of them, Ahmed – most men in Mauritania seem to be named either 'Ahmed' or 'Mohamed' – I came across at the roadside; his car had overheated in the extreme desert temperatures, and he and his assistant or servant were drinking tea under a little bush when I came up. Ahmed really was hospitable, to the point of insisting that I simply could not sleep in the desert but must spend the night at his house in Atar. The problem was that Atar was still 190 km away, and if I spent the night with him I would have to cycle back to where we had met, because the whole point of my trip was that I had to physically cover the entire distance.

Ahmed simply couldn't understand why I should want to do this, and I suppose that to a desert-dweller it made absolutely no sense. But I saw I was getting nowhere, and he was so insistent that I gave up trying for the time being and joined him in the car when it had cooled down enough. We had a late lunch, washed down with camel's milk and sweet tea, at a little village called Akjoujt, in a restaurant such as I had never patronised before – simply a big tent pitched in the desert – and then carried on. I tried once more to explain my logic, but only succeeded in confusing Ahmed even further.

By the time we arrived on the outskirts of Atar, however, he had reconciled himself to the fact that I was determined to refuse his hospitality and head back again, possibly because in the interim a genuine good excuse had presented itself – I discovered that I had forgotten my cycling shoes in Akjoujt and now had only a pair of leather sandals, which were very poor substitutes. So he dropped me off, slightly offended that I had spurned his offer of hospitality.

I set out early next morning and made fantastic time, thanks to the gale-force wind which was now propelling rather than obstructing me, so much so that I found myself unexpectedly breaking my personal record for fastest 100 km. The best 100 km stint I had done so far had taken me just over four hours, but now I clocked triple figures in no more than two hours and 45 minutes – an average of over 36 km/h on that heavily laden bicycle of mine ... and in sandals, too. Where were the Guinness Book of Records guys when I needed them?

I carried on till I got to where I had met Ahmed, and having covered the distance I could bum a lift back to Atar with a clear conscience. I relaxed by the roadside, and after about an hour a car came along, driven by another Ahmed who proved just as hospitable as his predecessor. This time I didn't try very hard to explain how I had ended up in these circumstances; it seemed I was the only person in Mauritania who understood why I wanted to cycle every centimetre of the way.

Ahmed didn't care. He helped me get my shoes back from the restaurant owner at Akjoujt, who could not speak a word of English or French, and invited me to stay over with him and some others at the house of a mutual friend in Atar, where, he said, I would be most welcome. We washed the grime off our bodies in some small pools of water we spotted just outside the town, after which he presented me with a new caftan he had bought in Dubai, which he intimated very tactfully would be more appropriate than the travel-worn clothes I was wearing.

When we got to our destination I understood his gift. Ahmed's host and friends were stinking rich. The host's house was carved out of stone, with the arched door of each room facing on to an enclosed courtyard with its own fresh water well (a sure indicator of wealth, I discovered). But they weren't snobs. All warm and deeply religious men, they welcomed me wholeheartedly with a generous hospitality which both impressed me and earned my deep gratitude.

There was one jarring note, though, that rather spoiled my enjoyment of the stay with them. One of Ahmed's business partners had a sort of manservant, a tall, very dark-skinned black man, whose main task was to keep serving us with whatever we needed or desired. For some reason I fascinated this character, and I noticed that when serving us meals in the main entertainment room during the two nights and a day I spent there he watched me closely to see how I was coping with the traditional Arabic way of eating.

One mealtime the black man brought in the main course, a leg of beef on a bed of couscous, then headed slowly towards the door with the plates which had contained the starters of olives and dates. At the door, however, he stopped and stared back at us, and that's when Ahmed produced his shock. Impatiently he waved the black man out, then turned to me and said with a broad well-we-know-how-it-is smile: 'The dog can't be in the room when we eat. You understand, hey, it's the same in South Africa, hey?' This shook me so much that even today I can recapture my exact feelings. During the apartheid years South Africa had become a byword for racial segregation, but this level of contempt was something I had never experienced in my years of growing up along the Natal coast. 'No, no, no, Ahmed, you can't talk like that,' I found myself saying, but he just smiled and repeated what he had said, obviously misunderstanding my reaction completely.

I was stunned, but I didn't pursue the matter. I would have liked very much to clear the issue up and explain that the recent past and the Truth and Reconciliation Commission had unfairly painted every white South African with the same brush. But this was not the time or the place, and anything I said would have sounded far too defensive. So instead of tackling Ahmed I tackled the beef, but for the remainder of my stay I made an effort to show the black man, who seemed to be little more than a glorified slave, what real open-minded South Africans were like. All this probably makes Ahmed sound like a pretty bad guy, but this is not so. As far as I was concerned Ahmed and his friends were genuinely good at heart; it was just that they were the product of a different milieu about which I was still very ignorant, although I hoped I would improve as I went on. As a religion Islam is pretty colour-blind, but social practices differ from country to country, and the Mauritanian culture is not like South Africa's. A Mauritanian's house is not just his castle but his kingdom, in which he is a god-like potentate who expects to be waited on hand and foot by the women and servants. That was the way they had all been raised, and none of them saw anything strange about it.

When it became time for me to leave, the generosity of my hosts showed itself again. I was given a guide and a luxury 4x4 to take me to the road north to Choum, and Ahmed's friend Mohamed – the owner of the 4x4 – insisted on saying a prayer for me. I stood in front of the 4x4, eyes closed and with Mohamed's hands resting on mine while he beseeched Allah to preserve me in the journeys that still lay ahead for me, and as the sincere words washed over me I could feel my heart softening towards everything that made up this strange land.

I got to Choum feeling more leathery than ever before in heat whose ferocity gave my camera a sort of digital nervous breakdown, so that everything it recorded was suffused with an orangey haze. I managed to summon up the energy to ask about trains to the coast, and it turned out that in addition to the renowned world-beating ore train there was also a sort of passenger train (I say 'sort of' because it was open and seatless). The next one was only due in three days' time, however, and I decided to take my chances with the ore train, although it had certain disadvantages. It was very slow, it was open to the extreme heat and cold of the desert's wildly fluctuating day-time and night-time temperatures, and the fine dust blowing off the cargo tended to damage everything a passenger owned, including his lungs.

I decided to chance it all the same, and a kindly policeman helped me to find a respectable turban which would help against the cold and especially the ore-dust, then gave me a lesson in the art of rolling and wrapping it around my head. We left Choum at sunset, and it was as long and cold a ride as I had been promised, but I survived it quite well by snuggling up with some goats that were also travelling westwards and burrowing into the iron ore. This got me through the night in fairly good shape, although my appearance and general effluvium left something to be desired when we arrived at the coast at sunrise next morning. A memorable experience in more ways than one!

I cleaned myself up a bit, touched sides with the managing director of a local fishing company who was a business partner of one of my Atar friends, then headed out of Nouadhibou, very conscious of the fact that I would have to pass through a most unpleasant no-man's land called the Western Sahara before reaching historically Moroccan soil. I say 'historically' because the Western Sahara has been in constitutional limbo since 1976: Morocco claims it's Moroccan, but the indigenous political party called the Polisario Front claims otherwise. How this affected me was that while there was no immediate threat of guerrilla war resuming, the Western Sahara was thick with indiscriminately sown and later abandoned anti-tank and anti-personnel mines. Mines are long-lived things that tend to become even more dangerous as time passes because their explosive charges become unstable, so although the ceasefire had been in place for more than a decade they were still capable of wreaking death and destruction on whoever or whatever set them off.

Everyone I came into contact with warned me not to diverge from the main road, not even on foot for only a few paces, if I wanted to stay in one piece, and when I got there I found warning signs posted at frequent intervals along the road that made it clear these were not just scare stories. One warning that remains vivid in my memory consisted merely of three simple but graphic illustrations. The first showed a normal two-legged man. The second depicted an explosion labelled KABOOM, and the third showed the man again, only this time with crutches and one leg. One would think that such stark warnings, combined with my experience in the extremely mine-conscious South African Army, would have been enough to keep me on the straight and narrow way, both figuratively and literally, but don't you believe it ... sometimes I think I have the mind of a goldfish.

This revelation about my likely mental state came to me at one spot *after* I had strolled casually off the road to position my camera so that I could film myself cycling past. I was nearly back on the road when I realised what a foolhardy thing I had done, in spite of all the warnings and personal knowledge. The casual stroll instantly turned into a series of very slow, very careful steps, each preceded by a scan of the ground ahead which was so thorough I could just about see the earthworms beneath the surface, while my mind's eye ran an endlessly repeated film of myself starring in the KABOOM scenario.

I reached the road unscathed, panted a bit till I had got my adrenalin under control again and then did my cycle-by, heartily grateful that I had been saved from the consequences of my foolishness. Then I realised that I still had to fetch the camera from where it sat smugly in death-and-wounds territory. It took some doing to force myself back off the road, very carefully stepping in the tracks I had made earlier, to retrieve the damned thing.

I didn't look back as I rode away; I had seen as much of that particular bit of landscape as I needed to, thank you very much. It was going to be a pleasure to get to Morocco proper. Granted, I was heading for the country we had beaten only days before in the pitched battle to host the Soccer World Cup in 2010, the first African nation to do so. But any hostility I might experience would be pretty small beer after my little off-road excursion into landmine territory. I'm getting ahead of myself, however: there would be some to-ing and fro-ing of note before I managed to say goodbye to the Western Sahara!

# CHAPTER 19

# DUST AND HONEY IN MOROCCO

*Much as I admire him, I do not believe Lance Armstrong would
have made it that far. The lack of close support would certainly
have played a part, but the essential thing would have been a
need to be as willing as I was literally to do or die. In my opinion he wouldn't have that sort of commitment. It isn't only
about the bike!*

Backtracking to before the mines in the desert ... I can't say that
my departure from Mauritania was very dramatic. Let's compromise and call it 'interesting'. The border post looked like the set of
a film about a ghost town. The tarmac road to the north ended in
a small, neat cul-de-sac in which slouched a battered roofless white
building with IMMIGRATIO – obviously dating from the Spanish-
speaking days – spray-painted on one wall. This was all a bit confusing: what was a traveller supposed to do when he had passed
through immigration and found himself facing a dead end? After
some minutes of shouting loudly in the hope of attracting the attention of an official (I was a bit worried about being gunned down
by an over-eager soldier mistaking me for a heavily disguised one-
man Polisario Front invasion force) I realised that in fact there was
no one to kiss me or anyone else goodbye on behalf of the Mauritanian government, and hadn't been for a long time.

In addition to all this there was no indication of the right way to
take to the Moroccan (Western Sahara) border, barring some tyre

tracks heading into the flat, barren landscape. I thought of getting my compass out, then decided the hell with it, I'd just follow the tracks. Where else could people be going when they left the retired border-post? There was nothing for me to orientate myself by, but as long as I could see signs of other people's movement I would be OK. So I tackled the world's largest desert in good spirits. But I mourned the end of the hard road that had died on me in the cul-de-sac, because it was impossible to cycle now. Dunes surrounded me on all sides, with only occasional patches of crusty rocks providing enough traction. That was it. No people, no road, no signposts, no nothing. So I slogged along in the tyre tracks, pushing my heavy bike through the soft sand and making very slow progress.

After a couple of painful hours I spotted a handful of sun-bleached cars and a panel van parked in a sort of laager formation about a kilometre to the east of the tracks. Reluctantly I temporarily parted company with the tracks and headed towards them, slightly concerned about the fact that they appeared to be deserted. At this remove it might sound like a fairly groundless worry, but after all, I had just passed through an abandoned border post, so it wasn't at all strange for me to entertain the possibility that this was a batch of vehicles which had been abandoned in the desert for reasons beyond my ken. I had long since lost most of my capacity for surprise.

As it turned out the forlorn little encampment wasn't deserted. It was a sort of desert workshop offering repair services to passing travellers, and before long I was trying to explain myself to a bewildered mechanic who seemed to become even more bewildered as we talked because he simply could not understand why I should be riding a bicycle through this inhospitable terrain. Eventually, though, the penny dropped and he pointed to a small building on the horizon, saying: 'Morocco there'. Actually the building turned out to be the Mauritanian border post, and I passed through it without regret because I was not sad to see the last of Mauritania; I had just had too many bad experiences there.

I started to see signs of life after I had passed through the border post. The southern part of Morocco seemed to be the gateway for European tourists bent on visiting the Sahara, and every now and then a car filled with foreigners would pass me. My progress at this stage was still painfully slow, even though some semblance of a road had reappeared. My bicycle's gears were worn and slipping, reducing me to the frustrating expedient of struggling along in one or two that still retained some grip, and on top of that, my chain was also giving problems. This was partly my fault. The premature component failure was clearly caused by the infiltration of the fine desert sand into the chunky old-fashioned grease I was using instead of more modern dry lubrication. Naturally this realisation did not help me at all as I struggled vainly to find some sort of interim solution.

And then – once again! – I experienced the kindness of strangers. I was squatting dismally next to my upside-down bike when a youth group, of all things, came driving by and stopped to offer assistance. What a relief! The people in charge, Patrick and Norra, explained that the French government sponsored the group, which specialised in taking youngsters between 15 and 18, all with records for petty crime, family violence or drug abuse, into the Moroccan and Mauritanian desert and mountains for creative therapy to help them to get their lives on track again.

I was filled with admiration for the purpose of the group and also for Patrick and Norra, extremely patient and experienced chaperones who handled their charges with a mixture of firmness, compassion and understanding. It was clearly not an easy task, but Patrick and Norra left me in no doubt that as far as they were concerned they had the best job in the world: they were able to spend time in what they considered the most beautiful part of the planet and at the same time had the opportunity of giving these troubled youngsters a second chance in life.

After considering my bicycle problem Patrick made an eminently sensible and kind-hearted proposal. He would take me to the town of Agadir, where a ranch-owning friend of his called Nadia Belvet would help me to get the repairs done; if she couldn't help, he would get me to the capital, Rabat. He knew many people in Morocco, Patrick said, which I discovered was no less than the truth, and he was sure that the parts I needed would be available in Rabat if they were not to be found in Agadir.

As it turned out, I couldn't find what I needed in Agadir, so I headed to Rabat, as suggested, where some more friendly South African diplomats came to my rescue. The ambassador, HE Mthuthuzeli Mpehle, received me in kindly fashion, and two of his staff really went the extra mile for me. One of them, named Roelof – a tall 'Simply Red' look-alike with lots of long, frizzy red hair – turned out to be a keen cyclist himself and was thus consumed with pity for my tenacious but travel-worn machine. His solution was to inspan the other members of his cycling group, who spent an entire evening giving my bike a royal once-over. By the time they had finished it had undergone a truly awesome change; it felt as if I was riding a brand-new set of wheels.

The other was Linda, the second in charge at the Embassy, a pretty woman who wore a tweed skirted suit and sported a longish, flowing bob hairstyle, and had the sort of stature that you have to be born with ... if you don't have it you can't acquire it. I was really impressed by Linda's personality, but what made me take her into my heart was something else altogether. I had arrived there wild, woolly and dirty from battling the desert, and she had Roelof bring me straight to her in her spacious, deliciously air-conditioned office. I slunk in behind him in a distinctly nervous frame of mind. What sort of trouble was I in that one of the embassy's heavyweights wanted a one-on-one with me?

I was staggered to find that I wasn't in any trouble; my wrecked appearance had filled Linda's heart with concern about my general health and hygiene, and she wanted to know if she could help. She didn't want to embarrass me, she said, but if I needed to have any washing and ironing done she would be happy to handle it (I realised then for the first time just how rough and ready, not to say downright intimidating, I must look to everyone around me). What a woman! A sophisticated diplomat of high rank, yet with a warm, down-to-earth South African heart beating underneath all that larney armour. I decided then and there that if Linda ever ran for president she would have my vote. With Linda in the top job we would certainly never go to war because we would be too busy concerning ourselves about things that really mattered.

Nadia Belvet had also arranged for her brother, Madani, to look after me while I was in Rabat. Madani was quite a big wheel, if you will excuse the fun, since he was national secretary of the Moroccan Rally championships and was also involved with the world-famous Paris to Dakar Rally. On our very first outing I found myself a VIP guest at the national Moroccan Rally championships function in the city of Meknes, and he laid on a dinner the night after with the current Paris to Dakar course director, Patrick Zanaroli.

Patrick was a veteran of the Dakar Rally, surely the world's most challenging road race – in fact, he won it in 1985 – so he knew all about eating dust in the African backveld, but even so he was astounded by what I had done so far and planned still to do. What amazed him most was that my only navigational tool was a compass; he believed that a GPS was a must-have for trip like mine. I didn't argue. If anyone knew what he was talking about, it must surely be Patrick Zanaroli. The only problem was that I didn't have a GPS or the money to buy one.

Madani also introduced me to a Moroccan cultural experience so amazing that it would have been enough by itself to make my visit to the country worthwhile, the annual Fantasia Festival. It's difficult to describe in words, but what it involved was dozens of musket-wielding horsemen charging across a dusty field about 200 metres long in such breakneck fashion that one could swear they were really involved in an old-time battle and not just a re-enactment.

The charge wasn't simply a wild gallop but a carefully synchronised and disciplined effort which took place under the critical eyes of a panel of judges and VIPs, with prizes awarded for the best-dressed and best-choreographed group of participants. The art, so I was informed, was for the galloping horsemen to stay in formation for the first part of the charge, holding back their magnificent horses – no easy task, because they were just as excited as their riders – up to a certain point, when they slackened the reins for the final sprint, culminating in a mass musket-volley. It was a gut-wrenchingly exciting affair which left me, and I suspect many others, keen on horses forever.

Further hospitality was showered on me by yet another of the

Top left: This isn't a swimming pool, it's the Red Sea!

Top right: Packed and ready to go in Alexandria.

Above: At the Alexandria City Museum: I can see where I come from – just the size of the ears makes me wonder.

Right: A puncture at the pyramids. (Photo: Reuters)

Bottom right: Le Meridien Pyramids, Cairo. A view from my hotel room.

Below: I can't remember where this was taken (joking only!).

Top left: One of my three goals ticked off: Lac Assal, Africa's lowest point – 153 m below sea level.

Top right: Marketing fish Khartoum-style. A Sudanese man attempts to peddle his fresh catch street by street, door by door.

Above left: 'If camels can't make this stretch then I'm surely in trouble.' Nubian Desert, northern Sudan.

Left: The Tortil Mountains of Kassala, Sudan. The tomb of Mahdi, the famous Islamic prophet, is at the base. Water from this oasis rock is said to be magical.

Far right: Kassala, Sudan: with the family of Yussuf Hijazi, Paul Azzo's employee.

Right: Yussuf Hijazi's pretty daughter pours 'jebena' (coffee).

Above and left: Sudanese desert/Nile traders at a town halfway between Wadi Halfa and Atbara.

Above: Big fall, big drama – lots of blood and lots of luck. The only car I saw that day carried the only doctor in the region, who gave me these Rambo-style stitches.

Top left: Women in Africa work, while the men enjoy being men. These young Ethiopian girls were up every day before dawn to collect firewood, carry it home, start the fire, then make food for the day ... for the men.

Top right: The night I used the body bag to keep me dry. Slip your sleeping bag in there, you follow, leave just enough of a gap for breathing and fall asleep to the hypnotic rhythm of the rain beating down on you in wild Somalian desert.

Left: I had multi-millionaire status in Somalia: one note gets thousands back at the exchange.

Left: Bulxaar, Somalia: a 102-year-old man puts me in my place. He wanted to arrange a 100-metre sprint between himself and our current world record holder.

Bottom left: Russian tank in the Somali desert.

Bottom right: Somali fun: target shooting in the main road, even when elderly donkeys are passing by.

Somaliland

Top left: This beautiful Ethiopian girl's hair has a mind of its own.

Top right: Introduction to new bugs in Ethiopia ... why not taste them too?

Left: The road into Ethiopia: the sharp curves indicate the change in altitude.

Above: A modern Ethiopian shepherd near the Kenya border: one AK-47, 200 bullets, 500 head of cattle.

Middle: The land gushes with life and there are always children around.

Above right: You, you, you ... I was pursued from one end of Ethiopia to the other by begging children.

Bottom right: On the way south from Addis – Orthodox churches look over your shoulder even in Rasta country.

Ethiopia

Top left: Moyale – Northern Kenya. The guy standing to my left is Solomon, the herbalist who attempted to expel the demons of evil from the pits of my stomach.

Top right: 'We fly to serve': my kind of restaurant in Kenya's northern desert.

Right: In this Turbi hotel rooms were named after famous South African places. I slept peacefully in the 'New South Africa' room.

Bottom left: Covered with biting yellow insects near Marsarbit.

Bottom right: Makindu: Sikh temple where the legendary lions of Tsavo slept after hunting the Indian labourers of the Lunatic Express.

Left: The indispensable mosquito net – I took my last malaria tablets in Ethiopia.

Kenya

Above: On top of Africa: Kilmanjaro, Tanzania.

Right: Scientists believe that the Kilimanjaro glacier will have melted away by 2020. Great marketing ploy? Nope. Pure fact.

Above: Debbie Yazbek interviewed me for 'The Star' at the Kenya–Tanzania border. (Photos: Debbie Yazbek)

Left: A pose of note. (Photo: Debbie Yasbek)

Above left: A helping hand near the Kenya–Tanzania border. (Photo: Debbie Yazbek)

Above right: Kilwa ma Soko, Tanzania. The lady who landed this awesome fish allowed me to pose with it in exchange for the moral support I'd given her.

Top left: Close, but still so far, in northern Mozambique. Cycling in talcum powder in 45 degree heat was not easy: 1 km/h on the downhills!

Top right: The 'breaching whale' rock formations near Nampula are majestic.

Above left: A bicycle carries much more than just the cyclist.

Above right: Heading for home: fellow cyclists and their weary pet.

Left above: So close ... so close.

Left below: A roadside rest – both the bike and I needed lots of down-time.

Bottom left: The Save River bridge near Vilanculos.

Bottom right: Missionary footsteps in Mozambique.

Mozambique

Above: The South African border, three metres from braai and boerewors country!

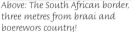

Top: KZN border – home territory!.

Middle: Cycling uphill out of Port St Johns with the Mzimvubu River mouth in the background.

Above: Plunging into the unknown: the world's highest bungee jump.

Above: Taken by an unknown journalist at Knysna, a week away from home.

Inset: At the end. What was going on in my mind? You're not the only one asking ... so am I.

Left: It's not every day you have a true legend look into your eyes with admiration. Mr Mandela probably has rooms full of photos presented to him by crazy people who have done extraordinary things ... but he treated me very kindly all the same.

seemingly endless number of hospitable French Patricks who came into my life. This one was a friend of Madani's, who turned his lounge into a temporary bedroom for me at his home in the area of Rabat where the exteriors for the film 'Blackhawk Down' was shot. This Patrick was a rather eccentric TV producer who took note of my first name and promptly christened me 'Soldier Ryan' in honour of the Tom Hanks movie 'Saving Private Ryan', on the grounds that my journey was something that only a crazy soldier would undertake. I didn't mind – Patrick was tickled pink with this flight of fancy, and I'd been called far worse things in my life.

Patrick was very proud of his Moroccan business partner, Khalid, who, he said, showed great diplomatic talent in his dealings with the various Arab rebel faction leaders. Among other things he had secured what was believed to be the first interview with the Polisario Front's leader in the Western Sahara, which was aired worldwide by the BBC. To be quite honest, however, what really intrigued me was the view from my temporary bedroom, every window of which gave me a fine look at the famous twelfth-century Tower of Hassan. Talk about the best address in town! And on top of that, it was in the same street as the South African Embassy, which was very convenient because I was pressed for time, due to my need to get back to where Patrick-the-chaperone and I had met originally in southern Morocco. In a way the making of a high-tech twenty-first-century film like 'Blackhawk Down' virtually in the shadow of the ancient Tower of Hassan pretty much symbolised the strange and sometimes uncomfortable make-up of modern Morocco. While it is a traditional Islamic nation, like most of its near and distant neighbours, its culture is a rich cosmopolitan blend of Arab, Berber, European and African influences, thanks to a coastline which runs from the Atlantic to the Mediterranean. It really is a land of contrasts, to use a very well-worn cliché, although I didn't realise the extent of the contrasts till later on.

My main concern at this stage was mainly with practical things rather than matters political. For one thing, my video camera had ingested a fatal dose of the fine iron-ore dust that had covered everything on my train ride through the Mauritanian desert and now wanted to be retired. I obliged, albeit with great reluctance, because my budget simply wouldn't stretch to buying any sort of photographic replacement except one of those cheap Kodak point-and-shoot cameras. Camera snobs tend to sneer at these little $10 contrivances, but I believed (correctly, as my results proved) that they were hugely underestimated when it came to the quality of the pictures they produced. The only inconvenience was that now I would have to scan in the hard copies to be able to show people back home how I was getting on. But a veteran of the West African jungle laughs at such little foibles of Fate.

My second concern was about which way to go. I could find transport back to the point just south of Dakhla from where Patrick had given me a lift to Agadir, or I could just start cycling back immediately and solve the transport issue once I was there. After some lengthy pondering I settled on the latter option, one important reason being that it would reduce my travelling costs – the Windhoek Light sponsorship would run out in just over four months' time, and I knew by now that my original time estimates had been totally wrong, so that I would not be able to make it home in the remaining time.

The route I settled on would take me from Rabat southwards through Casablanca to Dakhla in a 2 000-plus km slog along Morocco's Atlantic and Mediterranean coastlines that I aimed to complete in just 14 days, including two rest days. This meant that I would have to maintain a daily average of 166 km, which was really pushing it but was not, I thought, too ambitious, because I would have a good tail-wind. My only regret was that I would not have much time for the side-excursions that added so much extra spice to my wanderings.

It might seem strange that I planned to cycle southwards in the 'wrong' direction before heading northwards again, given the fact that I was already short of both money and time, but from my point of view it made perfect sense. I was not a tourist; my aim was to *cycle* through whatever country I was visiting, only using other means of transport when there was absolutely no alternative. I had passed through Casablanca – spent a night there, in fact – on my way to London, but making the trip by bicycle would be a brand-new experience; it would be like visiting the city for the first time.

And so it was. The Casablanca I saw this time was worlds apart from what I had experienced during my first visit, when my sightseeing had been confined mainly to the more modern section. Now I visited the Medina, or old city, dating back more than 1 000 years, with a huge surrounding wall which was breathtaking in its size and beauty, the sun giving it a golden glow that made me imagine the biblical Great Wall of Jericho. Just as fascinating was what lay inside the wall, a labyrinth of alleys housing everything from family homes to Internet cafés and linen stores. I had no difficulty in believing the conventional wisdom that if you wanted value for money in any Moroccan city, the only place to go was the Medina.

I was equally impressed by a visit to what is said to be the world's largest religious site after Mecca, the King Hassan II Mosque. Over 5 000 workers spent five years building this huge, beautiful structure, which can take up to 25 000 worshippers at a time under its roof and accommodate a whopping 80 000 more on its grounds. It was only when I walked across the outer area, dominated by a minaret which reaches up 215 metres, that I appreciated the sheer size of it. As I walked across the great expanse I couldn't help thinking that here, too, was another example of the contrasts one found in Morocco, because this most traditional of all edifices also featured state-of-the-art underfloor heating and an electric sliding roof to keep worshippers warm and dry in bad weather.

Casablanca brought me yet another slice of good fortune when the managing director of Transport Marocains (a Multiport representative), Mr Abdelaziz Mantrach, invited me for a traditional Moroccan lunch at his home. It was an unforgettable experience: together with his daughter we sat on woven pillows in a room with fantastic tiled mosaic walls such as I had not expected to see outside the pages of tourism brochures, working our leisurely way through five tasty courses of dates, vegetables, bread and tender meat. It was clear that the ancient Moroccan culture would never die as long as it was preserved with such love. Mr Mantrach insisted on making a personal donation to my sadly depleted store of travelling money. I was reluctant to accept his offer, given all the other kindnesses I had received, but there was no question of refusing. Firstly it would have been foolish, given the state of my finances (my income back home had been depleted radically in the last few months), and secondly it would have been discourteous, the last thing I wanted.

The result of all this was that I set out from Casablanca in pretty good shape, with a rejuvenated bicycle, a wallet that was distinctly fatter than it had been and some more good memories to take home with me. It was a pleasant departure: I pedalled my way along a very modern beachfront with kilometres of restaurants and places of entertainment. It was the weekend, and they were all doing a roaring trade in spite of the early hour, with cyclists, joggers and strolling family groups out in force to enjoy the truly awesome weather and views.

I passed through another pleasant place where I wouldn't have minded spending some time, a coastal town called Essaouira, which had an amazing old city section and a long beach, and was known as Morocco's hippy hang-out. Essaouira had been made famous in earlier days by temporary sojourners like Jimi Hendrix – the town's little coastal forts are said to have inspired his song 'Castles in the Sand' – and Bob Marley. I spent the night at the local campsite, which was pleasant but rather rocky, though fortunately the rocks were smooth, and actually gave my back and hips a sort of massage which undid the day's knots.

Next morning my great desert trek began in earnest, and the kilometres blazed by as I headed into the sea of sand and the craggy mountains of the lower Atlas range. The sections of cliff that fell into the sea were as majestic as those I had seen in Angola, the difference being that here the abrupt transition was from the desert to the sea rather than from the jungle.

I stopped off at the town of Tan-Tan to stock up on tins of its internationally famous sardines, which I had gone back to as a staple road diet to conserve my skimpy budget, and for the next fortnight I always had about 20 tins of Tan-Tan's best in my saddle-bags. I ate them for breakfast, lunch and supper, spread on bread I bought along the way. It had its drawbacks – between the sardines and extra water my bike was about 10 kg heavier than before, and any bread I bought soon staled in the dry desert heat – but it was a cheap and healthy diet, if somewhat monotonous. Tan-Tan's medina was just as fascinating as Casablanca's, the hand of the past so heavy on it that it gave me a distinctly peculiar feeling to step out of one of its ancient streets and enter the local Internet café. It was like going through a time-warp in a science-fiction novel.

Rather more mundane than this was my hassle with the local hospitality industry and its hangers-on. I had been warned by a number of people that in Morocco foreign women tended to be verbally harassed by lustful locals, while male foreigners were likely to suffer administrative nuisance, and this certainly happened to me. It started when I was checking into a little hotel whose reception area, like most public places in Morocco, seemed to have a number of people hanging around for no particular reason except to drink tea. The check-in manager questioned me insistently about why I was travelling through Morocco on a bicycle, and in a caftan at that. I didn't take this seriously, and with a laugh asked him how my dress and method of travelling could be a problem.

He didn't so much as crack a smile, and I stopped grinning myself when the assorted hangers-on surrounded us, all loudly chattering away in Arabic. Although the gist of the long, loud discussion was incomprehensible to me, I gathered that they had jumped to some nonsensical conclusion and were offering unwanted advice on what the check-in manager should do about me. At length some of them became so worked up that they tried to snatch my documents from my hands. At this stage I became pretty worked up myself; this cooled their ardour somewhat and the manager handed me my room key.

I thought that this would be the end of the affair, but when I opened my door the next morning I found a policeman slumped half-asleep outside my room. The squeal of unoiled hinges brought him to full consciousness, and he got up and asked politely if he could see my passport. I obliged, and after he had satisfied himself that it was in order I asked him for an explanation. In the usual mixture of French and broken English he explained that my self-appointed interrogators of the previous evening had reported that they had found a man who was acting like a spy and had a false passport, since everyone knew that there were no white men in South

Africa ... From a purist's point of view this was probably correct, seeing that South Africans of various ethnic backgrounds had been playing slap-and-tickle for at least 350 years, so that many modern officially white people share at least some genes with their darker compatriots, but no doubt participants in the anti-apartheid struggle would have been interested to hear that they spent three decades fighting against ghosts.

So who were these fervent but ignorant patriots who had blown a mistaken whistle on me? I decided that they were just bored busybodies who were desperate for a bit of excitement. You see them everywhere in Morocco, young and old and mostly unemployed, congregating in cafes, hotel foyers and similar places throughout the live-long day. It crossed my mind that perhaps the bunch in my hotel should be encouraged to lay off James Bond films and other highly-coloured espionage epics. The fact was that what South Africans would regard as loitering was something like an occupation and very nearly an art form in Morocco.

I caught up on my e-mail for the last time and then left Tan-Tan late that afternoon, intending to do a night ride of 70 or 80 km to make up the time I had spent in the sardine kingdom. Alas for my good intentions, I had one puncture after another almost from the start. By the time I had done 20 km I had repaired eight punctures and it had become too dark to fix another one, so I gave up the night trip as a fruitless enterprise and started looking for a place to sleep which was sheltered from the cold, gusty wind. The best I could manage was an old ruin on top of a hill, which was roofless but had partly intact walls made of medium-sized boulders that would keep the wind away. Wearily I pitched camp and fell asleep on a bed of stones and scorpions.

When I got to Agadir I contacted my benefactor Nadia Belvet, who insisted I stay over at her ranch. This suited me fine, because I needed a day of rest after my scorching (in all senses of the word) efforts of the past few days. By now, incidentally, I had acquired a valuable psychological booster in the shape of my sponsored Nike adventure watch, whose bells and whistles I had begun to use for the first time.

One of the Nike watch's features is its ability to provide barometric readings and also one's height above sea-level at any time. This was very valuable to me, because being able to see how I ascended and descended during the day's ride kept me focused and prevented me from giving in to pain and self-pity. In very basic terms, once you reached the top of a hill it wasn't very difficult to work out that the fun part of going down lay right in front of you, and enjoying the cruise bucked you up for the next uphill grind. This might seem pretty crude, but such mind games can play an important role in keeping your determination at a consistent level.

I was concentrating so hard on maintaining my daily average that I forgot that Morocco's peace was a fairly fragile thing. Just before reaching Nadia's ranch I stopped near a bridge to take a photograph of the sunset. I had noticed that each bridge I crossed had a sentry-post but had not taken any particular note; now as I aimed my point-and-shoot a soldier actually came running down towards me, shouting: 'No photo, no photo!' All my old fight-or-flight instincts jumped into gear and I rode away as quickly as I could, realising too late that this was just the sort of furtive-looking action that was likely to encourage him to fire a few shots in my direction. Luckily for me he didn't, and so I lived to arrive safely at Nadia's operation, the REHA Equestrian Centre.

Nadia is some woman, so small and dainty that few people would realise what a tough business person she is, and has to be, since her ranch is the most respected horse-training and group-ride outfit in Morocco. Her daughter, Safia, meaning 'Purity', could easily be Miss Morocco one day, and I reckoned her son Tarique was obviously going to go places, to judge by the network of friends and contacts he had cultivated ... at the age of just 17! Special people, those Belvets.

After leaving Agadir I covered seemingly endless kilometres of desert coastline, almost uninhabited except for the occasional fishing family, each with its small army of anything-but-friendly dogs. I retain vivid memories of a pack of six which spotted me as I passed one such habitation and came charging out, each leaving an individual dust-trail like the ones of the cars in the Dakar Rally's advertising posters. They were neatly spaced out as if they had rehearsed the whole thing, and from the way they snapped at my calves were obviously looking forward to pulling me down. If they hadn't attacked from the wrong angle they would have got their way, but as it was I found myself fending them off with kicks and shouts while I cracked on the speed to put some distance between us. But these were determined mutts, and although some of them looked distinctly elderly they kept up with me, even when I was doing a good 30 km/h.

What possessed them I don't know, since the average domestic dog would have given up after a while, and when we had covered about 10 km in this fashion without any slackening of the pursuit I began to wonder who would succumb to a heart attack first – the older dogs or myself. At this stage salvation arrived in a most unusual form, an old Land Rover coming from the north which obviously had a defective silencer, because it emitted a stupendous engine-roar which gave my dogged (sorry!) pursuers pause for thought. By now I had collected my thoughts and so applied a bit of dog psychology I had learned from my own pets. Instead of shouting at them I called and whistled with every appearance of confidence, patting my thigh as if encouraging them to come closer. This unpreylike behaviour obviously baffled them, and they finally abandoned their quest. I recommend this Plan B approach to any reader who ever finds himself facing a pack of unfriendly Moroccan muggers of the canine variety.

Bee farming is big business in the general Agadir area, so that there are hundreds of stalls selling honey along the road, and I was introduced to another unforgettable delicacy when one of the local producers put me up for the evening. He was an interesting guy who had undergone the rite of passage into manhood at the age of just 17 by swimming unaided from Agadir to his place of birth, the town of Tamri – 28 tough kilometres through seas whose roughness I could attest to. This fellow (who, as it turned out, was a major player in the industry), treated me to a supper in which honey was part of just about every dish served to us. The endless sweetness eventually got a bit much even for me, but one of the dishes I just couldn't stop eating was the typical flat Moroccan bread which was dipped into a honey-and-almond mixture – very simple, but delicious beyond description (I also got hooked on custard pies, by the way – Coca-Cola and the New Testament have yet to make an impact in Morocco, but custard pies are for sale everywhere, and I did my best to contribute to the local economy by eating them to the limit of my daily food-budget).

I found myself firmly in the shadow of the decades-long quarrel over the Western Sahara when I arrived at the town of Laayoune, smack bang in the middle of the disputed area and full of soldiers on perpetual stand-by in case of attacks by the Algerian military, the Saharawi rebels or both. At the time of my arrival things were pretty tense between Algerians and the Moroccans, who were convinced that their neighbours were supplying the Polisario Front with weapons and training in addition to refuge. As a result diplomatic ties were non-existent and all borders between the two countries were closed, while people I spoke to warned me to be very tactful in my dealings with the military, whose members would be very likely to suspect me of being a spy in the Algerians' pay. Well, after my experiences in places like Equatorial Guinea I knew all about that sort of thing and paid serious heed to the warnings.

My immediate problem, however, was not the Moroccan military but a wind sweeping through Laayoune at 40 knots-plus. I arrived just in time to battle my way through three huge sandstorms that brought all traffic to a halt, and for the first time I really appreciated my turban, a life-saver that kept at least half a kilogram of sand out of my ears. The visibility was so bad that some photographs I took to illustrate the severity of the storms didn't come out at all, and I trudged right past a gendarmerie (semi-military police) post on a hill just outside the town without seeing it. This meant that when I realised what I had done I had to turn around and trudge all the way up the hill into this ferocious wind to explain myself to the gendarme manning it. He was very patient about it all, but I was feeling pretty disgruntled at having to make this painful extra effort. On the other hand, I found I could grumble out loud because the gendarme and his colleagues couldn't hear a thing above the screaming of the wind. It was not much of a consolation, but you have to take what comfort you can.

Still, Morocco wasn't all sandstorms, and in fact I set a new personal best for daily distance during this leg of my journey, a whopping 215 km. When I left Laayoune a gust of wind turned in my favour for a small stretch down a long hill and I set up my new land speed record too – 77 km/h, and under the distinct impression that I was about to lift off! Admittedly the conditions were just about ideal – generally flat terrain and a gentle tail-breeze for most of the day in question – but even so it was quite something for me, and when my bike's clock ticked over the double-century mark I celebrated with a loud whoop of joy, the first such cry of triumph since I had hit the 1 000 km mark in Namibia.

People who have not travelled through a real desert have no conception of the extreme changes in temperature between day and night resulting from the general lack of moisture and undergrowth, but I learned that lesson very thoroughly. One night in particular I will never forget. I had put up my tent and secured everything against the gale-force wind before turning in, then realised that I had left my sleeping-bag on the bike. Being very tired and reluctant to face the icy blast outside the tent again, I persuaded myself that actually it wasn't *that* cold, and that my small plastic tarpaulin would be enough to keep me warm. Well, needless to say I was dead wrong. It *was* that cold and my tarpaulin was *not* enough to keep me even lukewarm. So I tossed and turned on the rocky floor of the tent, convulsive shivering ensuring that I wouldn't fall asleep.

Around 5 am I finally admitted defeat and crawled out to fetch the sleeping-bag so that I could get in at least an hour or two of slumber to prepare me for what I knew would be a full day's work. It was a short but unpleasant excursion, but very worthwhile. I fell into blissful sleep almost as soon as I crawled into the bag, and woke up a couple of hours later feeling absolutely wonderful – it was as though I had had a massage, a long hot bath and a full night's snoring in a soft king-sized bed. Why? Who knows? I should have been scratchy-eyed, woozy and irritable. Instead I felt ready to take on the world without boxing gloves. It made me think about that advertisement for a mattress that gave you the equivalent of an extra two hours' sleep a night. Ha! My sleeping-bag was just as good.

Good news from home reached me while I was battling with the heat, cold and wind of the Western Sahara. My latest despatch from the bundu had just been published in the *Cape Times*, and a wonderful lady named Janine Nagel, the owner of a company called Nagel's Transport, had been so moved by my adventures that she had deposited some desperately needed funds in my account almost before the ink had dried on her copy of the newspaper – and she wasn't the only one, then or later. I don't believe Janine and my other benefactors realise even now just how important their help was, especially at that time. With most of my money having to be sent home to cover expenses there, I was living entirely off what Windhoek Light had made available on a monthly basis for visa expenses. But it wasn't just the money, it was also the realisation that in faraway Cape Town people were inspired by my quest and wanted me to complete it.

I crossed the Tropic of Cancer on my way to covering over 1 000 km in just seven days, excited and inspired by the Tour de France, which was being run in Europe while I was engaged in my personal race. I kept myself informed as best I could because I was very interested in seeing if Lance Armstrong could do it again ... and of course he did. What an athlete! Naturally I wasn't his only admirer. I recall meeting a Canadian woman, a diehard Armstrong fan if ever there was one, who got the stony needle when she misunderstood a joking comment I made which, she felt, reflected on his abilities. She had asked me if Lance would have been able to do what I had done thus far. Light-heartedly I replied that there was no way he would have made it this far, especially without his masseurs and chefs. 'I don't know about that!' she snapped, clearly horrified, not to say flabbergasted, at my arrogance in comparing myself with her hero – and to his disadvantage, mind you.

I patched things up between us, but on further reflection decided I had not been all that far from the truth. Much as I admire him, I do *not* believe Armstrong would have made it that far. The lack of close support that I brought up in my conversation with the Canadian fan would certainly have played a part, but the essential thing would have been a need to be as willing as I was literally to do or die.

In my opinion he wouldn't have that sort of commitment. It isn't only about the bike! His ability to cycle 15 500 km is not in question. But he is a professional athlete, willing to test his skill and endurance in any contest, while I was not a 'pro' athlete and I was not engaged in a formal contest. I was a man with a self-imposed mission, the outcome of which would affect my entire life. That's a huge difference.

I didn't spend too much time pondering our respective philosophies, however. Doing my daily stint absorbed most of my attention and energy, and what was left was expended on irritations like dealing with the Moroccan gendarmerie, some of whose members gave me the usual run-around.

One gendarme in particular I remember for his uncouth and ignorant treatment. I was in the junction town of Tamayye, sitting near the police station eating my usual sardine sandwich, when this character came up and demanded to see my passport. I couldn't make out why – he couldn't speak English, although he seemed to be carrying quite a lot of rank – but handed it over, assuming he wanted to check my visa. Holding it upside-down, he examined it carefully, then confiscated my bicycle and said I would have to go with him to the town of Dakhla. Why? Well, either he didn't know himself or I couldn't understand what he was saying, but the upshot was that I sat on a bench outside the Dakhla gendarmerie chief's office for more than three hours while my nemesis and his colleagues leisurely chatted away about me inside.

Finally, bereft of patience and ready to engage in a heated discussion, I knocked firmly on the chief's door and asked to speak to him. This got me the attention of the chief, an educated man with a gentle manner, and I wasted no time in waiting for explanations. If they were not planning to arrest me on some charge, I said, I would like to be set free. If this was not possible I would like to telephone the South African Embassy in Rabat. This was taking a bit of a chance, but the chief did not get on his high horse. He apologised profusely, explaining that the gendarme in question had been too enthusiastic in doing his job, and had been confused by the fact that my passport had more than one entry and exit stamp for Morocco.

I suppose I should have shut up at this point, but I was furious.

I ranted about how ill-considered actions like these frustrated law-abiding tourists who only wanted to have a good time, and so on and so on. Now, this outburst would have seen me flung into the nearest cell in at least three of the countries I had passed through so far, but the Moroccan officer must have been used to handling irate tourists, or maybe he was just a nice guy. He let me rave away till I ran out of steam, apologised again and saw that I got taken back to Tamayye. All in a day's work for him!

With all that behind my back I could get on with my immediate requirement, which was to first complete the remaining kilometres I still owed and then get back to Rabat to pick up my visas for Algeria and Tunisia. This involved another 200 km stretch through the dunes towards the Mauritanian border till I got to where I reckoned Patrick had originally helped me. Now my immediate need was to find a lift northwards. I put my bike on the ground, and like a good Arab wrapped my turban around my head to keep out the sand while I lay in wait for any wheeled traffic moving northwards. I knew this might take some time, but in the meantime I would sleep a bit, and – Inshallah! (God willing) – something would come along in due course, perhaps an early-morning traveller heading for Dakhla.

In fact, however, divine intervention took only about 15 minutes to manifest itself, in the form of two Saharawians in a yellow Land Rover. We had a few laughs and a scrambled French/English discussion about the troubles in the region and then set off, and before very long they dropped me right outside the same building where I had had the altercation with the chief gendarme the day before. I chanced my arm and went in to see him, this time asking for help; he was still as diplomatic as before, and went to the length of helping me to get to the departure point for the Agadir bus.

When I got to Agadir Nadia Belvet not only welcomed me back to her ranch but, knowing how nearly broke I was, actually paid for my bus trip to Rabat. She and Safia dropped me off at the bus station, we said heartfelt goodbyes and they drove off without waiting for the bus to depart. Scarcely a couple of minutes later they came back, and the reason for their return really touched me. At Safia's urging she had turned around, Nadia said, so that they could extract a promise from me to both of them that one day I would return to visit them. As I said earlier, the Belvets are very special people, and that day I felt very much as if I was among family.

I arrived in Rabat to find the city in a distinctly festive mood. The loss of the 2010 Soccer World Cup to South Africa was forgotten; the EUEFA Cup was in full swing, and when David Beckham missed a sitter of a penalty by accidentally kicking into the ground I could have sworn the very walls of the buildings trembled with shock, horror and (in some cases) delight. Morocco is full of life at all times, but now the vibe bordered on frenzy. Any person who looked at all foreign was likely to be dragged into the nearest roadside coffee bar and asked to share his 'professional' views with the locals. I was no exception. I entered into the spirit of things and gave freely of my opinions, both good and bad, although frankly my knowledge of soccer is strictly limited. The locals didn't seem to worry much about the quality of my inputs, so I didn't either.

In between these impromptu sessions as a lamentably inexpert 'expert' I managed to collect my visas for Algeria and Tunisia, and after a few days' rest and recreation I was on my way again, heading for the border town of Oujda. I was taking a bit of a chance – the latest newspaper reports said that the Moroccan and Algerian foreign ministers had met and agreed that the borders should be re-opened, though no dates had been set as yet – but I had taken bigger ones in the past and things had worked out. Maybe I'd strike it lucky again.

In the meantime I had plenty to keep my mind occupied. First of all I had to get to the Algerian border, which was still a good distance away – Morocco is such a big, stretched-out place that I had spent more time within its borders than in any of the 21 other countries I had visited up to now. But I felt good as my wheels ate up the endless kilometres stretching westwards to Oujda. Five days, all going well, and I would be there.

My first night's stop was at Fès, the only big urban centre on my route. I rode in expecting ... well, I didn't know what, but something unusual. This was mainly due to the fact that back in Cape Town there was a hugely successful nightclub with the same name, crammed with exotic-looking Moroccan funk. The reality turned out to be quite different. So it would be fair to say that I did, in fact, spend an unusual night in Fès, although not of the kind I had vaguely envisioned.

My first priority after arriving was, of course, to find shelter for the night, and with my finances in such a precarious state there was only one likely affordable option, the local camping site. To my dismay its tariff was out of my reach – thanks, no doubt, to all those visitors from prosperous Europe just over the water. This led me to the dismal conclusion that if even the camping site was out of my reach, I could forget about finding an affordable hotel either. In any case I was pretty tired and an icy wind had started to blow, and I just couldn't bring myself to start fossicking around for accommodation. Then a rather unorthodox solution presented itself. Just over the road was a construction site with all sorts of heavy excavation machinery standing around, so I made my number with a couple of sleepy watchmen, climbed into the scoop of a large, muddy grader and made my bed there. I don't know of anyone else who has ever made his bed in a grader's scoop, but it was roomy and kept the wind off me, and I had a very satisfying night's rest. Chalk up another first for Manser of Africa.

The following night's accommodation was yet another personal first. I had stopped off at a roadside café and spent a very convivial evening with the owners, which they enjoyed so much that they allowed me to sleep over in a small adjoining room where customers went for their daily prayers. I would have thought that letting an infidel bed down in one's prayer room would be a strict no-no, but my temporary hosts apparently didn't share my opinion, and I wasn't complaining.

I reached the large town of Oujda in the late afternoon; I had expected to see signs of economic distress, since border towns live largely off the passing traffic, but it was vibrant and populous in spite of the closure of the border. The streets teemed with food stalls, families, show horses and even a proud falconer with his even prouder-looking hawk perched on his gauntleted forearm, a wonderful touch of the old Morocco. I realised that there were many things in this meeting-place of the old and new that I hadn't seen yet. This was real corner-of-the-eye observation because the border post was another 15 km further and I wanted to get there as soon as possible, hoping desperately that all the reported diplomatic interchanges had taken effect since my departure from Rabat. What I found there, however, was not an open border-gate but the most openly and humorously corrupt immigration officer I had encountered so far.

He was sprawling comfortably in a chair next to the gate-boom, a mere 30-odd metres from a similar gate which, I presumed, was the entry-point to Algeria. To my relief he spoke reasonably fluent English – surely this was a good omen! But no. When I had explained what I required he asked in a distinctly sarcastic tone how it could be that I was not aware of the closed border and had not taken an alternative route. We fell into a long dialogue, not without its flashes of humour, about what it would take to get me through the boom. I had not paid any bribes up to this point and had no intention of doing so now, so I concentrated on a discussion of why he couldn't let me leave his country, which I felt would not be illegal, and also why he, as a Moroccan, should care if I entered Algeria, especially considering I had a valid visa to be there.

My official friend wasn't interested in logical argument, however; his response to this slightly dubious logic angered me at the time, although nowadays I laugh when I think about it. Leaning back even further, he said lazily: 'What you are asking is a very, very, *very* expensive exercise ...' Translation: let's see the colour of your money, preferably in dollars. That was pretty much it. It was a matter of principle with me not to pay bribes, and in any case I couldn't afford to bribe a church-mouse (or perhaps I should say 'mosque-mouse') just then. I gave what must have sounded like totally insincere thanks (they were) and rode off immediately. He didn't call after me to haggle – either he was too lazy or he knew I was a pretty unlikely prospect.

Riding back to town, I realised that my only option now was to undertake a complicated dog-leg that I had not contemplated up to this point. I would have to enter Algeria from Spanish territory. The best scenario was that I would be able to catch a coastal ferry connecting the Spanish enclave of Melilla with an Algerian port, which I had heard was a possibility. In the worst scenario I would have to go to Tangier, take the ferry to Spain, then turn around and cross back to reach Algeria. After all that I would have to travel westwards till I reached the Algerian side of the Oujda border post so that I could resume my journey eastwards. I did my sums and sighed. Instead of paying an unofficial $20 exit fee and crossing 30 metres of no man's land, I would have to travel more than 1 000 km and spend the bulk of what I had in my wallet.

I consoled myself by stopping over at a fancy roadside restaurant and hotel – since my carefully calculated budget was now shot to hell, I reckoned, I might as well find a bit of enjoyment among the ruins. I didn't regret it. The food was wonderfully tasty, and there was some pleasant company. The consensus of opinion was that it was dead easy to cross illegally into Algeria. I considered my companions' suggestions, but not for very long. The fact was that Morocco and Algeria were at daggers drawn; how would the Algerian officials react if some strange-looking foreigner rolled up on their side of the border after having crossed in obviously illegal fashion? So when a friendly policeman advised me against doing anything foolish I didn't hesitate to accept his counsel. It would have to be the legal way, no matter what that involved.

# CHAPTER 20

# A MAN SUSPENDED BETWEEN
# TWO WORLDS

*This trip had taken me a long way on the road of spiritual dis-*
*covery. People seemed to be good and bad, kind and cruel,*
*crooked and honest in the same proportions, regardless of their*
*geographical origins, their language, their religious faith or*
*their skin colour. All that really divided them was ignorance of*
*one another, past events which had never been laid to rest and*
*venial leaders who did not hesitate to exploit their fears and*
*grievances. Was all this so difficult to understand? Surely not.*
*And yet that seemed to be the case.*

A quick bus trip to Melilla proved that my favoured scenario for
beating the closed border didn't exist. I discovered this as soon as I
reached the border town of Nador and met a handful of Nigerians
who were headed for Europe. They made no bones about the fact
that they planned to smuggle themselves to Spanish territory, then
catch a ferry to mainland Spain or France. A ferry along the Moroccan coast to Algeria? There was no such thing, they said.

So it would have to be Plan B, involving a ferry ride to Spain via
Tangiers, which in turn would mean going back to Rabat and getting a visa from the Spanish embassy there. This would be more
easily said than done, I knew, because Spain was a favourite entry
point to Europe for Africans fleeing unemployment, wars and corruption. The result was that the Spanish embassy had a more or
less permanent crowd of visa-seekers camping out around it. Apart

from anything else, it made me wonder how long it would take just to get to the right desk to apply for a visa.

An added complication was that things were not too amicable between the Spanish and Moroccan governments just then. There was the earlier row about Ceuta and Melilla, and now the shadow cast by the deaths of 191 people in the recent Madrid train bombings. Of the 15 people arrested and charged, 11 were Moroccan nationals, and the Spanish government believed the attacks had been the work of fundamentalist Moroccan suicide bombers. Given this situation, I tried not to think about the problems that might arise from my appearance and manner, because by this time I looked a lot more like an Arab than a good South African boy from Cape Town, and had even fallen into the habit of saying 'shukran' instead of 'merci'.

Not that any Moroccan would have been fooled by my appearance, of course, and in Oujda I had encountered another side of Moroccan life which proved that. Oujda was a deeply conservative country town which was wedded to the old ways, and I was intrigued – and at times offended and angered – by the reaction of some of its women to me, a foreign non-Muslim male. On one occasion, when I was taking a bus through the town, a woman who was covered from head to foot in a djellaba refused to sit down next to me in the only seat that was still empty. At first I didn't understand what was going on, because when another seat became vacant she hastily occupied it, in spite of the fact that her new next-door neighbour was also a man. Then the penny dropped. He was a local man. That was the difference.

On another occasion two young women came walking towards me in the street, but as soon as they saw I was a foreigner they stepped off the sidewalk while I passed, then stepped on to it again, although it was crowded with local men. What I was being told in these and some similar incidents was that the local women considered me unclean because I was not a Muslim. It was laughable. If only they knew what some of their own men probably got up to, I thought angrily, recalling the pious pornographer I had met in the Internet café in Nouakchott – a pillar of the community, no doubt, and virtually a permanent fixture at the mosque when he was not engaged in trawling through the filth of the world..

After a fairly fierce struggle with myself, because I felt immensely insulted and discriminated against by such public disdain, I managed to accept that it was not something about which I should get upset. This was not a deliberate effort to humiliate me; it was just the outcome of a lifestyle which differed greatly from my own and no doubt would gradually evolve, but in its own fashion and in its own time. It all reinforced one of my core beliefs, namely that we human beings, regardless of where we come from, should not judge and discriminate but rather experience one another's cultures at first hand, then make friends and accept that we are all cut from the same cloth and all want the same things at the end of the day: health, love and happiness.

But be all that as it may. My looming problem with the Spanish embassy evaporated when the South African embassy came to the rescue once again, intervening so successfully on my behalf that within 24 hours I had a five-day transit visa whose time-limit would only start operating once I had actually entered Spain; this would give me more than enough time to get to the Algerian ferry's departure point at Almeria. This sort of VIP treatment, I decided as I contemplated my miraculously swift visa, was definitely something I could get used to.

I wasted no time in heading for Tangiers, where I was plunged almost immediately into the surprises and lessons that seemed to await me at every turn in my trek from Cape Town. When I arrived I decided to give myself a personal bicycle tour of the city before finding a place to sleep, and I was meandering down the busy main street when I started hearing a voice in my head, insistently calling 'Soldier Ryan! Soldier Ryan!'

Soldier Ryan? The only person I knew who called me that was my eccentric friend Patrick, the TV producer. But he was in Rabat! Obviously I was hearing things. Maybe I was a little desert-crazy. But there it came again, very faintly. I stopped and looked around wildly in all directions, the way (I couldn't help thinking) in which lunatics look around when they hear voices in their heads. Then the shouts of 'Soldier Ryan! Soldier Ryan! Soldier Ryan!' began to get louder, and I realised they originated from somewhere above me. I started scanning the surrounding buildings, no doubt looking crazier than ever, and finally I spotted Patrick, not at a window but on a roof, screeching and waving frantically with both arms. What a surprise!

Patrick was in Tangiers on what he described with some embarrassment as a paparazzi assignment, shooting scenes for a tabloid documentary, and had been casting an eye on the main street to work out some good scenery angles when, as he said dramatically, he nearly had a heart attack at seeing 'Soldier Ryan' come cycling casually into the frame.

Patrick did not neglect either his paparazzi assignment or his hospitality. Lunch-time was devoted to staking out the third-floor flat of a Spanish woman, just deceased, who had gained renown for devoting her life to assisting needy Moroccans. Her family in Spain had sent a delegation of prominent Spanish people to Tangiers to wrap up her affairs, and Patrick wanted them on film. Not a man to do things by halves, he had booked out an entire restaurant across the road from the deceased philanthropist's flat to use as an observation-post, and here we spent an entertaining lunch-hour eating and talking. The only interruptions came when Patrick saw or thought he saw some movement in the flat. Then he would lunge forward with his camera at the ready, nearly choking on his mouthful of falafel sandwich. The whole thing was better than a cabaret. Never mind 'Soldier Ryan', I thought – meet 'Papparazzi Patrick'.

With the day's work over, Patrick took me for a drive around the city which opened my eyes to two other aspects of Morocco of which my knowledge was strictly second-hand. One was the huge windmills that produced much of Tangiers' electricity. I had seen them on TV, but there we were, driving past a whole mountainside neatly decorated with these gawky monsters, not just pieces of highly practical industrial art but an example to the world of how mankind could tap into clean, renewable energy that would never run out.

The other thing was the all-pervading extent of the drug trade in Morocco. Everyone seemed to be involved in one way or another – and nobody seemed to care. I discovered this before we even set out, in fact, when Patrick drew my attention to some of his local film crew, who had bought a block of hashish and were openly heating it up, preparatory to smoking it, in blatant disregard for anyone who might see them doing it.

How could the police claim that it was impossible to disrupt or at least contain such open trafficking and use of a highly illegal substance? Hell, even a foreigner like me would be able to infiltrate the process that brought this evil stuff from producer to user! I said as much to Patrick, and he laughed loudly but slightly nervously. Interfering in the drug world of Morocco, he said, was a very dangerous business – 'You would be surprised to know who uses hash! Everyone does!'

I understood why when we drove along the coast, and admired some of the palatial houses I saw. Patrick explained that at one time or another most of the larger ones had belonged to drug lords who had waxed fat smuggling hashish between Morocco and Europe. I didn't pursue the matter. Drugs were big business, and the trade was going to look after its interests at any cost.

The gods of good fortune smiled on me once more when the largest ferry company in Tangiers, Comarit, kindly sponsored my ticket for the 50 km journey to the Spanish port city of Algeciras, thus pulling me a little further away from the abyss of total poverty, and off I went.

My departure was slightly marred by a strange and rather unsettling encounter with a Spanish woman who turned her hand into a pistol shape and put it to her head. While I goggled at her she explained in Spanish that I would definitely die in Spain, letting off two gunshot sounds to underline her remark. I was puzzled and a little shaken. Why would she say something like this to a total stranger? And what did she mean? Later I was to understand her actions more clearly, but just then they were a total mystery.

But the weird encounter did not damage the magic of my journey to Spain. My departure from Tangiers was the beginning of a memorable and unexpected trip. The sun was setting over the African land mass as if it was melting into the continent where my home lay, but at the same time I had only to turn my head through less than a half-circle to see the lights of Europe twinkling at me across the expanse of calm sea. For a short time I was a man suspended between two worlds, equally old in geological terms but so very different in every other way. I took up that famous Titanic-style pose in the bow, breathing in the air of my good fortune. It was one of those rare times when everything in the world seemed perfect.

The moment of perfection, I knew, would stretch out to just over two hours. Then we would be across the Strait of Gibraltar and I would be having my passport stamped on Spanish soil, proof that my circumnavigation of Africa had bulged out to include a bit of Europe as well. Slowly the sparkling lights of Algeciras moved closer. I peered into the gloom for a sight of the Rock of Gibraltar, that byword for enduring solidity. But it was too dark, and all I could make out was its huge dim shape with its necklace of lights. I was not disappointed. Time enough to see the Rock for real in the morning; I might be impatient, but I could wait till then.

The immigration staff didn't chivvy me towards their office, and for once I was in no hurry to get there. It was 10 pm, far too late to do anything, and if I went through before midnight the clock on my five-day visa would start ticking immediately. That I didn't want, because I was not sure of what delays I would encounter and I planned to hoard my available time. So I hung around the floodlit harbour area, exchanging English/Spanish lessons with the workers in the food-stalls, till a nearby clock struck midnight. Then I saved myself the cost of a night's lodging by curling up under a food-stall trailer in the parking lot. Things were that desperate. I had left Oujda with just $250, which would have to last me till I finally reached the Algerian capital of Algiers, where, I was given to understand, there was an international ATM. After exchanging my remaining dollars into Euros I did a few sums. Minus a bus-ticket to Almeria and the ferry expense to Algeria, I had only 20 Euros left to play with. It was going to be a razor's-edge sort of thing for the next couple of days.

Well, that was just too bad. I dismissed the whole thing and went in search of breakfast. This consisted of some milk and a sandwich which, to save a little money, I assembled myself from separate purchases at a grocery of bread, cheese and ham. I was quite proud of this penny-pinching till I noticed while walking out that I could have bought a made-up sandwich for less than the two euros I had just spent. That taught me a lesson: Riaan, you're not in Africa any more. This is Europe, the land of mass production. Once again I didn't get my water hot. I ate my sandwich and drank my milk while looking out over Algeciras's harbour, which was very busy, and towards the neighbouring Rock, which seemed pretty inactive. Then I mooched around, rubbing shoulders with the locals, till the bus to Almeria left that afternoon.

It was an interesting interlude. The recent Madrid train bombings became part of every discussion I entered into, not just then but later on. I had been so busy dealing with lesser crises during the past weeks that I had not absorbed many facts, but now I got a crash course, not only about what had happened but also about the Spaniards' mood. The terrorists responsible for the bombings had made a huge mistake in thinking that their horrific actions were going to crush the spirit of their 'enemies'. The Spaniards are a tough-spirited nation, forged by centuries of brutal warfare, upheaval and hardship, and all that the bombings had done was to make them very, very angry, even the large number of people who had actually had some sympathy for the bombers' general grievances and objectives. The hatred I sensed when both old and young expressed their opinions was almost tangible, and I quickly decided that I would not try a Heathrow-style 'Muslim experience' at Algeciras (I was going to have one anyway – I just didn't know it yet).

I enjoyed the bus trip to Almeria. The road wound its way through some of the prettiest countryside I had ever seen, and I felt a little homesick because it reminded me so strongly of the Cape, barring the absence of vineyards and the native 'fynbos', that conglomeration of native plants whose charm defies exact definition. I remember we stopped at one lovely little town with whitewashed walls which looked as if it had been built especially for photographers from travel magazines. The girl sitting next to me was getting off there, and explained that this was a popular holiday destination for young southern Spaniards, and I believed her when we stopped briefly. Close up the town looked as enticing as it had at a distance, crammed with cafes and bars filled with relaxed-looking people.

We arrived at Almeria late that evening and I started looking for the port buildings, where I would be able to get information about departure times and ticket prices. That was as far as my planning went. I had no money to spend and all my thoughts were concentrated on surviving till the ferry to Algeria departed with me on it.

Finding your way around a strange unfamiliar city at night is not all that easy, but some friendly locals on the bus had given me a briefing, and for once I had no trouble getting to where I wanted to go. The departure building was closed, of course, but the parking lot was full of people, many families sleeping on the ground next to their overloaded cars. Every one of them was clearly of North African descent, and it was the same in the little canteen near by. We were all in the same boat, so to speak, except that the reasons for our departure differed.

I had heard the Spaniards' views about the bombings; now I was given a short lesson in Spanish history from the Muslim perspective. Many Arabs are very conscious of the fact that Spain was ruled by Muslims till they were thrown out by Christian armies in the fifteenth century, and still harbour a grudge about it. One middle-aged guy who sat across from me at a table in the canteen explained this history at length and then rounded off his tirade by telling me, I think, what racists the local Spaniards were. I couldn't follow his line of reasoning all that well, but his dislike of Spaniards was clear from the way he kept repeating the word 'racist' while flicking his thumb sharply forward from the base of his chin. What I didn't quite understand was why he obviously had not given a moment's consideration to the fact that there was a link between the current racism towards Muslims, as he saw it, and the murder of hundreds of innocent Spaniards by his co-religionists.

My own thought was that if some people in my own country went off and murdered hundreds of innocents, I and most other South African citizens would have been filled with suspicion and intolerance – lamentable emotions, maybe, but quite understandable in the circumstances. I didn't express this thought, however. It wouldn't have made a blind bit of difference and it might well have been literally life-threatening, given our company in the canteen.

I spent the night like the down-and-out I was, sleeping on a sheet of old cardboard between two parked cars, then deposited myself at the doors of the ferry offices and waited for them to open (you tend to get up early when sleeping rough). By now I knew what I had to do, which was to take the ferry to the Algerian port of Ghazaouet. The bad news was that it was only leaving in four days' time, 15 minutes over my legal stay, and would cost me the vast sum (reckoned by my straitened circumstances) of 90 euros. The good news, on the other hand, was that I had made provision for the 90 euros, and Ghazaouet was only 50 km from the Oudja border post.

I looked forward to leaning against that boom that had been so tantalisingly close during my discussion with the corrupt Moroccan official. Perhaps he would see me standing there and grind his teeth. That would make up for the fact that he had bankrupted me ... not that he'd know that, of course. Ha! It was an unlikely but pleasant prospect, and my arrival at the Algerian boom would be something of a small personal victory. While he had squandered the last few days in his chair, scratching his backside and staring vacantly at the same old scene, I had visited Tangier, met up again with 'Paparazzi Patrick', crossed the Med twice and seen a bit of Spain.

Almeria is a wonderful city, but surviving in it was not quite so wonderful, as I discovered on my second day there. I had ventured into the ferry departure hall again, my bike firmly by my side, to ask some more questions of the woman at the long, cigar-shaped information counter. While she was answering me a uniformed policeman who had been drinking at a table in the adjacent open-air bar came over, fixed me with a baleful glance and broke into curt Spanish, totally ignoring her. I gathered from his words and gestures that he had taken offence at the presence of my bicycle, and that both of us must get out right away.

Reluctantly – because an argument with a slightly drunken policeman is one that you are surely going to lose – I tried to explain that I had just come in to get some information, and when I'd got it I would leave right away. He wasn't at all interested, and simply shouted down every attempt at explanation. I was so astounded by this completely unwarranted harassment – after all, most of the other travellers had twice as much kit with them as I had – that I didn't move immediately. The information lady was now fairly nervous about his growing aggressiveness (perhaps she had had dealings with this unpleasant cop herself) and confirmed that he wanted my bicycle out of the building immediately, if not sooner.

I decided that in the circumstances I should get out while the going was still good, so I took the brochures the information lady held out to me, greeted her and said my thanks. This was when I made a bad mistake: instead of saying 'gracias' I absent-mindedly said 'shukran', and when the policeman heard that he blew his top in no uncertain terms. He charged around the long counter, shoved his face into mine and tried to grab my bike, blasting me with a fierce combination of alcohol and garlic fumes, like a bar-brawler getting ready to fight. I pulled my bike away from him, repeatedly asking: 'Por que?' (why?). He was quite a hefty fellow, I realised now, shorter than me but a lot stockier – he must have weighed something like 120 kg. It was most definitely time for me to go; Vasti's words rang loud: Lose the battle and win the war.

I packed up as quickly as I could, watched now by a huge crowd which had gathered to watch the fun, and doing my best to ignore the cop, who was shouting louder than ever, As I started turning my bicycle around he blew his top again, shoving me with his chest and holding one of his big hands next to my face, punching it repeatedly with his other fist to show me what he intended to do to me.

I was fairly nervous by this time, but unwilling to give him the satisfaction of flinching. In fact I was so unwilling that I did something I should rather not have done – I lowered my hands to my knees and moved them from side to side to show that I was so scared of his threats that my kneecaps were knocking. Needless to say, this bit of sarcastic performance art didn't sweeten his mood. He carried on shouting, hitting his hand with loud fleshy smacks that echoed through the hall, his fist passing so close to my face that I could feel its slipstream against my cheek. And then I had

had enough. I had progressed about five metres towards the entrance while all this was going on, but now I turned and deliberately wheeled my bicycle back to its original position. This spoiled his day even more.

In the meantime the drunken cop's partner, a much younger man who spoke fairly good English, had arrived on the scene and was pleading with me to solve the problem by leaving the building. I explained to him that the problem had been on its way out but that his partner had intervened. I was in a fair temper by this stage and said I wanted to see the port's chief of police. This immediately put the kibosh on the drunkard's performance; he went dead quiet and eased himself back into the front rank of the spectators.

Now one of the security guards decided to get involved as well, and put his flattened hand in my face in standard military fashion. I laughed at him (very nervously, although he didn't know that) and told him to think up his own intimidation techniques, not copy the army's. This wasn't very tactful either, but I was beyond caring. My blood was up, and it was me against them now. At the same time I didn't lose my head. The crowd was growing ever larger, with even the shopkeepers in the hall deserting their stalls to see what the commotion was all about, and it was clear that the whole thing was getting out of hand.

I didn't want to get embroiled in something that would leave me at the mercy of the authorities and possibly delay my departure; I was in enough difficulty as it was because of the time-restriction on my visa and my lack of money. So the only logical thing was to get out as soon as possible. But I was bitterly angry about the way I had been treated and I wanted to see the drunken policeman brought to book. At the very least it would wipe out some of the bad memories and retain the good ones. So when I got out of there, I decided, I would report the drunkard to the nearest police station. I told the younger policeman what I intended doing, then collected my bike and headed for the doors. As I pushed my way through the nearest element of the crowd I happened to look directly into the face of the drunkard, who had gone back to cursing me again. I had cooled down a little since deciding what to do, and couldn't resist giving him a smile and a wave, as if he was no more of an irritation than a persistent fly.

Bad mistake. As I got to the door I looked back and saw him running towards the bar where he had been sitting. This shook me a little. Was he going to fetch his pistol and let off a couple of shots at me? Then I saw he was only retrieving his cap. I gave a small sigh of relief and got out into the open without wasting any time. But I had sighed too soon. I was going over a zebra crossing outside the building when the drunkard came sprinting out, still screaming abuse, and when he was about two metres away he launched himself into a full-scale karate kick Eric Cantona-style at the bicycle.

This was the last thing I had expected, and the impact of this big, heavy man was a powerful one. The bike smashed into my right knee and wrist with such force that I found myself down in a crouch. Before I could get up again he was back on his feet and charging straight at me. Now I was really angry as well as frightened by this illogical violence. I wanted to hurt him, not just defend myself. I couldn't believe I felt that way – he was the law, after all, and I had been raised to abide by it. But now I wanted to make him suffer, and so when he rammed me with his chest, as he had done earlier, I met his head with similar force.

Heaven knows where all this might have gone if the younger partner hadn't arrived in time to wedge himself in between us. That stopped the fighting, and he managed to talk his ferocious partner back to the departure hall. I assessed the damage – the bike was OK and so was I, although my right knee and wrist were both swelling up already and gave promise of becoming fairly painful – and considered my next moves. I was still determined to report this guy, so I looked around for witnesses to the incident. One likely prospect was another policeman sitting on his parked motorcycle near by, but he either had seen nothing or was not willing to admit that he had. I was also still in need of the information I had been seeking at the information counter when the altercation with the policeman started. Since there was no way I was going back into the departure hall, I took myself off to the local tourism office.

A very nice girl was behind the counter there, and when she heard what had happened she arranged to have me checked out at the government hospital, suggesting that I get a report on my injuries which I could use when filing a complaint against the policeman. The doctors at the hospital were very kind and gave me some first-class attention, including the report the tourism girl had suggested. Armed with this, I went off to the police station to make my complaint.

This turned out to be rather frightening experience. The cops on duty not only refused to take a statement but threw me out and wouldn't let me back in again; then, when the tourism girl telephoned to find out what had happened, they told her that I had lied to them, and then misunderstood them when they had told me to come back later. I didn't make anything easier by trying to write down one constable's name and badge-number, which really got up his nose. It was Equatorial Guinea all over again, except that there were no eventual apologies. Long live First World law enforcement!

Well, thanks to the tourism girl's influence I finally managed to get a case number. I knew it was pretty futile, since the cops were not going to take any steps against one of their own and I was scheduled to leave in a day and a half anyway, but at least I had bolstered my self-respect and – maybe – motivated the drunkard to behave a little better towards Muslims. Because that's what it had been all about, and the fact that the country was in uproar about the train bombings was no excuse.

Anyway, all I wanted now was to maintain a low profile till it was time to leave. I felt very alone just then. It was no fun sleeping in a parking lot each night, homesick and fearful of being robbed, and with one eye always open in case you fell foul of an unsympathetic policeman (or possibly even a hostile one, as I knew from painful experience). I was particularly nervous about the police, given the fact that I had managed to irritate the entire local presence and was, moreover, quite recognisable. In particular I didn't want to run into my drunken acquaintance of the departure hall again. But I wasn't that lucky.

I was cycling inconspicuously (I hoped) through the town on my way to a coffee shop I'd visited earlier when a silver Citroen pulled up alongside me and stayed there, matching my speed. That was bad enough. Then the electric window whined down and I heard a deep voice shouting at me. I couldn't understand what was being said, but it was definitely threats and curses rather than idle chatter. I didn't look into the car right away because I was busy trying the keep the bike from mounting the kerb. When I did have a moment I was horrified to see that the source of the shouting was none other than the drunken policeman.

All I could do was ignore him completely and then turn into the first side-street I came up to. The Citroen didn't follow, and I straddled my bike for a few minutes to get my mind back in order and fight down a panic fit. I couldn't get rid of the thought that he had activated the cop mafia, so that the entire local police force was now bent on harassing me. If that was the case, my last day in Almeria was going to be an uncomfortable one indeed. When I had pulled myself together I ventured on to the main street again ... and there was the same silver Citroen parked about 50 metres away, with the drunken cop sitting behind the wheel and scanning the streets like a sniper looking for a target. No way was I going to go past him, or even within long-distance eyeshot of him! So I sneaked away through the back streets. Actually he did me a favour, because the result of these evasive tactics was that I saw some wonderful old cobbled streets and ancient buildings that I would have missed otherwise.

In this roundabout way I finally got to the coffee shop for a last fragrant cup, went to say goodbye to the tourism people and gave details of my encounter and the case number to the South African Embassy in Madrid – not to try to nobble the troublesome cop (I wasn't that much of an optimist) but to make sure that the embassy would have some clues to follow up in case I should happen to get into further trouble or even disappear. I thought the guy from the embassy would laugh at what suddenly sounded like a fanciful notion, but he didn't. Instead he told me about a similar scenario, involving a senior diplomat who had recently visited Spain, and urged me to put my experience in writing. I did that and mailed it off, then spent the rest of the day hiding out in the workshop of the Multiport representative for Almeria, making use of its shower to have a leisurely soaking.

Then, when the offices closed for the day, I said goodbye to the Mult-iport people and headed back to the port. Along the way I bumped into missionaries – South Africans, can you believe it? – preaching Christianity to Muslims arriving from North Africa. I passed my last couple of hours in Spain watching them beavering away, handing out inspirational tapes and cassettes to all and sundry. It struck me as being something of an exercise in futility in the circumstances, and I wondered what had brought them all the way to Almeria when there was still plenty of work to be done in Africa. But I didn't ask them; missionaries march to their own drum, and if they wanted to sow their seeds in such unpromising soil, that was their concern.

The ferry started warming up and reluctantly I handed over my carefully hoarded 90 euros' worth of ticket money, then sweated out those 15 illegal minutes. But nothing happened, and just after midnight we steamed out of Almeria, seven hours away from landfall on the Algerian coast. It was a moment of unmatched relief to know that at last I was out from under the Spanish police in general, and my drunken acquaintance in particular. Which is not to say I didn't regret leaving Spain. Cops aside, I had really enjoyed what I had seen of it – awesomely pleasant weather, extremely friendly people, gorgeous girls to look at and food that smelled near irresistible (I say 'smelled' because I hadn't been able to afford much to eat).

This crossing was not just far longer than the first, it was also much colder, so that I was caught off-guard with only a shirt to keep me warm. As a result I didn't sleep much, which gave me a lot of time to ponder the events of the last couple of days, and likely reasons for the drunkard's behaviour. With hindsight I was able to acknowledge that he might have been under all kinds of stresses that I didn't know about – for all I knew he had lost an old friend or loved one in the bombings – and had found his relief from the build-up of pressure by acting in a way that he never would have contemplated under normal (and sober) circumstances.

Having come to this conclusion, I parcelled up the thought and stored it away at the back of my mind. I could do nothing about it and I was not going to spend weeks and months with it lying sourly on my soul. It was just another ingredient in the stew of wildly varying experiences that I was cooking up. I needed all of those ingredients to make me stronger for whatever trials still lay ahead. An old Afrikaans saying just about summed up my attitude: 'Wat nie dood maak nie, maak vet': if it doesn't kill you, it'll make you stronger. That was about the size of it. So, consoled by this bit of folk wisdom, I waited impatiently for the moment when I would set foot on Algerian soil.

# CHAPTER 21

# CAKES AND KINDNESS IN ALGERIA

*It was clear that news of my arrival had spread through the town and stirred the populace out of their daily hibernation. Before too long there were literally hundreds of them sitting or standing outside the restaurant and staring at me. Barring a few people, the crowd wasn't hostile; in fact they appeared to be quite shy. But it was unnerving, all the same, so that at one stage I actually moved seats to avoid the hundreds of peering eyeballs glued to me.*

I watched the Algerian coast approaching with mixed emotions: partly the keen expectation with which I arrived in each of the countries I had visited ... and partly plain old-fashioned fear inching towards outright terror. The reason for the fear was that Algeria was firmly linked to the global war on terror, to use the American phrase – and not on the Western side. Everyone I talked to at the South African Embassy in Spain had the same message for me: 'Be careful – the Algerian Muslims are known to be the most vicious and ruthless of all in their treatment of infidels.' Each warning included a mention of the extreme brutality the Algerians had exhibited during the war for independence during the late 1950s and early 1960s, and the fact that the current sporadic civil war between the government and fundamentalists had shown that the Algerians' proclivity for violence and cruelty had not mellowed at all, one reason why more of them than ever before were arriving in Europe.

By way of proof they cited the case of the 'Groupe Salafiste pour la Prédication et le Combat', or GSPC, a splinter of the ultra-violent Islamic extremist group GIA, which had broken away in protest against the horrific massacres of the late 1990s ... and then, in 2003, pledged allegiance to Osama Bin Laden's Al-Qaeda terrorist organisation. The GSPC's motto was 'the best infidel is a dead infidel', which didn't leave much room for a peace-loving, multi-cultural South African like me. So my fears were legitimate. These were not characters to mess with. In fact, the best thing was to avoid them like the plague, which, of course, was easier said than done in view of my intention to ride right through their country.

Having been warned many a time about the alleged viciousness of this or that nation, only to find it was not true, I didn't accept these warnings at face value and did some research by way of the Internet. But the entries on the Internet sang the same tune. Between 1997 and 2001 thousands of people, many of them women and children, died at the hands of Islamic extremists. In 2002, the year in which a massive earthquake hit Algeria, the GSPC abducted 40 tourists and held them hostage in the south-west part of the country for nearly two months before intervention by the Malian government got the terrorists to release their prisoners, by which time one woman had died.

Recently, however, the attacks on civilians had decreased, although many bloodcurdling threats were still being made in public. I hoped that large numbers of the terrorists were Tour de France fans and would stay their hands when they ran across me. I would keep growing my beard and speak more Arabic, with the right accent if I could manage it, and just generally try to fit in. Perhaps all this would help to get me through the next couple of weeks. Perhaps. And, I reminded myself, I'm not going near the deserts! I should be OK. It was pretty thin, but it was all I had, and I spent most of the eight hours it took to get to Algeria reminding myself that not all people are bad and that if I died I would at least die doing something special.

I found myself constantly recalling a chance meeting with two Senegalese I met in the desolation outside Oujda – how long ago that seemed now! They were very dark-skinned and stuck out like sore thumbs, just as I must have stuck out for the opposite reason, and we soon established a rapport: all three of us were outsiders, just because we looked different from the people around us.

The Senegalese didn't seem afraid or intimidated by their precarious situation, and were quite willing to describe their journey to this remote outpost. It was an amazing story, next to which my own paled into insignificance. They had left Senegal months before on foot, slogging their way through Mali and then Libya and Tunisia, from where they drifted into Algeria and finally got to Morocco. Sometimes they would manage to cadge a lift, and when they couldn't they simply walked. Since they had no passports, visas or any of the other oil needed to make the bureaucratic wheels turn, they avoided border posts and made their way across mountains, rivers or even the desert, as the circumstances demanded. There was nothing harum-scarum about this long wandering. The Senegalese had a very clear aim and plan of action. By hook or by crook they would get on to a ship in one of the Moroccan harbour towns and arrange to be dropped off on one of the nearby Spanish islands. There they would throw themselves on the doubtful mercy of the authorities, so that the Spanish government would have to look after them. It was going to be easier to plan than to do, but there was no doubt about their determination.

It was getting dark by the time they had finished their story, and I asked them where they were going to sleep that night. They replied that that did not concern them; they would keep walking till they couldn't go any further, then find a place to sleep at the roadside, just like me. We said goodbye and I rode off. What had happened to those two tough-minded young men? In the light of my own experiences I feared for them, but I knew that I would never know.

The sun rose behind us as we approached the magical honey-coloured cliffs of the port of Ghazaouet, gloriously chiselled into the rocky coastline of North Africa. Big boulders jutted out of the water near the harbour entrance like huge unsleeping sentries, and a compact tug came out to guide us in to safety. I enjoyed these new sights, although acutely aware that the resolve I had been pumping up during the night hours was steadily seeping away again.

All my finely honed instincts were sending out loud warning signals. I was heading into danger, possibly more danger than I had encountered anywhere since Liberia; I was going to be completely alone, virtually defenceless and a foreign unbeliever to boot, travelling through a country which was not only bubbling over with religious and political turmoil but had a long-established tradition of brigandage as well. Potentially, anyway, I was like Ishmael in the Bible, who had every man's hand turned against him. I would literally have to live by my wits. I reminded myself once again that it couldn't be as bad as that, that all people weren't bad or looking to kill or rob a stranger, and reminded myself of all the unexpected kindnesses I had received so far, sometimes from the most unlikely people. Then the forebodings would move in again and I would start fighting them all over.

I was still engaged in this internal struggle as I disembarked with the other passengers and lined up for my passage through the official sausage-machine, doing my best not to be among the first in the queue. It didn't help, because almost immediately there were bellows of 'Touriste, touriste, touriste!' from the officials at the front of the queue. Hoping against hope, I kept my head down, pretending I was adjusting my bike's bags and panniers. I hoped in vain. A podgy, barrel-chested immigration official came briskly down the line towards me, pointing at me with his riding crop and shouting: 'Viens touriste! Viens maintenant!' Oh, shit! Ten minutes in Algeria, and I was in trouble!

But I was wrong. The fat man turned out to be the chief immigration official, and he was delighted to have his front door graced by a real, live, genuine tourist, which I gathered was a pretty rare item in that part of the world. Proclaiming to all and sundry his delight at having a tourist, he jumped me to the front of the queue, ordered his underlings to leave off what they were doing and attend to me first – there was no way that a VIP was going to be kept waiting at his harbour! – and personally took down my details with such enthusiasm that his grizzled moustache positively bobbed.

I was flabbergasted by this treatment. Half an hour ago I had been steeling myself to face some flinty-eyed xenophobes full of bad intentions, and here I was being welcomed with everything but a brass band and guard of honour! The only fly in my ointment was a slight apprehensiveness about how the other passengers felt about all this preferential treatment. But when I left the hangar-like immigration building, I got smiles and greetings of 'Bonne arrivée' from everyone. I could barely believe my ears and eyes.

And it got better. Relief had brought my appetite back, so I did my usual getting-to-know-the-place stunt of breakfasting at a local café before setting off. I reckoned I could spring for coffee and the traditional Algerian breakfast cake, but I was down to jingling coins rather than crackling banknotes, and although the fare was surprisingly cheap I still had to negotiate with the waitress about the price of two slices of cake while I absorbed two cups of coffee. But it turned out better than I had expected, because she told me my coffee had already been paid for by a man sitting two tables away.

Thanks to that kind stranger I could sit back and really enjoy those two slices of cake. When I had finished I left, feeling really uplifted. Our interaction had been minimal, to say the least: a couple of smiles, an exchange of greetings. Yet a bridge of human fellowship had been created in those few minutes which, to me at least, is as solid today as it was then ... and this, mind you, at the hands of one of those supposedly blood-thirsty Algerians. Now tell me that there's no hope for the world!

My passage through the Algerian part of the border post was a bit of a disappointment, since my unpleasant acquaintance wasn't occupying the chair on the Moroccan side. Too bad – I had quite looked forward to rubbing his nose in my appearance on the Algerian side. Oh, well ... I suppose it was a little immature of me to look forward to such a petty victory. But what the hell, everyone has the right to be a little childish at times, and I reckoned I had earned it.

The road eastwards was swarming with military personnel, their motorcycles and cars painted in the striking green and white of the national flag. Time and again I was stopped and asked where I had come from and where I was going, but always with a smile and a 'carry on' wave when I had explained. Then when I stopped for lunch at a roadside café, the owner not only served me himself but wouldn't let me pay for anything. All he wanted in return, I think, was to have me leave his café with a positive image of the Algerian people and to learn something about me, even if my fractured French took a bit of understanding.

And things kept getting better. Near sunset that afternoon I pulled in at a boldly branded Pepsi-Cola roadside restaurant and garage in a village called Ain Temouchent. The owner was highly impressed with me for some reason, and he not only called in all his friends from the village to meet me but pumped me full of Pepsi Light and allowed me to make a selection of his cheeses and cold meats for my dinner – free of charge! On top of all that he gave me a place to pitch my tent in his garage forecourt and instructed the attendants to watch over me during the night. All I could do in return was give him a signed copy of my favourite photograph, the one showing me chatting with the Senegalese cart-driver, of which I had a supply printed up to hand out to people I met along the way. This seemed to tickle him, and he placed the picture in a prominent place on his wall for all to see. One day, perhaps, I'll meet someone who will say: 'Oh, yes, I know about you – I saw your picture on the wall of the truck stop at Ain Temouchent in Algeria!' I would really love that.

I spent a pleasant night, full of good cheer and good food, and in the morning was woken up by a cacophony of Arabic chatter from customers pulling up to buy petrol and, I suspected, to peer in wonderment at the somewhat battered tent and equally weather-beaten and overloaded bicycle parked in the forecourt, neither of them a common sight in a place like Ain Temouchent. The noise and attention didn't worry me; I just felt too good. So I lay there for a few minutes more before easing myself into the new day.

It turned out to be an exceptionally tough one on both my tyres and my energy-levels, with extreme heat and constant punctures. What with all these things I put in only 60 km – my shortest day of official planned cycling so far – before calling it a day when I reached a roadside fruit-stall. I consoled myself and rehydrated my parched tissues by eating so many melons and paw-paws that it felt as if my stomach was going to burst. That night I shared the accommodation with the workers at the stall, very poor but generous people, bedding down with them between the rows of melons and paw-paws. It must have looked really odd and would have made a good photograph.

While I was packing my sleeping bag away next morning an early-bird customer fell into conversation with me. When he heard where I hailed from, he said I simply could not pass through the port-city of Oran, just 25 km away, without visiting the South African construction workers who were building the new military hospital there. Naturally I quite agreed with him, and the result was that I found myself having a braai with the guys from the Group 5 Construction firm, watching some of the rugby matches they had videotaped on the past two Saturdays. One of them was particularly chuffed to hear that I was not only born and bred in Zululand but also supported his provincial team, the Sharks. He had a photo taken of us jointly holding up some Sharks paraphernalia, and posted it to the official team website and magazine for publication. Small world!

Other kindnesses were showered on me before I left, having joined my new-found friends for a group photograph. The Group 5 management offered to put me up at the firm's staff home in Algiers, and on my way out of the construction site the resident Algerian security team presented me with a national flag. I decided to drape it over the baggage on the back of my bike; I reckoned that the small South African flag waving from the handlebars and the large Algerian one at the back would make my feelings and allegiance clear to anyone I encountered.

My immediate goal was to cross the Greenwich Meridian, seeing that I had already crossed the horizontal equivalent, and that is exactly what I did next. No bands or fireworks, but it was a good feeling to stand there on the line and spend a moment thinking about where I had been. The meridian was roughly the half-way point in my journey – 18 000 km – and this meant that from here on I was on the way home. However long the second leg of my trek might take me, every turn of my wheels brought me that much nearer to Cape Town.

Apart from hitting the homeward stretch, what had I achieved so far?

Well, so far my lone trek had delivered more in terms of experiences than I had originally anticipated. I had been abducted by rebels in war-torn Liberia and nearly trampled by a stampeding kudu in Namibia. I had suffered innumerable run-ins with the law and had been almost eaten alive by ferocious tsetse flies in Angola. And so on and so on. As a result I had racked up a set of unparalleled memories with which I would one day be able to fascinate (or bore) my grandchildren – all going well, it would be the first rather than the second.

The trip had slowly transformed itself from the predominantly physical to the broadly spiritual. Not that the physical aspects were unimpressive. I had fined down from a bulky 102 kg to a lean 88 kg. I had averaged 111 km per cycling day, a distance roughly equivalent to that of the famed Cape Argus cycle tour. I had averaged an overall speed of about 20 km/h, which equates to six or seven hours in the saddle every day, and I had been doing that for *nine months*. I had suffered extreme heat, biting cold and forbidding terrain, the lack not only of money but sometimes of food and water,

But the physical challenges, I saw now, had been and would be merely the gateway to my exploration of the really important things. Having nearly lost my life, I now savoured every moment to the full. Having been separated from all my family, friends and normal relationships for the better part of a year, I now appreciated them to the full, seeing the true beauty of the love displayed by those who cared for me. Having shed the irritating but essentially unimportant loads, I was thinking more clearly than I had ever before, enjoying a perspective that I had never imagined existed.

I reckoned I had sorted my mind out pretty well during those long hours on the bike which I had spent thinking about everything that had happened to me, blissfully divorced from the daily issues of normal civilisation that keep our world in turmoil, conflict and confusion. They seemed easier to understand, now that things I had once considered important had revealed themselves as the trivial things they were.

Then, wiser if not wealthier, I got back into the saddle, put my head down and set off on the next leg of my journey to Algiers. It went well, barring one rather off-putting, not to say downright scary, experience at Mostaganem, a pretty but very traditional harbour town.

The towns I had passed through so far had had even more loitering men than the ones in Morocco, so that every café was crowded with dozens of nosey coffee-drinkers, all intent on making your business their business. I was sitting in one of these cafes having a custard slice and coffee when Al-Jazeera, the Middle Eastern equivalent to CNN, showed the notorious video of journalist Daniel Pearl being beheaded. I don't think they showed the entire gory sequence, but I saw enough to horrify me, particularly the part where Pearl's severed head was held aloft by his murderer. My horror must have been clearly visible to the bunch of loiterers clustered spellbound around the TV, because they all turned around to look at me, then started to laugh and pass comments I couldn't understand but which were obviously derogatory. Emboldened by their numbers like the true cowards they were, they then started to jeer at me, enjoying the fear I must have been showing. And fear it was, the fear of Algeria I had felt the morning when the ferry was entering Ghazaouet. Stomach churning, I finished my snack, bade everyone a polite farewell and got out of there with all decent haste.

If anything, this made me even more careful about conforming to local customs than I had been before. One time, I remember, I saw the oddest swimmers in my experience, the shape of a number of Algerian women launching themselves off the rocky beaches into the sea. One might ask what was so peculiar about that. Well, they were all fully clothed. I must say I envied them, since the temperature was somewhere in the mid-40s, so that the thought of a quick sea-water dip was quite enticing. But I would certainly not go swimming with all my clothes on, and the consequences of a half-naked man – a white foreigner and a Christian at that – disporting himself among all those pious bathers would most likely have consequences to shudder at.

Another odd thing was that the closer I got to Algiers the more I got to see traditional Algerian weddings in their different stages:

people driving along in lengthy festive motorcades, playing loud music, singing songs, filming the bridal car and generally celebrating the way any crowd of drunken wedding-guests would. Except, of course, that in this strictly Islamic culture they were drunk on the spirit of each occasion rather than on hard liquor ... something of a novelty for a visitor from South Africa, where wedding celebrants like to be full of both the spirit and the spirits. It struck me that the Algerians must be the marryingest people I had ever encountered, till I learnt that getting hitched in Algeria was a three-day affair at the minimum. The wealthier you were, I was told, the earlier you started the count-down, so that a plutocrat's festivities would start on a Monday and keep rolling till the actual ceremony on the Saturday. Most people, though, my informants said, couldn't afford more than a Thursday-to-Saturday bash. Algeria seemed to have a good economic mix, because at some point during almost every night I spent in the country I was awakened by wedding guests whooping it up.

I reached Algiers after an exhausting passage through a beautiful but steep range of mountains that even cars struggled to cross. One carful of holidaymakers did me a great favour by driving to the nearest town to buy me two litres of Pepsi and two litres of frozen water so that I could make up my own energy drink, a mixture of the two which diluted the sugar and gas so that I could drink continually without suffering from a dry, sticky mouth.

Getting to the South African Embassy required some more serious effort – apart from having to navigate slowly through the unfamiliar streets, which is surprisingly hard on both the nerves and the muscles, the embassy was located high up in the city's hills, right next to the heavily guarded United States embassy. I managed to find the US embassy, but didn't know where to turn off to reach South Africa's, and finding out wasn't all that easy.

When I stopped in front of the US embassy's gate its three guards (the ones I could see, that is) immediately cocked their automatic weapons and shouted to me to move on. In spite of this unpromising start I tried to ask for directions, but it was strictly a one-way conversation, and they didn't calm down or lower their weapons till

I gave up and started cycling away at a reasonably fast pace. I carried on till I had put a safe distance between us and then used my cell phone to call Jaco, my contact at the embassy, who talked me in. I was a bit relieved. It would have been a real anticlimax to be gunned down by an overwrought American gate guard in the heart of Algeria because I hadn't thought of using my cell phone.

Thanks to Group 5's kind offer I had no worries about finding reasonable accommodation, and I got on like a bomb with the other people living in the staff home, an extremely diverse bunch which included very traditional Afrikaners, a real Johannesburg English couple, two Xhosas and a coloured guy from Cape Town named Malcolm, with whom I really hit it off. I became really fond of him, and we spent hours chatting – I think because I was missing my home city and I enjoyed Malcolm's Cape Town accent. Malcolm was a truly interesting character who had worked in New Zealand for a couple of years before coming to Algeria; it seemed this country provided him with what he wanted most, which was a continuous round of challenges to get his teeth into. The Johannesburg couple did me the greatest favour, however. Not only did they convince me that Algerians were good people, they gave me $150 US, which happened to be their entire monthly entertainment allowance. This was like manna from Heaven. To say I was grateful and deeply moved by their kindness is putting it mildly.

Thanks to Jaco, my embassy contact, I got a Tunisian visa in a flash, tried but failed to organise one for Libya as well – the Libyan diplomats said I would have get it in Tunis, capital of Tunisia – and inadvertently introduced myself to the most beautiful girl I had seen on my journey thus far. At the direction of the ambassador, Mr Super Maloi (so-called because he was as amazing as Superman, according to some of his staff – I expect you could translate this as 'being held in high regard') – Jaco arranged for me to be interviewed on Algerian TV on the 'Bonjour de Algerie' breakfast programme. This turned out to be quite an unusual experience, since the show took place not in the studio but in the playful environment of a travelling circus.

The hostess was a tall brunette Algerian girl who positively radiated charm and warmth. It had been some time since I had encountered an unveiled woman or one who didn't shy away from me because I was a foreigner, and I wasn't prepared to meet up with such a flawless beauty. I am not one to goggle in complete adoration, but this was clearly the sort of exception that proves the rule, and it was a bit of a battle to keep my wits about me and concentrate on the subject at hand. One of the show's viewers that morning was the ambassador himself, and when I went to see him afterwards he expressed his admiration at the way I had handled the interview, describing me as a perfect example of what our country is all about. I expressed my thanks, thinking: Mr Maloi, you have no idea of what was going on behind that calm face of mine!

All of my temporary housemates gathered to say goodbye to me the morning I left. With one exception their farewells and good wishes were fairly formal – the exception being my friend Malcolm, of course, who abandoned his normal standard South African English for a moment and sped me on my way with a high-pitched 'Hey, chain's a bit dryyyy, isn't it?' in the rich slangy accent of the Cape Flats. Well, of course my chain wasn't dry, but it was just the sort of cheerful heckling you could expect in Cape Town, and for weeks afterwards I grinned every time I recalled Malcolm's farewell. It was the next best thing to having a send-off from a couple of banjos playing a 'moppie', or traditional comic song.

I needed those grins. Most Algerians might have been friendly, but their mountains were not, and proved to be a major challenge. Sometimes the jagged passes literally reached into the clouds, and in places the heights were so steep that the road-builders had had to bore tunnels. Going through one on a bicycle was a hair-raising business. At first it wouldn't be too bad, but soon it would become darker and darker as I left the entrance behind, so that eventually I couldn't see where I was going except when the headlight of a passing car or truck briefly showed the way. The only thing I could do was aim for the proverbial distant light at the end of the tunnel and hope it wasn't a bus with only one headlight.

On top of that the daily temperatures were as unforgiving as the mountains themselves; the highest I recorded was 46 degrees Celsius, which is hot, hot, hot even when you're sitting still, never mind shoving a heavily laden bike up a steep incline. The heat and constant exertion finally began getting to me in a way I hadn't experienced so far. One day I began suffering spells of dizziness and faintness, during which I couldn't see straight and had to struggle to keep my balance. I soon found that the only remedy was to pull off the road and sit with my head resting on the handlebars while the cars screeched past in both directions, and I was so knocked out that sometimes I could feel myself drifting off to sleep as I sat there. Strangely, though, I could feel myself getting stronger with each mountain pass I topped; apart from the dizzy spells and such I had never felt in better shape.

I got a bit of a fright one evening that brought my earlier fears back to the surface. I had stopped at a roadside filling station, and the staff there had no objection to letting me pitch my tent safely close to the pumps. The only one who took exception to my presence was a strange-acting loiterer who seemed to have emerged from the mountains not long before. He kept shooting dirty looks in my direction and voicing loud but incoherent disapproval of my presence – from the look and sound of him I suspected he was brain-damaged. I crawled into my tent, intensely conscious of the fact that he was watching me intently all the while. Was he just slightly touched, or was he capable of going into a psychotic episode and trying to kill me? Anyway, that night I slept with my electric shocker firmly in hand on my chest, the safety switch in the 'off' position. The wild man didn't make an appearance, however, although I scared the daylights out of two stray dogs which were sniffing around my kit by charging out of the tent on all fours, shocker in hand. Looking back, I am surprised I didn't electrocute myself that night.

In due course I came to Constantine, perched majestically high up on the roof of what looked like a thousand hills. Thought to be the oldest continuously inhabited city in Africa, its distinctly un-Arab (or Berber) name is a legacy of its extremely unruly history. It was founded around 203 BC by King Micipsa, a Numidian, or what we would now call a Berber, who called in some Greeks to help with the design and construction. He ended up with a city of great splendour and a powerful army that made the Numidian empire a force to be reckoned with, but in subsequent years it changed hands and ruling cliques on a number of occasions. One of its long-time occupiers was the Romans, and in 311 it was totally destroyed during a civil war between Emperor Maxentius and the usurper Domitius Alexander. It was rebuilt in 313 and subsequently named after Constantine the Great, who had defeated Maxentius in the meantime. Then, in the seventh century AD, it was taken by the Arabs.

It was just the sort of place in which I could happily spend a couple of wandering days, visiting the ancient sites and drinking in the general atmosphere, but at this stage I just didn't have either the time or the money – frustrating, but there was no way around it. Before I left I went to the local Internet café and met a young student called Nadir who epitomised the unconditional and selfless hospitality I had encountered almost everywhere I went in Algeria.

We got to chatting in between our Internet activities, and I soon realised that he wasn't one of those locals who would attach themselves to a foreign tourist in the hope of scoring a free beer and lunch. Nadir was genuinely interested in making sure that I had everything I needed, and also that I left Algeria with the fondest memories possible. He proved this when, after about an hour of this sort of back-and-forth conversation, he invited me to have dinner with him. Thinking that I would treat him for being so kind to me, I suggested we have pizza and ice-cold Coke – I reckoned I deserved to spoil myself a little, and a genuine Algerian pizza shared with a kind Algerian wasn't a bad way of doing it. I was still busy sending some e-mails, so I asked Nadir to wait for a few minutes till I was finished, and then we'd head into the streets and find a good place. He smiled, which I took to mean agreement, and I went back to my e-mailing. A little later an intoxicating smell of cheese filled the room, and I realised that Nadir had seated himself next to me with a box of warm pizza, which he handed to me with an apology: 'I am sorry, Mr Riaan, I did not have enough money to buy you a Coke. I am very sorry. Please forgive me.'

I couldn't believe it. He had spent all the money he had to buy a stranger dinner – and then was embarrassed because he couldn't provide as much as he'd wanted to! Earlier I had seen him counting a handful of coins on his lap, but had not taken any particular notice of it. I was so deeply moved that I didn't know what to say. And worse was to follow: Nadir refused to touch the pizza; it was all for me, he said, and would not be budged. I finished every crumb, but with a very bad conscience, because in my book there is surely nothing more cruel than to eat to your heart's content in full view of a hungry person. But that was how it had to be in this case. I guess this incident goes a long way towards proving the truth of the old saying that there is much more pleasure in giving than in receiving.

I was in good spirits for a variety of reasons when I left Constantine next morning. My heart was filled with the memory of Nadir's kindness, I could feast my eyes on the magnificent setting ... and I knew I had 17 km of uninterrupted downhill to look forward to. After all my toiling through the mountain passes I really enjoyed that downhill stretch, and I stopped only once, to feast my eyes on the first pig I had seen in eight months. This comes under the heading of 'unusual sights' because pigs, needless to say, aren't exactly welcome in Muslim countries. This one certainly hadn't been, since he had obviously been run over and was very definitely dead. I should have been saddened by the pathetic porcine corpse, but to tell the truth, all I could think of was a plate of bacon and eggs.

I learned an interesting thing about Algeria as I went along. Most Algerians were very surprised to see me, not because they had never seen a tourist before, but because they were acutely aware of their country's tarnished image in the tourism industry as a result of terrorist activity. Instead of sitting back and waiting for the politicians to repair the damage they took it upon themselves as individuals to alter the negativity – and from what I saw, they were generally doing a good job. I reckon that if there was a 'friendliest person' award, the surliest Algerian would beat the friendliest person in, say, Mauritania – hands down.

Meeting Algerians was not difficult, and getting to know them was even easier, with language never the obstacle it might have been in other countries. Talking about language, I had a funny encounter with a fellow named Hamid in the small town of Chelghoum El Aid. He heard me use the words 'Genoube Afrique' ('South Africa' in Arabic) and came over to introduce himself, and it turned out that, of all things, he had actually lived in the Cape Town suburb of Valhalla Park for a year and a half. Hamid had picked up a little Afrikaans, which was hardly surprising because it is the majority home-language in the Cape, and he tried it out on me. I was amused to note that none of the words he remembered were curses, given South Africans' lamentable fondness for teaching swearwords instead of polite phrases to unsuspecting foreigners. This was something of a first, in my experience. Of course, it could also be that they were lousy teachers or he was a lousy student. Oh, well, it was one of those Arabian mysteries.

Chelghoum El Aid was a town that left me with some of my favourite memories. I remember one incident in particular, which started when I tracked down the local Internet café deep inside the residential area. It was run by a beautiful young girl who assisted me with a unique tranquillity and kindness, and was so intrigued by me and my bike that I showed her my website and where I had been to date. She was amazed, and next thing I knew I had her father standing in front of me, a large, sweaty man. I was a little worried at first, thanks to my experiences with women in Morocco, but he had a big smile on his face (the sweat, I was relieved to learn, derived not from rage but from the fact that he had just returned from his daily run). He introduced himself as Mohammed Meddour and said he was very glad to meet me, and although his English was about on a par with my French we communicated very well. Before I knew it we had not only eaten a home-cooked dinner right there in the Internet café but I was booked into a local hotel at his expense – a luxury I wouldn't have been able to afford just then. To make it even better, he refused to let me pay my Internet bill. I suppose he considered all this generosity a fair exchange for my travel stories and the general conversation they sparked, but I think I got the better part of the bargain.

Mohammed's hospitality did not end there. Before I left next day he arranged for me to have lunch with him and a few friends, and even found me a tailor to repair my torn pants, which had reached an embarrassing stage of dilapidation. This was a pretty straight-forward process: we went to a little shop in the market, where I took off my pants and then hid my nakedness under a sheet while the tailor did some on-the-spot surgery on all the rips and chafes. Then, when I had been restored to decency, Mohammed took me to another shop, owned by his good friend, Lachtar Salih. Lachtar was a character of all characters and very well known throughout Algeria. He had once studied in America, but now he ran a sort of multi-purpose shop which was a vehicle for his many talents and enterprises. Among other things he was a barber, an English teacher, a seller of pets and a music teacher, and I got a taste of his technique when he whipped out his guitar, stuck some song-sheets under my nose and asked: 'What do you want to sing?' as casually as if I came in to see him every day in search of a musical career. Now, people who know me will tell you that I am not much of a singer or dancer, and especially not in front of strangers, but before long I was singing 'Hotel California' with gay abandon, toes tapping and head bobbing. I should have been embarrassed out of my mind by making such a public spectacle of myself, but in fact it was very liberating to do something that out of sheer cowardice I would never, ever, have tackled back in South Africa. But right then, thanks to Lachtar's personal magic, my customary anal retentiveness about personal public jollification evaporated completely.

I left Chelghoum El Aid for my trek eastwards with a sturdy patch on the seat of my shorts and great warmth in my heart for Mohammed and his family and friends. The further east I went, the more rural and religious the people became, and my somewhat improved Arabic and fast-growing beard helped me to melt into the background, to the point where the ever-vigilant coffee bar-flies couldn't decide who I was or where I came from. I didn't tell them either. I would just smile, eat my slice of custard pie, drink a few shots of strong coffee and get back on the road. It didn't happen every time, but I was definitely making headway in the camouflage stakes.

My crossing of Algeria went quickly. Africa's second largest country, fortunately for me, doesn't have as lengthy a coastline as Morocco, and I was able to maintain a daily average of over 100 km in spite of the mountains and heat: my secret in dealing with the oftentimes excruciatingly tough going was to take it day by day and session by session. This worked well from a psychological point of view, and physically I was in top shape, barring renewed troubles with my third set of toe-nails since Cape Town. As before, the toe-nail trouble resulted directly from the necessity of pedalling standing up from the saddle. This put heavy pressure on my toes, resulting in ruptured blood-vessels under the nails which caused them to slowly detach themselves. There was nothing I could do about it except trim all the excess nail away, then remove the bits which were still attached with a firm yank of my pliers ... a painful experience, believe me.

One town where I encountered problems with religious busybodies had an odd, dusty, Wild West feel, with people peering at me from behind their curtains, as if I was some well-known gunslinger riding in out of the desert. The first few people I spoke to as I set about finding accommodation ignored me – more out of fear, I think, than hostility. Later I met up with a younger student type who spoke some English and offered to help me in my quest. Soon afterwards we were joined by some of his friends, who sat around, cracked jokes and discussed the singular stranger who had cycled unexpectedly into their midst. The subject of my accommodation didn't come up, however, and I must have looked a bit worried, because the English-speaker said they were waiting for a well-known resident who was coming to help me. So I relaxed and enjoyed the laughter and joking, the only thing being, of course, that they could understand the jokes and I couldn't.

In due course the well-known resident arrived and took me to the edge of the town, where a friend of his owned a traditionally tiled coffee shop and restaurant. The friend said it was OK for me to sleep on the restaurant floor after he had closed up, which would be around midnight. I didn't complain – I had had far worse accommodation than this, and it gave me some down-time. I spent it reading up about the countries still to come and eating far too many falafel sandwiches. Unfortunately I also attracted some very unwelcome attention. It was clear that news of my arrival had spread through the town and stirred the populace out of their daily hibernation. Before too long there were literally hundreds of them sitting or standing outside the restaurant and staring at me. Barring a few people, the crowd wasn't hostile; in fact they appeared to be quite shy. But it was unnerving, all the same, so that at one stage I actually moved seats to avoid the hundreds of peering eyeballs glued to me.

The exceptions to the rule were dressed as conservatively as an orthodox Muslim would be, complete with long, thick beards, and they were openly aggressive in their actions and body language – the very picture, in fact, of what the average Westerner thought an Islamic extremist looked like. These types came right in and sat next to or opposite me, giving me the evil eye. Just what irked them I didn't know till they started an argument with the owner when he told them I was a South African on a year-long cycle tour of Africa and asked them to lay off the eye-balling. They disagreed loudly, saying that I was no South African but an American, or maybe British. With dismay I noticed many of them using the same thumb-flick I had seen when the Muslim at Algeciras had been telling me about the iniquities of the 'racist' Spaniards.

The owner of the shop explained: 'These guys hate America and believe that you are American. They do not want you to stay in the town tonight. But I have told them to leave you alone.' That was a bit of a relief. What was not a relief was his explanation of what that forward flick of the thumb meant. 'They make the movement of a dagger into your throat and out again,' he explained hesitantly, obviously reluctant to upset me, 'the same as they will do when slaughtering a goat.'

It was pretty shocking to me, and not just because of the immediate implications. I wasn't surprised that people like this still existed in modern Algeria or anywhere else – I mean, racist white and black people still make up a sizeable chunk of my own country's population. The lessons passed on by parents stay with their children right through to adulthood, and only experience and a willingness to learn can sift the lies from the facts. The people in these mountain villages mostly stayed in the same place all their lives and had never had the opportunity to broaden their experience. So philosophically I could understand the whole thing, but that didn't help to lower my adrenalin production.

Eventually the owner chased the evil-eye merchants out of his restaurant and told me not to be concerned, but his assurances didn't help much as he guided me up a flight of stairs and on to the roof of his building, saying: 'You will sleep here. Lots wind, but little problems.' That suited me just fine: it was about the safest place in the whole damned town. So I spent the night on the roof while my bike slept in the kitchen, and very early in the morning we were both on the road before the first 'salaah' (prayer) was broadcast over the loudspeakers. The only eyes to witness my departure belonged to a drowsy watchman, and I was happy with that.

Two evenings later I had a slightly similar experience. The sun had overtaken me, and I found myself pedalling towards some twinkling lights in the distance, painfully aware of the fact that arriving in a strange town after dark was exactly what I should *not* be doing. But there was nothing for it, so I kept going. The lights came nearer and then I found myself riding down a street on the outskirts which had fires on either side where goat's-meat was being grilled for the crowds of people – women included, now that it was dark – strolling around in the (strictly relative) evening coolness. I didn't stop to sightsee or buy myself a snack. What I wanted was to get to the police station as quickly as possible, just in case this place, too, harboured a bunch of beards who would condemn me as an American in spite of anything that might be written in my passport.

Actually finding the police station was not as easy as it might seem. In South Africa there are always little signboards bearing the police badge and directions, but not here, so I stopped at the first corner café I saw, which was decorated with a Pepsi (did the local extremists make a distinction between flesh-and-blood United States citizens and bottles of an iconic American soft drink? There was definitely something screwy here. But right now I had other things to worry about). I greeted everyone in the café and explained what I wanted. No reaction: either they couldn't understand me or didn't want to. At length a young boy seemed to get the idea and gestured to me to follow him. I did so reluctantly, running the gauntlet of various 'you're not welcome here' stares from the usual café loiterers, since I didn't know where he was taking me. I became even more reluctant when I saw that some of the loiterers had followed me out into the street. But I was really out of options just then, so I would simply have to take my chances with the boy, to whom I kept repeating 'ena cairu policia tafadali' (I want police, please).

He led me deeper into the town, my apprehension increasing with every step, till we finally came to some large gates guarding an old colonial-looking building. To my immense relief a policeman came to see what we wanted, and the boy spoke to him in fast Arabic that I couldn't follow; since the cop didn't draw his gun or handcuff me on the spot I assumed that the boy was simply giving him the facts of our encounter. So I just leaned on my bicycle and let them get on with it. By now we had lost all our café escorts except one skinny fellow with a moustache, who was lurking behind a tree about 40 metres away. Good riddance, I thought.

When the policeman had finished with the boy he ushered me inside. He couldn't speak English, but he was very friendly and we got along quite well in sign-language, not only agreeing that I could pitch my tent on the lawn but also giving me part of his dinner, which his wife had just dropped off. While we were eating the solitary café stalker walked in and started up a lengthy discussion with my host. I looked on, baffled by all this. Was he a policeman? If so, there was no sign of it. The discussion came to an end and the policemen informed me by way of gestures that I was to go with the stalker, hauling out one of his few bits of French, namely 'Chef de Police', and indicating that I must take my documents with me.

I was furious, and understandably so, I think. I deduced that this busybody had actually gone to the real police station (what was this place, then?) to report me to the top cop, and all the way to the real police station I made my dislike of him as clear as I could without actually clipping him across the earhole. Clearly he didn't understand a word of what I was saying, but only an idiot would have missed my meaning. What I didn't realise was that he had actually done me a favour, albeit unwittingly. When we arrived at the real police station I was approached by the duty officer. I greeted him and then beat him to the punch by handing him my passport before he had even had time to ask for it. The cop went off with the passport and left me standing there like Lot's wife, with the busybody pushing into my personal space and throwing sneering remarks about me every time a passing policeman came over to look at my bicycle and ask my nationality.

After some time had passed I began to get angry. I had had a long, hard day, and all I wanted was to be left to put my little tent up and go to sleep. On the other hand, I knew that tantrums wouldn't help. I had to remain visibly calm at all costs. I started asking every policeman who came to look me over what the problem was. Nothing happened, except that I started to irritate them. Right! Time for Plan B, and damn the consequences. I waited for the next cop to come out from behind the counter's glass divider, latched on to him and explained loudly in French and English that I wanted to speak to the chief of police, and if I couldn't speak with him I wanted to call the South African Embassy in Algiers. For good measure I stated several times that I was not a thief. The busybody, meanwhile, was naturally enjoying every moment of the fuss. I could imagine him entertaining his fellow coffee-slurpers for weeks with his highly embroidered version of the story.

The whole unedifying spectacle got some action. A plainclothes policeman sitting on the other side of the divider got up, came over to me and said in English: 'Please, my friend, please be calm. My policemen are making some arrangements for you. There are some dangerous people in this town,' twitching his eyes in the direction of the busybody. The town was historically linked to the Al-Qaeda terror movement, he explained, and during the recent Algerian civil war had been the scene of many atrocities. As a result the police were concerned for my safety and were busy arranging safe accommodation at the local hotel, as well as transport for me to get there.

I calmed down fast, feeling a little ashamed. Here they were trying to save my skin and I was getting frustrated with them! Once again I realised that lack of communication was the key problem on this planet. The cops simply hadn't thought of telling me what they were doing, and so I had come to the conclusion that they were doing nothing. It was a small but frightening lesson in how easily a chain of cataclysmic events can be triggered simply because people didn't talk to one another. Naturally I apologised most sincerely to the top cop, and his minions then not only took me over to the hotel but organised me a complimentary dinner and room. Tremendous! I couldn't help wondering how many other police forces would have done all this for a scruffy, belligerent and almost incomprehensible foreigner who threw tantrums in their charge office.

Admittedly they probably didn't have to fight very hard to get me free room and board, because the hotel proprietor was so delighted to have a foreign guest, even a freeloading one, that he personally showed me to my room. But my night's adventures weren't over yet. All I wanted to do was eat my dinner and catch an early night, but this was not to be. During my dinner the owner's son came over to invite me to the bar after I had finished eating. Yes, the BAR! I told him I wouldn't mind at all, I just needed to shower first. Getting to the bar proved a trifle more difficult than I expected, however, because I attracted the attentions – or perhaps I should say passions – of another guest who was gay and thought I was, too, because I had given him a polite smile into which he had read the wrong indications. As luck would have it, he occupied the room nearest mine, and after I had showered made it plain by means of ultra-suggestive hand movements that he would like to forge a closer acquaintance. I got so worried about this that I called the reception desk and the owner's son arrived and escorted me to the bar.

The bar was underground in both the literal and figurative sense of the word, so that to reach it we had to go down a steep flight of stairs into the very bowels of the earth. And it was some bar. I couldn't believe that it was smack in the middle of a town so conservative that women weren't allowed out in daylight. The stairs took us through a doorway that would not have been out of place in a Western night club. Inside was a stage where Algerian pop singers were raising the roof while women in skimpy dresses and rather sloshed men gyrated on the dance floor. I sank a delicious beer or two and listened to the energetic, very vocal music, deciding that I liked the Algerian genre as much as I liked the beer. Much as I had enjoyed the long stretches of solitude, I also revelled in this loud, wild stuff; after all, man is a gregarious animal, as the experts say. I wondered what the beards in the coffee shops elsewhere in the town would say if they could see all this. No doubt we would all be regarded as sinners of the deepest dye.

The only slightly uncomfortable aspect was that my gay acquaintance turned out to be one of the singers, and made no bones about directing his more romantic songs at me. I felt a bit embarrassed by this serenading, but when all was said and done, an adventurer should not spurn any adventures, no matter how unusual, should he? I realised now that I was helping the hotel proprietor simply by being there. I was part of the entertainment. To the local people a foreigner represented unbridled freedom and all the fun things that the beards considered sinful. No wonder my singer acquaintance had come on so strongly to me!

But I wasn't the Riaan I used to be before my travels through the Muslim regions of Africa. I had gained considerable respect for both the people and their faith, and as I sat there, drinking beer and watching the cavortings of my fellow guests, I thought: It's fun, but it's not something I'd like to see devout Muslims doing. Sure, it was a total contradiction in terms, but it was evidence of what a sea-change my trip had brought so far, and would continue to do as I travelled down the east coast of Africa. I was still evolving; I'd sort out that contradiction in due course. How fortunate I was!

When I left next morning the police chief and some of his cops were on hand to pose for a souvenir photograph for the police station's wall before seeing me off. I made a further contribution to their interior decoration with a copy of my Senegalese horse-and-cart picture, thanked them all for their efforts to make sure I didn't leave feet first, then hit the road.

I was in a slightly thoughtful mood as I ate up the kilometres towards the Tunisian border. At this stage I was receiving plenty of e-mail support from back home, and one from a supporter had made me both smile and frown with the comment that I had cracked the 'after-dinner discussion' top-10 list. My first reaction to this news was: 'I can go home now – I've achieved what I needed to.' Actually, though, this particular e-mail got me to thinking about a few things. One topic was the attempt by three brave South African micro-light pilots to circumnavigate Earth. I had followed their attempt as part of my own motivational process, and had been saddened to hear that one of them had been killed in a flying accident in China, and his replacement in a similar accident in Mexico. I mourned with the families who had lost these two special people, and my thoughts went out to the remaining pilot, now bereft of his two friends. My unsought and unsent advice to him was just this: Now, more than ever, follow your heart. You will doubt whether it was all worth it. Of course it was! Those partners of yours believed in what you and they were trying to achieve, and you owe it to them to finish and then come home to tell us about it. I myself know what it means to risk what I am not willing to risk, if that makes sense to anybody. I knew his parents would not agree with me. But that's the way of any true adventurer.

Algerian kindness continued to dog my footsteps. In Azzaba, a student who was on holiday from his school in France took me to meet his cousins, one of whom was a baker who overloaded my bicycle with a cornucopia of cakes and sweetmeats – including my favourite custard slices – for the road ahead. All these treats were squashed into a box which I strapped to the rear baggage, and which I dipped into as the fancy took me. I must have looked like the proverbial baboon with the calabash when I took a roadside break and sat fishing out bits of mushy squashed cake, but that didn't worry me. The mixture of cakes was unbelievably delicious, and, being designed for a notoriously sweet-toothed race, brought me to the verge of a sugar hang-over each time.

On my last day in the country, having spent the night at the Muslim equivalent of the YMCA in the town of Annaba, I did a muscle-burning 125 km because I wanted to cross over into Tunisia that night. At sunset I arrived at the foot of the mountain that separated Algeria from Tunisia, took a breather and then headed up the pass connecting the two countries. The mountain, needless to say, was high – 1 500 feet, according to my map – and the 10 km of continuous climbing was the steepest uphill stretch I had encountered anywhere on my journey so far.

Passing through the Algerian border was a pleasure because the immigration officials were exceptionally friendly in spite of the fact that they were very busy through-processing travellers, but the same couldn't be said for the Tunisian side, which lay another 10 pitch-black kilometres away. I got there at 10 pm, confident that I had ample time to go through the formalities and then ride down to the coastal town of Tabarka and catch some sleep. But then everything ground to a halt. This was partly my own fault. I had followed my usual approach of telling them all about my trip before they had stamped me through, and the result was that the chief immigration official wouldn't let me in because I didn't have a visa for Libya, no doubt to avoid any possibility of my being stranded in Tunisia if the Libyans cut up rough about issuing one to me.

I could have kicked myself for prematurely running off at the mouth, but the Algerians had been so friendly and helpful that it had never struck me that I might encounter a different attitude among the Tunisians. I was still pretty optimistic, though, after all the good things that had come my way in Algeria, and I stayed that way till the blow fell when the foreign affairs department in Tunis backed up the immigration chief official.

I expressed my disappointment in eloquent terms and then exercised my only option, which was to cycle back to the Algerian border post and beg the chief immigration official to let me back into his country so I could sort out my problem. He agreed and let me sleep on the concrete floor of his office that night before heading back to the pretty coastal town of El Kala, where I spent a week-long involuntary holiday while the South African Embassy in Tunis laboured to persuade the Tunisian foreign affairs department to let me in.

The accommodation in El Kala was in a pleasant establishment run by a woman called Fatima, but it was not till the Tunisians had relented and I got a lift back to the border post with a rather drunken man that I found out about other home comforts I had been blissfully ignorant of. This I discovered when my companion asked with a broad smile: 'You stay Fatima's?' Yes, I said, to which he smiled even more broadly and asked: 'You make with the girls? Ha ha ha ha!' It was then that I realised that Fatima's doubled as a brothel. Whether I was very naïve or Fatima and her girls had been very discreet I wasn't sure, but either way it was another personal first, although a rather inglorious one.

The friendly drunkard also told me something else which made me blush rather more than the revelation about Fatima's entrepreneurial efforts. I had fallen into the habit of using a certain gesture to indicate extra effort when telling my stories, clenching my fist and moving it horizontally back and forth at chest height. Now, my bibulous friend revealed, in this part of the world that identical gesture was the universal sign-language for copulation. Good grief! I thought back to how many people I had entertained recently with stories of how tough the going was, complete with the copulation sign, and I couldn't help smiling.

The Tunisian border officials were still a bit suspicious, and I had to wait for five hours while they confirmed with Tunis that the letter I showed them was genuine. The time was not wasted, however, because it taught me about another facet of Algerian life and showed why Algerians were so fond of holidaying in Tunisia (I had been told that they accounted for fully 10 per cent of all the visitors to their neighbour). Car-load after car-load of returning Algerian girls would roll up at the Tunisian border post in shorts and T-shirts, then change into the traditional all-enveloping burka before carrying on, very prim and proper, to the Algerian side.

The Tunisians finally relented and stamped me through, and I left Algeria behind me with a real sadness such as I hadn't felt on leaving any other country so far. Why? At first I wasn't quite sure. Then I realised that never before had a nation so completely and utterly embraced me with kindness. From the moment I landed at Ghazaouet port to the last moments at the Algerian border post, I had always felt as though I was surrounded by people who were genuinely concerned about my well-being. Granted, there had been a couple of unpleasant moments, but they paled into insignificance before the great wave of unselfish goodwill that had carried me along from beginning to end.

In my book, that put Algeria in the Number One spot out of the 22 countries I had visited thus far. And it had done something else of far greater significance. It had made Islam less scary and definitely more appealing in its entirety than it had previously been. So the Algerians might never know it, but they had acquired an unofficial and self-appointed ambassador to tell the world about them and the wonders of their country.

# CHAPTER 22

# LAST-MINUTE REPRIEVE IN TUNISIA ... AND A FAITHLESS TRAVELLING COMPANION

*I must have looked like a total madman as I darted around, hunched over like Quasimodo, snatching at thin air. I was being watched by a large crowd which had assembled outside the shop's entrance; there were even some people inside the restaurant who had their faces squashed against the window-glass. What a nut case! I thought to myself. It's not a joke any more. You're slowly becoming a real nut case!*

Getting to my first destination, Tabarka, was as easy as freewheeling down a mountain, which is actually what I did – all the way. It was slightly less easy to grasp that I had arrived in a tourist's paradise, suspicious immigration officials notwithstanding. There is no other way to describe Tunisia; nowhere else on this fascinating but often wild and woolly continent is there any other place which is so visitor-friendly. The eager willingness to accommodate tourists was almost overwhelming, people spoke English, information offices abounded and the locals did not hound you to buy a curio. Overlaying all this was a general atmosphere which was relaxed beyond anything I had experienced up to now. And all this just 10 km into the country!

Maybe (to be facetious for moment) this was partly because in a sense the Tunisians have been dealing with foreign visitors, welcome or otherwise, since the time of the Phoenicians (the forefathers of today's Lebanese) as long ago as the tenth century BC. But they obviously ended up doing pretty well for themselves, even though 40 per cent of their land is desert. A sure pointer was the fact that there was universal compulsory education, with kids being taught French and English in addition to Arabic from pre-teen level. All that language teaching paid off for me right away when I arrived in the town of Beja in total darkness. I barely had time for a couple of glances up and down the main street before three students came up and asked how they could help me, which was just what I wanted – students always know everyone worth knowing and also tend to make first-class tour guides.

Within five minutes my need for Internet access and a bed for the night had been solved – I wasn't interested in dinner, because since leaving Tabarka I had eaten so much fruit at the many roadside farm stalls that at one stage it had actually been uncomfortable to keep cycling. My helpers gave me a thumbnail sketch of Beja's history culminating in the town's efforts in effecting international reconciliation towards the end of World War II, of which they were very proud. Next morning, as I set out for Tunis, I saw what they meant when I passed well-groomed war cemeteries for both the Axis and Allied dead. The people of Beja played no favourites: all the dead were accorded the same respect. There's a lesson there for the world and particularly for South Africans, who tend to remember only the bits of history they like or that provide them with a grievance to nourish.

It was only about 100 km to Tunis, and when I toiled over the last tall hill and caught sight of the lakes surrounding the capital I paused to enjoy a very special moment. 'You've cycled from Africa's most southern city to its most northerly one,' I said out loud and turned to look to the south, trying to summon up a picture of Cape Town in my mind's eye. And it's a funny thing, but at that moment Cape Town and Tunis didn't seem all that far apart.

Having finished congratulating myself, I headed into the heart of the city, and after some friendly advice from the locals ended up at a neat but tiny hotel in the middle of the Medina. This one was like a tourist's vision of what a medina should look and feel like – frantic, crowded and almost frighteningly confusing, with a plethora of cobbled streets separating small double-storey buildings no more than about two metres apart; it wasn't at all difficult to imagine what it must have looked like 500 years earlier ... much the same, I thought, except that clothes and vehicles were different and there were no blaring radios. All of which left me slightly out of phase when I went through the one and only exit and in the blink of an eye stepped out of ancient Tunisia into the modern version, as represented by the Rue de France with its glass-fronted hotels, Continental-style bars and trams zig-zagging graciously up and down. There was even a miniature version of the Arc de Triomphe.

The memory of the long period of French colonial rule did not seem to weigh as heavily on the Tunisians' shoulders as it did on the Algerians', I concluded as I stood in front of the huge Roman Catholic cathedral; I could have been in any of a dozen First World cities anywhere in Europe. Yet only a few steps away was the quintessentially Tunisian medina ... It was clear that Tunisians didn't allow themselves to be weighed down by emotional or political baggage. The French period had been only the latest colonial interlude in their long history (and a pretty brief and benign one, compared with most of the others), and when it ended it simply became yet another chapter of their long history. It was a refreshing thought. A nation is only at peace with itself, and its various groups are only at peace with one another, when all concerned accept the country's common history, good or bad, as their own.

As usual in Muslim countries (Tunisia has a number of small minorities, including a 600-year-old Jewish community, but it's 99 per cent Islamic), most of the people in the streets were men, often congregated in large groups in the streets and coffee bars. Women were much more visible than in Algeria, however, and favoured modern Western clothes, with the top-to-toe traditional hijab a rare exception to the rule. Later I was told that Tunisia, along with a couple of other Muslim countries like Azerbaijan and Turkey, actually prohibits females from wearing hijabs in government buildings, on pain of being fired from their jobs or, in the case of school pupils, being expelled. The new Riaan regretted such a draconian approach, but the old Riaan found it suited him just fine. The Tunisian girls with their beautiful hair, their exotic Mediterranean beauty and their magnificent unforced grace of movement were a feast to the eye.

Both men and women made no secret of their goodwill and eagerness to interact, and it was great fun to stroll around and submerge myself in what was going on around me without feeling at all out of place. I was amused to see that acting macho in everything was a pastime beloved of males both young and old. It manifested itself in a number of ways – including heckling passing women, who did not get their water hot about it – but one of the most obvious things was the way they smoked their cigarettes, like so many clones of John Travolta in the movie 'Pulp Fiction'. Was it Hollywood's influence or something else? Well, it didn't really matter, I decided. Tunis was truly a place of rich diversity. But later I found that this sort of thing was distinctly less common in the more rural and traditional areas. So perhaps it *was* Travolta's fault after all.

The South African Embassy staffers in Tunis were as friendly and helpful as their colleagues in all the other countries I had visited so far, and went out of their way not only to be personally kind to me but also to make the Tunisian immigration process easier to deal with. My primary goal was, of course, to get that elusive Libyan visa. Ambassador Mfabe told me that it was a very difficult item to acquire, and that less than a month earlier all his efforts to obtain one for a prominent South African businessman had failed. But, he added, he was willing to give it another try.

One of the embassy employees, Herman, insisted that I stay at his house while I waited for a response from the Libyans. So I found myself eating South African food lovingly prepared by his wife and listening to Afrikaans music, which made me feel about as close to home as I was going to get. He and one of the local staffers, Mirriam, and her husband arranged an excursion to the famous holiday spot of Hammamet and Herman rounded off my time with him and his family by taking me to the most northerly point of the entire African continent, Bizerte, with its ancient and colourful district of Sidi bou Said. So far I had stuck to my commitment to refrain from accumulating souvenirs, but Bizerte was obviously an exception, and so I kept my eye out for something that would help me to remember it for ever. I found it eventually, but not in a curio shop. I was standing at the water's edge, at a spot Herman calculated was absolutely the northernmost point of Africa, when a flat piece of driftwood came floating past. It was slightly out of reach, but after some effort I had it in my hands; I would wrap it up carefully and take it home with me, I decided, and there it was going to keep my memories of Tunisia and Bizerte bright and clear for the rest of my life.

Sidi bou Said was an amazing place, with colourful doorways and authentic Tunisian coffee shops where you sat on pillows like some old-time sultan. That said, my first attempt at drinking a shot-glass full of authentic Tunisian coffee wasn't all that successful: the coffee was as thick as mud and I ended up chewing a large part of the glass's contents ... what I didn't know at that stage was that you are not supposed to chugalug the lot in South African style, just sip off the runny part at the top. Anyway, with fine coffee-bean fragments spread evenly across my teeth I smiled broadly and said goodbye to the owner of the coffee shop concerned, thanking him for his hospitality and assuring him that I would like to come back again sometime. I imagine he often saw tourists making a spectacle of themselves like this, because he managed to keep a straight face during the entire farewell process.

Ambassador Mfabe was just as good in the personal hospitality stakes as his staffers, and invited me to join him for a night-time football match at the impressive national stadium, as a guest of the Tunisian football association. And not just any match, mind you, but one in which our countrymen from the Supersport United football club would take on Tunisia's best, the highly rated Esperance team. Alas, our lads went down to a convincing 2–0 defeat. But I thoroughly enjoyed the evening, and consoled myself with the thought that at least it was a slightly better defeat (if there's such an animal) than our 4–0 loss at the Cup of Nations in Lagos.

I saw a lot of another local staffer, Hayat, because she was the embassy's media contact person and therefore responsible for making sure that I received coverage on the national TV and radio stations. Hayat was an absolute star (she looked like one, too, being one of those graceful Mediterranean beauties I mentioned earlier). For some reason I brought out her motherly instincts, so that she was genuinely concerned about me, my problems and my future safety, and she went far beyond her official duties. On her own initiative Hayat arranged a small sponsorship for me from a businessman who happened to be very fond of South Africa, then she tackled the South African ambassador in Libya, Mr Ebrahim Saley, and persuaded him to become personally involved in my visa negotiations. Mr Saley, bless his heart, waxed so enthusiastic that he not only made a contribution to my exchequer from his own pocket but actually got our Minister of Foreign Affairs, Dr Nkosazana Dlamini-Zuma, personally involved in the paper-work. For all I know Hayat oiled some other wheels as well. An incredible all-round woman! I guess her husband knows he is a lucky man.

In spite of all these efforts there had still been no result after 10 days. This was both good and bad news – bad because the visa hadn't been granted, good because so far it hadn't been refused either – and I decided to take some positive action instead of just hanging around. I would carry on towards the Libyan border, hoping that the visa problem would be resolved before I got there. If and when it was, I would find a good place to store my bike and go back to Tunis to pick it up. I didn't even want to think about the possibility that the Libyans would turn me down. I simply had to have it, or I would be likely to fail in my self-imposed and completely non-negotiable goal of cycling through every single coastal country in Africa.

I left Tunis feeling glad to be on the road again to new adventures and heading in the right direction to get home to my loved ones. I got off to an unexpectedly bad start, though, with one puncture after another, even though the highway surface was among the best I had encountered anywhere. Even the jungle roads of the Congo hadn't caused such damage to my tyres. Why? I couldn't figure it out, and still can't. But there it was. I retain another less than pleasant memory from that time, a stomach-churning taste of the old Tunisia. I rode into the town of Bir Sheba just at the daily goat-slaughtering hour. It was a horrible sight: the goats bleating wildly while their fellows were having their heads cut off on the concrete slabs in front of the little butcheries, blood spurting in every direction as the beheaded bodies were hung to bleed while the hooves were removed and the skin expertly peeled off, while the severed heads began piling up on the tables outside the shops. The butchers seemed to take pride in their work, because every time one of them saw me looking at him he would smile and straighten up, as if posing for me to take a photograph. I didn't, but I forced myself to watch, firstly because it was an education like all my other experiences and secondly to fine-tune myself philosophically. This was an everyday event in Tunisia, as it was in the neighbouring countries, and the fact was that I loved eating the grilled meat sold by the roadside from stalls like these.

It was along this stretch of road that I acquired the first pet of my journey, a field mouse. It was on the second day out of the capital, when I was battling my way through icy rain of such intensity that I was soaked to the skin, even though I was wearing my trusty rain-resistant First Ascent jacket. Numbers of little field mice were shivering by the side of the road, while others had actually moved on to the tarmac to pick up some of its residual warmth. One mouse was sitting right on the yellow line, shivering uncontrollably, and I knew that he was a dead duck as soon as the next car came along, just like any number of his colleagues I had seen. Without really thinking about it I scooped him up, a pathetic sight, dried him off with my oily chain-rag, christened him 'Russell' (the name simply popped into my head as I picked him up) and stuck him into a relatively dry pocket of my jacket. Russell seemed very content with his new situation in life and didn't attempt to run away later on when I took him out for a chat and some pictures.

Anyway, Russell immediately became part of my journey. He shared my food and even sat with me in the fancy roadside garage restaurants, and I was soon so fond of him that in my mind's eye I could see myself riding into the Waterfront in Cape Town, holding him aloft for the cheering crowd to see. But Russell had other ideas. He was standing up on his hind legs and nibbling on a piece of carrot in his front paws at one of these snack-breaks when he suddenly decided it was time to go. He took off like a rocket, landed on the concrete, rolled on to his stomach and scurried away. I ran after him to save him from himself, dodging between the petrol pumps with the cleats on my cycling shoes clacking loudly. I must have looked like a total madman as I darted around, hunched over like Quasimodo, snatching at thin air a couple of inches above the concrete and loudly giving instructions to Russell while simultaneously upbraiding myself.

Eventually I managed to scoop him into my hand, then straightened up to see that I was being watched by a large crowd which had assembled outside the shop's entrance; there were even some people inside the restaurant who had their faces squashed against the window-glass. What a nut case! I thought to myself. It's not a joke any more. You're slowly becoming a real nut case! – But you know what? I was so relieved to have Russell back that it actually didn't matter to me at this stage if I was going mad. So I sat down on the ground next to my bicycle and fed Russell another piece of carrot, while the crowd continued to goggle at me. But the final parting of our ways was not far off. Russell became more and more disobedient, even though I had long discussions with him, explaining that if he ran away he wouldn't have a soul to speak to or a place to lay his head – surely he could see that he was best off with someone like me, who cared for him and looked after him?

But Russell was adamant. One day he bit me and then jumped out of my hand, but I caught him in mid-air and thereby saved him, as I explained, from certain death in the passing traffic. He didn't say anything, but he must have disagreed with me, because a little later he bit me again and took another jump. This time he was too far away to be caught, and after landing on the ground he scuttled under the freeway and ran into some mud-pans. I went after him and caught him eventually, not without some pain and suffering, in a small plantation of what looked like thorny cycad plants.

But he slipped out of my grasp, and when I slid and went down on my back in the mud I lost sight of him. I searched and called for nearly an hour, but he was gone for good, so I headed back to the road, disappointed in him and bereft of faith in my ability to bond with the animal kingdom. I didn't even have a decent photograph of him because the bad light had ruined the ones I had taken of him that first day.

OK, in cold blood that's a pretty crazy story. But it gives an indication of my state of mind just then. No doubt that same hypothetical psychologist I talked of earlier would be able to formulate a clear explanation of what was going on in my mind. But when you think about it, I had spent most of a year taxing my physical and emotional strength to its utmost, isolated from my loved ones and often completely alone for long stretches at a time. The unremitting strain hadn't broken me, but I had certainly bent a little in places.

Fortunately there was much to distract me from the shock of Russell's desertion. I had a sort of long-distance knowledge of places like Sousse and Sfax from following South Africa's recent unsuccessful bid for the African Cup, and I was keen to see them in the flesh, so to speak, by actually cycling through them. They were fairly modern industrial towns and turned out not to be all that interesting, but some of the smaller places I passed through were unforgettable. The greatest moment of all was cycling into the town of El Jem at the best time of day, sunset. In itself El Jem was not very remarkable, a sprawling, humble sort of place – but smack in its centre was a smaller version of Rome's Colosseum, its honey-coloured stone walls glowing in the fading light. I unlimbered my Kodak point-and-shoot and snapped away, mourning the demise of my video camera (the pictures came out very nicely, incidentally) and for the rest simply enjoyed the wonderful old structure. Some scenes of my favourite movie, 'Gladiator', were shot here, and I couldn't help wondering what the shades of the ancient gladiators might have thought of it.

Tunisia, of course, has made its magnificent scenery and sites available to film-makers for many years, the early 'Star Wars' series being probably the most famous in recent times. I was intrigued to find that the wide-awake Tunisians had not allowed the sets George Lucas had built to fall into ruin, but had turned them into popular tourist attractions. The top 'must-see' on every 'Star Wars' fan's list, I was told, was the bar where Luke Skywalker found Han Solo among a crowd of the weirdest-looking drinkers I hope never to meet.

In between all this sightseeing I made daily checks with the embassy in Tunis to find out if there had been any progress on my visa application. The closer I came to the Libyan border the more concerned I became. So far I had refused seriously to contemplate the possibility that it would be refused, but now I couldn't evade the facts any longer. What would I do if it was? In my spare moments I pored over my maps, considering other options. I simply *had* to go through Libya, and if I couldn't get the visa I would have to find some other way of getting in. By this stage I don't believe that I was thinking too clearly, thanks to what had become something close to an obsession. Libya was a dangerous place to try bending the rules, and if I fell foul of the law in Muammar Gaddafi's dictatorship the hands of my diplomatic friends would be tied.

When I reached the town of Medenine I decided to stash my bicycle and go back to Tunis to see if I could expedite the visa. Once again I fell among friends. The young guys who worked at the Internet café were enthusiastic about helping me and chained up my bicycle inside the shop, assuring me that it would be exactly as I left it when I returned, which I calculated would be in about four days' time. That settled, I got on the train to Tunis.

The following afternoon I walked into the embassy, apprehensive but still hopeful in spite of nearly three suspenseful weeks of negative news. And three days after my arrival it arrived! I had so many heroes and heroines to thank that I scarcely knew where to start: Ambassador Mfabe and his amazing staff, of course, particularly Hayat; Ambassador Ebrahim Saley, who had made my application his personal quest; and Foreign Minister Nkosazana Dlamini-Zuma in faraway Pretoria, who had personally intervened with her Libyan opposite number. People complain, with justification, about all the things that go wrong in South Africa, but I can affirm from personal experience that the diplomatic service isn't one of them. And where else in the world would a cabinet minister take the time amid hosts of other concerns to intervene personally on behalf of an obscure lone cyclist pursuing a quixotic quest like mine?

So, heart singing with joy, I hopped on the train back to Medenine. My bicycle was waiting for me exactly as I had left it, and I wasted no time in getting going. One day's ride later I was at the Libyan border. Under the stony stare of a five-storey poster of Gaddafi, I was stamped through by somewhat confused and intrigued immigration officials, and there I was, in the land of the little Green Book.

# CHAPTER 23

# LIBYA – HUNGRY HYENAS AND A GREAT MAN-MADE RIVER

*The bike was to be on display as a conversation piece in the mansion's foyer, but it took us a while to discover that it was parked in front of a bright light next to the swimming pool. It was only later that I discovered what had happened. The bike had indeed been parked in the foyer, looking thoroughly disreputable from all its hardships, with an old pair of underpants draped over the baggage as a final touch. Anyway, after a frantic appeal from his wife the ambassador had shifted it to the swimming pool and also had one of his staff tuck the underpants into one of the bags. That's what you call hardcore diplomacy.*

I was in a much more tranquil state of mind when I entered Libya than I had been when arriving in Algeria. While planning my trip (how long ago it seemed now!) Libya had been one of the countries that had really worried me. But after my Algerian experience, I wasn't going to get ahead of myself again. I would take Gaddafiland as it came. My arrival, as I've said, was pleasantly smooth. The immigration officials were clearly not familiar with customers like myself, but one who spoke some English eased me through in such a spirit of co-operation that he nearly approved my request to take a photo of the 15-metre-high portrait of the 'Great Leader' glaring down on us ... nearly, but not quite, since taking pictures of Muammar Gaddafi or even of his portrait is highly illegal in Libya.

The border post was quite a sight. There weren't many people or vehicles heading for Libya, but the line of 18-wheelers waiting to cross over into Tunisia stretched back for several kilometres. One of the immigration guys explained that Libya didn't produce anything of its own except fuel. This meant that it imported everything it needed, and the international trade embargo had only been officially lifted one month back. Talk about huge business opportunities! No wonder those truckers were so keen to get over the border.

After the good start to my day I couldn't wait to pick up some first-hand experience of this rather odd country and its equally eccentric leader. Libya did the 'land of contrasts' story better than anywhere else. For one thing, what Libya mostly consists of is achingly hot desert. But thanks to huge oil reserves and a tiny population (just under 8 million, all told), it is said to have more wealth per capita than any other nation in Africa, and the statistics bear this out. Male Libyans have an average life expectancy of 74 and women 79, the population is 82 per cent literate, the average family has just over two children and the HIV prevalence rate, if official figures are to be believed (decide for yourself), is one-third of one per cent.

Gaddafi has acquired a reputation for being the world's biggest sponsor of Islamic and left-wing terrorism, but this doesn't deter him from owning a stake in the famed Italian Juventus soccer club, and in fact one of his sons played professional football there at the time of my visit. Other children of his pursue similarly interesting and diverse careers, among other things in the fields of arts and charities, while one is a lawyer who was on Saddam Hussein's defence team at the time. You have to say this of the Gaddafis: they're a versatile lot.

Gaddafi also does not lack self-confidence. He has always seen himself as a revolutionary and visionary leader, and his 'Green Book' is, he says with a great lack of false modesty, the solution for Libya's problems. It is based on his 'Third Universal Theory', which claims to be based on a combination of socialism and Islam derived in part from tribal practices, the idea being that this ideology is supposed to be implemented by the Libyan people themselves in what he terms 'direct democracy'. When the slim volume appeared for the first time in the 1970s it was savagely criticised in the West, not that this worried him, and since there are absolutely no opposition parties in Libya, 'direct democracy' either enjoys universal popularity or doesn't exist outside the pages of the Green Book. Take your pick. Then again, when I was there I saw what he had been busy with for about two decades – creating the world's first man-made river, the plan being to bring underground water from deep within the desert to Libya's towns and cities, as well as to desert communities (Libya is so dry that one of its major sources is desalinated water from the Mediterranean Sea).

Needless to say, what greeted me as I cycled away from the border post was desert – plenty of it. It is true that the terrain had been changing while I was still in eastern Tunisia, but pedalling into a proverbial sea of sand was a bit of a shock, and I decided that the only way I would make it to Tripoli ('Tarabulus' in Arabic) would be by flagging down passing vehicles when I ran short of water. The problem with this, of course, was that traffic from the border to Tripoli appeared to be minimal – given my difficulty in obtaining a visa, I could understand why – although not the other way around. Still, that was the only option available, and I got down to making the best of it.

People always want to know what I thought about during those long, lonely hours on the road when I wasn't engaged in distractions like fighting potholes, fixing punctures, dodging bandits, fending off hostile dogs or forcing my way through jungles, and how the things I thought about popped into my mind. Well, this one was typical of the process. As I slogged along I couldn't get the thought of those long lines of 18-wheelers out of my head, and I found myself turning all sort of ideas for business opportunities. It was simply a question, I concluded, of working out what the newly unembargoed Libyans needed, and determining if they could afford to pay for it. The answers were equally simple: firstly, 'everything'; secondly, 'yes'. As soon as I got home, I decided, I would have to find an investor who would be willing to set up a factory in Libya to fill in one of those myriad niches in the local market, even if it was for something as mundane as toilet-paper.

My first stopover was the town of Zuwara, which proved once again how wrong first impressions usually are. Zuwara lay comfortably in the desert, apparently consisting of the usual small, square sand-coloured houses, but when I had passed through the outskirts I found myself in the brightly lit central area, surrounded by posh-looking Italian shoe and suit shops, as well as other twenty-first century conveniences. These included an Internet café, to which I immediately made my way. I wanted to send some e-mails, and I also needed a local SIM card for my cell phone for the 12 days or so that I intended to spend in Libya.

The owner, a kindly fellow called Amr who spoke fairly good English, proved very helpful in easing me into the Libyan lifestyle by giving me a temporary roof over my head and helping me to hunt down the SIM card I needed. This latter should have been a simple affair, as it had been in all the other countries I had visited, but not in Libya. Here, I found, only citizens could buy a SIM card, and to make it even worse the going price was about R3 000, which was as far beyond my budget as a Mercedes-Benz. SIM cards seemed to be a scarce item generally – one of Amr's friends owned a cell phone shop, and even he didn't have a loan card for me. It was a great disappointment, because up to this stage communication via SMS had been a powerful way of keeping in touch with the people back home. But there was nothing to be done about it, and I re-signed myself to the fact that they would not be hearing from me while I was in Libya.

My acquaintance with Amr helped me to understand the Libyan view of the West. Like many other good-hearted Muslim people he made use of our conversations to try to persuade me about the evil nature of the George Bush administration in the United States. I was amazed once again at Muslims' tendency to lump all Caucasian-looking people together and drop them into the American bucket, so that there were only two sides: for and against the war in Iraq. The idea that some Caucasians might deplore both terrorist acts and the deaths of innocents in Iraq didn't seem to have any relevance, although Amr was not uneducated and spent a fair amount of time travelling outside Libya – as a matter of fact, he was scheduled to be in Alexandria in Egypt at the same time I planned to pass through there. I didn't get involved in too much argument about the matter because, in fact, we weren't arguing; Amr certainly didn't rant or rave about it, but was quite sincere.

Amr helped me to finalise my arrangements for meeting with a team from 'Carte Blanche', the TV documentary programme, when I arrived in Cairo. This hadn't been possible before because of the uncertainty of my timetable, but now the crunch had come. The producers had set a specific date and booked the crew's flights and hotels, and they wanted an assurance that I would be there on time. I said I would, not without a few qualms – not because I couldn't average the 100 km-a-day stints that would be necessary but because a tight schedule was vulnerable to time-wasting unforeseen misadventures. On the other hand, this was a date not to be missed.

Once again the South African Embassy pulled out all the stops in welcoming me. As in Nigeria, it was considered best that someone meet me at a given point and escort me for the last few kilometres into the city centre. Ambassador Saley sent a staffer called Conradie Kok to meet me, which proved more difficult than either of us had anticipated (a tip here for people planning a stunt like mine: make sure you have communication with your escort, and do not plan a meeting during lunch-time prayers).

I pedalled along through foot and vehicle traffic which became busier and busier the closer I came to the city, searching with ever-increasing desperation for an Internet or telephone café and mourning the absence of a working cell phone. I finally found a place to call from when I was just 10 minutes away from our arranged meeting-time, and Conradie confirmed that he was on his way in a large white Mercedes with green number-plates. I was a bit worried about the number-plates, because I am partly colour-blind, in the sense that I can usually see colours quite clearly, except when there is little contrast between them. So I wasn't confident that I would necessarily be able to distinguish between, say, a dark green and a dark red number-plate. I didn't mention this to Conradie, though – we had enough complications already, and in any case there were surely not all that many large white Mercedes vans in Tripoli.

Then real disaster struck. Before I could tell him where I was –

not that I really knew, but at least there was no doubt that I was on the outskirts of the city – all the telephone lines went down. I did the only thing I could, which was to carry on and hope that Conradie would somehow spot me ambling along towards him. That was the theory of it, anyway, but I knew that the practice was bound to be more difficult, because by now the road was very busy indeed, with trucks on either side obscuring the view in every direction. I kept going, watching both the traffic heading in my direction and the rest whizzing past me in the other. It was a dangerous pastime, because it meant that I had to focus on what was way ahead, rather than what was directly before me. It didn't help very much. Moses in his wanderings in the desert didn't lust more after the Promised Land than I did for a sight of that white Mercedes.

After about 30 minutes of this I decided to duck into the first telephone café I came across while I was still alive and in one piece. The lines were up again now, although they weren't working too well, and there followed another conversation with Conradie which consisted mainly of repeatedly shouting 'Where are YOU?' at one another. Then, before this question was settled, the lines went down again. Hot, tired and frustrated, I paused to give my predicament some thought before setting off again. It was quite possible that somehow Conradie and I had missed one another earlier, and that he was actually behind me now, rather than somewhere ahead. This being the case, I decided, it made more sense for me to stay put by the roadside, making sure I was as visible as possible, and let him find me.

After a bit I saw a white Mercedes van heading towards us; I couldn't identify it by its number plates because my particular species of colour-blindness tends to become worse with distance, but surely it couldn't be a coincidence. At last! I edged up as close to the roadside as was possible without getting taken out by the passing traffic and stood by to attract Conradie's attention with a vigorous wave or two. The van came nearer and nearer, till it was only about 100 metres away and I could see the occupants; if I could see them, I thought happily, then surely they could see *me*!

It didn't work out that way, however. A truck began overtaking the van, and at precisely at the same time a double articulated mechanical horse and trailer slowly moved out in front of me. Between them they left me in total eclipse, effectively kraaled off in all directions. I couldn't believe my bad luck. I shouted and waved frantically as the van drove hurriedly in the direction I had come from. Soon it was gone, leaving me in total despair, straddling the bike with my feet deep in the roadside sand. I remember letting off the deepest 'I can't believe this' sigh of my life. All my energy and motivation seemed to have evaporated. I leaned forward till my chest rested on the front bags of the bicycle and stared at the ground just ahead of the front tyre, numb to the heat rising from the ground. If I go and try to call them now, I thought, wallowing in self-pity, you can be sure Conradie will have turned around and be on his way back, and he won't see me because I'll be inside the café. That is, if the phones work! I was in such a feeble-spirited state that it actually felt quite good to give up and just sit there.

But after a bit I grew some backbone again. I was not going to hang around like this, feeling sorry for myself; I would continue cycling into town – Conradie would surely find me somewhere along the road! I took a deep breath, lifted my head and seized the handlebars ... and as I looked across the road I saw a big, smiling, unmistakably South African face protruding from the side-window of another white Mercedes van, just like the one which had passed me earlier. That could only be Conradie! And so it was. Conradie signalled to me to stay put while his driver did a U-turn and a minute later I was in the van, bike and all, and heading for the embassy.

We went straight to the embassy, which was pretty much deserted because this was Friday, the Muslim Sabbath. There Conradie gave me a parcel he had personally brought back from South Africa for me which contained the digital stills camera I so desperately needed, let me telephone home and gave me free use of the embassy's Internet facilities, all of which I needed because I had to send off another newspaper article and confirm some radio interviews. This done, Conradie put me up at his house and then took me on a quick tour of the city.

It was instructive in more ways than one. For an African country there were few black people to be seen – the result, Conradie said, of a government crack-down on illegal immigrants. Because Sicily was only a short boat trip away, Libya had always been a favourite way-station for refugees and undocumented aliens heading for Italy. Now many had been rounded up, and those who had not tended to maintain a very low profile.

I also discovered that Libyan street butcheries were even more gory than their Tunisian equivalents, and another of my tips for prospective visitors to Libya and its neighbours is to avoid shopping for braaivleis meat while you're there if you are at all squeamish: the freshly slaughtered animals' heads – even cows' heads - are displayed on wall-hooks outside the butcheries like the stuffed and mounted trophies you see in studies in South Africa and elsewhere. Conradie wasn't squeamish, however, and neither was I after all this time, and the braai he laid on for me got my full attention. It was wonderful, and I discovered that Libyans, like South Africans, like their slices thicker than Europeans do. We washed it all down with beer, which was a pleasant surprise in this very teetotal Muslim country, and which I enjoyed as much as the meat.

The next couple of days were an eye-opener. The general world-view of Libya is of a backward little nation, walled off from the rest of the world by international sanctions and the eccentric Gaddafi political doctrine, but I soon found out that Tripoli was anything but that. There were certainly huge posters of the 'Great Leader' everywhere, but in between them were designer shops which looked like the ones I had seen on TV in Hollywood's up-market Rodeo Drive, offering the best clothing and other goods from Europe and elsewhere.

The one difficulty Libya had had during the sanctions period was in obtaining new cars. This wasn't a problem any more, though, now that sanctions had been lifted, and I could see late-model cars among the hordes of trusty old Mercs and Peugeots from the 1970s that filled the streets. I also managed to talk someone into taking a photo of me in front of one of those gigantic Gaddafi posters, a somewhat rash act about which Conradie wasn't happy – many foreigners had been jailed for less, he said. But not this one, and so I was able to enjoy Tripoli by night, which was a fun experience. The city looked really pretty, with strategically placed floodlights illuminating the old buildings and enhancing the atmosphere; it has had a long and incredibly varied history, the vibrations of which seemed to come alive as I strolled through the cobbled streets, rubbing shoulders with jovial families who were chaffering with the flocks of stall-holders.

Ambassador Saley asked me to extend my stay slightly so that he could have me as a guest at a function he was hosting at his residence for the outgoing ambassadors of Zimbabwe and Algeria; just about the entire diplomatic corps would be there, he explained, and he could introduce me to them. Naturally I fell in with this excellent idea, and agreed in a flash when, on the afternoon of the ambassadorial function, he asked if I would mind putting my bicycle on show as a conversation-piece. I was a bit worried that something might happen to it, so when Conradie and I arrived at the party the first thing I did was look for it. Conradie's impression was that the bicycle would be on display in the mansion's foyer, but it wasn't, and it took us a while to discover that it was parked in front of a bright light next to the swimming pool. It was only later that I discovered what had happened. The bike had indeed been parked in the foyer, looking thoroughly disreputable from all its hardships, with an old pair of underpants draped over the baggage as a final touch (for the record: those underpants were *clean,* and I was only trying to dry them out in my usual way). Anyway, after a frantic appeal from his wife the ambassador had shifted it to the swimming pool and also had one of his staff tuck the underpants into one of the bags. That's what you call hardcore diplomacy.

I found myself getting a bit of on-the-job training in diplomacy as well after I had been handed the microphone to share some of my stories with the other guests. When I had finished singing for my supper, so to speak, I mingled with the crowd, and to my surprise was buttonholed by the Zimbabwean ambassador, of all people. At that time South Africa was heavily involved in the debate about whether its official policy of 'silent diplomacy' was achieving anything in preventing Zimbabwe's swift decline into authoritarianism, famine and bankruptcy. The Zimbabwean ambassador, who was the guest of honour, literally cornered me, not to discuss my journey but rather to ask my opinion on the question of why his country should be expected to take remote-control orders from the British government.

Why me? Perhaps there was some higher reason, or perhaps he thought I knew the right people in spite of my generally dishevelled appearance, and he hit me right between the eyes with a long tirade, often couched in analogies, about the actions and policies of his government and 'His Excellency' (aka Robert Mugabe). Some of it was pretty far out. He was convinced, for example, that Zimbabwe was the coming powerhouse of Africa, going on to say that his government aspired to hosting the next Soccer World Cup and perhaps even the Olympic Games. Given Zimbabwe's dreadful state, I was completely flabbergasted. But, like the born-again diplomat that I was, I kept my mouth shut and nodded at the correct points while he elaborated on his theme. Ambassador Saley was watching all this from across the room, slightly worried about the chances of my foot landing squarely in my mouth, and was relieved (so he told me later) to see the one-way discussion end with the Zimbabwean Ambassador standing arm-in-arm with me and sharing a few laughs.

I wonder whether my diplomatic impassivity would have stayed in place today, when Zimbabwe is even worse off than it was then, the only constant being that 'His Excellency' and his government are as unashamed about what they are doing as they were then. I don't know how all that is going to end, but without getting involved in a debate about the matter I'll only say that Africa has got too many Zimbabwes already and doesn't need another one.

Barring that little encounter the evening went smoothly, and after the last of the guests had left I spent a while chatting to the ambassador and his very pretty wife (OK, she hadn't liked my bike and my underpants, but in all fairness they were more than a little out of place at a glamorous bash for Tripoli's diplomatic big). They were interesting people and so naturally it was an interesting conversation, and I made sure to thank Mr Saley most sincerely for the generosity and kindness with which he had supported me and furthered my aims. Till then I don't think he realised how much his support had meant to me.

Next morning I set off again. Conradie came out to see me on my way and make sure I had a full supply of water. Be strong, he said, be strong right to the end. I promised I would, neither of us realising that I was on the threshold of an unexpected test, although fortunately only a small one. Then Conradie drove off back to Tripoli and I headed for Egypt, via the town of Al-Khums, where friends of his were waiting to feed me and show me one of the most amazing archaeological Roman sites on the planet, the 2 000-year-old Roman city of Leptas Magna. But first I had to traverse a long stretch of the barren desert, and I mean *barren*; which started almost immediately after I left the vicinity of Tripoli. I couldn't help being overtaken by the feeling that the whole of Libya was like Mauritania: long stretches of sand with a few buildings here and there.

That little test Conradie and I hadn't anticipated came along just 10 km later. A taxi sped past me, and as it did so one of the occupants slung a plastic shopping-bag full of dates at me. The bag hit the left side of my back with such force that it knocked all the breath out of me; I was lucky that I wasn't knocked off my bicycle and sent sprawling into the traffic. I spent the next 10 minutes painfully getting my breathing back to normal, then ate some of the dates that had burst from the bag – food is food, after all, even if it has nearly killed you – and got on my way again. While battling with my bruised and semi-collapsed lungs I had noticed that the taxi had slowed down and turned off the road a little way ahead, and now I saw why: there was a mosque by the side of the road, and these thugs had pulled off to pay some lip-service after brutally attacking an innocent stranger. The hypocrisy of it was staggering. Not that they were worried by either the brutality or the hypocrisy. As I cycled past I saw them standing around the car, rocking with loud, unashamed laughter, not only accepting responsibility but doing so with pride. I could understand that: bullies always feel secure when they are in a pack, and especially when their victim is one who can't afford to retaliate. What I could not understand was why they would have wanted to do something like that.

A little later I experienced another unsettling encounter at the hands of a shopkeeper whose motivation was even more obscure than the date-throwers' had been. I had stopped off at a roadside shop to buy some fruit, and when I had made my purchases I struck up a conversation in elementary English and broken Arabic with some of the workers. Next thing I knew, the young shopkeeper came up and demanded: 'You finished? You finished?' Not grasping his state of mind, I smiled in all innocence and said 'yes' in Arabic. To my surprise he started chivvying me towards the door, shouting: 'Out! Out! Out!' Completely puzzled, I asked: 'Mushkela? Mushkela? (Problem? Problem?)' as he shoved at me. I didn't get any sort of reply till, as I stepped outside, he put his thumb to his chin and flicking it forward, made the throat-slitting gesture I had seen in Algeciras and Algeria. I felt a chill run down my spine. Why did he have such hate for me, a total stranger? There was no answer to that except getting on my bicycle and eating up the kilometres to Al-Khums, which I knew I could reach by nightfall if I cracked it on.

There were no further unpleasant surprises on the way, although during one water-break I saw a genuine flat dog – not a crocodile, which South Africans jocularly call 'flat dogs', but an actual bit of canine roadkill. I mention this unappetising sight because it was so extraordinary. The dog had been killed while in the act of running and had literally been flattened like a pancake, the thickest part of it being the incisors. The dog's lead, a length of wire, was perfectly positioned as if it was still being held by the unfortunate animal's owner. What had happened to *him*? Had he run away or been similarly flattened, then removed for burial? That was something else I would never know, so I photographed the pathetic but unique scene and moved on.

I made Al-Khums on schedule and was welcomed by Conradie's friends, one of whom was married to a Moroccan woman who happened to be a great chef, so that I had a pleasant reminder of the marvellous cuisine in her home country that night. The trip to Leptas Magna was as amazing as he had promised it would be. The city had only been about 25 per cent excavated so far (thanks to a deterioration in diplomatic relations with the home countries of the archaeologists who had been engaged in the excavations), but that was quite enough to make it an unforgettable experience.

Leptas Magna had been a place of some consequence in ancient times because it was the birth-place of Emperor Lucius Severus in AD 146, and what made it so unusual was that the complete city had been preserved during the next two millennia. It was like going through a time-warp as I walked under arched entrances and strolled past temples with chiselled stone floors and bas-relief carvings on the pillars. In my mind's eye it wasn't difficult to see Leptas Magna as it must have been, its streets crowded with people – vendors, children, soldiers, civilians of high and low degree, congregating in pillared corridors just as we would do today, except that the jaywalkers were dodging chariots instead of Mercedes-Benzes and there were no McDonald's or Internet cafés in sight. This, I vowed, was something else I'd show to Vasti one day ...

The ghost of Lucius Severus must have been smiling down on me, because after leaving Al-Khums I experienced a minor miracle. Normally I let my eyes roam about to absorb as many of the sights as possible, but this day I was battling with a strong head-wind and kept my head down so that I would know at all times exactly where my front wheel was. As a result I knew exactly what I had just gone over when the wheel crunched on some bits of plastic: the casing of a Nokia 5110 cell phone, the innards of which lay with the battery still attached in the sand not more than 30 cm or so from the road's edge. I stopped to pick up the remains, vaguely hoping that the battery would be intact and could be pressed into service for my own Nokia, a 3210. But the battery turned out to be damaged and unusable, so I gathered up the chunks of broken casing and dropped the various bits and pieces where I had found the phone's working parts. This bit of pointless tidying-up paid immediate dividends. I was watching the lighter bits of plastic fluttering to the ground when my focus moved to the slot that usually holds the phone's SIM card and was seized by a wild idea. Might there still be a functional card still in the phone? Surely not!

I checked all the same, and believe it or not, there it was. And not only that, it actually worked when I put it in my phone. Suddenly, and completely unexpectedly, I was in communication with the outside world again! I called Vasti right away and asked her to distribute the number to my media contacts at home, and it wasn't long before the calls started coming through to me. How the phone came to be lying in a dismembered state by the roadside with its SIM card still inside was a complete mystery, of course; I assumed it had somehow fallen out of a moving car without its owner knowing. The likely accuracy of this surmise was confirmed when SMSs in Arabic started to pour in at an alarming rate. I couldn't understand them, but ever more desperate messages aren't difficult to spot. I called my friend Amr, who had tried to find a local SIM card for me in Zuwara, and arranged to hand over the SIM card to him when we rendezvoused in Alexandria so that he could return it to its rightful owner. But in the meantime that worthy was going to be my unwitting sponsor till I crossed over into Egypt. I suppose it was a bit unethical, but my need was truly great.

By now it had become clear that the Libyan coast wasn't all barren desert, because every 100 km or so I would come upon an oil town with a refinery, each one the end-point of one of the thousands of kilometres of large pipelines that carried in oil from one or other well in the desert. Those pipelines kept me company for most of my Libyan trip, and the great circular structures of the refineries, filling the sky with bright lights by night and looming in the distance by day, became my lodestone. I felt a bit like Moses following the pillars of fire and smoke as he led the children of Israel out of bondage. In places the coast was a veritable hive of activity as a result of Gaddafi's river project. Now I realised for the first time what an awesome undertaking it was. Every day I passed kilometres-long convoys of trucks laden with giant concrete pipes, four metres wide and seven metres long, which were to be buried seven metres below the desert's surface; when the pipeline was finished, it would be 1 200 km long and bring millions of cubic metres of water to the drier parts of Libya.

The oil towns were my regular stopping-places where I would pause to rest or eat – usually only the latter, because after the date-bag and shop incidents I usually slept in the desert to avoid getting involved in some less-than-friendly social intercourse with the locals. On the other hand, sleeping in the open had its advantages. I went to sleep at sunset and was awoken by the rising sun, so I got more than enough sleep and travelling time. But my negative feelings towards Libya as a whole were ameliorated a little when I stopped at one small town which, to my surprise, had a large, dilapidated and unpopulated old hotel right in its centre. The tariff seemed a bit steep in view of the facilities on offer, but I badly needed a long shower, whether hot or cold, so that I could scrub the accumulated grime off my body (it turned out I couldn't have either because there was no running water). When the owner heard about me he came over to practise his English, in the course of which he invited me to stay as long as I wished, with everything, meals included, absolutely free of charge. It was a great kindness, but I didn't intend to stay a moment longer than necessary. Firstly I was on a tight schedule, and secondly the hotel was, frankly, a little creepy. I was on the fourth floor, which I was given to understand was the best accommodation available, but the only electric illumination was on the ground floor; with only the odd shaft of light struggling through the dust at the ends of the 50-metre-long corridors on the other floors.

Sleeping in the desert didn't eliminate *all* contact with the local inhabitants; it made it possible to avoid the local humans, but I was constantly plagued by the attentions of hyenas. Most people would associate hyenas with the bushveld further south, but there were plenty of them in the Libyan desert, and they were a perpetual nuisance. Perhaps the fact that I stopped erecting my tent at night had something to do with their unwelcome attentions. Basically it was from laziness born of fatigue. The wind would blow furiously, and struggling to get the tent up when I was worn down by a long day's run was both tiring and frustrating. So I would just lay my bike down on its side as a windbreak and crawl into my First Ascent sleeping bag in its lee.

The way to sleep comfortably through those freezing desert nights, I soon discovered, was to bury myself totally in the sleeping bag, leaving open only a gap about the size of my palm for breathing. The First Ascent bag was remarkably efficient at retaining the heat my body generated, so I would lie there as warm as toast with only part of my face exposed to the crisp, cold air outside. Making camp like this took no more than five minutes, once I had got into the routine of it. The problem was that there was a very good chance of a hyena grabbing a take-away snack from my face through the breathing-hole while I was asleep. But after a bit of thought I devised an effective anti-hyena device: I twisted my spare tyres into circular conical shapes which, when placed one on top of the other, formed a reasonable shield around my head. At the top end of the cone I attached a few criss-crossed spare bicycle spokes to prevent the predators from sticking their heads in to attack me. As an added precaution I resurrected my old technique of urinating around the perimeter of my sleeping area, but this didn't work here. I would wake up every morning to find dozens of hyena footprints around me; there was no doubt that, urine or no urine, they would creep up during the night and prod my recumbent form with their noses in an effort to work out whether I was something they could eat. In hindsight I can only think that the urine attracted rather than repelled them.

Water management, too, soon became one of my strong points, and obtaining refills was no longer an insurmountable problem. When my water-supply dropped to less than 500 ml I would slow down to maintain some sort of control over my hydration level and drink no more than 50 ml at a given time, swilling the scanty amount of water around in my mouth before swallowing it. I also made it a practice to flag down any passing vehicle and ask if its occupant or occupants had any water to spare, bottled or not. Usually they did and were willing to share it with me, one of these generous donors being no less than the head of the Libyan judiciary. He and his colleagues were intrigued by my presence in this barren waste with nothing but a bicycle and a cup of water to my name, and he not only gave me what I wanted but tried with all his charm to persuade me to return with him to Tripoli and enjoy some more of the city's sights.

In Sirte, the birthplace of Muammar Gaddafi, I had one of the most memorable contacts with a non-English speaking person I had enjoyed thus far. The sun had set by the time I arrived, but in this fairly modern town that didn't mean shut-down for the night. Everything was lit up, and it didn't take me long to find an Internet café. The routine I planned for the night was my normal one – find something to eat after finishing my Internet business, then make my way out of town and find a sleeping-place in the desert. But this night turned out to be different from the others. The manager directed me to a café on the other side of the double-lane main road, a large, neat establishment with a TV set suspended overhead, which at that moment was empty except for three attendants. I bought two tins of sardines and a sachet of milk for my frugal but filling evening meal and headed for the door. Before I reached it, however, I noticed that the TV was running a documentary about Nelson Mandela, and stopped to watch.

It wasn't long before the three assistants spotted my interest in the documentary, not to mention the small South African flag I always wore on my chest in Muslim parts to show extremists that I wasn't an American, and soon the four of us were dancing arm in arm underneath the TV. Libyans, it turned out, simply loved Mr Mandela, and these three not only enjoyed sharing my admiration for him but were much taken with meeting someone who 'knew' (well, by general proximity anyway) the legendary man that Gaddafi had been telling them about all these years. We spent so much time on these impromptu festivities that eventually the Internet café's manager arrived, concerned that something might have happened to me; judging by his expression when he walked in, the scene that met him was very far from what he had feared. He thanked the café guys for looking after me, then led me back across the road, explaining that in my absence he had spoken to his house-mates, and they had agreed to let me sleep over with them. It turned out that the three-storey house they were occupying was only half-completed, with unplastered walls and wind gusting through all the open holes and glassless windows. But the staircase had just been finished, and we all slept on the second floor. It wasn't five-star accommodation, but I was sincerely grateful. I was reasonably comfortable after all those days of living rough, there was no hit on my slender wallet and I was temporarily free of those damned hyenas.

I was passing through the town of Ajdabiya when something suddenly struck me: women were rarely to be seen on the street, even more rarely than in Algeria, although I was not sure whether this was due to religion or local custom, or both. The few women I did see were completely covered in black from head to toe, complete with face-veils and sometimes even gloves; what this meant in terms of comfort during the hottest time of day was something to speculate about. I was actually a little intimidated by this; wearing only the barest minimum of clothing, I felt almost vulnerable and over-exposed. What made me smile, though, was to see the behaviour of some of the youths sitting outside on the street's walls, decorously whistling at or calling to the girls passing by on their way to school. Their culture and mine might be far apart in so many ways, but one golden thread connected them: boys liked girls and girls (although more discreetly) liked boys. It was a strangely reassuring thought as I watched these kids' surreptitious courtship.

But of course social contact between the sexes is a little more difficult in rural Libya, where Islamic sharia law is strictly adhered to, than it would be in, say, South Africa. And I didn't want to think of the likely consequences of a foreigner making advances to a Libyan woman, or even speaking to her with no evil intent. The foreigner would probably only be warned and given a mild application of the frighteners, but the woman would automatically be labelled as unclean and immoral, and if she was lucky she would only be ostracised. Ghastly unfairness, of course. But women's rights still have some way to go in rural Libya, where the way of life might have been a little more technologically sophisticated, but has not changed all that much otherwise.

I also discovered that openly discussing the 'Great Leader' wasn't a very healthy thing to do. This I was told in no uncertain terms by one of my new Internet café friends while we were walking in the street. I asked him what people in this province thought of Gaddafi, using my normal speaking voice, as I would have done when putting the same question about President Mbeki at home in Cape Town. To my surprise he immediately brought his index finger to his lips and let out a long warning 'shoosh'.

'We do not speak of his name. It is danger,' he explained. 'The police, they will fetch you and put you in the prison. They will think you are spy. If me, the Libyan man, is talking to the stranger, they will think we are making plans for spying.'

Shoosh indeed, or rather 'sheesh!'. There was something wrong in the Great Socialist People's Libyan Arab Jamahiriya if citizens (and even foreigners) had to whisper when they mentioned the national leader's name. There were questions waiting to be asked here, if only I had the time. Were Libyans happy or unhappy with this, bearing in mind that they had no great domestic tradition of Western-style democracy? Or were they willing to accept it as a trade-off for the undoubted benefits Gaddafi had brought to pass? I had the feeling that any answers I got, if people were willing to respond and I didn't get slung in jail for asking the questions, would not be simply 'yes' or 'no'.

Radio 702's legendary talk show host John Robbie was now interviewing me for his breakfast show at regular intervals, but he did not know the lengths to which I went sometimes to stick to his schedule. For example, when I left Ajdabiya I had to reach a certain node where there was believed to be a cell phone tower so that Robbie could do a morning interview. My problem was getting to the node in time, and neither of the two choices of route I had were all that good.

Essentially they came down to this: I could cycle 365 km to the seaport of Tobruk, a place of bitter memory to South Africans who fought in the Western Desert in World War II, or I could take the more scenic route to Benghazi, which was longer and more mountainous. After some consideration I decided to try my luck with the Tobruk route, although my new friends in Ajdabiya warned me against it. Traffic was thinner, they said, and at times virtually nonexistent, and there were no roadside villages. But I had made up my mind, so I stocked up on water and food, then headed off into the desert in the late afternoon. My aim was to cycle late into the night, put in another long stint the next day which, with any luck, would bring me to that node with the cell phone tower in time to chat to John Robbie the morning after.

The desert lay flat and mysterious before me as I rode into the setting sun, which was as beautiful as it always is in the barren lands along the Libyan coast. I spent the last moments of daylight repairing a puncture and mentally preparing myself for the night's cycling. What I did *not* prepare myself for was something I had not anticipated but, with hindsight, I should have been ready for: harassment by over-zealous local inhabitants. They were the occupants of the only car to pass me, a Peugeot station wagon going in the opposite direction. As it approached me it slowed down, obviously to allow its driver and passengers to have a good look at me. Naturally this also allowed me to have a good look at them, and an unprepossessing bunch they were, swathed in traditional robes and headdress so that all I could see of them was a row of grim, unsmiling faces. Not so good, if my earlier experiences were anything to go by. When the Peugeot had passed I kept an eye on it in my rear-view mirror as it slowed down even more, crawling along till it finally dropped out of sight in the gathering darkness. I didn't like any of this, but when the car had finally disappeared I began to feel a little easier in my mind. Maybe I was shot of them after all!

No such luck. About 45 minutes later a car suddenly appeared quite close behind me – clearly it had crept up on me with its lights off till it was on my heels. It was the Peugeot, I saw as it came up to me; some of the robed humorists were gone, but the occupants now included a nattily uniformed military official of some kind. Now I was not afraid, just very angry. This bunch of paranoiacs had actually driven at least 60 km to fetch someone in authority to deal with the serious risk to national security posed by a somewhat tattered lone cyclist heading *out* of the country! Controlling my anger, I showed the official my passport, which he examined in the Peugeot's headlight beams. Heaven alone knows what the beards had been pumping into his head while they were catching up with me – maybe they told him I had made the sign of the cross at them, or even worse, the Star of David – because he was as unsmiling and suspicious as they were and ordered me to get off the road immediately.

I demanded to know the reason for this order. He ignored me, preferring to discuss the matter with his friends the beards. I persisted, and eventually he responded by claiming that under Libyan law it was illegal to ride a bicycle at night. This was such transparent rubbish that I decided a little bullshit-baffles-brains exercise would yield results, particularly since the official didn't seem to have a firm grasp of English. So I asked him a question to which there was no real answer because it wasn't a real question: 'How about speaking to Mr Robbie on Tuesday morning? He's expecting me, you know.' This stopped him in his tracks, all right, because he didn't have the foggiest notion of who 'Mr Robbie' was. But he didn't move, and he and his chums stood there staring silently at me while I sipped at my water, fiddled with my bicycle baggage and stared back. After a while the whole thing became ridiculous: he obviously didn't know what to do, and he wasn't getting any helpful suggestions from the beards. I decided to take the bike by the handle-bars, so to speak. 'Ma salaama' and 'Tesbha alegher' (Good night), I said firmly and started pushing my bicycle off the road into the dark dunes, leaving them glaring at my departing back. I'd just have to do the entire 185 kilometres that remained next day in order to reach my telephonic rendezvous with John Robbie.

I got away to a very early start, and by lunch-time I was well on the way to reaching that node which, so I hoped, had the telephone capacity I needed. My main problem now was not hostile busybodies but the weather. I spent hours battling a strong headwind, and late that afternoon ran into the worst rainstorm of the trip. My first inkling of what was to come was an enormous dark black weather system about 20 km away, which was heading straight for me. Then suddenly the wind died and almost as quickly the air became extremely humid. For a few minutes silence reigned, broken only by the sound of my tyres on the tarmac. Raindrops began to drum loudly on the sand and the road surface, getting nearer and nearer; then there was a gust of cooler air, followed by violent rain.

I turned my bicycle side-on so that I could sit on the crossbar, and covered both it and myself with my tarpaulin. That was all I could do, and it wasn't enough. The rain came at me at a 45-degree angle out of a grey-black sky which was shot through with sparks but did not utter the thunder-claps and flashes of lightning I expected. It was so fierce that it managed to penetrate the robust plastic covering, the roar of raindrops hitting the tarpaulin so loud that

I saw a large truck pass like a ghost, the sound of its mighty diesel engine completely drowned out.

I reflected on how insignificant man and all his works were, compared to the forces of nature, and couldn't help thinking sadly that this marvellous gift from the sky was totally wasted on the searing-hot and almost lifeless desert. But at the same time I was feeling more refreshed than I had been for days as my parched body soaked up all the moisture it had needed so desperately for so long. By the time I could carry on cycling I was feeling good. My body ached from the undue stress I had subjected it to in the last couple of days, but I was full of energy and sure I could make the rendezvous in good time.

And I did. But that was the good news. The bad news was that the node was nothing more than a T-junction on the road with a few trailers that housed everyone from doctors to mechanics. A traveller could fill up with fuel (the last thing I needed) or stay over in one of a number of very basic bedrooms. But cell phone reception? It didn't exist.

Hell-bent on doing the interview next morning, I persuaded one of the doctors to let me use his satellite telephone. He agreed wearily, and I went to sleep feeling pretty chuffed with myself for displaying such ingenuity. If only John Robbie knew! But my joy was premature. I got up in good time next morning and went in search of the satellite telephone on which Robbie was supposed to call me. To my horror I couldn't find it. Eventually, well after the time for the interview, we found it tucked away under the duvet of one of the other off-duty doctors, whose sleep had been so profound that its ringing had not been enough to wake him up. I was deeply disappointed, but could not find it in my heart to blame this overworked medical man, whose exhausted body had finally rebelled and put him into such a deep sleep that he would not have heard the last trump if it had sounded outside his front door.

I have a vivid recollection of a small, sad experience I had during one of those long stretches of slogging through the coastal desert. Dogs were a familiar sight around homesteads and larger settlements, but out in the desert itself it was only rarely that I saw one wandering about. I was pedalling hard, head down, when I clearly heard puppies yelping. Puppies in this bare expanse of sand, where there wasn't even a sun-bleached twig for shelter from the blazing sun? How could puppies – very young ones, by the sound of them, too – survive here?

I soon found them, eight scruffy but cute little white-and-brown fellows, not more than about 14 days old and obviously desperate for water. My head told me to walk away, that nature should always be allowed to take its course, but the sun must have been affecting me slightly, because I listened to my dog-lover's heart instead, which told me that I couldn't simply leave these little desert waifs to their fate. So I did something which verged on the suicidal and gave them a share of my remaining 300 ml of water. They slurped it up with heart-rending eagerness.

There was little else I could do for them. I couldn't take them with me, and I knew that the little water I had given them would do little more than prolong their lives by a few hours in the 50-degree heat. Yet I couldn't prevent myself from making a further futile attempt to help them. I scavenged up two lengths of derelict plank, each about a metre long, and a tattered piece of black plastic which I used to build a little shelter for them between two low dunelets, then urinated into an old oil-tin which had been cut open and thrown away and placed it within reach before abandoning them to their fate.

It was difficult simply to ride away from those pathetic little creatures. What would happen to them? As I pushed at the pedals I forced myself to accept that there was nothing more I could have done – that in fact I had done too much for my own good, because now my own water supply was down to little more than about a cupful. That was soon gone, too, but once again my luck held out, because after about 40 increasingly thirsty kilometres I managed to flag down a passing truck and get a refill.

On my second-last day in Libya I cycled 165 km into Tobruk and slept over in a normal bed for the first time since leaving Ajdabiya. The town was full of traditional folk of the older type, all of whom seemed to be puffing like mad at their shisha pipes, to the point where my hotel's reception seemed to be full of smog. It was a tranquil scene, though, accentuated not only by the slothful movements of the patrons but also by the pipe-smoke drifting gently out of the building. There was nothing slothful about the growling of my stomach, however, and I managed to lay hands on the local version of the triangular deep-fried sandwiches I had grown to love in Algeria. The sandwiches looked a lot like the Malay samoosas I love to eat in Cape Town, and the meat, egg, vegetable and cheese mixture inside was one of the tastiest things I had put in my mouth while in Libya.

I hoped that my exit out of Libya would be plain sailing, but again I was wrong. At the forlorn border post everything went well at first: an official wearily stamped my passport and I headed down the officially demarcated route between the last few buildings on this isolated border site. I couldn't help noticing as I went that most of the other people congregated there were streaming across at will, without being processed or even asked for their passports (which, I suspected, they didn't have anyway). I wasn't going to take any chances of another delay in my passage into Egypt, however; I would stick to the straight and narrow path, both figuratively and literally. But I got the delay anyway. I was only about 10 metres away from the actual crossing when there were sudden aggressive shouts from a young official who wanted to inspect me and my bicycle. The result was that I spent the next hour and half unpacking and re-packing everything I owned for no good reason except to massage his ego, while around us hundreds of people with bags of unchecked luggage swarmed through the border gates. I was so furious that I did not attempt to make conversation, and when he finally let me go I didn't even greet him.

I had headed for the border with a tarnished but truly salvageable opinion of Libya, but in one fell swoop this fool had filled me with such loathing that I couldn't help thinking how glad I was to get out and how I would never, ever, come back again. Harsh feelings, I know, but my frustrations had been boiling inside me for some time, and now they simply overflowed. I pushed my bicycle through the remaining formalities, desperately eager to bid farewell forever to Green Book country and wheel into the fabled land of the Pharaoahs. Like a true tourist, my abiding thought as I trudged through the darkness towards the Egyptian border post was: 'I'm going to see the pyramids!'

# CHAPTER 24

# ADVENTURES IN LOWER EGYPT, AND A PERSONAL DREAM ACHIEVED

*All this caused quite a commotion, and I finally emerged under the gaze of a group of giggling spectators. I exited the infernal machine in as dignified a fashion as possible (which wasn't much) and set about cleaning my hand and everywhere it had touched, no easy task because of my limited supply of water. I wasn't angry or embarrassed so much as strangely disappointed, because somehow I hadn't expected the descendants of the Pharaohs to have such sordid living conditions.*

I headed for the flamboyant Egyptian border post in a state of high anticipation, because at last I was going to enjoy one of the milestones of my 14-month-long journey, a sight of the 4 500-year-old pyramids of Giza – something I had dreamed about since childhood. And from here on I would be heading southwards in the direction of home. I don't know which prospect excited me more.

The sun had set by the time I reached the Egyptian border post with its large terminal building, about the size of the average South African school hall. Immediately I was plunged into a new culture about which the ornate exterior had given no warning. Egypt is densely populated – Cairo is the most populous city in Africa, with about 17 million inhabitants – and when I entered the terminal it looked as if about a million of them had arrived before me. I wasn't worried about this, having got used to crowds during my journey, and in any case I was too excited about having entered this new and mysterious way-station on my wanderings. The mystery soon faded in the face of a grim reality. In Egypt, I soon discovered from watching my neighbours in the queue, it was OK – in fact, commonplace – to clear your throat and then spit out the product on to the floor right next to whoever was in front or behind you. I fixed a faked smile on my face and shuffled along, occasionally sliding on the gobs of expelled mucus under my feet. I managed to stay upright, however, and after being hassled at great length by a tout claiming to be a plain-clothes policeman, was taken by some merciful officials to the front of the cue for processing.

I wasted no time in hitting the road because I planned to get to the first town of Saloum, 30 km away, before stopping for the night. This turned out to be easier said than done because the night was one of the darkest I had encountered so far, the road was very narrow and the passing vehicular traffic was impatient to the point of being downright dangerous. Eventually I saw that it was simply impossible to travel safely, so I gave up on my aim and made camp in rocky terrain about 100 metres off the road, not bothering to pitch my tent. That was a mistake. The dew was so heavy that it went right through my sleeping-bag, so that by midnight I was completely soaked, and to make it worse the wind picked up as well. At length I decided that I might as well use the wind to dry out my sleeping-bag and clothing, while I huddled under my plastic tarpaulin to try and retain what little body-heat I had left. It wasn't a pleasant experience – it's amazing how much sharper rocks feel when the mercury starts heading towards zero – but on the other hand it also provided me with a great incentive to get off to an early start.

Saloum nestled right on the coast, with giant golden dunes building up to the high plateau that surrounded it. I decided right away that whatever ailments the Saloumites might suffer from, rat-race stress wasn't one of them. The town was pervaded by a remarkable 'no worries' attitude that didn't seem to leave room for planning anything. Whether it was because the town was gearing itself up (or down) for Ramadan, or whether that was just the way Saloumites confronted the challenges of day-to-day life, I never discovered.

What I did find out was that Saloum had the filthiest long-drop toilet I have ever had to use. I made its acquaintance after breakfasting on a grubby cupful of coffee and then requesting the use of the nearest facility. I was given a jug of water for sluicing myself off and directed to a lean-to of corrugated iron, which looked awful from the outside and turned out to be even more awful inside.

The loo was tiny; the interior wooden frame was griplessly slimy with grease or worse, and a buzzing cloud of insects arose from the business end to envelop me as I lowered my shorts and went into the now-familiar squat which is usual in Muslim countries, although there was so little elbow-room that I couldn't even let my arms dangle. I resigned myself to my fate and got down to business, leaving the door open a crack so that I wouldn't be in pitch darkness. The main horror didn't come till I had finished and tried to get up out of my crouch. My worn-out cycling shoes slipped as I rose, my attempt at grabbing at the framework failed and I went down again, feeling one hand sink into the soft sludge of the muddy base and the other slowly slide through the slime to the bottom part of the toilet's frame. All this caused quite a commotion, and I finally emerged under the gaze of a group of giggling spectators. I exited the infernal machine in as dignified a fashion as possible (which wasn't much) and set about cleaning my hands and everywhere they had touched, no easy task because of my limited supply of water. I wasn't angry or embarrassed so much as strangely disappointed, because somehow I hadn't expected the descendants of the Pharaohs to have such sordid living conditions.

But Saloum wasn't all ghastly toilets. I was deeply moved by a stroll through the World War II cemetery, where many South Africans were buried. Some of the messages left on the South Africans' tombstones were extremely touching, and I photographed each one till my memory card was full. This was not the last of the war cemeteries I encountered as I worked my way eastwards across the coastal desert. The most famous, of course, was at El Alamein, which we had learned about at school. That was where the Eighth Army under Field-Marshal Sir Bernard Montgomery – which included thousands of South Africans – turned back the Germans and Italians under Field-Marshal Erwin Rommel and forced them into a retreat which did not end till they had surrendered. Many believe it was one of the battles which eventually brought an Allied victory over the Nazis. A pity, though, that it took so much young and precious blood.

I was now under the gun as far as time went, because I had to get to Cairo in time for my meeting with the 'Carte Blanche' television crew, and the urgency of the matter helped to keep me going through some very heavy physical effort. I took a break, though, when I reached Alexandria, the first big city before Cairo, and had a double stroke of fortune when I found a hotel room with a balcony overlooking this magnificent sight ... and for just $3 a night, dirt cheap even when translated into South African currency. The only drawback was that it was eight floors up a spiral staircase, a bit much when it came to my heavily overloaded bicycle. But this was a minor matter, all things considered, and I was happy to lock up my bike in a store-room at the bottom of the staircase before going out exploring on foot.

I had a lot to do, so much that I spent two days in Alexandria instead of one. A 'must' was to meet up with my Libyan friend Amr and hand over the roadside SIM card so that he could return it to its rightful owner. Amr laughed till his round belly shook as he read the SMS messages from the owner. The card's owner started by enquiring if anyone had found his card, then the enquiries turned into pleas for its safe return and finally into threats. I was glad to hand it over to Amr because I hadn't felt good about using the card. All I can do is plead extreme necessity, and of course I had not been able to understand the Arabic in which the SMSs were written!

Good fortune favoured me again when I fell in with a German named Torben, who turned himself into a tour guide for my benefit. Torben not only spoke English, he had been in Alexandria for six months and so knew his way around. He was a man with a mission, busy finalising arrangements to study Arabic at the local university. I gathered that his parents disapproved of the fact that he didn't want to come home just yet, and had disowned him, and he had fallen in love with a local girl.

This was only the top level of Torben's situation, however. The girl was a Coptic Christian, an extreme and very rigid form of Christianity which forbade its adherents to marry outside their faith. Torben had addressed this problem by enrolling in conversion classes and was already halfway to being anointed by the time we met. Like a good Coptic Christian-to-be, Torben took me to visit the beautiful church in the centre of the city which by repute has the head of St Mark – the New Testament Mark, who also founded the Coptic faith – buried beneath it.

The story went, Torben said, that during the Arab conquest of what is now modern Egypt the invaders hitched the corpses of Mark and his fellow-priests behind horse-carts and dragged them through the city to show the population what was likely to happen to people who persisted in espousing Christianity. But after the grisly show was over and the crowds had dispersed, a few die-hard Christians managed to make off with Mark's remains. In later years, Torben added, Mark's head was stolen several times by religious fanatics and treasure-hunters, but today it was safely buried beneath the altar, with access restricted to a handful of ordained priests. I reflected on this entire gruesome tale and decided that whereas I was no great supporter of religious conversion, my views might have been a little different if I had been one of those Christians watching Mark and his ecclesiastical colleagues being dragged through the streets.

I had a few of my own surprises for Torben. One which took him distinctly aback was my purchase in the older part of the city of some top-quality raw beef for an experiment in making biltong, that staple South African trail food. I had never made my own biltong before, but I felt strongly that my body craved some of the salty dried meat that has sustained endless generations of South Africans during hard times. Torben goggled as I rubbed salt and pepper into the strips of raw beef and then proceed to place them into women's stockings. The idea was that the packed stockings would hang on either side of my rear baggage, swiftly drying out in the heat and my slipstream, without flies being able to lay their eggs in the meat. It was a perfectly good idea, I thought, but Torben clearly wasn't so sure.

I truly loved Alexandria, but I had to leave no later than lunchtime on the third day if I wanted to cover the 230 km leg to Cairo in good time. Torben suggested I enquire about the buses going that way in case I ended up lagging behind my estimated time of arrival. This sounded like a good idea, but the bus company people simply could not understand why I didn't want to go all the way on their buses, or why I wasn't sure whether I actually needed their help or not. In the end I gave up and decided to ride through the night – the road was very good and the 'Carte Blanche' crew was only due to see me the following afternoon.

The riding went well. I passed more roadside billboards than I had ever seen before in one place, and was sped on my way by the hospitality of various Egyptians I encountered. I stopped off to camp on a small patch of lawn adjacent to a combined petrol station and café, then got off to an early start to complete the last 130 km before 1 pm. I was going to see the pyramids today! The thought drew me along like a magnet.

The 'Carte Blanche' team finally found me about 15 km short of the pyramids and hooked me up with microphones and other gear so that they could capture a biker's-eye impression of the moment the great structures came into sight. I don't think it turned out as dramatically as they had hoped, because I was so overwhelmed that I said very little except some stretched-out 'gees' and 'wows'. The pyramids reached into the low-lying clouds and at first seemed less colourful, somehow, than I had expected. But by the time I had cycled another five kilometres or so the clouds had lifted, so that I was actually standing in their shadow, and all of a sudden they looked like postcard pictures come to life. Man, I was excited.

John Webb interviewed me here, just before I went into Cairo, and I remember telling him that I was so excited that my legs were shaking. There was a strangely unreal feeling to the whole thing. Was I really standing in the shadow of the great pyramids? Had I really cycled along the entire westerly and northerly coasts of Africa, been held by rebels, nearly died of privation, been thrown in jail and everything else? If somebody else had told me he had done all this I wouldn't have found it easy to believe such a far-fetched story. But I enjoyed every morsel of the moment. I had got my well-earned reward, and it was a great one.

John noted my open-mouthed wonderment and used it – rather unfairly, I thought – for a humorous comment involving the popular theory that the pyramids were built by aliens from another planet. As a matter of fact I *do* believe in extraterrestrials, but this was certainly not the time and place for a discussion about my beliefs. He started the ball rolling by saying: 'Humans could never have built this. It had to be aliens,' as we stood in front of the Sphinx.

'You think so?' I responded, trying to strike the right note – we had just met, so I wasn't sure how his mind worked.

'There's no way that humans would have had the intelligence, skills and equipment to put something like this together,' he said, his face absolutely expressionless, so that I had not the faintest inkling of whether he was serious or joking.

This left me with two options. I could contest his theory or go with the moment. Like an idiot I went with the moment and said, glancing up to the peak of Khufu's pyramid, the largest of the three: 'Gee, John, it's amazing, hey? Aliens actually did build this. It's unbelievable!' At this John started laughing, and man, was I embarrassed. He really should not have taken advantage of me while I was in such a vulnerable state.

Thankfully, the other interviews were easy for me in my present frame of mind. The team's producer, Seamus, a large guy with the look of a rugby player, made sure we were continually taking footage in the truly beautiful Egyptian scenery, and arranged a coffee-shop interview with John in a bustling Cairo street that night, with a follow-up next day which took place while we sailed up that most Biblical of rivers, the Nile, in a graceful traditional felucca.

The coffee-shop interview was responsible for one of the funniest moments of the 'Carte Blanche' shoot. John wanted me to smoke one of the traditional shisha pipes while we were talking. A shisha is simply a pipe that draws flavoured tobacco-smoke through a water filter before the smoker inhales it, and according to most users is far gentler on the throat and lungs than traditional cigarettes, but

I said I was afraid to do it on film because I was a non-smoker, and every previous attempt at this pastime had left me coughing my way through the entire exercise.

John, an extremely well-travelled and experienced Africa hand, explained in his fatherly manner that smoking a shisha was as simple as breathing. I must have looked a little doubtful, because he proceeded to give me a demonstration. John exhaled, raised the pipe's flexible mouth-piece tube to his lips and began to inhale with controlled vigour. So far, so good ... but then things went pear-shaped with a vengeance. Instead of enjoying a cool, smooth smoke John started to splutter and cough furiously, eventually managing to say: 'That's *not* how to do it!' in a strangled croak which, I think, I was the only one to understand. But like the good sport he was, he had a long laugh after getting his breath back. So did I. Payback for his crack about aliens and the pyramids!

It was hugely beneficial for my state of mind to rendezvous with Seamus and John, two great guys who were very supportive. What made it even better was the knowledge that now people back home were going to get the real picture about my journey, and Vasti and our friends would be able to see how I was and where I had been, and so would Gran and my aunt, who I knew would feel proud. Yep, 'Carte Blanche' was going to be doing much more than merely entertaining South Africans on the prime-time Sunday evening slot.

Seamus had brought me a pair of new cycling shoes from the sponsors, Shimano, and with a twinge of sadness I said goodbye to my old cycling shoes, which were now at the very end of their tether after 21 000 km on the road. These old shoes were not going to be chucked away, though, I decided; they were historical items that had carried me through some of the toughest places on Earth. The shoes were not the only items in the parcel Seamus handed me. To my delight Vasti had crammed it with all sorts of treats for which I yearned: Liquorice Allsorts, ProNutro, Jungle Oats and Game energy-drink sachets.

A great disappointment came from a place where I had least expected it, the South African Embassy. I called the embassy with pleasant anticipation, because up to this point all the South African diplomats I had met had gone out of their way to help me and pass the word about me and my mission to their colleagues in the next country. I knew that Conradie Kok and Ambassador Ebrahim Saley had called ahead to their counterparts in Egypt, and I looked forward to more diplomatic kindness. But after a few telephone calls I realised that this time it was going to be different. The second-in-charge at the embassy seemed to have some very negative preconceptions about me which were so strong that it was extremely difficult even to conduct a conversation with him. When I asked if he could facilitate my application for Sudanese and Eritrean visas by notifying their diplomats of my unique circumstances he flatly refused and actually started yelling at me, asking me who I thought I was to make such a request. His open contempt left me deeply offended and even more deeply astounded, but I stopped myself from getting caught up in a verbal battle. Instead I explained succinctly that at all the other embassies the staff had understood my circumstances and had volunteered the additional assistance. It didn't work. Needless to say I was very disappointed, but when I had cooled down I decided to give him the benefit of the doubt – considering we were in the tourist hot-spot of North Africa, he was probably inundated with requests for assistance from guys like me.

Fortunately I still had the letter of referral to help me with the Sudanese and Eritrean embassies, and before I left one of the other staffers, who was familiar with my journey, came out to apologise for his colleague's failure to help me and also to offer his personal assistance. As if this was not enough, he ran back to his office to gather all the money he had with him to give me – manna from Heaven, for sure, because I was down to a few hundred dollars and my sponsorship with Windhoek Light was about to end – and on top of that also introduced me to the manager of Shoprite supermarkets in Egypt, Mark Copeland.

Shoprite Checkers is a very large supermarket chain in South Africa, of course, but I was surprised to find it flourishing in Cairo, about as far away from South Africa as it was possible to get without falling into the sea. It has spread throughout Africa and has enjoyed huge success in the traditionally competitive Cairo market-place. South Africans do well at providing sustainable services and products in what most Europeans would see as the most chaotic of the world's markets, and what Shoprite did, I think, was to identify the positives and harness them to its own benefit.

Mark was more than keen to assist. He not only sponsored me financially but allowed me to stock up on food supplies that I would normally only have got back home. His manager took care of another urgent need by finding an appropriate mechanic to carry out repairs on my bike, one Hussein, who was very patient with my insistence on quality of work. It was astounding to think that this unexpected largesse – cash sponsorship, free food supplies and expert technical attention – all came about from the kindness of just one man, my diplomat friend who had been shamed by his superior's oafish behaviour. It just proved once again how much damage or good one person can do.

Great kindness from various other Cairenes also helped to assuage the hurt in my heart. The Le Meridien Pyramids hotel, a swanky five-star establishment, offered me a free room for three nights while I pursued my visas and the long-suffering Hussein repaired my bicycle. This was really something special, because I had a wide-screen view of Khufu's pyramid from the balcony of my room (from this angle the Khafre pyramid looked taller because Khufu's one is sunk slightly into the ground). I just couldn't keep my eyes off Khufu's pyramid, or stop thinking about the expertise of its builders – 230 metres long on each side, and there was less than a 0.1 per cent difference in length between them; the more I read about the pyramids and their construction, the more I'm amazed. I found myself sitting on the balcony, repeatedly sending Vasti the same SMS: 'You won't believe where I am now', and, like the good sport she is, she indulged me in my madness by replying: 'I don't know, WHERE?' The only thing that could have made it better would have been to have her there with me.

The net of hospitality that had swept me up in my previous encounters with Multiport members was thrown out with a special flourish by Mr Said, the owner of Dominion shipping. His son, Khalid, took me out for a sumptuous dinner with a few friends on a five-star floating restaurant on the Nile which we all enjoyed, particularly my host and his chums, because Ramadan was in full swing now and the evening meal was their first of the day. They had all been educated in the United States, and it was good to get a balanced view of Islam from smart young people like this.

Mr Said himself invited me to be a guest at his company's combined yearly 'Iftar' (breakfast) meal, more or less the equivalent of a corporate Christmas dinner back home. It all took place at his head office in Port Said, and apart from enjoying the traditional meal I had an opportunity to see the Suez Canal at close quarters (Mr Said, who was something of a humorist, suggested that I do a side-trip to the Sinai Peninsula through the tunnel underneath the canal, thereby becoming the first man to cycle from Africa to Asia. I was tempted). He went even further by personally fattening my wallet to the extent of $600, a substantial sum in that part of the world which I needed desperately to secure the best possible spares and service for my bicycle. To be frank, I don't know what I would have done without it. I had been informed that south of Cairo I could expect hard times. Population centres were fewer, and both the environment and the people would be hostile. I still desperately needed a sponsor to assist me with my expenses for the rest of the trip home, but I would deal with this question once I returned to Cairo.

My new accommodation was in the hustle and bustle of downtown Cairo – and I mean 'hustle and bustle'. My surroundings only went quiet for a couple of hours out of every 24. I remember walking along the road to get something to eat and being almost struck dumb by the fact that families were walking around enjoying themselves although it was 2.30 in the morning. I could only conclude that many people spent the daylight hours sleeping. This impression was reinforced when I went to a little shop I frequented to buy some batteries. The shopkeeper was so fast asleep that I actually had to nudge him awake to make my request. He glanced drowsily at me, waved to the batteries, mumbled 'Mafe mushkela' (no problem) and passed out again. I helped myself, placed the correct amount of money on the counter alongside his head and left him to his travels through dreamland. Talk about laid back!

I started to fall into the same mode myself. I spent so many night and early-morning hours in a café called El Shams that they should have charged me chair-rent. It was a friendly little place, the shisha pipes and tea were cheap and good, and the hygiene bordered on clean, which I reckoned would train my stomach to resist the evils which were said to lurk in the deceptively crystal-clear Nile water. I had heard all the horror stories about dreadful intestinal problems, but my philosophy was 'don't be alarmed, rather be prepared'. The chief waiter, a gentle soul called Sherief Abd Al Rahmin (this is the shortened version of his name) grew very fond of me, and whenever I entered he would start shouting a mangled version of my name by way of greeting. It was like a home from home for a lonely traveller, and if you are ever in downtown Cairo, pop in there – the murals that cover every last inch of the walls are worth a visit by themselves.

The marvellous Mr Said, who had already done so much for me, now rendered another enormous service. Having got wind of the South African Embassy's refusal to help me with my visa applications, he sent his personal assistant all the way from Port Said to escort me from one embassy to the other so that I would have someone who could speak up on my behalf in Arabic when things became difficult. Mohamed was a natty individual in a tight-fitting grey suit, and he was definitely over-qualified for the task of interpreter and general nursemaid, since he had previously worked for the former American Secretary of State, Colin Powell, when he ran the Halifax oil company. But it gave me great peace of mind after all the doom-and-gloom stories about visa applications I had been picking up.

By all accounts the Sudan was a particularly tough nut to crack. At this time it seemed to be estranged from virtually all other nations, with the international media portraying it as a country caught up in xenophobic chaos. As a result the Sudanese were hyper-defensive about anything said about them, especially if the comments involved the Darfur region.

Mohamed went into the embassy offices, exuding nobility and charm in equal measures, while I shuffled anxiously along in the customary queue. One of my neighbours was an American girl who had been told she would only receive a visa if she paid $250 US, over and above the $150 I was expecting to pay. I was sorry for her, but made it my business to put some space between us as soon as the queue-shuffling allowed, because the last thing I needed was for any suspicion to be cast on me: experience had taught me that most embassies were paranoid about a guy wanting to cycle into their country without a clear route or exit-schedule. But I needn't have worried. About 15 minutes later Mohamed returned and told me we had to return after lunch to collect the visa. Having feared the worst after hearing all the ghastly tales of frustration and disappointment, I was dumbfounded. Could it be true? It was, Mohamed assured me, and then took me across the street for lunch at a convenient McDonald's.

Somewhat to my surprise there were a lot of other people in the restaurant in spite of Ramadan, and Mohamed explained that Islam allows those with good medical reasons to break the fast in an organised fashion. I had not considered the McDonald's chain as a medical facility of sorts before, but I didn't worry about it too much, because the only symptom I had was starvation-level hunger. I devoured a Big Mac while Mohamed sat and watched with benign pleasure, and then we went back to fetch my visa.

I remember him with fondness and gratitude, my saviour and a true gentleman in all his dealings with me. If he reads this he'll be glad to know that the lurid tartan Velcro wallet he bought me in the Cairo market is still where I keep my money, so that every time I pay for something I am reminded of him.

Money, I might add, was a major cloud on my horizon just then. In addition to staying too long in Cairo, I had also spent much more on things like visas, accommodation and bicycle repairs than I had anticipated – my first attempt to leave Cairo had failed when my entire rear wheel had collapsed because the food freebies from Shoprite Checkers had added another 10 or 15 kilos to my load. Hussein and his colleagues were perplexed and reluctant to carry on working on the wheel because they feared it would collapse again.

On top of that I had bought a video camera for $200 from a guy

I met at a coffee shop – he said it had been discarded by his cousin. He was very secretive about the deal, to the extent that he wouldn't even tell me his surname, and it was only later that I realised that the camera had probably been stolen from someone. And then he even talked me into buying a chicken for his family dinner that evening! A reward to himself, I suppose, for a dodgy job well done.

It wasn't the best camera but it would work well enough for me to record the rest of my journey ... if I could set out on it. I was now almost at rock-bottom as far as money went, with no more than about R50 – less than $10 – in my pocket after settling my hotel and bike-repair bills. It was true that I would still have one more payment from the Windhoek Light sponsorship, but that would be swallowed immediately by my home expenses. And I still had to stay one more night in my hotel.

So I decided on a gamble, the most desperate one of my life. I would spend 15 Egyptian pounds on food for the day, £30 on buying an international phone card and the remaining £5 or so on an evening meal. With the phone card I would call my early benefactor at Namibian Breweries, Dixon Norval, and ask if he would be willing to extend the sponsorship for another year. The chances of his saying 'yes', I thought, might well be slim. Windhoek Light had been firmly committed so far, but I didn't know if this had changed, seeing that I had been on the road for such a long time. Somehow, though, I didn't believe at this critical stage of my journey that this was going to be the end of the line for me.

In due course I put the call through to Windhoek, filled with worries. Just say he wasn't in his office? I had £30 worth of telephone time, and that was it. But he was, and in a moment I was put straight through to him. I had been so wrapped up in my problems that I had not even thought of a good opening gambit, so I found myself asking: 'How's the weather in Namibia?' A really original way of opening a conversation, especially as crucial a one as this.

Dixon didn't think anything of it and we chatted a bit about my progress – like many other Namibians, he had seen the 'Carte Blanche' story on DSTV, and he told me that it had provided the material for many dinner-table discussions. By now I was getting worried again, because the meter on the telephone's digital display was ticking away enthusiastically, so I got right down to the matter in hand: 'Dixon, I'm so grateful for you guys' support and could never have done this without your help. I know that this ...'

'Riaan,' he interrupted me, 'it's not you who needs to be grateful. *We're* the ones who are honoured to be involved with someone like you. You've done something people dream about. Something that forces people to look at what they can achieve with their own lives. We think that what you're doing is incredible.'

Now, that was exactly what I needed to hear. Vasti had always told me that I should remind myself of the reality of what I'd done and then, with that very feeling in my heart, approach people for help. What she meant, in fact, was that I must not discount my achievements through humility, because people treated you the way you saw yourself. I had, up to now, done something that no other cyclist had yet done, and still had the determination to make the journey a truly epic one by completing it. It was a considerable achievement which I should not diminish by being too modest about it.

'Gee, Dixon, thank you,' I said with absolute sincerity. 'That means a tremendous amount to me. I've told you from the outset that I'll deliver on the support I have received from you. I know the journey has taken longer than I had intended, but I'm determined to complete what I set out to achieve. But I need sponsorship to finish this. With your help over the final 12 months I'm sure I'll succeed.'

Dixon didn't hesitate. He asked me what I required and asked me to e-mail him with a breakdown, and as we said goodbye the timer ticked down to zero. Phew! I shot off the e-mail, and an hour later Vasti called me on my cell phone to say that Dixon had approved 60 per cent of my request for the next year. I can't describe my feeling of relief. Now I knew that there would be no more financial worries back home, and only my daily food and accommodation would need to be taken care of. Mafe mushkela, I told myself, like a good neo-Egyptian. And mafe mushkela it was. Vasti transferred 300 Egyptian pounds into my account for an emergency fund, and at last I was ready to set off on Stage Two of my trip – the downhill stage!

As a final kindness from the Saids, Khalid took me to the best soccer match I've ever attended, featuring the most successful African club of all time, El Ahly. The crowd at the military stadium where the match was played wasn't huge – about 10 000 all told – but it made more noise than the airport traffic passing overhead. Khalid explained that the match was a Cairo derby, something similar to the Pirates/Chiefs clashes in South Africa, and attracted huge interest from the city's fans ... which explained why the contingent of riot policemen present seemed nearly to equal the number of spectators. Sitting there, I realised once again how important it is to venture out and discover things that might seem odd or unusual; you will never learn anything new if you do not stray out of your comfort zone from time to time. I'm a rugby player, and many people in rugby circles see soccer as a boring game played by hooligans. Yet here I sat, astounded that I could enjoy a soccer game so much.

Saying farewell to the very kind staff of the hotel staff was a wrench, particularly in the case of a Nubian boy from the south named Alex who was the general help. Now, I don't know whether it is a fact, but many of the Nubian people, who look more African than Arab, tell stories of being marginalised and discriminated against in northern Egypt. I would have liked to leave him with a decent tip, since his pay was not very good, but being flat broke, I gave him my Kodak 'look and shoot' camera, plus two rolls of film, which left him in ecstasy.

# CHAPTER 25

# A LOCUST PLAGUE IN UPPER EGYPT ... AND I BECOME A CITIZEN OF THE RED SEA

*Time after time, till I became used to them, I would get the fright of my life when I approached a bush near the road and suddenly found a swarm of screeching locusts bursting out of it. This would trigger off the same thing on the other bushes in the vicinity, and I would find myself inside a veritable storm of agitated marauders. And could they eat! Overnight even densely foliaged bushes would grow perceptibly barer.*

My travelling plan through Egypt was simple. I would head straight east till I reached the coast, then turn south, camping out whenever possible and progressively lightening my load by eating the extra food I had stockpiled at Shoprite. The easiest route to the Sudan, I had been told, would be to follow the Nile down to Aswan. From Aswan I could take a ferry across Lake Nasser, a huge body of water created by the building of the Aswan High Dam in the 1960s, which would take me to the Sudanese border post at Wadi Halfa. This was the normal way of entering the Sudan and thus also the simplest as regards entry formalities.

But I had other plans. I wanted to work my way down the coast, passing through the resort town of Hurghada, and then keep going further south till I reached the border on the coastline. I was told I had no chance of getting through the military-controlled coastal area at the junction of the Egyptian and Sudanese coastlines, but I decided to aim for Port Sudan anyway – the whole purpose of my journey, after all, was to follow Africa's coastline as far as humanly possible.

Once I had left Cairo behind it wasn't long before I was surrounded by desert again and sweating fountains in the heat. Twice I was stopped by passing cars, each occupied by a mother-and-daughter team who seemed to have marriage as well as kindness on their minds. One team actually came back with a basket of groceries they had bought for me – an embarrassment of riches, considering my haul from Shoprite – took my cell phone number and asked if they could call me sometime. The daughter in this duo was huge of frame and wore very dramatic make-up, blue eye-shadow and dark red lipstick, and after they had climbed into their car again she leaned out and asked the same question as the previous team: 'Are you Muslim?' I said I wasn't, at which the girl gave me a provocative look and replied: 'Don't worry, we'll solve that.' *Wow*, I thought, *I'd better cycle hard and stay out of reach.*

Still, I'd be a liar if I said that this sort of attention wasn't flattering. I had swopped cell phone numbers with an extremely beautiful girl I'd met at the Dominion shipping dinner in Port Said, and now she started to call me very regularly as I worked my way down the coast. She had been dressed in distinctly fundamentalist style, and I had assumed she was looking for a husband of the same ilk, but now she kept calling me for in-depth discussions about my views on marriage and Islam, and eventually she implored me to make a turn up the coast and visit her family in Suez: she wanted me to spend some time with one of her brothers, who was very religious; it would be the only way, she explained, in which we could continue our relationship and possibly get married.

Since this was obviously not part of either my travel or social game-plans – I was travelling south rather than north, and back in Cape Town Vasti was waiting for me – I persuaded her that there was no chance of a detour.

Generally speaking, Arab girls are very good-looking, particularly the Egyptian and Lebanese pop singers – most guys I know who have never been in that part of the world would froth at the mouth just watching their music videos (the locals obviously felt the same way, because everywhere I went in Cairo I saw crowds of men, young and old alike, crowded around TVs showing the videos). Sexy but tastefully clad stars like Nancy Agram, Elissa and my favourite, Ruby, featured on advertising billboards all over Cairo. There was much controversy about the billboards at the time, with conservative Muslims complaining that the girls on them were dressed inappropriately and too provocatively. Well, shame on the Mother Grundies.

I managed about 80 km the first day before making camp by the roadside – not a long stretch, compared to some of my previous performances, but I was very tired and out of condition after the fleshpots of Alexandria and had been battling a head-wind all day. Obviously I was not going to have an opportunity to ease myself back into the swing of things, as I had hoped. The desert was so cold once the sun had gone that I put on extra clothes for warmth before climbing into my sleep bag. I slept like a tree-stump, my earlier bugbears the hyenas being kind enough to stay away. My advice to anyone undertaking this sort of trip is to put up with the extra 10 minutes needed to pitch your tent, which will help you against both night winds and bugs.

As it happened, I ran into serious bug trouble in the morning after I had set off for my next destination, the seaside resort at Ain Sukhna. I had barely got into my stride when I found myself surrounded by swarms of large locusts. I don't like insects, and particularly ones as forward as these. They crawled over me and brazenly plonked themselves down all over my body, some even clinging to my face. To make it even worse, they were just as haphazard about alighting as the West African flies had been – they either landed with a solid bone-jarring smack or, which was even worse, splattered on impact.

I found myself riding through a landscape blanketed with smoke from the fires local farmers and resort-owners had lit to repel the locusts. Time after time, till I became used to them, I would get the fright of my life when I approached a bush near the road and suddenly found a swarm of screeching locusts bursting out of it.

This would trigger off the same thing on the other bushes in the vicinity, and I would find myself inside a veritable storm of agitated marauders. And could they eat! Overnight even densely foliaged bushes would grow perceptibly barer.

I learnt later that the swarms had already decimated the crops in the Sudan and were now heading north to pastures new. I recalled a very true remark made by my friend Paparazzi Patrick about the similar plague which periodically hits the Moroccan–Mauritanian area. 'Moses', Patrick had told me, 'would have been in awe.'

Le Meridien Hotel chain gave me another night's free board and lodging when I arrived at its local establishment just south of Ain Sukhna, somewhat ragged at the edges from my travels. From there I headed southwards again for Hurghada, sleeping in the desert for several nights.

Setting up camp was an unpleasant business. I liked to camp near something dark, like a large rock or bush, which would make me less conspicuous in the moonlight to any passer-by who might harbour evil intentions. Inevitably this meant that I first had to check for locusts, and if necessary chase them off whatever bush I had selected for camouflage. I took to throwing a stone at any such bush before approaching it, to warn me if there were locusts on it or – in the best scenario – chase them away entirely. No doubt it looked totally insane, a ragged, bearded man stoning an innocent desert bush and then lying down next to it.

Both good and bad fortune visited me on that leg of the trip. The good fortune consisted of my encounter with Mr Faisal Neg Maldien, proprietor of the glorious seaside Menaville Hotel at the town of Safaga. A Britisher I'd met at the Egyptian rugby club in Cairo had referred me to him as just the man to give me a free meal and bed when I passed through the town, and so when I got there I went straight away to present myself to him. The Britisher had not called ahead to warn Faisal, as I had understood he would, but this was no problem for him. The idea of simply giving me a plate of food and a bed for the night he regarded as preposterous, and for starts he whisked me off to the hotel's spa for a full body treatment –

massage, bath and a therapeutic hose-down (this consisted of being sprayed on all parts of my body with high-pressure jets of water). By the end of Faisal's five-star treatment I felt positively guilty – I was supposed to be pitting my body against man and nature, and instead I was being coddled like some visiting potentate!

Little did I know, as I rolled into bed, that this was merely the start of an incredible little interlude. Faisal and his right-hand man, the charming Mahmoud, had decided to make a real meal of my arrival and put together an elaborate schedule of ceremonies and entertainment which would have done honour to a visiting cabinet minister, never mind a lowly passing cyclist. I ended up being granted the freedom of Safaga, meeting all the mayors of the coastline towns and – most spectacular of all – receiving the freedom of the entire Red Sea region from no less a dignitary than the Governor of the Red Sea himself, General Saad Aburida. Unbelievable!

General Aburida, who spoke quite good English, although with a distinct Egyptian accent, was a retired Army man who had fought in all of Egypt's modern wars, and we had a pleasant meeting in his plush office in Hurghada, where he reminisced about past exploits and asked me to spread the good word about his land when I got back home. I was happy to do this, although not too sure about what Egypt in general and the Red Sea region in particular had to offer. Being a sharp-witted character, he picked up on this right away, and, although I didn't realise it, quickly formulated some low-profile planning. He asked if I had gone diving at the Sharm El Shaikh resort at the southern tip of the Sinai Peninsula. I replied: 'No, I haven't, sir, but people say that it has the most beautiful and famous diving places in the world.'

His immediate response was: 'You go then.' This left me in a quandary. I would have to tell him, in the most diplomatic way possible, that I had a time problem – I had got ahead of the clock in the past week, and simply couldn't throw my gains away, and in any case I couldn't afford to spend an extra day at Hurghada. I decided that honesty was the best policy.

'I can't go, sir, because time is a problem. My visa will expire shortly. Also I don't wish to spend too much money; I must save that for emergencies. But I'll come back with my wife one day.' He looked at me, deep in thought, and said: 'No, no, no, you are my guest. You go.'

'Thank you, sir, you Egyptian people are too generous, and I see that you and Mr Faisal are the same men. Thank you, thank you, but no thank you,' I said. General Aburida didn't pursue the matter and moved on to another topic. I thought that had settled the matter, but generals don't give up that easily, and while coffee was being served he had a lengthy discussion with Faisal and his personal aide, Mohamed. Faisal was wearing his customary slightly naughty smile, but I thought this was merely because he genuinely loved bringing people together.

We had coffee, went outside for photographs to mark the occasion, toured the building and then returned to General Aburida's office to wind up the visit. Before Faisal and I could take our leave, however, Mohamed returned with a sheaf of documents which General Aburida perused and then handed to me. 'Tomorrow.' he announced, 'you go to the harbour at 9 o'clock, then you go to this hotel and speak to my cousin, then you go to the mayor for dinner. Call these people who will take you to the island for diving. OK? If the visa is a problem, then you call me, OK? You enjoy, OK?' That was it. What could I say except 'OK'?

Faisal's grin on the drive back to Safaga told me that he was as impervious to my objections as General Aburida had been, and when I raised the matter he brushed it aside, telling me firmly that if I wanted to be a wise man one day, I must learn more about people. To refuse the generosity of a great man like General Aburida, he said, would be like spitting in his face.

I thought the analogy was a bit strong, but I took the lesson to heart. When in Rome you do as the Romans do, and classic Arab hospitality laid obligations of respect and courtesy on the guest as well as on the host. So I resigned myself to my fate (a much pleasanter one than many others I could think of), and next morning I was on the ferry that would take me out of Africa and into the official Middle East.

The trip on the ferry was not part of that pleasant fate. There were something like 100 other passengers, mainly tourists from

Russia or various other parts of the former Soviet Union, and 99 per cent of them seemed to be competing for a gold medal in a sort of vomiting Olympics. They spent just about the entire two-hour trip tossing their cookies into the paper bags the ferry company thoughtfully provided, and the smell and sound-effects brought me close to joining in. I stuffed napkins up my nose and into my ears, but they didn't help much. Putting my fingers in my ears worked better as far as the retching went, but there was nothing I could do about fellow-passengers moving away from the heavy action to sit next to me. Their internal convulsions didn't have the same intensity as the gold-medal competitors, but they were in what I suppose you could call full-volume 'vibration mode', so that I could feel every jolt of nausea that racked them as it travelled through the frame of the joined seats.

I reflected dismally that I had now seen, smelt, heard and felt the vomit; my only unused sense was that of taste. Allah forbid that things would descend to such a level! And Allah was kind, because we reached the shore before I joined my fellow-passengers in the ultimate misery. People say I have a strong mind. They have no idea!

I staggered ashore, and the situation improved dramatically. The Red Sea really was a diver's paradise. We sailed along the coast in a luxury yacht which anchored at intervals so that we could go over the side to enjoy the wonders under the surface. I had never bothered to become a qualified scuba diver, and couldn't believe what I had missed out on up to this point in my life as I snorkelled about while the other tourists went down to depths I couldn't reach.

I must have spent about eight hours in the water, which was over 20 degrees and so clear that anyone seeing the video of me taken that day would have thought I was in a swimming pool back home … except for my considerable beard, which had reached the stage where it could have doubled to sieve out plankton like a whale's baleen. The only times I climbed back on board were to have a sandwich or empty my bladder – somehow it would have been like sacrilege to piddle in that marvellously clear water with its colourful hordes of eels and angel fish.

That evening I met the mayor of Sharm El Shaik, Mr Abdel, a very kind and gentle man who nevertheless, I could sense, commanded respect. He told me proudly that he presided over what was known as 'the city of peace', and that recent talks between Israel and Palestinian representatives had actually taken place not far from where we were sitting. We joked a lot and then exchanged gifts: he hung his personal prayer-bead necklace on me, and I gave him a lapel-badge depicting the South African flag, so that he would remember me every time he saw our flag waving somewhere – just as I would remember him whenever I handled his prayer-beads.

Sharm El Sheikh was positively crawling with current and former Russians. They all seemed rich, and probably had to be, seeing that everything was very expensive. Things had certainly changed on the other side of the former 'Iron Curtain' since the end of the Cold War.

We left Sharm El Sheikh at sunset, and the ferry-trip back was much better than the earlier one, at least from my point of view, perhaps because I snoozed all the way and so was unaware of any cookie-tossing. On arrival at Hurghada I felt much refreshed and was the first off the boat but the officials decided to strip-search me, and I ended up at the back of the customs queue.

General Aburida's PA, Mohamed, was waiting when I finally emerged from customs, and told me he had orders to book me into a hotel and entertain me for two days. I tried once more to explain that I was short on both time and money, but it didn't work. This was a bit worrying, but on the other hand he took me to the famous 'Alf Leila wa Leila' (Thousand and One Nights) for a truly wonderful horse show and genuine 'whirling dervishes'. The horse show was superb, with the riders performing amazing tricks against a backdrop of fire and lights, but the dervishes were even more amazing. Whirling dervishes are stock cartoon characters in the West, but the dance they perform is actually a deeply spiritual one which represents a person's rebirth, a cleansing of mind and thought which brings them before God in a state of purity.

The dervishes' dance consists basically of one continuous spin on the heels and toes, starting slowly but growing ever faster, their Frisbee-shaped robes – they wear two – rising higher and higher till they are flying parallel with the ground. Without slowing down or stopping, each dervish then removes first one and then the other robe and folds it up into the shape of a new born-baby in its wrappings to symbolise his re-birth. Mohamed was amused by my open-mouthed astonishment, which was quite genuine – I simply couldn't understand how they not only managed to stay upright throughout but also calmly walked off the stage in the correct direction at the end of the dance. I had to shake myself out of the trance-like state into which I had fallen within a minute or two.

Bravely I refused another day of entertainment and made Mohamed stuff me into a taxi which took me back to Faisal. This didn't speed things up, though; I had lost a filling and was suffering from toothache, and as soon as I mentioned this to Faisal he got on the telephone to book an appointment with the best dentist in town. I protested, but feebly, because the tooth really was hurting and Faisal pointed out with unassailable logic that I would have a problem if my tooth got worse after I reached the Sudan; I knew nobody there, he pointed out, and might have difficulty finding a good dentist (I gathered he did not have a high opinion of Sudanese dentists anyway).

We filled in some of the remaining time chatting and smoking shisha pipes. Faisal had a fund of funny stories, one of the funniest being about how he broke his leg after buying a new mountain bike. He misjudged a sharp turn somewhere in the mountains outside Hurghada, he said, and ended up careering at speed into a rock-face, leaving him with a few cuts and bruises plus one very sore knee. His friends rushed him off to the local hospital, where the doctor on duty in the emergency room sent him off for his knee to be run through the institution's very old roof-mounted X-ray machine. He was spread-eagled on the steel X-ray table, Faisal recounted, when he saw, as if in slow motion, the entire X-ray unit tear loose from the ceiling and crash down on him. The machine was wrestled back into position and two X-rays were taken. The first showed that he had damaged the ligaments in his knee, and the second that the rampaging X-ray machine had broken his femur in three places! Eventually he had to be flown to Germany, where 24 steel pins were put into his leg. Fortunately he had health insurance there, he added, which meant that he had not had to sell his house to pay for the treatment. I imagine this is the only recorded instance in history of a man's leg being broken by an X-ray machine. No wonder Faisal was so fond of telling the story.

That was the good fortune. The bad fortune struck me at Ras Gharib, south of Safaga, where I parked my bike outside the Internet café late one night while I sent off some e-mails and came out to find that a group of street-children had stolen some of my belongings. I wasn't too worried about the clothes they had taken, but grieved over the brand-new bicycle computer Seamus had given me in Cairo.

The loss of the bicycle computer was more serious than it might seem, because on this sort of long-haul trip it is mentally excruciating not to know how far you've gone or how far you still have to go. I had first learnt about the importance of goal-setting during rugby training. I was always first in line for the hard fitness work, asking only that the coach outline what the torture would entail. Once I knew that, I could get my body and mind to work together for maximum results, regardless of how much I suffered in the process.

My disappointment was softened a little by an unexpected act of kindness from a policeman named Khalil who was in charge of a roadblock outside the town, and who cleared out one of the rooms in his police station so that I could spend the freezing-cold night there instead of lying huddled up next to a locust-ridden bush in the desert. Next morning he gave me a new stick toothbrush – the very same kind, he assured me, that the Prophet Mohamed had used when he walked the earth. I hope someone who reads this will tell Khalil that I still have the Prophet's toothbrush as a treasured memento of my trip and the many kind Arabs I met during it.

Now that I was on the way at last I fell back to watching my pennies. One night I ended up sleeping in the back of a con-man's ancient, rickety Land Rover that didn't quite measure up to his tall tales about how rich he was. Over dinner and a few beers, which I ended up paying for, he claimed he owned an island in the famous oasis town of Siwa (were there islands at Siwa? I wondered), as well as a Porsche Carrera, a Hummer 2 and the latest Range Rover, not to mention a house he had inherited from his father and which was located in Spain, Italy or Hawaii (the venue changed with each telling). Naturally he was also a veritable sexual acrobat when it came to foreign women.

The evening ended with me pushing the Land Rover up the main street of Hurghada towards the petrol station. My reward for this effort was his promise of a piece of land on his island at Siwa, since I was a good man and deserved more than the world had bestowed on me (well, I couldn't argue with that). He apologised for our having to spend the night in the Land Rover, explaining that his uncle was using his house as a gambling den that evening, and he didn't want to upset the punters. OK, then, I thought. I had the aluminium roof over my head and a silver sun visor over my back for warmth, and that beat the desert any day.

Next morning I parted company with my allegedly plutocratic friend and carried on. Now my unscheduled burst of hospitality at the hands of Faisal and General Aburida paid further dividends. I stayed over at the diving resort of Wadi Lahmi and was given one of its shocking-pink pink T-shirts, and at Marsa Alam the mayor put me up at the luxurious Khaharamara resort, which looks as if it was hewn out of the mountainside (one of the hospitality touches was a 'Swing Kit' which had nothing to do with wife-swopping – it was meant to be 'sewing kit').

Wadi Lahmi consisted of an encampment of large tents next to the sea, my idea of an ideal holiday, and I met a sweet German girl there called Katrin whose story pretty much symbolised the grip a place like this could get on you. She had arrived there more than a year ago for a two-week diving course and, as she put it with eloquent simplicity, simply couldn't get herself to leave.

My new acquaintances also proved a great indirect help in me getting off lightly after I fell foul of the military at three o'clock in the morning while trying to cycle through the night into the Sudan. This was all my own fault. Almost everyone I had spoken to had warned that it would be impossible to cycle into the no-go military zone near the coastal border with the Sudan; the only exception had been General Aburida, who had told me I might as well try my luck, because he had not heard of any violence in the area for a long time.

That was good enough for me, so I threw caution to the winds and headed south. I nearly made it, too. There were numerous road-blocks along the route, but I went unnoticed through all of them. Admittedly this was a little nerve-wracking; normally I would have used my electric torch to see where I was going, but this night I kept it off so that as few people as possible would be aware of me, and to prevent the desert dogs from barking and attracting their own-ers' attention.

Eventually I got to a major roadblock at Shalatin, the last major town before the border, which was famous all over the Horn of Af-rica as a place for buying and selling camels and other livestock. Mi-raculously unnoticed, I slipped past behind the building guarding the road, my heart pumping much harder than the pace merited – I expected a burst of gun-fire at any second. But there was none, and I settled down to a few hours of solid cycling. All went well till about 3 am, when I was suddenly surrounded by armoured vehi-cles sporting machine-guns and laden with shouting soldiers who wanted to know who I was and what I was doing there. I put my hands up and stood there half-blinded by the glare of their lights, acting the innocent-puzzled-cyclist-caught-up-in-a-military-zone with every bit of histrionic skill in my body. The soldiers were un-moved and hustled me back to Shalatin, where they woke up their commander and his deputies.

The commander and his colleagues put me through some more aggressive questioning about my intentions. One of them took the line that I had no idea of how dangerous it was near the border, while another kept likening the area to the USA's Area 51 of flying saucer fame – as if either of us knew what Area 51 was like. I decided that the only logical thing was to pull some non-existent rank, so I told them that General Aburida had been my host further north and had suggested I try this route.

The rank-pulling didn't get me through to the border, but I did score a camel steak – the market was well-stocked because it was just before Eid El Fitr, the feast-day marking the end of Ramadan – plus a bus-ticket back to Marsa Alam. This was my first camel steak, and I found it pretty much like the other meats I'd eaten on my trip so far. It was tougher than lamb, but with considerable potential, I thought, if well-done and cut into beef stroganoff-style strips. There was no time to explore the local cuisine any further, however, because the military wanted to get shot of me as soon as possible, so I was sent off to the bus station with an armed escort which made sure that I was safely on board when the bus pulled away.

My plan was now to get back to Marsa Alam, find my way back to Aswan and then use the Nile route down into the Sudan. This way I could re-route via public transport back to the corresponding site on the Sudanese side; I estimated that I had been only about 50 km from the border when I was nabbed, and I could try back-tracking as far as possible from the Sudanese side.

While I waited at Marsa Alam for transport to Aswan an elderly Frenchwoman came cycling up to the bus stop, and we began to talk. She said her name was Sophie and that she had been travelling along the coastal route as well, but had now decided to use public transport because the traffic she had encountered was too dangerous. By way of evidence she showed me grazes on her knuckles and knees, the result of a close call earlier that day, when a truck had passed so close to her that its slipstream had literally blown her off the road; luckily for her she had landed on a mostly sandy patch.

I was really inspired by her commitment and bravery. She was in her late fifties, but she was risking everything to achieve something that most women her age would not even contemplate trying. We bused together to Aswan and spent a few days waiting for river transport to the south. Now I met more Nubians like my hotel acquaintance, Alex, and with a few exceptions they were just like him, humble and giving. Naturally their hustling sometimes got on my nerves, but Aswan depended on tourism and the Nubians had not become such out-and-out hustlers that they had forgotten how to be genuinely kind to a stranger.

Kindness wasn't in short supply at Aswan. The proprietor of the coffee shop Sophie and I frequented supplied me with free tea, and the people at the ferry company gave me a discount of nearly 60 per cent on my ticket after I told them about what I was doing and where I was going. It just showed that people don't mind helping those who are making an effort to help themselves. 'No food for lazy man!' as my bike's number-plate said.

I had some interesting conversations about Islam with the young men who also patronised the coffee-shop, conversations which went well beyond the usual George Bush tirades. I took the opportunity to lay out my own thoughts about Islam's international image. Every Muslim would tell you that Western people did not understand the real and peaceful side of the religion, but how were they supposed to see that side if all they experienced was Twin Tower bombings and the beheading of an innocent journalist in Iraq – all in the name of Islam?

From this, I said, the non-Muslim world could only make one logical deduction, which was that this sort of thing was supported by all Muslims. If Islam's most prominent leaders didn't stand up and denounce every action of this kind, then who would? The United States? If someone was denouncing the name of my religion directly and 99.99 per cent of its members knew this, I would expect public announcements by my leaders distancing us, the real religious members, from any actions taken by criminals. Even if I did not like the person they targeted, I said, I had to have a pure and godly heart about the way I saw these abhorrent deeds. Any god of any religion would never condone murderous action of this nature on innocent people.

Some of the young men listened to my words and nodded, but I sometimes felt that their desire to protect their religion was too strong for logical reasoning like this. Certainly a number of my listeners were clearly angry at what I had said, and some actually stormed out after listening to me.

I didn't get so wrapped up in my philosophical discussions that I forgot to board the ferry when it finally left on the following Monday morning, and in good time I stowed my bicycle below and then went up on deck to join the other passengers in seeing the sights as we sailed away from Aswan. It is a beautiful town with its many islands and dozens of sailboats, one of the various places I left behind me on my journey with a quiet promise to return one day in the future.

It took the ferry 24 hours to travel the length of Lake Nasser, and it was an uncomfortable period. The alleged meal which came with the ticket was, I discovered that evening, not even worth walking to the galley for – if food like this was to be served even in South Africa's toughest prison there would be an instant riot. The only foreigners who could bring themselves to taste the sour mush of beans and stale bread were a Japanese couple I had noticed earlier. Since Japanese appreciate good food, I can only think that they were extra-experimental or extra-hungry.

I had eaten some funny stuff so far, but I simply couldn't face this fare, so I traded my food coupons for extra tea chits. The steaming sweet tea helped to counteract the effects of an increasingly chilly breeze which arrived with darkness, and which I hadn't known about. The regular travellers had made themselves comfortable as soon as they had boarded, but all my bedding and extra clothing was locked away with my bike below decks. As the hours passed I became so cold that eventually my body was being shaken by involuntary tremors. Then Sophie the French cyclist came to my rescue and invited me to share her sleeping bag. Co-piloting a sleeping bag with a virtual stranger who was old enough to be my mother was something I had never expected to do, but I was deeply grateful to her. So all in all the night could have been far worse, and the following morning I woke up to the grandest and most opportunely timed sight I had ever had.

The temple of Abu Simbel was coming into view, the rising sun gilding the faces of the enormous statues guarding it. Every Egyptian tourism brochure features a picture of this great wonder of the ancient world, and I thought with gratitude of the gigantic UNESCO project of the 1960s which had carved up the temple and re-assembled it 60 metres higher so that it would not be covered by the rising waters of the then newly completed Lake Nasser. There is a common belief that other astounding artefacts of the ancient world are hidden below Lake Nasser's waters, and it's not impossible: elsewhere in Egypt new archaeological discoveries are made almost every year, even after more than a century of extensive excavations.

Late that afternoon we went ashore at Wadi Halfa, a dusty and dreary place. I didn't care what it looked like; my immediate aim was to get to the Sudanese capital of Khartoum, obtain the necessary visas and head to where the military had turned me back just north of the border.

# CHAPTER 26

# THIRST AND FRUSTRATION IN THE SUDANESE DESERT

*The beard would not be denied. He burst into an anti-Ameri-can tirade, spattering me with saliva, then ran out after me when I left the shop to shove a handful of pictures in my face depicting a variety of dismembered and beheaded corpses. 'This will happen to you!' he shouted. 'Before you leave our coun-try, this will happen to you, you filthy American!' He was liter-ally foaming at the mouth by this time. Just then a bus came past and I jumped on it. Undeterred, he ran next to it for about 100 metres, haranguing the other passengers in Arabic, while I sat there with my stomach cramping with horror as I remem-bered some of the pictures.*

Wadi Halfa was deserted when we landed. I decided to make a dash off the ferry ahead of the others to snap up the first available trans-port out of there – the day was almost gone, and I didn't want to waste what was left. It was very close to Christmas, and a multitude of delays in Gabon the year before had taught me to avoid holidays when applying for anything, or you were likely to end up waiting for the right person to get back from leave. According to my 'Lonely Planet' guide there was a train service to Atbara with a connection to Khartoum, and I reckoned that if I could get there before Christ-mas Day I would be able at least to submit my application to the Eritrean embassy before it closed.

At first it seemed that my frantic dash had been for nothing, since it turned out that the train wouldn't be leaving for two days, but then it paid off when I found myself at the front of the queue to get a mud-walled hotel room. It was nothing to write home about, but the twice-weekly ferry's passengers quickly soak up what accommodation there is. Next in the queue were the Japanese man and woman I had seen on the ferry. Actually they were not a team – they had been travelling separately and had met on the ferry. The man, Akira, was an experienced cyclist, although I didn't think he was properly equipped, since he had a racer-style bike with drop handlebars and thin-tyred 26-inch wheels. The woman, Sakurako, was on a lone tour down to Ethiopia via Egypt. This struck me as being a somewhat hazardous trek for a lone woman, but she scoffed at the mere thought of her being unable to protect herself. Akira planned to reach South Africa in about three months, and it would have been nice to team up with him for the home stretch, but he was set on following the conventional tourist cycle-route, whereas mine lay eastwards through Eritrea and Djiboutii towards Somalia, a place he wanted to steer clear of, for which I couldn't blame him. I would just have to hope that I could link up with someone south of Somalia.

In the Sudan all tourists have to get a travel permit within three days of arrival, but Sakurako and I decided to travel to Khartoum before getting ours because the price of $25 we were quoted at Wadi Halfa was suspiciously high (we were wrong, incidentally). Our tickets were pretty extortionate, too, considering that each of the train's carriages consisted of little more than a holey metal frame with broken windows through which large quantities of desert dust constantly blew in. Our fellow-passengers lolled around, obviously used to all this, but Sakurako and I were very uncomfortable. Fortunately she had a couple of surgical masks, like the ones people wore when the deadly flu strain had hit Asia, and these helped to keep most of the dust out of our lungs.

From time to time I went to the back of the train to see if my bicycle was still in one piece. This entailed running the gauntlet between groups of men who had gathered there to do some dedicated drinking and were sometimes distinctly aggressive towards me – mainly, I think, because they were upset at a stranger catching them in the act of boozing, something a good Muslim was not supposed to do. As if all this was not bad enough, our plans took a serious knock as a result of what can only be described as an act of God. One of the passengers died, and – unbelievable as this might sound – the train stopped at the next village so that burial preparations could be started and the necessary prayers offered up by the imam at the local mosque. This cost us six hours' travelling time, with the result that when we finally chugged into Atbara on the evening of 24 December the connecting train was long gone.

Sakurako and I spent a memorable (for all the wrong reasons) Christmas Eve on the freezing concrete floor of the railway station in a sort of tent which I constructed by leaning my bicycle against the wall and lashing my plastic tarpaulin to it. The only good thing about this humble abode was that we got a free Christmas present next morning, in the shape of an early awakening by a goods train that rumbled in and set the whole platform vibrating. To my surprise the goods train was emblazoned with the remains of what appeared to be the old South African Railways badge, and later on I was told that once upon a time, apartheid or no apartheid, the South African government had built up a very efficient rail service for the Sudan.

Our most urgent requirement was to get our travel permits at the local police station and then find some other transport to Khartoum, since the next passenger train would not be leaving for 10 days. However getting the permits proved impossible because the police station was closed for Christmas Day and Boxing Day – rather odd, seeing that the Sudan was a staunchly Muslim country. No doubt this was a distant hangover from the pre-independence times … a holiday is a holiday, after all.

My main feeling was one of frustration. How was I ever going to make it home? It was a ridiculous situation. The townspeople we spoke to about this warned us that the police had been known to arrest tourists without travel permits, yet they had made it impossible to get the permits. In any case, who had ever heard of police stations closing down on public holidays? But that was our problem, and it was quite a serious one. Travelling through the Sudan, especially the way we were doing it, was a tricky business because it was an unstable country – more unstable, in fact than any place I had encountered since leaving West Africa. To get to Eritrea, my next stop, I would have to go through some potentially sticky places.

Travel permits were a vital necessity in a country as war-jittery as the Sudan. But it was obvious that Sakurako and I were not going to get anywhere in Atbara within the three-day grace period, so we managed to buy tickets for a bus leaving for Khartoum on Boxing Day. We arrived in the early hours of 27 December, found ourselves a cheap hotel and later that day finally got our permits. Obtaining them was simple: you paid your cash and were given the permit, without so much as a question about where you intended to travel. This seemed rather illogical, considering the insistence on getting the permits in the first place; actually it wasn't, because unbeknown to us they were for Khartoum and its suburbs only. It was all too reminiscent of my experiences in Mauritania, and I began to feel uneasy.

I was also suddenly bereft of enthusiasm, which was not like me at all. I should have been excited at the prospect of arriving at the confluence of the fabled Blue and White Niles, and chatting to the locals about the situation in their country (at that time Darfur had dominated discussions in the world's humanitarian community for at least a year). But I just couldn't work up any eagerness. Looking back, it is clear that I was suffering from a sort of battle fatigue after well over a year of working my way through more problems, dangers, hardships and general vicissitudes than most people would face in an entire lifetime. The human spirit is a vastly dynamic and powerful thing, but it is not a bottomless well, and I had drunk very deeply from it in my long journey along Africa's coast.

Khartoum itself was not an impressive place. In the city centre there were uninteresting high-rise flat complexes, but elsewhere the architecture was what one could call 'Arab traditional', so that you didn't know whether it was old or new. The dust was universal, though. Technology did not seem abundant, with everything operating manually, and the airport was potentially life-threatening because it had no safety zone around it, so that it was slap bang in the middle of housing developments and industrial areas. Where else would you have aeroplanes landing literally inside a city?

My spirits got a wonderful boost when I went to the South African Embassy to make my number and met the second-in-charge, Mr Ebrahim Edries. My shabby treatment at the hands of his Cairo opposite number was still fresh in my memory, but Ebrahim proved to be a different kettle of fish altogether. He and his staffers were extremely helpful, even though they were up to their ears in work because President Thabo Mbeki was flying into Khartoum that very evening, preparatory to signing a peace treaty in Nairobi. In fact, Ebrahim made my day by asking me to meet with President Mbeki if this could be arranged, something I really wanted to do … clearly Khartoum had more in store for me than I had expected! Naturally I agreed, and Ebrahim put me on stand-by because Mr Mbeki was on a very tight schedule because of his date in Kenya.

The forthcoming meeting excited much interest among the locals with whom I discussed it. One of them (who told me to call him 'Mr Moon' because his Arabic name was so difficult to pronounce), very smart in a khaki safari suit and ivory-handled walking stick, asked me to convey his personal thanks to Mr Mbeki for his efforts in bringing peace to the country. I promised to do just that, and also prepared my own tale about how his portrait had literally saved my bacon in Liberia.

Alas, the much-anticipated meeting never came off. I got squeezed out of Mr Mbeki's tight schedule, thanks to the unexpected delays which are virtually part of the itinerary in that part of the world, not to mention the end-of-year holiday season. Mr Mbeki was a conspicuous exception to the general holiday fever, incidentally, as he made clear at a press conference when a journalist asked whether he would be doing anything special for New Year's Night. His reply was that New Year was just another day for him, and that as president he could not confine himself to dates on a calendar. But this particular New Year's Day, Mr Mbeki, *was* something special for the Sudanese people. A numberplate reading NO FOOD FOR LAZY MAN would have been a suitable gift for him, I thought.

In between all this excitement Sakurako and I, sticking together as a team, roamed around Khartoum, tracking down the embassies at which we needed to apply for visas. Both of us needed them for Ethiopia, but I also had to get ones for Eritrea, Somalia and Djibouti. Once again Christian holidays kept getting in our way in this Muslim city. But we kept going, frequently getting lost among the featureless flat complexes in the city centre (well, I kept getting lost, a situation Sakurako didn't fail to comment on. 'You go so far, so long, around all of Africa, by yourself,' she would say in her clipped Japanese accent, 'and now I ask where is hotel and you get lost every day? This is crazy!' My ego was slightly rattled, but I had to admit that she had a point).

Lost or not, we usually ended up passing the best fruit-juice restaurant in town. Although almost every fruit shop sold cold pureed juice, which really helped to flush away the layers of dust that had built up in our throats during the day, this one had a bigger variety than the others and also offered various sweet porridge-type meals. A tasty staple item was 'fool', fava beans with olive oil, tomatoes, onions, chillies and grated eggs, sprinkled with goats' cheese. This mixture was usually mashed a bit with the side of a Coke bottle and served with hunks of dry bread which doubled as the diner's eating utensils.

No doubt the affluent ate all sorts of other Sudanese dishes, but what I could afford was fool, and I ate it every day, and enjoyed it. The only problem I had with it was with the table manners, so to speak, of the locals who sat alongside me on the ground outside the shack from which the food was served. These characters espoused the wide-open-mouth eating technique, and the squishing, slapping and slobbering was awful to listen to, not to mention terrible to see. There was absolutely no reason for this disgusting way of eating. If the food had been tough or hard to break apart, it might have been excusable, but soft little beans and bread? I kept my peace, however, because interfering in an entrenched cultural usage is a waste of time. Aaaaaagh, international dining etiquette could be a thorny path! The other roadside entrepreneurs I patronised on a regular basis were the jebena (coffee) ladies, who sold coffee milled, brewed and strained directly into tiny little shot glass-type china cups. The coffee was good, cheap and helpful in creating more opportunities for me to practise my ever-improving Arabic.

My daily encounters with the fool-eaters were nothing serious, of course, but I was a bit shaken by something infinitely more sinister. One day I went to a roadside supermarket near the embassy to get a cool drink. The staff knew me from previous visits and, as usual, gave me a friendly reception. This day, though, there was a stranger present, dressed entirely in Western fashion but sporting a very long beard and very short-cropped hair, who wanted to know where I came from. I told him I was a South African, to which he replied: 'I know you are American. I can see and smell you are American.'

I tried to lighten the tone of what was obviously about to turn into a very heavy conversation, but the beard would not be denied. He burst into an anti-American tirade, spattering me with saliva, then ran out after me when I left the shop to shove a handful of pictures in my face depicting a variety of dismembered and beheaded corpses.

'This will happen to you!' he shouted. 'Before you leave our country, this will happen to you, you filthy American!' He was literally foaming at the mouth by this time. Just then a bus came past and I jumped on it. Undeterred, he ran next to it for about 100 metres, haranguing the other passengers in Arabic, while I sat there with my stomach cramping with horror as I remembered some of the pictures, hoping that he wouldn't succeed in working anyone up.

That wasn't the last of it. I encountered him three more times before leaving Khartoum, and each time he followed me to whichever place I was going to drink tea, then rant on and on about America's iniquities while handing his horrible photographs around. If this had been South Africa I would have dealt with him, but I wasn't going to try anything in a foreign and repressive country like the Sudan. His efforts weren't successful: one shopkeeper came out to chase him away, but otherwise all he achieved was to provide some amusement for the other locals.

Just how out of touch I had got with events elsewhere in the world was brought home to me when I happened to catch a news broadcast on a small TV in the Eritrean embassy's foyer and found out for the first time about the great Asian tsunami disaster that had taken place four days earlier. When I asked the others present what it was all about they were as surprised as I was that I knew nothing about this huge disaster in which hundreds of thousands of people had died. I mourned for the dead and felt ashamed that I had been so wrapped up in my own little world, so far out of touch with reality.

Of all the wonderful people I had dealings with in Khartoum, pride of place must go to the incredible Paul Azzo, whom I met quite by accident. Paul was a one-of-a-kind man if ever there was one. A Lebanese citizen but a Sudanese businessman, to use his own description, he was 70 years old but looked much younger and packed an unbelievable amount of vigour, intelligence, humour and passion for life into his diminutive frame. He had been knighted by the Italian government for services rendered and when I met him was furiously busy on his latest challenging task, compiling the first-ever Sudanese business directory.

Paul did so much for me out of the pure goodness of his heart that it is difficult to describe how much it meant to me. After a meal or two – which invariably stretched out into hours of conversation – he had me sized up. He knew exactly who I was, what I was trying to do and how seriously I needed financial help (a 'pat on the back', as he put it). Being Paul, he then started doing something about it. He persuaded me to stay on for another week, moved out of his office bedroom to a friend's home so that I would have a place to sleep and gave me pocket money along with instructions to 'discover' Khartoum while he negotiated with various of his business friends. Some of them were South Africans, and two in particular, one from Capo Dairy and the other from Coca-Cola, were of immense help. Capo Dairy and Coca-Cola were among the biggest business enterprises in the country, and hooking up with such heavyweights really smoothed my path.

Peter Meiring, the man from Capo, gave me some financial sponsorship, while another Pieter from Coca-Cola expedited the issue of a travel permit for the coastal areas, then arranged for me to fly to Port Sudan, from where his area manager would arrange transport northwards to the vicinity of the spot at which the Egyptian soldiers had turned me back. Without Pieter's intervention I would have spent a week just getting the permit, never mind the time and money I would have expended getting back to where I'd been.

Peter was a great guy, and we discovered we had a couple of things in common. As a young boy he had lived just two streets away from where my current house was, and we had played for the same rugby club, although at different times. He had played many games with famous Springboks like Calla Scholtz and had become quite renowned himself (he showed me newspaper clippings in which he was nicknamed 'Boy George' because of the long hair he wore at the time).

Among the things Peter helped me to 'discover' was one of the most interesting sights in Khartoum, the ruins of the Shifa Pharmaceutical factory which was blown up in August 1998 by American missiles launched from a submarine in the Red Sea, 600 km away, because it was believed to have been a chemical-weapons factory sponsored by Osama Bin Laden and the Al-Quaeda terrorist organisation. I marvelled at the accuracy of the missiles, which had flattened the rugby field-sized building without even damaging the fences around it. Peter said that the United States government had now agreed to pay compensation to the owners of the factory. I looked at the wrecked factory, which had once employed 300 people, and decided that it was the end-result of a mixture of factors: mutual arrogance, the bombing of the US embassy in Nairobi and Osama Bin Laden's very strong ties to the Sudan, where some of his family still lived. Still, the more I see of America's aggressive involvements with some foreign countries the more I understand how the laymen there can build up serious resentment, so that all the good things the Americans do are negated by their diplomatic disasters.

The South African Embassy's 2005 New Year bash, which Sakurako and I attended at Ebrahim's invitation, was a truly memorable one for a variety of reasons. The party was to take place at one of the staff residences, the main guests being Mrs Mbeki (the President was still in Kenya) and the Deputy Minister of Energy and Mineral Affairs, Lulu Xingwana, who was there to see about strengthening economic ties with the region. As it turned out, Mrs Mbeki could not make it because she got stuck in such horrendously gridlocked traffic that her trip was finally abandoned. This was just as well, because the party soon became pretty wild, thanks to a delegation of South African businessmen and women who let their hair down with a vengeance. The Deputy Minister resisted with admirable dignity a number of attempts to draw her into the ever more uninhibited revels on the dance-floor; another guest who kept his shirt on and his gentlemanly persona intact was the eloquent Mr Phillip Malebe, who took the time to quiz me very thoroughly about why I had undertaken my trek and why I didn't value my life enough. I laid it out to him in all the necessary detail so that he could understand exactly what was motivating me, and I obviously succeeded, because when I finally dried up he took me to one side and asked: 'Do you need some help? I mean, would you appreciate some support from my side?' and without even waiting for my reply took out his wallet and gave me $200 – completely unaware, like so many of my earlier benefactors, of what a great thing he was doing for me. It is at moments like this that one sees how much people want to connect with each other and offer their help.

Then it was midnight. The clock struck the hour, we all congratulated one another in the usual way, and Ebrahim came to me with a very special New Year's gift. Would I like to telephone Vasti? I didn't have to think about it twice, and next moment he was on the telephone and dialling. The call went through instantly, and I was talking to Vasti. It was a wonderful moment, and without warning the tears began to well up in my eyes. Ebrahim saw them when he came closer to check if I had got through, and he put his arm around my shoulders and gave me a gentle hug and a smile before going back to the crowd so that I could be alone with Vasti and my emotion. That simple gesture was the final proof that I was not alone on this trip, that many people did care.

A couple of days later Ebrahim provided further proof of his caring spirit, although a singularly unorthodox one with an unintentionally humorous ending, and I hope he will not mind if I tell the story here. On a visit to his office we fell to discussing the right way to use a long drop, and Ebrahim decided that I had not mastered the technique of the essential crouch. Nothing would do but a demonstration right there – fully clothed, naturally – and down he went in spite of a bad knee to show me exactly how to attain the position of greatest stability. Then a small disaster struck: his bad knee went on strike and I had to help him up again. This elicited a couple of bad jokes from me which Ebrahim, needless to say, fielded with professional aplomb

In the meantime Paul Azzo was still going out of his way to support me in my usual visa hassles – I am convinced that I reminded him of his sons, who were a little older than me, so that he was as proud of my efforts as he would have been of theirs, and just as determined to see that I succeeded at what I was doing. Having grown up without a real father figure I am inclined to be drawn to displays of affection, and I think he realised this.

Paul's guidance and support also gave me something else which was just as important, although it was invisible to everyone except myself: a sort of stability which enabled me to handle my mounting frustration with bureaucratic systems bogged down in red tape and the general holiday spirit. Among other things he arranged some media interviews. One was with a team from the national TV station, in the course of which the producer had me scoop up and drink a couple of mouthfuls of brown river water because there was a Sudanese saying that if you drank from the Nile you would always return to it. The other was with newspaper journalists at the Sudanese Olympic team offices. To my surprise I was besieged on arrival by bystanders, but it turned out that they had mistaken me for an Italian soccer player who had just been signed by the city's biggest team. Mischievous devil that he was, Paul made no attempt to deny it, just smiled and kept pushing me through the crowd.

Then it was time to head for the border, the poorer for the theft of my new cell phone which the Ericsson people had donated as a replacement for my old one. I left it at the local internet café, realised what I had done and was back within 10 minutes, by which time either the café's manager or the only other customer had pocketed it.

Ebrahim and his wife, Nachua, had me over for a farewell dinner, and then I was ready for the flight to Port Sudan that Pieter had arranged for me. My travel plan was simple (in theory anyway, although I knew that actually carrying it out might prove a little more difficult). Once I reached Port Sudan I would head northwards till I was more or less opposite the point at which the Egyptians had turned me back. From there I would cycle south-eastwards as though I had just crossed the border, in the direction of Eritrea, Djibouti and finally Somalia.

Pieter's area manager, Ahmed, collected me at Port Sudan when I finally emerged after the obligatory search through my baggage and then spent three days negotiating with the local military commander to get me on to a truck that was headed for the border, since I didn't have a military permit to travel anywhere in the frontier area. I ground my teeth more than once at this delay. Would this sort of time-wasting ever end? All I wanted was to be allowed to hit the road for the trip southwards.

My time was not totally wasted, however. In Khartoum a South African businessman who supplied the Mustad brand of fish-hooks to a general dealer in the port had suggested that I contact his client when I got there. I did just that, to my great benefit, because this fellow stocked a wide range of bicycle spares and attachments. I told him I needed a new bicycle computer and also a seat cover, and he made me a present of both, along with a siren and a headlight. The siren and headlight didn't last the distance, but the cover of mock leopard-skin is still on my bike. It is now tattered and torn by hard use, but that's where it will stay as a constant reminder of the kind merchant of Port Sudan. And although I have no need of hooks right now, Mustad will be the only brand I'll buy if my situation changes.

I also had some ... well, interesting ... brushes with the local cuisine. Ahmed and his friends stood me to a meal called 'maraara', which consisted of raw beef or camel liver, cut into little cubes which were embedded inside chunks of onion and flavoured with chillies. I found that the little portions slid down the throat like oysters; the liver was tasteless, of course, but the chillies and onions made up for that. I also had dealings with a self-confessed 'naughty Muslim' who liked to meet with his friends and get slightly plastered on bootleg liquor distilled from dates in the local township. I tasted this stuff, an innocuous-looking clear liquid whose fumes made my eyes water – and that was before I'd drunk any! I managed one sip and then politely but firmly turned down further hits from this home-made weapon of mass destruction. Needless to say, drinking this jungle juice was strictly a no-no in a deep-dyed conservative Muslim country like the Sudan, and he told me that 10 years earlier he had been caught red-lipped, so to speak, and flogged at the local police station. Nevertheless, he added, everyone drank, even the policemen who arrested the drinkers.

Eventually the north-bound lorry rumbled out of Port Sudan with my bike and myself tucked in between various greasy metal parts in the back for the 300 km trip to Halaib, my destination. It wasn't the most comfortable trip I had undertaken, but I didn't complain because I was taking no chances on being sent back. About 15 hours later we arrived at Halaib, an untidy sprawl of tents, shacks and wandering livestock which looked as if it didn't belong in the expanse of white desert sand. Some soldiers came over to the driver as soon as they spotted me. He explained that the commanding officer at Port Sudan had given permission for him to bring me along, but they weren't having any of this and told me to get going southwards right away. I was happy to comply, and in no time at all I was pumping at the pedals on my way to Somalia.

But not for long. I was passing through a nameless little settlement consisting of shacks and one brick building when a soldier in a creased and dirty uniform flagged me down in a very aggressive fashion. I handed him the travel permit that the commanding officer in Port Sudan had given me, but he just shook his head and demanded my passport. I gave it to him as well and he shook his head again and told me to unpack all my belongings.

This was going too far and I deluged him with polite but insistent questions. Who was he? Why was he harassing me like this? Had I done something wrong or made him suspicious in any way? His reaction was to shout: 'I know you white South Africans. I know how you are. Don't think I am stupid. I am not stupid. I know the law and I will lock you up for two weeks before I must tell anyone. I will show you, white man!'

Man, did this guy have a serious chip on both his shoulders! But I didn't have the time to sit down and work through his issues with him, so I suggested that he call his superior in Port Sudan, and while he was at it, the South African Embassy in Khartoum as well, so that they could tell him what sort of man he had arrested. All this, mind you, with a smile and a jovial manner which I was far from feeling.

'We have no phones here,' he replied. 'This is Nubian country. No telephones. You South Africans are disrespectful and arrogant. You better be careful.' But I could sense that he was softening, and after a while he also began to smile and said that I was lucky that he was in a good mood, otherwise he would not have been so forgiving. Then, of all things, he apologised for threatening me, explaining that he had thought I was being disrespectful.

I nodded continuously and thanked him, and after an hour of this senseless exchange I was out of his office and back on the road, furious at yet another experience of Sudanese officials' inability to deal with foreigners. This guy had created the whole scenario, convincing himself that I was a racist to justify what he must have known was a completely unjustified action. I thanked my lucky stars that at least he could speak some English; I might have found myself being accosted by some officious gun-wielding official who couldn't understand a word of what I was saying.

The desert was flat and had tracks I could follow to back to Port Sudan, so I made good time in the next three days – days of absolutely awesome scenery and sleeping under the desert sky at night. I also met some of the best people in the Sudan. The first night I had found refuge from the onshore wind in an outcrop of scorpion-infested volcanic rocks, but on the second night the village policeman at a little place called Mohammed Qol, about 150 km north of Port Sudan, gave me his outdoor metal bed for me to sleep on.

Mohammed Qol wasn't much to look at, but its population had a distinctly exotic air. All the males, including the policeman, sported bushy haircuts which strongly resembled the 1970s-vintage 'afro', and most of them carried large broadswords of mediaeval pattern which were dashingly slung over their shoulders in decorated scabbards. The only person who could speak English was, I discovered, also the very first inhabitant to go to university. He was in his second year of business studies at the University of Khartoum, he told me, and added that it was popular among South African Muslims who wanted to further their religious education.

The villagers invited me to stay on for a few days and go fishing with them. I would have loved to, but I couldn't. Before I left the student enlightened me as to the afros and swords. The haircuts were regarded as 'cool', he explained, and the swords were for protection against desert lions and the ever-present hyenas. Personally I thought the whole package – massive afro and equally massive sword – was pretty cool.

That day I had a very tough ride. The tracks were very sandy now, forcing me to leave them and find harder ground. This was a strictly relative term: 'hard ground' in this context meant places where there was a crust about an inch thick on the surface of the loose sand. If I maintained enough momentum I could ride in patches like this: the problem was that following the crusty patches meant I was slowly moving away from the tyre-tracks that pointed the way to Port Sudan.

Every hour or so I would spot a truck going north or south, from which I could gauge how far I had wandered away from the formal route – a real 'beaten track' in every sense of the word – but then there was a gap of a couple of hours during which no vehicles passed, and I began to worry, because I was very tired and I was running out of water. Where was I? My compass could give me the general direction in which I was heading, but what I needed soon was proof of other life, and some more water.

By midday I had no water left at all, and I knew that within a few more hours I would be so dehydrated that I might die. I recalled seeing dead camels sprawled at the roadside earlier; what chance did I have if even these ultimate desert survivors couldn't hack it? This was it, I concluded. I had taken one chance too many, and now I had run out of lives like a bankrupt cat facing death number 10. With surprising calm, considering the circumstances, I decided that the only logical thing I could do was film my own obituary while I still had the strength, to thank the people who had believed in me and, more importantly, people who didn't deserve to be hurt because I died doing stupid things like cycling through war zones and tackling deserts without enough water! The recording would also serve to wrap up my story to some degree if it truly was going to end here in the Nubian desert. I spoke my piece into the camera in a surprisingly jovial manner, considering I was about to snuff it. Man, what a strange thing to have to do, I remember thinking.

It should be noted that I didn't do this in a defeatist frame of mind. I had no intention of sitting in the desert and waiting for death. I planned to keep moving in as near to a south-easterly direction as I could manage, 50 metres east for every 100 metres south, going as far as I could. I set off at a steady 15 km/h, careful not to over-exert myself and eating the dry powder in two of my sachets of Game energy drink as I went. It didn't help my thirst, of course, but I calculated that at least the vitamins and carbohydrates in the powder would provide some sustenance. I don't know whether that happened, but the grape-flavoured powder certainly turned my teeth purple. Then after two hours came deliverance of a sort. Far away, near the horizon, I saw a dust-cloud slowly approaching. A vehicle! I knew I had a small window of opportunity, because in that part of the world trucks couldn't travel at more than 50 km/h at most, so I dropped my bike and started to run along an intersecting course with my two empty water-bottles.

I was a bit delirious by now, so that no matter how far I ran it felt as if I had not moved more than about 100 metres from my bike. But there was no time to worry about that now; this might well be my last throw in what was literally a game of life and death. So I just kept going, waving my arms every 20 steps or so in the desperate hope that the people in the truck would spot me. And they did! The truck turned off the track – a risky business, since it was clearly overloaded with passengers and cargo – and came up to me.

The driver and passengers helped me as far as they could, but the haul was meagre because the only water they had was brown-red in colour, with a pungent smell of diesel fuel to it. Perhaps it would be more accurate to describe is as diesel that tasted a bit like water. I thanked them and started trudging back along the trail of footprints back to my bicycle, feeling despondent after my sudden surge of expectation, because with water like this my chances of surviving the day had actually got worse. I decided to film myself sipping this water, but I didn't actually drink much of it, although I knew that if things got really serious I would consume the lot without a second thought.

Fortunately I didn't have to. Towards sundown I managed to flag down a van travelling southwards; the occupants were horrified when they saw the 'water' I had got from the truck and gave me two unopened bottles of mineral water, one of which I drank down almost immediately. That was the last vehicle of any kind I saw till the next day, but it had probably saved my life.

My last day of travel through the desert was the easiest, with occasional patches of clay over which I made good time. One of the highlights was a massive coincidence when the Multiport representative for Sudan – who had actually been ill when I attempted to visit him in Khartoum – drove past me on his way to a local fishing spot with his family. As flabbergasted as I was, he stocked me up with a plastic bag of large and juicy mangoes which, in my present dehydrated state, were positively addictive.

The surviving mangoes gave me a bit of a problem at one place, where the tracks turned into a cat's cradle because passing drivers had had to find their own routes up and over some huge, very soft-surfaced dunes. The dunes slowed me down to about one kilometre an hour. I persevered, however, although not knowing how much more of these impossible conditions lay ahead – or whether I would be able to see it through – was pure mental torture. While going up one exceptionally big dune my bicycle kept heading in a different direction to where I wanted to go, and the two of us toppled over time after time, the mangoes rolling out of the bag. After about the twentieth fall I called a temporary halt, righted my bike and sat on the crossbar so that we were holding each other erect, then grabbed the nearest mango. I tore the peel off with my teeth and got stuck into it. It was like ambrosia; the flesh was firm but ultra-juicy and slipped effortlessly down my throat.

My duneside rehydration didn't do my appearance any good, however, as I discovered later. A mango is a messy fruit to eat in the best of circumstances, and these definitely were less than ideal. Excess juice ran down my neck to mingle with my plentiful coating of dust, and little bits of flesh which escaped my mouth tracked down and found refuge in my beard. Not that I would have cared if I could have seen myself in a mirror, though; I was far beyond worrying about the social niceties.

I was still engrossed in mangling my second mango when a Land Cruiser with tinted windows came flying over the top of the dune, not 20 metres from me. My only reaction was to sink my face into the mango again. The Land Cruiser went past, the occupants obviously having failed to see me, but then it slowed drastically – a big risk in such soft sand – made a U-turn and pulled up right next to me. I was so far gone that I stayed propped up against the bike, paying no attention to anything except the mango. It wasn't till the electrically operated window on one side started whining open that I broke out of my thirst-induced trance and saw there were three people inside.

The one sitting in the back, who was obviously some sort of big shot, started asking me all the usual questions. Was I all right? Where was I from? Where was I was going? I don't blame him, because this was the real Riaan-the-Explorer he was speaking to, not the cleaned-up version who attended meetings with VIPs. I was sunburnt to a crisp and covered in sand, juice running down my face, food clinging to my beard and sweat dripping from my eyebrows, propped up against my overloaded bike against the enormous dune as if I had been there for years.

The big shot turned out to be the governor of Port Sudan himself, and he couldn't have been nicer once he had satisfied his official and personal curiosity about the bedraggled pilgrim he had run across. He was heading north and would be away for four days, he said, but I was welcome to stay over at his house when I reached Port Sudan. I expressed my very sincere gratitude at this bolt-of-from-the-blue hospitality and took down his address, although I knew that I would be staying with Ahmed for just one day before heading south again.

The second highlight of this extraordinary day was a lunch to be remembered at a village whose name I have forgotten. I had been somewhat cynical about the stories I had heard of how gentle and kind the ordinary Sudanese people were, since – with the exception of those at Mohammed Qol – I hadn't met many so far who were not rude or officious. Now I became a believer. I thought about this and concluded that a visitor to a country like the Sudan should put things into their right context and understand the dynamics of what a white tourist represents to the everyday poor man, of whom Africa has no shortage. Here things like a bank account and a visa were meaningless; these people had a fraction of what Westerners are willing to exchange their entire lives for, but they were the happiest individuals I'd ever seen in my life.

The food was terrible – sour and rancid fool that had probably been reheated 30 times – but it was a token of their hospitable spirit, and I could not do less than reciprocate that respect by eating it. So I choked it down while the kids (some were chewing tobacco, believe it or not) milled around me. They were fascinated by my hair, stroking their fingers along my head and pulling at the fluff on my legs. In some circumstances this might have creeped me out, but it was all completely innocent.

The video I took of my hilarious lunch-time party clearly shows how comfortable we were with one another, even though none of us could understand a word of what the other was saying. The men staged a traditional war-dance and jokingly chased me with their long swords, and I returned the favour by teaching them to sing the South African sports anthem 'Shosholoza', which they enjoyed even though they didn't understand a word. I expect that this was the first time Zulu had been sung in the Sudan.

I was welcomed back to Port Sudan by a serenade from a mega-phone-rigged pickup which was advertising the latest 10-year-old movies to reach the town cinema. I hooked up with Ahmed as scheduled and spent a day getting my bike in shape for the next leg, which would take me to the port of Suakin on – thankfully! – a tarmac road. From Suakin I would have to peel away inland and head for Kassala, because I didn't have a permit for the coastline to the south and there was no border post near the sea anyway. One of Paul's employees would be waiting for me in Kassala to render help if I needed it, and I felt quite optimistic about getting through to Eritrea in spite of warnings that I would not be allowed to cross the line.

I passed through Suakin without incident and headed for my next major destination, a town at the very top of a high plateau, aptly named Summit. My original plan was to ride into the night, but after a bit I began to feel uncomfortable about the fact that passing cars would slow down or even turn around so that the oc-cupants could get a look at me. I didn't like this, because my earli-er experiences had shown me the danger of someone telling highly coloured stories about me to whatever authorities existed further along the road. I kept going, but each time I saw a vehicle approach-ing I switched my headlamp off and flattened my bike and myself a few metres off the road till it had passed. It was inconvenient but better for my peace of mind.

On the second day out of Port Sudan, just before I tackled the final haul up to Summit, I found a farewell gift that Katrin and the other instructor from Wadi Lahmi had stuffed into my bag, a whole salami. I thanked my lucky stars that no fundamentalist had happened on it during my various baggage-searches, and decided to eliminate any future risk by eating it then and there. So I sat down on a rock almost hot enough to grill my impromptu lunch on and shovelled slice after slice into my mouth. It was a good salami, I hadn't had any for more than a year and it tasted amazing as I worked my way through it while feasting my eyes on the uneven landscape around me. The scenery was barren and deserted, but I really enjoyed my view because I was filled with a satisfaction that most people would think was a little crazy. Surely no one else in the world had ever sat on that precise rock, eating a luscious salami after a journey like mine!

'This is my view for lunch.' I thought aloud. 'I cycled here to come and have my salami lunch.'

I was also looking forward to seeing a familiar friendly face when I arrived in Summit. After my departure from Port Said Ahmed had found a jacket I had left behind at his house, and at this very moment he was bringing it to me. We had decided to meet at Summit in the mid-afternoon, since there was so little cell phone coverage along the road that we might well miss one another. That jacket and most of my other clothes were sponsored by First Ascent, and I can't remember how many times I put it on and thought how lucky I was to be using their brand. The First Ascent stuff was amazingly durable. In the past I had had some adventure vests falling apart after no more than 10 wearings, but the First Ascent clothes had literally taken a sunrise-to-sunset beating for more than 450 days and were still in good shape, even if they did look very well used by now. Or perhaps I should say 'full of character'. I had missed the comfort of my jacket during the ride from Port Sudan, so was very glad that Ahmed was making the effort to bring it back to me.

I had plenty of time before my rendezvous with Ahmed and stopped off for a rest at the village of Sinkat, just north of Summit. Here I came face-to-face, so to speak, with the terrible custom of female circumcision. I knew about it, of course, thanks to the worldwide lobbying by people like the famed Somali model Iman, but the full horror of it didn't hit me till I sat down in the grass-roofed restaurant to have some tea.

There I struck up a conversation with a Sudanese doctor, a well-spoken, thoroughly modern (to the point of being clean-shaven) 28-eight year old who was performing his compulsory year of community service. We started off chatting generally about qualifying as a doctor and what happened afterwards. Then he told me that 80 per cent of his daily patient intake were women from the village and its environs suffering from complications resulting from circumcision. To my shock he added that in spite of their life-threatening infections, these very women continued to practise the ritual on their children – the grandmothers apparently were the most insistent – which they believed would ensure that girls stayed chaste till they married.

This was bad enough, but then he got into the details. I had only a vague idea of what female circumcision actually entailed, and I think the doctor realised this, because he proceeded to describe it in detail – the excision of all external genital features, usually with a rusted and unsterilised razor-blade on a dusty floor, then the sewing up of the labia except for an opening to allow urination. Then on the girl's wedding night the labia would be opened again, either by penetrative sex or 'surgical' (if you can call it that) excision with the rusty but trusty old razor-blade. To conclude this gory and heart-rending tale, the doctor told me that 98 per cent of all the women and girls I saw around us had been circumcised, not one of them by choice.

I rode away from Sinkat with a maelstrom of thoughts running around in my head. Female circumcision was not required by any religion, so traditionalists could only justify it as a cultural phenomenon. But was forced ritual mutilation of this severity actually culture or simply a savage form of male domination? Sometimes 'culture' involved a complete lack of reason and compassion, I concluded bitterly. Then I put it in the back of my mind. This was the way of life that the women of Sinkat had inherited; we don't always have a choice. In my world things like that were abnormal and shocking, but not in theirs.

I reached Summit without difficulty soon afterwards, retrieved my jacket from Ahmed and was back on the road to Kassala again. En route the next day I had another brush with ultra-conservative Sudanese life when my water ran low and I stopped off in a roadside village's market to top up. It soon became clear that I wasn't welcome here, apparently because the locals had instantly concluded that I was an American. Children who had gathered around me were soon pulled away by their parents and ended up watching me from a distance, their little faces screwed up in anxiety, and the only shopkeeper willing to serve me asked me to leave his premises after I had bought a warm Coke. Groups of young men in dusty cloaks stood around, discussing me in what was obviously not a friendly manner. The general air of tension was so strong that it was almost tangible, and I realised how very vulnerable I was to kidnapping or worse. I got going without wasting a second more than was necessary, weaving between the sun-bleached clay huts with my heart pumping overtime and my eyes fixed on the roadside military radio tower that would guide me back on to the road. I was so shaken that when I came to some travellers' stalls about a kilometre and a half further I sped right by, thirst or no thirst.

The mountains of Totil come into view, great round mustard-coloured shapes that looked like gigantic bullets bursting through the desert's flat surface, and before too long I was within easy reach of my destination, Kassala. But rumblings from below my belt warned me now that my entry would not be plain sailing. My enforced drinking-water experiments in the desert had come home to roost, and it was quite obvious that if I didn't take the appropriate steps – and soon – my entry into Kassala was going to be a messy one.

When I came to a line of shack-stalls on Kassala's outskirts I flung myself off my bike in front of the nearest one and got right down to business without going through any of the customary greeting ritual. 'Min fadlak wain el-hammam?' (where is the toilet, please?) I cried out to the first person I saw. Confused by this abrupt introduction, he went off to get help while I hopped from one leg to another. Then one of the stall-owners came over, having obviously comprehended my problem. He handed me a bucket of water and pointed into the bare field across the road that lay between the stalls and a cluster of houses.

I laughed incredulously at the thought of attending to my needs in full view of the hundreds of people in the vicinity, not to mention their camels, donkeys and dogs, and illustrated my intentions with the customary squat just in case he had misunderstood me after all. He returned my laugh with equal gusto and pushed me encouragingly across the road and down the bank. I took the hint, unhappily conscious of the fact that my bright blue anti-fly shirt made me even more visible to all concerned. But then I went back into Riaan-the-Explorer mode and remembered my toilet experience in Guinea. It hadn't killed me and this wouldn't kill me either, so off I strolled with my bucket of water, while from the corner of my eye I could see small groups of people gathering to watch the fun. Repeating 'when it's over, it's over' like a sort of sanitary mantra, I dropped my shorts and got down to business, painfully aware of the watching eyes.

It goes without saying that I wasted no time getting rid of my problem, but my ordeal wasn't over yet. I still had to sluice myself down, and at this stage a handful of young men came walking past within five metres of me. All except one gave me a quick look and then walked on, but the exception kept turning to monitor my progress. This prurient interest infuriated me as I sluiced away, and the prayerful mantras turned into mumbled curses. Why was he staring at me like that? Hadn't he ever seen someone dropping a wad? What was he saying to his buddies – 'Aaaagh, look, the white man's finished shitting'? My advice to anyone caught up in a similar situation is that the only way to avoid near-terminal embarrassment is to concentrate on those prayerful mantras, or otherwise to settle for angry grumbles and curses. In my opinion the anger works better.

It was a relief in all senses of the word to haul up my shorts, return the bucket and get going into Kassala itself. Almost immediately I ran into problems when I came up to a police roadblock at a turn-off about 200 metres from the shacks. The cops were not interested in my travel permit. It might give me permission to cycle to Kassala, they said, but not into the town itself; at present even United Nations staff were prohibited from entering. I would have to go back to Khartoum and solve the problem there.

I wasn't having any of this, so I asked to see the local police chief and told him that the governor of Port Sudan had personally overseen my permission (this was shaving the truth slightly, but it *was* a fact that my permission had been given via his office), and if the top cop would be so kind as to contact him the governor would be sure to back me up. The upshot of all this was that my bicycle and I were loaded onto the back of a military pickup and taken to the area's military commander. He issued me with a week-long pass for the town, but flatly refused even to discuss the subject of crossing into Eritrea and warned me not to attempt going near the border. This was no empty warning, because while I was being processed at the adjacent police station another van arrived with a glum-looking Japanese in the back who had been caught trying to slip over.

The Japanese told me that he had tried to cross in the guise of a Bedouin, since many local men covered their heads with scarves to the point where only their eyes and noses were visible. Obviously the eyes didn't have it in this case, so to speak, and he was grabbed. Now he would spend some time in the police cells before being deported. No wonder he looked glum! I was amazed all over again by the Sudanese attitude to tourists. He wasn't a terrorist or criminal. He had entered the country legally, and now all he wanted was to leave again. What did the authorities have to fear from him? Surely it would have been much better and simpler just to let him go and prove to the world that they had nothing to hide.

Paul's man in Kassala was called Yussuf Hijazi, a distinctive-looking character with the three slanted scars of the prominent Hijazi clan on each cheek. Paul had told me that Yussuf was a big man in Kassala, and he hadn't been fooling. I realised almost immediately that I was in the best hands in the town; power is good, but influence is always better, and Yussuf had plenty of that. He took me into his house for the duration of my stay in Kassala, and we discussed ways of getting me over the border into Eritrea. It gave me some cautious but very welcome optimism, because I was full of instant faith in this formidable leader.

I also became aware of the political complications of the local situation. Yussuf explained to me that for years the town had had to withstand many challenges from the central government, and more recently there had been tension and open violence about the issue of autonomy for the Kassala province. Another complication, he added, was that many of the local families were separated by the border with Eritrea, which dated from colonial times. Half of his extended family, he said, lived only 35 km away in the town of Tessenay, but Tessenay was in Eritrea, and he had to have special government permission to visit them there. On the other hand, the Eritreans were even more unreasonable, and most of the blame for the violence fell on their shoulders.

Yussuf's main desire was for peace and a family which was not so severely separated. He didn't support violence as a means of achieving this end and had condemned the fighting between the government troops and rebel militiamen, but he was powerless to do more, and the very day of my arrival had brought the sound of gunfire from behind the smaller of the mountains north of Kassala.

I was privileged to sit in on a meeting he had convened with other prominent tribal leaders to discuss their plans for the coming year. They were unhappy about the increasing tension and violence, although they understood the reason for it. Khartoum was becoming more aggressive and opposed to negotiations, but the common people did not like it. It was clear to me that some sort of trouble was brewing, and I looked forward to my low-profile exit on the coming Saturday night. Kassala was no place for a foreigner to be in if fighting broke out.

On the Saturday morning I had an interview with Cape Talk Radio in South Africa, and would have liked to share my exciting plans about getting over the border with the presenter, Charmaine Noy, but naturally that was impossible in case it jeopardised my departure. But I did share something extraordinary I'd seen the previous evening. While lying on my wooden bed under the night sky I had spent time marvelling at the Milky Way, which seemed to be much brighter here than in most other places, even after moonset. As I lay there I spotted a spectacular shooting star, a huge ball of flame that lasted at least twice as long as a normal one and then suddenly broke into two smaller streaks of light.

I had never seen anything like this before, and I remember wondering whether anyone in South Africa had seen it too. If Vasti had,

I thought, it would have been nearly as good as having her there with me. But then I dismissed the thought. It would be impossible to find anyone back home who had seen this incredible sight. But when Charmaine Noy invited listeners to call in about this story and others I had told her, a man in Cape Town telephoned to say yes, he had seen the same thing. Charmaine and I were stunned, and she asked the man what time he had witnessed the spectacle. About 10 pm his time, he replied, and that fitted in as well. So we had seen the same thing, thousands of kilometres apart!

That was the last good thing to happen that day. That very morning there was an outburst of violence in Port Sudan in which government soldiers shot and killed 19 protesters, no more than 500 metres from where I had been staying with Ahmed. The immediate effect of the shooting was that Yussef firmly ruled out any ideas we might have had about sneaking into Eritrea because the military had been authorised to shoot at anyone trying to cross the border illegally, no questions asked. He called Paul and they decided that the best thing would be to put me on a bus back to Khartoum so that I could regroup, he and the Coca-Cola representative sharing the cost of the ticket.

I returned to Khartoum in a daze of unreality. Surely this couldn't be happening three countries in a row! But it was, and I would have to go through the same rigmarole of finding my way into Eritrea the long way around, then going back to a spot on the Eritrean side of the border near Kassala town, to start afresh – and, more importantly, join the dots of my journey. How I was going to manage this I didn't know, and just then didn't care either. I had almost no money and not much determination left in me, and I castigated myself for disappointing everyone who had helped me, particularly Paul.

But Paul was not disappointed in me. He knew exactly how depressed I felt and came up to scratch once more. He spent $200 of his own money on an airline ticket to Eritrea and organised a car to the airport, sending an employee named Joseph along to smooth the way for me. And then, after we had said our goodbyes and I was getting into the car, he slipped another $200 into my shirt pocket.

What more can I say about this great-hearted man which has not already been made clear by his actions?

But I had not yet finished with Paul, as it transpired. Joseph and I arrived at the airport in good time, only to run into an incredibly obstructive airline official who threw up every possible obstacle, real or made up on the spur of the moment – right down to requiring that I dismantle the bike and pack its component parts in cardboard boxes – so that in the end I missed the flight, to his visible joy and amusement. But for Joseph I would have assaulted him then and there. I boiled inside with anger.

It's difficult to describe the mixture of emotions I felt as we left the terminal building with all my bits and pieces, searching for a taxi back to Paul. What was I to do now? Paul had paid for this flight, and now I had gone and missed it! What would he think of me? How could I have let him down again? I didn't deserve the kindnesses Paul had given so freely. We got my bicycle and kit into the taxi and Joseph climbed into the front seat, next to the driver. He had spoken to Paul on the telephone, he said, and Paul had replied that everything was going to be fine, we would solve the problem when Joseph and I got back to his office. I felt guilty all over again; Paul had enough problems of his own, and here I was, heaping mine on his shoulders as well!

I slumped down in the back seat, and suddenly I just couldn't hold it all together any more – the anger, the frustration, the disappointment, the guilt. I leaned back and covered my face with both hands, with Joseph looking on with concern, and began to cry. I tried vainly to control myself. I was always so big-mouthed about how I could press through regardless of the challenge, about walking the talk. But here I sat in the back of a taxi, crying like a baby. I felt useless and pathetic.

Joseph laid his hand gently on my shoulder and whispered: 'Riaan, it's going to be OK. Mr Paul is going to make it OK. Believe me; everything is going to be OK.' His voice was as comforting as his touch, and although I was so down that I didn't want to believe him, I knew *he* believed it, and that was good enough for me. If Paul had so much faith in me, I had to show the same faith in him. If I didn't, *that* would be reason for disgrace. *That* would be something to be ashamed of. He had taken me to his heart like a son and never failed me in any way. Suddenly my spirits started to revive, and by the time we stepped out of the taxi at his office I was resolved that he would see only the determination that he knew was in me, the determination to overcome anything.

Paul was calm and organised, as always. He called the airline and rescheduled the flight for the Thursday, a couple of days away, then told me to take the afternoon off to get my mind right, starting with a visit to the Sudan's only shopping mall for a traditional Lebanese lunch (sort of like the 'retail therapy' that cheered women up, he joked). Paul knew that I was quite happy on my own and that a dose of down-time would do me a power of good. So I enjoyed my Lebanese lunch and then settled down in the well-organised and dust-free surroundings of this tiny First World outpost to plot my departure from Africa's largest country. I was going to Eritrea, no matter what. Challenges strengthen you if you see them exactly for what they are, not for how they make you feel! I felt happy again. The old Riaan was back after that disgraceful collapse in the taxi. The Thursday flight was all of 36 hours away, but I was ready today.

# CHAPTER 27

# BOUNCING OFF THE ERITREAN BORDER, AND CHEWING THE LOCAL FAT IN DJIBOUTI

*'I shoot,' the soldier replied eagerly, and I knew it was no good. This guy wasn't bluffing. Filled with propaganda and fiery home-made liquor, he would have shot me down without a second thought. I gave up and in due course was heading back to Assab in the bread van.*

The runway of Asmara's airport inclined upwards at the far end, as if its designers had realised that it was fairly short and needed something drastic to slow incoming aircraft down. That was just one of the out-of-the-ordinary things about Africa's second-highest capital city after Ethiopia's Addis Ababa, and one of the most lofty in the world. Approaching Asmara by air in the late afternoon was an experience. The hitherto flat desert terrain became ever more undulating till it suddenly reared up and turned into a plateau with the city and its airport on top. It was all quite impressive.

I disembarked without problems for once and made my way into Asmara itself, a small, spotlessly clean city with huge palm-trees shading tarred or cobbled streets lined with graceful old buildings and manicured gardens. It was teeming with cyclists, almost all of whom offered to race me. Ha! There was obviously not going to be a problem with finding a good mechanic to do some badly needed work on my bike. I knew that from now on the need for on-going repairs would be a constant factor in my trek, because new parts were not lasting as long as they had before. It is very important for a bicycle's moving parts to be more or less the same age. A new chain, for example, might work well for the first 500 km, but after that the extra stresses it takes because it does not mesh naturally with the worn sprockets will cause it to wear exponentially faster. Conversely, when all moving parts are replaced simultaneously there is a greater chance of a comfortable 'fit' and therefore considerably less wear and tear.

An early stop was at the office of Cynthia Daniels, the South African High Commission representative in Eritrea, an eloquent lady who reminded me a lot of Linda who had helped me so much in Morocco. Cynthia arranged for a night's stay in the same fancy hotel where she had her office, immediately started the ball rolling on my Djiboutian visa request and introduced me to most of the local South African community, some of whom were especially hospitable.

The South African guys from Mechem, who were in charge of the UN de-mining operation in western Eritrea, gave me a room for the duration of my stay, while a Danish UN worker named Steen Larsin was so enthused by my story that within a few hours of meeting me he made a personal donation towards my expenses. But the stars were two girls who were working for the UN, a universally popular South African named Adri Fourie and a Greek, Marianti, who was responsible for recruiting and placing volunteers within needed areas of the country. I admired their efforts: people like them were the UN's worker-ants, the ones who actually made things function by getting their hands dirty at the sharp end instead of shuffling paper in air-conditioned offices in New York.

I was particularly touched by a gesture from Marianti at a braai the Mechem guys hosted for me: an envelope with a small note of encouragement ... and $500 out of her own pocket. Her note said simply that she admired what I was doing because she was like many other people all over the world who would love to do the same but were not able to, and so she wanted to support my efforts in an appropriate way. I knew this came out of her heart because Marianti wasn't a frustrated 'wannabe' but a delightful person, one of the funniest girls I have ever met.

A parcel from Vasti awaited me, containing some new clothing as well as spare parts for my bike. Sad to say, the clothes were too small (she must have thought I had lost even more weight than was the case) but the spares were perfect, and within a day one of Asmara's expert bicycle mechanics had got my old faithful back to near-new functioning condition. One of the bits that had to go was the rear wheel rim, the spokes of which had begun to tear through the outer shell. But I couldn't complain. That battered old wheel had carried far more than its design weight over 23 000 km of tough terrain before finally calling it a day.

In the meantime I enjoyed Asmara. In architecture and general design the city had a strong Italian air to it – hardly surprising, considering how long Eritrea was an Italian colony – complete with an impressive cathedral in the main street which overshadowed everything around it, not only by its size but in its meticulous details.

When I finally arrived there things were still pretty much balanced on a razor's edge after decades of war against Ethiopian imperialistic designs. The three-year-old peace was holding, mainly because the UN was patrolling a security zone between the two countries to prevent any further border incidents, but the Eritrean economy was in ashes. All development had been seriously stunted by the decades of almost continual fighting, and now recovery was hampered by the fact that thousands of economically active people were rendering conscript service in the armed force. Food stocks were clearly beginning to run out, and fuel supplies were so low that motorists had to get written authorisation in order to buy any petrol. Cynthia was only able to fill her car's tank because she had a special diplomatic permit.

In spite of this Asmara was by far the neatest, cleanest and prettiest little city I had seen in my travels so far. It seemed that the Eritreans, unlike most other former colonies, had not allowed their colonial patrimony to decay through neglect. Yet it could have been a ruin if the Ethiopians had decided to bomb it during the long war. That they didn't was not out of love, the locals told me, but because they didn't want to inherit a ruin. So the death and destruction never came closer than Massawa, along the coast. It also soon became clear that Eritrea was hardly a bastion of democracy. Things were so tense underneath the surface that a while before my arrival 76 Eritrean athletes had hijacked an airliner and forced it to land in the Sudan, where they applied for asylum and refugee status. Thinking back on my experiences of the Sudan, I decided I would have chosen some other country to seek asylum in. It just shows how desperate they were.

Military service seemed to be pretty unpopular, but the government apparently didn't easily take 'no' for an answer – just before I got to Eritrea, Cynthia told me, army trucks full of soldiers had raided the city's bars and nightclubs to catch servicemen who had sneaked away from duty on the border. Just why it was so unpopular I soon discovered after talking with locals. Young Eritreans were badly frustrated. They wanted to travel the world, see new places and study abroad, but first they had to complete their conscriptive service, sometimes not even as soldiers. It seemed that many of Eritrea's hotels and other businesses belonged to the government in one way or another, and young people conscripted for military service might well end up doing their time as waiters and the like.

Some young Eritreans I spoke to said openly that they would dodge military service and be out of the country the next day if they could, but they were worried about what the government would do to their families. When I heard them say this, I thought of an Eritrean I had met in the air-conditioned mall in Khartoum, and whose family I planned to visit if I had the opportunity. This man had received asylum from the South African government 10 years earlier and was now running a successful clothing business there; I had thought him a bit of an opportunist, but now I could understand how he could have become so desperate that he had been willing to abandon his family and escape from his own country to find freedom and opportunity.

Adri made arrangements for me to meet up with the South African peacekeepers at Assab in the south, whose commanding officer, Colonel Charl Chromhout, was also commander of the entire

UN contingent. To me it sounded like positive luxury. I would start off from one node of measurable security and end up in another, which would surely make the in-between part's problems easily manageable. But before heading south down the coast I had to keep my travel-lines connected by backtracking inland to the Sudanese border and then covering the area over which I had flown. Talk about making your life difficult! But the integrity of the trip demanded it.

The road north-east out of the city plummeted almost immediately, weaving sharply left and right between lush terraced farmlands with villages huddled in between the cultivation. My first night's stop, after lots of long, steep upward stretches, was at Keren, where I negotiated a very affordable and decent place at the local hotel, spent a pleasant night (the hotel staff were incredibly friendly) and left early next morning.

It was like plunging down a mine shaft, just one long, heavenly stretch of down-slope, and I prepared to enjoy myself. But before I could do that I had to endure the ignominy of being attacked and robbed in broad daylight. I had only gone about 100 metres past the last police roadblock when I was jumped by 15 or so excited youths, drunk to a man. One of them, who looked about 15, pulled my bicycle to the ground and tried to get into a fist-fight with me. While I was fending him off the others grabbed anything and everything they could get their hands on, including the hamper containing my day's food and some of my clothing, including my prized First Ascent jacket.

There is no telling how all this might have ended, but a passing Red Cross worker screeched to a halt, jumped out of his car just as I got ready to commit some mayhem, and shouted at the youths in Tegra (one of the three Eritrean official languages) till they went away. There was no doubt that an awkward situation had been avoided, because my attitude towards people like this had changed to some degree. Till not long before I had been willing to consider the possibility of my bike being hijacked, but the way I felt now was that anyone who wanted to get my wheels would have to fight for them. And it would have been quite a fight. I was leaner, tougher and stronger than I'd ever been, full of determination and awash with adrenalin just waiting to be released.

Indeed, I had lost a chunk of my sense of humour at this time. It felt as if all I did during the day was go through the motions. My enthusiasm had waned, for both people and my journey.

The Red Cross man apologised for the youths' behaviour and assured me this was not what Eritrea was all about, but I wondered, because I had seen the reaction of the adults sitting on the porches and buildings along the road. They hadn't showed any sign of indignation. Instead they laughed and described the robbery to others who had not seen it. Some role models! They were simply leaving the children to work out their own notions of right and wrong. Children tend to do what adults do, and I couldn't help thinking that this was the start of a collapse in moral responsibility within a community setting such as I had not seen since Liberia.

The remnants of the adrenalin and some more endless downhills helped to speed me on my way to my next destination, Agordat, which was only 82 km away in any case, so I got there with lots of time to find a comfortable and affordable hotel. I am not saying it was exactly five-star accommodation, but by this stage my previous minimum standards had become modified to an extent which would have shocked some of my friends – I certainly would think twice about introducing Vasti to some of the places I slept in and considered quite decent.

At Agordat, I knew, I had entered rural Eritrea, with drastically different terrain and people. Eritrea has a large Christian community, but around here it was strongly Muslim, two very visible signs of which were the scarcity of women in public and the difficulty in getting a drink. When I wanted a beer with my dinner that evening it was brought to me from the darker side of the building in very discreet fashion. Dinner consisted of njera with mince and vegetables. A njera is a large savoury pancake with the same texture and surface as a crumpet, and a slightly sour taste that combines perfectly with the chilli-laden mince. Eating it was simple: you tore off a piece of the njera and used it to scoop up the mince and vegetables. Delicious!

The daily temperatures and humidity rose drastically as I ventured westwards, and the droopy vegetation didn't seem to appreciate the conditions either. I arrived at the town of Barentu at lunchtime, but decided to maintain my momentum and hopefully gain a day on my time budget by carrying on towards Haykota, passing through frequent military roadblocks whose soldiers were surprised at my mode of transport. At times I was told I couldn't go any further because of security concerns, to which I would reply that I had stayed in Kassala for a while and was only going to see what the other side of the mountains there looked like. This always did the trick.

I camped among some large desert boulders and set off early next morning for the border town of Sebderat. The inhabitants of the border region were not as openly welcoming as the people elsewhere in Eritrea, but I couldn't see any of the things that the Sudanese had warned me about. The villagers were dressed like the ones I had seen in Kassala, complete with tribal scars on the men's cheeks and large gold rings in the women's noses (and the children were better-behaved than the ones at Keren!) Near Sebderat I was stopped by a patrol of soldiers and told to turn back because it was unsafe near the border. When I gave them the story about wanting to see the other side of the Kassala mountains, the soldiers pointed at one in front of us and said that this was it. I had to believe them – so I started heading back immediately, hoping for a lift so I wouldn't cycle the road twice!

I made Tesseney before sunset and went looking for accommodation. Sleeping outside was not an option around here, now that I had seen the distrust and tension; in a situation like this, an innocent explorer could easily be mistaken for a threat of some kind. But getting a place to lay my head proved easy. The chief of the UN office, a Sri Lankan named Taliq, welcomed me with open arms, made sure I got a comfortable bed in the UN hostel and prepared a fish dinner for the two of us plus another UN worker, a young Pakistani. The Asian tsunami of which I had been so ignorant hit home again, hard this time, when Taliq showed us some photos he had taken just after the tsunami had destroyed his home town. Now it was very real to me.

Next morning Taliq arranged a lift for me on one of the UN trucks that was going to Asmara. As we passed through the town of Dedda I had an illuminating bit of instruction in the local customs. The driver, Tsegay, mowed down a goat that dashed across in front of us but then halted suddenly for some reason when he was well on the way to making a safe crossing. Tsegay had no time to stop and the goat was instantly transformed into roadkill. Right – in my world back home – was quite clearly on Tsegay's side, but local custom dictated that he had to stop, find the goat's owner and pay him. Tsegay didn't have enough of the local currency on him and had to leave his drivers' licence as collateral with the police. All this took about an hour, and when he returned I asked why he should take the blame when it was clearly the fault of the owner for not keeping the animal out of harm's way. Tsegay agreed, but said he wasn't going to go up against the area's informal laws, and no doubt he was right. I am sure that hell hath no fury like an Eritrean whose goat has been squashed by a UN lorry.

My first destination was Cynthia's office, and Tsegay insisted on dropping me right in front of the fancy hotel in which it was located. No doubt this provided the regular customers with something new to talk about, since people who patronised this establishment never arrived in dusty chauffeur-driven trucks. I found that in my absence Cynthia had cut out the middlemen and gone straight to the Djiboutian ambassador, with the result that my visa had arrived that very day. The Department of Foreign Affairs had scored again.

I took the visa with a mixture of excitement and anxiety. Djibouti was the last step to a place I really would have preferred to steer clear of, Somalia. But to Somalia I simply had to go if I was to make good on my plan to circumnavigate Africa. I decided to travel a bit lighter than usual, however, and made up a parcel of some of my clothes, food and money, which Adri promised to take to Addis Ababa for me.

This part of my travel-plan, such as it was, required that I get through from Djibouti to Somalia somewhere along the coast, which everyone I spoke to said was impossible, then get through

Somalia itself and enter Ethiopia at a suitable place – just where, I wasn't sure yet. But whichever route I took, I would at all costs avoid Mogadishu, the Somalian capital and arguably the most life-threatening and chaotic city in the world. Not for the first time I found myself thinking that the best thing might be to avoid Somalia altogether. But that was simply not on if I wanted to maintain the integrity of my quest.

First things first, however. I had to get from Asmara to the port of Massawa. Cynthia had told me that the view from the top of the mountains towards Massawa was breathtaking, and she was right. It was a strangely surreal sight, the sort of vista that makes it necessary to remind yourself about where you are. I was reminded of the famous scene in the film 'The Gods Must Be Crazy' where the unsophisticated Bushman, !Xi, comes to a massive cliff which rises above the clouds and believes that he has truly reached the ends of the world.

It was only 100 km to Massawa, mostly downhill, and I made it in just three hours without much of an effort; my biggest problem was not to pick up too much speed in case I flew off one of the many embankments. This nearly happened once, as a matter of fact. I was leaning into a corner at 60 km/h and felt my back tyre start wobbling uncontrollably and squeaking as it went flat and rolled in under the rim. Some heart-pounding stuff followed as I tried to brake and control the bicycle at the same time. Fixing the puncture gave me time to calm down again while enjoying the amazing views. I remained amazed by the way the nomadic people lived within the very fabric of the mountains. There was something enviable about the harmony between them and their surroundings – and in turn they thought that *we* were the fortunate ones. Life is one big circle of unsatisfied confusion.

Massawa was bland compared to Asmara, and the locals' sole topic of conversation seemed to be the battle fought there years earlier. Consequently it didn't break my heart that I had no time to sniff around. I caught some sleep and early next morning got on to the dirt road leading south, knowing that the wind was going to be my biggest concern, starting early in the day and building up to such serious proportions in the afternoon that my progress would be seriously affected.

The hyenas were huge, and so numerous, noisy and nosy during my first night in the desert that I gave up and broke out my tent. That helped, but not very much. They were louder than any I had experienced before and constantly woke me up. It is an indication of how tired I was after the fell battle with the day's wind that I wasn't too scared when I found one of the awesome creatures fossicking around my tent's flap, just annoyed at being disturbed. Next day I came across two that had been run down by passing vehicles during the night, and I was sorry in spite of my nocturnal hassles with them. They had been here a long time before any human beings, after all.

The bulk of the Eritrean coastline was created by volcanic activity millions of years ago, give or take a few months. Lava rock that is formed in cold water has a totally different texture and weight to the stuff that sets in air: I had always imagined lava to be heavy and indestructible, but the contrary now proved true – this version was light and as brittle as your gran's favourite crystal champagne glasses, and I took plenty of video footage to show on the home front, when I finally got back there.

I was now in the desolate Danakil depression, where some of the hottest temperatures in the world have been recorded, and this time I carried plenty of water. One of the places where I intended to stop off was the town of Thio, home to a remarkable Australian named Dirk. He had spent most of his life as a teacher for Volunteer Service Overseas, educating children in some of the remotest parts of the globe. In between he had cycled coast-to-coast through both Australia and the United States – all this in spite of the fact that he had only one leg. One of Adri's friends had told me about Dirk and suggested that I drop in on him. There was no way of calling ahead to warn him of my impending arrival, but as Adri's friend said, 'Dirk will appreciate the company.' Well, he certainly did, but if truth be told, mine was the greater pleasure. I reckon that if I could put across a mere tenth of how this one-legged dude from Oz inspired me, I'd set the stages of South Africa and the world alight.

Dirk decided to see me off the next morning by accompanying me to a rusty 30-metre-high lighthouse built by the Italians. The lighthouse was about 25 km out on a route which was rather challenging for an able-bodied individual, never mind someone with one leg missing, although it obviously hadn't slowed Dirk down very much. It was an interesting journey back through time as we climbed an almost endless spiral staircase to the top. In its heyday inspirational Fascist slogans had been painted on the interior walls, and in spite of the passage of years parts of them were still visible, although 'Il Duce' (the leader), namely Benito Mussolini, had been in his grave since 1945. It provided some food for reflection as we reached the top and sat down to enjoy the view from the best seats in the house while eating slices of Dirk's last tin of bully beef, laid on pieces of crispbread. Nearly a lifetime ago Mussolini had set out to create an African empire, using the long-established colony of Eritrea as his launching-pad. Now he and his short-lived empire and his colony were long gone, and all that remained were some exhortations, once bold but now only partly decipherable, in which one could still make out 'Duce' here and there.

Further along this rocky and wind-ridden coast I met an interesting duo of students who were doing a study for an international aid company which was interested in the viability of wind-generated power in Eritrea. I was willing to give them a blow-by-blow account of my battles with the coastal winds, but like good junior scientists they weren't interested in dodgy anecdotal material and relied on data collected from a number of small windmills alongside the road. I liked the idea and imagined how the wind farm I had seen on the mountains outside Tangiers would look here. Not too bad, I thought. But, as they explained, it would cost $10 million to set up and maintain each one, so we were definitely not talking about any backyard operations.

I had a pleasant surprise when I reached Assab to find that Adri had just arrived for a visit. She introduced me to the South African military observers who were attached to the local UN office with the task of monitoring the military movements of both Ethiopian and Eritrean military personnel. They were glad to see us, and Charl

Chromhout and a major named Alan gave me a real bed (not an army cot), a few good meals and some good laughs. Charl did not stand on his rank. He was a full colonel, while the highest notch I had reached during my time with 1 Parachute Battalion at the Tempe base in Bloemfontein had been lance-corporal, which is a pretty low form of military life by comparison. Yet he personally scrubbed my filthy clothes back to a semblance of their original colour. I knew no one would believe this, particularly not my old Army friends, so I made a point of recording the unusual event with my camera.

There was a distinctly unusual farewell gift from the military observers in my baggage when I cycled away from Assab. The UN had issued them with 248 plastic body-bags, just in case everybody's nightmare came true and the Eritreans and Ethiopians started killing one another again. Now they had only 247, because Charl made me a present of the 248th bag to use as a waterproof cover for my tent when I reached the rainy highlands of Ethiopia. I had never thought I would ever be zipped up in a body-bag, something soldiers try not to think about, but I had been wet and cold too often to worry much about this strictly unorthodox alternative use.

Actually getting to the border from Assab proved to be much more challenging than I could ever have imagined. Three days in a row I got to within sight of the border, only to be cut off by a military patrol for not having the 'correct paperwork', whatever that was, then loaded bike and all into a military bread van doing its daily run to Assab. The problem, it turned out, was that they had been given blanket instructions that no civilian movement was to be allowed in the border zone, and not even a hand-written letter on an official letterhead from the army colonel in charge of immigration that I brought along on my second try made any difference.

The third time I tried I was accosted by a bunch of soldiers who were sitting under a shade-tree drinking themselves silly on some horrible booze they had made from the tree's roots. I was feeling fairly rebellious by this stage, and when the bare-footed sergeant in charge told me to desist and wait for the bread van I refused. We got into a tugging match for the bike's handle-bars, in the course of which I told him that I had a visa for Djibouti, his colonel had personally given me permission to move unhindered, and if he wanted me to stop he would have to arrest me.

The sergeant – who was flanked by one of his troops by this time, a small angry-looking man carrying an assault rifle – wasn't interested. I decided to call their bluff and swung my leg over the crossbar, saying: 'You must shoot me, then,' and clipped one cleat into the pedal as if about to ride away. They didn't reply, and a few seconds that felt more like minutes slipped away. I leaned forward into cycling mode and asked in undisguised disgust: 'You shoot?'

'I shoot,' the soldier replied eagerly, and I knew it was no good. This guy wasn't bluffing. Filled with propaganda and fiery homemade liquor, he would have shot me down without a second thought. I gave up and in due course was heading back to Assab in the bread van once again (it was tasty bread, I must admit). My snack didn't calm me down, however, and when I got there I insisted that the colonel be woken up so that I could complain.

He apologised profusely (once again!) and asked me not be too negative about what had happened. I agreed, of course, but I thought his attitude was wrong, and I still think so. One of this continent's greatest problems is the tendency to accept the unacceptable simply because it's Africa. It is this sort of approach that leads outsiders to talking of an 'African mentality' which is seen as consisting of a mixture of incompetence and inefficiency. This is not an 'African mentality'. It is a cop-out for leaders who are too lazy to do their job, which is why I – like so many others – found myself again and again in frustrating situations with uneducated, badly trained, badly disciplined and frequently intoxicated people wielding powers they were not fit to handle. Africans of all races are not inherently incompetent, lazy or inefficient, any more than people anywhere else in the world. The problem is that the leaders are not doing their job. Till they focus on the realities and start doing so, Africa is not going to pull itself out of its dire problems.

Next morning I set off once more in the direction of the border, but this time the colonel had made sure of a smooth passage by loading me into a military van, along with an excessive number of others, whose driver had explicit instructions not to let me off his vehicle till we had arrived at the border with Djibouti. That was more like it! The only other foreigner among the multitude crammed into the van was an elderly British woman, a cancer survivor, who had been part of a group of cancer-beating women who had climbed Kilimanjaro the year before; the trip was documented by a TV team and received world-wide acclaim. Suddenly everything I was doing was put into perspective once again.

I got through the Djiboutian border post without any hassles (hallelujah!). The French policeman in charge promised to look after my bicycle while I got a free lift to the town of Obock, from where a ferry for the capital, Djibouti city, would be leaving the following morning. I wanted to catch this without fail, because I had some complicated work ahead to get myself into (and out of) Somalia. I would make contact with the diplomatic staff and plot my route into Somalia, and hopefully also enlist the help of the Multiport representative in Djibouti. Then, once all my ducks were in a row, I would go back for my bike and cycle straight past the capital into Somalia.

What would happen after that ... well, I tried not to think too much about what could go wrong. I had travelled so far in a spirit of anticipation and optimism, but I was afraid of Somalia, a classic failed state, and a highly lethal one, too.

It was only 90 km from the border to Obock, but it took us hours and included three sessions of digging ourselves out of the soft river-beds a ('free lift' for you!). I was the only one with a torch, which probably saved us a few more hours. At Obock the British woman and I had something to eat and drink, then unrolled our sleeping bags next to a building which overlooked the pier from which the ferry would depart, just to make sure that we didn't miss it in the morning. It was not a comfortable night's rest, thanks to the hordes of mosquitoes and dozens of arrogant stray dogs which came to check us out, but we got on the ferry all right, and in due course arrived in Djibouti, where I was welcomed by the Multiport chief representative, Jean-Pierre Guadierre, and his lovely wife Christine, who put me up for my entire stay and said that if I came back again a bed would be waiting for me.

Bad news came from South Africa's diplomatic representatives, Yvonne Modiaghotla and Themba Nyathi, who didn't want me to enter Somalia because of concerns for my safety. This took some working out, because their fears were legitimate but (as far as I was concerned) so was my broader aim. Eventually I asked them as diplomatically as possible if I could go even if they advised against it. Themba found it difficult to understand why I was so insistent on diving into such a hellhole and at one point thought me arrogant when I explained to him that *not* going to Somalia was not an option for me, even if I ended up dying there. That was the easy part. I was to get involved in negotiations so complicated that they beat anything I had experienced so far, and that was only one aspect of the problems I was to pick up at Djibouti.

I also made my first acquaintance with qat (pronounced 'chat'), to which it seemed the entire native population was addicted. I had read a good deal about qat, a soft, small-leafed plant that is chewed like tobacco for its stimulant effects, although they are not the same and there is no 'high' of the classic kind. I tried some – after all, any good explorer tastes the wine of the country he is visiting, and I suppose this was the Djiboutian equivalent. The leaf has a bitter taste and takes getting used to, but before long you are past worrying about that as you become increasingly detached from your sense of time and your surroundings. Eventually you reach the point where you have almost no interaction with the world, although you remain acutely aware of all that is going on around you. But you are not involved in any of it; you are just an analytical observer.

The city's streets are lined with people looking pretty much like hoboes spread out on pieces of cardboard with a big bunch or two of qat close to hand. As the day progresses and the qat diminishes, the chewers go from an extremely talkative state to a sort of distant calm. Noon always brings some excitement, though, because that is when the day's fresh shipment arrives by air from Ethiopia, and if it is late one can see people in the souk (market) trotting around making anxious inquiries about what has happened to the happy green stuff. To illustrate how serious the average Djibouitan is about qat, I quote a story which a most reliable person vouched for as the truth. Colin Powell had arrived in Djibouti to meet with the president and also to visit the American military base. His aircraft landed a few minutes before 12 noon, and as a standard security precaution all other air traffic was kept in a holding pattern till he had arrived and been picked up by a suitably grand motorcade for the drive into the city.

To Powell's surprise his entry into Djibouti received a most unwelcoming reception from the populace, who screamed insults, slapped the vehicles' sides and even pelted them with rotten fruit and vegetables. A hostile demonstration against the US and its policies was the last thing Powell and his entourage had expected in Djibouti, of all places, and he and they were naturally confused by the whole business. In fact the Djiboutians did not give two hoots about Powell, the US or its policies at that moment. Their problem was that one of the aircraft orbiting overhead while Powell moved through the city was an Ethiopian flight containing the day's consignment of fresh qat, so that they were going cold turkey while Powell was pressing the flesh and handing out 'God bless America' T-shirts.

I would go to sleep while the downtown part of Djibouti carried on chewing, and next morning the very same people I had seen the night before would still be stretched out in exactly the same places and getting ready for the new day, albeit a bit groggily. I decided that the customary afternoon siesta provided them with the strength – or life-force, or whatever it was – to take them through. One wise old (well, old, anyway) man asked me how many kilometres I normally covered in a day, but before I could answer he added: 'Don't worry; just add a zero to that, that's how much you can cycle with qat.' Tempting thought! But I didn't take him up on it. Losing touch with reality wasn't a luxury you could afford while cycling through the wilder parts of Africa.

If I were to pass judgement on qat, I would say that it seems less dangerous than alcohol, although it is, after all, a narcotic drug. No doubt, through, it is a great aid to any dictatorial regime, not just because it distracts people from petty tyranny but also because it inculcates the laziest life-style I have ever come across. To give an example, the time-schedule of the native Djiboutian (this is one who works rather than lies on a piece of cardboard in the street) is more or less as follows: Nominally your office opens at 8 am, closes for an hour at lunch-time and then re-opens till 5 or 5.30 pm. In fact you only get there at 9 or 10 am and close from noon to 2 pm, and if the lunch-time qat-chewing is going particularly well you don't bother to go back at all. If you do, however, you close your doors at 4 pm or 4.30 because you have to get back to your qat den, where you and your friends lie around to chew qat and drink sweet tea. If that is particularly congenial – well, it's going to be another late night.

To a South African this lackadaisical attitude was both incomprehensible and irritating, but after thinking about it I decided that it was due largely to the stultifying quality of life. What did the average Djiboutian have to look forward to? The country could not and would not be able to produce anything, but lived off the necessities of other nations, and it did not even have any inner political dynamism. I saw this when a presidential election took place, complete with motorcades, loudspeakers in the streets and so on. Then I discovered that the president had banned all his competitors. One man, one vote, one candidate. It was enough to make you rustle up a piece of cardboard and a heap of qat.

After four days in Djibouti city I returned to the border post to pick up my bicycle from the French cop who had been guarding it and set off for Obock. The desert wasn't as challenging as I had thought – there were hard and crusty patches like the ones in the Nubian desert, but the tracks were more defined and thus easier to follow – and I managed to cover this tank-littered stretch in one day.

One of my three major aims was to visit the lowest point on the entire continent, Lake Assal, but there was a surprise in store for me first, and it wasn't a pleasant one. It happened while I was travelling through the passes of the mountain of Tadjoura between Obock and the town of Tadjoura. The inclines and declines here were like the worst sections of Lesotho's Sani Pass. In some places the road faithfully conformed to the jagged edges of the mountain, creating some very acute angles, and the road itself was extremely rocky, with many large, loose stones which sometimes reduced my traction to zero. I was extremely patient for the first 45 km, but when I came to one of the few sections which was straight and slightly downhill I could not resist pushing things a bit.

I could hear the smaller stones flying up, hitting the frame of the bike and ricocheting away, and for once the dust I was churning up was being left behind, so that it didn't cake my sweaty face and turn into a fine muddy paste as it had been doing all day. It might well have been the first sub-4-minute mountain mile, but whether it was or not didn't matter. It just felt pretty good. But good things usually don't last, and this one certainly didn't. All dirt roads have what South Africans call a 'middelmannetjie' (middleman), a central ridge between the tracks that vehicle tyres have eroded into the surface, and this one was no exception. I was approaching a slight bend and decided to cross the middelmannetjie to avoid some particularly jagged rocks protruding from the wheel-track I was on, my belief being that the other wheel-track was smoother and would ease my entry into the bend. What happened then is a bit of a blank. I greeted a man leading a camel with the customary 'salaam aleikum' (peace be with you), and the next thing I recall is lying next to my bicycle under a blanket of dust, cloaked in an eerie silence.

It was my first really serious fall since the time in Gabon, and once again I remained surprisingly calm. I did a quick body check to see if everything was still where it was supposed to be. There was the usual assortment of grazes and bruises, but there was also a deep, dull pain in my chest, and I knew I had a problem on my right elbow, which had apparently made direct contact with a protruding rock. I consoled myself with the thought that since the tough First Ascent shirt was not actually torn the arm was probably not all that bad. But when I painfully rolled up the slightly damaged sleeve I found a deep gash, right down to the bone, two inches long. I probed the gash with one dusty finger, although to judge by the blood pouring along my forearm and creating tiny dust clouds of its own as it hit the dry ground it was already clear that I had suffered more than your average cycling injury, and that I had to act quickly.

Which I did, Manser-style. I took out my camera and recorded the event with a quick self-interview, as further proof to future scoffers who might believe that cycling around Africa's perimeter was plain sailing. At this stage the camel man came up and helped me to swill out the wound with my drinking water, then ran off at top speed to his hut somewhere in the mountains to fetch more water. I was touched: this total stranger really was sharing the pain with me. In the meantime I got out my medical kit and took the most immediate steps to treat the wound. I stopped the bleeding, made certain that the larger foreign bodies had been removed, then – vitally important – immediately started a high-dosage course of penicillin. I couldn't do anything about the pain in my chest, which I later found was caused by a broken collar-bone.

The main problem, now that I was more or less patched up, was how I would manage to get to Djibouti. It was almost impossible to cycle, and so far (it was now around 3 pm) not one vehicle had even passed by that day. And then, as I waited for the camel man to return and pondered my scanty options, a car became visible in the distance, picking its way slowly down the same route I had used before going airborne. As it crawled past the driver asked if everything was OK. I said it was, but at the same time instinctively also lifted my elbow for him to see. The spectacularly gory sight inspired instant action, the car coming to an abrupt stop and all its occupants jumping out. I asked if one of them was, perhaps, a doctor, although I didn't think there was much chance of such a stroke of luck ... and next thing I knew I was being inspected by a very concerned Syrian medical man who was currently serving a nearby rural area. Truly, I was blessed with more luck than a man deserves!

The doctor had a suture kit with him, but no gloves. I had no suture kit but I did have gloves, so we pooled our resources and he got busy stitching me up. No anaesthetic, of course, but that was nobody's problem except mine, and it was hardly the most serious. So I sat there like a veritable Rambo while he sewed me together again – although in all honesty it wasn't really all that bad. I think the mere thought of having a needle and cotton piercing your skin and pulling the edges of the wound together is worse than actually having it done to you ... not that I would enjoy a repeat performance, mind you.

Anyway, the doctor finished his stitching, bandaged the arm and told me to have it thoroughly checked out when I got to Djibouti, and I thanked him and the camel man and got going again. But it was a painful business which got ever more painful. I was in serious trouble by the time an elderly American couple drove past an hour later, took one look at me and loaded me into their Land Cruiser for the last 5 km into Tadjoura town. With the pain in my chest I was a man of few words at this stage, but I had not planned to include this section of road around the bay of Ghuobet, so I didn't feel any ethical twinges about missing out on the ferry ride from Obock to Djibouti.

The American couple dropped me at a hotel run by an Italian-Eritrean family, where I asked for a quiet place to recuperate. They must have been touched by my dreadful appearance and obvious pain, because they gave me an air-conditioned room for free. I took more antibiotics and pain pills, set my alarm and went straight to bed. I didn't fall asleep right away because my body hurt all over, but it wasn't long before Nature and the drugs took their course and I passed out.

Next morning I was ready – though only just able – to carry on. I still hurt all over, but Lake Assal beckoned and the combination of a good night's sleep plus the pepper-upper effect of the Game energy drink I knocked back had had such a good effect that I didn't see why I shouldn't reach the lake by nightfall. So I set off, although not before the proprietor's son had made sure I stopped at the local clinic for an anti-tetanus injection.

Lake Assal is three times more saline than normal sea-water, and it was even more impressive than I had hoped. For me, it was not just a question of standing at Africa's lowest point and staring out over the salt-plains. It was about being an astonishing 153 metres below the level of the seas which occupy 70 per cent of our planet. It was a strange feeling to know that the surface of this great mass of water was far above my head and only seven kilometres away, on the other side of a slender mountain. If I hadn't set out from home on this bicycle over a year ago, I thought, I would never be standing here today. That was the bottom line.

Getting back up the 18 km incline back to the main road that night proved near to impossible, mainly because there was a gale-force wind which made forward movement out of the question and would have blown me clean off the bike if it had hit me sideways on. It was by far the most powerful gale I had yet encountered, even worse than the wind in the Moroccan desert, and eventually I spent two pain-filled hours dragging heavy boulders around to build a wall behind which I could pitch my tent. My first attempts to lie inside the tent were futile because the wind squashed the whole of the roof down on to my face and body, but eventually with the wall I managed to make my improvisation work. I just hope subsequent visiting tourists don't get all worked up wondering about which primitive civilisation erected that wall.

Back in Djibouti Jean Pierre's Christine, who is a nurse, looked with concern at the damage to my arm and decreed that I should ask the doctors at the French military hospital for an opinion. In the meantime Jean-Pierre got on to the colonel who commanded the hospital, who happened to be a golfing buddy. It helps to know the right people, because within the hour I was being attended to by the best.

The hospital's surgeon inspected me, confirmed that I had broken my right collar-bone, then opened up the wound, trimmed away some gangrenous flesh (the Syrian doctor had sewn up the wound with the lips of flesh pointing inwards and not outwards, which had hindered circulation) and dug out some dirt that we had missed. Too little flesh now remained for him to stitch the wound closed in the customary manner, so he put a drain in the centre of the wound with a stability stitch across it to make sure the new skin cells grew in the right direction. The doctors, not to mention Christine, were concerned about my taking that kind of injury along to a place like Somalia, so they insisted on my staying on for a few extra days of observation and care. I couldn't argue with that, given the state both Somalia and I were in; getting through it in one piece might well demand an effort that I would not be able to make with an open wound in my arm and a broken collar-bone.

I loafed around Djibouti for a week while I healed, then had a final check-up at the hospital and headed off past the golf course with its clay greens and sandy fairways. Next stop Somalia! I made sure my hard-won visa was within easy reach. But the border post was as far as I got, because a situation which was bizarre even for Africa (where we do some pretty strange things, often without realising it) opened up under my feet. I had a perfectly valid visa for Somalia ... the central, UN-recognised Somalia, that is. The trouble was that Somalia had split in three, and the pieces weren't speaking to one another; in fact they were declared enemies. The northwestern part of the country, which was where I had hoped to enter, had seceded and set itself up as the independent Republic of Somaliland, and another northeastern area had renamed itself Puntland and also taken over control of its own affairs. The irony of all this was that the toothless government of the chaotic central part of Somalia was internationally recognised, while Somaliland, which was relatively stable, was not. My visa was useless!

The Djiboutian army captain at the border agreed to look after my bicycle as I headed back to the capital to tackle the Somaliland representative with the help of Themba and Yvonne. Strangely enough, I wasn't as frustrated as I had been before because I felt I was clearly dealing with serious geopolitical issues, not just simple incompetence and officiousness. Well, I was partly right about that. My plan was for us to launch a full diplomatic effort on the Somaliland representative to convince him that the best course was to make the visa problem go away. Themba agreed with this approach, although he never stopped suggesting that I cut my losses and give up on the entire country. The negotiations started off well, with the Somalilander telling me what the conditions were under which he could grant me a visa, one of which was a letter from Yvonne supporting my cause. Yvonne had to run this past the South African High Commission in Ethiopia, and after nearly $70 worth of faxes and telephone calls I had the support document in my hand. But when I took this to back to the Somalilander, expecting my Somaliland visa to be issued forthwith, he immediately denied everything he had laid out to me and said he needed a letter from Yvonne and nobody else.

Yvonne and I both explained to him that such a letter had to come from her superiors in Ethiopia, but he wouldn't budge. I swallowed my rage at his double-dealing and kept up my polite harassment campaign till he said that he had spoken to his interior minister and had been told that I could enter Somaliland as long as I had a return air ticket out of Somalia. That was more like it! With Yvonne's support I successfully approached Djibouti Air for a return ticket, and three days later I was back with the Somalilander, confident that now, at last, my visa would be in my passport by lunchtime. But now he claimed he had told me that I would have to leave my bicycle behind – which was a damned lie – and did I still insist on taking it along?

It was obvious by now that actually he didn't want to give me a visa to Somaliland and would keep finding new reasons to frustrate my efforts. I was so desperate by this stage that I was willing to go without my bike, then find some way of retrieving it once I had arrived in Somaliland, so I asked Themba to apply a little more official pressure which would include an undertaking that I would leave my bicycle behind. But Themba had had enough of my obduracy and was beginning to worry about my wrangle with the Somalilander turning into a diplomatic incident, and he refused. The fact was, he said, that the Somalilanders weren't sure of my bona fides and didn't want me in their country. I was stunned: what now?

I needed to get my bicycle back again, and got ready to walk the 40 km back to the border post to collect it, but in spite of their exasperation with me Themba and Yvonne kindly offered to drive me there. This was just as well, because when we got to the border the immigration staff wanted to detain me on the spot when they noticed that my visa was due to expire the next day. I managed to get out of that by promising to renew it in the city, with Themba giving his official assurance that he would see it was done.

I was running out of money at this stage, because Djibouti is notoriously 'budget traveller'-unfriendly; every night I spent there was costing me about $25 dollars, including accommodation and food.

Vasti had to transfer $50 to me urgently (at this stage I didn't realise what a run-around I was still going to get from the Somalilander). Normally I would have used Western Union, but Djiboutian controls against money-laundering were so severe that the organisation had closed its doors. My alternative was Moneygram, but here I, too, fell foul of the law. The owner of the Moneygram office told me it was forbidden to transfer money directly to a South African citizen; I would have to find a local to act as the recipient. I said the Moneygram office in Cape Town had told us that proof of identity was all that was needed, and showed him my passport, my ID document and the original letters from South African embassies all across Africa. He was unmoved and actually called the police to check if I was a criminal, but would not contact Moneygram South Africa to see if I was who I said I was.

Rescue came in the form of a larger-than-life character called Said Mokbel, an employee at the United States embassy who moonlighted as a bouncer. Said calmed things down and persuaded the Moneygram man to help me out. But it was a grudging and short-lived relationship, because thanks to the Somalilander's delaying action I had to go back for several more $50 drafts. This got too much for him, and after the fourth transfer he asked me to take my business elsewhere because he did not want to get into trouble with the law.

By now I had had enough of lies, deceit and general shilly-shallying. I would not let myself be stopped from achieving my goal, and if I couldn't get into Somalia by fair means, I would do it by foul. My revised plan of action consisted of three stages, each one dodgier than the last. First of all, I would let no one know what I planned to do. Secondly, I would sneak on to a flight bound for the airport at Hargeysa, using the ticket from Djibouti Air. Thirdly, on arrival I would apply for a visa to Somaliland, on the grounds that I was stranded there, so that the authorities would have no choice but to issue me with one.

I was acutely aware of what might happen, apart from the possibility of getting the chop from ill-intentioned locals. Just for starters, the South African diplomatic representatives might be so irritated by my rashness that they would toss me on to the first flight home, thereby wrecking my entire trip when it was so near to completion. On the other hand, if I didn't risk everything my trip would be a failure anyway. All in all, I was glad that I had purged my system of its pent-up frustration in the Sudan. I needed to be emotionally tough and resolute now, ready to handle literally anything without blowing my top or giving in to despair, because I would be strictly on my own.

I implemented the first stage of the plan by informing a relieved Themba and Yvonne that I had changed my plans: I would probably cycle into Ethiopia and then make my way into Somalia. If not, I would skip the country altogether, as they had suggested; this would protect them from any official backlash. That was it. I didn't even tell Said, probably the only guy I felt I could trust in this city, what I really intended to do.

Disaster nearly struck during the second stage when I got to the airport and had two shocks in rapid succession. Firstly, I found that I had got the departure date wrong and was a day early. Secondly, just about the only other person present was none other than my nemesis the Somaliland representative, ever-present cigarette hanging from his lips, who was there on other business. I stood there with my bicycle by my side, frozen with shock. How could I explain my presence here? Then I collected myself. I would not be intimidated by this purveyor of lies. 'Salaam aleikum,' I said with a suitable air of confidence, telling myself that I had nothing to fear from the arch-prevaricator.

'Waleikum salaam,' he responded around the cigarette. 'Where are you going?'

I thought fast. 'To Ethiopia, I'll apply for a visa there, maybe.' I didn't know if there was an Ethiopian flight that day, but desperate situations require a little risk-taking. He accepted this without demur, no doubt glad to get me out of his hair, so obviously I had guessed right (there was one leaving that very morning, I discovered).

I hid away in the airport building till the Somalilander had left. This unscheduled dress rehearsal made one thing clear. I couldn't take my bicycle with me out of Djibouti; it attracted too much attention and took too much time to process through customs. I would have to leave it behind and then find a way to come back and fetch it.

Next morning I was at the airport nearly two hours before departure, and made sure that I passed through customs before anyone else. Now I had one more obstacle to overcome, namely the Djiboutian immigration people, who would obviously want to know where I was headed and then check my passport for the relevant Somaliland visa, which, of course, I didn't have.

My salvation came in the shape of a young Ethiopian woman in the lobby who was waiting for a flight to Paris to visit her husband. We got to chatting, and I realised that this extremely attractive, constantly smiling girl could be a very good way to distract the attention of the immigration official at the check-in counter from my missing visa.

I bought her a drink at the waiting-area restaurant and then we headed for the check-in counter. My plan was to let her hand over her passport first, then have her wait around while the immigration official cleared me through as well, so bedazzled by her beauty and charm that he would not give my papers more than cursory attention. It worked exactly like that. The official was clearly smitten and kept on looking up and smiling at her as he checked my particulars. I waited, heart in mouth, till he had finished and handed me my passport and ticket with a last smile at my lovely companion.

All I had to do now was avoid the Somaliland representative. Quickly I scanned the destinations board and saw that there was a flight scheduled for Addis Ababa. Right! If I had the bad luck to run across him, I would simply tell him that I had nearly boarded the wrong flight after our last encounter and was actually due to leave today. Well, that was absolutely true, barring a few small lies.

My nerves wound up tighter and tighter as I said goodbye to my Ethiopian guardian angel when she went to catch her flight, and then headed for the boarding gate myself. I was so near to my flight that I could just about smell it, but I wasn't out of the woods yet. Just say the Somaliland representative had smelled a rat and put out an alert for a bearded white man with a bicycle? I shuffled along, expecting some security goon to grab me at any moment and drag me away to the lock-up. Maybe they were scanning the passenger lists at this very moment! I was in the grip of raging paranoia by the time I passed through the boarding gate.

But it was a waste of good adrenalin. I climbed on board with the rest of the passengers, buckled myself into my seat and sat back to enjoy the take-off. The aircraft headed down the runway, tilted its nose and kissed the soil of Djibouti goodbye. I sat back to enjoy a bird's-eye view of the hot and dusty landscape over which I had cycled on my abortive ride to the border, watching the semi-desert of Djibouti turn into the pure desert of Somalia. The Manser Freedom Flight was on its way!

# CHAPTER 28

# SNEAKY STRATAGEMS IN SOMALILAND, AND A NIGHT IN A BODY-BAG

*The nearer I got to Zeila, the more desolate and deserted the terrain became. Now and then I spotted hundreds of camels being herded in the distance, and every so often I would come across one of the battle tanks the Russians had abandoned when they pulled out of Somalia … a reminder, like the peeling Fascist exhortations in that rusty old Eritrean lighthouse, of things done long ago, and ill-done.*

The aircraft landed at Hargeysa and we were ushered to the main airport building, a small structure with goats and sheep grazing peacefully on the lawn around the entrance. There were about 30 passengers, most of whom seemed to be East Africans of one variety or another, a rather scanty number for my purposes.

The aircraft on which I had arrived simply *had* to take off before I reached the counter and the officials discovered my visa problem. If it didn't, my plan to take Somaliland by crook rather than hook was doomed to failure. The international rule was that if you were deported you were sent back to your point of departure, or, as a last resort, your country of residence. I knew that the next flight from Djibouti and back would only arrive in two days' time. So if I ran into problems I would have at least that amount of time to wriggle out of them. It wasn't a very good plan, just better than nothing. But it would not work if that damned aircraft was not off the ground and heading for Djibouti by the time I reached the counter ... and the short line of passengers ahead of me was getting shorter with dismaying speed.

A long wrangle between a passenger and an official would have come in quite handy just then, but of course there was no such crisis, now that I needed one. I decided that I would have to create a distraction of some kind to give the aircraft time to leave, and I would have to move fast: by now there were only two unprocessed passengers left, and on the tarmac the aircrew were *still* milling about and writing on clipboards.

My off-the-cuff plan involved approaching one of the airport staff who was standing among us inside the arrival lounge and asking him how to exchange my money for the local currency. Then I would get into that queue and delay my visit to the immigration desk till the damned plane took off. Now fortune favoured me. The guy's English was very bad, so he told me wait while he fetched someone who could help me. In normal circumstances I would have been irritated by the delay, but not this time. May your steps be slow, brother, I prayed. In due course the official returned with another man in civilian clothes who could speak broken English. I repeated my question about exchanging money, taking my time about it, and he told me that the regulations required all foreigners to exchange a minimum of $50US at the airport before entering the country.

My inner tension subsided slightly now as I saw the aircrew begin boarding the plane at last. But I wasn't out of the woods yet. This stage of the plan would only click in properly once the Djibouti flight had actually left the ground – and in the meantime the immigration official had finished processing the last of the passengers bar myself and was clearly impatient to pack up and leave. I had to stretch things out a little more. Accompanied by my impromptu interpreter, I worked my way into the finance office and addressed the official who was actually exchanging the money. I made a couple of jokes about how broke I was, and how they were forcing me to eat qat for the rest of my life, before producing my crisp $50 note. The money-man joked back, signalling to the immigration official to be patient while he dealt with me.

The plane still hadn't taken off, so I did some more stretching. I asked how many East African shillings there were to a dollar, then got on to the question of whether the rate of exchange outside the airport was different from the one inside. But I had run out of time. The money-man cut the conversation short with the assurance that the rate was the same for the whole country and added I must hurry now, his colleague was waiting.

'Mafe mushkela,' I replied as I was conducted to the glass counter behind which the young immigration guy sat, despondently aware that the plane was still on the ground.

'Passport?' the immigration official asked.

'Oh, my passport! I'm sorry, it's still in my bag,' I said, as convincingly as possible. 'Wait one second for me to get it.' I bent down to scratch around in my bag, as if I didn't know exactly where it was. I suppose I gained all of 10 seconds, and then I was completely out of time-wasting opportunities. The official started to write my passport information into a logbook, but before he had finished he started to page back and forth through my stapled-together collection of temporary passports. At most borders the proof of where I had been validated my story to anyone suspicious of my reason to visit their country, but he was looking for something specific, and I knew what it was.

'Where is the visa?' he asked. I could see he was now impatient and was looking around for someone, probably his superior. I had another quick but desperate inspiration and said that the Somaliland visa must be there somewhere, although I knew very well that this would be strictly a short-term diversion. It didn't hold his attention for more than a moment, and then he sent someone to look for the airport manager.

When the manager arrived I modified my story slightly, apologising for confusing the official at the counter by showing him the Somalia visa and explaining that I had now remembered that the South African Embassy in Addis Ababa had directed me to collect my Somaliland visa here at the airport. How else would I have got through customs at Djibouti? The airport manager was no fool. He stuffed the passport back into my hand and hurried towards the door heading to the runway, shouting something or other as he went. I followed him more slowly and to my immense relief saw the plane lifting off the tarmac and banking away. Saved! For the moment, anyway.

The manager sped back inside and made a quick telephone call before returning to demand my passport. When I had given it to him he told me to remain in the waiting area and rushed away. I obeyed, maintaining my temporary persona of the innocent traveller who had been dropped in the dwang through circumstances which were not only beyond his control but positively incomprehensible to him.

While waiting for the official machinery to grind into life I got to talking with two men who were to become the Somaliland branch of my gang of saviours. One of them was called Xassan (pronounced 'Hassan'), a Somali who had spent 15 years in London running a chauffeuring business with his father. When he learnt of my predicament he summoned a couple of his friends who worked at the airport. One of them was named Shirwa, a cheerful soul with a permanent naughty grin on his face who apparently knew everyone worth knowing in Somaliland and was a personal friend of the son of the governor of Hargeysa. When Xassan had briefed him he started making some calls on his cell phone.

Now the airport manager returned, also glued to a cell phone with which he was conducting an animated discussion. He chatted to Shirwa and then explained that I would not be allowed into Somaliland and had to get out as soon as possible. Shirwa assured him, however, that he would solve the problem; he knew the Interior Minister, the person who decided if people could visit Somaliland or not. This worried me a bit, seeing that the Somaliland representative in Djibouti had claimed that the Interior Minister had been the one who had rejected my original visa application. But Shirwa called the minister to explain who I was and where I came from, and that I had been told to pick up my visa at the airport.

The minister said he wanted to speak to the airport manager, and blasted him with a set of shouted instructions that were audible to everyone in the room. I didn't know whether this was good or bad. Was he saying 'let this man go' or 'clap him in irons'? But Xassan explained that the minister knew all about me and had been expecting me: 'They are privileged to have you in the country, and will make all the effort to make your stay memorable and pleasant.' Next thing I was being chauffeured into Hargeysa and put up in a hotel at the minister's expense. Unbelievable, considering how unpromisingly the whole business had started!

Comfortably and legally settled in, I worked out what was necessarily a complicated travel plan. I would rent a bicycle and travel to the coastal town of Berbera 150 km away, an easy day's ride. From Berbera I would head back to the border with Djibouti, a whopping 300 km which I would have to foot-slog because there were no roads and the tracks were barely negotiable even for a 4x4. All going well, I would arrive in one piece at the town of Zeila, near the border. I would then organise a lift back to Hargeysa and use the other half of my return ticket to return to Djibouti. Having retrieved my bike, I would head straight for the Ethiopian border, from where I would aim for the Ethiopian side of the Somaliland border near Hargeysa. Complicated, yes, but at least the dots would be joined again.

There was no doubt about the fact that this back-and-forthing was going to be a rough trek that would use up two or three extra weeks of my time, but I was in a rebellious state of mind at having to depend so much on the kindness or otherwise of strangers. I needed to get some control over my life again, and in addition the detours would ensure that I stuck to my goals.

Mohammed, the hotel owner, had become fond of me and organised a cheap bicycle rental. It was a little garish for my taste, since it had purple and yellow plastic flowers adorning the handlebars and crossbars, but otherwise it seemed to be in reasonable shape, except that the front and rear shock-absorbers were worn out. I knew this would make my cycling twice as hard, because in such a situation most of the cyclist's power is transmuted into shock absorption rather than forward motion. But needs must when the devil drives.

I set off towards the coast on a full stomach of camel liver and onions, with Xassan's and Shirwa's promises to show me around Hargeysa on my return ringing in my ears. They were two real gentlemen, expecting nothing for their great kindness except my friendship. I hadn't done more than 40 km, however, before I began to vomit continuously. I didn't know what caused this, but suspected the liver. I've never been a great liver fan, but I had always followed the theory that things that were good for you didn't always *taste* good as well. Liver was good food and therefore should be enthusiastically consumed. Well, right now I was enthusiastically reversing the consumption part. At one stage I decided to do some self-filming, but the liver came back to haunt me some more, and what the viewer sees is a revolting sequence showing me leaning forward on those gaudy handlebars with my bulging pack on my back and periodically projecting a spray of nastiness. My only remedy was to drink a large amount of water to prevent dehydration, always a major concern.

After another 60 km the bicycle started to give trouble. As if cycling on a constantly wobbling piece of metal with my knees around my ears was not enough, the front bolt holding the left crank in place kept loosening and had to be tightened up every kilometre or so. This I had to do by hand because my tools were back with my own bike in Djibouti, and it soon became clear that I needed help to get to Berbera.

Once again – how often had this not happened? – I had a stroke of good fortune about 40 km from Berbera when I came across a truck-driver doing repairs of his own. He helped me repair the bike, advised me that it was as well to be off the road after sunset and offered me a lift, seeing that it was almost sunset. I accepted with gratitude; I could come back and cycle this last stretch early next morning.

On arrival in Berbera I presented myself to the area governor, another friend of Xassan and his circle. The governor was very pleasant and helpful. He instructed his police chief to look after me (which among other things included arranging for an air-conditioned mosquito-free room in a friend's hotel) and took me to dinner at a locally famous seaside restaurant where we ate a meal of fish and rice, as typically Somali as the courtesy I had been shown.

I was up early, and in no time had covered the 40 km out to where I had called it off the day before. Within 10 minutes of arrival I was on the way back to Berbera after a passing truck-driver noticed my outstretched thumb and stopped to take me on board. I pondered the universality of signs and gestures as we sped back. How universal were they really? In Nigeria, for example, I had been told that the hitch-hiker's outstretched thumb was a very rude gesture. But apparently not in Somaliland.

I had hoped to start my foot-trek up the coast that afternoon, but the need to repay hospitality could not be denied. The hotel's owner invited me to join him and some friends, rich businessmen who had travelled extensively in places like North America and Europe, for some congenial qat-chewing. I couldn't very well say no, so I spent the afternoon chomping away at a double armful. I decided to pack some for my desert walk the next day: admittedly qat could make you drift away from reality, but it also had this ability to keep you alert and awake. It would be interesting to see how it worked in the field, so to speak.

I was a little sneaky about leaving Berbera. Both the governor and the police chief had strongly advised me against the desert trek, and in fact had told me that they would not allow it. So I was on the road before dawn with 17 *very* heavy litres of water, some tins of sardines and two bags of fresh qat crammed into my backpack. All I needed was to do 60 km a day, so if I kept a steady and relaxed pace of 7 km/h, an average 8–10 hour day would more than suffice. What else would there be to do out there anyway except walk?

I had covered just 15 km when an over-zealous passing taxi-driver, convinced I was a spy of some sort (considering where I was, how I looked and the difficulty of explaining what I was up to, I couldn't really blame him) forced me go with him to the local airport and handed me over to the security staff so that they could take me back to Berbera. The police went over things with me and eventually let me go, the top cop's parting words being: 'It your life, you can do with it what you want. Even if it crazy things.'

I walked on, at one point crossing the longest aircraft runway in Africa, stretching all of 4 140 metres, which had been built by the Americans as an emergency alternative landing site for the space shuttle. Finally I reached the coastal town of Bulxaar (pronounced 'Bulhaar'), about two kilometres from the shoreline. The inhabitants were shocked at my sudden appearance out of the desert with nothing but my bag on my back, thinking I was some sort of apparition, and the children sprinted away from me as fast as they could. But a young man who owned a small house in the town took me under his wing. He understood English fairly well and had interesting stories to tell, among others of the days when, aged just 14, he had used his own boat to run guns from Yemen to the future Somaliland liberators. Now he was retired from the gun-running business and had become a general trader ... and he was still only 21!

Bulxaar was full of other characters, including a 102-year-old man who insisted that I film him running (and he really *could* run, as the video shows) after hearing that a South African held the 100-metre record in the category for centenarians and above. I must bring that man to Bulxaar, he said, so that he could run against him. Not a bad idea, I thought, and asked for proof of his age. The Bulxaarians scoffed good-naturedly at this. People his age who live in deserts didn't have such things, they joked.

Bulxaar was both an old and a new town. Old in the sense that there had been a town named Bulxaar in that area for a very long time; new in the sense that a year or so earlier the original town, which had lain at the sea's edge, had been flattened by a tidal wave. The retired gun-runner took me on a tour of the old town's ruins; the destruction had been so complete that the only structure left standing was part of what had been their new mosque. Did they suffer again on the day of the great Asian tsunami? I asked. Well, they said, the wind had dropped suddenly to a dead calm before returning with gusts such as they had never seen before, and the water had risen slightly more than usual, but it was nothing compared to what had happened to them before. Would the world ever know about the total destruction of old Bulxaar? I doubted it. This really was the back of beyond. The people of Bulxaar would re-tell the story for many generations, but it would never make the pages of the world's media.

Another time I spent the night at a nameless collection of mud huts which housed about eight people, all members of an extended family, I think. Some of them were shocked when I came walking in from nowhere, but calmed down when I indicated in my few words of Arabic that I was on the way to Zeila and wanted only some water and a place to sleep. I spent the night in the open air of the dusty courtyard, my next-door neighbour an old man who appeared to be a criminal of some kind, since he was chained to a large log. He seemed pretty relaxed about it, presumably because he had accepted the community's judgement for whatever crime he had committed. Maybe he had got off lightly and so wasn't complaining. What exactly he had done I didn't discover, because we had too few words in common.

It was wonderful to travel on foot for a change, rather than lug around a bicycle with 45 kg of baggage, but I soon found that temperatures of over 50 degrees Celsius made walking impossible during most of the daylight hours. The way to do it, I discovered, like generations of earlier desert trekkers, was to dig a hole under one of the many big thorn-bushes and lie low during the daylight hours. Around 4 pm I would emerge and walk through to about 3 am, navigating by keeping to the existing tyre-tracks. I also discovered that it was better to stay close to the sea, where it was noticeably cooler. Proof of this was a dramatic reduction in my consumption of water. Walking inland during the day, I would drink about seven litres, but hugging the shoreline and moving in the late afternoon and night brought it down to no more than three litres. I replenished my supplies when and where I could – once from a passing truck – but didn't drink much from the wells of the shoreside settlements I passed through because the water tended to be brackish. And the qat? I never did discover whether it was an aid or a hindrance because, what with one thing and another, I clean forgot about it till I was out of Somaliland. Obviously I just didn't have it in me to be a dedicated qat-masticator.

Spiritually I was not as steady as I had thought, in spite of my self-purging in the airport taxi in the Sudan, and the intense loneliness of the desert probably damaged my fragile balance even further. My true state of mind manifested itself one day when I pulled out my camera for a diary session and had a moment of partial collapse when I started speaking to the camera. I remember making a joke about the Pope being able to watch his own funeral from heaven that day, and commenting on how important he was to world peace. Then I became more serious as I started to recall how I was feeling. I had been very sad the night before – sad because I had not seen Vasti or my best friend for so long, sad because I had tried to call them but neither had answered the call, sad because I was homesick and wanted some familiar people and things around me.

I felt tears well up in my eyes as I tried to articulate all this. My first reaction was to stop the camera and leave the diary session for later. Then I decided to carry on for the same reason that had impelled me to film the blood pouring from my arm after my accident. I wanted to take back a true account of what I had seen and done, and what it had done to and for me personally. 'I just want to go home,' I ended in a strained, crumbling voice. That small handful of words said everything in a nutshell.

The nearer I got to Zeila, the more desolate and deserted the terrain became. Now and then I spotted hundreds of camels being herded in the distance, and every so often I would come across one of the battle tanks the Russians had abandoned when they pulled out of Somalia ... a reminder, like the peeling Fascist exhortations in that rusty old Eritrean lighthouse, of things done long ago, and ill-done.

After four days had ticked by I arrived early in the morning at a transport node which provided rest and refreshment for truck-drivers and other travellers. I found a place that served njera and tea. The owners were very friendly, and through those who understood some English found out where I was from and what I was doing here, namely that I was on my way to Djibouti via Selac. In return I took a few photos of the people and the animals. Some of the locals came to see me for themselves, and suddenly things began turning sour. Before long there were about 30 men watching me drink my tea, and I noticed various distinctly unwelcoming stares. The stares morphed into heated debate, with some of the crowd shouting: 'American, American' in a tone of voice which made it obvious that they were unhappy about my presence. It actually got to a point where the village policeman and some others had to use force to hold back the crowd, some of whose members had taken to shouting insults and spitting at my feet.

Clearly it was time for me to leave, and quickly at that. The policeman wouldn't let me go, though, and took me to a secluded area: one of his supporters explained that he had communicated with his chief in Selac and had been told to keep me safe till a police vehicle could fetch me. The vehicle arrived just after lunch, driven by a policeman who, thank goodness, could speak some English, and after 30 km of severe hassles with various big dunes he delivered me at the front door of the police chief. The police chief explained that the inhabitants of the settlement where I had stopped were supporters of Al-Qaeda and the Islamic Jihad movement, and the more extremist types had begun talking about taking me hostage when the village policeman had intervened.

I was shaken. Man, it's at times like these that you realise how brainwashed some people on this planet are ... and you also realise how naïve some other people are, who do not listen to wiser heads warning them about situations like this. But for that village policeman and his friends I would now be a prisoner, or even a corpse.

The chief handed me a wad of Somali shillings, 50 000, I think, and explained that I had two choices. I could be put on the first truck to Hargeysa; or his men could escort me to the border and explain to the officials here that I wished to collect my belongings in Djibouti city. I thought about it. Going to the border was the riskier of the two options, but if it came off the possibility of returning to Hargeysa with my own bicycle was stronger than ever (considering I now had a visa. So it was obviously worth the risk.

To my pleased surprise the immigration officials on the Djibouti side allowed me through with a firm instruction to revalidate my visa when I got to the capital; perhaps my earlier border hassle had created some sympathy for me. I didn't wait for them to change their minds but struck out on foot for Djibouti city right away. After my trek from Berbera to Zeila I wasn't walking for the enjoyment but to save a little money I might otherwise have spent on transport.

In Djibouti I renewed the visa, collected my bicycle, greeted the people I knew and then negotiated with Djibouti Air about exchanging my unused Hargeysa–Djibouti ticket to one for a flight in the opposite direction. The airlines people didn't kick up a fuss about this unnecessary irritation, just did it, to my everlasting gratitude. The fact is that Djibouti Air played a vital role in the solution of my Somali visa problem. The whole rigmarole had been a waste of energy, and more importantly, time, but it had saved the entire effort to which I had dedicated myself.

I returned to the airport, bike and all, with the serenity that comes of doing something perfectly legal. My only disappointment was the absence of the Somaliland representative who had been the author of all my problems. It would have given me great satisfaction to see his confused little face with its ever-present cigarette goggling at me. Was it immature of me to thirst after such petty revenge? You bet! I had grown to like Somaliland and the Somalilanders, but I didn't like him, and a spot of harmless vengeance is often good for the soul.

This time there were absolutely no visa problems at Hargeysa. Both Xassan and Shirwa were waiting to facilitate my passage through immigration, and a prominent, very influential businessman with whom I had struck up an acquaintance on the aircraft threw his weight behind me as well. The businessman, who owned the largest cigarette-distribution agency in Somaliland, among other things, was much taken with my story and promised to spread the word about me among his associates.

Xassan and Shirwa introduced me to a legendary local character called Mohammed, whom I nicknamed 'Gangster' because of his great fondness for American slang and colloquialisms. Mohammed was partly paralysed in the legs and walked with a cane, the result of being shot in the spine during a gun battle with rebels in the streets of Hargeysa. He actually took me to the spot, next to a dried-out tree, where he had been gunned down and left to die. Taking me there was not something most people in his situation would care to do, but he made light of his physical problems and did not let them slow him down. He put together a television interview deal for me and arranged for it to be sponsored by Dahab Shill and the cigarette company. Dahab Shill was one of Somaliland's best-known business concerns and a pillar of the economy, because of the amount of foreign currency it remitted back to its homeland every year: 'Somalians are all over the world,' as I was repeatedly reminded, which happened to be quite true.

Dahab Shill not only sponsored the TV show, its representatives took me to dinner at a fancy restaurant at the best hotel in the city. All they asked from me in return for their support, they said, was that I tell the world some good things about their country. If only all of us would follow their example and make it our personal responsibility to market our countries to the world! And it's not difficult or expensive either, because the best and most convincing 'sell' stems from your generosity to strangers.

I was also privileged to meet the governor of Hargeysa before cycling out of the city towards Ethiopia. He was genuine and generous, despite our discussion hovering at one point over how South African pilots had apparently been used to bomb Hargeysa in the 1980s. The marks of this destruction were still very visible. Somalis as a group have a certain reputation for deviousness among other East Africans, yet the only devious one I had met had been the liar in Djibouti. It's a place I would like to come back to, and I even made a commitment to Xassan that I would open a business with him one day. Maybe that will really happen.

Somaliland might be mainly a dry place, but on the way to the border post at Tog Wojale I discovered that it could also get awesomely wet. I was hit by a storm of rain which can only be described as 'torrential', so that at one place the floodwater covered the road to a depth of four metres and nearly swept me away. It was simply unbelievable. An hour earlier I had been cycling through bone-dry desert;

now I was faced with what looked like a cousin of the mighty Zambezi. Needless to say, I was soaked to the skin and freezing cold.

I had hoped to cycle a considerable stretch at night, but as this was obviously no longer an option, I pulled in under a large tree which was already sheltering several vehicles. The rains had pulled the temperature down and it was getting cold and dark, but I didn't bother to cover myself up just yet, because I had worked up a good appetite which needed immediate attention. Eating with my hands, I devoured a delicious tinful of oily tuna while torch-beams from the vehicles played on me as their occupants tried to see what I was doing. It could have been a miserable night, but now I deployed my secret weapon, the body-bag Charl Chromhout had given me in Assab. I set up my inner tent portion, which had no protection from the rain but was fitted with gauze netting to keep mosquitoes out, then climbed into my sleeping bag and pulled on the body-bag, zipping everything up except for a small breathing-hole. The rain beat down loudly and so copiously that when I woke up the next morning half the tent was under an inch of water. But thanks to the body-bag I was both dry and warm. If I hadn't had it, a very pitiful creature would have crawled out from under the frame of my old tent next morning.

Tog Wojale consisted of a rather peculiarly placed bamboo boom gate at a river-bed which separates Somaliland and Ethiopia. The boom sat squarely in the road to stop cars, but on either side of it dozens of pedestrians were casually passing back and forth from one country to the other. I suppose I could have tried doing the same, since a cyclist is simply a wheeled pedestrian, but as a matter of protocol I stopped at the frail boom and reported to the sheet-metal office next to it so that I could check myself out of Somaliland and into Ethiopia. One must play the game, after all ... except perhaps if one is lacking a certain visa.

# CHAPTER 29

# FLOODS AND PESKY CHILDREN IN ETHIOPIA

*The calls behind me would fade away as I outdistanced some of my pursuers, but the ones keeping up would continue their shrilling, and they would be echoed up ahead by children (and adults) who had not yet even sighted me. It was strangely frightening to hear the screams of 'you, you, you, you!' from people so far away that they couldn't even see me yet, but who knew from the shrill baying of my pursuers that an unknown sucker was approaching.*

The rain did not abate in this part of the world for two days. Tog Wojale's main street was flooded that morning as I was leaving and the president (as they term him) of the Somali region of Ethiopia was arriving. He was on a campaign trail and received an enthusiastic welcome despite the wet conditions. The route ahead did not get easier, although the sun had dried up the ground near some of the road-verges. I was obviously approaching a natural water-catchment area, and everything else was knee-deep in mud and water.

The roads were almost totally impassable for wheeled traffic, and on several occasions I stopped to help with digging out a vehicle which had sunk down to its chassis. I managed to make some progress by riding slowly on the raised verges when I could and pushing the bike when I couldn't, which was most of the time. In the process I lost my footing numerous times and soon was caked in mud.

One particularly bad stretch nearly defeated me altogether because it was so deep that my bike would have been completely cov-

542

ered by the water, but the kind-hearted driver of a passing UN Land Cruiser came to my help. We loaded the bike and myself into the Land Cruiser and the driver went at the flooded stretch with his foot on the floor. We were about half-way through when he lost control, and the Land Cruiser spun around twice before coming to a stop, securely bogged down. But Land Cruisers are impressive vehicles and the driver was obviously an old hand, so after some manoeuvring he found his way out, although at one stage I could see the water seeping in through the doors' lower edges.

Conditions improved drastically on the last 15 km to Jijiga, but I still needed to concentrate in order to keep going, and often had to get off for some strenuous pushing. Jijiga is a fairly small town, considering its regional importance, but I achieved another short burst of instant fame when people swamped me for autographs after seeing the local newspaper and BBC correspondent taking photographs of me. I also had the privilege of meeting the president of the Somali region, whom I had passed the day before. This was quite flattering, but what really pleased me was finding a room for $3 a night at the local hotel.

Jijiga might be small, but it is not remote in terms of modern communications, as I discovered next morning, when I asked the man in the next room where I could find an Internet café. He told me that he knew of three and offered to guide me to them. We had no luck with the first two, one of which was closed while the other did not have a connection, so we walked into the centre of the town to visit the third, deep in conversation about South Africa and Somalia. I was explaining something or other when he gasped and swivelled his gaze to the area just behind me. I turned to find out what he was looking at, just in time to see a boy of about 10 falling on to his neck and head, then rolling away in a ball of dust as a car sped down the street, presumably after knocking him down. He was conscious and breathing, but I couldn't get him to respond directly to me as I ran my hands over him, checking to see if he had broken anything. A passer-by horned in, grabbing the boy and pulling him to his feet, which was the wrong thing to do, because the boy collapsed immediately. I managed to catch him, but as soon as

I had laid him on the ground his eyes rolled back in his head and he went onto convulsions. I gave my bag to my companion and rolled him into the recovery position, making sure his tongue was out of his throat. This seemed to help, and the convulsions stopped.

At this stage my companion explained that the boy had not been knocked down but had fallen off the back of a speeding pickup. All the young boys who didn't go to school ran errands for businessmen around the town, he explained; they got around by hitching lifts on passing vehicles, and 'they fall all the time'. This was all very well, but I was in a quandary about what to do next. I couldn't see any obvious injury, but I wasn't a doctor. Then, as I felt for the boy's pulse, he started to convulse again.

'Where is a doctor? Call a doctor, someone. Hurry!' I shouted to a group of young men standing to one side. They looked blankly back at me. 'Stop a taxi,' I shouted as I lifted the boy's limp body off the sand-covered concrete, feeling the blood from his grazes seeping into my clothes. 'Where is the hospital? *Is* there a hospital?'

Now a taxi stopped, and I put the boy on the back seat and told the driver to take us to the hospital. Luckily he understood and headed straight there, my companion sitting next to him in front while I stayed at the back with the boy. I still couldn't get any direct response from him, and I was starting to feel panicky. I would probably have felt even worse if I had known that I was about to be exposed to a very ugly face of Africa, the same one that, unfortunately, usually reaches the media.

Things started to go wrong as soon as we arrived at the hospital and discovered that the weed-infested emergency room had no electricity – 'The light only from 8 o'clock,' the duty nurse explained to me as I put the boy down on an ancient examination bed whose white enamel was chipped in many places. Again I made sure he was in a safe recovery position. The nurse was not much concerned about this; what she was really interested in was who was going to pay for the boy's treatment.

With this response it was impossible not to be rude to her. 'Call a doctor,' I told her abruptly. She went off to get him, then returned to her primary interest, namely who was going to pay for the boy's treatment. My companion explained that I was a tourist and that she must not be so concerned over the bill; he and I would help to pay it. At this stage the doctor came in and hooked the boy up to a drip. I tried to tell him what had happened to the boy. But he wasn't interested at all and interrupted me, his palm raised towards me, with: 'Don't explain to me. You can tell police when they come.' Then he handed me a damp piece of cigarette carton with a figure written on it: 100 birr, the equivalent of about 100 South African rands. I was infuriated. Quite apart from the fact that he had not rendered service worth 100 birr, most of the drugs and equipment in the hospital had been donated by agencies from across the world. And he still wanted 100 birr! What for? I told myself to keep my focus on the child and not the money, so I paid him, much as it went against the grain, and continued to sit next to the boy's bed.

An hour later the doctor returned to replace the drip ... and to hand me *another* scrap of cardboard, with '200 birr' on it. 'What for?' I asked. 'Medicine and for stay in hospital,' he responded. This was the last straw. I told him I would pay later, because I wanted to discuss this with my Somali friend first and see what he would do. (The answer was that he would probably have brought the boy to the hospital, but would never have come in with him.) We confidently returned to the nurse and told her that we were not liable for the bill, but that she and the doctor were liable for the child's health; if they had a problem with this, they could call the police, as the doctor had threatened to do at our first encounter. When she relayed this to the doctor, who was now reclining in another room and reading a magazine, he stormed out to ask me why I was not going to pay.

I explained calmly that I was not in any way responsible for the child's injuries and that in fact, although a foreigner, I had helped the boy when no one else in the street had been willing to do so. If he ever came to South Africa, I said, warming to my theme, he would receive free medical treatment at any government hospital if he needed it, not a call to the police. The doctor didn't take the matter any further but turned to my companion and started questioning him in Amharic. My friend started to scratch around in his pocket and I asked what he was looking for. The doctor had ordered him to give him his identification documents, and told him that he would have to deal with the police on my behalf.

Stunned and angered by this cowardice and misuse of authority, I told my friend to put his wallet with his ID card away and go back to the hotel at once. Keeping my eyes fixed on this so-called doctor, I told him that my companion and I barely knew one another and demanded that he telephone the police immediately to come and resolve the matter, and while he was about it also to produce a receipt for my payment with a breakdown of the costs. I made a last check of the boy's condition and then left, saying I would be back next morning to see how he had been treated. A few minutes later I caught up with my friend, and we hailed a donkey cart back to the hotel because, as I explained to him: 'Saving Ethiopia is a pricey business. I have to save money where I can.'

When I returned to the hospital at seven o'clock the next morning the boy's bed was empty. The nurse – the same one I had had dealings with the day before – told me that the doctor had discharged him an hour after my friend and I had left. I left it at that, relieved that the boy was OK, but I couldn't help thinking that the doctor would have tripled his treatment if he knew I was shelling out the cash.

A husband-and-wife business team I met at the roadside when I headed out of Jijiga towards Harar washed some of the bad taste out of my mouth. I'm hard when it comes to lazy people who expect help all the time, but I can't help coming to the aid of those who, as the cliché goes, help themselves. The husband was a bicycle mechanic and his wife a tea-lady, their stalls right next to one another, so while I enjoyed the wife's dumplings and sweet tea, he repaired my chain, which was beginning to fall apart. I made a mental commitment as I sat there: I would try to get sponsorship to provide this humorous and hard-working man with professional bicycle-repair tools and a decent covering for his work area.

I left Jijiga in the late afternoon. The rain had now been well and truly left behind, and dust filled my throat on the gentle but apparently endless climb that lay ahead. It was up and down all the way as the road dodged in between rocky outcrops. I spent the night in a tiny mountain town with a distinct Wild West atmosphere which rejoiced in the name of Babile, pronounced 'baaabli', and I found the solution to a small misapprehension I had not known I was labouring under. Starting in Somaliland, I had been drinking a mixture of Coke and a type of carbonated water which was sold everywhere in large 500 ml bottles. I thought it was called 'Bubbly', and nothing had happened to make me change my mind – every time I went into a bar and ordered a small Coke and a bottle of 'Bubbly' they knew exactly what I was talking about. Not having a map, I usually didn't know exactly where I was unless it was clearly spelled out, and it was only when I arrived here that I realised my current favourite drink was actually called 'Babile', because this was where it came from. So visitors to Ethiopia who order 'bubbly' and get soda water, be warned – the locals aren't trying to crook you, they're giving you exactly what you asked for.

The road from Babile to the third holiest town in the Islamic world, Harar, was pure torture, not just because of the never-ending inclines and gripless dirt roads but also because of the excessive Algerian-style heat, which climbed into the mid-40s and was accompanied by great humidity that had me sweating out a few litres every morning before I even stopped for brunch. And this was not the only challenge I encountered.

At one point, as I struggled up a steep, winding road towards a small village, I caught up with a bunch of cattle being herded by a wrinkled old hunch-backed lady armed with a long stick of sugarcane, only to be charged and butted right off my bike by a young bull who had decided to take matters into his own hands. Then, having knocked me down, he stood over my bike and tried to force his nose into one of the panniers, while the herder beat him on the nose with such wild enthusiasm that she nearly gave me a thrashing as well. I managed to dodge the swing of the sugar cane and jumped back on the bike, indicating that I was OK. Then the bull decided to charge me again! Oddly enough, I wasn't concerned for my safety – I was more interested in getting it all on videotape. This was the reality I wanted the people at home to see!

En route the weather changed abruptly once more, and I arrived in Harar in pouring rain the following day. There I found a journalist who was hoping to interview me for the local newspaper. I obliged, as long as they found an affordable hotel with a warm shower for me. They found a hotel, but it didn't have warm water, so I did the interview still covered in travel-dirt.

I was trying to get to grips with Amharic now, which was no joke – try casually tossing off 'amassegeneloh' every time you want to thank someone. Having prided myself on my ability to pick up snatches of the languages I had encountered so far, it hurt that 'amassegeneloh' defeated me, and every attempt amused whoever I was saying it to. I wondered morosely why there couldn't be a universally accepted rule that general greetings and niceties be restricted to one or two syllables only.

I worked hard at that one diabolical word during the 750 km ride to Addis Ababa – mainly in sopping wet conditions – but only acquired a sore throat and a Rod Stewart voice for my pains. On the other hand, I was back on a tarmac surface, my body felt good and the mountain-ranges of eastern Ethiopia were spectacular, with views that made every drop of sweat I expended worthwhile. It felt like years since I had last averaged over 20 km an hour during a day's ride. I felt upbeat, too, because I sincerely believed that the infuriating delays of the northern African region were a thing of the past. I would be home almost before I knew it!

I was in a hurry now, because I had a date in Addis Ababa. Originally I had intended to turn southwards at the town of Mojo (that's right, 'Mojo') and by-pass Addis, which was another 200 km down the road, because I had been told that I would be able to get a visa for my next country, Kenya, at the actual border post. But H.W. Short, a keen 4x4 adventurer who was the South African minister to the African Union, had invited me to be a guest at our embassy at the yearly democracy celebrations. I really wanted to do this, as it meant that I would be in Addis by midweek. I would be able to get my passport in at the relevant embassies before the Friday and not waste a weekend, as I had so many times before.

So I was pressed for time. I would have just a day and a night to

cover the 200 km through mountainous terrain along a road littered with police anti-smuggling roadblocks. I decided that I would
be able to do it, though, if I set out on an all-nighter; I was confident that if I could get fairly near to Addis I would be able to cadge
a lift for the last hour or so of travel. When I had finished with
Addis I would have to backtrack to Mojo and re-start my journey
southwards. This was a nuisance, but backtracking was nothing
new to me.

Thanks to my mapless state I started off by wasting an hour's
worth of time and energy on the wrong road, but then I got back on
track, so to speak, and slogged my way through the mountains and
the persistent rain, taking the downhills more slowly than I would
have liked because I was determined not to fall again any time soon.
There was a never-ending stream of trucks heading eastwards to
Addis, but the road was getting better as I approached the capital,
although also steeper and more slippery, and became much quiet-
er as night fell. But I enjoyed cycling through the night. Each lorry that approached from either side would somehow segment the
pain and fatigue I was enduring, and I kept up my motivation by
setting small goals to be completed and imagining the subsequent
rewards in vivid colour. The final reward would be arriving in Addis
and indulging in whatever luxuries presented themselves to me.

So time and distance gradually marched on, my progress unbro-
ken except for the time my over-full bladder provided me with a
small but unique memory to take home with me.

Absolutely desperate for a pee, I stopped at a village whose buildings literally – and very dramatically – hung out over the steep cliffs
and banks of the mountain range I was passing through, held up
only by thin bamboo stilts. I asked the first shopkeeper I saw where
the nearest toilet was, and he directed me to a narrow alley in between his shop and his next-door neighbour. Little suspecting what
awaited me, I forced my way through it and found myself teetering
on the rocky edge of a precipitous drop. I was risking a fall to my
death because of my brimming bladder! I backtracked as quickly as
the claustrophobic alley allowed, making no secret of my feelings
about this near-fatal attempt to splash my boots.

The shopkeeper found this fairly hilarious, shared the joke with the other villagers and then waved me back to face my demons and do the necessary. I was so desperate by now that I went back, looked those demons in the eye and made my donation to the Ethiopian water table. But that is not the unique memory I mentioned earlier. Precarious though it was, my perch gave me the best view anyone has ever had while taking a roadside piddle: a network of valleys, running together so that the end of one was the beginning of another, weaved between the green mountains far below me, the sun's shadows turning it all into an incredible three-dimensional image. It was one of those scenes beyond the ability of any camera to capture in its entirety. Relieved in both mind and body, I couldn't help thinking that although it had been a somewhat nerve-racking experience, there was surely no other place in the world where a roadside urinator could come closer to the majesty of nature. Maybe, I thought with a rush of crazy humour, I should establish a website about this place to share my thoughts with like-minded people. I could give it an address like www.theworldsgreatestspot2pee.com.

Around midnight, after cycling for nearly 12 hours flat, I got to a roadblock at a town called Awash, from where I planned to hitch a ride through to Addis, 165 km away. Fortunately the policeman at the roadblock happened to be the most senior one in the region, and he instantly organised a lift for me by the simple expedient of picking out a lorry-driver and instructing him to get me to Addis that very night, and no arguments. The driver was quite amenable (for reasons I discovered much later), and soon we set off on what one could call an interesting trip in its own right. The driver and his assistant chewed up bag after bag of qat, and whenever we came to a drinking-hole they pulled off for a couple of beers with various other drivers who were doing likewise. The fact that drinking and driving was a criminal offence just about everywhere in the world didn't seem to bother anyone.

As a result of these frequent pauses for refreshment it took us five long, tiring hours to get to the point where the sprawling capital came into view in the first light of day, the scores of tall, beautiful old churches elegantly catching the first rays of sunlight on their steeples. Instantly I took Addis to my heart, because for some reason it had the most comforting and welcoming feeling of any of the cities I had passed through up to now. As we drove into the city I noticed runners everywhere. Of course! They were contenders for the Olympics, where Ethiopia has more or less had squatter's rights on medals for running since before I was born.

In spite of having been press-ganged by the cop at Awash the driver was kind enough to drop me off at the gates of a small hotel very near the embassy as soon as he and his mate had made a quick business stop in a dark and secluded residential area. There they armed themselves with long screwdrivers, and for a moment I thought my last moment had come. But I need not have worried. These guys were businessmen, not muggers, and I soon saw the nature of their business when they unscrewed the door panels and radiator grille, hauled out about 200 boxes of 35 mm Kodak film and stuffed them into a black plastic bin liner. No wonder he had fallen in so readily with the top cop's demand at Awash! I sat on the front seat while all this was happening, making a maximum effort to portray a man innocently minding his own business and shooting reassuring smiles at them, since they were obviously worried and kept glancing nervously up and down the street as they worked. I realised that I was an accessory in a way, but I wasn't too upset, seeing that a live accessory was better than a dead victim any day of the week.

I remembered having heard that Tog Wojale is the gateway to Africa for contraband items from Dubai via Somalia. In Berbera the shelves of the market stalls had been packed with digital cameras, 35 mm film and CD players. I had bought a Nokia 1100 for $40!

The celebration at the Inter-Continental hotel was fine but something of an ordeal, as I was now rather run down after a sleepless night, 40 straight hours of travelling by bicycle and truck, five beers and two smugglers. But our people in Addis could not have been more generous in temporarily adopting this rather ragged pilgrim whom circumstances had washed up at their door. H.W. Short was an influential guy and exactly the right general to wage war on my remaining visa problems (it also turned out he was a friend of Vasti's father, who was the South African ambassador in Jordan and regularly travelled to Addis Ababa for African Union meetings).

My good fortune just went on and on. A husband-and-wife team at the embassy, Albert and Mandy, not only put me up but pulled off something so miraculous that I had difficulty in believing that it was really happening. I had told them at length about how I had not seen Vasti for more than a year and how homesick I was, and how much I would have liked to meet her somewhere along the rest of my trip back to Cape Town. This sad tale really went to Mandy's tender heart, and she took direct action without wasting any time on delicate manoeuvring. She literally cornered the ambassador at an official function they were attending and asked him if they could use some of the embassy's accumulated Voyager miles to help out. Aware of my journey and its associated tribulations, he didn't hesitate to give his approval, which Mandy triumphantly announced to me on her return from the function.

To me it was like a dream. I had so little money that buying an air-ticket for Vasti to visit me was merely a lovely vision that I had played and replayed in my mind when I needed some perking up. And now, all of a sudden, it was actually going to happen! I had been to 30 countries in Africa and we could only share stories about two of them, Senegal and Mozambique. Now the legendary land of Ethiopia would be added to the list.

Mandy made the booking for a date that suited Vasti, incidentally including her birthday! She was a very junior member of the law firm where she had been articled and in normal circumstances might have had problems in getting away for eight days at short notice, but luckily her bosses had been following my journey in the newspapers and felt somewhat compelled to let her go. H.W. and his colleagues also got in on the act by arranging with the local Hilton Hotel in the capital to treat us to five nights of luxury when Vasti arrived (I couldn't help grinning at the thought of how surprised Vasti would be, since she knew that I had just about no spending money). She would be even more surprised with her birthday present, a visit to a most peculiar tourist attraction at Harar. It would be a tough surprise, a 17-hour ride (one way) by minibus taxi from Addis to Harar, but there was so much I wanted her to see. I wanted to show her how I was living, suffering and missing home, which was hard to communicate in an SMS or during a two-minute telephone conversation. In the meantime I prepared to fill in the blank spots on my itinerary by getting me and my bicycle back to the other side of Awash as soon as possible, cycling the bit I had traversed with my boozy, qat-chewing smuggler friends. If all went well, I'd then continue south till a day before Vasti arrived before re-tracing my steps to meet her at Addis's airport.

The terrain after Awash had now levelled out drastically and allowed me to make rapid time on the good Ethiopian roads. The Awash area, incidentally, was where they found 'Lucy', the oldest known humanoid fossil, which dated back about 3.2 million years. Why the most un-Ethiopian name of Lucy? Well, it seems that someone kept playing the old Beatles hit 'Lucy In The Sky With Diamonds' while she was being uncovered. Things like this, and the famous hand-carved churches in Lalibela, would have made great sights for Vasti to see when she came, but I knew we wouldn't have the time. I reckon that Ethiopia could make tourism earnings an easy 10% of its GDP. Coffee was already earning the country a stable income, and, of course, many farmers did well out of raising the tons of qat which kept Djiboutians in their pleasant daze.

Ethiopia conjures up images of famine in many people's minds, and I had psyched myself up to be strong when I passed through this country of dying and starving millions. Having a soft heart for children, I did not know if I would be able to handle it when the first bloated-stomached, bulging-eyed child lifted his arms toward me. Fortunately this is exactly not what I encountered.

Up to this stage I had been too preoccupied with the question of getting home to take in as much of the country as I should have, but now I was more relaxed and began to notice things ... and two of them were fairly negative.

The first was the Ethiopian children's unrelenting begging. Children who were clearly not abjectly poor, and were healthy and fit by African standards, begged non-stop whenever they saw a white foreigner like me. It would start with a painfully loud, monotonous chant of 'You, you, you, you, you, you, you, you, you, you, you, you' till eye contact was made, when the chant would turn into something more specific: 'Money, money, money, money, money, money!'

Ethiopia's juvenile beggars – and their tendency towards hostility if they do not get any money – are notorious in world cycling circles. While researching about cycling through Ethiopia in preparation for my trip I had come across story after story in which foreigners expressed their dislike of the country, and I think it was mainly because of the child-beggars.

The children were just the lowest layer of a culture of begging that starts right at the top. I suspect the begging culture was begun and fostered by the government during the horrific famine of the 1970s, when the UN came to the rescue. I don't intend to get into a blame game which would inevitably end up as a colonial-versus-colonised argument, even though Ethiopia is the only African country except Liberia that was never colonised. All I'll say is that in my opinion the automatic begging has become a habit which is based on a culture of false entitlement, the basic tenet of which is that 'The white man has everything and will give it away because it means little to him.' It infuriated me to realise that these children's parents openly encouraged them to chase after me, demanding money.

I blame the nation's leaders for allowing Ethiopians with their traditional culture of reliance on solving their own problems to metamorphose into a nation of mendicants whose comfortable, well-fed rulers' greatest talent lies in their ability to compile yearly cash wish-lists. There is no way that a child learns the art of begging while building sand-castles or herding goats, and adults don't succumb to the something-for-nothing allure all on their own either. Someone shows and encourages them, indirectly or otherwise.

Nowhere in any of the 29 countries I had visited so far in 18 months of travel had I come across land as fertile as what I was seeing now, the soil virtually bubbling with vitality as the ploughs carved their way through the fields. The moisture and life in the air was crisp and tangible. The cattle were fat and had gleaming coats, a stark contrast to the ones I had seen elsewhere. I was shocked at how far the real Ethiopia was removed from the one I had learned about as a child. Two sayings that were drummed into my generation while we were growing up were: 'Don't waste your food, think of all the hungry children in Ethiopia,' together with 'This looks like something out of Beirut' when you wanted to describe a battered old building. But now it was all beginning to make sense to me. Beirut, so I had discovered from my friend Paul Azzo and others, was an incredibly modern and developed city. The areas damaged in the civil war had been rebuilt, so that it did not consist of the bombed-out set of ruins we had seen on TV as children. As an African I had anticipated being shocked by the famine conditions that allegedly existed in Ethiopia, but the shock was actually seeing well-fed kids begging as if they had not had a square meal for a month ... and being encouraged by their parents.

I pitied those kids, knowing that the belief that people should give you something for nothing simply because you demanded it would become engrained into their psyches and cripple their spirits forever. I thought of my own intermittently difficult childhood, in which I had had to fend for myself because I had known that no one was going to do things for me, that I had no one I could count on unconditionally. The result was that I did not grow up with a something-for-nothing mindset, and the 'make a plan' attitude manifests itself in everything I do. I realised now what a valuable gift it had been, no matter how sad it had made me feel at times, which is why I wanted to see people standing up and doing things for themselves, like that bicycle mechanic and his tea-lady wife in Jijiga. I wanted my continent to pull itself out of its pit by righting itself and encouraging its people in places like Ethiopia to change their own lives themselves, without waiting for someone else to fill their outstretched hands with food or money or both.

I had met many selfless United Nations field workers who had dedicated their lives to improving the lot of their fellow humans, but I also realised that higher up the tree the UN was a bloated, directionless organisation whose funds were more likely to go towards lining the pockets of certain individuals than to help the desperate people who needed assistance. As originally envisaged it had been a wonderful concept, but in most cases it has not been successful in achieving its goals (let me be the first to add that there are some shining exceptions to this), so that instead of solving problems it has either given up on them or merely provided temporary relief without trying to bring about a permanent solution. The war in Iraq would never have taken place if the UN had faced up to its responsibilities regarding Saddam Hussein's blatant flouting of the oil-for-food programme to line his own pockets, and something concrete would have been done about the plight of the people in Darfur and Zimbabwe a long time ago.

Perhaps I sound a bit too vehement about this, but my experiences on the ride to Addis are very vivid in my memory. Every time I approached a mountain village I would be greeted by shouts of 'You, you, you, you!' This would build into an ear-splitting chorus as children with their schoolbooks under their arms would start running next to me, sometimes for kilometres at a time, falling behind on the downhills but catching me again on the uphills.

The 'you, you, you, you' would start turning into 'money, money, money, money' in a sort of relay. The calls behind me would fade away as I outdistanced some of my pursuers, but the ones keeping up would continue their shrilling, and they would be echoed up ahead by children (and adults) who had not yet even sighted me. It was strangely frightening to hear the screams of 'you, you, you, you!' from people so far away that they had couldn't even see me yet, but who knew from the shrill baying of my pursuers that an unknown sucker was approaching.

As I headed down to Shashamane on the final stretch to Addis the shrieking changed to chants of 'ferangi' (Amharic for white man, one of the first words an Ethiopian child learns), 'ferangi, ferangi, ferangi!' in between the calls of 'money, money, money, money!' I had been critical of the harsh reports I had read about Ethiopia on the Internet and in cycling magazines, believing that the writers were ignorant of African ways. Now I saw that I was wrong, and although I wasn't stoned, as some writers reported had happened to them, I couldn't wait to get out of the country.

Now and again some children would leave off chanting to ask: 'What is your name?' or 'How are you?' At first such interludes were a pleasant break in the non-stop pan-handling. Then I saw their blank stares when I replied. Clearly they did not have a clue about what I was saying; they had learnt the greetings parrot-fashion as part of their begging technique.

What made it even worse was that I was having serious trouble with my bike's chain. Locally available ones were poor quality and simply not up to handling the stresses resulting from the exceptional hills and the heavy load, so in town after town I would have to stop and fit a new chain, invariably surrounded by a crowd whose members either stared at me or chanted 'You, you, you, you ... money, money, money, money!'

My second negative impression came from the prostitution I found at every hotel I stayed at. It was so blatant and unapologetic that I was flabbergasted. The girls, some very attractive, did not approach foreigners easily, but wrestled each other to get to any local truck or car stopping outside the entrance. On the other hand, I must point out in all fairness that thanks to my slim purse I had to stay in the cheaper 'hourly' hotels, which were the prostitutes' natural stamping-grounds. They all had exactly the same look and modus operandi, and I became so attuned to my environment that before long I could spot a 'my price' kind of hotel from afar; 'my price' meaning an establishment with a room for about one US dollar a night, which meant that I could afford a decent dinner.

Naturally there were certain disadvantages, since the hotels' main source of income obviously wasn't from their rooms. The hotel I stayed at in Mojo, for example, had a raucous disco attached which kept me awake till about 10 pm, in spite of the fact that I was very tired. Then flesh and blood would not be denied any longer and I passed out, but around 3.30 next morning there was a loud banging on my room's thin wooden door. I woke up alarmed and disorientated, then gathered my wits and shouted: 'Go away, I am sleeping!'

This had no effect and I repeated myself several times, louder and louder. Then I heard a woman's voice from behind the door, saying: 'Please, please!'

'Go away, go away!' I responded.

'But I am cold and I want to get warm,' she replied. Later I was able to laugh about this ingenious approach, but just then I wasn't in the mood for Ethiopian prostitute charm and suggested she get her own one-dollar room – a silly suggestion, of course, since as a house employee accommodation was not her problem. But that did the trick and I could get back to my brutally interrupted rest.

The 'bar girls', as they were called, were such an integral part of the scene that everyone who heard where I had slept asked if I had seen them pursuing their trade. It created a perception in my mind that was not an accurate reflection of Ethiopian society.

But now the time had come to take a break from bar girls and biking to return to Addis for Vasti's arrival. Mandy and Albert drove me out to the airport in lots of time; I was in a daze as we checked on the arrival time of the Ethiopian Air flight from Johannesburg – I still couldn't quite believe that I would soon be seeing Vasti in the flesh. Mandy was in a justifiably good mood at seeing all her hard work about to culminate in such a grand fashion, and she was obviously savouring every moment of the occasion.

I wish I could say I thrilled Mandy by collapsing with overwhelming emotion the moment I spotted Vasti, but I didn't. I stood behind the glass separating us, thinking about how much we needed this meeting to lift our spirits. It was a tough burden that I had laid at her feet, something that most relationships would never survive. But ours had survived, and leaving Vasti back home, all alone and never knowing from one day to the next whether I was even alive, was the only thing I regretted about my journey.

The Hilton hotel provided the most amazing luxury I had experienced so far. I know that everything was relative in respect to my drastically lowered current standards, but even so, we had an unforgettable time. It is the older of the two five-star hotels in Addis, but it was definitely the more alluring, with a character all of its own. You felt as if the very chairs and tables had a charming history attached to each of them.

Like many other people, Vasti and I both believe that essentially any hotel is just a room to sleep in; what puts some apart from the others is the breakfast it offers ... and the Hilton's breakfasts were unmatched by any we had ever had before. All this time later, I can still almost taste those morning repasts – a wide array of fruits and cereals, then warm dishes, whose contents seemed crisper and more intense in taste and flavour than we had experienced at any other hotel: fresh-picked fruits, juice that had just been squeezed, omelettes delicately wrapped around fillings of green peppers, onions, mushrooms and ham.

We didn't spend much time talking over breakfast, just ate, drank, smiled and held hands, savouring the fresh 'just rained' smell of the gardens which ran down from the dining area to the hotel's warm baths. Then we would work off these massive breakfasts by playing putt-putt, swimming in the steaming heated pools or knocking a ball around on the tennis courts. We would have spent more time outside the hotel, but the elections were coming up soon and the streets were crammed every day with hundreds of thousands of demonstrators marching for or against one or other issue.

The day that the government allocated to a march by the official opposition was an amazing spectacle for both of us. From our balcony we could see how jammed every road leading down to Meskel Square was with peaceful demonstrators, mostly young people and students. The newspapers estimated that there were hundreds of thousands coming together, and it certainly looked like it. Vasti and I, ignorant of all the implications, went down to the foyer with the intention of taking part in the march, but we decided not to get involved when some of the hotel staffers warned that we might be in danger, not from the marchers but from the police. They explained that the government was embarrassed by the level of the public's discontent with its leadership and would respond in one of two ways. In the first scenario the police would 'oversee' the march to show the world how considerate they were of true democracy, but if the crowd lingered too long it would be dispersed by brute force, the government justifying its actions by claiming that it had been forced to step in because of the anarchic nature of the opposition.

When we went to walk about a little later we had some friendly and entertaining interactions with the marchers as they streamed back past us after being dispersed by the ever-present police. They were still in high spirits; everyone was showing the famous Churchillian 'V' sign, and they kept on pretending to spray us with an aerosol bug-killer, accompanied by a broad smile and the necessary 'ssshhhhhhhhh'. It turned out that the ruling party's symbol was a bee, and as far as the students were concerned, this particular bee was a pest which it was their job to eradicate. They were confident that it could be done; after the election, many told us, the government's bee would turn into a fly.

That day and the following three we spent on exploring the city. I introduced Vasti to awesomely tasty Ethiopian dishes like 'tibs' (mince) and njera, and showed her how cheap everything was by our standards. Vasti enjoyed what she experienced of Ethiopia, more than she had enjoyed Senegal. The country had a culture, she said, which was evident in everything its people did, be it singing, eating or dancing. It was all Ethiopian, through and through. If Vasti had not been there with me I wouldn't have seen Ethiopia as I did now. The music alone would have been just another way to describe the culture, but now we searched the market for cassette tapes featuring the famous Ethiopian singers Gigi and Teddi Afro. I would never have done anything like that if I had been alone and frustrated.

Then it was time to set off for Harar so that Vasti could get her surprise birthday present (it was a surprise for me too, as it turned out), something that I hoped she would remember for ever. Just getting to it was something of an experience – a day-long ride in a crowded mini-bus taxi, followed by a sleep-over at the town of Nazareth in a hotel room which also accommodated thousands of small cockroaches (still, better than what I was used to!).

The fun part included giving her a chew of qat, but the main attraction would be seeing what is probably Africa's most peculiar tourist attraction, Harar's famed 'hyena men'. These gentlemen had cultivated a special relationship with the huge hyenas that lurked on the city's outskirts, and those tourists brave or crazy enough to go out on their excursions are given the opportunity of feeding raw meat to wild, fully grown, foul-breathed hyenas ... mouth to mouth. I admit that this was not the sort of birthday present one would ordinarily give to your ordinary South African girl, but then Vasti was no ordinary girl.

As we retraced the route I had cycled I was able to show her exactly what it took for me to get around the continent, and I saw immediately that her understanding of my daily suffering was taking on another dimension. Creating a vague idea of your experience in people's minds through the written word is one thing, but having them witness it at first hand is something else altogether (incidentally, Vasti also became the only other person in the world to have the privilege of seeing where I had had my nerve-racking but inspiring 'pee with a view').

On arrival in Harar we booked into a small hotel and found a guide who would take us and a handful of other tourists to the steep-sided ravine on the outskirts where the hyenas were fed after being lured out of the deep shadows they liked to use for their approaches. It was a strange business, which started with a seated 'hyena man' calling to them by name, recognising each one because of its unique markings. There was a sort of relationship or mutual understanding between man and beast; it seemed to me I could see the two hyenas who cautiously approached responding to the change in his tone of voice.

The hyena man invited any bold spirits to come and join him as he draped some meat on the point of a bamboo stick about 10 cm long and started feeding the bigger of the two, which I guessed was a female, since females are said to average 10 kilos heavier than the males, which normally weigh in at around 55 kilos. I wouldn't have put my head on a block about this because hyena sexuality is a strange business – I remembered reading about how hyenas were the transsexuals of the animal kingdom because the female genitals resemble those of the males, with some parts taking on positively phallic proportions.

I didn't get the chance to confirm this now, though, and didn't even try, because I had more pressing matters to worry about. Being a card-carrying adventurer, I felt obliged to step forward when the hyena man called for volunteers, although I wasn't too happy when I thought back to my earlier encounters with their desert colleagues. I could also not help noticing that except for Vasti, who was close behind me with the video camera at the ready, none of the others had taken up the hyena man's invitation.

I started off by holding out the meat-draped piece of bamboo in my hand. This worked out all right, but then I found myself nervously clenching the stick in my mouth while the hyena returned for another snack. The thought of the hyena snatching the meat from the bamboo stick, her beady eyes a mere 10 cm from my face, wasn't a happy one, but adventurers have to do what they have to do. This hyena was just as suspicious of me as I was of her, though, and I remembered being told that they were considerably more intelligent than dogs and therefore built up a memory of their interactions with humans. That suited me fine: with any sort of luck this particular hyena had been involved in the tourist trade for a long time and knew better than to eat the paying customers.

The hyena took her time sizing me up, then lunged forward and snatched the meat off the bamboo, moved off a few paces and set about eating her meal, her eyes staying firmly on me. It was a wasted effort, since I had absolutely no intention of trying to get it back.

Considerably relieved with the happy ending to my ordeal, I offered Vasti a chance to take my place. She declined twice, politely but firmly, but I persisted, because I really wanted us to share this strange experience that we had travelled such a long, hard way for. Eventually I prevailed, helping her with a few encouraging pushes to get her in front of the only remaining hyena, the other having sloped off. I don't believe that Vasti was afraid: it was more a case of her logic telling her that this was an unnecessary risk which was not going to prove anything to anyone, which was quite true. But when her face lit up with excitement as the hyena snatched the first piece of meat from the point of her stick I knew I had been right to insist.

Her excitement continued to buzz long after we were done, and I believed she was feeling the kind of energy which had helped me to survive during the more gruelling parts of my journey, and I was deeply grateful that I had had an opportunity to make this selfish journey of mine more memorable and real to her. And it really did. The visit and the encounter with the hyenas made her understand why I had left everything to do what most people thought was crazy, and in which she had loyally supported me because she had realised how important it was to me.

The chewing of the qat, on the other hand, was a non-event. The fact that it held a sizeable chunk of Africa in thrall and probably influenced political events didn't impress her. She chewed a few leaves and then gave up because, she said, it just plain tasted too bad. So in an instant qat's legendary powers of enslavement evaporated before the taste-buds of one down-to-earth girl from Cape Town.

We returned safely to Addis the following day after another gruelling taxi ride, and put the Hilton's warm baths to good use to get the knots out of our overtaxed muscles and brain. I lay there, filled with a mixture of emotions: sadness because Vasti was leaving next day, joy that I had had the immense good fortune of seeing her, gratitude towards the South African diplomats who had made it all possible and in the process done more for me than they would ever know.

Vasti and I went especially early to the airport so that we could take our time about sharing a last meal of Ethiopian njera, meat and vegetables before she boarded her flight. Unlike Dakar the airport building would not allow me to watch the take-off, so I said goodbye to her in the terminal and promised to be home in a few months. Then she was gone, and I returned to my ever-present visa worries. But our people in Addis had the visa situation well in hand, and a few days after I had handed on my passport it came back with the visas in it. These days, I was told, entry requirements for a South African visiting various countries in East Africa tended to be little more than a formality, so much so that a visa to enter Mozambique would soon be waived altogether under new Southern African Development Community rules (I just hoped the rules would come into effect before I reached the Mozambican border).

The aim of these rules, I knew, was to allow a free back-and-forth flow of travellers such as one finds in the European Union, but I didn't know whether the idea would please ordinary South Africans, who tend to worry about floods of economic refugees, an unpleasant prospect in view of the country's high unemployment figures. As it was, there had already been many incidents of strong hostility to foreigners in black communities.

Thinking about things like this made me wonder whether I was going to recognise my country when I returned: for all I knew, her political, sporting and economic landscape had altered drastically in my all-but-two years of travel. With these thoughts, I was back on the road after renewing my Ethiopian visa with the help of kind Ethiopian people like Hewan Retha, a girl I met at the Department of Foreign Affairs.

Both my bicycle and I looked a bit different. I had had a barber in Addis trim off the bushy beard I had cultivated for nearly a year, which had got so long that during Vasti's visit I had been reduced to the embarrassing stratagem of pinning it under my chin with hairclips. My bike too had had a face-lift; among other things she had a new aluminium rear baggage rack, because after 25 000 km-plus of tough going the old one had reached the point where all the cable ties and chewing gum in the world could not hold it together any more. I thought to myself that whereas I might not be a perfect poster-boy for a sunscreen ad, I was certainly the guy you wanted for promoting that particular brand of carrier.

The first thing I had to do was catch a lift to where I had temporarily halted my southward journey in order to peel off to Addis and Vasti. Normally such a retracing of my steps was rather irritating, but not this time. What was a bit of backtracking, compared to what I got out of the detour? I was now heading to Kenya, only 500 km away. I looked forward to arriving at Shashamane, an unusual town I had heard much about from the locals and whose whole identity was integral to the decades-old link between Ethiopia, Jamaica's native reggae music and the Rastafarian religion (in fact Bob Marley's posthumous sixtieth birthday celebration had taken place less than a month earlier in Addis, and had been attended by tens of thousands of 'believers' from across the world).

The love affair began in the 1930s when Haile Selassie I, the last Ethiopian emperor, paid his first visit to Jamaica. The country had not had rain in years, but the moment the emperor's feet touched the ground, so it is said, a downpour started, which so impressed the Jamaicans that they founded the Ras Tafari religion. Rastafarians accorded divine status to Haile Selassie as 'Jah', or God, the name being derived from his title and appellation before he assumed power in 1916 – Ras (Chief) Tafari Makonnen. The funny thing was that Haile Selassie was not a Rastafarian but an Orthodox Christian and most certainly never wore dreadlocks or smoked cannabis, little extra touches that seem to have originated in Jamaica.

For decades Haile Selassie preached freedom for Africa's nations. He encouraged Jamaicans to remain in their own country and gain independence as a first priority, but in the 1970s, Jamaica having duly become independent, about 2 000 Jamaicans emigrated to Ethiopia and settled on a special piece of land he gave them in Shashamane. Not surprisingly, dreadlocked Rastafarians fill the streets there, each ready to take time out for story-telling, like the one about how the settlers ceremonially burned their passports on arrival to demonstrate their allegiance to their new country and ensure that they would not simply be turned around and sent home again. In turn I delighted the bearded and dreadlocked locals with my story about the famed South African rugby-playing Rastafarian, Ncgobani Bobo.

I also picked up some decidedly less pleasant local knowledge, namely, that visitors need to be very careful about offers to show them around and introduce them to the 'true' Ethiopian culture. I met some students at an Internet café and they offered to show me the town; we ended up at a bar/restaurant where they drank a huge amount of beer and then slipped quietly away before anyone noticed, leaving me to the mercies of the owner and his bouncers. The bill was far beyond my means and I refused point-blank to pay it. Fortunately for me the owner had seen my crooked companions and said he would extract the money from them ... painfully, I hoped ... or I could have been in a very sticky situation. As I made haste to put the bar behind me I remembered that earlier in the evening an elderly man had called me over to warn me that I needed to be careful of the guys I was with, or I would end up going home in my underpants. I'd laughed it off, but it had nearly happened.

During this last leg of my journey through Ethiopia I also learned about the true power of qat. I had tried it in Djibouti and written light-heartedly about it in one of my newspaper diary articles, and so I made the mistake of thinking I knew all about it. But then one day I had a strange experience which taught me not to scoff at the potency of this innocuous-looking bush.

I had done over 130 km that day, and at sunset arrived at the town of Agere Maryam, a well-organised place with a neat main road bisecting it. I checked into a reasonable hotel on the main street, headed off to find something to eat and by 7 pm was on the way back to the hotel again, looking forward to an early night. But along the way I gave in to the friendliness of a tea-lady who, along with a qat salesman, served the continuous stream of truck drivers passing through the town. As I sipped on my first cup of boiling-hot sweet tea the qat salesman gave me a few twigs as a gesture of friendship ... and that's practically all I remember of the next 12 hours. I can recall glancing at my watch and seeing it was now 1 am, then glancing at it again, seeing the hands at 7 am and realising that I hadn't had a wink of sleep yet. And that's all.

I finished off my last few sips of tea and went straight to my hotel, where I set my alarm for 8 am and then got back on the road with 110 km to cover on just one hour's sleep. Fortunately the severe mountainous areas were now behind me, but inevitably my lack of rest eventually started catching up, and lunch-time that day saw me sprawled out on the floor of a busy restaurant, enjoying a two-hour siesta while more active diners continued with their meals around me – and it's no secret that I slept even better than usual that night.

At another village I took a refreshment-break unlike any other I had had so far. Taking a break usually involved stopping for a cool drink and perhaps snapping a few pictures. But in this village it meant playing a game of table tennis on the worst 'court' I had ever come across: some slippery rocks only a few metres from the edge of the road on which the table perched precariously. I couldn't help but think of what an advantage 'home' players would have in an inter-village match: they would know which of the rocks underfoot to avoid and also the effect each type of passing vehicle would have on wind conditions. No doubt this was at least one of the reasons why I lost. But I was sure the guy I had asked to film me had caught me winning at least one point.

I wasn't feeling too good at this stage, and I knew what it was. I was supposed to take a weekly malaria tablet, as I had on the west coast, but had failed to adhere strictly to the regime. Now I felt sick each time I took the tablets and had constant migraines. But my time-budget had no rest days scheduled till after I arrived at the Kenyan border town of Moyale, which was still a good few hundred kilometres away, so I persevered and stuck as strictly as possible to my 7.30 am daily starting time. The rain was pelting down, but the land had flattened out now, giving a welcome reprieve to my chain. That meant I could manage a steady daily average of 115 km, but the unremitting effort in the heavy rain was beginning to take its toll: the headaches were constant now, and I could feel my body starting to weaken.

If any of my readers ever happen to be travelling in this part of the world, there are two ways of knowing if you are approaching the border. The first sign is that the terrain becomes drier and drier. The second is the increasing number of AK-47-wielding shepherds you come across. AK-47s are the preferred tools of the modern Ethiopian cattle herder. Theoretically they are for protection against lions and other big predators, but in reality – as everyone will tell you – they are for protection against rival cattle-herders and thieves, all Kenyans. I reckon stealing a head or two of cattle is a risky undertaking in these parts. If I were a border criminal I would rather concentrate on banks and old ladies' purses.

I posed for a few pictures with some of these guys, something I would not have even contemplated while going up the west coast. The ones I met were friendly enough, but the bottom line is that if people are allowed to carry weapons like this so brazenly it will not be long before you have them in the wrong hands. A rifle's muzzle against my head and the confiscation of my bicycle was an all-too-easily imagined scenario.

Sick though I was, I looked forward to arriving at Moyale. Ethiopia had been a highlight of my journey, but Kenya would be my third-last country and there I would have a common language at last; most of all, however, it would mean an escape from the never-ending, suffocating attention from everybody around me. People who have toured through Ethiopia on bicycles will understand this desire; I would certainly have gone mad if I had stayed there another week.

And then I was there. On the last day I took it easy on a 100 km-long descent, and suddenly found myself in Moyale, the gateway to the endless plains of Kenya.

# CHAPTER 30

# TIME TRAVEL IN KENYA

*It had been a long, hard slog, but I had finally completed the
second dimension of my adventure. A huge pride filled me.
But not just pride. The world took on another perspective for
me as I stood there, freezing by inches in the minus 13 degrees
Celsius temperature. Here I seemed to understand things about
myself and the world itself that I had never understood or even
thought of before. Like finding the places to put difficult pieces
of a giant puzzle. Nothing flashy happens but inside you know
and understand that the puzzle is nearly completed. I don't
think it could have happened anywhere else on the planet.*

The border post was at the northern end of a bridge, and I hurried to
get through before it closed so that I could find some decent accommodation and Internet access on the Kenyan side. It didn't work that
way, however. For some reason I had been under the impression that
Kenya would be more progressive and developed than Ethiopia. Instead, all I found was camels, cattle, candles and chaos.

Perhaps my misperception resulted from having spent time under
the Julian calendar still used in Ethiopia, which differs by a substantial margin from the later Gregorian system to which most of the
world – including Kenya and South Africa – adheres. One strange result of this had been that I had aged instantly by eight years when I
crossed into Ethiopia, and another was that the Ethiopians had yet
to reach the kick-off of the new millennium, which they had scheduled for 11 September 2007 by our reckoning. We Gregorians had
awaited the millennium in a state of controlled panic, but Y2K, Ethi-

opian-style, was being planned as a celebration. I liked their style, if not their calendar, which seemed to me to be 50 years behind the times, not eight. But at least I had got my eight lost years back as soon as I cycled over the border. That was the only benefit, however.

The Kenyan side of the border was a complete contrast to Ethiopia in every way. Travellers' accommodation was scarce, the first town with electricity laid on was 575 km of rocky dirt road away and communicating with the people back home was almost impossible because there were no landline telephones or e-mail access and cellphone reception was patchy at best. The general atmosphere, too, was different, stricter and less welcoming. Because this was a heavily Islamic region very few women were to be seen, and people were not as friendly and jovial as they had been just one kilometre further back. But atmosphere was the least of my preoccupations just then. My luck had run out after travelling 28 000 km through 30 countries without once falling seriously ill – something of an achievement, considering the conditions I had encountered at various places en route.

I had not been able to shake off the migraines which had been plaguing me for more than a week now. I had thought I could overcome them, as I had in Guinea and Angola, but these were far more formidable, and sapped my will and determination. When I finally found a tiny hotel I decided to hole up there for a day's rest. The day's stopover became several, since it soon became clear that I wasn't in a fit state to go anywhere. I spent the days eating liver and rice, drinking fresh warm mango pulp and sleeping. But nothing helped. After each nap I felt much worse than before. I battled to stand upright because of the pain in my joints and the flashes of agony going through my head and into my eyes. At times it got so bad that my vision went blurry. What made it even worse was that I didn't have any idea of how to doctor myself. It felt as though I was dying.

The people running the hotel were mainly interested in seeing that I paid my bill in advance, but a Kenyan sangoma or herbalist named Solomon who was staying in the courtyard room opposite mine took me under his wing. Solomon was truly concerned about my condition and did what he could to heal me. He massaged animal wax and oils into the back of my neck and head, and carried out traditional healing rituals which I was too sick even to take note of: all I remember is that he circled me and laid his hands on my head, while his wife ground up more ingredients for his medicines. But Solomon's best efforts couldn't heal me. I would wake up each morning feeling slightly better, but by lunchtime I would be groggy, disorientated and full of pain again.

Eventually I decided to see the doctor at the town's government hospital. It turned out to be a waste of time, because the doctor did not turn up, although about 30 other people of all ages had come for treatment. It was yet another first-hand lesson in the lot of poor and uneducated people in so many parts of Africa. We sat there for four hours, staring at one another while babies and small children cried loudly. I was not just sick now, I was angry. It was so absolutely unfair. What sort of doctor could be so unfeeling towards the sick and needy? Had Kenya abolished the Hippocratic Oath? But at least I had a choice which my fellow-sufferers did not: I could afford – just – to consult the one private doctor in Moyale when my patience finally ran out.

This wasn't much better. I spent a solitary hour in his dirty reception room while he had a leisurely lunch, and when he finally deigned to roll up his examination was anything but thorough. He didn't check my vital signs except for taking my temperature and spent five minutes asking me about my trip. Then, without even telling me his diagnosis, he wrote out a prescription for pain-killers and antibiotics and instructed his nurse to give me an injection of some unknown medicine. I could scarcely believe it. In South Africa even a bad doctor will find out whether you are allergic to any medication, especially penicillin, before prescribing anything. This one obviously didn't care whether I lived or died – and if I had been allergic to penicillin Moyale would have been the end of me, as I discovered when I questioned the nurse while the mysterious liquid flowed from the syringe into my vein.

Rather sarcastically I asked her what it was. 'Medicine,' was her cryptic response.

'What medicine? What is the name of this medicine?' I persisted, trying to get her to tell me it was penicillin, and she promptly obliged: 'Oh, it is penicillin, for infection.'

'I'm allergic to penicillin.' I said very calmly, to see her reaction. 'I must never have penicillin, my doctor in South Africa said to me.'

She looked at me, presumably to check the sincerity of my statement, but didn't stop pressing the syringe's plunger till she had pumped all of its contents into my arm. Then she cleaned the injection site, gave me a cotton-wool swab to hold over the wound and went outside to look for the doctor. A couple of minutes later she returned to say that she couldn't find him. But he would be back later, and I must return if I experienced any serious problems, which she assured me I wouldn't.

I paid her, left and never returned. This excuse for a doctor, and the helpful incompetent one who had sewn up my arm in the mountains of Djibouti, wouldn't survive in the 'real' world because they would spend so much time in court defending themselves against malpractice suits that they wouldn't be able to get around to treating their unfortunate patients.

When I got back to the hotel I gave myself a malaria test. The test came up negative, which was not all that comforting because I was feeling worse than ever, even though I had spent four days doing nothing but sleeping and resting. What the hell was wrong with me? It had become so bad that I could barely keep my eyes open and even battled to speak, and I was so disorientated that someone had to help me undo the padlock on my room's door and guide me onto the bed.

Solomon decided that the time had come to give me his full medicine-and-magic treatment, starting with a grainy, lukewarm concoction that I had difficulty getting down. When I had finally succeeded, between the gagging, I said good night to him and the rest of the small crowd which had congregated in the courtyard – by this time the news about me had spread not just throughout the hotel but further afield as well, so everyone wanted to know what was wrong with the strange white bicycle man – and promised I would call him if I needed help during the night.

I went to my room and slowly crawled on to my bed, fully clothed, tucking the fringes of its large hanging mosquito-net in under the mattress with the last remnants of my energy. Lying with my head back gave me mild but instant relief from the pounding that was going on inside it; it felt as though my brain was too big for my skull and was forcing itself out at my temples and eye sockets, and when I blinked it seemed that the skin all over my head moved as well. But now a new problem arose. My stomach was not happy with Solomon's lumpy mixture and wanted to get rid of it. I fought down wave after wave of nausea, washing the taste out of my mouth with sips from a bottle of water I kept next to me. I hoped against hope that I would fall asleep and wake up feeling OK, but of course I simply delayed the inevitable, as I found out when my stomach started to convulse.

Holding one hand tightly over my mouth to win a little more time, I tried to open up the mosquito-net with the other. It didn't work, and at the next convulsion I sprayed the inside of the net, the bed and myself with Solomon's medicine and everything else that had gone down my throat that afternoon. The mess was indescribable, but anybody who has been that nauseous will understand when I say that I was past caring, even about the small triumph of getting my head out through the net in time to deposit the next load of vomit on the floor instead of on myself.

All this must have been accompanied by some loud sound-effects, because Solomon started knocking on my door and asking me if I was OK. I couldn't speak right then, but Solomon must have known this, because he didn't go away but waited patiently till I could eventually open the door for him. He took one look at me and my self-created mess, and said I needed to get to Nairobi as soon as possible. I agreed and asked him in a whisper which was all that was left of my voice to find someone who could drive me there right away, night or no night. I would pay $380, I said after counting all the money I had to my name.

Solomon went out and found two drivers, each of whom was willing to take me, but only for $400. I was in no position to argue and said I would pay the remaining $20 when we arrived. That seemed to settle things, but my relief was short-lived, because within an hour both drivers pulled out – earlier that day unknown gunmen had ambushed travellers on this road and killed several of them, and the police had advised against any movement after dark. I wasn't going anywhere after all!

I was now feeling a little better, though – not much, but better than a man would feel on his deathbed. So it seemed that the vomiting had helped, although I didn't believe Solomon when he said he had expected it and that it was a sure sign that I was being healed. Still, I was grateful for the respite. I sent an SMS to my South African Embassy contact in Nairobi, Izak Barnard, who had earlier offered to help me if anything should go wrong, told him about my condition and added that I would be coming through with the first available transport. Izak replied that he was standing by and told me that the first thing we had to do when I arrived was to get me straight to the nearest hospital.

Early next morning I arranged to store my bicycle at the hotel and finally got away from Moyale on an Ethiopian cattle truck Solomon had found. The driver knew I was sick and made sure I had the most comfortable of the uncomfortable spots available in his front cabin, but it was a long two days before we arrived in the sprawling, over-populated hive of Nairobi ('Night Robbery', as the locals called it) around 11 o'clock in the morning.

Izak had roused himself from his weekend rest and took me back to his house. I was feeling much better now, but he still insisted on getting me to hospital for blood tests and a CT scan. I would never have done this if I had been alone; I would certainly have convinced myself that I was OK and that it would just be an expensive waste of money. But Izak would not take 'no' for an answer, and I'll always be indebted to him for his help, which he gave freely in spite of the fact that some of his colleagues had advised him not to get involved.

Izak turned out to be an interesting guy. Among other things he had a special bed in his house which, as I understood it, emitted waves of energy that were supposed to rejuvenate the body's tired cells and boost the immune system. Very sceptically I had a few sessions on this bed while staying with him. I can't say that I felt any drastic change, but I did get all my original energy back.

The CT scan cost 13 000 Kenyan shillings, the equivalent of about $200, and the blood tests a further 2 500 shillings, or $34. Being a man who likes to get his money's worth, I awaited the outcome with some anticipation: I must surely have something pretty bad wrong with me! But all the doctors could tell me was that they couldn't find out what had struck me down – possibly a viral infection? So it could have been anything, I thought, somewhat disgruntled. Maybe even a common cold that went bad.

The good news was that Windhoek Light had kindly decided again to extend their support for a few more months. It couldn't have come at a better time. Looking back now, it is clear that their steadfast support was what had made my entire trip possible. Nairobi was a case in point. Without their continued support I would probably have done without the CT scan and half of the blood tests, and if my problem had been anything worse than some mysterious viral infection I might have died as a result. Izak's deadpan comment on all this was that the brain scan might stand me in good stead in the future: if ever I were to be questioned as to whether I had a brain or even a reasonable level of intelligence I would be able to produce documentary evidence which would confirm beyond doubt that I actually did have the first, if not necessarily the second.

There were plenty of South Africans in Nairobi, and Izak suggested that I make use of the opportunity to sound some of them out about sponsorships in exchange for media coverage – the national TV channels and newspapers had already confirmed that they wanted interviews, while the CNN 'Inside Africa' programme had booked me for an interview in the coastal town of Mombasa. I was particularly keen on the CNN story because the head presenter would be the exceptionally talented Tumi Makgabo, a well-known South African TV personality before she was head-hunted by CNN. My own belief is that we need to keep amazing people like her in our own country at all costs (something that really impressed me about her was that she spoke her second and third languages, English and Afrikaans, better than some people who spoke them as their first languages).

One of the South Africans, Pierre, was from the East Africa Kodak office. He must have thought I resembled the Frankenstein creature in a famous series of Kodak advertisements of a few years earlier (I have to admit I wasn't looking my best) and took pity on me in the form of a $1 000 sponsorship; what it came down to was that he was aware of what I had done and endured in the past 15 months and wanted to contribute to something historic – and I wasn't asking for something I hadn't worked for. Sewing another company logo on my shirt wasn't something I did easily, considering the wonderful help I had had from Windhoek Light. But I was very grateful for Pierre's help, and the Kodak logo with its trademark yellow colour stood out like a beacon against the bright blue of my First Ascent shirt.

Half of the Kodak sponsorship went immediately into professional repairs on my bike. This solved my most pressing problem, but I still wanted to find someone willing to provide another $1 500 sponsorship so that I could climb to Africa's highest point, Kilimanjaro. This was a long-standing personal ambition and would also be an opportunity to shoot some interesting video footage.

I had a bit of luck when Izak directed me to the local branch of South Africa's famous Spur steakhouse chain. My main aim was to get a smell and taste of home again, but the owner-manager, a South African named Tom, turned out to be a great benefactor. He promised me free meals for as long as I was in Nairobi (which meant that I tucked into Spur's justly famous spare ribs for breakfast, lunch and dinner every day during my stay), and also suggested that I speak to a friend of his called Adrian Penny, another South African who was general manager of the Holiday Inn group for Kenya. It turned out that Adrian was away, but Tom got on to his deputy, who gave me free accommodation for the next four days. This was great news, because it meant I did not have to impose on Izak any longer, and also that I would have a tranquil environment to recover in – I was feeling better, but had developed flu symptoms which left me with a hoarse voice and a runny nose.

I planned to use the recuperation time to get my documents checked and renewed for the last time, particularly my temporary passport, and see about entering and re-entering neighbouring Tanzania. My journey was on the point of becoming somewhat complicated. Remember, I didn't have my bicycle with me! I had to fetch it at Moyale and cycle down to Nairobi, and from there go down to Mombasa for the CNN interview. Then I would cross into Tanzania to climb Kilimanjaro – providing I could raise the cash, which I intended to try doing in Dar es Salaam – and return to Nairobi to have my bike fitted with locally unobtainable parts Vasti was sending up from Cape Town. When all that had been done I would carry on with the slog to Mozambique and South Africa.

I planned to set this in motion by finding some transport to Moyale that Sunday, but my friends strongly recommended that I stay on to meet Adrian Penny, who was due on the Monday. I fell in with their suggestion because I wanted to thank him properly for his company's kindness, but I wasn't looking forward to it, because by all accounts he wasn't the hail-fellow-well-met type – he didn't warm instantly to people, didn't like meaningless chit-chat and didn't take nonsense from anybody. I was packed, ready to go and waiting nervously outside this scary man's office at 7.45 am, a good quarter-hour early, wondering why I was putting myself through this ordeal after everything that had happened to me lately. I would thank him, I decided, shake his hand firmly, give him a photo with my signature and thanks on it and then do a sharp military about-turn out of his office. I reckoned he would appreciate this economical use of his time. And then he arrived, and it turned out I had been about as wrong as I could be. I gave him a few minutes to settle in and then presented myself to his secretary. She went to tell him, and he came right out of his office to greet me. He didn't know who I was, but he shook my hand (firmly – at least I had got *that* part right) and sat me down in his office to listen to my story. I explained who I was, what I was doing and how he had unknowingly helped me already, then thanked him for everything and said that I was on my way back to Moyale.

Adrian would have none of this. He had my bags sent back to my room and instructed me to meet him for breakfast in half an hour. He was exactly as people had described him, firm and forthright, but I took to him right away because our general approach was much the same. He wasn't rude or impatient; he just knew what he wanted and seemed to know what I wanted too – I had the clear impression that he had already made some sort of decision while we had been talking, but instead of wasting time would discuss it with me at breakfast.

Adrian, his wife Jill and (during school holidays) their daughter Tarryn had lived in Kenya for four years, during which time he had turned the Nairobi Holiday Inn into one of the most successful hotels in the group, and it was not difficult to see why. He was goal-orientated and wanted to see results daily, if not hourly. I loved his energy and approach to everything. At breakfast I saw him in action. He thought I was mad to go first to Dar es Salaam, then back-track for 20 hours to climb Kilimanjaro, which was no more than two hours from Nairobi. All I needed to do, he said, was obtain the necessary multiple-entry visa to Tanzania, and the rest he would take care of.

He was as good as his word. He inspanned Kobo Safaris, Spur, Holiday Inn, the SAWAS (South African Women's Association) branch in Nairobi and the Marangu Hotel in Tanzania, the starting-point of the climb. Each organisation threw something into the kitty, with Kobo Safaris contributing a hefty $500, and by the time Adrian was finished there was enough money for my venture to the continent's highest point, right down to tips for the guide and porters I would need for the climb. All I had to do now was get my body to the top.

I was duly grateful, because by now I had realised that climbing 'Kili', to use the local term for the great mountain, was not as simple as I had thought. I hadn't given much thought to how I would actually get up and down, but ascending Kilimanjaro wasn't a lazy afternoon stroll – which was, of course, one reason why it is an adventure that attracts people from all over the world. It would take five days of climbing to reach the summit (many climbers, including the more elderly and the nervous types, often added another day at the 3 700 metre camp to acclimatise, although there was nothing to prove that this actually helped). One needed to be reasonably fit, capable of enduring some severe climatic challenges and prepared to deal with altitude sickness, which was liable to strike at any time and could be deadly if not professionally responded to. Being an incurable optimist, I was not worried by any of this. Barring my struggle with the mysterious virus infection I was incredibly fit, and I reckoned I was suitably altitude-adjusted after my arduous wanderings between and over Ethiopia's mountain ranges.

I had a pleasantly eventful mini-bus trip to the Marangu Hotel. The road into Tanzania was packed on either side with herds of giraffe, zebra and even some rhino; every now and again we would pass a sleepy Masai village whose inhabitants would casually watch the day and the traffic go by, unmoved by the fact that less than a kilometre from them the veld was teeming with potentially dangerous game animals.

The whole Kilimanjaro experience starts when you see its cloud-covered peaks actually coming into sight and realise that photographs pale by comparison with the real thing. This, I knew as I craned forward in my seat, was the real beginning of the adventure that would culminate with the moment when I finally stood on the summit.

The final leg of my trip involved changing transport at Arusha, where our official ride ended, although there was still nearly 100 km to go. My old companion, good fortune, clicked in again at Arusha in the form of a fellow-passenger, himself a Tanzanian tour operator. He said that a friend was due to pick him up at Arusha's transport hub and offered me a free ride, as long as I was not in a rush, because he planned on stopping for a meal and a few beers on the way. I *was* in a bit of a rush because I was due to start climbing the next day, but this was the best offer on the table.

The trip took considerably longer than he had expected because we had two punctures along the dark, deserted road and finally had to swop cars to get to where we were going. The result was that I arrived at the Marangu Hotel near midnight, literally on the eve of my climb. This was hardly ideal timing, since many climbers prefer to arrive a few days early to familiarise themselves with their surroundings before easing up the mountain, but there was nothing to be done about it. The Marangu hotel staffers were not fazed at my late arrival, although it had meant that they had had to remain on duty till I finally pitched up; given the transport situation from Arusha, I suppose that late arrivals were not a novelty. They checked me in, served me a hot meal, dessert and all, and said that breakfast for my climbing group would be at 6.30 am, after which its members would be briefed about Kilimanjaro and kitted out with the necessary climbing gear.

I was very tired indeed, but the adrenalin was pumping and I could hardly wait as I climbed into bed. After breakfast the members of my group gathered in the courtyard of the old hotel and I went off to find my contact, Seamus, a direct descendant of the family which had founded the Marangu Hotel and organised the first guided trips up Kilimanjaro more than half a century earlier. I found him in the original hotel building, which now housed its offices, and he said that I shouldn't expect to leave with the early-morning group, since he and I still had to go through a lot of preparation. But I would be able to catch up with them quite easily later in the afternoon.

This contradicted the advice I had received from Adrian and Jill, who had recently climbed Kilimanjaro and had told me that the key to a successful ascent was 'pole, pole' ('slowly, slowly' in Swahili). I didn't mention this to Seamus, but later I understood what he meant when he gave me a detailed one-on-one briefing on Kili and its geography. The first two days, he said, would be relatively easy – no more than an 'enthusiastic stroll'. The last two days were much harder, with the final haul to the summit being the worst. Seamus reiterated what I had heard elsewhere, that fitness was no guarantee of success. Symptoms of cerebral and pulmonary oedema, he warned, would not be tolerated by the guides, and if I showed any such signs of altitude sickness I would be taken back down, whether I liked it or not.

Geez, I thought, imagine travelling from the other side of the world to climb Kilimanjaro, and then being forced to come down by the very people you're paying to get you up to the top in the first place! But I couldn't disagree with Seamus when he said that although an ascent of Kilimanjaro involved spending a considerable amount of money, effort and sacrifice for many people, the climbers' lives were surely worth more. I didn't take any of this personally, because it didn't feel as if any of these things were likely to happen to me. They might happen to other people, but I would be OK – I was going to get to the top of Kilimanjaro, otherwise why was I here?

The briefing over, I went to the hotel's quartermaster so he could issue me with suitable gear for the ascent, which he did ... except for boots and the gloves, because they didn't have anything big enough for my X-large hands and feet. The quartermaster then did some intensive further scratching and finally managed to find a pair of boots that fitted, but my hands still defeated him. In the end we had to settle for two sets of stretch fabric-style gloves which could be squeezed over one another and then forced into painfully tight mitts. I wasn't too happy about this. If I was uncomfortable now, what would it be like up there? So my advice to would-be climbers of Kilimanjaro is to bring their own gloves (not mitts) and waterproof boots.

Around 2 pm Seamus declared me fully prepared – which I was, in more ways than one, because I had had time to buy a souvenir T-shirt which I hoped to wear on the summit itself. It was a dark blue round-neck one with a spoof of the well-known Nike slogan on the front: KILI – JUST DONE IT! I suspected that most people bought the T-shirt after they had 'done it', but I wanted actually to be wearing it as I dragged myself to the top.

With my guide and porters I set off to the Marangu National Park gateway in an old Land Rover and paid the exorbitant entry fee of $400 (the park made a good thing out of Kilimanjaro, I reflected after a quick calculation, considering that about 20 000 tourists go there every year, not all of them to climb the mountain). By now it was 3 pm, and I was in a hurry to set off for the first night's accommodation; I had paid for today and the clock was ticking. 'Pole, pole' would have to wait till the following morning.

The first leg was a gentle, manicured stretch which, I was told later, had been build and donated to Tanzania by the Danish government. As a result we soon reached the half-way mark for the day, and the guide told me that we had more than enough time to reach our camp before nightfall. So far, so good! During this first stretch I met up with a Canadian of Chinese extraction, a medical student named Jesse Cao, who was also on a five-day climbing plan and, like me, had started late. Jesse told me he was doing practical work at a rural hospital and would later complete a similar stint somewhere in Uganda before going home. We hit it off and agreed that we would climb together and assist each other if it proved necessary. Another bit of advice to would-be Kilimanjaro climbers: don't climb alone. You and your guide can only spend so much time discussing topics like the customary tip for him if you made it to the top, his hard life and how corrupt the government was. Sometimes you and your climbing partner need to give one another some moral support.

The next four days were truly magical. The first day took us to about 2 700 metres above sea level, out of the cultivated lower slopes and through the belt of dense rain-forest that encircles Kilimanjaro. On the second day we hiked up almost to the 3 750 metre mark, through much drier terrain with small shrubs sharing the surface with ancient volcanic rock. The third day consisted of a long, gradual climb through barren desert; the air was markedly thinner from about 4 000 metres, and the struggle to get enough oxygen into my lungs seemed to increase exponentially.

At 2 pm, after six hours of tough hiking, we finally got to 4 700 metres and the stone building that was to be our base camp for the final leg, a night trek up to the summit. Jesse and I settled for the slightly longer version of the standard trail because it would take us past the jagged cliffs of Mount Mawenzi to the base of Uhuru Peak, Kilimanjaro's highest point. I didn't regret this choice, and I recommend it to any Kilimanjaro climbers; the views we had were incredible, and the video footage I took with my guide's assistance along this stretch was most definitely some of the best I'd ever managed.

On arrival at Kibo we settled down to make last-minute preparations to our kit (such as donning the 'done it' T-shirt, in my case) and catch some sleep before the guides came to roust us out around midnight. This was when I realised the value of having a climbing companion. Or perhaps I should say that Jesse did. He was racked by headaches and vomiting constantly, and said that if it went on like this he would not attempt the final push to the summit. He just curled up in his sleeping bag, mumbling that he wasn't hungry. I almost always have extra energy and ideas, even in adverse conditions, and now they were obviously going to be needed; I would have to re-motivate Jesse about the climb to the summit and also get him to take some liquids and, if possible, solid food. I sat down next to him and did what I hoped someone else would have done for me in the same circumstances. I gave him a simple motivation argument and asked him to do one more thing before he slept, which was to have lunch with me. If he still was not feeling well after that, I would personally arrange for his evacuation. Jesse agreed, although he wasn't thinking too clearly by now.

Our lunch consisted of popcorn and soup, and I gave Jesse twice what I thought he could handle, just in case. It worked, and by the end of the scratch meal both his colour and his attitude had begun to improve. We got dressed in all our summit-climbing gear, ate a chocolate each and squeezed into our sleeping bags. After a year and nine months on the road I should have been able to pass out like a light, but my expectation was so intense that at first I couldn't sleep a wink.

As an aside, I was unimpressed by our guides. Jesse's guide never once spoke to him, the reason being that he didn't know any English, which meant that Jesse had no one to jolly him on when he was down. Mine, on the other hand, sulked all the way up because I had made it clear that my tip wouldn't be a fat one because I simply didn't have enough money, and on top of that he complained endlessly about a painful knee. I felt sorry about the knee (although perhaps it was related to my nearly empty wallet), but I had to focus on my own challenges. Everything was new and intimidatingly unfamiliar to me – for one thing, I had never seen a glacier or dealt with snow before – so I didn't know what to expect and needed to concentrate on each task as it confronted me. On the other hand, the porters who carried most of the food and baggage up the mountain, prepared our meals made the food and generally cleaned up, were a very helpful and pleasant bunch. They smiled throughout the entire trip, making me wish I had more money to tip them with.

We got up in such cold that it was painful to touch the hut's stone walls, even with gloves on, then stepped outside into a silent darkness which, to me, was the perfect setting in which to bottle up my excitement and prepare mentally for what lay ahead. Jesse, I was glad to note, was a different man and eager to get going. Because the earlier arrivals left first, it was 1.30 am before Jesse and I actually stepped on to the steep path of scree which started right outside the hut. From here on, we were given to understand, it would be a six-hour march to the summit 1 250 metres above us.

Scree is bad stuff on a steep path. It consists of tiny chips of volcanic rock that have been ground fine by thousands of years of erosion, and going up that path was like ascending a kilometre-high desert sand dune, so that we slid back one step for every two taken. Not very motivational! This was where mental endurance really came into play. 'Pole, pole!' Just keep trudging on, concentrating not on the big picture but on the next step, and eventually you'll get there.

Jesse and I were feeling all right, but my guide, the very person who was supposed to be keeping an eye on me in case of altitude sickness, was clearly under the weather. During our half-way stop at Hans Meyer Cave ('Maya' to the locals) he wandered off into the darkness and I distinctly heard him vomiting. When he returned he denied this, though, saying he had just gone to investigate something. It was a practical illustration of the ever-lurking danger of random attacks of altitude sickness. This particular guide had climbed Kilimanjaro 12 times and should have been thoroughly acclimatised, yet here he was, exhibiting a classic symptom of altitude sickness. I didn't push the issue because I knew this was his bread and butter, although I was worried about his health being endangered. So here was I, keeping watch on *his* condition instead of the other way around!

The funny thing was that in my determination to reach the summit I had actually worked out a strategy to prevent an over-hasty evacuation if I got altitude sickness. Seamus had told me that cerebral oedema was the most dangerous kind because it affected a person's brain and therefore his motor senses, so that he wobbled around like a drunkard and talked nonsense. So on our first and second day I 'acclimatised' the guide by singing and talking to myself about things he didn't understand, to make sure he would have no clear benchmark against which to measure my sanity or lack thereof. It must have worked, because I can remember getting long, thoughtful glances from him in those early stages, so I was confident that if I did start involuntarily wobbling and babbling as we approached the summit he wouldn't automatically assume that I had altitude sickness. With hindsight it was damned stupid, of course, and my advice to would-be Kilimanjaro climbers is not to try to hide any oedema symptoms.

Because we were tail-end Charlies, Jesse and I decided to keep our stops to a minimum so that we could catch up with the other groups. We made such swift progress, scree or no scree, that we actually began to pass many climbers who had left an hour before us. At first we were worried that in fact we were going too fast and would shoot our bolt, but our assessment at the half-way mark was that we had hit on the correct pace. Meanwhile Kilimanjaro continued to take its toll, and more and more climbers were turning back before Jesse and I had even reached the rim of the crater. One was an American who had told us before our departure that we must respect Kilimanjaro; he had climbed many mountains in America and had only succeeded because of his respect for nature. But Kilimanjaro had not respected him; he said that he had run out of energy to such an extent that he couldn't even lift his legs.

We reached the rim of the crater after only four hours; now it was a mere 200-metre climb to reach the very top of Uhuru Peak. It was a very special and emotional moment for me when the great glaciers came into view a mere 30 metres from where I stood. As the sun hit these blindingly white shelves of ice I was enveloped by sadness that I was up here without someone special at my side, sharing all this truly majestic beauty with me. But I was here at last, and at

7.30 am on the morning of 3 July 2005, a date never to be forgotten, I saw the sun rise over our continent. I had seen it rise many times before, but never from the breathtaking viewpoint of Uhuru Peak, 5 892 metres above the plains.

It had been a long, hard slog, but I had finally completed the second dimension of my adventure. A huge pride filled me. But not just pride. The world took on another perspective for me as I stood there, freezing by inches in the minus 13 degrees Celsius temperature. Here I seemed to understand things about myself and the world itself that I had never understood or even thought of before. Like finding the places to put the difficult pieces of a giant puzzle. Nothing flashy happens, but inside you know and understand that the puzzle is nearly completed. I don't think it could have happened anywhere else on the planet.

Jesse, I am convinced, wasn't thinking any such elevated thoughts just then. The lack of oxygen was getting to him, and he literally fell asleep on his feet while filming me in front of the Uhuru Peak sign. This sounds like a tall story, but the video footage proves it. The camera moves slowly from my head right down to my feet as Jesse loses his sense of time and nods off, then returns to my face, which bears an expression of disbelief.

This was very funny at the time, but actually it was no joke. We had been there for 35 minutes – way beyond the norm – and he had to get down to thicker air as soon as possible. We photographed each other in front of the peak sign, I pinned a small South African flag to the battered wooden frame and then jumped about 40 cm into the air so that I could say in all truthfulness that I had gone a little higher than any of the climbers who had made it to the summit. So it could be that I set a new altitude record for Africa, namely 5 892 metres ... and 40 centimetres.

Then we started down. It took us about two hours to get back to the Kibo base camp, where our ever-friendly porters welcomed us with bread and bowls of hot soup. I didn't enjoy either the descent or the soup as much as I might have, not because going down the scree path was difficult (although it was) but because altitude sickness had finally got to me. I was nearly paralysed by such a monumental headache that any sideways movement of my head was so painful that it brought me to the brink of shutting down entirely. I had to fight off an intense desire to lie down and sleep, but somehow I kept going, repeatedly telling myself: 'I will never, ever, ever, ever climb a mountain again' as I slid down the scree. But I lied. For the record, I can't wait to climb a big mountain again. My problem was dehydration, I think. Up there you don't feel hungry or thirsty.

We returned to the main gate of Marangu and received our certificates from the park rangers. At the small souvenir shop I marvelled at length at the large high-resolution images of the top of Kibo's volcanic crater. *I've stood there*, I reminded myself, hardly believing my own words. Next morning I said goodbye to Jesse, who was staying on for a few more days, and got myself on to a bus for Nairobi. Looking back now, I can honestly say that I had just lived through one of those weeks that I really did not feel I had deserved. I had experienced more personal development than I had ever bargained for, and I knew that not a day would go by on which I would not remind myself of the saying that without challenge there was no achievement.

That trip up to Africa's highest point, which had been made possible by so many people, would be a focus of any public speaking I might do when I got home. Just getting across in words what had happen to me during this experience would be a challenge. But it would not be a major challenge. The main one remained the circumnavigation of Africa, and I still had a way to go.

At the Kenya–Tanzania border I ran into an interesting recent acquaintance, a tall veterinarian from Liverpool named Anthony Chadwick whom I had met, of all places and times, on the slopes of Kibo while he was on his way down and I was on my way up. Anthony, who had gone from pasty to well-fried virtually overnight, as Englishmen exposed to the African sun tend to do, was touring East Africa and was also on his way back to Nairobi. It was a happy meeting because Anthony proved to be an extraordinary character. He delighted the bus passengers by singing Liverpudlian soccer songs at the top of his voice and charmed the locals on board by speaking a fair bit of

Swahili that he'd picked up. He also proved to have lots of ingenuity, as he demonstrated when we broke down 20 km outside the city boundary in the busiest section of road imaginable. Anthony spotted a taxi, flagged it down before any of the locals could react and got us home before midnight. All things considered, he deserved the solid South African meal I stood him to at the Spur when we arrived.

Now that I was back in Nairobi I could get down to the main business at hand. For starters this meant a return to Moyale so that I could cycle to Nairobi, which I hoped I could manage before my now seriously rackety bike fell apart entirely. Then, having had the bike repaired with the parts Vasti was sending up to me, I would head for Tanzania and points south.

I went to the city's transport hub and found a mini-bus which could get me as far as Isiolo, the town where the tarmac ended. I arrived after an uneventful day-long ride and then hopped on to a large cargo-type truck taking a load of passengers to Ethiopia via Moyale. This trip was exhausting, with breakdown after breakdown which kept me from my sleep for 30 hours, but surprisingly enjoyable. One of the best bits was spotting a cheetah at sunrise. We had just passed a small town called Turbi (meaning 'Seven Hills') at about 5 am when I saw a distant object moving along the edge of the rocky road at roughly our speed (about 35 km/h), but much more gracefully. When we were about 100 metres away I saw it was a cheetah, glancing back periodically at us as it ran. Then, when it realised the truck was catching up to it, it gently shifted into another gear, briskly pulled clear of us and soon dodged through a gap in the thick bush. What made the sighting especially meaningful to me was that this cheetah was completely wild, not one that had been coerced into living in a fenced area for the benefit of tourists. It was 'wildlife' in the fullest sense of the word.

To my great thankfulness my bicycle was exactly where I left it. I paid the storage charge and laid my plans for an early-morning departure. This meant I had time to spare, and I decided to spend some of it on a last visit to Ethiopia to enjoy the cuisine one last time. I know I said earlier that I was glad to leave it, but I realised now that the country had got under my skin, and I had begun to miss the wonderful 'macchiatos' (latte coffee) which were not to found among the dedicated tea-drinkers of northern Kenya.

According to the Moyale locals this would be easy – everyone in the town simply crossed back and forth as they pleased, so why didn't I do just that? I took this somewhat dodgy advice and joined a bustling herd of schoolchildren who were heading north, walking with a confident air which was meant to indicate that I did this every day. The problem, of course, was that a six-foot-tall white guy stands out a little when all his companions are about 400 black children who are a good deal shorter and are staring at him in undisguised fascination. So my presence didn't escape the notice of the Kenyan border officials, but after I had explained what I was doing they said there wouldn't be any hassle about getting back in on my return. But their Ethiopian opposite numbers at the northern end of the bridge were a different story.

I was already on Ethiopian soil when I heard some loud shouting and turned to see a couple of border policemen running after me in agitated fashion. I stopped and the man in charge, who spoke reasonably good English, asked me the obvious question. I told him exactly what I was there for – the food, the coffee, Internet access and so on. This got me nowhere. I had only a single-entry visa for Ethiopia, he pointed out, and ordered his guards to escort me back to Kenyan territory without delay;

'Fair enough' I told him, 'but what about all the people who are streaming through the border post at will?'

'No, no, you don't understand,' he said impatiently. 'They are all Kenyan and Ethiopian people.' Since the unhindered border-crossers were at least 100 metres away, I concluded that this arrogant fellow must be a psychic, and expressed my admiration for his very rare and under-utilised skill. But this sarcastic flattery didn't get me anywhere either, or maybe he just got irritated at my sleep-deprived grumpiness, because next moment his guards seized hold of my arms and frog-marched me back over the line. It would have made some eye-catching humorous reality TV, the border guards dragging one crosser back to where he had come from while droves of others calmly strolled over, hardly more than a pistol-shot away.

The road out of Moyale into the surrounding volcanic desert started fast and downhill, but neither lasted, and if it had been bumpy in the truck it was unspeakable on a bicycle, undoubtedly the worst I had encountered thus far. It was 'paved' from side to side with rocks the size of golf-balls, and this didn't agree with my heavily overloaded and as yet unrepaired bicycle, which bounced violently from one to the next, so that I was averaging four or five kilometres an hour at best. It didn't agree with me either. I soon realised just how tender and fragile that undercarriage area between one's legs is – I was literally bruised black and blue, which made sitting down awkward.

There were other irritations besides the rocks. The heat was around 45 degrees Celsius, forcing me to stop just about every passing vehicle to replenish my liquids, and a new species of insect came to pester me, yellow things that descended on me in a biting cloud. Earlier in my journey, I think, I would have panicked, but my travels had hardened me and I pushed grimly on, since there was nothing I could do about them and their bite was not nearly as bad as a tsetse fly's.

A local who pulled up his luxury 4x4 about a metre away from me at one stage got me a bit worried, though, when he failed to recognise them. Rolling his window down half a centimetre or so he shouted: 'What are those things on you? Bees?'

'Nah,' I replied calmly, 'but they do bite.'

He slipped me a bottle of water and then sped off in air-conditioned, pest-free luxury. Covered by these little yellow insects I stood and watched him disappear, feeling grimmer than ever.

After considerable suffering I was back at the unmemorable village of Turbi, where I found that another new arrival was none other than my friend Solomon, who had looked after me so energetically in Moyale. I spent the night in the humble and only accommodation, a lonely little building on the desert flats. One of its dusty rooms was named 'Soweto' and the other, in which I stayed, 'The New South Africa'.

News of my arrival spread quickly among the villagers, thanks partly to Solomon, who explained at great length to all and sundry about our sickbed adventures in Moyale, and both young and old inhabitants of this tiny desert village came to watch me devouring the worst meal of the journey, goat's brain and heart stew on rice. But I discovered that news had also filtered through about my meeting with a white Catholic priest who had passed me near Sololo, about 30 km from Turbi. He and I had chatted for a while, and then he pressed me to spend the night at his house. I was agreeable, but when we got to the turn-off to his home I discovered that the detour would take me 10 km off my route. In my view a total 20 km detour would be crazy for someone who was now counting every kilometre. Even the lure of a bath and hot food wasn't strong enough to tempt me off the road; it would be better to cover 20 km in the direction of an eventual permanent hot shower and home-made eatables. The people in Turbi were much taken with this story, and joked that it was bad luck not to visit a priest who had made such a kind offer.

The desert might have been arid but it was not unpopulated by either man or beast. Just before I reached Marsabit I saw two herds of elephant roaming around outside the town, no more than 500 metres from me, swinging their huge trunks from side to side while feeding off a lush hillside, the only greenery for hundreds of kilometres. It was an odd feeling to think that soon I would be pitching my tent by the roadside, right in the vicinity of these great grey creatures which loomed so large as I sat on my bicycle.

These wild elephant lived practically shoulder-to-shoulder with the local Masai inhabitants, and I was sorry that the chances of watching these descendants of warriors tackling a lion in their traditional style were small to zero. I was still holding thumbs that I would have some more direct interaction with the wilder wildlife en route – after all, adventurers have to have adventures. By the time I got to Marsabit, however, it was clear that the adventures would have to go on hold for the time being. The alleged road from Moyale had mortally injured the bike's back wheel and worn-out sprocket. The sprocket had now given up the ghost to such an extent that when I came to any sort of gradient the chain would just slip around as if it was entirely stripped, reducing me to pushing the bike. There was nothing for it – I would have to interrupt my trip and get my bike to Nairobi again to be properly repaired with the parts I had ordered from South Africa, then hitch a ride back to Marsabit so that I could cycle the rest of the way. AGAIN!

It was incredibly frustrating, to say the least, but there was no other way, because I simply couldn't be late for my date with CNN in Mombasa. This had now become an all-star occasion featuring the Mayor of Mombasa, the Kenyan national cycling team and (which was not to be missed) two nights of luxury accommodation. Then, at last, I would be able to transport my repaired bicycle back to Marsabit and complete the two-wheeled trek to Nairobi, whereas what I really wanted to do at this stage of my journey was simply to keep cycling southwards till I saw Table Mountain rising up in the distance.

Just before leaving Nairobi for the coast I had an extraordinary magazine interview in which I was asked to give opinions on a subject that I really knew little about, although I had strong feelings. A South African freelance journalist named Darren Taylor believed that my observations about Africa's farming problems would make an interesting feature for the *Farmer's Weekly*, a serious magazine which had been required reading for generations of South African farmers. Always ready to investigate new territory, I obliged (what the professional farmers made of my opinions I never discovered), after which I hit the road for Mombasa.

It was an interesting trip, full of new sights and sensations. The countryside became more fertile as I neared the coast, and the air smelled different as I pedalled along, stopping here and there to see particular sights. One of them was the famous Sikh temple at Makindu, which had been described to me by a friendly hairdresser of Asian descent at the Holiday Inn in Nairobi. It was built on the site of the original temple, which had been erected by labourers and artisans brought in from India a century earlier to build a railway line which would link Uganda to the coast at Mombasa. I didn't realise just then what a remarkable line this was, or how it had changed the face of East Africa.

When the British started building it in 1896 its detractors called it the 'Lunatic Express', because it would have to run for 576 miles through very difficult terrain which included a semi-desert, lofty highlands and the bed of the Great Rift Valley before reaching Kisumu on the shores of Lake Victoria. They imported materials and got to work with thousands of labourers and experienced artisans from India's enormous railway system. It was a tough business. The line became known as the 'Hell Express', with good reason. There was a lack of water in the early stages, floods frequently washed away newly laid lines, termites ate the sleepers, tsetse flies ravaged the herds of draught-oxen and workers fell ill by the thousands of everything from malaria to amoebic dysentery.

As if this was not enough, work was stalled for nearly a year in the Tsavo area by a pair of clever man-eating lions which killed 28 Indian workers and an uncounted number of black workers (some say more than 100), plus one senior British official. Eventually they were shot by an engineer named J.H. Patterson, whose subsequent book *The Man-Eaters of Tsavo* became an African classic and inspired at least three films, the latest one starring Val Kilmer and Michael Douglas.

Altogether it cost the British five years and the massive sum of £5 million to finish the line with its 1 200 bridges and 43 stations (one of them being Nairobi, which started off as the line's headquarters). It took the line 58 years to pay for itself, but it opened up East Africa to the outside world.

The people in charge of the temple were the first Sikhs I had ever met, exotic-looking men with high turbans and curly twisted moustaches, and they were very hospitable. They took me on a guided tour of the temple and its grounds – among other things showing me a spot where, it is believed, one of the man-eaters used to sleep during the day – fed me, gave me a souvenir T-shirt and offered to put me up for the night, which I had to refuse because of time constraints.

From Makindu it was straight into the Tsavo National Park. No lions tried to eat me, but I had an interaction with the local wildlife which was not what I had envisaged – at one spot I was concentrating so hard on my cycling that I nearly rode straight into the hind end of a grazing zebra, one of a sizeable herd. I managed to set up my camera on the other side of the road and film myself walking among them like a real bushvelder. The zebras didn't seem to mind, although they were definitely not the eat-out-of-my-hand tame types found in zoos.

Fifteen kilometres outside Mombasa I was met by the Kenyan cycle team and a film crew. I was deeply grateful for the company, because the passing traffic was just about the most lethal I had ever seen. Trucks flew past us and one another at breakneck speed, and the road had no shoulders on to which one could dodge. The Kenyans and the film crew took it all in their stride, though, and one of them swopped bikes with me. It was a pleasant arrival, all downhill, and although the Kenyan's bicycle was far too small for me, it was so pleasantly light and manoeuvrable that I barely raised my pulse-rate on the trip into Mombasa. The diminutive Kenyan cyclist riding my bike, on the other hand, had a real battle to maintain the pack's 35 km/h pace.

The welcoming party and festivities were arranged by a South African woman named Charlene who had settled in Kenya with her husband. With patriotic pride I basked in her energy, charm and influence – there's your typical South African girl, I thought. It was people like her I had had in mind when, at earlier stages of my trip, I had told my new friends: 'Give me one person's $9 000 United Nations salary and I'll bring you four South African "mover and shaker" girls to make things happen ... and with better results.'

To my regret Tumi Makgabo couldn't be there to interview me. CNN's resident East African correspondent, Gladys Njoroge, did a good job, but somehow I felt that I had failed to convey the uniqueness of my trip during this huge international opportunity, especially the fact that it wasn't just a social saunter around Africa but rather a pioneering world-first trip through places to which even soldiers in armed vehicles frequently would not go. The description of my journey on the final televised show apparently was something along the lines of 'this crazy guy, zig-zagging his way across Africa'. I mean, crazy, maybe, but zig-zagging? 'Zig-zagging' implies an aimless meandering, and my route was anything but aimless –

for one thing, if it had been I would not have got involved in all that frustrating backtracking. On the other hand, Gladys had booked me into what was reputedly the best hotel in Mombasa, the four-star Silversands. The hotel's food was definitely up to the four-star rating, and I really tucked in when Grace took me to eat there – I was so busy with my knife and fork that for once my dinner partner did more talking than me!

With the CNN story done, it was back to Marsabit for my latest piece of backtracking, which was so indescribably frustrating that even my iron determination started wavering, so that I kept asking myself: Why can't I just continue? I could be home weeks sooner than expected if I did. And I just knew my bicycle would suffer some damage and have something go wrong with it at the worst possible time, even though I had spent nearly $600 to get it into shape again. But I managed to put that little croaking voice behind me, and soon was heading for Marsabit again in a big truck driven by a kindly preacher called Pastor Moses. Along the way he also gave me the latest news of the stretch I would be passing through, none of it good. In the past fortnight there had been violent attacks in the Turbi region, and specifically in Turbi itself, by gunmen who were believed to be from another local tribe.

According to Pastor Moses the gunmen killed 90 inhabitants, mainly children and old people because most working adults were out herding or fetching water. The gunmen had been armed with automatic weapons and had shot the children down as they fled out of Turbi's one-roomed school building, Pastor Moses said; elderly people had been beaten to death with rocks. I felt very sad. No one deserved to die before their time, and so brutally, and especially not innocent children. In another incident, Pastor Moses said, a vehicle ambush along the very road we were travelling on had resulted in two people having their throats slit because they were suspected of belonging to the 'wrong' tribe. I couldn't help wondering what would befall me when I set off from Marsabit. I decided that I ought to make it in one piece because the danger was limited to tribal conflict, but Pastor Moses didn't agree. Foreigners were targeted as much as possible to make a bigger statement, he said.

Oh, well ... I would just have to take my chances, although I wasn't exactly happy about any of it. As it turned out, though, I had a tranquil journey. Once I had passed through the mountains around Marsabit the road was smoother and much more conducive to two-wheeled travel. There were more roadside villages and a definite increase in human movement, and water was easier to come by. So I pressed on with enthusiasm, because I knew that after my next stop, Isiolo, I would have 300 km of glorious tarmac under my wheels, and I would be free to stop off where I wanted to.

One such stopping-place was the equatorial line at Nanyuki, just past the neat slopes of Mount Kenya. I had deliberately ignored it during my four truck-borne crossings, but now I got off and stood right on it, my thoughts going back to when I had done the same thing in the pouring rain of Gabon on the other side of the continent. Had it really been more than a year and a half ago? Yes, it had. Wow!

Since I had already cycled from Nairobi to Mombasa I took a bus to the coast, although I couldn't help thinking (and my friends agreed with me) that it might well be safer to go under my own steam. Just a few days earlier a bus from this very company had crashed on this very road, killing 29 passengers.

Before leaving for what we all hoped would not be a death-ride I had an encounter which showed why Nairobi was known as 'Night Robbery'. I had long since learned to be very vigilant and convey the impression of being exactly the wrong sort of person for a mugger to tackle, but this time I was caught unawares. I was about to head for my hotel early one evening when I decided to stop off for something to eat at a respectable pub-style restaurant. The people inside were friendly and most looked as if they had just finished work, so I relaxed with a plate of 'nyama choma' (well-done grilled meat) and rice. When I had finished I sent an SMS to Vasti, left the money for the meal on the table and made for the door, which was no more than three metres away.

Just then a group of young men came in, and two of them headed straight to my table. The others remained clustered together at the door, although it was clear I was on my way out, shooting hostile glances at me and mumbling comments at one another. I edged past them into the street, then remembered I had left my cell phone on the table and hurried back inside, less careful about inching through their unresponsive ranks than I had been a minute earlier. They gave way to a chorus of assorted racist remarks and invitations for me to fuck off back to my own country. I ignored them – all I wanted was my cell phone.

When I got back to my table I greeted their two chums in Swahili and asked in English if they had seen my cell phone. They looked at each other, laughed and told me that it had not been there when they had sat down. This was clearly a lie, since the fact that my money was still lying there proved that the waitress hadn't returned to clear the table in the few seconds that it had taken me to return from the street. I went down on my hands and knees, just to make sure that the telephone hadn't perhaps dropped on to the floor, but I knew I hadn't. They had laid hands on it. Now the bigger of the two decided to pull the race card. He asked me where I came from; I replied politely that that was not important right now, all I wanted was for them to help me to find my cell phone. I knew this type only too well.

There is considerable hostility towards South Africa because it is one of the few countries on the continent which is relatively prosperous and progressive, and I knew that as soon as they saw the 'Proudly South African' logo on my shirt the penny would drop and these two thieves would try to save face by becoming aggressive. And so it was. 'You think I fucking steal because I am black? You racist pig! I will fucking kill you!' the bigger one shouted, getting to his feet. This was the signal for his fellow-thugs at the door to start pushing me around and telling me to fuck off. I was clearly outnumbered and so I fucked off, rather than end up dead at the hands of a bunch of racist petty thieves who would still be paddling along in Nairobi's gutter life long after I had ridden into the record books. Not, of course, that this made me less angry at the way I had been treated. 'Night Robbery' indeed!

I suppose an equally apt colloquial name for Nairobi would be 'Numerous Riots', at least for the period I spent there. A number of violent protests took place because, so the very vocal opposition proclaimed, President Mwai Kibaki had made many promises to the electorate during the last general election but had not delivered on them. So they took to the streets in demonstrations which soon became violent and tended to degenerate swiftly into strictly non-political looting. The day before my unpleasant encounter over the cell phone, mobs had ransacked shops and restaurants, one looter being killed in the process. This sparked even fiercer protests from the opposition, and I soon got a first-hand taste of what was happening.

I was sitting in a coffee shop frequented by many of the city's TV journalists when crowds of people came streaming down the cobbled walkway outside. The shop staff didn't need to be told what was about to happen. They rushed out between the tables and began closing the doors and lowering the external security fences. Across the road the same thing was happening. People were sprinting in all directions, trying to find refuge in the shops before they closed, fast and slow getting in one another's way, with the weaker being trampled underfoot to a chorus of screams.

Things got even worse with dismaying speed. Rocks and other rubble started flying through the air and were soon joined by large metal dustbins which clanged against the security mesh screens which had hastily been rolled down over the shop-windows. Now the first of the rioters came into view – mostly homeless or street people, to judge by their appearance, rather than solid citizens or students. My heart raced as the rioters drew closer. What did they want? What would they do to us if they got in here? It was rather frightening, even though I knew I was relatively safe behind the coffee shop's security fence.

But it didn't last long. All of a sudden the Kenyan police in their black riot gear appeared opposite the crowd and went swiftly and aggressively at them. All sorts of makeshift missiles began bouncing off their Perspex shields and helmets, but these were resolute men, professional and unwavering. It was good to see, except from the point of view of the rioters, who wavered and were soon in full flight with the cops on their heels. I decided that I really wouldn't want to be a Kenyan riot policeman unless the medical benefits were fairly spectacular.

The oddest thing about all this was how quickly everything returned to normality as soon as the rioters had been chased away. The shop assistants conducted lengthy sign-language discussions with the police, opened the glass doors, rolled up the security mesh and went around asking the remaining customers if they wanted refills for the coffee which had grown cold during the riot (mine certainly had – I had been too interested in what was going on to take even a sip). Not a minute after the mesh went up new customers appeared, ordered their drinkables and sat down to chat about day-to-day things or read newspapers. One would swear that absolutely nothing had happened.

This episode highlighted something I hadn't realised before, how distanced I had become from my turbulent surroundings because I was so intensely focused on my own affairs, to the extent that I hadn't noticed how the pressure had been building up over the past fortnight. It was like seeing that TV broadcast of the tsunami, four days after the actual event.

One could throw in a heavy dose of naïvety as well, stemming from the same source. For example, I spent three nights in the suburb of Eastleigh, which was notorious among Nairobians as 'Little Mogadishu' because it was crammed wall to wall with fugitive clan warlords who had been driven out of neighbouring Somalia by the Islamic militia which ruled the chaotic non-state for a while – tough, ruthless people who expected the same deference they had enjoyed while swaggering around Mogadishu with their thugs. Needless to say, Eastleigh had a rough, nasty vibe to it, but I didn't grasp its true notoriety till I telephoned Izak Barnard at the South African Embassy and he, obliging fellow though he was, told me bluntly that there was no way he was coming anywhere near Little Mogadishu, and that if we were to meet I would have to get some transport into the city centre.

I shudder now when I think back on one instance of foolish behaviour which could have led to lethal consequences. I had wandered out of my little hotel just after sunset one rainy evening to get some tea from one of the roadside tea-ladies, just as I had done all over coastal Africa. I was drinking my tea and chatting in Arabic to the tea-lady when a scrawny, wrinkled man, his head shrouded, appeared out of the rainy darkness and warned me: 'You leave our women or we kill you.'

With a species of friendly aggression (I was half-smiling) I replied: 'Fuck off, you idiot. Who are you?'

'We are the Somalis, and we will stab you if you talk to her again,' he said from the shadows of his shrouded head. Now I noticed that the pedestrians around us wore shocked and fearful expressions. I wasn't going to give him the satisfaction of scaring me off, so I chatted a little more with the tea-lady and then set off down the muddy street to my hotel with all my senses hyper-alert and my finger curled around the trigger of my electric self-defence shocker.

I left Nairobi without regret and bused safely to Mombasa, where my bicycle picked up what would now be called 'bling' from a friendly storekeeper by the name of Murtaza Kitabwalla, who was much taken with what I was doing. He not only gave me a rear-view mirror but insisted on brightening things up with some colourful additions. These included supplying a new mock leopard-skin cover for the seat to go over my old one from the Sudan, which was getting rather battered, and decorating the front and rear wheel-rims with vividly coloured little things like miniature feather dusters. He said they were called 'dust-busters' because they cut down on dust accumulation. It was all a little bright for my taste, but I went with it because these extra frills came out of the goodness of his heart and helped to wash away the bad taste left by the cell phone thugs. And maybe the dust-busters actually would work! That would be a bonus on the many kilometres of dodgy road-surface that I was sure still lay ahead.

It was in Mombasa, too, that I belatedly learned the meaning of one of the few internationally-known Swahili phrases, 'Hakuna matata', which became famous all over the world because it was the name of one of the songs in the 'Lion King' film. I have always liked to sing out loud – sometimes at slightly inappropriate times, like when out in public with my friends – if I know the words of the song. In this case, though, I hadn't realised till I reached Mombasa that 'Hakuna matata' was actually Swahili for 'no problem'. Well, we live and learn. Hakuna matata!

I was also involved in thinking about another (albeit much more complicated) cultural matter: the various ways in which locals all over the continent had absorbed outside influences into their own lives and cultures. All along my journey I had observed how the earlier explorers, adventurers and/or colonialists (take your pick) had left their distinct footprints, and by this stage I had seen enough to realise that a regional change in culture was not simply the result of traditional internal developmental forces. As a result I was able to link each country's general vibe to the specific outside cultural influences to which it had been exposed. For example, I had gone from the un-colonialised mountains of Ethiopia to 'English' Nairobi and then to 'Arabic' Mombasa, and now I was on the way to 'Swahili' Tanzania. In each case I could feel – just about on a daily basis, from village to village – an almost tangible difference in the people I encountered, which affected their interaction with the rest of the world. Perhaps it had been happening all the time and I had been unaware of it, but I was certainly very conscious of it now.

Mombasa was a particularly clear example of this absorption and interaction process. Huge numbers of seafaring travellers had called in here over the centuries, some to visit and others to stay, and each new culture had left its mark on some local aspect, from architectural styles to language and religion – particularly religion. Belonging to a specific faith is like membership in a club; it makes a person feel safe and gives him a sense of righteousness. Yet this usually works out badly, although the belief in a Maker should unite us, not divide us.

In the past few weeks I had spent a lot of time asking myself how I would feel, as a local, knowing that my religion or language or both had been inherited from some energetic seafarers who had come calling. It was obviously a touchy subject. Most people I talked to about this between Mombasa and Tanzania were extremely defensive and went to great lengths to explain that they had no links with Arabia and were pure Kenyans or Tanzanians.

I didn't think the people I spoke to had a problem with being Arabic per se, but it seemed to me that an African feels less African if history shows that he and his people were exposed to one or other external influence. My personal conclusion is that people conveniently forget to follow the time-line back far enough. We are all settlers to some extent, because we all originated from somewhere else if we follow the time-line back to its roots. In the process we have all experienced external influences which affected our individual and group development – a prime example is the Ethiopians' Julian calendar, which was introduced by Julius Caesar in 46 BC. What causes all the trouble is that we only go back as far as we want to and try to ignore the rest of our common history.

On the other hand, the locals obviously didn't spend their time worrying too much about time-lines and such while there were tourist dollars to be earned, as I saw when the manager of a large holiday resort near the Tanzanian border invited me to a dinner-dance. It took place around a huge pool, surrounded by large palm and coconut trees, and the manager had pulled out all the stops and put me at a table right next to the dance-floor. I spent about two hours with a permanent smile on my face, not just because there was a vast array of food with which to satisfy my usual ravenous appetite but also because most of the dancers were doing the good old 'langarm', or 'long arm', a sort of cha-cha much loved in many of the more traditional areas of South Africa – all to the strains of a Kenyan version of 'By the Rivers of Babylon'. It was hilarious in a surreal sort of way, and I wished I could summon up my friends Bollie and Tanya, who are dyed-in-the-wool langarm experts, to give some expert tuition.

Next morning I indulged myself in a silly but entertaining masquerade. As a child I had always enjoyed role-playing with strangers, and I now I had such a marvellous opportunity that I simply couldn't resist the temptation. I was having a coffee-and-scones breakfast after a leisurely couple of hours checking my e-mails and such when I was besieged by some locals who were obviously drunk in spite of the fairly early hour. I spent a while politely fending off their continual requests for beer and money, then decided to have a little fun. For my victim I chose the drunkest of the lot, who had sat down close to me for a bit of one-on-one bonding, preparatory to putting the bite on me. I listened to the sad story of his life, suggested that he stop drinking (advice he allowed to pass without comment), encouraged him to improve his circumstances and then asked him what he did for a living.

'I cannot talk about it,' he whispered.

Now I was really interested. Surely he couldn't hope to extract something for his throat or pocket from me without explaining about his pitiful dead-end job or (best of all) no job at all. I was still thinking about this when he asked: 'What do *you* do?'

Aha! This was a moment not to be wasted. Many of the people I'd met along my route had found it hard to believe that I was merely a white guy riding a bicycle because most of what they knew about white people derived from Hollywood movies or what their governments wanted them to believe. So instantly I turned from Manser the Bicycle Man into Manser the Indiana Jones knock-off.

'I'm smuggling oil,' I said, looking very serious in spite of my desire to roll around laughing. I leaned into the miasma of beer fumes and sweat enveloping him and added: 'I need a man who can buy this from me.' To add an extra bit of atmosphere I glanced nervously around and then up at the slowly spinning ceiling fans above us as if afraid of observers or recording devices.

Instantly he adopted the same furtive manner and even asked some of his closer associates to move out of earshot: 'You cannot trust them,' he explained. By now, obviously, he had appointed himself my right-hand man and trusted confidant.

I fought another battle to keep a straight face and whispered: 'The ship is landing tonight; I need 10 donkeys, 5 camels and 35 goats. Can you help me?' Perhaps 35 goats was going a bit far, so I hastily added: 'The goats are a gift for the captain.'

That was good enough for him. 'No problem, no problem,' he replied with drunken nonchalance. 'What time?'

Might as well see how far I can string it out, I thought. 'But very importantly, I also need five machine-guns, plenty bullets. I don't want people to steal from me. When can I have them?' To my surprise this didn't shake him. 'The machine-guns I can have for you also, no problem, just buy me a beer now first. Then you will have them by five o'clock.'

A herd of animals and a cache of machine-guns in exchange for a litre of ice-cold beer! Now I couldn't help laughing, and of course I had to tell him I had been having him on. But I was also laughing at myself. I had been making a joke about something that, it seemed, actually could take place. I suppose it all came down to supply and demand. Or to put it another way, how many beers would a machine-gun cost?

I left my beery 'friend' behind and set off southwards towards the Tanzanian border post again. My short-term aim on this leg was to get to Dar es Salaam and find some place which had South African digital satellite TV reception, because I was starved for a good game of rugby which featured our national Springbok team. In Nairobi a fortnight earlier I had heard our national anthem sung on TV by the players at the Nelson Mandela Challenge, and it had made me more emotional than the average Oprah Winfrey audience guest. I wanted – needed – more of the same fix.

But first I had to deal with a much more mundane matter. While I was standing in the queue at the Tanzanian border post a forthright female immigration official approached me with outstretched hand and asked: 'Your vehicle documents, please.'

'Vehicle documents? Do I need *vehicle documents?*' I stuttered, absolutely amazed. Were these characters planning to confiscate my bike because it weighed too much, or something? This really would be the last straw! But the official knew what she was doing. 'Where is your vehicle?' she asked.

'My vehicle is outside your office window.' I replied.

She leaned out of the window and glanced up and down, obviously confused, since the only 'vehicle' parked outside certainly wasn't a two-wheeled car. Then the penny dropped and she smiled. 'You waste my time,' she said, pointing to another line of people. 'You are in the wrong queue. Go over there.'

I did just that, heaving a sigh of relief. My 'vehicle' and I had taken another small step in the direction of Cape Town, home and Vasti.

# CHAPTER 31

# SOUL FOOD AND WHEEL-WOBBLES IN TANZANIA

*I found myself sharing a table with three fierce-looking Ma-
sai warriors – spears, short swords, traditional dress, stretched
ear-lobes and all – straight out of the National Geographic at
first glance. But not at second glance. The three alleged sons
of old Africa spurned my unsophisticated local dish of meat
chunks in favour of omelettes and ordered up bottles of the best
lager, which they drank while one conducted a long conversation on his cell phone and the other two puffed away at filter-
tips – 'Marlborough Man', African-style.*

My second-last country! The very thought was unreal. I had come
so far on a journey that sometimes had seemed endless, and suddenly here I was, just two countries and two sets of border-crossings
away from South Africa. To make it even better, I had some knowledge of Tanzania, which I had visited as a tourist two years earlier,
so that I was free of the nagging apprehensions about what might
lie ahead which I had felt when entering just about all of the countries I had gone through so far. That knowledge was based on actual observations, not on perceptions created by the media or by
politicians. There are so many sensationalists and spin doctors in
the world these days that the only unalloyed truth derives from personal experience.

I spent longer in Tanzania than I had planned, but the time went
by so swiftly that suddenly two whole weeks had passed. Unfortu-

nately this wasn't matched by the number of kilometres I could theoretically have cycled in that time. I don't adhere to the old belief that time only flies when you're having a good time; it can go by just as fast when you're not, and what happened to me in Tanzania provided ample proof. It's not that the fortnight was so excruciatingly bad, it's just that I don't know what consumed all those valuable penultimate days of my journey. All I know is that I covered roughly 800 km, watched some good rugby, ate some 'pap and wors' – that good old traditional South African meal of savoury porridge and beef sausage – and fixed my bike a few more times, local style.

My choice of route for the first leg of my foray into Tanzania wasn't the most comfortable one, because to stay true to my concept I ignored all the advice I received and set off by way of the coastal dirt roads instead of the smooth tarmac ones inland. This would be no great hardship, I calculated. According to my understanding it was only a short 66 km to the village of Tanga, after which there would be tarmac all the way to the capital of Dar es Salaam, a place of which I retained fond memories from my previous visit. My plan was to reach Dar in one stretch without rest days or delay, recharge physically and watch the upcoming Springbok rugby match against Australia if I could find the right TV facilities. Then I would complete the stretch to the Mozambican border, come hell, high water or horrendous roads.

But, incredibly, my bike's rear wheel was showing signs of acting up again. The chains, sprockets, new brake-pads, cables and other replacements which had been fitted in Nairobi were running beautifully, but there was a problem which, in due course, was revealed as a broken internal spring ratchet inside the rear wheel's 'free hub', or bearing capsule (the spring-loaded mechanism is what makes that rolling trrrrrkkrrrrrkkkrrrrr sound when you back-pedal while freewheeling). As I understand it, when you are pedalling forward the spring-loaded clip expands to latch on to teeth inside the wheel, thus allowing the energy you have created to be efficiently transferred to the sprockets and chain. Because of the broken spring this was not happening properly, particularly when I tried to apply heavy force (which had been the reason why I couldn't pedal uphill in the Marsabit section). An additional danger from this slipping motion of the rear hub, as many male cyclists will know, is that when it gives way as you start forcing the pedal down your gonads meet with the central stabiliser bar in a way that doesn't help to lift your spirits, although you might find it lifting the pitch of your voice to a painful yodel. I had a few close calls but managed to avoid any permanent damage in the fatherhood stakes. But that was as far as my luck extended: at the very least I had to find someone qualified to carry out repairs.

The ideal solution to this problem would be an entire (and expensive, needless to say) replacement of either the free hub or preferably the entire rear wheel, but that would be a serious drain on my remaining scanty finances. Meanwhile, all I could do was struggle on and hope that the bike would make it to Dar es Salaam, where I would surely be able to find a professional bicycle mechanic. An additional worry was that I wasn't at all sure my diagnosis was accurate; what was happening inside this part of the bicycle was largely a mystery to me, my only real source of knowledge being the mental pictures I had formed from descriptions I had been given by various mechanics.

Thanks to my late departure from the border it was dark by the time I arrived at Tanga, a relaxed, touristy town full of squarish old Arabic-style architecture. I had a bit of trouble finding affordable accommodation, because when you arrive at a place looking the way I did it is immediately assumed that you are desperate and will pay whatever price you are quoted. The first few places had faded official government tourism department letterheads bearing fake prices which, as I was to discover, were something like 10 times more than the norm. I couldn't afford such prices, and so I went on searching till I found a hostel whose tariffs were only reasonably inflated. As a South African – and especially one with a thin wallet and a malfunctioning bicycle – I was infuriated when I discovered that I was expected to pay more simply because I was white. One could put this discrimination down to racism, but it was more likely simply a result of the widespread misperception that all whites were foreigners and therefore rich.

In Tanga I had a real 'small world' experience, and then some, while breakfasting on pie and coffee at a small pastry shop the morning after my arrival. I was reading a copy of the local English-language newspaper, and after wading through all the political stuff I saw a boxing photograph which interested me, being keen on the sport myself. It was about the career of a local fighter named Matumla, holder of the Commonwealth middleweight title. The name seemed very familiar, although I wasn't sure why. Then I got to the part where mention was made of his great fight against South Africa's best middleweight, my friend Troy Mitchell (whose birthday I'd gone to London for!) He was considered by many knowledgeable boxing people to be South Africa's most promising fighter at that time. This was hardly surprising, because I knew how much effort and determination he put into both his training and his fighting.

I was aware that Troy had fought once in Tanzania but couldn't remember the details, so I sent him an SMS right away to ask if he remembered fighting Matumla. I didn't expect an instant reply but got one all the same. Yes, he said, he remembered the fight. He had been in the best condition of his career and would easily have won except that a cut to the eye gave the fight to Matumla on a technical knockout in the second round. It was certainly a great coincidence that the first newspaper I had bought *anywhere* along the route should have a story about him, but when I sent another SMS to say what a surprise it had been for me he came back with the cherry on top: 'You know what the really amazing thing is? The day me and him fought was exactly this day 10 years ago. Can you believe it?'

On my way out of town I decided to stop at the Tanga Cement factory, which apparently had South Africans on its staff. It took me a while to make contact, but eventually I was whisked off for lunch and invited to spend the night so that I could meet the Chief Financial Officer, Lafras, who was down in Dar on business. A refusal, it was made clear to me, was not to be contemplated. So I didn't contemplate it, which led to a bit of sweet revenge when I was booked into one of the hotels I had been shown out of the night before because the inflated price had been too high for me!

The extra day's stay turned out to be well worthwhile, apart from the fact that I ate and slept well. I made a good new friend in the shape of Lafras. He and his staff loved my story and asked if I would re-tell it to the pupils at the local Catholic school, which was one of the company's social community projects and apparently a role model for many other Tanzanian schools. South African companies and their expertise were very involved in the Tanzanian economy, Lafras explained, adding that I would bump into many more of our fellow countrymen on my way south. My biggest 'score', however, was a donation of $400 from the company – obviously Lafras's work – which would go a long way to getting my bicycle in shape again. Lafras even offered to have me driven to Dar es Salaam to have the bike fixed and brought back again, but I decided to take the chance that it would last for the 360 km trip. I should have known better.

I spent the first day passing through a wondrous landscape which was intensely green but unfortunately also very hilly, so I did a lot of pushing. The second day brought further problems, so that it became impossible even to use a bigger gear. My average speed dropped to about 13 km/h, and when I reached the town of Mkata I reluctantly tossed in the towel and called Lafras. He said he had a vehicle due to take one of his staff members to the airport at Dar, and told me to be ready to be picked up before sunrise. So I ended up getting to Dar rather sooner than I had thought. My game-plan stayed roughly the same: find some accommodation, track down a good bicycle mechanic, watch the rugby game, see if I could scare up some sponsorship and then get a ride back to Mkata.

The accommodation was no problem because Adrian Penny had asked the manager of the Dar es Salaam Holiday Inn, Adam Fuller, to look after me – which he did in spades. He welcomed me warmly and asked if it would be OK to call a media conference with me as the star. Naturally I agreed immediately, even though I got the impression it would take place very close to that rugby match I was looking forward to. Then I got down to seeing if I could source some sponsorships. Dar es Salaam was the last major city I would encounter for the next 3 000 km, so I needed to secure enough money to keep body and soul together for this entire stretch. My costs would be rock-bottom, because I intended to forego all pleasures of the flesh and do things as I had done them at the start of the journey, eating my own food and sleeping in my tent by the roadside most of the time. That would keep my costs down to about $5–10 a day, which included three Cokes (ice-cold if possible) for my daily treat.

I struck it lucky right away. The local Sony-Ericsson operation gave me one of its fancy late-model P910i cell phones to replace the one I had lost in my 'Night Robbery' experience, and DSTV Tanzania, which is run by a South African called Nic, with a surname that will tell you he is Greek, gave me $200 and asked me to do a Supersport interview for a private Tanzanian TV station's sport channel (I was happy to oblige, because DSTV had been good to me at various times during my trip). Air Tanzania was keen to negotiate a deal with me, but this had to be scheduled for when I returned to Dar after re-starting my journey from Mkata.

Finding an expert bicycle mechanic turned out to be a mission, though. According to the driver of the Holiday Inn van who was taking me on my search there were no professional cycling shops or mechanics in Dar es Salaam, and I soon came to believe him when I had met some of the local talent. Every alleged expert I came across swore blind he knew just how to fix my bike before it had even been unloaded from the van for him to inspect it. This was nerve-wracking for me, because I had no idea of precisely what was needed and had to go by instinct and first impressions. Most of these self-proclaimed mechanics disqualified themselves right away when I saw what they had for workshops and tools. This is not even to mention the responses to my questions. Most of the time our negotiations would go something like this:

'Where will you work on my bike?'

'Here on the street.'

'In the middle of all these people, selling vegetables and cool drinks and food?'

'Yes'

'Where will you leave my bicycle when you go to mosque?'

'Here.'

'Where?'

'Here.'

'You must be joking.'

'No, I'm not joking.'

'But it will be unlocked, lying in the open road in the centre of a city. Someone will steal from my bags or even steal the bicycle itself.'

'No, no thieves here! They will not like your bicycle.'

'Can you fix it?'

'Yes.'

'Have you seen a part like this before in your life?'

'No.'

'How much?'

'How much you want to pay?'

'You can fix this?'

'Yes, I can fix this.'

'Where are your tools?'

'It's OK, I don't need tools.'

Most people will understand why I didn't fling myself on the mercy of the first bike mechanic I came across, ignorant though I was. Anyway, I persevered till I found a mechanic who was basically the only guy who didn't scare me off at first sight, and the wheel looked and felt good after he had re-spoked and serviced it.

The 'pap and wors' experience I mentioned earlier was definitely a highlight of my stay in Dar es Salaam. Anyone who has travelled outside their own country for an extended period of time will know what I am talking about; food, even more than language, is what allows you to close your eyes and experience the sensations of home as strongly as if you were actually there.

The media conference – co-hosted by the South African High Commission, to my pleased surprise – went exactly as planned; the only odd thing about it was that every so often a pretty young blonde woman in a traditional chef's outfit would peek through the door at the rear of the room, then vanish again. When the interviews ended after a total of about three hours I was worn out and contemplating strategies for a graceful exit. But this was unnecessary, because the blonde chef lady, having leaned into the rear doorway for about the hundredth time, decided she had waited long enough. In a very gentle voice she introduced herself as Maryna, explained that she worked in the hotel's kitchen, asked me if there was anything specific I would like to eat and then suggested pap and wors. I was too flabbergasted to give her the emphatic 'yes' which was all that the occasion demanded. Instead I found myself croaking feebly: 'You're not joking, are you?'

But no, Maryna definitely was not joking. Three-quarters of an hour later I was blissfully tucking in. By this time she had also informed me that she had intervened to make sure that I would be able to catch the rugby game, which she also wanted to watch. She had arranged to join Nic, his wife and me at the opposition hotel's ladies' bar for the purpose. All this only added to my appetite, and what a meal that was! Maryna not only provided the pap and wors (the genuine article, imported from home) but topped them off with the 'braaibroodjies', or grilled sandwiches, which are an essential part of a true South African braai – two crispy toasted slices of bread with a thick layer of melted cheese, onion slices and tomato in between. Some famous braai experts add spices as well, but in whatever form the 'braaidbroodjie' has got a large number of South Africans securely hooked.

While I did my patriotic duty and ate non-stop, Maryna explained to me that after seeing me on CNN and also the first 'Carte Blanche' documentary she had become convinced that there was no way that I could pass through Dar es Salaam without bumping into the South African contingent there, and had therefore planned this treat for me. She could not have been more spot on. So far most of the people I had encountered had tried to solve my increasing homesickness by treating me to luxuries (which, let me hasten to add, I needed and appreciated), whereas this simple South African staple would have done the trick 10 times over. Maryna was the farm girl that all South African guys talk about as being the ideal woman to marry – sweet, pretty and a demon cook as well. Just perfect! Oh, yes, and the Springboks beat the Australians. That was one perfect day, all right.

When my bike had been repaired the same Tanga Cement driver who had brought me to Dar took me northwards again and dropped me off exactly where he had collected me in Mkata. I wasted no time in getting on the road, my heart filled with a mixture of joy at resuming my journey home and gratitude towards Lafras, Nic, Adam, Maryna and all the other people who had taken me under their wing out of sheer kindness. Lafras in particular had turned what could have been a truly demotivating exercise into an absolute breeze.

How would it be possible to show my appreciation? 'Thank you' just wasn't adequate; it had been worn out by repetition, like 'I love you'. Something more was needed, some sort of extra-sensory message. A few people had this gift, but I didn't seem to be one of them. I remember thinking how I wished I had the ability to let people know that my gratitude came from my entire body and soul, not just the bottom of my heart; that I would lie awake at nights, trying to convince myself that I was worthy of such personal kindness, support and involvement. Two years on, people still ask me if I learned anything about myself on this trip, and I think: too much to work out in just two years, my friends.

In the meantime the road ahead lay waiting for me to eat it up, and I did, although it soon became evident that while my chosen mechanic had improved the rear wheel's performance, he had not managed to eliminate the problem. The terrain had flattened considerably and the wheel was not being tested as severely as it might have been, but I still had that nagging worry. I might get to Dar without major problems, but at the same time I wouldn't know just how reliable the bike really was for the stretch after that.

Just how important tourism is to Tanzania became steadily more apparent as I got closer to Dar es Salaam, with tourist stalls and groups of authentic-looking 'Masai' warriors everywhere along the roadside. Many other countries on the continent can offer wildlife experiences, but none on Tanzania's grand scale. The annual animal migrations, most noticeably the wildebeest, up and down the Serengeti plains are one of the wonders of the world. I reflected as I rode along that in some countries I had passed through, especially the more undeveloped ones, the Minister of Tourism's job was actually more vital to the national well-being than the Minister of Finance's.

Needless to say, this concentration on tourism has brought strange contrasts, sometimes rather hilarious ones, such as the time I stopped for lunch at a rather scabby local eatery and found myself sharing a table with three fierce-looking Masai warriors – spears, short swords, traditional dress, stretched ear-lobes and all – straight out of the *National Geographic* at first glance. But not at second glance. The three alleged sons of old Africa spurned my unsophisticated local dish of meat chunks in favour of omelettes and ordered up bottles of the best lager, which they drank while one conducted a long conversation on his cell phone and the other two puffed away at filter-tips – 'Marlborough Man', African-style. They left before I did, but a little later I passed them entertaining a crowd of very pale-skinned tourists in a luxury 4x4, bouncing up and down on one leg, just like in the documentaries. The tourists in their stiff new khaki clothes were so impressed by this taste of the real, raw Africa that they tumbled out to take lots of photographs, for which they were quite willing to pay a fee, of course. I wondered what would have happened if that one warrior's cell phone had started ringing amid all the jumping around.

Having enjoyed a good laugh, I couldn't make up my mind about the morals of all this. Were the tourists being tricked? My first conclusion was that they were. But after further consideration I wasn't so sure. Tourism isn't about mere sightseeing any more, but about having an experience. If these tourists felt they were having a real African experience, was any harm being done to either side? One could make the accusation that if it hadn't been for the tourists the true Masai warrior's lifestyle would not have become merely an act. On the other hand, the tourism created work where few other opportunities existed, especially for the Masai. Finally I decided that I didn't know what was right and wrong in this case. The fact was that the genuine Masai warrior lifestyle had been in decline long before Tanzania became a world-famous tourist destination. People moved on from their traditional folk ways as circumstances changed, and the best they could do was preserve their traditions. After all, two centuries earlier my ancestors had worn big hats and corduroy trousers, and had ridden about the veld with long muzzle-loaders cradled in their arms. Here I was in ragged shorts, riding a cutting-edge bicycle with a cell phone in my pocket. Should I have stuck with the corduroy trousers and the muzzle-loader? But one way or the other, I concluded, I would be very surprised if I ever met a genuine, untarnished, unmodernised Masai warrior in my lifetime.

The last 70 km into the city indicated that there were lots of South Africans in Dar, just as Lafras had said, judging by the numerous vehicles with back-home registrations passing me in one direction or the other. This made me feel really good, and I waved to all of them, although I don't think many noticed that I had a South African flag flying on my handlebars.

I arrived late that evening in Dar es Salaam with its hustle and bustle and smiling faces that give it a unique carnival-like atmosphere. People here seem to be having fun doing whatever they are doing. But I didn't have time to submerge myself in the general spirit because I intended to make my stop-over a brief one. I met with the guys from Air Tanzania, and attended a black-tie function with Nic, the DSTV managing director – a lavish five-star dinner at the Holiday Inn, plus entertainment of the same standard, featuring the well-known South African hypnotist, Max Kahn. But there was a lot of action attached to both.

The Air Tanzania guys were willing to fly Vasti over for a few days' visit, but to my enormous regret I had to turn this down. I simply did not have the money to fly her from Cape Town to Johannesburg to connect with a Tanzanian flight, not to mention covering the various airport taxes and so on; in addition it would cost five days of valuable cycling time and use up money that could see me through to the end. As a substitute, however, they agreed to fly a very charming and famous South African photo-journalist, Debbie Yazbek, from Kenya to Tanzania for a photo-shoot. They also said they would arrange for the African affairs writer Hans Pienaar to join her. This was something of a coup. Debbie had just won the CNN photo-journalist of the year award when I met her in Nairobi, although this had not swelled her head at all, and Hans Pienaar was virtually a legendary figure in his field.

The function with Nic and his wife Nicky was wonderful for two reasons. Firstly, I got an unexpected boost for my ego. Naturally I didn't have a tuxedo, nor anything else remotely suitable, so Nic loaned me a black suit, a pale pin-striped cotton shirt and smart black shoes (fortunately he had big feet like me). I thought I looked OK, what with the contrast between my chic borrowed clothing and the wild and sun-blackened look of the rest of me. Apparently at least one other person agreed with me, a lovely Russian expatriate woman who informed me: 'You are very, very handsome man ... You are the most handsome man I see.' I ducked out of this encounter, which obviously had heavy overtones, but I have to admit I enjoyed it while it lasted.

The second high point was when I bumped into Maryna, the blonde pap-and-wors magician. She had been so busy working on a new menu for the hotel that I had not seen her at all since my return. By chance she walked past our tented function and saw me talking to Max Kahn. Immediately we arranged to meet, this time together with an Ethiopian friend of hers called Sonait Mekonen, who owned a popular restaurant called 'Addis in Dar'. I couldn't wait to eat Ethiopian again – I enjoyed Tanzania's cassava dishes, limitless cashew nuts and grilled meat, but wished I could take pre-cooked Ethiopian 'tibs and njera' with me on the road – and I said as much to Sonait when we met. She was an interesting woman who had travelled the world with her former husband, a UN official; now she and her son ran the restaurant, serving food that I thought tasted even better than the real deal I had had in Ethiopia itself. Sonait couldn't grasp that I had actually done what I said I had done, but appreciated my admiration of her country and its food so much that she wouldn't let us pay – when she opened her dream restaurant in Cape Town called 'Addis in the Cape', she joked, we could pay her back by coming to eat there.

Then I loaded myself and my bike on to the jam-packed ferry that plied southwards across the bay from behind the very aromatic fish market to Dar's renowned beaches. I didn't avail myself of them, however, because I wanted to get going. Thanks to the leisurely ferry-ride I only made it to the Kipepeo ('butterfly' in Swahili) lodge and campsite by evening ... and by now I had had an unpleasant taste of things to come, because my rear wheel was already pulling out of shape.

I spent a day at Kipepeo re-aligning the wheel, but after no more than 30 km the spokes started to snap. I limped back to Kipepeo and spent another day repairing the spokes, so successfully (in my opinion) that I believed the worst was over. It wasn't. I managed to cover 55 km and reach the main road heading south when the wheel made trouble again and the gears started slipping as badly as they had in northern Kenya. I didn't want to believe it, but there was no denying the facts. I would have to find transport back to Dar. Even this went badly, so that the best I could do was hop a succession of short-distance lifts as far as Kipepeo.

I contacted Vasti and we discussed the problem. It was plain that trying to head southwards through largely uncycled territory with a chronically ailing rear wheel was not a proposition: what I needed was a new wheel, free hub and all. Vasti would therefore have to contact Mongoose South Africa to see if they would be willing to supply a replacement. I also contacted Maryna to tell her about the problem but said I would be able to sort it out, which was a flat-out lie. She couldn't get away but had Sonait drive out to Kipepeo to help. Sonait and I sat on the campsite's beach lawn with some hippy-looking local travellers, taking the entire back wheel and free hub apart in the hope that somehow we could engineer a miracle. We couldn't, but it was good to have someone like Sonait around, because although she knew nothing about bicycles she was enthusiastic in searching for a solution. Her 'can do' spirit was refreshing – it becomes tiring after a while when you are the only person who thinks like that.

Mongoose South Africa didn't react immediately to Vasti's request, so I decided to try one more time. I gave up after 40 km; I could have struggled on a little further, but the snapped spokes and crumbling rear wheel were enough to convince me that it would be an exercise in futility. I felt utterly dejected. Would I never be able to get going on the last stretch to Cape Town? I was so down that I avoided making contact with the people who had helped me earlier because I felt they would see me as a failure. It didn't make sense and I was truly shocked at myself for thinking like this, but I just couldn't snap out of it. So I vegetated at Kipepeo, waiting to hear from Mongoose South Africa via Vasti.

Adam Fuller broke through this self-destructive mood when I slunk over to Dar to send some e-mails. When I had finished I broke temporarily out of my self-imposed exile to go and say hello to Maryna before catching the ferry back across the bay, and Adam saw us chatting in the Holiday Inn foyer. He didn't greet me, just asked why I didn't want to stay at the Holiday Inn and then, before I could respond, told the receptionist to book me into a room. I wanted to object, but he interrupted: 'Don't be rude. We want to help, and you're refusing. That is *rude*, my boy.' Then he strode away with a smile. What a man!

Now it was easy to send and receive e-mails, ands I pushed Vasti for a response from the Mongoose South Africa people, who eventually came back with a great offer: would I like a totally new bike? Naturally I was very grateful for the offer, but I said 'no' for two reasons. Firstly, I had become attached to my boon companion of two years' standing. Secondly, and this was the most serious reason, when I arrived back home I wanted children across South Africa to be able to touch and see the bike that had made it around the earth's most famous continent.

Mongoose fell in with this and said a new wheel would be available for free; all we had to do was courier it up to Dar. This was an extremely expensive exercise, but Vasti and I knew that we would not regret spending the money – I would certainly not shed a tear to see its predecessor roll away into the bush. And that is exactly what happened. I unclipped my old wheel and rolled it forcefully down the road and out of my life, and the new one was already in and spinning before the departing one had lost momentum.

I didn't feel guilty about littering. Children in Tanzania love to play with loose bicycle wheels, so I knew that it would soon find a home and a new lease on life.

I sent SMS messages to all those good people in Dar. All ended the same way: 'See you in South Africa'. This time there would be no turning back, and it felt great to be on the road again. OK, I would have to re-do about 100 km of road that I had done twice already, but so what? I had to get to Cape Town, and I knew it was going to be a testing time. Earlier in the trip I could afford to lose my concentration at times and choose wrong routes by the seat of my pants. But now that sort of thing was becoming risky. I had the feeling that my bicycle was getting tired, new wheel or no new wheel. Side-excursions would now be an unaffordable luxury rather than an option. Keep focused! That was the only way to go.

I soon needed all the focus I could get. Before long the road southwards narrowed and in many parts disintegrated into little more than soft pools of fine sand which made it almost impossible even to push my bicycle in the right direction, never mind ride it. At one stage I got a misery-loves-company boost for my morale when I saw a tractor battling to get through a nasty stretch ahead of me. At least I was still moving!

I found myself in the middle of an all-out election campaign again, starring one Jakaya Kikwete from the ruling CCM party, who billed himself as 'the president in waiting'. He and his supporters also seemed to be heading south, and every so often I would be passed by a convoy of speeding 4x4s. At other times I would find myself in the middle of handouts of T-shirts bearing Kikwete's face and slogan. I wasn't sure how much this would mean in terms of votes, because the people weren't interested in the speeches, it was the T-shirts they were after. I managed to get hold of one by buying a recipient a cool drink and literally giving him the sweaty shirt off my back in exchange.

It was very much the very basic politicking you see in countries where most of the people are uneducated. In my opinion it is archaic and wrong for politicians to sweep people up with entertainment, free food and colourful T-shirts aimed at creating the perception that they love the people and the people love them. The fact is that when you hand out clothes and food to people who do not earn even a dollar a day it's easy to get them excited. If one banned all this cheap razzmatazz and concentrated on simple pamphlets to educate the people there might be fewer voters at the polling stations, but they would be a lot more knowledgeable. Am I saying that many people in Africa vote blindly for one party or the other, without an ounce of an idea about what the party can or should or will really do for them? Yes, that's exactly what I'm saying. An easily solved problem, therefore, but I'm not holding my breath.

One night I slept in the reception area of a small roadside guest house because all their rooms were full. I had wanted to pitch my tent outside, but the proprietors were so insistent that I stay inside that I really could not refuse. The problem was that this meant the mosquitoes could make merry on me all night. And they did, so that next morning I was just as itchy and scabby from over-vigorous scratching as I had expected to be. Yet I felt good, because personal kindness is contagious and invigorating. Tanzanians are mostly gentle, kind, loving people, and I shudder when I think of the damage that Western technology and values are going to do – and are already doing – to the deep-rooted traditional values I saw around me in this isolated part of the world.

I would have welcomed more Western technology as far as roadmaking was concerned, though. One 30 km push between Ndundu and Somanga was as tough as anything I'd encountered thus far – although very high, the temperature was not the worst I had experienced so far, but in addition I had thick sand and the usual discomfort-level tropical humidity to contend with. I had been relatively fortunate when it came to the weather so far, all things considered, even in the Congo jungles, the southern bit of Cameroon and the North Africa desert stretches. But on this stretch it all came together, and things were grim for a while.

Tony and Gaby Dunn, owners of a bayside lodge at Kilwa Masoko, were expecting me and welcomed me with open arms. I was so focused on my trip that I was actually wary of getting too friendly with them, because making friends is the best way of deciding to break your journey, and I didn't want to lose momentum. Naturally that was not how it worked out. Tony and Gaby came from my Cape Town stamping grounds, Hout Bay, and there was just no way of not getting chummy with them.

They were busy turning their piece of seaside paradise into what they were determined would be the finest fishing destination on Africa's eastern coastline, and it was working, too. One of the prominent people who had visited them very recently was the 'next president in waiting' in whose wake I had cycled southwards. One who was still there was South Africa's renowned explorer, Kingsley Holgate. He had inspanned his whole family for the purpose of promoting an anti-malaria campaign by sailing a traditional dhow from Durban to the Kenyan border, handing out thousands of impregnated mosquito nets while simultaneously educating the local public on malaria prevention. Malaria killed more Africans than AIDS every year, I was informed – shocking when one considered that 40 years ago it had been well on the way to being eradicated.

I named my fortnightly South African newspaper article 'Cuda, Kilwa and Kingsley' in honour of my stay at Kilwa Masoko. The Dunns took me to visit the twelfth-century Arab ruins on a nearby island and then, after hearing that my most adventurous piscatorial experience had been as a kid in the small craft harbour of Richards Bay on the KwaZulu-Natal coast, deposited me on a fishing boat to spend an afternoon catching my dinner. My fellow-anglers were one of the lodge managers and two of the other guests, a Portuguese professional hunter and his girlfriend.

The rule, so I gathered, was that when trolling for fish the lady on board gets to handle the first strike, followed by any 'virgin', such as me. When the first strike came the hunter's girlfriend wasn't keen on taking it and nearly missed the experience of a lifetime, because at the other end was a large sailfish. Sailfish are awesome sea-animals whose trademark is 10-metre leaps into the air; this one weighed 32 kilos and put up such a fight that Kilwa Masoko's catch-and-release policy couldn't be applied – the struggle had gone on too long, and it was so exhausted that it would not have survived.

When my turn came it was a comparably small 12-kilo yellow-fin tuna which I eventually brought on board and posed with for the video camera. The film doesn't show the unpleasant part of the proceedings, when a last-minute struggle meant that I ended up with the tuna's blobby coagulating blood splattering over my face and even going into my mouth. As a dedicated animal-lover I felt bad about this and resolved that next time I would stun my catch personally, but I have to admit that the sashimi tasted so good that night that I actually turned the starter into my main course.

It was sublime to sit there under the stars with the waves breaking only a few metres away, the bar and restaurant so close to the water's edge that guests would get their feet wet at spring-tides. As we sat there I reflected on the variety of people, each with his or her life and as-yet unknown destiny, who had enjoyed Kilwa Masoko's hospitality so far. The 'president in waiting' had passed through, holding thumbs for the election. Kingsley Holgate was getting ready to carry on up the coast. I was about to head southwards again. The lynch-pins of all this were Tony and Gaby Dunn, who knew that their own little paradise would still be there long after we had left.

The landscape south from Kilwa Masoko was a privilege to be in, wild, tough and hilly, peopled with that quintessentially African tree, the baobab. I passed through swarms of Chinese who were building the first-ever highway down to the Mozambican border (Tanzania's percentage of tarmac roads is among the lowest in Africa) several hundred kilometres away. On the way I spoke to a couple of South African engineers who told me that the Chinese had made a hash of the multi-million-dollar project because they had prepared the under-surface of the entire stretch of road before tarmacking it, but were then caught with their pants down when torrential rains washed out great potholes in the smoothly manicured surface. Since the damaged patches could not be repaired on a piecemeal basis, the whole thing had to be re-done from scratch. The result was that over-all management of the project had been handed over to South Africans, who are old hands at dealing with the obstacles the continent tends to throw at man-made constructions.

The Chinese are very visible in Africa from about the Sudan southwards, and many people I spoke to were suspicious about this high-profile presence. The Chinese government's strategy, they said, was to buy into Africa in order to get a hold on its oil, timber and other resources; some even claimed that China was a new-style coloniser. Personally, I thought that that was victim talk. Any country's government has the responsibility for bartering the nation's wealth for the good of its people. The problem is that there is considerable doubt as to whether the people were actually scoring from this, as opposed to politicians with numbered foreign bank accounts. It was certainly true that in various countries I had passed, the ordinary people did not seem to have derived any benefit from resources like oil. But the only way to deal with such accusations is to pressure African governments to be transparent in their dealings and to actually deliver on their promises, something which wasn't happening in most of the countries I visited.

The bungled highway might not have been good for four-wheeled traffic, but dodging the potholes was no problem for a cyclist, and I made good time. The coastline before Lindi is really spectacular, a small bay surrounded by mountains, and I passed over the Rufiji River by way of an incredible low-slung bridge one kilometre long and spanning the river at its broadest.

The Rufiji was the scene of a famous South African military exploit of World War I. A German cruiser called the Königsberg sank a number of British ships, including the warship HMS Pegasus, and then holed up in the lower reaches of the Rufiji for repairs. A pursuing British naval force blockaded the river's mouth and despatched a famous Boer War commando soldier and hunter called Major P.J. Pretorius into the trackless bush to find the Königsberg and plot her position. Pretorius sneaked up so close to the Königsberg that he could hear her sailors talking and discovered that the barrels of her heavy guns had been replaced by wooden dummies. He deduced (correctly) that the Germans planned to use the guns in the ferocious land battles they were waging against British and South African forces, and after some hair-raising adventures he managed to return through the German lines with the information. The blockading force destroyed the Königsberg with long-range gunfire, and the missing guns were later captured too.

I remember Lindi well for two reasons. For starters, I took my first real tumble since wrecking myself on the way to Djibouti city. I was going down a very steep decline just outside Lindi when my front brakes locked and I was thrown over the handlebars. I had been taking the downhill at a conservative speed, however, and apart from a little pain and minor bloodshed, I was OK – and so, which was just as important, was my bike. Secondly, at Lindi's dilapidated guest house I got an eye-opening insight into how the NGO money game works in that part of Africa. My source of information was an auditor for a well-known international company who was engaged in looking at the books of a local NGO. I think he was starved for company; he was avoiding the NGO's dinner invitations so that no wrong signals were sent, and so we were soon in deep discussion

I asked him straight out whether he personally thought organisations like the UN and such-like were corrupt – did all that aid money actually go to those who really needed it? I followed this up with the comment that I thought that most people who worked for these organisations didn't have a real heartfelt desire to help anyone but themselves. Surely he must see the corruption and money-laundering that took place when he looked at the financial records? Yes, he said. That was exactly what happened.

I had another pointed question. Did the CEOs that these organisations put in place in each country provide false documents for him to audit at times? He laughed and said: 'The NGO's own staff provide me with forged documents so that they can look after their own jobs. If funding was pulled for fraud in any of the countries where they operate, they'd lose their jobs, and they'd do anything to avoid that.'

At this stage I was ahead of my schedule. I had only 200 km to cover in the next three and a half days to make my meeting with Debbie Yazbek and Hans Pienaar near Mtwara, on the northern bank of the Rovuma River, the border between Tanzania and Mozambique. But I didn't allow myself to slack off. I had no intention of missing our date, and I had been told that the roads got worse from Lindi onwards. My informants however forgot to tell me how the countryside would become even prettier now, with traditional Arabic-style houses dotted along the coast. This influenced my decision in Mikindani, just 35 km from Mtwara, to stay over at a well-known backpackers' lodge called Ten Degrees South, a wonderful place just 100 metres from the sea, and spend a day exploring the immediate area while my rear wheel received some fine-tuning.

The lodge was full of tourists, each with an interesting story of some kind. One was an Italian woman who told me she took a solitary holiday in Tanzania every year to unwind from the stresses of the preceding 11 months. Then there were some British girls from Nottingham who were travelling around East Africa, and a New Zealand couple who taught at the local hilltop school and also performed voluntary work at the 100-year-old Mikindani Boma hotel. Both the school and an old fort near by were interesting places to visit, they told me.

At breakfast the following morning I crossed paths again, sort of, with one of my recent acquaintances. The British girls recounted with great fondness the story of how a colourful stranger had appeared out of nowhere a few days earlier to get their broken-down rental car going again by repairing the radiator and providing distilled water for the battery. From their description it was clear who they were talking about. Big man? Long grey beard? Big belly? It could only be Kingsley Holgate!

'He's a legend in South Africa,' I informed them. 'You had a legend fix your car and didn't even know it! Did you get a picture with him?' They were suitably impressed, and I reckoned that a few of Kingsley's books would be flying off the bookshop shelves when they got back to Nottingham.

I got to Mtwara early on the day of our scheduled meeting, only to discover that Debbie and Hans had been delayed and would only be arriving the following afternoon. Bummer! If I'd known, I would have stayed on at Mikindani for another night. Still, the delay gave me time to look around Mtwara and check my e-mails. The town was small, but developing fast, and I knew things would speed up even more when the highway finally got there. And high time, too, since the present one was so bad that most travel in and out of the town was by air. And, of course, by the occasional mad cyclist like me.

I doubt if the inhabitants of Mtwara realised that when the road had eventually been laid over the meandering tracks left by my tyres it would be both a blessing and a curse. The old traditional way of life would be under constant pressure from the twenty-first century, and soon it would be more and more difficult to find pure traditionalist villages. I hoped that the southern Tanzanians would not forget how to smile at strangers.

My e-mails had often been energy-boosters at various stages of my journey, and at Mtwara it happened again. One was from the 'Getaway' TV show, whose producers wanted me to come and tell my story at their Johannesburg studio. I accepted gladly, but reminded them that they would have to get me to Johannesburg from wherever I found myself at the preparation for show-time. That would likely be the Mozambican capital of Maputo, a mere 45-minute flight from Johannesburg, or perhaps even somewhere in northern KwaZulu-Natal if the going had been really good.

The following afternoon I finally rendezvoused with Debbie and Hans, who found me fast asleep on the stoep of the border post with my hat tipped over my eyes like some loafer in a cowboy film. We went down to the river and Debbie took some great photos which made the most of the wonderful tranquil colours brought out by the fading afternoon light.

We had a humorous but enigmatic encounter with another cyclist who was also heading for the river, a local man of noble aspect who was dressed rather too smartly for cycling, right down to impressive heavy-framed spectacles. It was only when I caught up with him that I realised that his glasses had no lenses in them. I couldn't help speculating about him. Was he a great man who had come down in the world? Or a man of lowly station who was on his way up? Or perhaps a devout Catholic who had vowed to undertake a pilgrimage without lenses in his spectacles as a mark of his faith? Or even someone who had good eyes but just liked the horn-rimmed look? We didn't ask him, and in due course he left, bearing his secret with him.

The bank of the Rovuma was another of those magical places

I had encountered on my wanderings around Africa, and if I had been alone and not scheduled for an interview with Hans back at Mtwara I would have pitched my tent right there. The lambent orange soil was a striking contrast to the green of the reeds, the powder-blue sky and the miles of coffee-coloured water all around. It seemed to absorb every ray of sunlight and then feed it slowly back to us; I felt as though I was sitting inside a bright Van Gogh painting. It was definitely one of the five best camping sites of my entire trip.

But we had things to do, alas. At Mtwara Hans and I did the interview and then went on to the luxurious (for me, anyway) comfort of the hotel for a meal. There I got a quick reminder of how much my values had changed when Hans asked me if I would like to have a shower before we sat down to eat. I think his suggestion was mostly inspired by self-interest because I wasn't smelling too good – not that I had noticed, since the lone traveller gets too used to his personal pong even to notice it. There is, of course, BO and BO, as I had discovered. A man who subsists mainly on vegetables and water smells better than the fellow who eats pizzas and washes them down with brandy and Coke. But it is only a matter of degree, and I think Hans was slightly dismayed when I settled for leaving the shower till I had satisfied my customary ravenous hunger. But then the penny dropped, and I agreed to wash off some of the rubble before we sat down.

Next day, with Debbie and Hans on the way back with their material, I crossed the Rovuma into Mozambique ... the hard way, naturally. There is a ferry, but the Rovuma is a tidal river, and at low water the only way across was by means of a less than confidence-inspiring canoe made from a hollowed-out tree and propelled by a pole which the boatman dug into the riverbed at intervals. It would take about four times as long as the ferry, but I was too fired up to wait. It was a nerve-racking trip, though. The canoe-punt was small and fairly wobbly, especially after the bike had been loaded, and I wasn't comforted by the boatman's constant slapping at the side with his pole – the idea being, he explained, to warn the hippos and crocodiles that we were coming, so that we wouldn't run into them.

I sat frozen as he went on his leisurely way, knowing that hippos kill more people every year than any other African animal; if we came across a bad-tempered one it would not think twice before biting the canoe in half, either mangling us in the process or presenting us to the crocodiles for lunch. Was my trip going to end here, with myself in a croc's stomach and my valiant old bike gathering mud and weeds at the bottom of the Rovuma like a latter-day Königsberg? But the hippos weren't very interested in us and didn't come closer than about 30 metres, while the crocs did nothing more than give us a once-over as they sunbathed on the Mozambican bank – right where the boatman intended to land me, I realised.

The crocodiles should have scared me spitless, but instead I found myself full of adrenalin and looking forward to setting foot on Mozambican soil. If I ever came back to Tanzania, I vowed, revisiting the Rovuma would be a priority.

A few minutes' more poling and we reached the opposite bank. Under the crocodiles' cold gaze, the boatman and I unloaded my bike and set its wheels on the golden clay of my last country. I felt as if the great baobabs, those iconic African trees, were waving a welcome to me as I pedalled along the beaten track that led to the border post.

# CHAPTER 32

# A SERPENTINE SPEED-BUMP AND CRIES OF 'AY!' IN MOZAMBIQUE

*I jumped off and kicked the rear pannier bags so hard that the bike flipped over and skidded away. I charged after it to deliver the coup de grâce, but managed just in time to restrain myself and give the frame a sharp jab with my foot instead of kicking it to bits. Instead I turned away, tugging at my hair, then squeezing my balled fists against my body, screaming a jumble of curses and questions in a sort of controlled whisper. I had simply gone over the edge.*

I had travelled scarcely 10 km into Mozambique when I came close to satisfying my long-standing desire for some adventures with animals – not an elephant stampede, mind you, or a mauling by a lion (well, maybe a smallish cub), but an interaction that would result in something between a doubling of my heart-rate and a wetting of my pants. Humans had had that effect on me several times during my journey, but never animals. Now my chances were better, because I was travelling through country which was wild and unventured, if such a word exists. 'Unventured' might sound a bit arrogant, because of course people *had* ventured there before me, but what I mean is that northern Mozambique had not yet acquired any glitzy holiday resorts. It also hadn't acquired anything much in the way of roads, so I alternated between riding slowly over the better bits and pushing my bike through thick sand decorated with piles of warm, moist elephant dung.

Elephant droppings are impressive things, great grainy brown lumps with thick twigs sticking out of them. I calculated that the whales must be only the only creatures able to squeeze out larger turds, although I wasn't sure because I had never got this intimate with any whale. Their huge steaming pools of piddle were equally impressive. I stopped at the first scattering of droppings and stuck my left hand into one of them. It was warm inside, which was quite exciting, since the elephants must still be close by. From there on I spent most of the time moving slowly along, keeping my bike pointed in the right direction but scanning my surroundings instead of concentrating on the ground ahead, as I normally did.

Elephants can be fairly noisy – their stomachs tend to rumble and you can often hear them tearing off their food – but in this case the endless squadrons of flies circling my head actually blanketed out so much ambient sound that I had to track by sight. My aims were firstly to spot the elephants and secondly, if possible, to photograph myself in their presence (stills only, unfortunately, because that slightly dodgy video camera of mine had gone wrong in Tanzania and started chewing up every tape I inserted into it). It wasn't an easy way to make progress, since the soft, sandy track had begun to turn into an equally soft, sandy ditch. But it was that or nothing, so I just kept at it. And then my wish for interaction was answered ... although not exactly as I would have preferred.

I was still looking around at elephant height when the corner of my eye picked up a dark object spanning the entire track ahead of me. That got my gaze back to the view directly ahead, and I braked sharply. The bike slid to a halt about 20 cm from the thick body of a glorious jungle python, more than two metres of her, stretched out in front of me like a bushveld speed-bump. Jeez! I was happy and scared, all at the same time. Quickly but carefully I pulled the bike backwards, expecting the python to lash out at any moment, till there was a safe distance between us, then took out my camera and advanced on foot.

At this stage I still didn't know for sure what type of snake she was, and I couldn't help thinking that if she was poisonous and bit me it would mean yet another delay for medical attention when I had barely got going on the second-last stage of my journey. But that was the best scenario. The reality was that there was no medical attention available anywhere, so the delay would likely be permanent. All I could do was manoeuvre so that at all times we were separated by a densely leafed branch broken off a nearby bush, presumably by one of the elephants. Then if she struck her fangs would have to get through the foliage first before reaching my flesh. I got as close as I was comfortable with and then sat down, staring and taking pictures till she got bored and slid back into the thick bush that surrounded us. I was well-satisfied with the encounter. This was real *wild* wildlife, far from any game rangers, zoo fences and things like that. This magnificent serpent was in a different league altogether. This was *her* environment, not mine.

When I had fully savoured my chat with the python I pushed on to the village of Palma, about 65 km down the track. After a while the sand became so thick and fine that even pushing was nearly impossible, and walking in it was little better because I had near-zero traction. So I ended up walking next to the track and trying to push the bike along. It worked hardly at all. The slender tyres simply sank away as if the sand was a sort of thick liquid, and my back began to ache fiercely from all the bending over.

Every cyclist knows that even pushing a bike along a nice flat tarmac road will get him in the back before too long; now imagine what happens when your feet are sliding and the bike is not just bogging down but is about 30 cm lower than you are ... and all this in fierce heat. It got to the point where I had to stop every few hundred metres because I had actually become disorientated. Around noon I gave up for the time being and decided to let the worst heat of the day pass before I went on. I lay down with a tree-trunk for a pillow and slept for an hour and a half. In moments of wakefulness I realised that various bugs and spiders were crawling all over me, but I was just too clapped out to care. It was really a pity about the video camera, because these were the sort of conditions I needed to record for the people at home.

The sleep refreshed me and I carried on. To my relief the track firmed up slightly towards sunset, so that I made good enough time to see the large church outside Palma before the light vanished. I freewheeled down a long, steep, dusty road which took me right into the simple traditional seaside village and up to an establishment called the Hotel Fernando to which I had been directed by some locals I had passed on the way in.

Five-star the Hotel Fernando wasn't. In fact, I don't know if it even merited an asterisk. I gathered it belonged to a guy called Fernando who had put it up. Fernando had taken the minimalist approach. His hotel consisted of a shell of a building with a floor laid on beach sand and four large rooms inside. The rooms had hand-made wooden beds scattered around, each with a mosquito net which seemed to hover unassisted above it.

Fernando himself came to greet me, and as we stood in the golden candle-light I addressed him in my few words of Portuguese. I got a flood back, since he had obviously leapt to the conclusion that I spoke the language fluently. I was too tired and vocabulary-challenged to disillusion him, and so I confined myself to mumbling 'sim, sim' ('yes, yes') at intervals.

On the other hand, the shower I had was a great pleasure, and an unusual one as well. Like the showers in many other places I had passed through, it didn't have fancy things like taps and spray-nozzles – you got into the cubicle and then poured the water over yourself from a jug. Fernando's shower was different in two ways. Firstly, in addition to the customary jug of cold water (not that 'cold' was anything but relative in that oppressive heat), there was also a jug full of hot water, which, I was soon to learn, was the way they did things in Mozambique. Secondly, this shower was mechanised up to a point: there was a wooden staff about a metre and a half long with a metal milk jug nailed to the end, so that you could mix your water to the temperature you wanted before pouring it over yourself – simple but effective. I stood there in the dancing light thrown by the wildly flickering candle, luxuriating in the water streaming down over my aching body, and decided that this was by far the most enjoyable shower I had had for just about two years. I must have washed myself 10 times, and only stopped when the water ran out.

That night I slept like a log. The evening was warm and reminded me again of my very sweaty experiences in Angola, but here my net was more or less intact and kept the mozzies away, and in any case I was too tired to worry about anything except getting my head down.

The roads (apparently with some South African help) got better and better the further south I travelled. My next stop was Mocimboa da Praia (Mocimboa Beach) and before setting up my tent I was able to use the Internet facility at the local post office – proof that northern Mozambique was not as undeveloped as I had thought, although this was almost unknown in the outside world because not many foreigners ever got there.

But Mocimboa da Praia didn't run to any bicycle-repair facilities, and I had started having trouble with my rear wheel again. I had hit numerous rocks on the rough, hilly road between Palma and Mocimba da Praia, and I was not really surprised that they created problems with the new wheel, which had not had the time for gradual adjustment to the weight of the bicycle and the road conditions. So I had expected some trouble, although I certainly didn't welcome it; I had had more than enough of bike problems on this final stretch.

As far as I could make out, though, the worst scenario would require me to re-spoke the wheel, and the best was that I would have to manage each snapped spoke by readjusting the tension of the remaining ones. But I was a little too optimistic. By the time I had done 80 km from Mocimboa da Praia I seemed to have reached the end of my tether. I had used up all my replacement spokes and the ones on the sprocket side of the wheel were beginning to go as well. This was bad news, because these spokes only snapped when things were beyond bad. They also had to be replaced with the help of a special spanner, which I didn't have.

Help came from an unexpected source, three of the Chinese 'settlers' who were felling trees. They couldn't speak more than three words of either English or Portuguese, but they knew a broken-down bike where they saw one, China being a dedicated bicycle-borne nation. They gave me a lift down to Pemba, where I had been

led to believe there were many South Africans and – most important of all – bicycle-spokes to be had. Then, when the wheel had
been repaired, I would have to cadge a lift back to where the Chinese had picked me up. It was back to the bad old backtracking
days, and it was just as well that I didn't know that such crises were
going to be a feature of my entire 3 000 km journey through Mozambique.

On arrival in Pemba my first priority was finding Russell's backpacker site, a famous venue which was listed in the 'Lonely Planet'
guide. Explaining this to my Chinese benefactors was more than a
trifle difficult, given our serious communication problem. I found
myself resorting to the sort of thing I had always found embarrassing in other tourists who battled with language problems – raised
voice, condescendingly over-pronounced words and lots of confusing gestures. They thought it was all pretty funny, which I am sure
it was. Anyhow, the conversation went something like this:

Me: Do ... YOU (*frantic gesture*) ... know where ...Russell's ... campsite ...is?

Chinese: Ha ha ha ha ha ...ha haaaaa ha haaaaa ha ha.

Me: Russell's? ... Sleep, sleep (*more frantic gestures*)? ...Yes?

Chinese: Ha haaaaaaa ha ha ha ha ha haaaaaa haaa ha haa ha.

My frown became near-permanent under that street light in Pemba, and from their merriment I suppose it made me look even more
hilarious.

Everyone in town knew Russell, however, and somehow I managed to get to his establishment. Russell was an Australian who had
come out to tour Mozambique 10 years earlier and had decided to
stay on, and he introduced me to an assortment of other interesting people. One was Gustav, the local hotel's entertainment manager, whose mother, it turned out, lived only a kilometre away from
me in Cape Town (like Peter Meiring in Sudan! What are the chances?). Another was 'Johan Vanilla', a daring new vanilla farmer and a
character of characters. Yet another was Xali ('Charlie' in Xhosa, he
explained while introducing himself).

Charlie was one of the most interesting characters I'd met so far.
He spoke no fewer than nine languages, including fluent Zulu, was

also a good friend of Kingsley Holgate's – in fact, he had participated in the Mozambican stretch of the mosquito-net project – and had a large fund of stories derived from a life packed with experiences. The story of his life appealed particularly to me because it resonated with my own view. I wasn't interested in the rewards most people would expect to get out of a journey like mine. What I wanted most of all was personal fulfilment, the sort of thing that is difficult to categorise or even to describe. Charlie had had many such rewards, and that was what I was after.

As I had hoped, I managed to find the right spokes in Pemba and set about fitting them to the wheel and re-aligning it. I also took a chance and contacted the SuperSport 'Adventure Zone' people at DSTV through my contacts with Sony South Africa about the possibility of their sponsoring a replacement for my deceased video camera. To my delight and gratitude SuperSport came right back to say that Sony South Africa had really come to the party and had provided a top-of-the-range 3ccd camera, which incorporated the latest technology for hand-held digital video cameras and provided TV-broadcast quality.

Rodney Knight and Mike Richardson, who ran the 'Adventure Zone' website and TV programme – they were also the guys who had invited me to talk at the 'Getaway' show in Johannesburg – would make arrangements for the camera to arrive safely at the correct address, whatever it was. Pemba? Sure! I had the feeling that the more exotic the destination, the better they would like it.

With the bike in running order again, I got a lift back north on a truck carrying a load of supplies for Mocimboa da Praia, and after a tortuous battle with hordes of serious potholes the driver dropped me near where, so Mozambicans believe, the insurgency against Portuguese rule began. The actual spark, so I was told, was struck when an insurgent walked into the office of a high-ranking Portuguese official near the town of Chai and killed him.

It took me two days to get back to Pemba, and as I pedalled down the track winding through the dense jungle I kept coming across patches where the trees were being turned into charcoal – the way the locals did it was to set fire to the trees, then take the charred wood and dry it further in clay ovens. Some of the resulting charcoal they kept for themselves and the rest they sold. I was sad to see the jungle being despoiled in this way, but I didn't blame them. They were trying to keep body and soul together, and they had a thoroughly bad example in the form of the Chinese loggers, who were trucking out hundreds of immense tree trunks on a daily basis. By comparison, the damage the locals were doing to the medium-range flora was almost immaterial.

When I arrived at the turn-off to Pemba I begged for a lift into the town from one of these Chinese trucks. The driver was amenable, I joined another hitch-hiker on the mountain of giant logs in the back and we roared off into the darkness. What I didn't know was that I was soon to be given a graphic illustration of the ruthless Chinese approach to things about which I had heard.

Before long our journey was interrupted when we came on the scene of a horrific road accident. A medium-sized local truck full of passengers had just crashed into a much larger Chinese truck full of logs which had broken down on the road. The local truck's front passenger had been crushed, but the driver was still alive, sobbing and moaning with pain as dozens of people clambered around on the wreck, trying to help. The two trucks were so tangled together that the only way to get him out was by mechanical means. In South Africa this would have been done with the 'Jaws of Life', a hydraulic device which was standard emergency-services equipment, but obviously nothing like this was available in Pemba. The two Chinese drivers had an excited discussion and the one in my truck, who appeared to be the other's senior, decided that he would tow the vehicles apart.

There was now a sizeable crowd at the scene and its members were shouting at the Chinese to hurry up and get the injured man to hospital as soon as possible. My fellow passenger, apparently a natural-born pessimist, said that in his opinion it wouldn't matter, the injured man was going to die anyway, but at that moment I was beginning to be more than somewhat concerned about the chances of my dying as well. Some members of the crowd had been playing the beams of their torches over our truck's load and had spotted me. I could feel the mood turning even uglier, and I pretended to be having a conversation with my fellow passenger, employing my most eloquent body language to make them understand that I was as much of a helpless onlooker as they were; the last thing I needed was for them to channel their aggression towards me because they believed I was in partnership with the Chinese in some way. Before a lynching party could form, fortunately, my truck's driver hooked up to the other one and pulled it clear, the screams of the injured man as the trucks separated clearly audible in the cold night air in spite of the roaring of the engines.

What happened then was truly horrifying. The injured man would now be loaded in the front of our truck, I guessed, so that we could take him to the hospital at all speed. But I guessed wrong. The driver of my truck brusquely waved the locals back, threw the tow-rope up on to the logs and shoved the other driver back into his cabin, screaming at him in Chinese, obviously telling him to get going. They were going to leave the injured man behind! As the crowd realised this it exploded in rage. Some of its members started throwing rocks at the other truck, while some began to climb up on to ours. I stuck my head between my legs and hoped like hell. Clearly my time hadn't come just yet, because our driver had started up by now and we drove off, stones bouncing off the truck and us impartially.

I remember that moment very clearly, and I also remember noticing as we pulled away that the other truck, the one that had caused the accident, had no headlamps or indicators. I was still in a state of shock at our driver's brutality and my narrow escape when we reached Pemba. After this little episode my battle with the bike's rear wheel was minor stuff by any standards.

I hadn't intended to stay long in Pemba. There were still signs of wear and tear on the rear wheel's spokes, but I had convinced myself that it wouldn't result in anything that I couldn't handle, since the roads had already started showing patches of smooth(ish) tarmac, which was a good portent of things to come ... or so I hoped. But there were serious logistical concerns. I was already far behind my schedule, and to get to Johannesburg in time for the 'Getaway' show I would have to fly from Pemba to Maputo and Johannesburg, do the show and then come back to Pemba to pick up my camera and continue my road journey. The most immediate problem was that my air-tickets were only from Maputo to Johannesburg. Somehow I had to get on a flight from Pemba to Maputo, and I simply could not afford it. I began to give serious consideration to contacting Rodney and Mike to tell them that I would simply be unable to make it to Johannesburg. I hoped they would understand. I hated to even think about it.

My interesting friend Charlie aka Xali stepped into the breach. He went with me to the Mozambican airline office, explained my situation to them with great eloquence and effortlessly managed to wangle a large discount on the fare which made it possible for me to manage the rest of the price.

So there I was, coming in to land at Johannesburg International Airport for my first sight of a country I had last seen about two years ago. The talk went well and was well received, although personally I felt I would only have something to really open my mouth about when I had crossed the finish-line in Cape Town. It's one thing to talk about trying to do something, but what divides the doers from the tryers is the fact of seeing a project through to the end.

The 'Getaway' gig completed, I boarded the first flight back to Maputo and Pemba. I was in a curious state of mind, almost as if I was in another world mentally. I hadn't regarded the trip to Johannesburg as a homecoming, but there was a distinct difference in my attitude. Although still far from home, I was confident of where I was: it was no longer likely that I would need to negotiate my way through places.

Back in Pemba I had to turn down a very tempting offer. While I was in Johannesburg the South African office of the Pemba Beach Hotel, where my camera was to be sent, had offered me boat tours to the islands and a stay at one of the island resorts while I waited for it to arrive, but I just wasn't able to afford the time. A good example of my attitude change! I could smell home and would not be sidetracked for even a day.

During this time I met another interesting – and downright inspiring – person: Trevor Hutton, recent holder of the world free diving record. For those who don't know, 'free diving' is one of the most dangerous sports in the world. The idea is to dive as deep as possible on one breath, then return to the surface with the same weight that took you down (weight-belts, for example) and – most significantly for your health – still be conscious when you burst through the surface again. Trevor had dived to 83 metres, where the water pressure is so high that a fully oxygenated lung is squashed smaller than a Coke can. It was an experience just to speak to a guy who would do something so crazy and unbelievable. Most of us wouldn't even make 10 metres down before shooting upwards again for air. Quite rightly, he had featured internationally on TV and in magazines and even received the 2003 South African Adventurer of the Year award.

The story Trevor told me of how he realised he had a talent for free diving was rather funny. His brother had run a dive training school in Sodwana Bay on the South African east coast for a while and sometimes Trevor would go along to help. On one occasion his brother had a group doing their qualifying 30-metre dives, and Trevor noticed that most of the students were extremely nervous about going so deep, even though they were wearing breathing apparatus. Being at a loose end, he decided to swim down a bit and see how the students were getting on. He put on his Speedo and mask and headed downwards, passing his brother, who was hooked up to the safety line. His brother waved frantically at him and even tried to grab him as he passed, but he kept going till he reached the rocks on the bottom. There he hung around for a minute or so, got bored because no one else was down there and decided to go up again. On the way up he passed his brother again, who was in a state of excitement and kept pointing at his watch. It was only when they were all back on the boat that he realised that his brother had been at the 30-metre mark to prevent the students from going any deeper. How deep he actually went Trevor didn't know, but on another dive he was shocked when he did the same thing and another scuba diver tapped him on the shoulder and showed him that he was 38 metres down, gesturing that he must return to the surface immediately.

My earlier acquaintance Johan Vanilla did me two last favours before I left. Firstly he agreed to take me back to where I had to resume my journey, and secondly he undertook to personally track down my only pair of socks, which had gone missing at Russell's camp. The first was easy, but the second self-imposed task required more ingenuity, of which Johan had plenty – when he couldn't find my socks at the place where I had left them, he hijacked a pair belonging to another backpacker, explaining that he saw it as an international exchange programme of sorts. I suppose I should have ordered him to take them right back, but how could I spurn such a gesture? So, rather belatedly, I apologise to that unknown backpacker who unwittingly contributed to the success of my project.

My original surprise at the systematic destruction of the Mozambican forests turned to horror as I moved further south. Presumably the combination of professional logging and the local charcoal industry was still the main culprit, but the scale of destruction was totally different. Instead of a few hundred metres of burnt-out forest or barren areas of stumps every now and then I was seeing what looked like hundreds of *kilometres* of smouldering despoliation, and if anything was being done by way of regulation or reforestation there was no sign of it. I didn't even want to think about it, but because I was crawling along on a bicycle instead of speeding by in a motor vehicle I was forced to witness every inch of this crime against nature. Perhaps the wielders of the chain-saw or axe would take offence at such a phrase, and perhaps I was ill-informed about the bigger picture, but what I saw on the ground was shocking: the brutal transformation of Mozambique's ancient natural heritage into an apocalyptic wasteland.

A local inhabitant in the town of Nacaroa who happened to work for his government's department of agriculture made me laugh, albeit uncomfortably, when I raised this matter with him. He said that the systematic destruction of the ecosystem was being curbed by government-sponsored education, but I pointed out that the said education was obviously not working and then followed up by asking what the government would do once the situation had become irreversible. 'Blame colonists' he said. 'The Portuguese made us like this.' He meant it as a joke, because we both knew that all over Africa blaming the evils (real or imagined) of colonialism was an all-purpose cop-out to evade responsibility for greed, corruption and incompetence. But we also knew that it was quite possible that the lame old excuse would actually be trotted out at some stage.

In some ways Mozambique was a mirror-image of Angola, so far to the west. The lifestyle was almost identical, as were the friendly faces and the smell, mainly of charcoal ovens. In other ways it was very different, and visually there was little comparison; for one thing, there were far fewer baobabs, those beautiful symbols of Africa. Still, the ones I saw were as large and majestic as Angola's, and as before I marvelled at them. A local man told me that every nine metres of a baobab's girth represented about 1 000 years of growth; I don't know whether this true, but a baobab induces a sense of reverence in me that makes me want to believe a story like that.

On a more mundane level I was still having problems with the bike's rear wheel, a sort of reminder that my long journey would not be over till it was over, when I finally rolled into Cape Town. I had re-spoked the entire wheel, but the spokes continued to snap, including those I could not replace without the special spanner which I didn't have. So every 10 km or so I would have to stop and adjust the tension on the continually bending wheel. To say it was frustrating would be an understatement. But on the other hand I was still making it to each day's goal destination and remained on schedule, although each day I spent longer in the saddle than I had planned. I tried not to think about it, but it was beginning to look as if the bike wasn't going to hold out in spite of all the extra care and conversation (yes, conversation).

The glorious sights and scenery on the approaches to the town of Nampula distracted me from my troubles: enormous bullet-shaped boulders that seemed to be forcing themselves through the smooth flat land and reminded me of a southern right whale breaching after a long dive. By now I had become used to the interest that my bike, which was heavily loaded even by Mozambican standards, continually evoked among people I passed on the road. Mozambicans have their own vocal version of 'good', 'better' and 'best'. 'Huh?' meant good, 'eish!' meant better and a high-pitched 'ay!' was the ultimate expression of amazement and admiration. I got a lot of the 'ay!' accolade, and where possible I returned the compliment.

I passed one man who couldn't have been more than about five and a half feet tall and surely weighed no more than 60 kg, but was carrying two 50 kg bags of cement on his head. This was such a sterling effort that I gave him an 'ay!' as I passed, and although his neck vertebrae must have been compressed to the density of lead he still managed a broad smile and a bit of a glance in my direction.

I had an 'eish' moment myself in response to a story about a light aircraft that had crashed into a traffic circle right in the middle of Nampula town. A single-engined Cessna with a pilot and passenger had started experiencing engine trouble just after taking off from the local airfield. The pilot still had some control and aimed the doomed aircraft at the only piece of open space within reach, which happened to be the traffic circle. He made it, thereby saving many lives ... except his and his passenger's. Eish!

What made my arrival at Nampula even better was that it also had a small South African community whose members worked for Vodacom and a construction company. They proved hard to find at first, but when I finally tracked them down they were immensely hospitable and insisted that I stay with them (my house-hosts were Frans, who worked for Vodacom, and his wife Marie), braai with them and watch rugby with them.

The rugby part was a little difficult because it would interfere with my schedule, as I explained at the Friday evening meal when the question came up of where the next day's rugby-watching would take place. Frans and company wouldn't hear of this, but I stood firm, although it took all my rugby-starved resolve not to crumble. Undaunted, my new chums put their heads together and proposed to chase after me next day, bring me back to Nampula for the rugby, have another braai and some beer afterwards and then take me back early on Sunday to where they had picked me up.

This roundabout scheme suited me fine, because I had an easy stage planned, only 70 km to the village of Murrupula. Fine! I would get away early in the morning, and Frans would meet me at Murrupula between noon and 1 pm and bring me back to Nampula.

I got away early as planned, but I wasn't in very good physical shape because the previous night's entertainment had gone on a bit late, and I had only had about three hours' sleep when I got on the road. The beer I had drunk hadn't done me any good either – I like beer, but my body reacts to anything more than one at a time, and, of course, the effect was worse now because I was short of sleep as well. So I wasn't feeling very sparkly as I set off into the warm morning air. Then things got even worse. Every one of the charcoal-carrying bicycle taxis I came across wanted to race me, and, being competitive to the last drop of my sweat, I took on all challengers. I had a particularly tough contest with one fast fellow, who had the advantage of a distinctly lighter load. I slugged it out for about 20 km over very hilly terrain, lagging on the uphills but closing in again on the downhills. It was exhausting stuff, because it meant that I was making a 100 per cent effort all the way instead of spelling myself. Eventually this display of machismo caught up with me in a rather peculiar way.

At noon, when I was still about 15 km from Murrupula, Frans suddenly popped up in my rear-view mirror. His appearance didn't spur me on as much as might have been expected, because the midday heat was reflecting off every surface, especially the road, and I had begun to feel very drowsy, while a deep feeling of relaxation spread through me. What was happening, although I didn't realise it, was that I was actually falling asleep at the handlebars. Next thing, a horrified and helpless Frans watched me veering gently into the face of the oncoming traffic. Then, praise be, I woke up, possibly after going over a bump, and saw the Nampula-bound traffic coming at me like a herd of buffalo. Man, it was frightening! I swerved back to my side just in time, my heart pounding and so revved up by a sudden squirt of adrenalin that I stayed wide awake for the last few kilometres to Murrupela. It would have been a sad thing to brave and survive all the terrors and dangers of coastal Africa, only to be wiped out practically on the threshold of South Africa by a lorry loaded with chamber-pots or something similar.

By the time we got back to Nampula the adrenalin had dissipated again, however, and I passed out cold while sitting in front of the TV set with Frans and Marie. Very rude, of course, but my body had decided to shut down, and that was it. By the time I drifted away it was clear that my team had lost anyway, so I didn't miss much as I sat there and disturbed the afternoon with my snoring. Frans and Marie knew a sad case when they saw one and didn't take offence, in fact when we left to go back to Murrupula early next morning Frans presented me with a great gift, a Vodacom telephone number and some airtime. This was a wonderful kindness; I had had to tell Vasti that week that I could not SMS her as often as before because the budget was so tight: the bicycle was clearly going to cost me still more money before I got home.

That wasn't Frans's only gift. After making my acquaintance he had decided that his business colleagues should also be told about me and emailed most of them. One response in particular that I really appreciated was from Leon de Kock in Kimberley, who offered a contribution of $300 for running expenses, adding that all he wanted in return was that I visit this ground-zero of South Africa's diamond-mining industry one day and address the kids at the school his children attended.

The road soon became difficult again, and the rocky, weather-beaten surface exaggerated and compounded every movement of the 40 kilos I was carrying on my rear pannier. The spokes started snapping again, so often that that at times I had to change some every 5 km. By the time I had completed 100 km, with another 20 km to go before my next scheduled stop at the town of Alto Molocue, I had run out of spares, and the rear wheel was in such bad shape that the mere act of sitting in the saddle warped it. I did the only thing I could, which was to climb on to a small passenger truck, find a place to sleep and spend the following morning looking for more spokes.

It took some doing, because all of Alto Molocue's cyclist population seemed to ride the same make of bike, and it wasn't the same as mine. Eventually the general assistant from the lodge where I had spent the night made it his personal mission to find what I required, and after some effort eventually actually succeeded. I say 'eventually' because unfortunately I had arrived on the eve of a public holiday, which meant that for practical purposes Alto Molocue's collective heart stopped beating.

The upshot of all this was that I was stranded in Alto Molocue for two days before I had the wheel back in shape and could get a passenger truck to drop me off where I had had to interrupt my journey. And the bicycle was still not going well! I can't begin to explain the anger and frustration that was building up. But at the same time I was working a lot harder than usual because of the bad road surfaces and the bicycle problems, so I managed to bring my stamina levels up to near where they should be. I was recovering quicker and had far less lactic acid build-up than I had had only 10 days earlier; most people will tell you that for a cyclist, stamina is a non-negotiable ingredient. Strength is flashy, but it will take you only so far.

South of Alto Molocue my long-simmering pot of frustration finally boiled over. It was late afternoon and I had covered 100 km, an endless cycle of pedalling, stopping for repairs, cycling and stopping again for more repairs. I had laid in an enormous stock of spokes, but it was diminishing faster than I had thought, and the smaller it became the angrier I got. I began to go slightly off my head and believe that some malign influence was out there somewhere, taunting me, and I warned it aloud to stop, or I wouldn't be as calm (!) as I was at present.

Then I snapped. I jumped off and kicked the rear pannier bags so hard that the bike flipped over and skidded away. I charged after it to deliver the coup de grâce, but managed just in time to restrain myself and give the frame a sharp jab with my foot instead of kicking it to bits. Instead I turned away, tugging at my hair, then squeezing my balled fists against my body, screaming a jumble of curses and questions in a sort of controlled whisper. I had simply gone over the edge for a variety of reasons. My endless problems with the bike may have been the catalyst, but mainly it was the thought that here I was, on the very edge of success, and I simply could not get through this last country.

Eventually it was all out of me, and I could begin to take deep breaths of fresh air and get my thoughts in order again. The reality was that I was here in the bowels of Mozambique, and I had bike problems, money problems and time problems. But the objective remained the same: rolling back into Cape Town on my own two wheels, just as I had promised everyone – and myself – that I would. Getting angry and kicking my poor old bike would solve nothing.

Having successfully sold all this to myself, I settled down to make some contingency plans. I would dust off my bike, look it over to be clear in my mind what was needed to fix it, then get a lift back to Alto Molocue – that very night, if possible. If nothing north-bound came along, I would camp by the roadside. I would make it my business to get that special spanner I needed to replace the snapped spokes on the sprocket side of the wheel-bearing. Then I would carry on.

Right! I lay my bicycle neatly on the side of the road and waited for northbound transport. Nothing came past in either direction, and with sunset less than an hour away it looked as if I would defi-nitely be camping where I was. Then a truck appeared in the north and came grinding its way through the potholes. I flagged it down and addressed myself to the driver, a Portuguese man who intro-duced himself as João.

Communicating with João wasn't easy, since he spoke even less English than I spoke Portuguese, but he got the message after in-specting my bike. He couldn't go back to Alto Molocue, but I could ride along to the town he was headed for (Quelimane, which I con-firmed by consulting the maps Mandy had photocopied for me in Addis). Quelimane was a 'grande' place, he said. It was also, I re-called happily, the seat of some South African businessmen who were friends of Frans's.

João told me a little about himself as we struggled southwards, and I mean struggled – a man on a bicycle could actually move faster on that dreadful road than a big truck. He had grown up in Mozambique, he said, and had lived there for a while as an adult. But his place of residence now was Portugal, where his wife and children were; he visited them as often as he could. We had plenty of time for conversation because our progress was so slow that we had to spend the night at a dot on the map called Mocuba.

I arrived in Quelimane by lunchtime the next day and set off to find Frans's friends – Attie and Johan, who were scrap-metal dealers exporting to India, and a wheeler-dealer named Carl, who was in the process of opening a factory which would export fresh fish and other seafood to South Africa. My heart went out to Carl, who was very homesick and constantly spoke about his wife, a cancer survivor whom he was very much in love with. It made me sad to hear about her suffering, but her courage and his selfless love also motivated me.

Attie and Johan believed that the bicycle mechanics in the town would definitely be able to fix my problem and set out to find one. Meanwhile I got busy on the problem of acquiring that special spanner whose absence was my greatest immediate handicap. My greatest worry was that getting one sent from South Africa would swallow up all that remained of my ready cash. I consulted Carl, and he worked out a plan to get it on a passenger bus leaving Johannesburg that evening if someone could pick it up in Johannesburg. I called Rodney Knight from the DSTV 'Adventure Zone' to beg for help, and he responded in truly spectacular fashion. He persuaded a bike-shop owner of his acquaintance to donate a spanner, then jumped into his car and fought his way through Johannesburg's ferocious peak-hour traffic to fetch it. Then he plunged back into the traffic to get to the bus depot, only to find that the bus had already left. Undaunted, Rodney chased after the bus, flagged it down to an unscheduled stop and talked the driver into taking the spanner to Quelimane. Talk about literally going the extra mile!

While waiting for this tool to arrive Attie and Johan took me on a rather unusual night on the town, which among other things had me providing the back-up vocals for a local musician who was performing at the pub/club we went to, and then sleeping in the back of Attie's little Datsun 1300 pickup when he got bogged down in thick sand while on a scenic drive afterwards to show me the harbour. It wasn't the best night's rest I have ever had, seeing that I had thousands of voracious mosquitoes as bedfellows. But who was complaining?

My long-desired special sprocket spanner eventually arrived, and even though I had never used one before I had the wheel entirely re-spoked and balanced within a day. This done, Attie and Johan negotiated at length on my behalf with the local taxi-drivers but couldn't find a rate that suited me. I probably gave the impression of being ungrateful for their efforts, but the plain truth was that I was too embarrassed to tell them that I didn't have money to pay for a taxi, and knew that if I told them this they would insist on paying out of their own pockets.

Having made my way back to the point where I had left off I got going in good spirits, confident that at last my main transport worries were over. But they weren't, of course; problems that have been building up over 35 000 km do not get solved that easily.

# CHAPTER 33

# A PARTY IN THE BUSH ... AND A STRENUOUS DASH TO THE BORDER

*A fellow drinker was none other than the mayor of Zitundo,
who frankly disbelieved me when I told him what I had been
doing for the past two years. I didn't have the time to convince
him that I was on the level, and as I left Zitundo behind me I
reckoned that for a long time to come he would be telling people about this bedraggled-looking white guy who had rolled up
out of the blue and claimed to have done this and that while
riding around Africa on a bicycle.*

Back on the road to Quelimane, I was doing a respectable average
100 km a day in spite of the abysmally bad surfaces. Every 20 km
or so a spoke would snap, but with my new acquisition I could replace it whether it lay on the difficult side of the hub or not. Ideally I should also have trued the rim, which had been pulled and
stretched so much by now that it probably was not even perfectly
round any more, but for that I needed a professional balancing tool
which, needless to say, I did not have.

I had an interesting encounter with a group of hunters that not
only reminded me once again of how very basic and traditional a life
many Africans still lived but also gave me some food for thought
about how my own attitudes were changing as I neared the end of

my journey. It was about an hour before sunset and I was meandering along, keeping my eyes open for a suitable campsite, when I saw three very ragged men up ahead of me, each with a big muttoncloth bag on his head, a bow with a quiver of arrows slung over his shoulder and a mangy-looking dog trotting at his heels. I decided to pull up and chat a bit to find out more about how they lived.

They were a little alarmed at first, because they could not speak either Portuguese or English, but after a while we managed some sort of communication, or perhaps I should say 'miscommunication', because one of them interpreted my sign-language as indicating that I was hungry. He promptly lowered his bag and opened it for me. It was full of very crispy flame-grilled chunks of meat portions which seemed to have come from various species of small game. Being both hungry and an official anything-goes adventurer, I decided to try a piece and in return gave them 50 000 meticais, which was the equivalent of about one and a half US dollars. They were very happy with this, and I fished out the best-looking piece of meat I could find to take along for my evening meal. One of them allowed me to let off a few shots with his bow, after which I prepared to carry on with my chunk of grilled meat.

But as I was about to pedal away I noticed a familiar-looking shape in the very bag from which I had selected my meat. I had another look and saw a skinny little arm, fingers clenched as if waiting to hold a torch like the Statue of Liberty. I pulled it out and saw that it was what I suspected, one-quarter of a monkey. I joked about it with them, mentioning that we, as humans, share many physical features with this blackened grilled animal I now held before me. After this hearty laugh I summarily returned the meat I'd picked earlier. Now, this was interesting to me because I had eaten plenty of monkey meat during my wanderings without any particular qualms of conscience. But somehow I just didn't feel like it now. Was it because I was almost on the threshold of South Africa, where people didn't eat monkeys, and I was slowly casting off my adventurer mode? Whatever the case, I would be content with opening a tin of sardines when I made camp.

My encounter with the monkey-hunters helped me to realise that since entering Mozambique my bike problems had kept me at such a level of frustration that I had not become part of the environment, as I had earlier in my journey, and had not taken in as much of the people and the places I encountered. Every day had been spent carrying out countless roadside repairs, counting the kilometres to my next destination and then finding a place to sleep. So I made a deliberate change to my behaviour-pattern when I reached the junction town of Nicodala, near the half-way mark for Mozambique, where the road forked – south to Quelimane and south-east to Maputo. I found a dingy little room on the edge of the main intersection and went for a meal at the first eating-place I caught sight of. It worked, and I made new friends whose faces I remember to this day.

It was very, very hot and damp going, and I think I sweated more on this stretch than at any other time on my circumnavigation. The road itself was tarmac and an easy ride compared to where I had just come from, but the humidity level was beyond what I had imagined was possible. By nine o'clock every morning I was so drenched from head to foot that I could take off any piece of clothing, especially my shirt, and wring a stream of pure perspiration out of it (it was so amazing that, naturally, I filmed it).

At lunch-time I stopped off at whatever roadside stall was convenient, the main course almost invariably being guinea-fowl disguised and advertised as thoroughbred chicken. I was frankly sceptical about whether I was actually attacking a plateful of 'frango/galinha' (chicken in Portuguese) rather than a representative of the scrawny semi-domesticated guineas I saw scratching about. The drumsticks were suspiciously long, and it is a fact that cooked chicken meat is not bright pink and as tough as biltong. But although the preparation of the meal often took longer than normal (probably because it included hunting down the 'chicken'), that gave me a little more reason to rest up during the hottest part of the day.

Regular afternoon rainstorms were the norm now, and were refreshing to cycle through. All I would have liked was to see more tarmac and less dirt surface. I had to swing away from my desired coastal route for a while because of a severe flood in the Zambezi

River delta, which dominates this part of the Mozambican coastline (the 2001 and 2003 floods set a regional record for severity and destruction). After heavy rainfall on the higher land of Zambia and Zimbabwe the Mozambican section of the Zambezi becomes a disastrous bottleneck, with results seen live throughout the world when a woman gave birth to a baby in a tree, the only refuge she could find.

The bike's rear wheel continued to make trouble during all this time. Thanks to my special spanner the problem of snapping spokes had been contained, but the evil bicycle gods dreamt up another way of sapping my enthusiasm and willpower. The wheel had now apparently decided that it was not the standard 26 inches all the way round and started refusing to accept the standard-length spokes I had bought, so that they were either too short or too long. I tried the logical approach, namely 'this is a 26-inch wheel and these are spokes for a 26-inch wheel, therefore they belong together'. They did not, and I ended up with a mixture of spokes as taut as guitar-strings on one side and as wobbly as wet spaghetti on the other which continually pulled the tyre onto the frame of the bicycle.

My faith in the virtues of pure logic was severely dented, but I struggled on, because what those malign deities did not know was that I had made a pact with the *benevolent* bicycle gods that I would get home regardless of what was thrown at me in the 4 000-odd kilometres that still separated me from Cape Town, such as my rear wheel taking on eccentric dimensions that natural science could not account for.

My crossing of the Zambezi River was not what I had expected. A South African/Zimbabwean couple, whose names I have forgotten, I am sorry to say, took pity on me when they saw me squatting next to my upside-down bike about 30 km from the river while again re-spoking the entire rear wheel. They were going to a campsite and lodge just on the other side of the river, they said, which was owned by some friends of theirs. Why didn't I come with them for the night and return in the morning? Perhaps their friends would be able to provide some expert help. I had had enough of re-spoking for the day, and next thing we were on our way to the ferry.

Unfortunately the friends knew even less about bicycles than I had when I left Cape Town, but I found myself involved in some new interaction which was both graphic and sad. They were a counterpart to the couple I had met in Benguela near the beginning of my journey: they had recently lost everything in Zimbabwe during Robert Mugabe's crazy destruction of his country's vitally important white-owned farm holdings. Yet they saw themselves as fortunate at having escaped a worse fate and intended to stay on in Africa because, as the husband said, 'where else would I feel as if I belong?'

I spent a lot of time thinking about Mugabe's insane programme of so-called 'land reform' that had turned hundreds of profitable farms into presents for his cronies with little benefit for the ordinary people in whose name he had claimed to be acting. For years Zimbabwe had been just another item on the news at which I and many other South Africans would shake our heads. Now I was having dinner with the reality of what would go down in history as another African failure. A reflection on me, an African.

Three other couples staying over for the night were ex-Zimbabwe farmers who had relocated to Mozambique and either taken jobs at Mozambican farming estates or invested in business ventures like the lodge we were staying at. For the first time I grasped the extent of what had Mugabe had done to his country, just to stay in power. The other guests were quite willing to tell me what had happened to them, how they had had to leave their homes within a matter of hours, leaving all their belongings behind, and abandoning fields which were ready to be harvested. They had literally lost everything. What do you put into the little bag you are allowed to take after being told to leave the home your grandparents built? I didn't reply: I just didn't know, and I was humbled by their stoicism.

And stoic they were. They were quite matter-of-fact about what had happened to them and oddly philosophical about the second chance they had found in Mozambique to do what they knew best how to do. Above all they were grateful that they had not suffered death and torture like so many of their neighbours. But what shocked me most was the reply of one farmer of about 35 when I asked him about where he was currently living and what his plans were. Had he bought land in Mozambique yet? His response, and the others agreed with him, was: 'There's no way that I would invest in an African country ever again. I'll work as hard as my father did and deliver just as he did. My arrangement with the Mozambican government is to deliver for them. I will. In turn, they'll pay me well. That's all I want. Nothing more.'

It was awful to hear this. Even the most sophisticated farmer is a man of the earth, deeply rooted in the land he owns and husbands and where he will be buried one day. Yet here was a young man, an African born and bred who would not feel at home on any other continent and had once had that passion for the land, who had decided he didn't want roots any more. He had severed himself from what had once been the essence of his life and was now merely doing a job from which he could walk away at any time. I was sad for him, because I knew that his spirit had lost something special, and I was sad for Zimbabwe, the ultimate loser.

I completed a very messy and rushed re-spoking the following morning and set off back to the Zambezi ferry so that I could complete the 30 km I had covered in my new friends' car. Now, as I cycled past the riverside market, I noticed for the first time that both banks of the mighty river were virtually crawling with bicycle mechanics, and on my return I picked out an able-looking one to ask why he thought my spokes weren't fitting any more. The mechanic was very confident about his remedy, which consisted of trimming down some of my spokes to the wheel's requirement with his rusty pliers and digging out some longer spokes from his stock to replace the standard ones that were too short.

I wasn't really keen on the approach of treating the symptoms rather than the ailment, but I stuck to my re-minted philosophy of going with the flow and let it carry on. The result of his ministrations was that the wheel ran relatively well vertically, but from a lateral view was distinctly egg-shaped. The mechanic pooh-poohed my concerns and guaranteed that the wheel would make it all the way to South Africa. I paid him with lunch and a non-alcoholic malt beer (my favourite drink at this stage). It would have been cheaper to pay cash, but it's not every day that you get that sort of guarantee thrown in.

This time I crossed the Zambezi River the way it should be crossed, on a small motor boat, to get a true idea of just how powerfully it runs toward the ocean. I tried to imagine what it must be like when this great mass of water comes down in flood, and the mental picture I conjured up was positively frightening. That night I stayed at the lodge again, this time in a tent instead of a log cabin. I hadn't seen the tents the previous night and was mightily impressed with them: anyone with plans to set up some form of tourist bush camp would be well-advised to copy this model. A number of concrete slabs were scattered about, each measuring three metres square and possessed of its own electrical power point; a sturdy military-type tent would be erected on the slab and furnished with two beds, a small lamp and adequate bedding. It was as good as sleeping outside without the risk of waking up next morning to find a lioness chewing on your leg.

Something that definitely could not be copied, though, was a very special grave about 50 km away, containing the bones of Mary Moffat Livingstone, wife of Dr David Livingstone. I would have liked very much to take a detour to the grave – I had visited and been amazed by so many things on my way around Africa, things that I would probably never have the opportunity of seeing again – but I was now really under the gun as far as time was concerned. If I did not adhere strictly to my schedule I would not make it to South Africa by December. But in retrospect I am sorry that I didn't pinch off the time to go and visit this legendary adventurer's wife's grave.

Nearing the Gorongosa National Park, I had two options. I could stick to a brand-new tarmac road that would take me around Gorongosa Mountain (the park is inside its crater), or I could take a route through the mountain itself which was shorter but hilly and dirt-surfaced. I persuaded myself to take the shorter route and cycle through the night till I reached Gorongosa town, 43 km away on the other side of the mountain. Hey, how tough could it be after some of the alleged roads I had used in the past 30-odd countries? Why would it be any more difficult than what I'd faced and conquered before?

Well, once again I should have known better, as I soon discovered. My average speed dropped to under 10 km/h as I babied my wonky rear wheel over the smaller rocks and got off to push where the sand became too thick. The locals I encountered stared at me in surprise – the area is so inaccessible that the mountain people are still relatively uninfluenced by the outside world, although this had already begun to change, as I was about to discover. Sunset came before I had seen even one village, and now began the eeriest night trip I had made anywhere along my journey. As I negotiated my way up and down those dusty hills in the pitch darkness I could not rid myself of the feeling that I was being watched, and I became more and more fearful – not the naïve fear, born of ignorance, that I had contended with in Angola but a dread of the unknown springing from the knowledge that my chosen road bordered on a national park that was home to every man-eating creature to be found in Mozambique.

In the end I didn't make it to Gorongosa town that night – but my journey was interrupted by people, not animals. I was wending my way through the night when from somewhere ahead I heard the unmistakeable sounds of a drunken party. I carried on and eventually found myself among a few roadside shacks, in between which a considerable number of locals were dancing or wobbling, depending on their individual states, so enthusiastically that I couldn't see their faces. Loud music with a monotonous beat boomed out from a battery-operated hi-fi tape recorder, and to one side warm beer was being served from a shack. I rode in unnoticed and took a drink of water, but after about 20 seconds the penny dropped. A *white man on a bicycle* had come to the party! Far from arousing resentment about gate-crashing, my arrival actually increased the celebratory spirit. At the invitation of the village's young storekeeper I parked my bike next to a middle-aged woman who lay passed out on the powdery clay soil almost under the feet of the dancers, her dress pulled up virtually to her head and her breath sending up small dust-cloud bubbles with every exhalation.

I was mind-blown. I could imagine this sort of drunken orgy taking place in a seedy part of, say, Maputo or Johannesburg, but here in a remote part of rural Mozambique! It was a very friendly orgy nonetheless, at which I was obviously very welcome, although the reason for that – or for the orgy, come to think of it – was a total mystery to me. Just about everyone, mostly the men, propelled me here and there to introduce me or just show me off to their acquaintances. The storekeeper eventually came to my rescue – all the other solid, sober citizens had long since gone to bed, I gathered. He gave me his straw sleeping-mat and led me to the side of his shop-shack where I could lay down my bike and sleep without too much interruption. That was his intention, anyway, but it didn't quite work out like that. Every 10 minutes someone would wake me up, exclaiming 'Branco, branco, branco!' ('White, white, white' in Portuguese). The noise of revelry got even louder, so that at one stage it seemed as though the dance-floor had moved to within arm's-reach of me, and I had to cover my head with a cloth to cut down on the amount of dust I was inhaling from all the enthusiastic foot-stamping.

I hate to be a party pooper, but it gave me great pleasure when the tape recorder started to slow down and eventually stopped. There was a moment of stunned silence, and then a loud argument which, I guessed, revolved around the storekeeper's refusal to sponsor a new set of batteries. But that was strictly their worry, and I concentrated on trying to catch some sleep. It wasn't easy, because the guests included hordes of mosquitoes which not only interrupted my sleep but must have drunk at least a pint of my blood. For some reason my hands suffered the worst, so that when I got up in the morning they were entirely covered in large welts.

I didn't tarry in the village of party-goers but got back on the road as early as possible. It goes without saying that thanks to lack of food, lack of sleep and plenty of hills the last 25 km to Gorongosa town felt more like 250 km. Each time I got to the crest of a steep hill after labouring up the meandering track I would find an identical steep hill waiting for me on the other side. So it is hardly surprising that it was lunchtime before I got to the town. I took some refreshment and carried on to my scheduled destination 60 km further, Inchope, which lay at a large four-way junction that offered roads to Maputo, Zimbabwe, the harbour city of Beira and Tanzania. I was still suffering from the after-effects of the orgy, so I got in an early night after pitching my tent in the grounds of a roadside restaurant. I slept blissfully, unaware of the fact that I had a bed-partner in the shape of a furry brown spider the size of a small saucer. There was no malice in it, however, and it seemed to be as glad to get out of the tent as I was to see it go.

The evil gods had another go at me after I had left Inchope and hit the Maputo road. The rear wheel was pulling more and more to one side, to the point where the tyre was now rubbing against the bicycle-frame. I had loosened the brakes days before because the wheel was rubbing against them, raising the threat of a hole being worn through the tyre and tube. But now even this was not enough any more, and after about 100 km I had to resort to the most drastic action I had taken thus far. I couldn't adjust the spokes that countered the lean of the wheel any further because they were too taut already – so taut, as a matter of fact, that they were starting to pull out of the rim and permanently strip the spoke-thread. But the wheel kept pulling even further to one side, especially after even a little bump, so obviously I would have to take drastic action. The tyres I was using were 'semi-slicks', meaning that they had a flat surface for tarmac roads and large knobs on the sides to provide some grip on soft surfaces, and I used my Leatherman to cut these protrusions away and thus give myself another millimetre or two of extra space. I was that desperate.

The road wasn't much help. Although tarmac in some places, it was atrocious for long stretches; Chinese road-builders were involved here too, and I suspected that they were just as inexperienced about African conditions as the ones in Tanzania. I wasn't worried about the discomfort of this type of vehicular torture; my concern was about the inevitability of the rear wheel collapsing under the combined weight of myself and my baggage.

And the inevitable happened, all right. The wheel simply buckled and gave up the ghost. I had been anticipating this disaster and took it calmly. Earlier in my trip I would have been furious, but that wild tantrum of a little earlier had blown a lot of bad stuff out of me, so all I did was lay my bicycle down and sit next to it to wait for somebody to come driving by in whatever direction. If it meant that I would have to take a few days to travel down to Maputo, that's the way it would have to be. All I needed was correct-sized spokes and a new rim. I didn't mind starting the process all over again.

The first truck that stopped for me was headed back to Inchope. I decided to take it and then hop another lift to Beira, where I would look up Attie from Quelimane, who I knew happened to be there on business. That was how it worked. Later that day I arrived in Beira, a lovely colonial-looking harbour city and soon found Attie ... and someone else I really had not expected to see.

We were sitting over dinner and a beer in a pub-restaurant with a few of Attie's business friends when someone tapped me on the shoulder and said: 'Hello, Riaan.' I stared at the shoulder-tapper, a smiling guy with spiky blond hair and a familiar face. Then a second later I remembered who he was: André Olivier, from Mtubatuba in Zululand, someone I had played lots of rugby with – and against – in my schooldays. André had been by far the best school-level rugby player I had encountered on the field. He had been handicapped by the fact that he had been small for a rugby player, but he had made up for it with such heart and guts that he had often out-performed the bigger players. André was a good all-round sportsman, an absolute gentleman. That we should be at the same remote place at the same time was one strange coincidence, but there was another waiting. André took me over to his table to meet a stunning Spanish-looking girl, a school-teacher, whom he planned to propose to in about a week's time ... and she turned out to be with a group of people I had met at the Zambezi River lodge a few days earlier! It's a small world, all right – or perhaps the places to go to are just too few.

Attie and his friends made it their combined mission to scour Beira for the right bicycle spares. I went along, enjoying the city in between swoops on bicycle shops. It had the same sort of old, white-washed feel to it as Mombasa, and the locals told me about marvellous beaches and fishing spots. Beira was never on the tourist radar before, but as the roads improve I reckon that is going to change drastically.

With my bike back in running order (thanks, Attie and friends!) I got moving again. I was now under such pressure that I didn't care what time I hit the road. My best scenario was that I would get a lift directly to Inchope plus the additional 100 km I had covered before the rear wheel died on me. But just for once my luck was out in every way. I had two punctures before I even reached the outskirts of Beira, and I couldn't find anyone to pick me up – I think people were put off by the thought of having to load up my large, unwieldy-looking bike as well. I say this because it was 80 km later and well after dark before I got a lift after laying my bicycle down out of view. That got me straight to Inchope, and in the morning I got another lift down to my stopping-point right away. There I got going immediately. The wheel felt good and so did I. I was back in business!

I spent an interesting night at a truck stop in the middle of nowhere, with nothing either way for several hundred kilometres, which catered for drivers plying between South Africa, Beira and Zimbabwe. I gathered that the drivers didn't just rest here, they also liked to add a bit of recreation by throwing impromptu parties, complete with some working girls.

One of the drivers I shared a plate of food with was a South African who had some good horror stories to tell, like the one about the steep mountain pass on the Mozambican side of the border post at Komatipoort. He had driven non-stop from Johannesburg with 20 tons of cargo, he said, and was keen to get to Maputo, but what he hadn't noticed was that the brakes of his truck were beginning to fail. He only discovered this after starting down the Komatipoort pass. By the time he reached the second corner he knew that there was no way of piloting the truck to the bottom, so he did a Hollywood stuntman-style dive out of the cab and the truck went careering over a cliff.

'Your boss couldn't have been happy,' I joked.

To my surprise he replied matter-of-factly: 'No, it was no problem – it was my first accident.'

I was slightly flabbergasted. Had his boss considered the accident part of the normal learning-curve? Surely only an extremely lenient type would have been able to write off a R1 million driving lesson.

All went well till I got to the impressive arches of the Save River bridge. Then that blasted rear wheel warped again. Well, there was only one thing to do, as usual: get to some place where you can get help. In this case it was Vilanculos. At this time this was about the northernmost point in Mozambique to which South Africans travelled regularly, and I knew that several owned reputable lodges here.

Vilanculos was crucial in my schedule for two reasons. For one thing, it was in my non-negotiable time schedule. For another, and more importantly, my planned arrival date would coincide with the Rugby Currie Cup Final (the South African Super Bowl) between the Gauteng Province's Blue Bulls, the current champions, and the Free State Cheetahs, who hadn't taken the trophy for 30 years. It was a special occasion because the Cheetahs won, and the rest day I had scheduled for later in the week was used up that Sunday so that I could recover from the previous evening's celebration. Next morning one of the fellows I had met at the post-match celebration, Jaco, saved me some money – and, more importantly, time – by driving me back to the Save River bridge.

The wheel problem was still with me as I set off from the Save River, but I had convinced myself that I had learned to live with it. The way I saw the situation now was that it was only 900 km from here to Maputo. If the road was bad all the way I would have to re-spoke the wheel only three more times. And when I got to South Africa I would buy a new wheel and have a professional take a look at my bicycle. So I would just plug on and hope for the best. In between plugging on I found a new favourite in the Just Juice range, to which I have always been partial, when an Englishman stopped at the side of the road late one sweaty afternoon to chat with me and gave me two ice-cold cans of a flavour I had never come across before, mandarin and orange. I drank one right away and then couldn't help draining the second tin as well. I can't describe how good it tasted – in fact, I nearly kept the second tin as a souvenir.

The scenery was changing now. Things were dryer, I noticed, and the jungle's trees were shorter and shrubbier. But to tell the truth, I wasn't paying much attention to the scenery, or even the construction taking place on the road. Instead I hardly took my eye off the rear wheel, apart from scanning the road ahead now and then to make sure I was not about to ram a bulldozer. I was in fairly familiar territory by this time, since I had visited southern Mozambique before, and knew which towns to identify for rest days because they had electricity and cell phone reception. One of these was Maxixe, which lies across the bay from Inhambane town, and was the ideal place for me to update my website and fulfil my newspaper commitments. Inhambane, though, was very different from the town I remembered visiting three years earlier. It still has my best-beach recommendation, even though resorts have sprung up all over.

My final target town before Maputo was Xai Xai, which I reached earlier than I had expected. Any good impressions I retained from my previous visit were dispelled by an incredibly rude restaurateur. I had just started to eat when he came up to me and started shouting at the top of his voice in Portuguese, telling me to move my bicycle away from a wall against which I propped it. Then, obviously realising that most of his tirade was going over my head, he told me in broken English to put the bicycle, with all my belongings, outside in the street so that his customers wouldn't be able to see it. I wasn't impressed by this because I was the only customer there (hardly surprising, if this was his normal attitude) and we ended up having a shouting match, arms waving – clearly my laidback approach applied only to bicycle rear wheels, not rude restaurateurs. Or it was because he was disrupting me during my meal? Some people are grumpy in the mornings, maybe I'm grumpy if I'm disturbed during a meal. Or maybe I was just offended by his disdain for my very special bicycle. Whatever the case, don't go to that restaurant. It's on the left side of the road as you enter Xai Xai from the north.

I left Xai Xai behind with few regrets and glided on to Maputo, which I thought was very similar to Luanda in many ways, right down to the fact that the outskirts became busier and busier the closer I got to the actual city, starting quite far out in distinctly rural areas. It was a surprise to see how many cars carrying South Africans stopped and sometimes even turned around to ask if I was the fellow on John Robbie's breakfast radio show on Radio 702.

I found myself saying: 'I think I am'. Think? Of course I was! For some reason I had to keep reminding myself that I was the only guy who had nearly circumnavigated the continent by bicycle. No doubt my reply made a lot of people think me a little odd. Perhaps it was because somehow I couldn't believe that my trip was nearly done, that the moment I had looked forward to for so long was just around the corner. Would there come a day when people would walk up to John Robbie in the streets and ask him if he was the guy who had interviewed Riaan Manser, the young man who went around Africa on a bicycle? I didn't think so, somehow. One bunch of questioners in a white Opel were on film-shoot assignment and heavily armed with video cameras. I asked for a cameo role and they filmed my progress at some length.

The Holiday Inn gathered me to its generous bosom once again for the few days I spent in Maputo (I think they might have ended up regretting it, because I didn't stop eating their glorious food till the moment I left). Coincidentally the full-page feature Debbie and Hans produced was published in *The Star* newspaper in Johannesburg, which naturally circulated in Maputo. This gave me a bit of celebrity status, because many of the hotel's staff recognised me and never passed up an opportunity to ask me about my journey. David, the hotel's general manager, took it on himself to make enquiries about the terrain I would encounter on my trip south to the border and even gave me a few referrals in case I got stuck. I thanked him with real appreciation for his efforts, but I had no intention of getting stuck anywhere. I was only a day's ride away from my homeland, wasn't I? Well, yes, I was.

Did I really believe that I was just one a day away from home? Nope, I didn't – not easily, anyway. I had mulled over it for longer than two years now. But believing it was finally going to happen? Well, I'd see about that when I crossed the border into my own country and sank my feet into the soil of the place where I was born and belonged.

As can be imagined, I set off from Maputo in a highly determined frame of mind. For practical purposes, this was the actual start of the final leg through to Cape Town. At the same time I didn't feel pressurised. There wasn't much room for manoeuvre in my schedule, but I didn't see why I couldn't relax and enjoy the ride, yet still make it to Cape Town on 25 November, as I planned.

I was so keen to get going that I didn't want to spend another night in Maputo, although by now it was late afternoon. So I decided to head south to the town of Bela Vista, a couple of hours away, spend the night there and then set off on my one-day dash to the border early next morning. The road to Bela Vista was unsurfaced but solid, and I got there exactly as planned. It was a neat little place that looked like a transplanted chunk of Portugal, but it was something like a ghost town still inhabited by living people. Nothing moved as I cycled down the neat main street; I didn't even see a curtain twitched open as I cruised around to locate its camping site. I began to think I must have sweated myself into a state of invisibility since leaving Maputo.

I found the campsite, put my invisible self to bed and hit the road so early that I was already 10 km to the south by sunrise, happy in the knowledge (imparted by my friends in Maputo) that I could look forward to a blissful 18 km stretch of tarmac. The downside of this was that after the tarmac ended at the town of Salamanga there would be a notorious stretch of sand, so bad that in some cases vehicles had ended up being permanently bogged down. I would see hundreds of tyre-tracks going in all directions when I got there, my advisors said, made by desperate drivers trying to beat the sand.

Not a little worried, I had repeatedly asked: 'How will I know which way to go?' and always got the same answer: 'Simple! Look for the most worn-out track; it will be going to Ponta do Ouro.' This isn't awfully good news for any cyclist. The most worn-out track would certainly show me the right direction, but it was likely to make the going almost impossible. It felt as if this huge country was determined to make me leave it just as I had entered, pushing my bike through thick sand in a cloud of sweat. The difference today, though, was that I really had the bit in my teeth because my home ground was just a hop and a skip away, and I was going to go full steam ahead till I got there.

The road after Salamanga – if you can even call it that – was as bad as my friends had said. I located the most beaten track and tackled it, head down, muddy sweat burning in my eyes as I leaned into my bicycle. The figures told the story. I had to cover about 50 km of this horrible terrain in the next 10 hours if I wanted to reach the Mozambican border post at Kosi Bay before it closed at 5 pm sharp. On a properly surfaced road, either tarmac or dirt, it would have been a snip, but this little stretch of hell made nonsense of time-scheduling, and I was reaching 6 km/h at the most. I battled on, the figures reeling through my mind, and stopping only for a sip of water now and then. This was serious elephant country, but the only way I would know if I encountered one would be if he or she trumpeted, I hoped before dancing a fandango on my bones, because I certainly wouldn't see it.

After a while my back began cramping, and it was clear that simply pushing the bike through the powdery sand of the well-worn track was not going to work. The only alternative to that was scarcely more attractive, namely to cycle through the waist-high bush alongside the track. It was a daunting prospect. This was the worst surface I would actually have to cycle on since the Congo. The power I generated would be equally shared between moving forward and bashing my way through the dense vegetation and negotiating the numerous little dongas which would be sure to appear at unexpected moments. It went without saying that this wouldn't do my wonky rear wheel any good either.

Well, that was the way it would have to be. The wheel would simply have to give of its utmost, and if it wasn't up to the strain I would just have to push my bicycle the rest of the way, regardless of the bush, the heat and the humidity; if I could keep up a constant four or five kilometres an hour I would still have a fighting chance of making the border in time. That remained my main goal, and as I've said, having a clearly defined goal is what makes it possible to achieve things that appear to be unattainable. But as the day went slowly by I began to lose my clarity about this major goal and knew I would have to set smaller ones to keep me going towards the first prize. The problem was identifying them in this well-nigh featureless wasteland.

The first minor goal was a surprise which presented itself. A handful of cars had passed me during that day, but usually on another of the less-travelled tracks. But then a small passenger bus came up behind me, hooting wildly, and to my amazement the passenger was none other than one of the Holiday Inn staff members I had got to know in Maputo. My amazement was nothing compared to his when he saw what I looked like after a day of track-bashing. He fed me some much-needed water, then pointed out a distant hill with a communications tower on its summit. That marked the town of Zitundo, he told me –the last urban concentration before the border.

Then off he went and so did I, although considerably slower. But I had my first intermediate goal. As I slogged on I could see the tower gradually coming nearer. This visible evidence that I was actually making progress was a shot in the arm that I needed very badly, because the going remained as terrible as ever, with the bush so dense at times that I was forced back on to the track. But I didn't stop, although I was suffering bad cramps now, especially in my back and hamstrings. If I could reach Zitundo by 2 pm I could get some food and more water, and easily reach the border post before it closed for the day. So it was Zitundo or bust ... and I was very nearly bust by this stage.

I was still struggling towards Zitundo when I was cheered up by another blast from the past. I had decided to travel light and beg liquids from passing vehicles. One of them was a Toyota 2x4 pickup which was hurtling along, to the extent that a vehicle could hurtle in that part of the world, the driver's only intention apparently being to skate along on top of the sand. But he was kind enough to risk his bakkie's permanent interment and stop to fill up my water bottles. He was well equipped against the environment with a hat and sun-glasses which pretty much disguised him, but somehow I recognised his voice – although where I had heard it before eluded me. Then, as he was saying goodbye and advising me to re-stock with water at Zitundo, it came to me. He was the owner of a legendary floating restaurant and bar that had been a favourite gathering place for me and my Richards Bay friends during our younger days. Unbelievable! And I was equally low down on the list of people he expected to encounter in the bush en route to Zitundo or anywhere else. He said that he had heard about my journey, but realised now for the first time just what a hard, unglamorous business it was.

We said goodbye and he went back to skating on the sand while I returned to grappling with the bush. But it was worth it. I got to Zitundo just before 2 pm and took my only scheduled rest and refreshment break, an important part of which was demolishing a cold Coke. A fellow Coke-drinker was none other than the mayor of Zitundo, who frankly disbelieved me when I told him what I had been doing for the past two years. I didn't have the time to convince him that I was on the level, and as I left Zitundo behind me I reckoned that for a long time to come he would be telling people about this bedraggled-looking white guy who had rolled up out of the blue and claimed to have done this and that while riding around Africa on a bicycle. He was very polite about it, though, and in spite of all his head-shakings he bade me a smiling farewell as I headed down the steep hill on which Zitundo was perched.

Now it was back to the sand and the bush that I had been battling for the last eight hours. A passing 4x4 group told me that the border was just over the next hill. It wasn't, of course; I knew it was still 12 km away, and that I had just two and a half hours to get there before closing-time. So the hills went on and on, and after about the tenth my old all-purpose manta, 'just keep going', wasn't working too well any more. But it retained enough power to keep me moving, and finally the magic moment arrived when I pushed my bike over one final sandy hill and saw the border post, not more than a kilometre or two ahead. Well, it *should* have been a magic moment, but I was too exhausted for any excitement, and I had missed closing time by only a few minutes.

I didn't let that stop me. I dragged my way up to the border post, determined either to make an official late entry or beg my way through. But my pleadings didn't help. The Mozambican officials stood fast, although they softened their stance after a while and explained that although they might be inclined to help, their South

African equivalents on the other side of the line wouldn't break any rules. It felt good to know our guys stuck to the law, although to myself I also admitted rather shamefacedly that if the Mozambicans had offered to let me through illegally I would have taken them up on it like a shot.

Well, there was nothing to be done about it, and I was too tired to get worked up. I would eat something and go straight to bed. It was an old trick from my childhood: if something exciting was going to happen the next day, the best thing was to have an early night. Then, when you woke up, all the time in between had passed like a flash. The immigration guys kindly offered to put my bicycle inside their offices for safekeeping while I went off to find some food at the only eating-place on the Mozambican side of the border, a pub masquerading as a restaurant.

I was ordering my meal in the disguised pub when I got a call from a man named André Snyman, the head of a community crime-prevention group called eBlockwatch. The group had an offshoot called Travel Buddy, he explained, which aimed to support tourists visiting South Africa; he had been following my journey and would like to assist me on my last stretch through to Cape Town. The aim was to use me as a test subject, not only to see how successful the communication between the participants was but also – more importantly to me, I guess – to determine how hospitable and friendly each of their members was.

Talk about the cruelty of fate! Here I was, ordering some chicken and rice which might very well be OK, but might not, and I had to sit listening to André telling me that on the other side of the border local Travel Buddy people were waiting to welcome me with one of my favourite meals, boerewors rolls with an onion and tomato topping. But there was no way to get to them, in spite of André getting involved in some serious personal negotiations with the Mozambicans. I stared at the lights twinkling on the other side of the border fence, a mere 100 metres or so away, and it was as if I could *smell* that delicious beef sausage that South Africans of all races start eating when they are barely off their baby's bottles.

In the meantime, André said, some people from a coastal resort near Ponto do Ouro were on their way through to fetch me. They would put me up for the night and then bring me back to the border in the morning. It was a tempting prospect, but I explained to André that I wanted to be right at the front of the queue the following morning. He assured me I would be, and so I agreed. But I was strangely unhappy about the plan. Backtracking over the hell run I had just had ('hell plod' might be a better term), even though in a powerful 4x4, and then coming back again was strangely unattractive, now that I was on the very edge of Mozambique and ready to plunge into South Africa. It was not very logical, but just then I was not in a very logical frame of mind. I just didn't want to pull back from that long-awaited border. And I didn't. What went wrong I don't know, but my would-be hosts never arrived. Every set of approaching headlights had me and the other drinkers – all of whom knew my story by now – waiting expectantly ... but it was always somebody else. By 10 pm I gave up and called André to tell him I was going back to my bicycle and would sleep outside the border post.

Some bad memories are better when they have aged in the wood a little, while others retain every bit of their original nastiness. My last night in Mozambique was definitely one of those nasty ones. Because my bike was locked up in one of the offices I couldn't get to my camping equipment, so I had to curl up in the freezing cold on the concrete slab of the immigration office wearing just my shorts and my faithful long-sleeved cycling shirt. To make the night even more memorable, hordes of mosquitoes came calling, as per the script.

The wind grew stronger and the temperature went even further down as time went by, and at least three times I stumblingly migrated between two spots on the concrete slab. One spot had a low side-wall which deflected most of the wind but facilitated the mosquitoes' assaults on my blood supply. The other was fully exposed to the wind, which discouraged the mosquitoes but left me frozen stiff. I would be chewed over by the mozzies, tell myself: 'Of course being cold is better than being bitten by malaria-carrying mosquitoes,' and stagger off. Then, after a while out in the open, I'd change my mind and tell myself: 'Being chowed on by mozzies is better than freezing to death.' And so on. Believe me, the night hours just couldn't pass quickly enough for my liking.

The video I took of myself next morning when I got my bike back is graphic evidence of my physical state. I was just another wretched African refugee, a sort of reverse refugee, in my case. I wasn't fleeing my home because of war, revolution or famine. I was fleeing *back* home from circumstances I had created myself. But I didn't care as I crossed the line, weary, scruffy, downright dirty and heavily decorated with lumps and bumps though I was. In 30 minutes I was going to be greeting people with 'Sawubona' and 'Goeie môre' and 'Good morning' instead of 'Bom dia' or 'Jambo' or 'Bonjour'. I was going to be paying in rands instead of meticais or shillings or lira or CFA francs, trying to figure out the exchange rate so that I would know whether I was exceeding my daily budget. Most of all, I would be flying along the thousands of miles of good tarmac roads that many spoiled South Africans bitch about because as far as they are concerned the maintenance is not up to scratch.

In a nutshell, I would be back where I belonged. 'Oos, wes, tuis bes', the old Afrikaans saying had it. East, west, home is best.

# CHAPTER 34

# BACK IN SOUTH AFRICA AT LAST!

*You did not have to look further than the battered mini-
bus taxi drinking in petrol in front of the garage shop and the
five top-of-the-range 4x4s, each hooked up to a trailer with a
10 metres-plus ski-boat, which stood in the parking area. They
were symbols of the sort of ostentatious prosperity you would
expect to see in a place like Monaco's millionaires' harbour,
and it really shook me, even though I had seen similar sights at
various places during my African trek. I gawked at the 4x4s, together with dozens of other people, including even the service-
station staff. They represented wealth beyond our the wildest
dreams.*

By the time the border post opened at 8 am it already had a solid
queue of people with 4x4s and boats, headed both north and south.
I got in line, patient now that I was about to be stamped out of the
last country in my journey around Africa. But for some reason the
Mozambican border officials got very excited and hung around me,
taking pictures with their cell-phone cameras. I was happy for them
but not worked up either way. I was about as mellow as a man can
be, so that in spite of the momentous occasion it was just another
border post to get through. But it turned out to have a special moment when a young South African who was travelling to Mozambique with a tour group also wanted to take pictures of me. He was
hugely impressed when I recognised him as one of the many people
who had chatted with me at one of the shopping centres at which I
had been beating the bushes for my trip, more than two and a half
years earlier. I remembered him because he had asked some in-depth

questions about my plans and had wanted to contribute to them.

Anyway, before I knew it many of the people in the immigration office were asking me if I was the guy who was cycling around Africa. The guy on John Robbie's radio show? That crazy guy? I admitted it. I was that crazy guy, all right. One young traveller came up and put R100 into my pocket. It is a humbling thing to take money from people, even when you need it as badly as I did just then, but it's easier when the giver looks you straight in the eye, as this one did, and says: 'You're an amazing man. We've followed your journey for a long time now. You've done an amazing thing.' My turn at the immigration desk brought another moment to remember. When the woman checking me in saw my bicycle parked outside she couldn't contain her amazement and called her colleagues to come and have a look at it and me. *This* was the welcome home I needed just then. No lights, bells and whistles, just smiling faces.

Once I was through immigration I wasted no time in reaching my rendezvous with those boerewors rolls at the little town of Emangusi, 18 km down the road, where my host, Johan, owned the Total petrol station and garage ... 18 km of tarmac! Johan was waiting for me, and in no time I was tucking into a huge spread. This really touching hospitality for a complete stranger didn't stop there. Johan gave me his cell phone as a spare and helped me to remake the 'no food for lazy man' number-plate I had found in Nigeria and subsequently lost. I had mourned the loss of that plate, which had expressed my personal philosophy so clearly, and had been carrying around a car's mud-flap I had found on which I intended to re-paint it as soon as I found some waterproof white paint. Johan found the right paint in his store-room but didn't have a brush. But this was only a minor challenge for a true-blue adventurer. I dug out a piece of wood, rinsed most of the dirt off it and then chewed one end into a scruffy but effective facsimile of a paint-brush. Thus equipped, it was a piece of cake to inspan my artistic talents and Johan's paint to produce my message to the world.

After I had finished a gargantuan number of boerewors rolls, Johan and a few of his friends packed some 'padkos' for me in the ancient South African tradition of sending off your guests with some food for the road, then had a whip-around to raise something towards my running expenses. As I say, I was really touched, and I would have loved to stay on for a while, but I had to keep a sharp eye on the clock now. I simply had to be at my starting-point at Cape Town's Victoria and Alfred Waterfront on the 25th, and I still had to do 90 km to the world-famous Phinda resort near the Mkuze Game Park, where a contact of André's at the CC Africa game lodge management company had offered five-star accommodation for the night.

I didn't make it. I was done in by an exceptionally strong headwind and the effects of my over-indulgence at Johan's overflowing table, and after 60 km I had to call it quits for the day. I called ahead to Phinda to say I just couldn't get there, then started looking around for a roadside camping site in the next 15 km or so. It was a wonderful 60 km, though. I greeted as many people as I could and felt rejuvenated by this simple social exercise. One thing that really caught my eye, something I never would have noticed before, was how neat and smart our school-going children looked in comparison to the rest of Africa's (with the possible exception of the Libyan kids in their quasi-military camouflage uniforms); an important point was that these children I was impressed with all belonged to what most South Africans would consider financially disadvantaged schools. In my opinion the much greater movement of people, and the consequent improvement in roads, have played a significant role in the upliftment of rural communities, although I wonder if those communities realise how much of the improvement in their personal lot is actually a trickle-down effect of general development. Railway lines and good roads always bring benefits to out-of-the-way communities all over the world.

The Phinda people had no intention of leaving me to sleep by the roadside, however, and sent out a guide to fetch me, then take me back to the 60 km mark next morning. I was pleased and relieved; right then a comfortable bed was something to look forward to ... perhaps it was part of my general wind-down as I got nearer to Cape Town and journey's end.

When we got to Phinda I was even more pleased, because as far as I was concerned it was worth every cent its guests paid. We South

Africans tend to take our country's majestic beauty and awesome wildlife a little for granted and gripe about prices, because we forget that whereas an elephant or a lion or a rhino is always fun to watch, they are virtually mythical creatures to people from most countries outside the continent. Phinda was a place where myth became reality right away. As soon as we drove through the gates of the actual reserve we came upon a herd of elephant and then a crush of rhinos casually hogging the right of way. The driver-guide said that I would have two options next morning: he could transport me right back to my starting-point, or he could take me on a game drive first – it was up to me. I wished it was; if this was what it was like virtually in the driveway of the park, I could just imagine how it must look a bit further in. But with great regret I had to decline his offer, because my time was just too tight.

I met some interesting guests at Phinda that evening. One was an American woman who arranged seminars and corporate talks for the renowned motivational speaker Anthony Robbins and, in fact, was at Phinda to check it out as a possible seminar venue. Her description of the level of preparation which went into Robbins's seminars, and the seriousness with which he took his role of influencing people's lives, opened the door to a new world for me. I want to do what he does, I told myself. I want to tell people about my journey and influence their lives for the better. Earlier in my journey I would never have spent time pondering possibilities like this one. Maybe it was that I was nearing home now and could realistically set new goals for myself. I knew that my thinking was noticeably different this side of the border. Previously my thoughts had tended to switch between the consideration of macro-issues and immediate things like how I was going to get to the next village, and when. But this new train of thought related directly to my future life and its opportunities.

I spent a blissful night in one of Phinda's luxury stilted cabins and was up before first light, drinking coffee with the other tourists as they prepared to go off on the game drive that the clock had forced me out of. Then the young resort manager and her husband, who ran the rhino-protection programme, personally drove me back to where I had been picked up the night before. I waved good-bye and watched them depart with a bit of a sigh in my heart – I wouldn't have minded spending another night in that cabin.

My bicycle's rear wheel, which had behaved itself for the past few days – or perhaps I'd simply been too distracted by the hectic pace of events – now reasserted itself. It started to pull exaggeratedly to one side again, and spokes began to snap. I didn't allow this latest betrayal to cast my spirits down: the money that I had been given at the border and at Johan's wasn't going to be spent on minor self-indulgences: I would spoil myself with the best treat of all, a new wheel, as soon as possible. But in the meantime that blasted wheel slowed me down so much that I was unable to catch up on the distance, as I had hoped, and my time-bind suddenly got worse when I was interrupted during some emergency roadside repairs by a call informing me that somehow the arrangements for my family and the mayor of Richards Bay to welcome me back to my home town had been scheduled for a day earlier than should have been the case.

This desperate situation demanded a desperate remedy, and I was up and scanning the passing traffic for a lift without even waiting to right my upside-down bicycle. Once more the benign gods of the road counteracted their evil brothers' efforts, and a young guy who worked for the Spar grocery chain got me to Zululand Cycles in Richards Bay a scant hour before the mayoral welcome. The Zululand Cycles people undertook to service my bike, replace its problem parts and re-spoke the rear wheel – free! – and wished me well on my final leg home.

I hadn't been back to Richards Bay for seven years, and my official welcome was really something to remember. My Auntie Margie and my Gran, Uncle Jimmy and Auntie Sue, other familiar faces like my old school principal (I could have chosen a far shorter route by which to come visit, he joked), Mayor Denny Moffat and a busload of school children were waiting for me on the City Hall steps. It was a very emotional moment for me. As a foster child I had had an extremely turbulent upbringing which had left me deeply cyni-

cal about the world and its people's supposed capability of unconditional love. Yet love was something I wanted more than anything.
Not just any love, but unconditional love. I had no clear idea of
what that meant, except that it would not depend on whether I was
a hero or not.

What I did know was that the first step had to come from me,
that I had to start by strengthening my relationships. I wanted to
tell my aunt, Gran and my other family members how grateful I was
to them, to let them to know I was an amazing person even without
achieving something which others admired. I wanted to be *wanted*
by my family, not the other way round. And so it was tremendously important to me to see the looks of admiration, especially from
those closest to me. I knew that my trip was not going to solve some
intricate emotional issues within me and my life, as I had sometimes dreamed it would. But this meeting had taken me towards
another platform of expression and introspection from which the
process could continue.

That night we had a family dinner, where I shared some of my
experiences and caught up on the lives of the people I cared most
about. This was in between wolfing down the food. My Gran had
made the meal I always begged her to make – that traditional South
African dish, bobotie, with its fluffy rice and wonderfully tasty cur-
ried mince. I had seconds and then thirds without a trace of shame.
Firstly, bobotie was one of my top favourite foods, secondly, I could
afford any weight-gain because I was a growing boy again, and
thirdly, I had 100-plus kilometres to cover the next day.

Rika and Dawid, friends of my Aunt Margie, offered to take us –
my aunt, my bicycle and me – out to Hluhluwe early the next morning. The offer gave me a real lump in the throat, because it meant
that my aunt, the nearest person in my life to a mother, would have a
special personal involvement in my adventure; a small one, perhaps,
but one which meant more to me than I could express in words. So
when I finally I said goodbye to them all and rode away it was with
that lump still in my throat, hoping she was proud of me.

By the time I got to Hluhluwe's petrol station I was back in
road mode and couldn't resist stopping off at the Wimpy Bar for

a breakfast cheese-burger to reinforce the good work that the previous night's bobotie was still doing, and while I was working my way through the juicy hamburger I had a ringside seat on yet another African experience which was taking place on the other side of the plate-glass window, not in some distant foreign country but right here in my own backyard. While a beggar stood staring sadly at me, a minibus taxi crammed with wildly gesticulating and shouting black people raced into the garage forecourt with the deafening music from its speakers shaking it to its very nuts and bolts and someone hanging more than half-way out of every window. When the taxi stopped in front of a petrol pump a seemingly endless horde of people rushed out and headed straight for the garage shop adjoining the Wimpy. Within seconds, so it seemed, every available space was occupied. All this noise, music, gabbling, arm-waving, dancing, singing and jostling painted a picture of complete chaos, but I wasn't fooled, although it raised some frowns from my fellow-diners and even the service-station staff. This was the ear-splitting exuberance with which a lot of Africa lived and went about its business, and that wasn't likely to change any time soon, irksome though it might be to the more sedate ways of the middle class, which is mostly white at this stage but is steadily transforming itself into a thoroughly multi-racial group.

The real point of all this was that it underlined the economic disparity that still exists in South Africa in spite of a prosperity that makes it a land of milk and honey in comparison with most of the other countries south of the Sahara – something a lot of us tend to miss or misunderstand. Yet it was there for all to see. You did not have to look further than the battered minibus taxi drinking in petrol in front of the garage shop and the five top-of-the-range 4x4s, each hooked up to a trailer with a 10 metres-plus ski-boat, which stood in the parking area. They were symbols of the sort of ostentatious prosperity you would expect to see in a place like Monaco's millionaires' harbour, and it really shook me, even though I had seen similar sights at various places during my African trek. I gawked at the 4x4s, together with dozens of other people, including even the service-station staff. They represented wealth beyond the wildest dreams of all the gawkers (including myself). How demoralising, I thought, a sight like this must seem to a man with almost nothing in the way of material wealth and even less chance of accumulating it.

It was as though the scales had fallen from my eyes, so that for the first time I could see the shabby clothes and worn sandals that the members of the ear-splitting mob in the garage shop were wearing. The only wealth they had was their smiles and their energy. But this did not blind them to the unbridgeable gap between themselves and the diners in the Wimpy. I could see some draw in on themselves and others whose body language spoke of discontent and even hostility.

It was not a uniquely South African situation; you can encounter the very same scenario in scores of other countries inside and outside Africa. But of course race played a role here. All South African whites are not rich and all South African blacks aren't poor, but that didn't matter. It would be very easy for some demagogue to say: 'They have and we don't. Let's hate them', and find ears willing to swallow his lies.

I would be a socialist if socialism were able to do what it preaches, namely to give people equal standards of life. But the reality is that it is more important to teach people how to stand up for themselves and use their own skills to improve their lot. A man who works for what he has, irrespective of how meagre it might be, is a proud man. A man who expects hand-outs for doing nothing is a beggar and will never be proud, and the only way he can improve his lot is by seizing that which belongs to others who are better-endowed than he is. The concept of teaching a man to catch a fish instead of simply giving him one is so well known that it has become a cliché, but I don't think it goes far enough. You also have to teach the man how to think up new ways of fishing on his own, because the ability to create your own opportunities as a solution to your problems is more valuable to a person and his or her community than simply being shown how to solve a problem.

As I finished my meal I asked myself why I hadn't had these

thoughts as strongly as this in the past two years. There was no easy answer, but one I came up with which seemed to fit the bill was that I now saw myself as blessed in many ways, and therefore responsible for helping people who were less fortunate than me. This was no theoretical thing: I was in my own country, and I had a duty towards my fellow-South Africans who were worse off than I was.

On this note I swallowed the last of my cheese-burger and set off again. The summer rain belted down as I passed Mtubatuba and approached Kwambonambi, which I think are two of the most beautiful place-names in South Africa. The road took me through vast expanses of commercial forestry plantations; many nature-lovers consider such plantations ugly, but these ones were luscious and green, with plenty of natural undergrowth. I observed all this in snatches, because the rain was so heavy that it collapsed my soft-brimmed hat about 10 km past Kwambonambi and started hitting me square in the face with such force that I was actually riding blind, blinking every two or three seconds to make sure I was still in the right place on the road. This was obviously a recipe for disaster, and so unenthusiastically I turned back to Kwambonambi to wait for the rain to abate.

I spent the night at a great backpacking lodge whose owner, a foreign woman in her mid-thirties, ran it in a way for which the words 'laid back' are inadequate. She had to take a bunch of tourists on a guided tour and left the entire set-up in the hands of the only other remaining guest, a Swedish girl, giving me a key to the dormitory and telling me to just lock up behind me when I left, and 'mark off your beers and leave the money when you go, thanks'. Wow! But after all, if you can't trust a backpacker, who *can* you trust?

Thanks to my unscheduled stop, I set off with a formidable distance to cover to Durban that day, all of 180 km, and the weather didn't help at all. A consistent head-wind slowed me down, and it was still raining hard, although it was to soften up that afternoon. On the other hand, I enjoyed my surroundings, especially the long, rolling hills, which I was convinced actually speeded up my progress. I was passing through KwaZulu-Natal's heartland now, the sugar-cane plantations which are the backbone of its prosperity. The plantations stretched as far as the eye could see, interspersed with others producing bananas for the entire nation – it's not a co-incidence that KwaZulu-Natal's inhabitants are jocularly known as 'the Banana Boys' to all other South Africans.

When I reached the toll plaza near Kingsley Holgate's home town of Mtunzini I pulled off the freeway and rode a few kilometres into the town itself to refill my water bottles and have a snack. With the prospect of the long haul to Durban awaiting me I did all this as fast as I could – so fast that it wasn't till I was back on the freeway that I realised I had forgotten to take on the water. I decided not to waste time retracing my tracks, since I was sure to find a roadside shop before long, and if worst came to worst I could always revert to my old stunt of flagging down a passing vehicle. Well, it didn't happen. There were no roadside shops anywhere, and passing mo-torists were definitely not keen to stop for a bedraggled, long-haired cyclist who strongly resembled a drowned rat.

There was a certain irony to the fact that I was desperate for a drink while all about me it was raining cats and dogs, but irony was the last thing in my mind. I got so thirsty that I squeezed my rain-soaked clothes out into my water bottle, and even constructed an elaborate but unworkable catchment device on the back of the bike. But necessity is the mother of invention, and after 60 km I tried an even more drastic approach. On most of the hills the freeway had a storm-water drain about four metres wide which, needless to say, was in full flood. I filtered my bottles with a double thick-ness of shirt, filled them up with the drain-water and then drank like crazy with my eyes closed in case there were floating nasties that I didn't want to know about. Now, if I had seen someone else drinking drain-water of such doubtful provenance I would have considered him insane. But you cut your cloth according to the cir-cumstances, and what mattered right then was that the water was sweet, the sieve did a good job (as far as I could see) and, above all else, it quenched a ferocious thirst.

André Snyman from Travel Buddy had arranged for me to stay over at a bed-and-breakfast in Salt Rock for the night, a great place with an awesome view of the Indian Ocean which the owners, David and Sue Stiles, had aptly named 'B&B By The Sea'. It was a wonderful stop-over. Sue was the epitome of charm and David had some amazing stories to tell. One of his best was about the day a playful killer whale about eight metres long had harassed him while he was kayaking just beyond the breakers. This might sound pretty unbelievable, but scores of people had watched from beaches and balconies while the killer whale chased David for several kilometres, bumping him repeatedly and eventually hoisting him into the air, kayak and all.

I set off along the smaller coastal road next morning in weather which was even worse than it had been, including such a furious head-wind that when David doubled back from his place of work to check up on me he was amazed at how little progress I had made towards Durban. I was dismayed rather than amazed because I was scheduled to meet the Mayor of Durban and do a radio interview, and I had no intention of missing either occasion. Naturally my rear wheel decided to act up just then to further complicate my progress, but the evil bicycle gods' intentions were thwarted when David came back to check up on me again, and with perfect timing found me carrying out emergency repairs by the roadside. That was it. David loaded up my bicycle and me and drove us to the nearest bike shop to have the wheel's tension professionally adjusted while I went about my other business.

My friend Duane Lodetti, a student of the culinary arts, and his friend Craig took me over from David and in due course brought me to the grand staircase of the city hall to meet with the Deputy Mayor, Mr Logie Naidoo. Years before I had stood on those steps and watched Queen Elizabeth II come driving by; now I was standing there as a guest of honour myself, rather than as an anonymous face in the crowd. Incredible!

With all my meetings and interviews out of the way, David picked my bike and me up again to spend another night at 'B&B By The Sea', and at sunrise next morning I was on my way again. I had some catching up to do because I was now about 70 km behind my schedule, but there were no distractions, the wheel was behaving itself and I didn't have to worry about hunting up some affordable accommodation – a former workmate and talented provincial rug-by player, Jonno Brayley, had arranged to meet me along the road and take me to his parents' retirement home in a village south of Durban for the night. I knew that it was going to be near impossible to cover the 100 km to the Brayleys in the space of two or three hours, but it spurred me on to make an all-out effort, even though I had to watch out for police patrols along the freeway – bicycles on national roads, especially at peak hour, are highly illegal.

I had hoped to avoid any unwelcome attention from the law, but this was wishful thinking, as I soon discovered when a youngish traffic cop halted his official scrambler ahead of me in a cloud of dust, right on the centre-line of the freeway. He was shouting something, but there was so much noise from the streams of passing vehicles between us that I couldn't hear what he was saying. I tried to indicate this in sign-language. It didn't work, and he began to get seriously angry, red face, jabbing finger and all. What probably saved him from popping a blood-vessel right there was a brief lull in the traffic, so that I could hear him screaming: 'Get your vehicle off the road! NOW! NOW!'

I wasted no time in turning my bicycle around and heading over to the old main road, which was now a secondary road; by all appearances the cop had lost it entirely and was contemplating assaulting me. The old road would make for slower going, but at least I would be safe from psychotic traffic policemen who did not seem to believe that basic courtesy was part of that 'serve and protect' ethos they were always talking about. All he had had to do, after all, was to tell me that for my own safety I must use the secondary road. But he carried on as if I were a fleeing cash-in-transit robber, and for the next 20 km he and his mates drove past me a number of times to make sure I didn't sneak back on to the sacred tarmac of the freeway. I shrugged off this fine advertisement for KwaZulu-Natal's law enforcement and enjoyed the scenery with its abundant banana plantations and full strong-flowing rivers. This was healthy-looking country that made you feel good just from looking at it.

My arrangement with Jonno was that he would meet me near his parents' house, and next morning bring me back to where he had picked me up. This gave me another opportunity to show how what a day of my life on the road consisted of, and while Jonno was helping me to lift the bicycle on to his car I handed my video camera to a passing schoolboy and asked him to film us.

My next overnight was one I had been looking forward to for a long time, since my hosts were my best friend Troy's parents, Vernon and Veronica Mitchell. I had worked for Vernon for a year and grown very close to him and Veronica and Troy. Like me, he was a former paratrooper – he had served in Britain's Parachute Regiment – and he was full of zest for life: his idea of retirement had been to relocate to Port Edward and buy a microlight aircraft, which he flew all over the place whenever the weather allowed.

The Mitchells had been expecting me for quite a while, because there had been so many unscheduled interruptions on my journey that I had had to re-schedule my date of arrival several times, and it nearly happened again because of all the unexpected distractions. Jonno had asked people he knew at the East Coast radio station to broadcast an appeal to everyone to assist me where they could, and since this happened to be the most widely listened-to provincial radio station in the country, the response was remarkable. Passing motorists hooted in support and some even hung out of their windows to wish me luck. One fellow, an Indian guy called Kevin, actually stopped a few kilometres ahead of me in the shade cast by a bridge (did I mention that it was very hot?) and offered me half a tin of warm Diet Coke, all he had with him.

I reached the town of Scottburgh to find that my local fame had preceded me. This was just as well, because I needed to cash a cheque for R500 that I had received from the Richards Bay tourism office, and it wasn't looking too good. I hadn't wrapped it up well enough and the rain had just about done for it. The signatures and most of the writing were visible, but South African banks have become so wary of rubber cheques that I anticipated some difficulty. But there was nothing for it, so I girded my loins and joined the queue in the local bank branch. I was standing there, getting myself worked up for some fast talking, when the woman behind me asked if I was that fellow who was cycling around Africa. It was a question I had been asked so often that answering it had become routine, but I couldn't help noting that my reply sounded odd, somehow. Then I realised that the question had not changed, I had. My journey was almost complete, and my answer just didn't sound the same as it had in foreign countries when I still had so much distance and unknown things ahead of me. I was now *almost* the guy who had cycled around Africa!

Thanks to my new-found fame I managed to cash my much-weathered cheque without any trouble, the branch manager commenting that she was proud to assist me. Financially fortified, I left the bank and was confronted by people from the local eatery, who invited me to have breakfast with them. This led to an interview with the local newspaper and an introduction to some prominent business people in the main street. What with things like this I was obviously not going to make Port Edward that night, or even the town of Margate, but in characteristic fashion Vernon wasn't prepared to take 'no' for an answer yet again, seeing I was now so close. With typical meticulousness he pinpointed the exact spot where we would meet, below a big billboard advertising a butchery, to make sure that he knew precisely where to drop me off again next day. Typically, too, he got there first, and when I had toiled up the hill I was so moved by the pride I could see in his eyes that I literally felt weak. It made me feel like a million smackers in any currency. 'We're so proud of you, my boy,' Vernon said as we drove away. 'Everyone has been following your trip, and they can't believe how well you've done. It's incredible what you've done.' Coming from him, that meant a great deal.

Supper that night was another 'family' occasion, but it was an early night for me again because I had to be off by sunrise. Vernon drove me back to the exact spot where he had picked me up, and I mean *exact*: when we had unloaded he took the bike from me and gravely rolled her back three metres, commenting: 'No cheating here. Here is the exact spot. Now you're OK to go!' It was a pleasant moment. Usually I was the one who was adamant about returning to within a metre of where I had been, and it was nice to see someone else grasp the logic behind my pedantic fussiness about starting-points.

Margate, my next stop, attracts thousands of tourists with its nightlife and pretty beaches, but I planned to stop for only as long as it would take me to have a quick snack. Further encounters with friends, however, meant that I left Margate considerably later than I had intended and got caught by nightfall about 30 km from Port Edward. Vernon and his daughter Tracy came out to escort me home, an arduous business because Tracy, who was driving, proved to be a hard taskmaster. She decreed that she would dictate the pace rather than me, and so we set off with me pedalling frantically to keep a little distance – about a metre! – in front of the car. It was probably the quickest 30 km of hill-riding I had ever done.

We had another fine evening, and I rode off next morning with a mixture of sadness and relief in my heart. Sadness because there would be no more family and close friends from here on till I got to Cape Town. Relief for the same reason, because at the rate I was going, I would never make it to Cape Town in time unless I kept up a stiff pace and didn't undertake any side-excursions.

I left KwaZulu-Natal behind and entered the Eastern Cape, formerly the Transkei Xhosa 'homeland'. I had travelled this route by car in previous years, and steeled myself for such perils as animals wandering around unhindered on the freeway and motorists' total disregard for all traffic rules – not to mention some steep mountain ranges and hills I would have to struggle over. But I was in for a pleasant surprise. At 20 km/h I had plenty of time to avoid the animals, and more courteous and friendly drivers would have been difficult to find. People waved to me as they passed, and whenever I was stationary everyone came over to ask politely where I was from and where I was going. What really amazed them, apart from the fact that I had just about completely circumnavigated Africa, was that I was a South African like them; they just couldn't believe a white man would be willing to undertake something like this.

The Transkeian countryside was breathtakingly beautiful. I remember one view in particular, a vista of endless smooth, rounded hills that looked almost unreal in its perfection, like a digitally manipulated film background. The tallest of the hills had a soccer field on its summit, and through a gap in the overcast sky a broad beam of sunlight reached down to cast a glorious golden spotlight on to the hill itself, the field, the players and the spectators. I have no doubt that anyone who believed in omens would have taken this as a sure sign that South Africa was the right choice to host the 2010 Soccer World Cup.

The mountains and hills often slowed me down to about 10 km/h, but it was worth it. As I cycled towards my next interim destination, the incredibly pretty coastal town of Port St Johns, I was very aware of how the dots and names on maps had come alive to me because I was travelling by bicycle instead of in a car. Port St Johns was a case in point. It was off the freeway, and if I had been travelling by car I might have decided to bypass it. Well, that didn't happen this time, and eventually I arrived at the little town in its beautiful setting between the mountains at the mouth of the broad Mzimvubu River. I spent the night at the Cremorne riverside lodge, a collection of chalets and camping sites, whose management not only put me up but invited a group of locals to a talk about my journey. They loved it and asked many questions, but what I remember the best about that evening was how I embarrassed myself afterwards when I was sitting at the bar and talking to an elderly man who had been in the audience.

The talk got on to fishing on the Transkei coast – an evergreen topic in that part of the world, as evidenced by various clippings and photographs of notable catches on the noticeboard – and I recalled one clipping of 1950s' vintage which had caught my attention. 'This local guy was fishing somewhere off the main beach in Port St Johns,' I recalled. 'The newspaper said he hooked this huge kob, fought it for a while and then reeled it in in waist-high water to within 10 metres of himself. It said he was battling with the fish, because it was a considerable size. Then a shark suddenly attacked the fish and bit a chunk out of it. The fisherman was still in waist deep water, only 10 metres away. He backtracked as quickly as possible and managed to reel in the remainder of the kob. The shocking thing, though, was that when they measured what remained of the kob they could determine that even in the shallow water the shark had been easily big enough to eat him.' The elderly man listened intently to my tale, and I was sure he had been entertained by it. And I was right, if for the wrong reason: my listener was Tony Oates, a legendary angler in those parts ... and the very man in the photograph published with that faded clipping nearly a half-century earlier! It must have been pretty funny to sit in the pub and listen to some young whippersnapper solemnly telling him about his own adventure. At least he was kind enough not to laugh in my face.

CHAPTER 35

# COUNTDOWN TO CAPE TOWN

*The common denominator for success in our country is the basic understanding that it takes sincere effort and consideration on everyone's part to make it happen. How could things work otherwise?*

I left Port St Johns knowing that I had a tough challenge to overcome. A family of cyclists who had attended my talk had told me afterwards that there was absolutely no chance of my being able to pedal such a heavily laden bike over the steep Mlengana Pass which lay ahead; I would end up pushing it at least part of the way, sure as fate, they said. Well, I wish they had decided to accompany me for the day's ride, because I was so hardened by my long trek that I crossed the incredibly steep but stunningly engineered pass without putting a foot to the ground except when I stopped to rest. It wasn't easy, but a dose of stubbornness and two years of pumping pedals will take you a long way.

Mthatha brought me an unexpected and very touching bonus. On arriving there I was approached by a woman who said she had heard about my trip and asked if there was any way in which she could help me. I said that I appreciated her gesture, but there wasn't anything I needed just then. But this was one determined lady. She gave my bike a careful front-to-back inspection and then pointed to my home-made 'No Food for Lazy Man' slogan. 'I'll make you a proper one,' she said. 'I own a sign shop in the town.' Can you believe it! That professional version of my sign is still in mint condition, because I kept it tucked away as a spare, which fortunately I never had to use.

The coastal area just south of Mthatha is renowned for its un-spoilt beauty at places like Coffee Bay, but just then, so I was told by various concerned locals, it was also notorious for attacks on tour-ists. This was a pretty bad situation for an area which depended heavily on out-of-area visitors, since tourists base their decisions al-most totally on perceptions – after all, what else can they use? – and it made me really angry to think that a tiny part of a population could spoil things for all the rest. The people I met in the town of Butterworth went to great lengths to explain that the perpetrators weren't locals but 'makwerekwere' ('black foreigners' in Xhosa), and that it was difficult to keep track of their movements because nobody really knew them; as a result, the blame landed squarely on the shoulders of the local inhabitants. Yet I had discovered that this was one of the friendliest places I had travelled through so far. It was so damned unfair.

For all I knew they were right about the perpetrators. Literally millions of illegal aliens had streamed into South Africa in the past decade to escape poverty or oppression or both elsewhere in Af-rica, particularly in neighbouring Zimbabwe, and this is likely to get worse before it gets better. Because they do not go through the laid-down procedures they are invisible and untraceable, and in a country with high unemployment among its own citizens, crime is a natural temptation – particularly because many of the illegals are former soldiers and policemen. True or false? No one can say for certain. All one can do is read the screaming newspaper head-lines describing yet another unnecessarily violent crime and make up one's own mind.

The bottom line, though, was that the crimes were taking place, not just here but everywhere in South Africa, and the solution rate was anything but spectacular. Everyone except the perpetrators (whoever they were) suffered as a result. Victims lost their posses-sions and frequently their lives, and the local population in tourist destinations saw one of their main sources of income dwindling. If most of the perpetrators are indeed makwerekwere, it means that because of the iniquities of many other African leaders South Afri-ca is being punished for the 'sin' of keeping itself in running order.

On the upside, though, this part of the Transkei has gained a new kind of fame in the past few years because just off the N2 freeway are the village of Mvezo, birthplace of Nelson Mandela, and the town of Qunu, where he grew up. I regretted not having the time to veer off my scheduled route to visit Qunu, where Mr Mandela's umbilical cord is said to be buried in accordance with traditional Xhosa culture, a symbolic linking to his ancestors. I also regretted being unable to fulfil the promise I had made 18 months earlier to our ambassador in Morocco, Mr Mpehle, who had asked me to drop in on his family if possible when I passed through. I felt very bad about both, particularly my failure to visit the Mpehle family. In hindsight I would sooner have passed on one of the grand sights I saw elsewhere than on this one.

My arrival at Idutywa sparked yet another of those innumerable acts of kindness I had received during my journey. I stopped at the town's Spar outlet for a cool drink and a pie, but I got a lot more than that from the manager, Mthunzi Ngozwana. Without any prompting on my part Mthunzi arranged for free accommodation at the Idutywa Hotel across the road, a modest place but the best accommodation in the town, gave me a couple of vouchers to use at Spar supermarkets further along my way and even called ahead to inform his colleagues further south that a South African madman was on his way to visit. Mthunzi definitely did not have to be this kind to me, but I think I know where he was coming from. He was just another South African who wanted to reach out and change our country for the better, and this was his best opportunity so far of doing so. It might sound as if I am trying to over-dramatise my journey, but I honestly believe that it was thanks to him and hundreds of thousands like him of all races that South Africa was able to confound the pessimists in 1994 and make a peaceful transition. The common denominator for success in our country is the basic understanding that it takes sincere effort and consideration on everyone's part to make it happen. How could things work otherwise?

Two more interesting characters who literally appeared out of nowhere one cold, drizzly, misty day were a sangoma and his assistant, a charming woman with a permanent grin, who also happened to be his wife. We didn't understand one another very clearly, but I gathered that they wanted me to arrange jobs for them in Cape Town. I felt for them, but I was somewhat at a loss about how a guy on a bicycle who was on a circumnavigation of Africa (I didn't know how to explain to them what I had been doing), would know where sangoma vacancies were to be found.

I had a date with some bird's-eye-view video coverage at the majestic mountain passes called the Kei Cuttings, thanks to Vernon's contacting an East London microlight pilot and budding cinematographer called Graham Coutts. Alas, it didn't work out because such strong winds were sweeping over the passes that Graham couldn't risk flying. But he took some good ground-level footage of me negotiating one of the steep inclines. This was a valuable addition to my video archive, and what made our encounter even better was that Graham promised to put in a word for me with various dairy-farmer friends along the route ahead. Since I love milk, this promised some pleasant wayside refreshment.

I had an encounter with another Graham, whom I had met in Vilanculos in Mozambique on the night of the Currie Cup final. I hadn't thought we would ever meet again, at least not in this manner, but suddenly he was there next to me on the freeway as East London came into view over my handlebars. I had planned to cycle straight past East London, but I found myself having lunch with Graham, who also arranged a picture-and-interview session with the local newspaper, the *Daily Despatch*. The only downside to it was that I lost another afternoon of cycling and ended up heading off into the night to catch up a bit.

Making night dashes was nothing new by now, of course, but I felt a strange reluctance this time. I was in a frame of mind that I found difficult to explain. I was getting closer and closer to that big elephant in my living-room; the end of my journey. I had been thinking and talking about it since the day I left Cape Town, but now it was difficult to accept that it would actually happen very soon. That last kilometre, that last metre ... how would it feel? Would it be a moment of personal glory – or a disappointing anti-climax? I decided not to think about it any more; this was no time to lose focus. What would happen would happen. In the meantime I just had to keep those pedals going around. I felt like a soldier going into battle with no knowledge of what the outcome would be.

The traffic police I encountered around East London were the mirror image of the apoplectic character I had run into near Durban. On one occasion I didn't notice that a patrol car had quietly caught up with me, and when the cop behind the wheel warned me away from the freeway over his loudspeaker I nearly fell off my bike in sheer startlement. The cop felt so bad about giving me such a fright that he insisted on buying me some lunch. Another cop, a pretty little Afrikaans woman, was so concerned about my safety that she gave me a detailed briefing on the best alternative routes to follow.

Using the secondary roads along the coast was not always easy, but it did afford me a very graphic insight into the process that ends with the act of casually pulling a carton of milk out of a supermarket fridge. One time I stopped off to get a refill of water and was promptly dragged into the bowels of the amazing world of dairy farming when the farmer, Andrew – the fourth generation of his family to be in the business – showed me around his operation. Milking machines sucked away at rows of patient cows, each providing its share of the 15 000-litre daily yield, which would then be processed to near-final state in the adjoining factory before being picked up by one of the giant dairy-products firms. Then came the best part of the tour – breakfast to feed the perpetually hungry hyena under my belt. It was literally the freshest meal I'd ever had. Andrew brought a large container of milk directly from the factory, and his wife raided the chicken-coop for newly laid eggs. If they had kept pigs we would certainly have had bacon with our eggs on toast as well. I really climbed into all that lovely fresh milk and must have finished off two litres of it during the meal. Andrew not only didn't bat an eye about this voracious consumption of his bread and butter but strapped a container holding another two litres on to my bicycle before I left just in case I felt like wetting my whistle later in the day (I did – frequently).

I didn't spend much time at Port Elizabeth, my next major destination, but I couldn't help noticing the vast construction work taking place on its outskirts on the Coega Harbour project. If ever a development scheme proved South Africa's importance as a maritime 'truck stop' between East and West, this was it. The harbours at major ports like Cape Town and Durban had been servicing East–West maritime traffic for hundreds of years, but Coega was far larger than either of them. I couldn't help feeling that somehow it was appropriate. Port Elizabeth has always lagged behind in the image stakes. It has been dubbed 'the windy city' – a lie, since it is officially classed as the *least* windy major city in South Africa – a pretty but dull little place. On the contrary, it has a thriving tourism industry, plenty of nightlife and all sorts of outdoor activities, especially water sports, and its industrial sector includes a large, long-established automotive sector. And as a keen sportsman I knew that it had hosted the country's first rugby and cricket test matches.

Historically it was just as interesting. Its recorded history goes back to 1488, when the Portuguese seafarer Bartholomeu Diaz landed at what he called the Bahia de Lagoa (today's Algoa Bay) while feeling out a sea-route to the East. As Port Elizabethans like to point out, he hadn't bothered to set foot ashore at the Cape of Good Hope ...

But I couldn't stop. I was in the last week of my long journey now. In five days, all going well, I would roll into Cape Town after more than two years on the road. I was already beginning to look back and reflect on my journey as I pedalled southwards, even though it hadn't ended yet. It had been not just a journey into Africa but a long, sometimes painful trek into own soul. Memories of special moments, and their significance, coursed endlessly through my mind: memories of people who had come to mean a lot to me in spite of our brief encounters; the scores of new acquaintances who had showed me kindnesses large or small, or gone out of their way to help me, a total stranger; the knowledge I had acquired of just how much tenacity I really possessed, knowledge which could only be gained by a long series of acid tests.

I didn't know how I would put all this into words when I finally got home. What would I say when I arrived at the Waterfront in Cape Town, where I knew my friends and supporters would be waiting to welcome me home? What would they expect to hear from me? What would my first words be to Vasti, who had understood why I had undertaken this long quest and then stood by me in word and deed throughout all those many months of absence in which each day could have been my last – sometimes for many days without hearing a word to tell her whether I was dead or alive? How many other women would have had this sort of understanding and resolution? I didn't know, but my guess was that they were thinly sown over this planet of ours.

I hastened determinedly on to the pretty little coastal town of Cape St Francis, right next to the world-renowned surfing paradise of Jeffrey's Bay, where the local branch of the Travel Buddy network stood ready to receive me. Getting there involved crossing the notorious 'death bridge' over the Van Staden's River gorge. At the time I crossed over it, no fewer than 66 people had committed suicide by throwing themselves off this awesomely beautiful arch. Why? Nobody knows, and the dead aren't telling. All I knew was that it was the only bridge in Africa with a 24-hour free link to Lifeline, the country's telephone hotline for people with suicidal tendencies.

I was pretty sure that tour guides invariably passed all this on to their clients as they drove over the soaring bridge, and when I stopped part of the way along and stood peering down at the river far below I couldn't help noticing how many cars and tour buses slowed down to give me the once-over. What sort of comments was I evoking: 'Oh, dear, that poor ragged boy's climbed off his bicycle because he wants to jump', perhaps? Well, I wasn't going to oblige, after everything I had seen and done. What I did, though, was ask myself what made me stop at the spot where so many people had killed themselves? What had I achieved by doing that? I couldn't think of a satisfying answer, so I got on my bike and rode on.

The Cape St Francis Travel Buddies were waiting with open arms and stood me to a stop-over of VIP standard in a fine B&B. A lot of people think that the average B&B specialises in adequate but budget-level accommodation, but here, as had been my experience elsewhere, many a five-star hotel would have had stiff competition when it came to service and luxury level. I had come to understand why most of the major hotel chains' advertising strategies were now focused on their personal interaction with their guests.

The next day, a Sunday, happened to be the day of Johannesburg's answer to Cape Town's Argus Cycle Tour, the Pick 'n Pay 94.7 Cycle Tour, and I did a sort of spiritual long-distance latch-on to provide me with a goal for the day. The '94.7' represents the frequency and name of Pick 'n Pay's partner radio station in the event, and also the exact distance to be completed, and I intended to do the same, even though the 25 000-odd cyclists officially taking part were 1 600 km away. This proved easier said than done. Normally it would have been an easy ride, but I got off to a late start and rode straight into a strong headwind, so that by late afternoon I had only managed about 70 km. My friend Graham from East London, who knew the area quite well, had been following my progress this day and became concerned about where I was going to spend the night.

I was concerned myself. I had stopped at one roadside house, which turned out to be a farm manager's, to ask him for a safe site to pitch my tent for the night. To my surprise this modest request got a negative response. The manager told me nervously that 'I don't do things like this', and ushered me off his property and back on to the night-bound freeway. I had no idea what he meant, but it was clearly no good pushing him, and at this late stage I couldn't be bothered to get worked up about it. Again I set off into the night. I would ride on till I had done the 94.7 km I had set myself, and then I would sleep wherever I happened to be.

In the meantime Graham was frantically calling around among his dairy-farmer friends, and one of them happened, of all things, to be the owner of the farm where I had been cold-shouldered. He was one of the country's major milk producers and had been away in Johannesburg on business that day, but after Graham had told him about me he sent off another of his farm managers – also named Riaan – to fetch me and put me up for the night. And yes, by the time I was on the way again the following morning I had drunk a lot of milk. A little lesson learned here: Don't tell a dairy farmer you love milk. Tell him it's OK or it's pleasant, but don't tell him you love it unless you can absorb a heavy load.

This day's journey was interrupted by something I had not got involved in at any other stage of my journey. I knew that one of my way-destinations on this day's leg would be the Blaauwkrans River Bridge, which at 216 metres above terra firma was the highest commercial bungee-jumping site in the world, and I had decided to give it a try if the company concerned would give me a free leap. I have never been very enthusiastic about bungee-jumping, but it would make some good footage for my film record, I thought. Actually doing something about it wasn't so easy when I reached the bridge. The prospect of throwing myself into thin air suddenly seemed even less attractive than it had been, and I had some difficulty talking myself into turning off the freeway to the jumping site. One of the things that persuaded me to take this step was a little voice in the back of my head which kept saying in a reassuring tone that the bungee-jumping company probably wouldn't give me a free ride. But the little voice lied, and 30 minutes later I was frantically pumping adrenalin as I shuffled nearer and nearer to the edge of the huge bridge, a thick elastic cord tied around my ankles.

Let me say only that it is amazing how your perspective of a pretty view changes when you know you're soon going to hurl yourself out over it with nothing but a cord around your ankles. The soaring height of the bridge changes from something spectacular into merely lots of thin air, and the picturesque rocks in the river below aren't picturesque any more, just jagged and lethal. My only sort of consolation was that the man jumping with me, a British tourist, was clearly more nervous than I was. I had expected to be frozen with fear, but as my date with lots of nothing approached I got a grip on myself. The thought of stepping off the bridge was terrifying because it went against every natural instinct, but I knew that bungee-jumping was much safer than it looked – and, after all, as a paratrooper I had done something very similar. When I compared it to some of the real dangers I had faced during my journey there was no comparison. So by the time I leaped off the edge I had my fears under control; I was still nervous, of course, but not afraid. The video footage that shows me charging over with every appearance of enthusiasm only lies a little.

Enough! I had 350 km to cover and three days to do it in. I got my head down and pumped the pedals, stopping now and then along the road to take in the vistas of farmland filled with sheep and ostriches. I realised again just how beautiful my country was. One vista was so beautiful that for a moment I was literally stunned. On the middle day of the three I cycled into The Wilderness, at the top end of the world-famous Garden Route from the Cape of Good Hope, and stopped at the bridge that would take me into the mountains ahead. I got off and stared speechlessly around me, more than a little convinced that I was actually asleep and dreaming a dream that was too good to be true. On my left was the Indian Ocean, where the great rollers crashed on to long, pristine white beaches. On my right rose the great mountains I would soon have to cross. Linking the two very different scenes were paragliders sailing off the mountain pass ahead of me and gliding down to land on the beaches below.

It was hard work crossing those mountains, but I can't remember one occasion on which I was conscious of being tired. I just kept going, with every turn in the road bringing me yet another view to savour and then leave behind. And now, as the kilometres slid past under my wheels, quickly and almost invisibly, I started thinking about my homecoming again (Vasti had warned me that there would be a lot of people to welcome me) and resurrecting the original expectations with which I had left Cape Town on that distant day.

I had not set out with the aim of eventually basking in the limelight. That would be the cherry on top, public acknowledgement and appreciation of the dangers and hardships I had suffered in the pursuit of my goal, but it wasn't the first prize. The first prize would be the knowledge that I had achieved something personally worthwhile and significant, something, I reminded myself, I could tell my grandchildren about one day and see their understanding of why I had gone on this incredible adventure.

When I registered this point again, all my feelings of anxiety about the moment of homecoming fell away. I had departed and now I would be coming back. I had done what I had set out to do. I didn't care what sort of reception I got at the Waterfront, whether it was a brass band or a vagrant trying to rifle my panniers. And yet in another way I *did* care, very much. I wanted to see Vasti and my friends waiting for me. They had seen me go and they must see me return, so that the wheel had turned full circle.

That ever-ticking clock forced me to give up on my intention to visit Cape Aghulhas, literally the very southernmost point of Africa. I promised myself that I would go back there and carried on. I would have to cover 120 km on the final day – the very next day, hard though it was to grasp – and I had to make allowance for the fact that about 100 km from Cape Town I would be met by a television crew.

I spent the night at a quaint stone-built B&B. As I left just before sunrise I paused to take a couple of mental snapshots of this final morning. 'Tonight I'll sleep in my own bed,' I told myself. It just didn't feel real.

Now the kilometres were really flying past. With my TV crew in tow and filming frantically, I went up and down the great Sir Lowry's Pass through the grand mountains that barred the way to Cape Town. At the top of Sir Lowry's Pass friends from the Helderberg Rugby Club, who had been following my progress from the start, turned out to welcome me back. It was wonderfully exciting, but now I was like a shark which had smelled blood, because I could see the unmistakeable profile of Table Mountain in the blue distance, welcoming me home as it had been welcoming returning travellers for three centuries and more.

I was in a strange frame of mind. The TV crew had been interviewing me at intervals ever since we had joined up, but I had had surprisingly little to say. It wasn't that I was tongue-tied by the thought of what lay ahead, it was a sort of numbness that had come over me, numbness and a flood of almost overpoweringly strong memories of where I had been. Soon the golden thread that bound me directly to those memories would be snapped because the journey would end. Now I just wanted to get it over with.

More kilometres slipped by as we sped through the green winelands of the Boland. I cycled in the slipstream of the TV crew's car, so that we averaged nearly 40 km/h at times as we approached Cape Town. I knew it wouldn't last once we got close to the Mother City when the freeway became engorged with streams of traffic from all the tributaries leading into it. The traffic-streams were frantic but friendly, with people hooting and waving at me as they passed. I waved back, but a little abstractedly, because I was seized with fear of being knocked off my bike five kilometres from the end of my journey. That would be embarrassing beyond all measure.

On top of this I had to face yet another trial. On the way to the Waterfront I stopped off at the studios of 567 Cape Talk Radio for an hour-long interview with one of its personalities, Lisa Chait. To say that I went through that interview with mixed emotions was putting it mildly. First of all, of course, I was grateful to Lisa. On the other hand, I could actually see the Waterfront every time I looked through the studio window! When the interview was over I thanked Lisa and jumped into the saddle again. A few minutes – too many minutes! – later I was freewheeling down the pretty road leading into the Waterfront. I had a last small panic attack, with 'What's going to happen? What's going to happen?' echoing over and over in my head. This I banished by answering: 'You're here to finish what you started. You're here to finish what everyone said couldn't be done.' Having crossed that mental bridge, I was ready for the actual one that would take me to the exact spot from which I had started two years, two months and fifteen days before.

Vasti was there with all my friends and a lot of enthusiastic strangers besides, and I shared a few of my feelings with them. But what sounded loudest of all in my ears was the voice within me, which kept repeating: 'Well done. Well done. Well done.' I was truly proud of myself.

I felt strangely purposeless. What would I do tomorrow, now that no new horizon waited to be reached? I had been so long on the road that I had almost forgotten what it was like not to be bound into an all-consuming quest. Well, I'd take the day off, I decided. And maybe the next couple of days, too. And then? I had some things to attend to, like knitting the long-interrupted threads of my life together again. And then? Well, I'd start planning my next adventure. That's what adventurers do, after all.

# LAST WORD

A story shouldn't go on past the happy ending. But before I disappear from your sight on the way to the next horizon, I think I should say a few words about what I learned from my circumnavigation of Africa, in the hope that it may help others who plan or dream about their own great adventure, whatever that may be.

Above all else, this journey taught me to back myself, even when there was an eminent possibility of failure. Failure is part of success, as long as you pick yourself up and keep going. Your greatest reward is that you personally discover your true value, regardless of what any of those around you might think, realising that you are worthy of more than you think you are worthy of, that you are better than you think you are.

The foundation of all your unwillingness to attempt what you have dreamed of, but never believed to be possible, is the fear of failure. When you sincerely believe that there is no limit to your value and your possibilities, your fear of failure is transmuted into an embrace of those very things. So do not fear failure: often it is the very cement that is needed to build a strong foundation.

# TRIP STATISTICS

For the benefit of anyone wanting to follow in my wheel-tracks, whether actually or vicariously, the following statistics might be of interest:

**Total distance covered:** About 36 500 km by the map. According to the bicycle's odometer, several thousand more were covered during zigzags, backtracking and side-excursions.

**Number of tyres used up:** About 120, the worst wear taking place on the tough roads of northern Kenya and Mozambique.

**Number of chains used up:** A total of 15. The first chain lasted 12 500 km, all the way to Abidjan, but the replacement lasted only 10 km. Ethiopia used up about 10 chains.

**Number of inner tubes used up:** About 90, some tubes having over 20 patches by the time they were discarded. There were far fewer punctures on the final leg, incidentally.

**Number of countries visited:** 33, not including the detour I made to Spain to avoid border problems in North Africa.

**Number of borders crossed:** 35.

**Number of roadblocks passed through:** Uncounted hundreds, if you include the unofficial ones.

**Number of bribes paid:** Not one – probably a record in Africa.

**Number of cycling days:** About 808 days over two years, two months and 15 days.

**Average distance covered per cycling day:** About 90 km.

**Longest distance covered in one cycling day:** 215 km in Morocco – thanks to a strong tailwind and the Western Sahara's very flat roads.

**Shortest distance covered in one cycling day:** 25 km at Oran, Algeria, after bumping into some fellow South Africans and staying over for the night (resulting in a very early start next morning to catch up).

**Average weight of bicycle:** 45 kg, plus over 5 kg of water (except in Mozambique, when dumping some items out of sheer necessity reduced the overall weight to about 40 kg).

**Number of toe-nails used up:** Two sets. The third set lasted all the way to Cape Town.

**Weight lost:** 14 kg, from 102 kg (my rugby-playing weight) to a steady 88 kg. My current weight: 90 kg.

**Number of meals per cycling day:** About eight, depending on circumstances such as availability and time.

**Most frequently consumed food**: Tinned sardines, with other food according to what was available: about 1.5 kg of rice a day in Nigeria and in East Africa 'nyama choma', or grilled goat's meat.

**Average water consumption per cycling day**: About six litres, plus whatever soft drinks were available, usually as treats. This went up to 12 litres and sometimes more during the desert sections.

**Highest temperature of trip:** Above 50 degrees Celsius in the Somali desert.

**Lowest temperature of trip**: Minus 12 degrees Celsius on Kilimanjaro's Uhuru Peak, Africa's highest point.

**Highest price paid for accommodation:** $45 (then about R270) in Nigeria.

**Lowest price paid for accommodation:** Apart from camping alongside the road – where accommodation was free, although there were always some peripheral 'in-kind' costs, such as fending off desert hyenas, or a sore back from a knobbly earth 'mattress' – the tip for camping on someone's property was usually around $5, but this varied: in Ethiopia the tip was usually $1 (R6 at the then exchange rate).

**Pairs of cycling shoes used up:** Two pairs. The first pair lasted till Cairo (21 000 km from Cape Town) and the second pair all the way home. I also had a pair of sandals to wear when not cycling.

**Worst bout of illness:** The mystery malady in northern Kenya – headaches, vomiting, general weakness – which baffled the doctors in Nairobi in spite of blood tests and a brain scan.

**Percentage of tarmac roads:** About 70 per cent of the roads were tarmac, at least to some extent.

**Most mountainous country traversed:** Ethiopia, although South Africa's Transkei provided some stiff competition.

**Clothes taken along:** I had two changes of clothes, an extra shirt which I washed whenever possible and two pairs of pure wool socks. When one pair of socks was stolen, I used the other pair all the way to Pemba in Mozambique, where I – ahem – 'inherited' another pair.

**Average daily expenses budget:** I budgeted for about $20 a day, but saved on accommodation where this was possible.